HIGH FLAVOR
LOW LABOR

HIGH FLAVOR LOW LABOR

REINVENTING WEEKNIGHT COOKING

J. M. Hirsch

PHOTOGRAPHS BY MATTHEW MEAD

BALLANTINE BOOKS

NEW YORK

To Parker, my son.
You are my world.

Copyright © 2010 by Jason M. Hirsch

All photographs, except copyright page
photograph, copyright © 2010 by Matthew Mead

Published in the United States by Ballantine Books,
an imprint of The Random House Publishing Group,
a division of Random House, Inc., New York.

BALLANTINE and colophon are registered
trademarks of Random House, Inc.

Copyright page photograph by Holly Ramer.

LIBRARY OF CONGRESS CATALOGING-IN-PUBLICATION DATA
Hirsch, J. M.
High flavor, low labor : reinventing weeknight
cooking / J. M. Hirsch.
p. cm.
Includes index.
ISBN 978-0-345-52229-0 (pbk.)
1. Quick and easy cookery. 2. Cookery,
International. I. Title.
TX833.5.H585 2010
641.5'55—dc22   2010014951

Printed in China
www.ballantinebooks.com
9 8 7 6 5 4 3 2 1
FIRST EDITION

CONTENTS

THE INITIAL STUFF

Weeknight cooking is no time for nuance. Meals must stand and be noticed. They must cut through the clutter of weekday chaos. And they must do it quickly and without fuss, mess, or toil.

It requires what I call blunt force cooking, a brash approach to cooking that cranks the flavor and rolls its eyes at bashful ingredients. It balances my desire for real and satisfying food with the demands of my real and overscheduled life.

It's a simple premise. Let high-flavor ingredients do most of the work. Foods that taste great going into the pot need less work from you to taste great when they come out. I'm talking about the Parmesan cheeses, balsamic vinegars, jalapeños, chorizos, and wasabis of the world.

A ham and cheese, for example. Fine as is, but swap out the provolone with manchego or aged gouda and put prosciutto in place of the ham, and fine becomes fantastic. Ditch the sliced bread for baguette smeared with chutney, pop the whole thing in the oven, and you have something seriously special. And all for about the same effort as a ham and cheese.

Spaghetti and meatballs are good, but spike the sauce with balsamic vinegar and finely chopped sun-dried tomatoes, and you get mouth-puckering greatness. Or lose the sauce altogether, pop some crumbled blue cheese into your meatballs, and toss the whole thing with melted butter and minced garlic.

Cooking this way requires no particular genius or skill, and certainly not much time. I lack all of these. It takes just a bit of thought about which ingredients can best ramp up the flavors of a dish.

As food editor for The Associated Press, it's my job to help Americans sit down to great meals. That means creating recipes for flavorful, beautiful food that don't infringe on the rest of our lives. It means showing that real food and real flavors can be convenient and satisfying.

My expertise is the same as yours. I'm not a chef. I'm just a dad with a six-year-old in constant need of feeding, cleaning, and ferrying; a journalist wife forever on deadline; and a demanding job with the pressure of a nation watching over my shoulder every time I stand in front of the stove. What I don't have is time to fuss over dinner. Meals must be fast, flavorful, easy, and real.

For many families, "real" is the stickler. We all need to nuke dinner now and again. But for the health of our bodies, our families, and our communities, it is better to prepare and enjoy food with our loved ones. This is how we connect, how we teach our children the value of family and food.

Not that I can spare much time for this. And no one has to. Grocers today are jammed with flavorful ingredients. What follows are nearly 150 of my favorite weeknight recipes that draw on those foods.

Blunt force cooking is an easy way to embrace family meals, a hectic lifestyle, and satisfying food. And despite the name, kitchen trauma is kept to a minimum.

THE PHILOSOPHICAL STUFF

Too many cookbooks kill off too many trees trying to micromanage your kitchen, instructing you on everything from the best time of day to grocery shop to the finer points of alphabetizing your spices. My eyes are rolling just thinking about it.

So while my patented technique for washing, sorting, and storing produce might prove titillating, I've kept such drivel to a minimum. Here, in as few words as possible, is my cooking philosophy. You're on your own if you need advice about organizing your canned beans.

- I buy organic. Reducing pesticides is better for my family and the environment.

- I buy local as much as possible. Supporting local businesses is better for my community and the environment, and therefore my family.

- I buy whole foods: the dairy, produce, meats, and grains found mostly along the outer aisles of the grocer. Processed foods are exactly what they sound like. So is real food. Not enough children know the difference. It's important that they do.

- I value convenience and shortcuts where and when they make sense. Packaged, processed meals don't fly for me, but canned beans, bottled lemon juice, and frozen fruit make total sense for time-pressed cooks.

- I shop broadly, trying ethnic and unusual items even when I haven't a clue what to do with them. This is often. This keeps cooking and eating interesting.

- I stock my pantry and freezer with stuff that keeps—beans, pasta, rice, meats, seafood, seasonings—because that makes it easy to prepare good dinners on otherwise bad nights.

- I involve my son in the shopping and cooking. It isn't always easy or fun, but nothing about raising children is always easy or fun.

- I let high-flavor ingredients do most of the work for me. Foods that taste great going into the pot need less work from me to taste great when they come out.

THE BASIC STUFF

In this book, ease and flavor rule. Even recipes that seem unfamiliar don't stray far from the everyday comfort cooking you know and need. Each recipe is either an easier, more flavorful rethinking of a familiar dish or an introduction to one that has lots in common with those you already love.

As in Doro Wat Chicken (page 94). Unless you're a fan of Ethiopian food, you've probably never had it. But it's just a well-seasoned one-pot chicken dinner. Likewise, the Deep-Dish Pesto and Prosciutto Tortilla Pizza (page 71) has everything you love about heavyweight pies, but with more flavor and less effort.

Not only won't blunt force cooking take you outside your comfort zone, it probably won't even take you outside your favorite grocer. Start in the international aisle. Nearly anything you grab is going to be jammed with flavor.

TECHNIQUES

I'm not big on fancy techniques, mostly because I don't know any. But there are some that are so ridiculously easy anybody can use them. These are the six I rely on regularly to amplify flavor.

Blooming and Toasting

These are fancy terms for heating your herbs and spices. It works because seasonings contain highly flavorful oils and heat draws out the oils. There are two ways to do this. The first is to toast spices, especially whole ones, in a dry skillet over medium heat for up to a minute.

The second, called blooming, is to briefly heat them in oil, butter, or another fat before adding other ingredients. This is good for ground and dried seasonings used in soups, chili, and sautés, such as my Bacon, Beans, and Beer Chili (page 54).

Hot liquids also can be used to bloom ingredients. Coffee often is used to bloom cocoa powder. This is great for cranking up the flavor of chili, mole, or brownies.

Broiling

Intense heat brings out tremendous flavor in vegetables and meat. And we are talking intense. The flame in a gas broiler burns at about 3,000°F; an electric coil reaches a relatively mild 2,000°F. Both are perfect for browning meats and caramelizing the sugars in vegetables.

But all that heat also can be a challenge. I've broiled to oblivion so many things that the folks in the AP test kitchen laugh every time I turn it on. And getting the inside cooked without torching the outside takes practice. That's why broiling works best with thinly cut meats and produce.

Deglazing

Another fancy term for a simple trick. When you sauté food (cook it with fat) in a pan, you get sticky bits on the bottom. These bits contain oodles of flavor. You want that flavor in your food, not stuck to the pan. So you toss some liquid into the pan while it's hot and scrape up those bits.

This most often is done to create a pan sauce. Sauté some meat and veggies, then transfer them to a plate. The skillet goes back on the heat, you toss in some liquid, scrape up the yummy bits, then add cornstarch to thicken it. Add seasonings and you've got an insanely flavorful pan sauce.

This trick also can be used with stews and chili. I usually brown some onions, seasonings, and meat, then splash in some liquid without removing the other ingredients. Once I've scraped up the tasty bits, then I continue with the recipe.

The liquid can be anything. White wine is common, but beer, cider (hard or otherwise), red wine, chicken or beef broth, water, or juices work. Try to select a liquid that complements the other ingredients, such as red wine with beef or beer in a chili.

Salting

Not as obvious as it sounds. Most people don't appreciate the power of salt to elevate simple flavors. For a quick demo, make a fruit smoothie. Taste it, then buzz in a pinch of salt and take another sip. You'll never taste the salt, but the flavors of the fruit come alive. This is true for nearly any dish. Just be sure to taste as you cook, especially when the recipe includes already salty ingredients, such as Parmesan or prosciutto.

And unless your doctor has warned you off all salt, don't sweat it. Americans eat too much salt, but little of it comes from what's added during home cooking or at the table. Most of the excess comes from processed food, which can contain astronomical amounts of sodium.

Searing

The principle is the same as broiling, but it involves thicker cuts of meat and is done in a pan on top of the stove. Meat is seared by browning it briefly on all sides in a very hot pan. The meat then is transferred to the oven to cook the insides slowly at a lower temperature.

Temperature

This is more an awareness than a technique. Few foods taste their best when ice cold, even beer. Cheeses, for example, are at their peak flavor closer to room temperature. This also is true for salads and most fruits and vegetables, dips, salsas, cured meats, and olives. Cold dulls flavor. Other than ice cream, don't serve things (including most drinks) directly from the refrigerator. Twenty minutes at room temperature can make a huge difference in flavor.

THE STUFF TO BUY

Physically and emotionally, bland foods just don't satisfy. If they did, we'd all be content stuffing ourselves with tofu. Hold your breath for that one.

We crave assertive foods—rich chocolate cakes, savory chilies and sauces, sharp cheeses, bright, citrusy desserts. These flavors comfort and satisfy.

Getting those flavors to the table, and fast, is the essence of blunt force cooking. And it doesn't require any special skills or hours at the stove. It's just a matter of taking good raw ingredients, adding intensely flavorful stuff, then eating.

As with any style of cooking, a stocked pantry makes on-the-fly blunt force cooking easier. These are my go-to ingredients.

COMMON

These are ingredients most people already have, but that often are underappreciated for the powerhouse effect they can have on flavor.

Cinnamon

In the U.S., cinnamon makes us think of sweets and baked goods. In the rest of the world, it's a savory seasoning that shows up in meat rubs, vegetable stews, and curries, as well as sprinkled over grains, such as couscous. And with good reason. Cinnamon imparts a mellow, delicious warmth and aroma. Try a little in your next batch of chili. Or combine it with garlic powder, cumin, and salt for an awesome steak or chicken rub.

Citrus Juice and Zest

Citrus effortlessly brightens and sharpens flavors. The juices are best in marinades, dressings, sauces, even soups (try a splash in chicken and tomato soups). The zest (the thin outer layer of colorful skin, not the white pith beneath it) is great in baked goods, sauces, and sautés (add it to a sauté of kale with garlic and grated Parmesan cheese). While fresh juice is nice, bottled is easier and often cheaper. As for the zest, you can use a vegetable peeler to remove it, but a wand-style grater (such as a Microplane) is better.

Ginger

Fresh ginger (sold as a funky brown root in the produce section) has a peppery sweet flavor and is essential to Asian cooking. Also try it grated over steamed and buttered potatoes or mixed into a vinaigrette. The best place to store fresh ginger is the freezer. Not only does it keep for months, it is easier to grate, and as long as you use a very fine grater, there is no need to peel it first. Dry ground ginger (sold with the other spices) is excellent in meat rubs, chili, and vegetable sautés. Its flavor is milder than fresh. Crystallized ginger has been candied. Sold cut into a variety of sizes, it can be eaten as is, or minced, diced, or ground. It's also wonderful finely chopped and simmered in homemade cranberry sauce.

Salt

Many foods—even sweets—simply taste flat without a pinch of salt. It doesn't take much, and it doesn't take the pricey gourmet stuff. The best bet is kosher salt, which is inexpensive and easy to pinch. Keep a bowl of it next to the stove.

Wine

It's all about getting sauced. Or is that making sauce? Whichever, wine is great for deglazing pans. When wine is cooked, it reduces and the flavors are intensified. If the wine tastes good, this is good. If the wine tastes bad, this is bad. So while you don't need to spend a fortune, skip the rotgut. Use whatever you drink. For cooking and drinking, I'm pretty happy with ten-dollar bottles. Use reds for beef- and tomato-based dishes; stick with whites for everything else.

ASIAN

Asian ingredients are great for adding sharp and salty notes to a dish. Soy sauce and rice vinegar, for example, are a brilliant combination with noodles, vegetables, rice, and most meats.

Miso
It's not just for soup anymore. Miso has a deep, salty, rich flavor that complements meats and seafood. Use it in glazes, marinades, and sauces. Generally, the lighter the color, the sweeter the taste. So stick with white or yellow miso. Keep miso in the refrigerator and it will last until the next ice age.

Rice Vinegar
Use it everywhere you'd use cider, white, or even balsamic vinegar. It has a deliciously sharp, sweet flavor that works well in salad dressings, marinades, and peanut sauces. It's usually sold in two varieties, seasoned and plain. Seasoned varieties tend to be sweeter; both are delicious sprinkled with soy sauce over warm rice.

Soy Sauce
Salty goodness in a bottle. Use it in place of salt in just about any sauté, or add it to marinades, soups, and barbecue sauces. Low-sodium versions taste just as good as conventional ones, so don't hesitate to try those. But avoid soy sauces labeled "dark" or "black," which are especially thick and strongly flavored. Those varieties are intended for specific uses in Asian cooking.

Toasted Sesame Oil
This is the cooking oil equivalent of smoked cheese. It tastes toasty, smoky, and savory all at once. Use it for stir-fries, or drizzle it over warm pasta, rice, and couscous. Combine it with soy sauce, rice vinegar, hot sauce, and chopped scallions for a dipping sauce for sushi, dumplings, spring rolls, and grilled meats. That same combination also makes an outstanding marinade.

Wasabi
Don't limit yourself to sushi. You also don't need to use sinus-clearing quantities. In mashed potatoes it offers pleasantly sharp flavors. Or blend it with the butter or oil used to cook fish, especially salmon. Whisk it into oil and use it to coat vegetables, chicken, or beef for roasting or grilling. But note, wasabi needs liquid for its flavor to shine. Don't sprinkle the dry powder directly onto food.

HISPANIC

Many of these ingredients can really crank up the heat. But as with many Hispanic foods, they are best when balanced with cooling ingredients, such as cheese, sour cream, or avocado.

Jalapeño Peppers

Jars of sliced jalapeños are my go-to heat source. They are convenient, tasty, and inexpensive. And unless you're a serious heat fiend, a jar will last months. Sprinkle the slices whole onto sandwiches and pizza. Or dice them up for use in sautés, sauces, ground meat (think Southwestern burgers), and chilies. You can find them at the grocer sold alongside pickles and olives. When making salsa, I prefer fresh jalapeños.

Chipotle Peppers in Adobo Sauce

Chipotle peppers are dried jalapeños. They usually are sold in small cans packed in adobo sauce, a thick, smoky, and spicy sauce. Dice the peppers and add them to sautés, meatloaves, stir-fries, and curries. The adobo sauce is incredible in chilies, pasta sauces, marinades, and barbecue sauces.

Hot Sauce

This is my secret ingredient in hummus and cheese sauces. Just a dash brightens the other flavors without adding significant heat. Try it in macaroni and cheese and mixed into burgers. Use it to perk up mayonnaise for a sandwich or potato salad. Also try it in vinaigrette on a hearty salad (something with meat and cheese in it). There are innumerable hot sauces; experiment until you find a favorite.

Cilantro

A sprinkling of chopped fresh cilantro, a brightly flavored and aromatic herb, can really make the meal. It also makes a damn fine pesto (especially when pureed with toasted pumpkin seeds and a splash of lime juice; page 180) and is essential to Argentina's wonderfully herbaceous chimichurri sauce (page 138; use it on chicken, steak, and roasted potatoes). Cilantro also does well with most Asian and Indian dishes, especially sprinkled over potato curries.

Chorizo

These spicy pork sausages are available in Spanish, Mexican, and Portuguese varieties. The main difference is that Spanish and Portuguese varieties use smoked pork, while Mexican uses fresh. Always remove the casing, then crumble or chop the chorizo into the pan. Use it in chilies, shepherd's pie, or any dish that calls for ground meat.

INDIAN AND AFRICAN

These regions offer so many seriously oomphy ingredients it's tempting to list many more. I resist only because of the limited availability of some of them in the U.S.

Chutney

This thick sweet-and-sour Indian condiment usually accompanies spicy curries. It also makes a fine sandwich spread, especially paired with roasted turkey breast and cheese. Or add it to a grilled cheese. Thin chutney with chicken broth and use it as a marinade or to glaze a baked ham. Bake it into tiny puff pastry tarts topped with halloumi (Greek grilling cheese) or feta. There are many varieties of chutney; mango is the most common here, and the best choice for these uses.

Cumin

Most commonly available ground, cumin also can be found as whole seeds. If you find whole seeds, toast them for a minute in a dry skillet, then add them whole or ground to curries, meat rubs, grains, and chilies. But there's nothing wrong with already ground cumin. Like most dry spices, it keeps for about six months, then loses potency.

Coconut Milk

Equally good in sweet and savory recipes. Coconut milk is deliciously fatty and creamy, making it a perfect partner for spicy foods. It's an essential element of many curries and can be added to virtually any rice dish or stir-fry. It also turns out wonderful baked goods, including banana bread. Use it in place of milk when making pancakes. Regular coconut milk separates inside the can, creating a dense layer of coconut cream at the top. To use the whole can, you'll need to mix this into the liquid under it. To be totally decadent, ditch the liquid and just use the creamy top.

Ghee

For intense buttery flavor, you can't beat ghee, Indian-style clarified butter. It has been melted to separate the milk solids from the water. The thick paste that results is a dream for stir-frying (it has a high smoke point). It also is the only way to go when buttering popcorn (ghee contains no water, so it won't make your popcorn soggy). Ghee is sold in jars (not in the refrigerator case with other dairy products).

Peppadew Peppers

Peppadews (the name of the product and the brand) are small red peppers grown and pickled in South Africa. They are insanely delicious, with a piquant, snappy, vinegary bite and a mild heat. They are delicious stuffed with feta for a simple hors d'oeuvre; diced and added to salads, pasta sauce, and just about any sauté; threaded onto skewers with meat and vegetables for kebabs; and even pureed and added to dressings and marinades. Peppadews are available at most large grocers. A smaller amount of jarred jalapeño pepper slices can be substituted.

EUROPEAN

Europe is the land of meats and cheese. Take a culinary stroll there and you'll never be at a loss for blunt force ingredients.

Anchovies

For many people, anchovies are a no-go zone. Too bad. They are incredibly savory, inexpensive, and easy to use. Best yet, you don't need to eat them whole to appreciate them. Place a few in a hot pan and stir around; they will melt into a flavorful paste. Now continue with your sauté. You'll never know the anchovies are there, but the taste will be tremendous. This is great with sautéed hearty greens, such as kale and chard, as well as for pan sauces tossed with pasta. They also can be pureed into salad dressing. Because they are salty, be sure to taste as you cook.

Balsamic Vinegar

A good balsamic can be breathtaking. It has an intensely sweet and mouth-puckering flavor that is awesome drizzled with olive oil onto a salad. It makes a great dipping sauce for chunks of Parmesan cheese and dark chocolate. When it comes to red sauce, it can make the difference between so-so and superb. For a great dessert sauce (over shortcake, angel food cake, and cheesecake) simmer equal parts chopped fresh strawberries and balsamic vinegar until reduced and thick. For most cooking purposes, inexpensive varieties are fine. For dipping, consider splurging on the good (aged) stuff.

Cheese

Broad, but true. Cheese works wonders, almost regardless of the cuisine. It balances heat and effortlessly lends an otherwise hard-to-get richness. For pungent, slap-you-across-the-face flavor, crumble blue or feta cheeses over salads, roasted vegetables, and grain dishes. For savory notes, grate Parmesan, pecorino, or manchego over pasta and chicken and into sauces. For creaminess with grains, sauces, and even salad dressings, go for the soft varieties, such as fresh goat cheese, Brie, or even cream cheese.

Cured Meats and Sausages

There's enough here to fill several books. Bacon is a fine place to start, especially the smoked variety. Crumbled cooked bacon enhances everything, from meatloaf and burgers to salads and stir-fries. Cured pork products, such as prosciutto and Serrano ham, also are phenomenal choices. Even better, they tend to be more flavorful than bacon, but (because they are thinly sliced) have much less fat. A little goes a long way with these, which is good because they can be pricey. Finally, sausages can pack a flavor wallop. Any will do, but I gravitate toward precooked chicken and turkey sausages. They are faster, healthier, and come in a wide variety of flavors.

Smoked Paprika

I totally abuse this. It's in way too many recipes in this cookbook. But that's because it is toe-curlingly good, lending deep, smoky flavor without heat. Use it in soups, meat rubs, chili, and any sort of sauté; toss it with pasta and oil or butter. Just about anything that gets roasted or broiled does well with it, including potatoes. Blend it with olive oil and crushed garlic for an amazing shrimp sauté.

FIRST UP

People tend to have a certain image of a food editor's life, mostly involving plenty of wining and dining, noshing with celebs, and whipping up multicourse gourmet meals.

I so do not have that life. I do have a six-year-old son. And that, combined with living in rural New Hampshire, tends to limit my fine-dining options.

As for gourmet cooking? Not quite. My knife skills amount to running a lawn mower over the food. I've managed to set fire to nearly every flammable ingredient (and several parts of my home). And any recipe requiring exacting measurements or fussy techniques lands in the recycling bin.

Celebs? I do have better-than-average access, but even that I tend to bungle.

As in the time I attended a dinner with Rachael Ray, Katie Lee, Mario Batali, Bobby Flay, and Bill Clinton. It was fine until I left and decided—with perhaps a bit too much wine influencing the decision—to call my wife. And loudly tell her how gorgeous Katie Lee was. And that she might have touched my arm.

I'm smooth like that.

But what I do have is a determination to eat well and eat real. Because after I've spent the first half of my day playing editor and the second half as the only dad at my son's playdates, I want food that sucker punches me with flavor. No matter how little effort, time, or skill I can manage.

As in these starters. Any starter that can't be made while drinking wine and chatting with friends is a nonstarter. Because let's face it, starters are for company. I wish I was the sort of guy who had the time and energy to make appetizers for my family, but they can dream on.

So most of these recipes take about 10 to 20 minutes and require no special skills or equipment. Not sure where to start? Try the Feta Cheese Drizzled with Honey, Walnuts, and Oregano (page 4). It's intensely good, ridiculously easy, and everyone will love it.

Crostini with Basil Goat Cheese and Crisped Prosciutto

Anytime you can play salty, crunchy foods against creamy, soft ones you probably have **a winner of a dish.** For a variation, substitute a slab of gouda for the goat cheese, then pop the assembled crostini in a 350°F oven until the cheese just begins to soften.

2 slices prosciutto
4-ounce log chevre (soft goat cheese), room temperature
2 large fresh basil leaves, cut into slivers
1 tablespoon extra-virgin olive oil
Ground black pepper, to taste
12-inch baguette, cut crosswise into 12 slices, lightly toasted
1 scallion, thinly sliced

Coat a large skillet with cooking spray. Add the prosciutto and cook over medium-high heat until just lightly browned and crisp on both sides, about 4 minutes. Transfer the prosciutto to paper towels to absorb excess oil, then cut it into small pieces.

In a medium bowl, use a fork to mash the goat cheese. Add the basil and olive oil. Mix well, then season with pepper.

Spread a bit of the cheese mixture over each slice of bread, then sprinkle with sliced scallion and bits of prosciutto.

➔ HOW LONG? **10 MINUTES**
➔ HOW MUCH? **12 CROSTINI**

Feta Cheese Drizzled with Honey, Walnuts, and Oregano

Feta keeps you thin. Or so went the advice of the diet counselor who helped me shed some serious pounds during high school. Her theory sounded good. Feta's assertive flavor meant you were less likely to eat as much as you would a milder cheese.

Nice try. But I was not lugging around a spare eighty pounds because of a bland diet. I tend to pack it in—bland, spicy, whatever. I can eat feta by the pound. And thanks to living in the test kitchen, I still manage a twenty-pound year-round yo-yo. **Maybe I just haven't eaten enough feta.**

Just about any nut (as long as it's unsalted) will work in place of the walnuts here. As with all cheeses, be sure to serve this close to room temperature.

12-ounce block feta cheese, cut into thin slices
$\frac{1}{3}$ cup honey
$\frac{1}{3}$ cup toasted walnut halves, crumbled
Leaves from several sprigs fresh oregano
4 to 5 fresh mint leaves, cut into thin strips
Grated zest of $\frac{1}{2}$ lemon
12-inch baguette, cut into 12 to 14 slices (toasted, if desired)

Arrange the feta cheese slices at the center of a large serving plate or platter. Drizzle the honey over the feta.

Sprinkle the crumbled walnuts over the top of the cheese, then scatter the oregano leaves and mint over it. Sprinkle with lemon zest.

Serve the cheese with the baguette slices.

➡ HOW LONG? **10 MINUTES**
➡ HOW MUCH? **4 TO 6 SERVINGS**

Spiced Cashew Hummus with Smoked Paprika

A former boss once told me I had to stop writing hummus recipes. Her loss. I can't get enough of the stuff. **Give me a tub of hummus and a loaf of bread, and I'm good.**

This delicious rethinking ditches the traditional sesame seed paste for ultra-creamy cashew butter (think peanut butter, but made from cashews).

Serve it with hunks of flour tortillas, nacho chips, or pita bread.

Like all hummus, this tastes best at room temp. Fresh from the food processor is ideal. If you do refrigerate it, let it stand, covered, on a counter for 20 minutes before serving.

15-ounce can chickpeas, drained
½ cup cashew butter
3 tablespoons cider vinegar
1 teaspoon hot sauce
¼ cup extra-virgin olive oil, plus extra to drizzle
3 cloves garlic
2 tablespoons water
½ teaspoon salt
¼ teaspoon smoked paprika

In a food processor, combine the chickpeas, cashew butter, vinegar, hot sauce, olive oil, garlic, water, and salt. Process until smooth. Transfer to a bowl, then drizzle with a bit more olive oil and sprinkle with smoked paprika.

→ HOW LONG? **10 MINUTES**
→ HOW MUCH? **4 TO 6 SERVINGS**

Grilled Bacon-Wrapped Figs
with Blue Cheese

This technique works with just about any **grill-friendly fruit,** such as spears of fresh pineapple, rings of cored apple, or slices of pear.

Not a fan of blue (a true gift to the blunt force kitchen)? Try finely chopped pieces of manchego, pecorino, or aged gouda. Or go for soft goat cheese, which has a mild flavor but an awesome texture, especially when warmed.

4 strips bacon
4 large fresh figs
Ground black pepper, to taste
¼ cup crumbled blue cheese
1 tablespoon chopped fresh parsley

Coat a grill rack with oil or cooking spray. Heat the grill to medium.

Wrap 1 slice of bacon around each fig, starting at the top and spiraling it down the length of the fig. If needed, secure the bacon at each end with a toothpick. Season with pepper.

Place the figs on the grill, close the cover, and cook for 2 minutes. Depending on the fat content of the bacon, there may be some smoke and flames.

Turn off one side of the grill and use tongs to carefully move the figs to that side. Close the lid and grill for another 3 minutes, or until the bacon is cooked through.

Use tongs to carefully transfer each fig to a serving plate, then sprinkle each with a bit of blue cheese and parsley.

➔ HOW LONG? **15 MINUTES**
➔ HOW MUCH? **4 SERVINGS**

Polenta Cakes Topped with Prosciutto and Peppadew Slivers

The mild taste and grainy texture of polenta is the perfect foil for creamy goat cheese and salty prosciutto. Meanwhile, sweetly sharp **Peppadew peppers add just the right bite.** If you're the sort who cranks the heat, use diced fresh or jarred jalapeño peppers.

18-ounce tube prepared polenta, cut into 8 rounds
4 thin slices prosciutto, halved crosswise
4-ounce log chevre (soft goat cheese), cut into 8 rounds
8 Peppadew peppers, cut into thin slivers

Heat the oven to broil. Coat a baking sheet with olive oil cooking spray.

Place the polenta rounds on the baking sheet and broil them for 3 to 4 minutes, or until lightly browned. Flip the rounds, then broil for another 3 to 4 minutes and remove from heat. Leave the broiler on.

Place a slice of prosciutto on each polenta round, then top each with a round of goat cheese. Return the polenta to the oven and broil for another 2 minutes, or until the cheese is soft.

Use a spatula to transfer the polenta cakes to a platter or individual serving plates. Top each with a small mound of slivered Peppadews.

➡ HOW LONG? **20 MINUTES**
➡ HOW MUCH? **8 SERVINGS**

Sun-Dried Tomato and Crème Fraîche Crostini

This **snappy little number** tastes like a killer pizza, but looks good enough to serve guests. Or turn the cheese topping into a pasta sauce. Just make it as directed, then toss it with warm pasta and about ¼ cup of the pasta cooking water.

8-ounce package crème fraîche
½ cup grated Parmesan cheese
6 oil-packed sun-dried tomatoes
**¼ cup green olives (any variety, such as jalapeño-
   or garlic-stuffed)**
18-inch baguette, cut into about 24 slices
Balsamic vinegar, to drizzle
¼ cup chopped fresh basil

Heat the oven to broil.

In a food processor, combine the crème fraîche, Parmesan, tomatoes, and olives. Process until chunky smooth, scraping the bowl several times.

Spread the mixture over the baguette slices, using the knife to make a slight indentation at the center of each. Arrange the slices on a rimmed baking sheet and broil for about 2 minutes, or until warmed through.

Drizzle a few drops of balsamic vinegar over the center of each piece, then sprinkle with fresh basil.

➔ HOW LONG? **10 MINUTES**
➔ HOW MUCH? **12 CROSTINI**

Sweet-and-Sour Meatballs

It's hard to make a pretty meatball, **so I focused on making a pretty fantastic one.**
These are tangy and sweet, and have just a hint of heat. Serve them with toothpicks as a party
food, tossed with heaps of pasta, or jammed into a sub roll with sautéed onions and peppers.

½ small yellow onion
4 cloves garlic
¼ cup Peppadew peppers or 2 tablespoons jarred
  jalapeño slices
½ cup apple jelly
2 tablespoons cider vinegar
½ teaspoon salt
¼ teaspoon ground black pepper
1 teaspoon soy sauce
½ teaspoon ground ginger
1 cup panko (Japanese-style) breadcrumbs
1½ pounds ground beef

Heat the oven to 400°F. Line 2 rimmed baking sheets with foil, then spritz
them with cooking spray.

In a food processor, combine the onion, garlic, and Peppadew or jalapeño
peppers. Process until finely diced, scraping the sides of the bowl as
needed.

Add the apple jelly, cider vinegar, salt, pepper, soy sauce, and ginger.
Pulse until well mixed, then transfer to a large bowl.

Add the breadcrumbs and ground beef, then use your hands to mix them
thoroughly with the onion and apple jelly mixture.

Form the mixture into about 30 meatballs, arranging them on the
prepared baking sheets. Spritz the meatballs with cooking spray, then
bake for 20 minutes.

➲ HOW LONG? **30 MINUTES (10 MINUTES ACTIVE)**
➲ HOW MUCH? **5 SERVINGS**

Ham and Cheddar Arancini

Arancini is Italian for **"little oranges,"** a reference to what these stuffed and fried balls of rice supposedly resemble. Traditionally, they are made using leftover risotto, but my version uses "ready rice" (the stuff you microwave in 90 seconds). Any leftover rice can be used, even the stuff you get with takeout.

Two 8½-ounce packages "ready rice" (about 4 cups cooked rice)
3 tablespoons butter, melted
1½ cups grated Parmesan cheese
¼ teaspoon ground black pepper
Ten ½-inch cubes extra-sharp cheddar cheese
Ten ½-inch cubes cooked ham (or chicken or other
  cooked meat)
1 cup panko (Japanese-style) breadcrumbs
Canola oil, for frying

In a medium microwave-safe bowl, combine the rice, butter, and Parmesan. Microwave for 30 seconds, or until the rice and cheese are just warmed and sticky.

Use your hands to mix well. Season with pepper.

Press about ¼ cup of rice into a bowl shape in the palm of one hand. Place 1 piece each of the cheddar and ham inside, then cover with a bit more rice and shape the whole thing into a ball. Repeat with remaining rice, cheese, and ham to form 10 balls.

Place the breadcrumbs in a bowl and roll each rice ball in it, packing it tightly with your hands.

In a small saucepan over medium, heat about 1 inch of oil until it shimmers and a grain of rice dropped into it sizzles.

Place 1 or 2 balls at a time in the oil. Fry on each side for about 10 seconds, using tongs to gently turn them. Transfer them to paper towels to drain.

➔ HOW LONG? **20 MINUTES**
➔ HOW MUCH? **10 ARANCINI**

Warm Mashed Cannellini Crostini

For a **Mexican-influenced** version, substitute black beans for the cannellini and add some minced jalapeños or hot sauce. Try manchego or Jack cheese in place of the Parmesan.

12-inch baguette, cut into 12 rounds
4 tablespoons extra-virgin olive oil
1 medium yellow onion, thinly sliced
2 cloves garlic, minced
½ teaspoon red pepper flakes
15-ounce can cannellini beans, drained and rinsed
1 tablespoon cider vinegar
Salt and ground black pepper, to taste
Parmesan cheese, for garnish

Heat the oven to 400°F.

Arrange the baguette rounds in a single layer on a rimmed baking sheet. Brush with 1 tablespoon of the oil. Bake until lightly toasted, about 5 minutes. Remove the bread from the oven and set aside to cool.

Meanwhile, in a large skillet over medium, heat the remaining 3 tablespoons of oil. When the oil is hot, add the onion, garlic, and red pepper flakes. Sauté for 5 minutes, or until the onions are lightly browned.

Add the beans and vinegar, then sauté until heated through. Remove the pan from the heat.

With a potato masher or fork, crush the beans until they form a chunky paste. Stir well to mix the beans with the other ingredients. Season with salt and pepper.

Arrange the bread rounds on a serving platter or individual plates. Top each round with a bit of the bean mixture.

Use a vegetable peeler to shave large strips of Parmesan cheese over each piece.

➲ HOW LONG? **30 MINUTES**
➲ HOW MUCH? **12 CROSTINI**

Chipotle Buffalo Wings with Blow-Your-Mind Blue Cheese Dip

Because if you're going to do buffalo wings, you need to do them right. **These are seriously intense.** The agave and chipotle sauce gives the wings a sweet-meets-heat bite that is tamed by the intensely creamy and rich blue cheese dip.

Don't have (or want) chipotle hot sauce and agave syrup (a honey-like syrup)? Substitute any hot sauce and honey.

5 pounds chicken wings and drummettes (20 to 25 pieces)
¼ cup chipotle hot sauce
2 tablespoons agave syrup, plus more, to taste
2 tablespoons butter, melted
1 tablespoon soy sauce
2 tablespoons finely chopped fresh cilantro
6 cups canola oil
Salt and ground black pepper, to taste

Use paper towels to pat the chicken pieces dry. Use many towels and try to absorb as much moisture as possible. Let the chicken sit at room temperature for 15 minutes.

Meanwhile, in a large bowl combine the hot sauce, agave, butter, soy sauce, and cilantro. Taste to check the heat level. If the sauce is too spicy, add agave. Set aside.

Place the oil in a large Dutch oven. Heat over medium until it reaches 275°F.

Divide the chicken into four batches. Working one batch at a time, fry for 8 minutes, transferring each to a clean plate or baking sheet when done.

Once the first round of frying is done, increase the heat to medium-high and heat the oil to 375°F.

Fry the chicken, again in batches, for 2 minutes, then transfer it to a baking sheet lined with paper towels. The skin should be brown and crunchy. As each batch finishes, season it with salt and pepper. When all the chicken pieces have been fried, transfer them to the bowl of prepared sauce. Toss to coat well, then transfer the buffalo wings to a serving platter.

⮕ HOW LONG? **1 HOUR (45 MINUTES ACTIVE)**
⮕ HOW MUCH? **6 SERVINGS**

Blow-Your-Mind Blue Cheese Dip

2 tablespoons olive oil
5 cloves garlic, minced
4 shallots, minced
½ teaspoon mustard powder
1½ cups sour cream
½ cup plain whole-milk Greek-style yogurt
2 tablespoons mayonnaise
1¾ cups crumbled blue cheese (such as Gorgonzola or Roquefort)
Pinch smoked paprika

In a medium skillet over medium-high heat, combine the oil, garlic, shallots, and mustard powder. Sauté until the shallots are lightly browned and very tender, 4 to 5 minutes.

Remove the skillet from the heat and let it cool for 5 minutes.

Stir in the sour cream, yogurt, mayonnaise, and blue cheese. Transfer to a serving bowl, then refrigerate until chilled, at least 45 minutes.

When ready to serve, sprinkle with paprika.

⮕ HOW LONG? **1 HOUR (15 MINUTES ACTIVE)**
⮕ HOW MUCH? **10 SERVINGS**

Smoky Fried Calamari with Zesty Tomato Sauce

With calamari, fresh is better than frozen, but **size is even more important.** Look for the smallest calamari you can find (about 1½ inches around). Large squid are tough. Your best bet is to get whole squid (bodies and tentacles) and cut them yourself.

½ cup tomato sauce
1 tablespoon hot sauce
1 tablespoon honey
1 cup all-purpose flour
1 teaspoon salt
¼ teaspoon ground black pepper
1 teaspoon garlic powder
1 teaspoon smoked paprika
1 egg
1 cup water
1½ pounds calamari rings and tentacles, thawed if frozen
Canola or vegetable oil, for frying

In a small saucepan over low heat, whisk together the tomato sauce, hot sauce, and honey. Heat until the mixture is just warm, then remove it from the heat, cover, and set aside.

Meanwhile, in a medium bowl, whisk together the flour, salt, pepper, garlic powder, and paprika. Set aside.

In a small bowl, whisk together the egg and water. Combine with the flour mixture and whisk just until smooth.

Add the calamari to the batter and toss until all the pieces are coated.

In a large, deep skillet over medium-high, heat 2 inches of oil to 365°F.

Working in batches, use a fork to lift pieces of calamari from the batter and set them into the oil. Fry for 2 minutes, then use a slotted spoon to transfer them to paper towels to drain. Serve with the dipping sauce.

➡ HOW LONG? **30 MINUTES**
➡ HOW MUCH? **4 SERVINGS**

Fig and Manchego Puff Pastries

Sweet, salty, flaky, cheesy, and ready in about 20 minutes. It's everything you want in a starter. Or do a savory mini pizza version, substituting a thin slice of plum tomato for the fig jam.

1 sheet frozen puff pastry, thawed according to package directions (each 17.3-ounce package contains 2 sheets)
3 ounces manchego cheese, cut into 12 chunks roughly ⅛ inch square and ¼ inch thick
¼ cup fig preserves
Ground black pepper, to taste

Heat the oven to 400°F. Line a baking sheet with parchment paper.

Unfold the pastry sheet and use a paring knife to cut it into twelve 2-inch squares.

Arrange each square on the prepared baking sheet. Use a 1½-inch round cookie cutter to lightly press a circle into each square without cutting all the way through.

Place a square of cheese in the center of each pastry square, then top with a dollop of fig preserves. Bake for 15 minutes, or until the pastry is puffed and lightly browned.

Sprinkle with black pepper and serve.

➲ HOW LONG? **20 MINUTES (5 MINUTES ACTIVE)**
➲ HOW MUCH? **12 PASTRIES**

Feta Crostini with
Tomato, Bacon, and Apple Jam

This recipe takes slightly longer than most of my other starters. But everyone who has tried it insisted I include it in the book. The jam has a **brilliant blend of savory, sweet, and tangy** flavors that go so nicely with the salty feta and crusty bread. It's worth the extra time.

The jam can be made ahead and refrigerated for several days or frozen for several months. Thaw frozen jam overnight in the refrigerator, then heat it briefly on the stove before using it.

The recipe also intentionally makes a bit more jam than you'll need for the crostini. Try spreading the extra on a bagel with cream cheese or on a grilled cheese sandwich.

½ pound smoked bacon
28-ounce can diced tomatoes, drained
1 apple, peeled, cored, and diced
1 small yellow onion, diced
1 cup sugar
2½ tablespoons cider vinegar
1½ teaspoons salt
¼ teaspoon ground black pepper
12-inch baguette, thinly sliced and toasted (about 18 slices)
8-ounce block feta cheese, cut into thin slices roughly the size
  of the baguette slices, or crumbled

In a large skillet over medium-high heat, cook the bacon until it is just browned, about 5 minutes. Transfer the bacon to paper towels to drain excess fat. Crumble or cut it into small pieces.

In a large saucepan, combine the tomatoes, apple, onion, sugar, vinegar, salt, pepper, and bacon. Bring to a rapid boil and cook, stirring often, for 12 minutes.

Remove the pan from the heat and set aside for 5 minutes.

Arrange the baguette slices on a serving platter, then top with feta and a dollop of warm tomato jam.

⮕ HOW LONG? **30 MINUTES**
⮕ HOW MUCH? **18 CROSTINI**

Fertilizer. Water. Industrial-grade aluminum foil. Sex toys.

My dad's gardening essentials. And when I was five, it made perfect sense. Blame his obsessive desire to grow the perfect beefsteak tomato. In the city. In winter.

Frustrated by our tiny city plot of hot top, Dad took his gardening ambitions into our basement, a dank, asbestos-filled hole he was convinced could be fertile ground.

Mom and I had doubts. The plants didn't. They grew phenomenally.

But for that to happen, Dad first had to hermetically seal the basement in foil, rig giant lights powerful enough to approximate sunlight, and devise a mechanized watering system.

Thankfully, he didn't also bring in a hive of bees to pollinate. He did that manually. With a vibrator. Flower by flower.

A short, pudgy electrical engineer (anyone shocked that he's an engineer?) crawling around a steaming, extremely well-lit foil bubble in our basement gently rubbing tomato buds with a sex toy. We're lucky he didn't get busted for . . . something.

But apparently a little loving can go a long way with tomatoes. And lettuce. They were delicious. Though it took years before I understood why he wouldn't let me help pollinate.

I don't believe in working quite that hard for a decent salad.

Baby Spinach with
Pears and Plumped Raisins

This salad is easy to keep seasonal. Simply swap out the pears with whatever is freshest, including apples, halved grapes, slices of melon, strawberries, or mango. And **if spinach isn't your thing, use whatever green you got.**

1 cup golden raisins
8 ounces baby spinach
2 pears, cored and diced
2 medium carrots, cut into matchsticks
3 tablespoons toasted pine nuts
1 teaspoon kosher salt
3 tablespoons balsamic vinegar
Extra-virgin olive oil, to taste
Parmesan cheese, for shaving

Place the raisins in a small bowl, then add enough warm water to cover. Allow to soak for at least 20 minutes, or until quite soft.

Meanwhile, in a large bowl combine the spinach, pears, and carrots. Toss, then sprinkle the pine nuts and salt over the salad.

Once the raisins have plumped, drain and discard the water. Gently squeeze the raisins to remove any excess water. Add the raisins to the salad.

Sprinkle the vinegar over the salad, then drizzle it with olive oil and top with Parmesan shavings.

➡ HOW LONG? **20 MINUTES**
➡ HOW MUCH? **4 SERVINGS**

BOILED BALSAMIC, ANYONE?

Don't want to spend big bucks on high-end aged balsamic? Make your own. Buy a cheap bottle, then simmer the vinegar until reduced by half. Let it cool, then return it to the bottle to use as you normally would. The flavor is intensified and the consistency becomes nice and syrupy.

Fennel and Avocado Salad with Cumin Vinaigrette

Fennel has a **pleasantly peppery flavor** that goes wonderfully with creamy avocado and acidic tomatoes. Turn this salad into a meal by adding crumbled feta and either chunks of grilled chicken or a can of chickpeas (or be wild and add both).

2 tablespoons extra-virgin olive oil
2 tablespoons balsamic vinegar
½ teaspoon salt
¼ teaspoon ground black pepper
½ teaspoon cumin
1 large fennel bulb, ends trimmed
2 large tomatoes, cut into wedges
1 firm, ripe avocado, peeled, pitted and cut into bite-size chunks

In a small bowl, whisk together the olive oil, vinegar, salt, pepper, and cumin. Set aside.

Cut the fennel bulb into quarters lengthwise, then cut each quarter crosswise into bite-size chunks. In a large bowl, toss the fennel with the tomatoes and avocado.

Drizzle the dressing over the salad, then gently toss to coat.

➡ HOW LONG? **10 MINUTES**
➡ HOW MUCH? **4 TO 6 SERVINGS**

Crab Salad Vinaigrette

Dressings should enhance already assertively flavored salads, not compensate for an uninspired toss. In this crab salad, the **lemony vinaigrette** cuts through the flavors of the crab and radishes.

2 tablespoons extra-virgin olive oil
Juice of 1 lemon
2 cloves garlic, finely minced
¼ teaspoon kosher salt
¼ teaspoon ground black pepper
1 tablespoon chopped fresh chives
2 red radishes, cut into fine matchsticks
16-ounce can lump or claw crabmeat

In a medium bowl, whisk together the olive oil, lemon juice, garlic, salt, and pepper. Mix in the chives and radishes. Add the crabmeat and gently toss with the vinaigrette.

Serve the salad over mixed greens or on a crusty roll.

HOW LONG? **20 MINUTES**
HOW MUCH? **4 SERVINGS**

Pronto Panzanella

For added flavor, get an herbed bread, such as rosemary or an olive loaf. But skip sliced sandwich loaves. **You want something rustic and hearty** for this satisfying bread and tomato salad.

6 thick slices sourdough or other rustic bread, cut into 1-inch chunks
6 tablespoons extra-virgin olive oil, divided
6 medium tomatoes, quartered, seeded, and chopped
1 medium cucumber, peeled, seeded, and chopped
1 small red onion, finely chopped
1 teaspoon kosher salt
¼ teaspoon ground black pepper
½ cup loosely packed fresh cilantro, tough stems removed, roughly chopped
2 tablespoons balsamic vinegar

Heat the oven to 400°F.

Place the bread in a large bowl and drizzle it with 3 tablespoons of the olive oil. Toss to coat well, then transfer the bread to a baking sheet. Toast for 10 to 12 minutes, or until lightly browned. Alternatively, the bread could be skewered and grilled briefly to toast.

Return the bread to the bowl. Add the tomatoes, cucumber, and red onion. Toss well.

Sprinkle the salad with salt, pepper, and cilantro, then toss again. Drizzle with the vinegar and remaining oil, toss, then serve.

➲ HOW LONG? **20 MINUTES**
➲ HOW MUCH? **6 SERVINGS**

Pesto-Drenched Tomato Wedges

This recipe makes what may seem like an excessive amount of pesto, but **the idea is to really slosh it over the tomatoes.** You want this salad seriously dressed.

To save time, the pesto can be prepped ahead. But be sure to let it come to room temperature (or nuke it in 10-second bursts until it is about room temperature) before serving it.

2 to 3 large beefsteak or other slicing tomatoes
⅓ cup extra-virgin olive oil
1 cup lightly packed fresh basil leaves
4 cloves garlic
2 tablespoons balsamic vinegar
½ cup grated Parmesan cheese, plus extra block Parmesan
  for shaving
Pinch red pepper flakes
1 teaspoon kosher salt
¼ teaspoon ground black pepper

Cut each tomato into 8 wedges, then arrange the wedges on a platter. Set aside.

In a food processor, combine the oil, basil, garlic, vinegar, Parmesan, red pepper flakes, salt, and pepper. Pulse until mostly smooth. To serve, drizzle the pesto liberally over the tomato wedges. Shave additional Parmesan over the tomatoes.

→ HOW LONG? **10 MINUTES**
→ HOW MUCH? **4 SERVINGS**

BASHING YOUR BASIL

In the rare event that I have extra time (so, about once a year), I like to use a mortar and pestle to make pesto. In addition to being a good upper body workout and a fun way for my son to help (kids love to smash things), pesto made this way has a chunkier texture and fresher taste.

If you're in the market for a mortar and pestle, look for one that has two qualities—size and weight. A small mortar (the bowl) is frustrating because the ingredients constantly shoot out at you. Lightweight models don't stay put on the counter.

I use a large cast-iron mortar and pestle made by Typhoon. You wouldn't want to lug it very far, but it makes fast work of whatever I put in it.

Spinach, Bacon, and Corn Salad

Bacon and its best friend, prosciutto, should be your top go-to meats when you need tons of flavor with little effort. Crisp some of either in a skillet, then add it to salad (potato, pasta, or fresh), soup (just before serving), or mashed vegetables (winter squash or potatoes). Bacon is even good baked into chocolate chip cookies. Trust me.

And, yes, the corn in this salad is eaten raw. Corn does not need to be cooked. It has a sweet, fresh flavor when eaten raw. But if you prefer it cooked, by all means have at it.

> **5 strips bacon**
> **½ cup chopped raw walnuts**
> **Pinch kosher salt**
> **3 ears corn, husked**
> **4 cups baby spinach**
> **¼ cup bottled blue cheese dressing (or Blow-Your-Mind**
> **Blue Cheese Dip on page 17)**

Set a large skillet over medium-high heat. When the pan is hot, add the bacon and cook until crisp, about 8 minutes. Leaving the bacon fat in the skillet, use a slotted spoon to transfer the bacon to paper towels to cool.

Return the skillet to the heat. Add the walnuts and toast, stirring constantly, until lightly browned and fragrant, about 2 minutes. Use a slotted spoon to transfer the walnuts to a bowl, then sprinkle them with salt.

Remove the kernels from the ears of corn. To do this, stand each ear on its wide end and use a serrated knife to saw down the length of the ear. Discard the cobs.

Divide the spinach among 4 serving plates. Top each with a quarter of the corn kernels. Crumble the bacon and divide it between the salads.

Sprinkle the toasted walnuts over the salads, then drizzle with dressing.

⮕ HOW LONG? **20 MINUTES**
⮕ HOW MUCH? **4 SERVINGS**

Warm Potato Salad with Red Onion and Bacon

The beauty of this potato salad is that it's good warm or cold. And **don't hesitate to add whatever you love**—hard-boiled eggs, chopped olives, more veggies, whatever.

Pickle juice (the liquid bread-and-butter pickles are packed in) may seem like an unusual ingredient, but it adds a delicious sweet-and-vinegary tang.

4 pounds red new potatoes
½ cup mayonnaise
¼ cup whole-grain mustard
¼ cup ketchup
¼ cup juices from a jar of bread-and-butter pickles
½ teaspoon ground black pepper
¾ cup diced bread-and-butter pickles
1 cup diced celery
1 small red onion, diced
1 red bell pepper, cored and diced
10 strips bacon

Lightly pierce each potato with a fork, then place it in a large microwave-safe bowl. Microwave on high until cooked through, about 10 minutes (timing will vary by microwave). Set aside to cool slightly.

Meanwhile, in a large bowl, whisk together the mayonnaise, mustard, ketchup, pickle juice, and black pepper. Mix in the pickles, celery, red onion, and bell pepper. Set aside.

Set a large dry skillet over medium-high heat. When the pan is hot, add the bacon and cook until crisp, about 8 minutes. Transfer the bacon to paper towels to drain, then cut or crumble it into small pieces.

When the potatoes are cool enough to handle, cut into large chunks. Add them to the mayonnaise and vegetable mixture, then mix without breaking up the potatoes too much. Sprinkle with bacon and serve.

➲ HOW LONG? **30 MINUTES**
➲ HOW MUCH? **6 SERVINGS**

BBQ Chicken Pasta Salad with Lime and Sour Cream

Not in the mood to clean the meat off a rotisserie chicken? Toss about a pound of boneless, skinless breasts on the grill, then chop them up or pull them apart for use in this **tangy, creamy melding of pasta salad and chicken salad.**

16 ounces bow-tie or spiral pasta
2 cups frozen peas
1 cup frozen corn kernels
1½ cups barbecue sauce
1 teaspoon hot sauce
2 tablespoons lime juice
Meat from 2½-pound rotisserie chicken, cut or
   pulled into bite-size chunks
½ cup sour cream
2 stalks celery, diced
1 medium red onion, diced
1 medium carrot, cut into matchsticks
4 tomatillos, chopped
¼ cup chopped fresh cilantro
Salt and ground black pepper, to taste

Bring a large saucepan of salted water to a boil. Add the pasta and cook according to package directions. During the final 2 minutes, add the peas and corn, stirring to ensure they don't clump together.

Drain the pasta and vegetables, rinse with cool water, then set aside to drain.

In a large bowl, whisk together the barbecue sauce, hot sauce, and lime juice. Add the chicken and toss to coat.

In a second large bowl, combine the sour cream, pasta-and-vegetable mixture, celery, red onion, carrot, tomatillos, and cilantro. Toss well to coat.

Combine all into one bowl, mixing well. Season with salt and pepper.

⟶ HOW LONG? **20 MINUTES**
⟶ HOW MUCH? **12 SERVINGS**

Warm Carrot and Asparagus Salad with Sesame Dressing

Lightly sautéed carrots and asparagus are dressed in a salty, savory dressing made from sesame oil, rice vinegar, and soy sauce. To turn this salad into a meal, add thinly sliced strips of cooked chicken and **call it a stir-fry.**

2 tablespoons sesame oil, divided
2 cloves garlic, minced
Pinch red pepper flakes
1-pound bunch asparagus, bottoms trimmed, cut into
** 2-inch lengths**
10-ounce bag shredded carrots
¼ cup rice vinegar
2 tablespoons soy sauce
2 tablespoons light brown sugar
½ teaspoon ground ginger
2 tablespoons toasted sesame seeds

In a large skillet over medium-high, heat 1 tablespoon of the sesame oil. When the oil is hot, add the garlic and red pepper flakes, then sauté for 30 seconds.

Add the asparagus and carrots, then sauté for 4 to 5 minutes, or until the vegetables are just barely softened. Transfer to a serving bowl.

Return the skillet to the stove, reducing the heat to medium. Add the remaining 1 tablespoon of sesame oil, the rice vinegar, soy sauce, brown sugar, and ginger. Simmer until reduced and thickened, about 3 minutes. Drizzle the dressing over the vegetables, then toss to coat.

Sprinkle the salad with sesame seeds and serve.

➡ HOW LONG? **15 MINUTES**
➡ HOW MUCH? **6 SERVINGS**

SOUPED UP

I suspect my son got a shock the first time he ate dinner at a friend's house. The family probably did something crazy. Like just sat down and ate.

"Where is the guy who takes pictures of your food before you eat it?"

Growing up in the test kitchen of the world's largest news organization has given Parker an odd—some would argue warped—relationship with food.

Not that I mind that the roar of the KitchenAid was all that would lull him during those colicky first six months (not sure why that trick hasn't made the parenting books).

And sure, he asked for (and received) a five-inch santoku knife for his second birthday (like you didn't cave when your kid asked!). And answered "Soup" when asked what he wanted to name a new stuffed animal, a chicken.

You can't help but love a kid who jams to Jimmy Buffett's "Cheeseburger in Paradise" and who was able to write *falafel* before he'd mastered his last name.

Okay, so the kid's a little peculiar.

I do wonder what growing up in the chaos of photo shoots is doing to him. Cooks bustle through the house at all hours, and photographers have been known to use his toys as light baffles while whining about spectral highlights on tomatoes.

"Daddy, when I grow up I want to be a knight and a chef," he explained to me one day. I didn't have the heart to tell him Daddy is so not a chef. Chefs actually know what they're doing.

Despite his culinary precociousness, he still can be a fussy six-year-old. He'll eat wasabi peas and sushi. Devours chimichurri and chicken mole. Has a passion for Parmigiano-Reggiano and prosciutto. And insists on making pasta. From scratch. Yet I can't get the kid to eat soup. On their own, the ingredients get no fight. Add liquid and it's a no-go zone.

Maybe he thinks I'm trying to serve up Soup.

Bread and Tomato Soup

This traditional Italian soup is **hearty enough to be a meal**. But for a thinner soup, stir in chicken broth until it reaches the desired consistency.

2 tablespoons olive oil
1 large yellow onion, diced
4 cloves garlic, minced
2 teaspoons fresh thyme leaves
Three 28-ounce cans diced tomatoes, with juices
2 tablespoons balsamic vinegar
3 cups slightly stale good-quality bread, cubed
  (not sliced sandwich bread)
Salt and ground black pepper, to taste
½ cup fresh basil leaves, torn
½ cup grated Parmesan cheese

In a large pot over medium-high, heat the oil. Add the onion and sauté until just tender, about 4 minutes. Add the garlic and thyme and sauté another 2 minutes.

Add the tomatoes and balsamic vinegar. Bring the mixture to a simmer, stirring frequently. Add the bread, stir, cover the pot, then remove it from the heat. Let stand for 20 minutes.

Uncover the pot and stir well to break up the bread. Season with salt and pepper. Stir in the basil and cheese. Serve the soup hot or chilled.

➡ HOW LONG? **30 MINUTES (10 MINUTES ACTIVE)**
➡ HOW MUCH? **6 SERVINGS**

Cider-Braised Beef Stew

This one's a little longer than most of my recipes, but a lot faster than most beef stews thanks to the cut of beef used. Don't substitute traditional stewing cuts, which are tough and require long simmers to tenderize. Bottom sirloin starts tender and stays that way. Serve this with a crusty baguette to **mop up the juices.**

2 tablespoons olive oil
1 large yellow onion, diced
2 cloves garlic, minced
4 sprigs fresh thyme or 1 teaspoon dried thyme
1 teaspoon smoked paprika
¼ teaspoon ground ginger
2 pounds bottom sirloin or skirt steak, cut into bite-size chunks
1 cup apple cider
2 large carrots, cut into thin rounds
3 small potatoes, cut into small chunks
14½-ounce can diced tomatoes, with juice
1 tablespoon cider vinegar
¼ cup cool water
1½ tablespoons cornstarch
Salt and ground black pepper, to taste

In a large Dutch oven over medium-high heat, combine the oil, onion, garlic, thyme, smoked paprika, and ginger. Sauté until the onion is tender, about 5 minutes.

Add the steak and brown, about 5 minutes. Discard the thyme sprigs. Add the cider, carrots, potatoes, and tomatoes. Stir, then bring to a simmer. Cover and cook until the potatoes are tender, about 25 minutes.

Stir in the cider vinegar. In a small glass, mix together the water and cornstarch, then add it to the stew. Simmer for several minutes, or until the stew thickens. Season with salt and pepper.

➡ HOW LONG? **45 MINUTES (30 MINUTES ACTIVE)**
➡ HOW MUCH? **4 TO 6 SERVINGS**

Shrimp and Tomato Peanut Soup

In southern and western Africa, **peanuts are an important seasoning and thickener.** They often are toasted and ground, then used to add rich, nutty flavor as well as velvety body to stews and soups. In this recipe, we save some effort by using peanut butter. Just be sure to use a natural peanut butter (which means the only ingredients should be peanuts and salt).

2 tablespoons peanut oil
1 large yellow onion, diced
1 green bell pepper, cored and diced
3 cloves garlic, minced
¼ teaspoon red pepper flakes
2 tablespoons grated fresh ginger
28-ounce can diced tomatoes, with juices
1 quart chicken broth
1 cup smooth peanut butter
2 cups baby spinach greens
1 pound raw large shrimp, shells and tails removed
Salt and ground black pepper, to taste
¼ cup chopped fresh cilantro
Chopped peanuts, for garnish

In a large saucepan over medium-high, heat the oil. Add the onion, bell pepper, garlic, red pepper flakes, and ginger. Sauté until the onion and pepper are tender, about 5 minutes.

Add the tomatoes and chicken broth, then bring to a simmer.

Add the peanut butter, stirring until dissolved. Transfer the soup to a blender, in batches if necessary, and puree until mostly smooth. Return the soup to the pot.

Add the spinach and simmer until wilted, about 3 minutes. Add the shrimp and simmer until cooked through, about 5 minutes.

Season with salt and pepper, then stir in the cilantro. Ladle into serving bowls and garnish with peanuts.

➲ HOW LONG? **30 MINUTES**
➲ HOW MUCH? **6 SERVINGS**

Spicy Carrot Bisque

This recipe also works well with other **root vegetables,** such as potatoes, parsnips, and sweet potatoes, as well as butternut and other winter squashes.

2 tablespoons canola or vegetable oil
1½ pounds carrots, cut into small chunks
1 large yellow onion, diced
6 to 8 Peppadew peppers, diced, or about 1 tablespoon
    minced jarred jalapeño peppers
½ teaspoon red pepper flakes
1 quart low-sodium chicken broth
2 to 3 tablespoons chopped fresh dill
½ cup (4 ounces) crème fraîche
Warm milk, if needed, to thin soup
Salt and ground black pepper, to taste

In a medium saucepan over high heat, combine the oil, carrots, onion, Peppadews, and red pepper flakes. Sauté for 5 minutes.

Add the broth and bring to a simmer. Cook until the carrots are tender, about 10 minutes.

Working in batches if necessary, carefully transfer the soup to a blender. Add the dill and crème fraîche, then puree until smooth. The bisque can be thinned by adding warm milk.

Season with salt and pepper.

➡ HOW LONG? **25 MINUTES**
➡ HOW MUCH? **4 TO 6 SERVINGS**

Rosemary and Ginger Vegetable Soup

When you buy real Parmesan cheese (the stuff that comes in chunks, not in a can, tub, or bag), it should have a thick, hard rind on one end. After you've eaten the cheese, keep the rinds in the refrigerator. When you make soups such as this, toss in a piece of rind. **It infuses the soup with deep, savory flavors.** Discard the rind just before serving.

3 tablespoons olive oil
Leaves from 1 large sprig fresh rosemary
2 cloves garlic, minced
2 tablespoons grated fresh ginger
1 large yellow onion, diced
1 green bell pepper, cored and diced
1 red bell pepper, cored and diced
2 carrots, cut into thin rounds
8 ounces (about 2 cups) white button mushrooms, stemmed and quartered
2 medium Yukon Gold potatoes, cut into small cubes
½ small butternut squash, peeled and cut into small chunks
1 quart chicken broth
14½-ounce can crushed tomatoes
Salt and ground black pepper, to taste
4 slightly stale sourdough dinner rolls, cut into cubes

In a medium stockpot, heat the oil over medium heat. Add the rosemary, garlic, and ginger and sauté for 1 minute.

Add the onion, both bell peppers, carrots, mushrooms, potatoes, and squash, then sauté 3 minutes. Add the broth and tomatoes, with juices, and bring to a simmer. Lower the heat, cover the pot, and simmer for 30 minutes, or until the potatoes and squash are tender.

Taste and season with salt and pepper. Ladle the soup into serving bowls and stir a quarter of the bread cubes into each.

➲ HOW LONG? **45 MINUTES (10 MINUTES ACTIVE)**
➲ HOW MUCH? **4 SERVINGS**

Rich Corn Chowder with Prosciutto Crumbles

Simmering the corn cobs in the milk draws out the juices—**and therefore tremendous flavor.** You could skip this and just use frozen kernels, but the effort is well worth it.

4 cups whole milk
7 ears corn, husked
3 tablespoons olive oil, divided
1 large yellow onion, diced
1 large Yukon Gold potato, peeled and diced
½ teaspoon dried thyme
4 cloves garlic, minced
4 slices prosciutto
½ cup heavy cream
Salt and ground black pepper, to taste

In a large saucepan over medium heat, bring the milk to a low simmer.

Meanwhile, cut the kernels from the cobs. To do this, stand each ear on its wide end. Use a serrated knife to saw down the length of the ear. When the milk is warm, add the cobs only and simmer for 10 minutes.

While the cobs simmer, in a large skillet over medium-high heat, combine 2 tablespoons of the oil, the onion, potato, and thyme. Sauté for 8 minutes, or until the potato is tender. Add the garlic and sauté another minute.

Remove the cobs from the milk and discard them. Add the corn kernels and the potato mixture to the milk. Simmer over low for 15 minutes.

Meanwhile, in a large skillet heat the remaining tablespoon of oil over medium-high. Add the prosciutto and cook until crisp, about 4 minutes. Cool, then crumble the prosciutto.

Just before serving, stir the heavy cream into the chowder, then season with salt and pepper. Sprinkle each serving with crumbled prosciutto.

➜ HOW LONG? **35 MINUTES**
➜ HOW MUCH? **6 SERVINGS**

Bacon, Beans, and Beer Chili

Don't be intimidated by the number of ingredients in this recipe. **This sucker comes together in no time** but tastes like you had it on the stove for hours. Blooming the seasonings—cooking them briefly in the bacon fat before adding the other ingredients—intensifies their flavors. To make this chili vegetarian, substitute 3 tablespoons of olive oil for the bacon and use additional canned beans in place of the beef.

The amount of jalapeño peppers I call for produces a mild chili. Adjust to suit your tastes. As for what to do with the other half of the beer… well, you can't let it go to waste, right?

6 strips bacon, cut into 1-inch pieces
1½ teaspoons chili powder
2 teaspoons cumin
1 tablespoon cocoa powder
1 tablespoon smoked paprika
2 teaspoons dried oregano
1½ tablespoons packed brown sugar
1 large yellow onion, diced
2 tablespoons diced jarred jalapeño pepper slices
   (or more or less, to taste)
4 cloves garlic, minced
2 pounds ground beef (85 percent lean)
Half of a 12-ounce bottle amber beer
15-ounce can kidney beans, drained
28-ounce can diced tomatoes, drained
Juice of 1 lime
¼ cup loosely packed fresh cilantro, chopped
Salt and ground black pepper, to taste
Sour cream, to serve

Set a large, heavy stockpot over medium-low heat. When the pot is hot, add the bacon and fry until it renders enough fat to coat the pot.

Add the chili powder, cumin, cocoa powder, smoked paprika, oregano, and brown sugar. Cook, stirring constantly, for 3 minutes.

Add the onion, jalapeños, and garlic, then sauté for 3 minutes. Add the ground beef and sauté for another 5 minutes.

Add the beer, beans, and tomatoes. Bring the chili to a simmer, then reduce the heat to low and cook for 15 minutes, stirring occasionally.

Just before serving, stir in the lime juice and cilantro. Season with salt and pepper, then serve with sour cream.

➔ HOW LONG? **35 MINUTES (20 MINUTES ACTIVE)**
➔ HOW MUCH? **6 SERVINGS**

Broiled Chilled Gazpacho

Broiling may seem an odd step in making a chilled soup, but **it deepens the flavors** by caramelizing the sugars in the vegetables. Cooking the vegetables also eliminates that raw taste that puts some people off gazpacho.

1 large red onion, quartered
15 pitted green olives
15 pitted Kalamata olives
4 large tomatoes, cored and quartered
15-ounce can corn kernels, drained
4 tablespoons extra-virgin olive oil, divided
1 cup tomato juice
1 tablespoon lemon juice
1 clove garlic
¼ cup lightly packed fresh cilantro leaves and
  thin stems, plus additional for garnish
Salt and ground black pepper, to taste
Crème fraîche, for serving (optional)

Position a rack in the middle of the oven and heat it to broil.

On a rimmed baking sheet, combine the onion, both olive varieties, tomatoes, and corn. Add 2 tablespoons of the olive oil, then toss to coat. Broil for 20 minutes, or until lightly browned in spots. Let cool slightly.

In a blender, combine the tomato juice, remaining olive oil, lemon juice, garlic, and cilantro. Puree until nearly smooth. Add the broiled vegetables except for about half of the corn kernels and olives. Pulse until chunky smooth.

Transfer the soup to a large bowl. Roughly chop the remaining olives, then stir those and the remaining corn kernels into the soup. Cover and refrigerate until chilled, 1 to 2 hours.

When ready to serve, season with salt and pepper. Garnish with cilantro and, if desired, a dollop of crème fraîche.

➲ HOW LONG? **2½ HOURS (30 MINUTES ACTIVE)**
➲ HOW MUCH? **4 SERVINGS**

No-Pain Chicken Soup

No long simmers needed for this deeply flavored chicken soup. Browning the chicken—as well as using the darker-meat thighs—keeps the flavor high and the labor low. This soup was a collaborative effort, for which deep gratitude is owed to Chris Kimball, Alton Brown, Barbara Kafka, and a few Jewish grandmothers.

1-ounce package dried porcini mushrooms
½ cup all-purpose flour
1¼ pounds boneless, skinless chicken thighs
2 tablespoons butter
1 tablespoon olive oil
1 large yellow onion, diced
3 large cloves garlic, minced
¼ teaspoon dried thyme
¼ teaspoon dried basil
½ teaspoon chopped fresh rosemary
1½ quarts (6 cups) low-sodium chicken broth
1 cup water
¾ cup frozen peas
2 carrots, cut into thin rounds
½ cup orzo pasta
2 celery stalks, chopped
2 tablespoons chopped fresh flat-leaf parsley
Juice of ½ lemon
Salt and ground black pepper, to taste

Place the mushrooms in a small bowl and fill with enough hot water to cover. Set aside.

Place the flour in a shallow bowl. Cut each chicken thigh in two. Dredge each piece of chicken through the flour to lightly coat on all sides. Set aside.

In a large stockpot over medium-high heat, combine the butter and olive oil. When the oil and butter begin to sizzle, add the chicken and cook, turning as needed, until lightly browned on all sides, 5 to 7 minutes.

Remove the meat from the pot and set aside. Reduce heat to medium and add the onion, garlic, thyme, basil, and rosemary. Sauté until the onions begin to brown, about 6 minutes.

Increase the heat to high and add the broth and water. Bring to a simmer.

Meanwhile, cut the meat into bite-size pieces. Drain the mushrooms, discarding the water, and squeeze any liquid from them.

When the broth is simmering, lower the heat to medium-high and add the chicken, mushrooms, peas, and carrots. Return the soup to a simmer and cook until the carrots are tender, about 5 minutes.

Add the orzo and celery and cook until the pasta is just tender, about another 5 minutes. Stir in the parsley and lemon juice, then season with salt and pepper.

➔ HOW LONG? **50 MINUTES**
➔ HOW MUCH? **6 TO 8 SERVINGS**

Lemon Grass and White Bean Turkey Chili

Lemon grass, which has a pleasant sour-lemon flavor and aroma, is sold in the produce section. It resembles a long, yellow scallion and has a woody texture. Treat it like a bay leaf—add it to a soup, chili, or casserole, **let it simmer to infuse the dish,** then fish it out and discard it. Before adding lemon grass to a dish, cut it into 2- to 3-inch-long chunks and gently bruise them with a rolling pin to break up the fibers.

**15-inch stalk lemon grass, cut into 4 segments
   and gently crushed
2 tablespoons olive oil
1 tablespoon diced jarred jalapeño pepper slices
1 large yellow onion, diced
3 cloves garlic, minced
½ teaspoon chili powder
1 teaspoon ground cumin
½ teaspoon cinnamon
1 teaspoon smoked paprika
14-ounce can coconut milk
1 cup chicken broth
1¼ pounds ground turkey (chicken or lean beef
   could be substituted)
15-ounce can cannellini beans, drained
4 cups lightly packed baby spinach
Salt and ground black pepper, to taste**

In a large saucepan or medium Dutch oven over medium-high heat, combine the lemon grass, olive oil, jalapeños, onion, garlic, chili powder, cumin, cinnamon, and smoked paprika. Sauté for 3 minutes.

Add the coconut milk, broth, turkey, and beans. Bring to a simmer, then cover, reduce heat to low, and cook for 20 minutes. Discard the lemon grass. Add the spinach and stir for 1 minute, or until it wilts. Season with salt and pepper.

➲ HOW LONG? **35 MINUTES (15 MINUTES ACTIVE)**
➲ HOW MUCH? **4 SERVINGS**

Creamy Sun-Dried Tomato and Thyme Soup

This recipe is based on one **I slurped almost daily** when I lived in Germany as a child. It was so rich and creamy and utterly tomatoey, I insisted on having it as my afternoon snack anytime I wasn't having my first choice, a giant mug of chocolate milk accompanied by liverwurst spread thick on crusty bread. Yeah, it's a little messed up.

The baking soda in this soup keeps the dairy from curdling. Fresh oregano, basil, and marjoram are great herb additions.

2 tablespoons olive oil
1 large yellow onion, diced
4 cloves garlic, minced
2 teaspoons fresh thyme leaves
28-ounce can crushed tomatoes
6 oil-packed sun-dried tomatoes, roughly chopped
2 tablespoons balsamic vinegar
½ teaspoon baking soda
1 cup half-and-half (fat-free also works)
Salt and ground black pepper, to taste

In a large saucepan over medium-high, heat the oil. Add the onion and sauté until just tender, about 4 minutes. Add the garlic and thyme and sauté another 2 minutes.

Add the crushed tomatoes and their juice, sun-dried tomatoes, and balsamic vinegar. Bring to a simmer, stirring frequently. Reduce heat to low and stir in the baking soda. Add the half-and-half, stir well, and bring to a simmer. Do not boil.

Carefully transfer the soup, in batches if necessary, to a blender and puree until smooth.

Season with salt and pepper.

➥ HOW LONG? **25 MINUTES**
➥ HOW MUCH? **4 SERVINGS**

I've been dreading this for several years, but it's time to come clean and come out of the closet. Mom doesn't know. She probably won't like it. My wife does know. She does like it.

I'm talking about meat. The animal type. I eat it.

A ho-hum revelation except that my first cookbook won 2004 book of the year from People for the Ethical Treatment of Animals. It was vegan. I was vegan.

Now I'm not. In a big way. And this book most definitely isn't. (Have you seen how much bacon and prosciutto I call for?)

The Associated Press is to blame.

Six years ago, my job changed. I went from doing a weekly vegetarian cooking column to overseeing food coverage for the AP. And since part of the job is developing recipes that appear in your local newspaper, staying the vegan course suddenly seemed a career hazard.

So I embraced meat. In a really big way. As in we recently hosted a pig roast party.

Not a big deal, except that I wrote that first book with Mom, who has been vegetarian since before I was born. I didn't have the heart to break it to her.

And so for the past few years, I haven't lied, but I also haven't confessed. She hasn't asked how I abstain while running a department responsible for everything from July Fourth burgers and Thanksgiving turkey to Easter ham and Christmas goose.

Willful ignorance meets passive deception? Sorry, Mom.

Head Case Pesto Chicken

This one is named for the head of garlic used in the pesto, which doubles as marinade and sauce.

This is a great dish to prepare in the morning and let marinate all day. The pesto can even be made a day ahead. Serve the chicken with plenty of pasta or rice to sop up the sauce.

If you have the time and own a mortar and pestle, use it instead of the food processor to make the pesto. The flavor is better, and **bashing garlic is oddly therapeutic.**

1 small head garlic (about 8 cloves), peeled
½ cup extra-virgin olive oil, plus 2 tablespoons for frying
1 cup packed fresh basil leaves
1 teaspoon kosher salt
⅛ teaspoon ground black pepper
2 tablespoons balsamic vinegar
½ cup grated Parmesan cheese
Pinch red pepper flakes
1½ pounds chicken breasts
1 cup all-purpose flour
4 tablespoons (½ stick) butter

In a food processor, combine the garlic, ½ cup of olive oil, basil, salt, black pepper, vinegar, Parmesan, and red pepper flakes. Pulse until chunky smooth.

Transfer half of the pesto to a glass or stainless-steel baking dish. Cover the remaining pesto and refrigerate until ready to serve.

One at a time, lay each breast on the counter and carefully slice across the center horizontally to create 2 thin halves. Place each half between sheets of plastic wrap and use a meat mallet, rolling pin, or heavy skillet to pound it to an even cutlet about ¼ inch thick.

Place the chicken in the baking dish with the pesto, turning it to coat. Cover and refrigerate it for at least 30 minutes, or up to 8 hours.

When ready to cook, remove the reserved pesto from the refrigerator and let it come to room temperature.

continued on next page

Place the flour in a wide, shallow bowl. Use a fork to lift each piece of chicken from the marinade and dredge it through the flour, lightly coating both sides.

In a large skillet over medium-high heat, combine the butter and remaining 2 tablespoons olive oil. Heat until the butter is melted and sizzling.

Several pieces at a time, fry the chicken until lightly browned, 2 to 3 minutes. Turn and fry for another 2 to 3 minutes, or until cooked through. Repeat with remaining chicken.

To serve, drizzle the chicken with the reserved pesto.

➡ HOW LONG? **1 HOUR (20 MINUTES ACTIVE)**
➡ HOW MUCH? **4 SERVINGS**

Deep-Dish Pesto and Prosciutto Tortilla Pizza

This fantastically easy rethinking of deep-dish pizza is **totally over the top in flavor.** Instead of piling toppings onto a single thick crust, this version layers them within a stack of flour tortillas. Adding pesto and tomato sauce creates a truly intense pie.

While the toppings called for are a great combination, substitute at will. Just be certain everything you use is very thinly sliced; this keeps your sky-high pie from toppling over.

**7 large (about 10-inch) flour tortillas
1 cup prepared tomato or pasta sauce
6 slices prosciutto (or deli-sliced turkey breast or ham)
1 small red onion, very thinly sliced
3 cups (two 6-ounce packages) shredded cheddar cheese
3 cups (two 6-ounce packages) shredded mozzarella cheese
7-ounce package prepared pesto
1 large red bell pepper, cored and very thinly sliced
3.8-ounce can sliced black olives**

Heat the oven to 350°F. Coat a baking sheet with cooking spray.

Place 1 flour tortilla in the center of the baking sheet. Spoon a third of the tomato sauce evenly over the tortilla, then top with 2 slices of prosciutto and a third of the sliced onion.

Sprinkle a bit less than ½ cup of each cheese over the pizza. Place a second tortilla on top and gently press the tortilla to compress and flatten it. This helps the pizza stack evenly.

Spoon a third of the pesto over the tortilla, then top with a third each of the sliced pepper and black olives. Top with more cheese, then another tortilla, pressing gently again.

Repeat with remaining ingredients, alternating the fillings for a total of 6 layers (3 of each), gently pressing the stacked tortillas before adding each new layer.

continued on next page

Top with a final tortilla, a bit more tomato sauce or pesto and the remaining cheese.

Bake on the center rack for 35 minutes, checking frequently during the final 5 to 10 minutes to make sure the top doesn't burn. If the top browns too quickly, tent it with foil.

Remove the pizza from the oven and let it stand for 5 minutes. Use a sharp knife to cut the pizza as you would a pie.

➔ HOW LONG? **45 MINUTES (10 MINUTES ACTIVE)**
➔ HOW MUCH? **6 SERVINGS**

Panko-Crusted Salmon Croquettes

Adding smoked salmon to the canned salmon deepens the savory flavors of these croquettes. Smoked trout, finely diced cooked shrimp, or chopped crabmeat could be substituted.

This recipe is a great way to use up leftover mashed potatoes. If you don't have any, just nuke 1 large or 2 medium baking potatoes, then mash them (skin and all) with some butter.

Resist the temptation to add salt while preparing these; the ingredients have enough.

14-ounce can salmon, picked over to remove any bones
4-ounce package smoked salmon
1 cup mashed potatoes
½ cup peas (thawed if frozen)
Zest of 1 lemon
1 tablespoon Dijon mustard
1 tablespoon hot sauce
¼ teaspoon ground black pepper
3 tablespoons chopped fresh flat-leaf parsley
1 cup panko (Japanese-style) breadcrumbs
Tartar sauce, for serving

Flake both salmons into a large bowl. Add the mashed potatoes, peas, lemon zest, mustard, hot sauce, pepper, and parsley. Mix well, then use your hands to form into 8 patties.

Spread the breadcrumbs on a plate. Set each patty into the crumbs, turning to coat both sides.

Coat a medium skillet with cooking spray and set it over medium heat. Add the patties, 2 or 3 at a time, and cook for 4 minutes per side, or until they are lightly browned. Serve with tartar sauce.

➔ HOW LONG? **20 MINUTES**
➔ HOW MUCH? **8 CROQUETTES**

Garlic-Lime Steak with Avocado Salsa

The goal here was to make a steak that was **mouth-puckeringly savory**. The secret ingredients are lime zest and soy sauce. This steak and salsa combo is wonderful as is, or nestled in a warm flour tortilla.

¼ cup extra-virgin olive oil
Juice and grated zest of 1 lime
¼ cup seasoned rice vinegar or cider vinegar
1 teaspoon soy sauce
2 teaspoons garlic powder
¼ teaspoon ground black pepper
1 pound flank steak, cut against the grain into ½-inch strips
1 avocado, peeled, pitted, and cubed
1 tablespoon chopped fresh cilantro
2 cloves garlic, minced
Salt, to taste

In a medium bowl, whisk together the olive oil, lime juice and zest, vinegar, soy sauce, garlic powder, and pepper. Set aside 2 tablespoons of the mixture.

Add the steak to the bowl and toss to coat. Cover and set aside for 15 minutes.

Meanwhile, in a small bowl, gently toss together the avocado, cilantro, garlic, and reserved 2 tablespoons of the lime marinade. Mix well, then season with salt. Set aside.

Heat the grill to medium-high and coat the racks with oil or cooking spray.

Grill the steak slices just until grill marks appear, 1 to 2 minutes per side. Arrange the steak on a serving platter and serve topped with the avocado salsa.

➲ HOW LONG? **30 MINUTES**
➲ HOW MUCH? **4 SERVINGS**

Chicken Satay with Peanut Sauce

Chicken satay also makes great party food and can be marinated up to 12 hours in advance.

Change it up by using country-style pork ribs instead of chicken. Just cut the ribs lengthwise into thin strips. And either meat can be broiled instead of grilled. Broil on the oven's middle rack for about 5 minutes, turning the skewers halfway through.

If you use bamboo skewers, be sure to soak them in water for about 30 minutes before threading the meat to prevent them from burning.

¼ cup soy sauce
¼ cup rice vinegar
2 tablespoons toasted sesame oil
¾ cup water, divided
1-inch chunk fresh ginger
2 cloves garlic
½ to 1 teaspoon hot sauce
1 scallion, roughly chopped
3 tablespoons honey
½ cup smooth peanut butter
12 boneless, skinless chicken breast tenders
  (about 1⅓ pounds)
2 tablespoons toasted sesame seeds

In a blender, combine the soy sauce, vinegar, sesame oil, ¼ cup of the water, ginger, garlic, hot sauce, scallion, honey, and peanut butter. Blend until smooth.

Remove ½ cup of the peanut sauce; cover and set it aside. Add the remaining ½ cup of water to the blender and puree until smooth. Set aside.

Thread each chicken tender onto a skewer. Arrange the skewers to lie flat in a large baking dish. Add the peanut sauce from the blender and turn the skewers so that all of the chicken is coated. Refrigerate for 20 minutes.

Once the chicken has marinated, coat a grill or grill pan with cooking spray and heat it to high. Place the chicken on the grill or in the pan and sear for 2 to 3 minutes.

Reduce the heat to medium and turn the skewers to cook for another 2 minutes on the other side. Transfer the skewers to a serving platter and sprinkle them with sesame seeds.

Serve the skewers with the reserved peanut sauce for dipping.

➡ HOW LONG? **30 MINUTES (15 MINUTES ACTIVE)**
➡ HOW MUCH? **4 SERVINGS**

DRINK UP!

Trashy Sangria

All the bold, fruity, winey flavor of sangria, but none of the work. This is what I sip—okay, gulp—while at the grill. Make it by the glass, pitcher, or trough. And don't break the bank when buying the wine. A South African or Australian red for five or ten dollars a bottle works nicely.

1 teaspoon lime juice
1½ tablespoons sugar
6 ounces red wine
Ice

In a serving glass, mix together the lime juice and sugar. Add the wine and stir until the sugar is dissolved. Add the ice.

➡ HOW LONG? **5 MINUTES**
➡ HOW MUCH? **1 SERVING**

Child's Play Spice and Brown Sugar–Rubbed Pork Tenderloin

This intensely savory pork came about thanks to child's play. Literally.

My son likes to help during photo shoots, so I'll sometimes let him mix whatever he can grab from the spice cabinet. One afternoon Parker came up with a mélange of salt, brown sugar, pink peppercorns, rosemary, and a few other seasonings.

One of my test kitchen cooks gave it a whiff. Then I did. **We were floored. It smelled unbelievably good** and was just begging to be rubbed on pork.

So we tried it on pork tenderloins, using half of the mixture as a brine and the other half as a rub. The pork was outstanding, especially when drizzled with a truffle nut vinaigrette the cook concocted to complement Parker's rub. Talk about teamwork.

It took some trial and error to figure out the ingredients and proportions Parker had used (we hadn't watched him closely when he made his batch), but with a magnifying glass and some tasting, we eventually sorted it out.

The pork can be brined for up to about 6 hours, and doing so produces an insanely moist and flavorful loin. But to save time you also can skip the brining entirely. Just use half of the spice blend as the rub and proceed with the recipe.

There is little hands-on work involved here, and the flavor is so intense you will be blown away. It's worth it.

FOR THE SEASONING BLEND:
⅔ cup brown sugar
4 tablespoons pink peppercorns
1 tablespoon salt
2 teaspoons dried oregano
2 teaspoons dried rosemary
1 teaspoon cinnamon
1 tablespoon black sesame seeds
2 teaspoons dried diced onion
2 teaspoons dried parsley

FOR THE BRINE:
3 cups water
¼ cup kosher salt
½ cup brown sugar
3 cups ice

FOR THE PORK LOINS:
Two 12-ounce pork tenderloins, silver skin removed
2 large yellow onions, diced

1 recipe Truffle Nut Vinaigrette (page 80)

To make the seasoning blend, in a small bowl combine all ingredients. Transfer half of the mixture to a large saucepan. Set aside the remaining seasoning blend.

To make the brine, add the water, salt, and brown sugar to the seasoning blend in the saucepan. Set the pan over high heat and boil until the sugar and salt dissolve. Remove from the heat, then add the ice and stir until cooled.

Place the pork in a large zip-close bag. Pour the brine over it, then seal the bag and refrigerate for 3 to 6 hours.

When ready to cook, heat the oven to 375°F.

Remove the pork from the brine, patting it dry with paper towels. Rub the reserved dry seasoning blend over both tenderloins.

Scatter the onions over the bottom of a roasting pan, then set the pork over them. Roast for about 30 minutes, or until the tenderloins reach 145°F at the center.

While the pork is roasting make the vinaigrette (recipe follows).

Let the pork rest in the roasting pan for 15 minutes before cutting into thin slices. Serve over the roasted onions and drizzled with truffle-nut vinaigrette.

➲ HOW LONG? **4 HOURS (20 MINUTES ACTIVE)**
➲ HOW MUCH? **4 SERVINGS**

Truffle Nut Vinaigrette

This is the most intense vinaigrette you will ever taste. You won't be able to stop eating it. If you're not in the mood for pork, skip the recipe above and drizzle it over roasted butternut squash and potatoes for a winter salad.

3 tablespoons cider vinegar
1 tablespoon Dijon mustard
1 teaspoon coarse salt
¼ teaspoon ground black pepper
4 tablespoons canola or vegetable oil
4 tablespoons white truffle–flavored olive oil
¼ cup finely chopped mixed nuts such as walnuts, pecans,
   and almonds, but not peanuts

In a food processor or blender, combine the vinegar, mustard, salt, and pepper. With the processor or blender on, slowly drizzle in both oils to create an emulsion.

Transfer the mixture to a small bowl and mix in the nuts.

➲ HOW LONG? **5 MINUTES**
➲ HOW MUCH? **ABOUT ¾ CUP**

KITCHEN PLAY

Want to buy yourself some peace during dinner prep? Buy some inexpensive spices. While I always want my son to feel welcome in the kitchen, sometimes I just need to get dinner going. That's when I break out his spice kit. I stock it with inexpensive dollar-store finds, as well as older spices purged from my own collection. I give him a whisk and a bowl, set him up across the cutting board from me, then let him go. More often than not, I've been amazed by the delicious seasoning blends he comes up with. When he has a hit, I try to work it into the next meal. Sometimes I mix his blend with breadcrumbs, then dredge chicken in it. Or I use it (and a bit of olive oil) to season butternut squash for roasting. Everyone wins. He has fun, I get to focus on dinner, and he feels he is contributing.

Lamb Kofta with Tzatziki

Adding cinnamon to savory foods is the norm in much of the world, and for good reason. It provides a **gentle warmth,** as in these Middle Eastern–style meatballs.

Tzatziki is a garlicky yogurt sauce seasoned with fresh dill. It goes great with grilled and broiled meats. Most grocers sell it next to the hummus. To make your own, mix plain Greek-style yogurt with minced garlic, chopped fresh dill, a bit of peeled and diced cucumber, a spritz of lemon juice, salt, and pepper.

Lamb not your thing? Ground beef or turkey work just as well.

2 slices white bread, lightly toasted
1 medium yellow onion, quartered
½ cup loosely packed fresh flat-leaf parsley
¼ cup loosely packed fresh mint
2 cloves garlic
½ teaspoon cumin
½ teaspoon cinnamon
½ teaspoon chili powder
½ teaspoon salt
¼ teaspoon ground black pepper
1 tablespoon grated fresh ginger
½ tablespoon Thai red curry paste (page 190)
2 large eggs
1¼ pounds ground lamb
4 large prepared or homemade flatbreads
Tzatziki or plain yogurt
Chopped fresh tomatoes (optional)
Diced fresh cucumber (optional)

Place a rack in the middle position of the oven. Heat the oven to broil.

Lightly coat a rimmed baking sheet with cooking spray.

In a food processor, pulse the bread until it forms fine crumbs. Add the onion, parsley, mint, garlic, cumin, cinnamon, chili powder, salt, pepper, ginger, red curry paste, and eggs.

Pulse again until the onion and herbs are finely chopped. Transfer the

mixture to a large bowl. Add the lamb and use your hands to thoroughly mash everything together.

Shape the mixture into 1½- to 2-inch balls and arrange them on the prepared baking sheet.

Lightly spray the kofta with cooking spray. Broil for 8 minutes, then use tongs to rotate each kofta and broil for an additional 8 minutes.

Remove the kofta from the oven and let stand for 5 minutes.

Meanwhile, turn off the broiler. Wrap the flatbread in foil and place it in the still-hot oven for 1 to 2 minutes, or until warmed.

Arrange 4 kofta down the center of each flatbread, then top them with tzatziki. If desired, scatter tomatoes and cucumber over all.

➡ HOW LONG? **40 MINUTES (20 MINUTES ACTIVE)**
➡ HOW MUCH? **4 SERVINGS**

Mustard-Thyme Chicken with White Wine Pan Sauce

The acidic flavor of mustard adds a nice tang to the coating on these chicken cutlets. That same acid acts as a nice tenderizer, so if you have extra time, let the chicken marinate in the mustard mixture for 30 minutes or so.

2 tablespoons Dijon mustard
1 tablespoon mayonnaise
Salt
1 egg
1 teaspoon garlic powder
¼ teaspoon ground black pepper
1 cup panko (Japanese-style) breadcrumbs
1½ teaspoons dried thyme, divided
1¼ pounds thin-cut boneless, skinless chicken breasts
2 tablespoons olive oil
2 tablespoons butter, divided
¼ cup white wine
¾ cup chicken broth
1 tablespoon cornstarch
1 tablespoon cool water
2 tablespoons heavy cream
Ground black pepper, to taste

Heat the oven to 350°F.

In a wide, shallow bowl, whisk together the mustard, mayonnaise, ½ teaspoon salt, egg, garlic powder, and black pepper. In a second wide, shallow bowl, mix the panko and 1 teaspoon of the thyme.

Use paper towels to pat the chicken dry. Dredge each piece through the mustard mixture, turning it to coat both sides, then do the same with the breadcrumbs. Set the breaded chicken pieces aside.

In a large skillet over medium-high heat, combine the olive oil and 1 tablespoon of the butter. When they are sizzling, add the chicken, in batches if necessary. Cook for 2 to 3 minutes, then flip the chicken and cook another 2 to 3 minutes, or until evenly browned on both sides.

Transfer the chicken to an oven-safe plate and place it in the oven to finish cooking.

Return the skillet to the heat and add the wine and broth to deglaze. Use a silicone spatula to scrape up any bits stuck to the bottom of the pan. Swirl in the remaining tablespoon of butter. Add the remaining thyme.

In a small glass, mix the cornstarch and water. Add the mixture to the skillet, then heat, stirring constantly, until the sauce thickens, about 2 minutes. Stir in the cream, then season with salt and pepper.

Serve the chicken with the pan sauce drizzled over it.

HOW LONG? **20 MINUTES**
HOW MUCH? **4 SERVINGS**

Chicken Mole

The sauce in this traditional Mexican dish is **unbelievably rich and mildly spicy,** thanks to a blend of garlic, cinnamon, cocoa powder, red pepper flakes, and almond butter (think peanut butter, but made from almonds). It begs for mounds of rice to sop it up.

The recipe is adapted from several by Chicago chef Rick Bayless, the man who has given Mexican cuisines the respectability they deserve. And several years ago at his Frontera Grill restaurant, he served me the best meal of my life.

2 tablespoons canola or vegetable oil
1 medium yellow onion, diced
6 garlic cloves, minced
¼ teaspoon ground cloves
½ teaspoon cinnamon
¼ teaspoon ground black pepper
½ teaspoon red pepper flakes
1 tablespoon cocoa powder
1 cup smooth almond butter
1 cup canned crushed tomatoes
2 cups chicken broth
¼ teaspoon salt
1 slice soft white bread, cut into small pieces
1½ pounds boneless, skinless chicken breasts,
    cut into ½-inch chunks

In a Dutch oven over medium-high heat, combine the oil, onion, garlic, cloves, cinnamon, black pepper, red pepper flakes, and cocoa powder. Sauté for 5 minutes.

Add the almond butter and mix until it melts into the other ingredients. Add the tomatoes, broth, salt, and bread and bring to a simmer. Add the chicken and return to a simmer.

Cover the pot and cook for 12 to 15 minutes, or until the chicken is cooked through.

➲ HOW LONG? **30 MINUTES**
➲ HOW MUCH? **4 TO 6 SERVINGS**

Peppery Pumpkin Risotto

A faster version of this dish can be made as a faux risotto by using orzo pasta in place of the rice. You'll need only about half the liquid called for in the recipe.

And while many traditional risotto recipes call for heating the broth before using it, I find this unnecessary. **As long as your broth is room temperature**, it's fine.

2 tablespoons olive oil
2 tablespoons butter
1 medium yellow onion, diced
1¾ cups Arborio rice
1 tablespoon grated fresh ginger
Pinch cayenne pepper
½ cup white wine
1 quart chicken or vegetable broth, plus extra, if needed
15-ounce can pumpkin puree
1 cup grated Parmesan cheese
Salt and ground black pepper, to taste

In a large skillet over medium heat, combine the oil, butter, and onion. Sauté until the onion is soft, about 5 minutes.

Add the rice, ginger, and cayenne; sauté for 1 minute. Increase the heat to medium-high and add the wine. Stir constantly until the wine has been absorbed.

Add half of the broth, stir once, then simmer until the liquid is mostly absorbed, about 7 minutes. Continue adding broth ½ cup at a time, stirring frequently and adding more liquid as it is absorbed. Once the rice has absorbed all the broth, reduce the heat to medium-low.

Taste to check the texture. The rice should be firm but cooked through. If it is too hard or dry, add additional broth, ½ cup at a time.

When the rice is ready, stir in the pumpkin. Cook, stirring constantly, for 3 minutes. Stir in the cheese, then season with salt and pepper.

➲ HOW LONG? **40 MINUTES**
➲ HOW MUCH? **6 SERVINGS**

Anchovy Butter Chicken with Fettuccine

Anchovies and Parmesan cheese are a powerful duo in Italy. When heated, anchovies melt away, leaving a deep savory, salty flavor without any fishiness.

Not in the mood for pasta? Toss some mozzarella cheese on the chicken pieces after they come out of the pan, pop them under the broiler for a minute, then slap them onto a bun.

½ cup (1 stick) butter, softened
4 oil-packed anchovies
Pinch red pepper flakes
2 boneless, skinless chicken breasts, each cut horizontally
   through the center into 2 thin halves
Ground black pepper, to taste
¼ cup all-purpose flour
½ tablespoon garlic powder
12-ounce package fresh fettuccine
2 tablespoons chopped fresh flat-leaf parsley
2 cloves garlic, minced
Parmesan cheese, for grating

Heat the oven to 200°F.

Bring a large pot of salted water to a boil.

In a food processor, combine the butter, anchovies, and red pepper flakes. Process until smooth, scraping down the sides of the bowl as needed. Set aside.

One at a time, place each piece of chicken between sheets of plastic wrap. Use a meat mallet or rolling pin to gently pound each piece to an even thickness of about ¼ inch.

Season each piece of chicken with black pepper.

In a wide, shallow bowl, whisk together the flour and garlic powder. Dredge the chicken through the flour, lightly coating both sides of each piece. Set aside.

In a large skillet over medium-high heat, melt a quarter of the anchovy butter. When the butter is bubbling, add 2 pieces of chicken and cook until lightly browned on the bottom, about 3 minutes. Turn and brown on the other side, another 3 minutes, or until cooked through.

Transfer the chicken to an oven-safe plate, cover it with foil, then place it in the oven to keep warm. Repeat with the remaining 2 pieces of chicken and another quarter of the butter.

Add the pasta to the boiling water and cook according to package directions. Drain and return it to the pot and add the remaining anchovy butter, tossing until it melts and coats the pasta.

Add the parsley and garlic, then toss again.

Divide the pasta among 4 serving plates. Slice each piece of chicken into thin strips, then distribute them among the plates. Top with grated Parmesan cheese.

➔ HOW LONG? **30 MINUTES**
➔ HOW MUCH? **4 SERVINGS**

POWDER POWER

I'm a big believer in fresh garlic (I even use an entire head of it in some recipes, such as Head Case Pesto Chicken on page 69). But powdered garlic has a place in my kitchen, too. When I'm working with lots of fresh veggies and herbs, or roasting meats, fresh cloves are where it's at. But when I'm doing sauces or coatings (such as breading for chicken or dry rubs for pork), powdered garlic is a must. It provides a more even and gentle flavor. And in the case of coating and rubs, it simply mixes and adheres better to the food.

Toasted Cumin and
Rosemary-Rubbed Lamb Chops

Other than overcooking, there's not much you can do to mess up lamb chops. And that makes them perfect for busy weeknights. Rub some seasoning on them, toss them in a pan with a bit of oil, and about 8 minutes later you've got dinner.

Use your imagination when it comes to the seasoning blend. Toss black peppercorns, red pepper flakes, and kosher salt into a spice grinder for a rub with kick. Or try cinnamon, black pepper, cumin, and paprika.

2 tablespoons cumin seeds
1 teaspoon kosher salt
¼ teaspoon whole black peppercorns
2 sprigs fresh rosemary, leaves only, finely minced
8 lamb chops
2 tablespoons vegetable or canola oil, divided

In a small, dry skillet over medium-low heat, combine the cumin seeds, salt, and peppercorns. Toast, stirring constantly, until fragrant, about 1 minute. Transfer the spice mix to a mortar and pestle or spice grinder. Pound or grind to a coarse powder.

In a small bowl, combine the cumin mixture and the minced rosemary. Mix well, then set aside.

Use paper towels to pat the lamb chops dry. Rub a bit of the cumin-rosemary mixture over both sides of each chop.

In a large skillet over medium-high, heat the oil. Add the lamb chops and cook until browned on the bottom, 3 to 4 minutes. Flip the meat and cook for another 3 to 4 minutes.

➡ HOW LONG? **20 MINUTES**
➡ HOW MUCH? **4 SERVINGS**

Chili Balsamic Marinated Sirloin with Fettuccine and Sun-Dried Tomatoes

I love the sharp bite of freshly ground peppercorns, especially on tender sirloin. But when you load on the pepper, **it's important to balance the flavor with something sweet.** In this case, that role falls to balsamic vinegar, which is sweetly acidic. For good measure, I also toss in a bit of hot sauce and sugar.

¼ cup balsamic vinegar
2 tablespoons olive oil
1 tablespoon sriracha chili sauce (or other hot sauce)
½ teaspoon kosher salt
1 tablespoon black peppercorns (or a blend), roughly crushed
1 tablespoon sugar
1¼ pounds sirloin steak, trimmed of fat and cut into thin strips
3 cloves garlic, minced
12-ounce jar roasted red peppers, cut into thin strips
Half of a 7-ounce jar julienne-cut sun-dried tomatoes
16 ounces fettuccine pasta
2 tablespoons canola or vegetable oil
1 cup grated Parmesan cheese, plus extra for shaving

In a medium bowl, whisk together the vinegar, olive oil, sriracha, salt, peppercorns, and sugar. Add the steak, mixing to coat well. Set aside to marinate for 15 minutes.

In a second medium bowl, combine the garlic, red peppers, and sun-dried tomatoes. Mix well, then set aside.

Bring a large pot of salted water to a boil. Add the pasta and cook according to package directions.

When the pasta is nearly finished, in a large sauté pan over medium-high, heat the canola oil. When the oil is hot, remove the steak from the marinade (discard the marinade) and, working in batches if necessary, cook the strips for 1 to 1½ minutes per side.

Transfer the steak to a plate and cover it with foil. Return the pan to the heat and add the red pepper and sun-dried tomato mixture. Toss until heated through.

When the pasta is cooked, drain and add it to the pepper mixture. Toss well, then add the grated cheese and toss until melted. Serve topped with steak strips and additional shavings of Parmesan.

➲ HOW LONG? **30 MINUTES**
➲ HOW MANY? **4 SERVINGS**

Doro Wat Chicken

I've been told that in Ethiopia men don't make doro wat, the national dish of slowly simmered chicken. But **I've never been one for glass ceilings**, or for food that takes particularly long to make. So, under the influence of testosterone, I came up with this much faster, but still impressively flavorful, variation.

Berbere (an Ethiopian spice blend that contains garlic, red pepper, cardamom, coriander, and various other spices) and fenugreek (a slightly bitter, celery-tasting spice common to curries) are a bit esoteric, but give doro wat its authentic taste. If you have trouble finding them, leave them out and up the smoked paprika to 1½ tablespoons. The taste won't be quite the same, but it will still be delicious. My favorite online source for berbere, as well as so many other awesome spices, is Kalustyan's in New York (www.kalustyans.com).

And be sure to serve this with warm flatbread or pita pockets. Most Ethiopian foods, even stews, are consumed by using bread (not spoons) to scoop the food.

**1¼ pounds boneless, skinless chicken breasts,
  cut into 1-inch chunks
Juice of 1 lemon
Kosher salt
2 tablespoons butter
2 medium yellow onions, diced
2 cloves garlic, minced
1 tablespoon grated fresh ginger
1 teaspoon turmeric
¼ teaspoon ground fenugreek
¼ teaspoon ground cardamom
⅛ teaspoon ground nutmeg
1 to 2 tablespoons berbere, depending on
  desired spiciness
1 tablespoon smoked paprika
¼ cup red wine
¾ cup water
Ground black pepper, to taste**

Place the chicken on a large plate and drizzle it with the lemon juice, then sprinkle it with salt. Set aside.

In a medium Dutch oven over medium heat, melt the butter. Add the onions, garlic, ginger, turmeric, fenugreek, cardamom, nutmeg, berbere, and smoked paprika.

Sauté until the onions are tender, about 5 minutes.

Add the wine and water, mixing well, and bring to a simmer. Add the chicken to the pot, turning it to coat it with sauce, and return to a simmer. Cover the pot, reduce the heat to low, and simmer for 15 minutes, or until the chicken is cooked through.

Uncover the pot and simmer for another 3 minutes to reduce the sauce. Season with salt and pepper.

➲ HOW LONG? **30 MINUTES (10 MINUTES ACTIVE)**
➲ HOW MUCH? **4 SERVINGS**

NO-WHINE WINE

My life doesn't leave much room for affectations. Wine, for example. I love it, but I don't sweat it. Which means I'm happy to sip, slurp, or chug it from tumblers, recycled jam jars, sometimes even a wineglass. I'll use a sippy cup if that's all I've got. I don't expend much thought on whether my "stemware" has the right "bowl" for the wine.

I'm equally laid back when it comes to pairing food and wine. I drink what I like and eat what I want. Sometimes they are wonderful together. Sometimes they merely tolerate each other. Either way, I got food and wine I like, so I'm pretty happy. And that is about as complicated as it needs to be.

Red Curry Beef

Think of this as a **Thai-inspired sloppy joe.** I usually serve this seriously seasoned ground beef over rice, but it's traditionally eaten scooped into lettuce leaves. If your style is more along the Manwich lines, spoon it onto a bun or baguette.

> 1 cup long-grain white rice
> 1½ cups water
> 2 tablespoons canola oil
> 1½ tablespoons Thai red curry paste (page 190)
> 1 tablespoon soy sauce
> 1 tablespoon sugar
> 1 pound lean ground beef
> ¼ cup coconut milk
> 6 scallions, thinly sliced
> 5-ounce bag baby spinach
> Juice and grated zest of ½ lime
> ½ cup shredded fresh basil
> ½ cup crushed unsalted peanuts, for garnish

In a medium saucepan, combine the rice and water. Bring to a boil, then cover, reduce to a simmer, and cook for 15 minutes. Remove the pan from the heat and let stand, covered.

Meanwhile, in a large, deep skillet over medium-high heat, combine the oil, curry paste, soy sauce, and sugar. Cook until fragrant, about 1 minute. Add the ground beef and sauté until cooked through, about 8 minutes.

Stir in the coconut milk. Return to a simmer. Mix in the scallions and spinach and cook until the greens are just wilted, 2 to 3 minutes.

Mix in the lime juice and zest and the basil. Serve the beef over rice, garnished with peanuts.

➡ HOW LONG? **30 MINUTES**
➡ HOW MUCH? **4 SERVINGS**

Panko and Parmesan-Crusted Cod
with Wilted Spinach

I learned this trick for adding **tons of flavor** to basic white fish when I was a kid. Apply "secret sauce"—a blend of equal parts mayonnaise, ketchup, and mustard. This sauce, which has a tangy, sweet, and creamy flavor, also makes a fine condiment on burgers and sandwiches.

Any hardy green works well here, including kale and chard. And just about any mild fish, such as tilapia or haddock, is great with this coating.

The breadcrumb mixture for this recipe is crunchy, with chunks of panko and pine nuts. If you prefer a finer crumb, run the mixture through a food processor before using it.

2 tablespoons ketchup
2 tablespoons Dijon mustard
2 tablespoons mayonnaise
1 cup panko (Japanese-style) breadcrumbs
¼ cup pine nuts, finely chopped
½ cup grated Parmesan cheese
2 tablespoons dried parsley
1 pound cod fillets (or other firm white fish)
1 tablespoon olive oil
2 cloves garlic, minced
1 medium yellow onion, thinly sliced
¼ teaspoon red pepper flakes
5 ounces baby spinach
Grated zest of 1 lemon

Heat the oven to 400°F. Line a baking sheet with parchment paper.

In a wide, shallow bowl, whisk together the ketchup, mustard, and mayonnaise. In a second wide, shallow bowl, combine the breadcrumbs, pine nuts, Parmesan cheese, and parsley.

Divide the cod fillets into 4 pieces. One at a time, dredge each piece first through the mayonnaise mixture, turning to coat both sides, then through the breadcrumb mixture.

Arrange the fillets on the prepared baking sheet. Use your hands to pack additional breadcrumb mixture onto the top of the fish.

Bake for 12 to 14 minutes, or until the fish flakes easily at the thickest part.

While the fish cooks, in a large skillet over medium-high, heat the oil. Add the garlic, onion, and red pepper flakes. Sauté until the onion is tender, 4 to 5 minutes.

Add the spinach and sauté just until it wilts, about 3 minutes.

Remove the skillet from the heat and mix in the lemon zest. Divide the greens among 4 plates and top each serving with cod.

➡ HOW LONG? **30 MINUTES**
➡ HOW MUCH? **4 SERVINGS**

GET ZESTY

If all you ever do with your lemons is juice them, you are depriving yourself of some serious flavor. Use an ultrafine grater to remove the zest (the thin yellow outer skin, but not the white part beneath it). Zest is jammed with flavor. Add it to baked goods, warm pasta with melted butter and garlic, and salads (or salad dressings). And if you need the juice and zest, be sure to do the zesting first. This all holds true for limes and oranges, too.

Middle Eastern Chicken and Veggies with Hummus

The Middle East is a rich source of flavor combinations we don't often see in mainstream American cooking. In this case, cumin, oregano, cinnamon, and smoked paprika create a warm coating for chicken.

This recipe also uses the **intense heat of the broiler to caramelize the natural sugars** in the vegetables, creating deep flavors in a flash.

1-pound bunch asparagus, bottoms trimmed
1 green bell pepper, cored and cut into about 6 wedges
1 red bell pepper, cored and cut into about 6 wedges
1 medium red onion, cut into wedges
6 tablespoons olive oil, divided
Kosher salt and ground black pepper, to taste
½ teaspoon ground cumin
¼ teaspoon oregano
½ teaspoon cinnamon
½ teaspoon smoked paprika
1¼ pounds boneless, skinless chicken breast tenders
10-ounce tub prepared hummus (or use homemade; page 115)
4 to 8 rounds flatbread or individual-size pita bread pockets

Position a rack in the center of the oven. Heat the oven to broil. Line 2 baking sheets with foil.

In a large bowl, combine the asparagus, both bell peppers, and the onion. Drizzle with 2 tablespoons of the olive oil and toss to coat evenly.

Transfer the vegetables to one of the prepared baking sheets, arranging them in a single layer. Season with salt and pepper. Set under the broiler on the center rack; broil until tender and browned.

Meanwhile, in the same large bowl, stir together the remaining 4 tablespoons oil, ½ teaspoon salt, ¼ teaspoon pepper, the cumin, oregano, cinnamon, and paprika. Add the chicken and toss to coat.

Arrange the chicken in a single layer on the second baking sheet. Broil until the chicken is cooked through, about 8 minutes. Remove both pans from the oven (the vegetables may finish first).

Divide the chicken and vegetables among 4 plates. Serve with hummus and flatbread.

→ HOW LONG? **25 MINUTES (15 MINUTES ACTIVE)**
→ HOW MUCH? **4 SERVING**

DRINK UP!

....

Strawberry Agave Mojito

A mojito isn't your typical accompaniment to Middle Eastern–style chicken and hummus, but it works wonderfully with it. The sweet and lightly acidic drink is perfect for cutting through the heavy spices and oil.

Agave is a honey-like syrup made from the desert plant of the same name. Though the taste is mild, it can be sweeter than honey and can be substituted equally. Widely available at grocers and natural food stores, agave is excellent in mixed drinks.

3 medium strawberries, hulled and quartered
3 large fresh mint leaves
1 tablespoon agave syrup
Juice of ½ lime
2 ounces light rum
Ice cubes
Club soda

In a tall glass, combine the strawberries, mint leaves, and agave. Muddle (mash) them until the strawberries are well crushed and the mint leaves are bruised.

Add the lime juice and rum, then stir well. Add enough ice to nearly fill the glass, then top with club soda. Stir gently.

→ HOW LONG? **5 MINUTES**
→ HOW MUCH? **1 SERVING**

Wasabi Miso Glazed Salmon

If you've only ever had miso in soup, you're missing out. The salty, savory paste most often made from fermented beans can be used to make outstanding marinades and glazes. It pairs best with other common Asian ingredients, such as ginger, sesame oil, rice vinegar, and scallions. In most grocers, miso can be found alongside the Asian produce and tofu.

⅓ cup yellow or white miso
2 tablespoons lime juice
1 tablespoon water
1 clove garlic, minced
1 teaspoon wasabi powder
1 teaspoon soy sauce
Four 6- to 7-ounce salmon fillets (about 1½ inches thick)
1 tablespoon toasted sesame oil
½ cup panko (Japanese-style) breadcrumbs
2 tablespoons chopped fresh flat-leaf parsley

Position a rack in the middle of the oven. Heat the oven to broil. Lightly coat a rimmed baking sheet with cooking spray.

In a small bowl, whisk together the miso, lime juice, water, garlic, wasabi powder, and soy sauce. Arrange the salmon on the prepared baking sheet.

Use a pastry brush to coat each fillet with the miso sauce. Broil the salmon for 3 minutes, then cover it with foil and continue broiling until it is cooked through, about another 5 minutes.

Remove the salmon from the oven and let it rest for several minutes.

Meanwhile, in a small skillet over medium, heat the sesame oil. Add the panko and toast for about 2 minutes. To serve, sprinkle each fillet with panko and a bit of parsley.

➲ HOW LONG? **20 MINUTES**
➲ HOW MUCH? **4 SERVINGS**

Ground Turkey Moussaka

Traditional moussaka calls for laborious salting and squeezing of the eggplant, followed by an hour of cooking. No time for that in the weeknight kitchen. This version speeds things up by taking advantage of the high-quality jarred roasted eggplant dips found in most grocers' ethnic aisles. The result is **an easy one-dish meal** that is excellent served with warmed pita bread or rice.

2 tablespoons olive oil
1 large yellow onion, diced
2 green bell peppers, cored and diced
2 cloves garlic, minced
¼ teaspoon cinnamon
⅛ teaspoon ground allspice
1 bay leaf
½ teaspoon smoked paprika
1 pound lean ground turkey
14½-ounce can diced tomatoes
2 tablespoons tomato paste
12-ounce jar roasted eggplant dip
Salt and ground black pepper, to taste
⅓ cup crumbled feta cheese
2 tablespoons chopped fresh mint
Pita bread rounds, warmed

In a large, oven-safe skillet over medium-high, heat the oil. Add the onion, bell peppers, garlic, cinnamon, allspice, bay leaf, and paprika. Sauté until the onion is tender, about 5 minutes.

Add the ground turkey and cook until just browned, about 8 minutes. Stir in the diced tomatoes and tomato paste. Bring the mixture to a simmer, cover the pan, reduce heat to low, and cook for 10 minutes.

Heat the broiler.

Stir the roasted eggplant dip into the turkey mixture and simmer for another 5 minutes. Remove and discard the bay leaf. Season with salt and black pepper.

Remove the pan from the heat and top the moussaka with crumbled feta. Broil it for 1 to 2 minutes, just enough to lightly brown the cheese.

Just before serving, garnish with mint. Serve with warm pita bread.

➔ HOW LONG? **30 MINUTES (15 MINUTES ACTIVE)**
➔ HOW MUCH? **4 SERVINGS**

American Chop Suey

This lunch-line staple of a different era gets new life, thanks to ramped-up flavor from the bacon. **Push it even further by stirring in some grated Parmesan** cheese at the end.

The best part of this dish is you get everything—protein, veggies, and whole grains—in one pot. And for anyone not sure about whole-grain pastas, this is the place to buy in. The other flavors are so powerful, you'll never know you're eating the good-for-you stuff.

4 strips bacon, cut into 1-inch pieces
3 cloves garlic, minced
1 large yellow onion, diced
1 green bell pepper, cored and diced
1 red bell pepper, cored and diced
1 teaspoon Italian seasoning blend
1 pound lean ground beef
14½-ounce can diced tomatoes
14½-ounce can tomato sauce
1 cup chicken broth
1½ teaspoons soy sauce
2 cups whole-wheat pasta (such as elbow macaroni
**   or broken spaghetti)**
Salt and ground black pepper, to taste

In a large skillet over medium-high heat, cook the bacon for about 2 minutes, or until it renders enough fat to lightly coat the pan.

Add the garlic, onion, both bell peppers, and the Italian seasoning. Sauté until the onion just begins to soften, about 5 minutes.

Increase the heat to high. Add the beef and sauté until lightly browned, about 5 minutes. Mix in the diced tomatoes, tomato sauce, chicken broth, soy sauce, and pasta.

Bring the mixture to a simmer, reduce the heat to low, cover, and cook, stirring occasionally, until the pasta is tender, about 14 minutes. Season with salt and pepper.

➲ HOW LONG? **30 MINUTES (15 MINUTES ACTIVE)**
➲ HOW MUCH? **6 SERVINGS**

Middle Eastern Beef with Apples and Couscous

Pears are great in this dish, too. Or for a more Polynesian take, try pineapple. Boneless, skinless chicken breasts could stand in for the beef.

1¼ cups water
1 cup regular or whole-wheat couscous
2 tablespoons olive oil
1 large yellow onion, thinly sliced
1 green bell pepper, cored and thinly sliced
2 cloves garlic, minced
1 teaspoon ground cumin
½ teaspoon cinnamon
¼ teaspoon cayenne
½ teaspoon smoked paprika
1 pound sirloin, trimmed of fat and cut into 1-inch cubes
2 green apples, peeled, cored, and cut into bite-size chunks
1 tablespoon cider vinegar
½ cup apple cider or juice
1 tablespoon cornstarch
2 tablespoons water

In a small saucepan, bring the water to a boil. Add the couscous, stir, then cover the pan, remove it from the heat, and set it aside.

In a large skillet over medium-high, heat the oil. Add the onion, bell pepper, and garlic. Sauté until softened, about 5 minutes.

Add the cumin, cinnamon, cayenne, and paprika. Cook for 1 minute, then add the beef and brown on all sides, about 5 minutes.

Add the apples, vinegar, and cider. Cover and simmer for 5 minutes.

In a small glass, mix together the cornstarch and water. Add this to the skillet and cook, stirring constantly, until the sauce has thickened.

To serve, top mounds of couscous with the beef mixture.

➔ HOW LONG? **30 MINUTES**
➔ HOW MUCH? **4 SERVINGS**

Beef Stroganoff with Egg Noodles and Sour Cream

Using deli-sliced roast beef in this version of the classic stroganoff saves serious time. Since the meat is already cooked, it just gets heated in the sauce right at the end.

12 ounces egg noodles
2 tablespoons olive oil
1 medium yellow onion, diced
4 ounces button mushrooms, sliced
2 cloves garlic, minced
½ teaspoon dried thyme
1½ cups beef broth
¾ pound deli-sliced roast beef, torn into small pieces
1 tablespoon cornstarch
2 tablespoons cool water
Salt and ground black pepper, to taste
¼ cup sour cream
1 scallion, thinly sliced

Bring a large saucepan of salted water to a boil. Cook the noodles according to package directions, then drain and set aside.

Meanwhile, in a medium saucepan over medium-high heat, combine the oil, onion, mushrooms, garlic, and thyme. Sauté until the mushrooms are browned and tender, about 7 minutes.

Deglaze the pan by adding the broth and scraping up any bits stuck to the pan. Add the beef, then return to a simmer.

In a glass, combine the cornstarch and water. Mix it into the sauce, stirring until thickened, 1 to 2 minutes. Season with salt and pepper.

Divide the noodles among 4 serving plates. Top each serving with the roast beef mixture, a dollop of sour cream, and a sprinkle of scallion.

➡ HOW LONG? **20 MINUTES**
➡ HOW MUCH? **4 SERVINGS**

Turkey, Leek, and Gouda White Pizza

No time to roll out the dough? Or just don't feel like making the mess? **Ditch the pizza dough** and use large flour tortillas. The pizza also will bake faster.

But if you do feel like doing dough, consider buying a ball from your favorite pizzeria. Most are happy to sell you some for just a few dollars. The quality is way better than what you find at the grocer.

> 1 ball prepared pizza dough, room temperature
>   (about a 20-ounce ball)
> 2 tablespoons olive oil
> 4 cloves garlic, minced
> ¼ teaspoon red pepper flakes
> 1 large leek, white and light green parts only, cut into
>   thin rounds
> 6 cups chopped greens (such as kale, chard, or spinach)
> Salt and ground black pepper, to taste
> ¼ cup heavy cream
> ¼ pound deli-sliced smoked turkey breast, chopped
> 8 ounces smoked gouda cheese, shredded

Heat the oven to 500°F. Line 2 baking sheets with parchment paper.

On a lightly floured counter, divide the dough in half, then use a rolling pin to roll each piece into a 10-inch round. Transfer the dough to the prepared baking sheets.

In a large skillet over medium-high, heat the oil. Add the garlic, red pepper flakes, and leek. Sauté until the leek is tender and just starting to brown, 4 to 5 minutes.

Add the greens and sauté until just wilted, about 2 minutes. Season with salt and pepper, then stir in the cream.

Using tongs, divide the leek mixture between the dough rounds, spreading it evenly.

Top the greens mixture with the turkey breast, then the cheese. Bake for 10 to 12 minutes, or until the crust and cheese are lightly browned.

➡ HOW LONG? **30 MINUTES**
➡ HOW MUCH? **2 SERVINGS**

GRILLED PIE

Just about any pizza can be done on the grill. Just be sure to cook the toppings before they go on the pizza; the dough cooks so quickly on the grill there isn't time for the ingredients to cook before the crust would burn.

It's also important to wait to assemble the pizza until one side of the crust has been cooked. To do this, place the rolled-out crust on the grill and cook until the bottom has nice grill marks. Flip the pizza, top it as desired, cover the grill, and cook until the bottom is lightly browned and the cheese has melted.

Pulled Pork over Soft Polenta

Pulled pork and polenta aren't as much of a culture clash as they sound. **Spicy salsa-spiked pork is a natural with corn**—think corn chips and corn tortillas.

Prepared polenta is widely available in tubes. It slices and grills easily, which would be another great way of preparing it for this recipe. To do so, simply cut the polenta into 1-inch-thick slices, coat both sides with oil, then grill them briefly until heated through.

½ tablespoon whole peppercorns
1 tablespoon fennel seeds
3 bay leaves
3 cloves garlic, lightly crushed
1 medium yellow onion, chopped
1-pound pork tenderloin, cut into 3- to 4-inch sections
18-ounce tube prepared polenta, cut into chunks
¾ cup whole milk, plus more, if needed
¾ cup grated manchego cheese
1 tablespoon minced jarred jalapeño pepper slices
½ cup spicy barbecue sauce
1 cup prepared salsa, drained
½ cup lightly crushed tortilla chips (optional)

Bring a large saucepan of lightly salted water to a boil. Add the peppercorns, fennel seeds, bay leaves, garlic, onion, and pork. Boil for 15 minutes, or until cooked through.

Meanwhile, in a medium saucepan over medium heat, combine the polenta and milk. Cook, mashing and stirring the polenta, until it is smooth and creamy. Add additional milk if needed to reach a smooth consistency. Stir in the cheese and jalapeño peppers. Cover and set aside.

When the pork is ready, remove it from the water. Discard the water and seasonings. Use forks or your fingers to pull the chunks of meat apart into strands and return them to the pot.

Add the barbecue sauce and salsa to the pork. Cook over medium-low heat until warm.

To serve, spoon polenta onto each plate, then top it with pulled pork. Sprinkle with crushed tortilla chips, if using.

➡ HOW LONG? **30 MINUTES**
➡ HOW MUCH? **4 SERVINGS**

Spicy Ground Lamb with Hummus

This classic Middle Eastern meal is easy and kid-friendly (**they can eat with their hands!**). Whip up a batch of hummus and spread it on a platter. Brown some ground lamb, then dump it on top. To eat, smear some of the hummus and meat over warm flatbread.

To save effort, you can substitute purchased hummus and just prepare the ground lamb. And if lamb isn't your thing, ground turkey or beef are fine substitutes.

Roasted vegetables (toss potatoes, asparagus, and carrots with olive oil, salt, and pepper) are an excellent and easy side for this dish.

FOR THE HUMMUS:
Two 15-ounce cans chickpeas, drained
¼ cup sesame tahini
3 tablespoons lemon juice
2 cloves garlic
½ teaspoon ground cumin
½ tablespoon hot sauce
1 teaspoon salt
3 tablespoons olive oil
2 tablespoons water

FOR THE LAMB:
1 tablespoon olive oil
1 small yellow onion, diced
¼ teaspoon ground allspice
¼ teaspoon cinnamon
¼ teaspoon ground black pepper
¼ teaspoon red pepper flakes
1½ pounds ground lamb
1 tablespoon finely chopped fresh flat-leaf parsley
½ teaspoon smoked paprika

6 to 8 pita bread rounds, warmed

continued on next page

To make the hummus, in a food processor combine the chickpeas, tahini, lemon juice, garlic, cumin, hot sauce, salt, olive oil, and water. Pulse until mostly smooth, about 15 seconds. Set aside.

To make the lamb, in a large skillet over medium-high, heat the olive oil. Add the onion, allspice, cinnamon, black pepper, and red pepper flakes. Sauté for 1 minute. Add the lamb and sauté until browned, about 8 minutes. Remove from the heat.

Spoon the hummus onto a serving platter, making a shallow well in the center. Garnish the hummus with the parsley and paprika. Use a slotted spoon to transfer the lamb, draining any fat, into the well of the hummus. Serve with warm pita or flatbread.

➡ HOW LONG? **25 MINUTES**
➡ HOW MUCH? **6 SERVINGS**

Baked Breaded Eggplant with Marinara

These crisp, cheesy eggplant slices are a lighter take on the more traditional fried eggplant Parmesan. It lets the savory flavor of the Parm and the satisfying crunch of the panko shine. This same recipe also works with sliced zucchini and summer squash.

When dredging the eggplant slices, don't be afraid to get your hands dirty. And really press that panko onto the slices. **The more breadcrumbs, the more crunch.** Panko can be found alongside the other breadcrumbs at the grocer, as well as in the ethnic or Asian aisle.

2 eggs
2 cups panko (Japanese-style) breadcrumbs
1¼ cups finely grated Parmesan cheese, divided
½ teaspoon ground black pepper
1 teaspoon dried oregano
1 large eggplant (about 1½ pounds)
1½ cups jarred marinara or other pasta sauce
1 cup grated mozzarella cheese

Heat the oven to 400°F. Coat a large baking sheet with cooking spray.

In a wide, shallow bowl, whisk the eggs. In a medium shallow bowl, mix together the panko, ¾ cup of the Parmesan, the pepper, and oregano.

Trim the ends of the eggplant, then cut it into ½-inch-thick slices.

Dredge each slice through the egg, making sure both sides are coated, then through the breadcrumbs, flipping it to coat both sides.

Arrange the slices in a single layer on the prepared baking sheet.

Spritz the eggplant slices with cooking spray, then bake them for 20 minutes. Turn the slices and bake for another 20 minutes, or until both sides are crisp and slightly browned.

Sprinkle the eggplant slices with the remaining Parmesan and return them to the oven until the cheese melts, about 2 minutes. Meanwhile, in a small saucepan over medium heat, warm the pasta sauce.

continued on next page

Divide the eggplant among serving plates and top with pasta sauce and mozzarella.

➡ HOW LONG? **50 MINUTES (15 MINUTES ACTIVE)**
➡ HOW MUCH? **4 SERVINGS**

Roasted Rosemary-Rubbed Chicken Breasts and Cherry Tomatoes

Roasting cherry tomatoes intensifies their flavor. **Tossing them with capers, balsamic vinegar, and kosher salt doesn't hurt, either.**

1½ pounds boneless, skinless chicken breasts
½ cup chardonnay or other white wine
Juice of 1 lemon
4 cloves garlic, minced
1 pint cherry tomatoes, halved
1 tablespoon capers, drained
2 tablespoons balsamic vinegar
Kosher salt
1 tablespoon whole black peppercorns, lightly crushed
2 tablespoons coarsely chopped fresh rosemary

Heat the oven to 400°F. Coat a rimmed baking sheet with cooking spray.

Lay each chicken breast on the cutting surface and slice across the center horizontally to create 2 thin halves. Place each half between sheets of plastic wrap and use a meat mallet, rolling pin, or heavy skillet to pound it into an even cutlet about ¼ inch thick. Set aside.

In a large bowl, whisk together the wine, lemon juice, and garlic. Add the chicken, turn it to coat, then set aside for 15 minutes.

Meanwhile, in a medium bowl, combine the tomatoes, capers, vinegar, and a pinch of salt. Transfer the mixture to the prepared baking sheet and roast for 15 minutes.

In a small bowl, mix together the crushed peppercorns, rosemary, and ½ teaspoon kosher salt.

Remove the chicken cutlets from the marinade and use paper towels to pat them mostly dry. Rub each with the peppercorn-rosemary mixture.

continued on next page

Remove the tomatoes from the oven, arrange the cutlets on top, then return the pan to the oven for 10 minutes, or until the chicken is cooked through (it should register 165°F on an instant-read thermometer).

➔ HOW LONG? **30 MINUTES**
➔ HOW MUCH? **4 SERVINGS**

Chili-Stuffed Twice-Baked Potatoes

This one's got it all. These twice-baked potatoes are packed to overflowing with cheese, ground beef, refried beans—**an overall package that screams comfort.** If you like it hot, add both tablespoons of the minced jalapeños. And maybe even a dash of hot sauce.

4 large russet potatoes
2 tablespoons olive oil
2 cloves garlic, minced
¼ teaspoon red pepper flakes
1 small yellow onion, diced
1 to 2 tablespoons minced jarred jalapeño pepper slices
1 pound lean ground beef
1 medium tomato, diced
16-ounce can refried beans
Salt and ground black pepper, to taste
1½ cups shredded cheddar cheese, divided
⅔ cup ricotta cheese
½ cup milk
½ cup sliced black olives (optional)

Heat the oven to 425°F.

Pierce each potato several times with a fork. Microwave on high for 10 to 12 minutes, or until cooked through (timing will vary by microwave). Allow the potatoes to cool slightly.

Meanwhile, in a medium saucepan over medium-high heat, combine the olive oil, garlic, red pepper flakes, onion, and jalapeños. Sauté until the onion just softens, about 4 minutes.

Add the ground beef and sauté until browned, about another 6 minutes.

Add the tomato and refried beans, then mix well and reduce the heat to low. Bring the mixture to a simmer, season with salt and pepper, then cover and set it aside.

Once the potatoes have cooled enough to handle, carefully cut each in half lengthwise. Use a spoon to scoop out the insides and place them in a large bowl. Leave about ¼ to ½ inch of potato flesh inside the skin. Arrange the potato skins on a baking sheet. Set aside.

continued on next page

To the bowl of potatoes, add 1 cup of the cheddar cheese, the ricotta, and milk. Mix well, then season with salt and pepper. Set aside.

Fill the potato skins to overflowing with the meat and bean mixture. Carefully spoon a bit of the potato and cheese mixture over the meat. You may have extra potato.

Sprinkle each with some of the remaining cheddar and the black olives, if using. Bake until the cheese melts, 12 to 15 minutes.

➡ HOW LONG? **45 MINUTES (30 MINUTES ACTIVE)**
➡ HOW MUCH? **8 SERVINGS**

DRINK UP!

To stand up to a potato like this, you need a seriously flavorful and refreshing drink. Bring on the frozen margaritas!

Lemon Mango Margarita

This same recipe is great with frozen raspberries or blueberries substituted for the mango. If you don't have agave, honey works fine, too. Also consider adding a banana.

4 ounces tequila
2 ounces orange liqueur (such as triple sec)
Juice of 2 lemons (about 2 ounces)
2½ tablespoons agave syrup
2 cups (10-ounce bag) frozen mango chunks
2 cups ice cubes
Pinch salt
Orange juice or water, if needed

In a blender, combine all ingredients and puree until smooth. If the mixture is too thick to pour, blend in several tablespoons of orange juice or water.

➡ HOW LONG? **5 MINUTES**
➡ HOW MUCH? **2 SERVINGS**

Bangers and Mash

Sausage, mashed potatoes, and beer. What is not to like about bangers and mash? This dish, which comes to us via the Brits, calls for sweet Italian turkey sausages, but really any sausage—including precooked—will work. Precooked will shorten cooking time by about 5 minutes.

2 pounds Yukon Gold potatoes, peeled and quartered
2 tablespoons olive oil
2 large yellow onions, thinly sliced
2 green bell peppers, cored and thinly sliced
1¼ pounds sweet Italian turkey sausages (about 6 sausages)
½ teaspoon smoked paprika
1 teaspoon salt, divided
½ teaspoon ground black pepper, divided
12-ounce bottle amber beer
1 teaspoon cornstarch
2 tablespoons cold water
½ cup sour cream
¼ cup whole milk

Place the potatoes in a medium saucepan. Add enough water to cover by 1 inch. Bring to a boil and cook until tender, about 12 minutes.

Meanwhile, in a large skillet over high heat, combine the olive oil, onions, bell peppers, sausages, paprika, ½ teaspoon of the salt, and ¼ teaspoon of the black pepper.

Sauté until the onions are tender, about 5 minutes. Add the beer, cover the pan, and cook for 5 minutes. Uncover and simmer for another 5 minutes, or until the liquid is reduced by half.

In a small glass, combine the cornstarch and water. Add the cornstarch mixture to the skillet and heat, stirring constantly, until the sauce thickens, about 1 minute.

When the potatoes are done, drain and return them to the pot. Add the sour cream and milk, and the remaining ½ teaspoon salt and ¼ teaspoon pepper. Mash well, then divide among 4 serving plates.

continued on next page

Place 1½ sausages, along with sauce and onions and peppers, over each serving of potatoes.

➡ HOW LONG? **30 MINUTES**
➡ HOW MUCH? **4 SERVINGS**

Pork Chops with Red Wine Cranberry Sauce

Juicy, savory chops meet up with a sweet and tangy sauce. For convenience, you can substitute an equal amount of canned whole-berry cranberry sauce for the fresh or frozen berries. If you do, omit the honey; the canned sauce is sweet enough. Jalapeños can stand in for the Peppadews, but cut the quantity in half.

4 center-cut, boneless pork chops (about 1 inch thick)
½ teaspoon salt, plus more, to taste
¼ teaspoon ground black pepper, plus more, to taste
1 teaspoon ground cumin
1 teaspoon garlic powder
3 tablespoons butter
1 medium red onion, thinly sliced
½ cup red wine
1 cup fresh or frozen cranberries
2 tablespoons minced Peppadew peppers
2 tablespoons honey

Heat the oven to 200°F. Use paper towels to pat the pork chops dry.

In a small bowl, mix together the salt, pepper, cumin, and garlic powder. Rub a bit of the seasoning blend onto both sides of each chop.

In a large skillet over medium-high heat, melt the butter. Add the pork chops and cook until lightly browned on the bottom, about 6 minutes.

Turn the pork chops, cover the pan, then reduce the heat to low and cook until the chops reach 145°F at the center, about another 6 minutes.

Transfer the chops to an oven-safe plate, cover them with foil, and place them in the oven to keep warm.

Return the skillet to the burner over medium-high heat. Add the onion and sauté for 2 minutes. Add the wine, cranberries, Peppadews, and honey.

continued on next page

Bring to a simmer and cook until the cranberries pop and the liquid forms a thick sauce, about 5 minutes. Season with salt and pepper.

To serve, drizzle each pork chop with the cranberry pan sauce.

➡ HOW LONG? **25 MINUTES**
➡ HOW MUCH? **4 SERVINGS**

INSTANTLY ACCURATE

Chefs and experienced cooks are great at judging when meat is cooked by how it looks and feels. I'm not one of those people. I live and die by my digital instant-read thermometer. For me this is the easiest way to avoid overcooking my dinner or spending my evening in the ER. Good models are widely available online for about $50 to $100.

Curried Haddock with Coconut Milk

Curry powder is a British invention intended to simplify Indian curries, which can be complex dishes sometimes involving dozens of ingredients. But **the powders lack the vibrancy of the real thing**. If you'd still rather substitute the powder for the seasonings called for here, toast it in a dry skillet for about 1 minute before using. That will deepen the flavors.

In this recipe, the haddock is cooked on top of the other ingredients. This prevents the fish from falling apart and turning mushy during cooking.

**4 medium russet potatoes, peeled and cut into
  1-inch chunks**
2 tablespoons olive oil
2 large yellow onions, halved and thinly sliced
2 large green bell peppers, cored and thinly sliced
¾ teaspoon ground cloves
½ teaspoon ground cardamom
½ teaspoon cinnamon
½ teaspoon turmeric
½ teaspoon ground cumin
14-ounce can light coconut milk
1 cup water
2 tablespoons grated fresh ginger
2 tablespoons jarred jalapeño pepper slices, diced
1 teaspoon salt
**1½ pounds haddock, cod, or flounder fillets,
  divided into 4 servings**
2 teaspoons lime juice
¼ cup chopped fresh cilantro

In a medium saucepan fitted with a steamer basket, bring 1 inch of water to a boil. Add the potatoes to the basket, then cover and steam until tender, about 10 minutes. Uncover and set them aside.

Meanwhile, in a large sauté pan over medium-high, heat the oil. Add the onions and green peppers. Sauté until softened, about 4 minutes.

Add the cloves, cardamom, cinnamon, turmeric, and cumin. Sauté another 3 minutes.

continued on next page

Lower the heat to medium and add the coconut milk, water, ginger, jalapeños, and salt. Bring to a simmer. Cook for 10 minutes.

Add the fish, setting the fillets over the onions and peppers; don't mix them in. Cover the pan and cook for 5 minutes. Uncover and cook for another 5 minutes, or until the fish flakes easily.

To serve, divide the potatoes among 4 plates and lightly mash. Top with cod, onions, and peppers. Sprinkle with lime juice and cilantro.

➔ HOW LONG? **30 MINUTES (10 MINUTES ACTIVE)**
➔ HOW MUCH? **4 SERVINGS**

Sweet-and-Savory BBQ Chicken

This barbecue sauce is way intense. It's got a great balance of sweetness and vinegary bite. Thin it with tomato sauce and use it as a killer cocktail sauce for shrimp.

If you want to save time, you can skip brining the chicken. But it's a great and easy way to keep chicken breasts from drying out on the grill.

In my life, a house is not a home if there isn't an open bottle of red wine around. So it was an obvious choice for the liquid in this barbecue sauce. If you don't have an open bottle of red handy, substitute white wine, beer, apple juice, or even water.

Because chicken breasts can easily dry out during grilling, this recipe calls for them to be cooked over indirect heat. One side of the grill is set on high, the other on low. Keeping the chicken on the low side lets them slowly cook through without drying out.

FOR THE CHICKEN:
2 cups water
¼ cup kosher salt
¼ cup sugar
6 boneless, skinless chicken breasts

FOR THE BARBECUE SAUCE:
6-ounce can tomato paste
1 tablespoon Dijon mustard
1 teaspoon Worcestershire sauce
1 teaspoon soy sauce
2 tablespoons cider vinegar
3 tablespoons olive oil
3 tablespoons red wine (see note above)
3 tablespoons light brown sugar
1 teaspoon ground cumin
1 teaspoon cinnamon
1 teaspoon garlic powder
1 teaspoon kosher salt

In a large bowl, mix together the water, kosher salt, and sugar. Add the chicken, turn the pieces to coat, then refrigerate them for at least 30 minutes or up to 6 hours.

Meanwhile, in a medium bowl, whisk together the tomato paste, mustard, Worcestershire sauce, soy sauce, vinegar, olive oil, and wine. Add the brown sugar, cumin, cinnamon, garlic powder, and salt. Whisk until smooth.

continued on next page

Heat the grill to high. When the grill is hot, generously coat the grate with cooking spray. Reduce the heat on one side of the grill to low.

Remove the chicken from the brine and pat it dry. Arrange the chicken on the low-heat side of the grill and cook, covered, for 6 minutes.

Use a basting brush to slather the tops of the chicken breasts with the barbecue sauce, then use tongs to turn them. Baste the second side, then close the grill and cook for another 3 minutes. Baste the chicken again, using up the remaining sauce, then cook for another 6 to 8 minutes, or until the breasts reach 165°F at the center.

⮕ HOW LONG? **1 HOUR (30 MINUTES ACTIVE)**
⮕ HOW MUCH? **6 SERVINGS**

DRINK UP!

Sparkling Watermelon Lemonade

Barbecue chicken begs for a sweet, summery drink. This vibrant lemonade is snappy enough to both refresh and stand up to the chicken. And if you wanted to splash some vodka in it . . . well, things can only get better.

5 cups cut watermelon flesh (about ¼ large watermelon)
1 cup lemon juice
½ cup honey
Pinch salt
12-ounce can (1½ cups) seltzer or soda water
Ice

In a blender, combine the watermelon, lemon juice, honey, and salt. Puree until smooth, about 1 minute. Transfer the mixture to a pitcher, then stir in the seltzer or soda water. Add ice.

⮕ HOW LONG? **5 MINUTES**
⮕ HOW MUCH? **6 SERVINGS**

Chinese Pie (What the Rest of the World Calls Shepherd's Pie)

There are all sorts of theories about why New Englanders call this dish Chinese Pie. My favorites include that Chinese railway workers enjoyed it while building the train lines in the region. There's also the (only slightly more plausible) suggestion that French Canadians popularized the Irish staple after moving to China, Maine.

Whatever the origins, this is my take on the Chinese pie my French Canadian great-grandmother used to make for me. I'm not a fan of gravy powder, but she swore by it. And after you try this, you'll understand why.

Don't be intimidated by the length of the recipe. **This deconstructed version of the traditional baked shepherd's pie saves time** by preparing the components—mashed potatoes, corn, and ground beef—separately on the stove, then assembling them on the plate. Ground turkey also works in this recipe.

FOR THE MASHED POTATOES:
4 medium Yukon Gold potatoes, peeled and
   cut into small chunks
½ teaspoon dried thyme
½ cup milk
4 tablespoons (½ stick) butter
Salt and ground black pepper, to taste

FOR THE CORN:
1 tablespoon olive oil
1 medium yellow onion, diced
15-ounce can corn kernels
14½-ounce can creamed corn
Salt and ground black pepper, to taste

FOR THE GROUND BEEF:
1 pound lean ground beef
¼ teaspoon red pepper flakes
1-ounce package chicken or beef powdered
   gravy mix
½ cup water
¾ cup grated Parmesan cheese

continued on next page

In a medium saucepan, add the potatoes and enough water to cover by 1 inch. Bring to a boil over high heat, then reduce to a simmer. Cook, uncovered, for 8 minutes, or until the potatoes are tender.

While the potatoes cook, prepare the corn. In a medium saucepan over medium heat, combine the oil and onion. Sauté for 4 minutes, or until the onion just softens. Add both corns, reduce the heat to simmer. Season with salt and pepper.

Drain and return the cooked potatoes to the pan. Add the thyme, milk, and butter, then mash until chunky smooth. Season with salt and pepper, then cover and set aside.

To prepare the ground beef, in a large skillet over medium-high heat, sauté the beef and red pepper flakes until the beef is cooked through and lightly browned, about 8 minutes.

Stir in the gravy powder and water. Stir in the cheese. To serve, arrange portions of potatoes, corn, and ground turkey on each serving plate.

⬏ HOW LONG? **30 MINUTES**
⬏ HOW MUCH? **4 SERVINGS**

Cheater Chicken Curry

Ah, **the rotisserie chicken. Consider it your blank slate.** Pull the meat off and toss it with barbecue sauce, then toss that on a pizza crust with gobs of mozzarella. Or add the meat to cooked pasta and sprinkle it with Parmesan. Or dice it, mix it with mashed potatoes and eggs, then form it into patties, coat them with breadcrumbs, and fry them as croquettes. Or, as in the case of this dish, mix it with curry spices and vegetables and serve it over couscous.

1 cup water
3 tablespoons olive oil, divided
1 cup couscous
1 medium yellow onion, diced
1 red bell pepper, cored and cut into thin strips
3 cloves garlic, minced
2 large carrots, cut into matchsticks
1 cup golden raisins
1 tablespoon curry powder
Meat from a 2½-pound rotisserie chicken
14-ounce can coconut milk
Salt and ground black pepper, to taste
3 scallions, thinly sliced
2 tablespoons chopped fresh cilantro

In a small saucepan, bring the water and 1 tablespoon of olive oil to a boil. Turn off the heat. Add the couscous, stir, then cover and set it aside.

In a large, deep skillet, heat the remaining 2 tablespoons of olive oil over medium-high. Add the onion, red bell pepper, garlic, carrots, and raisins. Sauté until the onions and pepper are just tender, about 5 minutes.

Add the curry powder and cook for 2 minutes. Add the chicken and coconut milk. Bring to a simmer. Season with salt and pepper.

Transfer the couscous to a serving bowl or platter. Spoon the chicken curry over the couscous, then garnish with scallions and cilantro.

➡ HOW LONG? **30 MINUTES**
➡ HOW MUCH? **4 TO 6 SERVINGS**

Spicy Black Bean, Sausage, and Rice Burrito

One part burrito, one part jambalaya, all good. If you want to crank the heat, splash some hot sauce onto the rice and beans, or sprinkle diced jalapeño peppers inside before rolling up the tortilla. This filling also would be good as a hearty rice dish served alongside spicy grilled chicken. Or add a quart of chicken broth, bring it to a simmer, and you've got a satisfying soup.

4 slices bacon, cut into 1-inch pieces
1 small yellow onion, diced
2 cloves garlic, minced
2 precooked spicy chicken sausages, cut into rounds
1 teaspoon smoked paprika
1 cup long-grain white rice
2 cups chicken broth
15-ounce can black beans, drained
1 cup jarred tomatillo salsa
Salt and ground black pepper, to taste
4 burrito-size flour tortillas
½ cup chopped fresh cilantro
1 cup shredded cheddar cheese
½ cup sour cream

In a medium saucepan over medium-high heat, cook the bacon for 2 minutes, or until it lightly coats the pan with fat. Add the onion, garlic, sausages, and smoked paprika. Sauté for 3 minutes.

Add the rice and cook, stirring constantly, for another 30 seconds. Add the broth and beans, stir well, and bring to a boil. Cover the pan, reduce the heat to simmer, and cook for 15 minutes.

Remove the saucepan from the heat and let cool for 5 minutes. Mix in the salsa, then season with salt and pepper.

Microwave the tortillas for about 15 seconds to soften them. Divide the rice and beans mixture among the tortillas, then top each with chopped cilantro, cheddar cheese, and sour cream.

➲ HOW LONG? **30 MINUTES**
➲ HOW MUCH? **4 SERVINGS**

Chicken Chimichurri with Roasted Asparagus and New Potatoes

Chimichurri is the national meat marinade and condiment of Argentina. **The tangy, mildly spicy green sauce** resembles a loose pesto but gets its fresh, lively flavors from parsley and cilantro rather than basil. Be sure to try chimichurri on grilled steak.

FOR THE CHIMICHURRI SAUCE:
1½ cups packed fresh flat-leaf parsley
¼ cup packed fresh cilantro
1 cup extra-virgin olive oil
⅓ cup red wine vinegar
2 tablespoons dried oregano
1½ tablespoons ground cumin
1½ teaspoons salt
3 cloves garlic
¾ teaspoon red pepper flakes

FOR THE CHICKEN AND VEGETABLES:
1½ pounds boneless, skinless chicken breasts
1 pound new potatoes, quartered
1-pound bunch asparagus, ends trimmed
2 tablespoons olive oil
1 teaspoon salt
½ teaspoon ground black pepper
1 teaspoon dried oregano
1 teaspoon ground cumin

In a food processor or blender, combine the parsley, cilantro, olive oil, vinegar, oregano, cumin, salt, garlic, and red pepper flakes. Puree for 2 to 3 minutes, or until very smooth.

Pour half of the chimichurri sauce into an 8-inch square baking dish. Pour the remaining sauce into a bowl, cover, and set aside.

Slice each chicken breast lengthwise into strips about ½ inch thick. Place the strips in the baking dish and turn them to coat with chimichurri. Cover and refrigerate.

Meanwhile, heat the oven to 400°F, positioning racks in the upper third and the center. Line 2 rimmed baking sheets with foil.

In a large bowl, combine the potatoes and asparagus. In a small bowl, whisk together the olive oil, salt, pepper, oregano, and cumin. Drizzle the mixture over the vegetables, then toss to coat.

Arrange the potatoes and asparagus in an even layer on one baking sheet, then place it on the upper rack. Roast for 25 to 35 minutes, or until the potatoes are cooked through. Remove the pan from the oven and set the oven to broil.

Arrange the chicken in a single layer on the second baking sheet. Place it on the center rack and broil for 5 minutes, then turn the chicken and broil it for another 5 minutes. Serve the chicken and vegetables with the reserved chimichurri sauce for dipping.

➲ HOW LONG? **45 MINUTES (15 MINUTES ACTIVE)**
➲ HOW MUCH? **4 SERVINGS**

White Wine Braised Chicken

The red wine version of this classic French dish was delicious, but the wine turned the chicken an unappealing purple. **If you're color-blind, have at it.** Otherwise, stick with white.

2 tablespoons olive oil
3 to 3¼ pounds bone-in, skin-on chicken legs and thighs
6 cloves garlic, minced
1 large yellow onion, diced
1 large carrot, chopped
1 red bell pepper, cored and diced
1 cup pitted and chopped green olives
1 teaspoon dried thyme
1 teaspoon dried basil
1 teaspoon smoked paprika
1½ cups chicken broth
1½ cups chardonnay or other white wine
1½ tablespoons cornstarch
2 tablespoons cool water
Salt and ground black pepper, to taste

In a large Dutch oven over medium-high, heat the olive oil. Add the chicken and brown lightly on all sides, turning as needed.

Add the garlic, onion, carrot, bell pepper, olives, thyme, basil, and paprika. Sauté until the onion is just tender, about 6 minutes.

Add the broth and wine. Mix well, bring the liquid to a simmer, then cover, reduce the heat to low, and cook for 10 minutes. Uncover the pot, increase the heat to medium, and cook for another 15 minutes. Use tongs to transfer the chicken to a plate and cover it with foil.

In a small cup, mix together the cornstarch and water, then add it to the Dutch oven. Cook, stirring constantly, until thickened, about 1 minute. Season with salt and pepper.

Serve the chicken with sauce ladled over it.

➲ HOW LONG? **45 MINUTES (15 MINUTES ACTIVE)**
➲ HOW MUCH? **6 SERVINGS**

Porcini Chicken with Wilted Spinach

If spinach isn't your thing, **try this chicken over rice or couscous,** either of which would be great tossed with the same lemon–olive oil mixture.

Two ½-ounce packages dried porcini mushrooms
1 tablespoon smoked paprika
1 teaspoon garlic powder
½ teaspoon mustard powder
½ teaspoon ground cumin
½ teaspoon black peppercorns
2 teaspoons kosher salt, divided
2 boneless, skinless chicken breasts
2 tablespoons butter
4 tablespoons extra-virgin olive oil, divided
Juice of 2 lemons (about ¼ cup)
2 cloves garlic, minced
10 ounces (about 6 cups) baby spinach
1 red bell pepper, cored and thinly sliced

Heat the oven to 200°F.

In a food processor, combine the mushrooms, paprika, garlic powder, mustard powder, cumin, peppercorns, and 1½ teaspoons of the salt. Process until reduced to a fine powder. Transfer to a shallow bowl.

Carefully slice each chicken breast across the center horizontally to create 2 thin cutlets. Flatten each with a meat mallet to an even thickness, about ¼ inch.

Dredge each piece through the mushroom mixture, coating both sides.

In a large skillet over medium-high heat, combine the butter and 2 tablespoons of the olive oil. When the butter is melted, add the chicken and sauté until lightly browned on the bottom, about 4 minutes. Flip it and sauté for another 4 minutes, or until cooked through.

Transfer the chicken to an oven-safe plate and keep it warm in the oven.

continued on next page

Wipe the skillet clean, then return it to the heat and add the remaining 2 tablespoons olive oil, the remaining ½ teaspoon salt, the lemon juice, garlic, spinach, and bell pepper. Sauté until the spinach is wilted.

To serve, divide the greens among 4 serving plates. Top each with a piece of chicken.

➔ HOW LONG? **30 MINUTES**
➔ HOW MUCH? **4 SERVINGS**

WHICH CAME FIRST?

So perhaps it doesn't matter which came first. My son, when asked how chickens make eggs:

"First you put a yolk in half of a broken egg shell, then you put the other half on and glue it together. Then the chickens hide them. Then they do what they have to do."

Barbecue Pulled Chicken Nachos

Also try this chicken over baked and smashed potatoes. Nuke large baking potatoes, then use a masher to crush them flat.

12-ounce bag tortilla chips
16-ounce can refried beans
2 tablespoons minced jarred jalapeño pepper slices
1 cup shredded mozzarella cheese
1 cup canned or thawed frozen corn kernels
Meat from a 2½-pound rotisserie chicken, pulled into
   small strips
⅓ cup bottled spicy barbecue sauce
1 teaspoon hot sauce
1 tablespoon cider vinegar
14½-ounce can diced tomatoes, well drained
1½ cups shredded Monterey Jack cheese

Heat the oven to 400°F. Arrange the tortilla chips in a single layer on a rimmed baking sheet. Set aside.

In a medium microwave-safe bowl, combine the refried beans, jalapeño peppers, and mozzarella cheese. Heat until the cheese is melted.

Pour or spoon the refried bean mixture evenly over the tortilla chips. Spread the corn in an even layer over the beans.

In the same bowl used for the refried beans, mix together the chicken, barbecue sauce, hot sauce, and vinegar. Microwave until just warmed through, about 2 minutes.

Spread the chicken evenly over the corn, then top with the diced tomatoes. Sprinkle Monterey Jack cheese over all.

Bake for 10 minutes, or until the cheese is melted and bubbling. Serve immediately.

➡ HOW LONG? **30 MINUTES**
➡ HOW MUCH? **6 SERVINGS**

North African Grilled Chicken

After searching the spice cabinet for dinner inspiration one day, I tossed a bunch of seasonings in a bowl with some olive oil, dredged some chicken through it, then threw it on the grill. **It was so good my son and I ate the entire pound of chicken.**

Too bad I hadn't been smart enough to write down what I did. It took me about twelve attempts to re-create just the right blend of seasonings, the combination of which is reminiscent of North African cooking. Lesson learned—I no longer experiment without taking notes.

This chicken also can be cooked under the broiler. Arrange the meat on a baking sheet, then broil it on the center rack for about 5 minutes, flipping the chicken halfway through.

½ tablespoon ground cumin
½ tablespoon ground coriander
½ tablespoon turmeric
1 tablespoon cinnamon
1 tablespoon smoked paprika
1 tablespoon mustard powder
½ tablespoon kosher salt
2 tablespoons olive oil
1½ pounds boneless, skinless chicken breast tenders

In a large, dry skillet over medium heat, combine the cumin, coriander, turmeric, cinnamon, paprika, mustard powder, and salt. Toast the seasonings, stirring constantly, for 1 minute, or until aromatic.

Transfer the spices to a plate to cool. Once they have cooled, transfer the mixture to a zip-close plastic bag. Add the olive oil, seal the bag, and gently shake and knead the seasonings until they are well blended with the oil. Add the chicken, close the bag, and shake until well coated.

Coat the grill grate with oil or cooking spray. Heat the grill on high.

Grill the chicken for 3 to 4 minutes per side, or until the meat reaches 165°F on an instant-read thermometer.

➲ HOW LONG? **30 MINUTES**
➲ HOW MUCH? **4 SERVINGS**

Prosciutto-Baked Tilapia Stuffed with Sun-Dried Tomato Tapenade

While other white fish can stand in for the tilapia in this recipe, the fillets need to be thin enough to roll. And whatever fish you use, **be sure to have toothpicks handy** for pinning the rolls together before cooking them. Once cooked, the rolls hold up fine and the toothpicks can be removed before serving.

8 slices prosciutto
4 tilapia fillets (4 to 5 ounces each)
Salt and ground black pepper, to taste
1 teaspoon garlic powder
Extra-virgin olive oil, for drizzling
**2 jarred roasted red peppers, drained, patted dry,
    and finely diced**
4 oil-packed sun-dried tomatoes, finely diced
1 tablespoon capers, minced

Heat the oven to 400°F. Lightly coat a rimmed baking sheet with cooking spray.

Arrange the prosciutto on the baking sheet in 4 stacks of 2 slices each. Set a tilapia fillet over each pair of prosciutto slices.

Season each fillet with salt, pepper, and a quarter of the garlic powder, then drizzle with olive oil.

In a small bowl, mix together the red peppers, sun-dried tomatoes, and capers. Spoon a quarter of the mixture over each fillet, using the back of the spoon to spread it evenly.

Starting at one end of each fillet, carefully roll it up, holding the prosciutto so that it wraps around the fish. Push a toothpick through the center to hold each roll together.

Bake for 20 to 25 minutes, or until the fish is firm and flakes easily.

➔ HOW LONG? **35 MINUTES (10 MINUTES ACTIVE)**
➔ HOW MUCH? **4 SERVINGS**

Hummus Meatballs

Serve these **North African–style meatballs with warm flatbread**, tzatziki (a blend of yogurt, diced cucumber, fresh dill, and lemon juice), and sliced tomatoes.

3 slices whole-wheat bread
½ small red onion
¼ cup packed fresh flat-leaf parsley
¼ cup packed fresh cilantro
1 teaspoon ground cumin
½ teaspoon cinnamon
¼ teaspoon ground allspice
½ teaspoon smoked paprika
½ cup prepared or homemade hummus (page 115)
1 egg, beaten
1 teaspoon salt
½ teaspoon ground black pepper
1 pound lean ground beef (ground turkey could be substituted)

Heat the oven to 400°F. Coat a rimmed baking sheet with cooking spray.

In a food processor, pulse the bread until it is finely ground. Add the onion and pulse until it is finely chopped and blended with the bread.

Add the parsley, cilantro, cumin, cinnamon, allspice, and paprika. Pulse several times, or until thoroughly blended. Add the hummus, egg, salt, and pepper, then pulse until blended.

Transfer the mixture to a large bowl. Add the beef, then mix well.

Use your hands to form the mixture into balls by the tablespoonful. Arrange them on the prepared baking sheet. Spritz the meatballs with cooking spray.

Bake for 20 to 25 minutes, or until cooked through.

➲ HOW LONG? **35 MINUTES (10 MINUTES ACTIVE)**
➲ HOW MUCH? **22 MEATBALLS**

Three-Chip Baked Chicken Cutlets with Cranberry Sauce

The goal here was an **ultra-crispy** chicken cutlet without the mess of deep frying. The solution? Start with ingredients that already are crunchy, add high heat, and we've got a winner. For even more intensity, use flavored chips, such as sour cream and onion or sweet potato chips.

Canned cranberry sauce isn't just for Thanksgiving. I doctor it up to make all sorts of pan sauces, including for pork chops. It works well with spicy ingredients, and also can be jammed under the skin of chicken to add flavor during roasting or grilling. If you prefer less heat in your dish, cut down or eliminate the red pepper flakes.

2 cups plain potato chips
1 cup thin pretzel sticks
1 cup tortilla chips
½ to 1 teaspoon red pepper flakes
2 eggs
1 teaspoon low-sodium soy sauce
2 boneless, skinless chicken breasts
2 tablespoons canola or vegetable oil
½ cup chicken broth
2 tablespoons cider vinegar
1 small yellow onion, diced
1 teaspoon grated fresh ginger
2 cloves garlic, minced
1 cup canned whole-berry cranberry sauce
Salt and ground black pepper, to taste

Heat the oven to 450°F.

In a food processor, combine the potato chips, pretzels, tortilla chips, and red pepper flakes, then pulse until reduced to fine crumbs. Transfer the mixture to a wide, shallow bowl and set it aside.

In a second wide, shallow bowl, whisk together the eggs and soy sauce.

Carefully slice each chicken breast in half horizontally to create 2 thin cutlets.

continued on next page

One at a time, place the chicken pieces in the egg mixture, turning to coat both sides, then dredge each through the chip mixture, turning to coat both sides. Set aside.

In a large, oven-safe skillet over medium-high, heat the oil until very hot. Add the chicken breasts and cook until they are browned on the bottom, about 2 minutes. Turn the breasts, then place the skillet in the oven. Bake for 8 minutes.

Transfer the chicken to a serving plate. Cover it with foil to keep warm.

Return the skillet to the stovetop over medium-high heat. Add the broth and vinegar, then bring the mixture to a simmer, using a spoon to scrape up any bits stuck to the bottom of the pan.

Add the onion, ginger, and garlic and cook until the liquid is mostly evaporated, 2 to 3 minutes. Add the cranberry sauce and return to a simmer. Season with salt and pepper.

Serve the chicken drizzled with the pan sauce.

➔ HOW LONG? **30 MINUTES**
➔ HOW MUCH? **4 SERVINGS**

Ginger Tomato Shrimp Curry

One of my favorite uses for a bag of frozen shrimp is an adaptation of a Paula Deen recipe (whom I once interviewed as she showered, but that's another story).

Toss the thawed shrimp with several tablespoons of melted butter, a couple tablespoons of ground black pepper, and a sprinkling of salt. Arrange them in a single layer on a rimmed baking sheet, then roast at 450°F for 5 to 7 minutes, or until pink. Eat.

3 tablespoons ghee (clarified butter), divided
1 pound large shrimp, peeled and deveined
1 medium yellow onion, diced
1 jalapeño pepper, diced
3 cloves garlic, minced
½ tablespoon turmeric
½ tablespoon chili powder
½ tablespoon grated fresh ginger
14-ounce can diced tomatoes, with juices
1 tablespoon tomato paste
Zest and juice of 1 lime
¼ cup chopped fresh cilantro
Salt and ground black pepper, to taste

In a large sauté pan over medium-high, melt 2 tablespoons of the ghee. Add the shrimp and cook for about 1 minute per side. Transfer the shrimp to a plate and set aside. Discard any liquid in the pan.

Return the pan to medium heat and add the remaining tablespoon of ghee. Once the ghee is melted, add the onion, jalapeño, and garlic. Sauté for 2 to 4 minutes, or until the onion is tender. Add the turmeric, chili powder, ginger, tomatoes, and tomato paste. Simmer for 5 minutes.

Return the shrimp to the pan, mixing and heating thoroughly. Stir in the lime zest and juice, and the cilantro. Season with salt and pepper.

➡ HOW LONG? **20 MINUTES**
➡ HOW MUCH? **6 SERVINGS**

Panko-Coated Chicken Cutlets with Roasted Tomatoes and Garlic

Getting **impact-worthy flavor** out of chicken cutlets and out-of-season cherry tomatoes can be a daunting task. This recipe delivers, thanks to a spicy panko breadcrumb coating for the cutlets and a high-heat roast for the tomatoes.

3 pints cherry tomatoes, halved (if large, quartered)
Kosher salt
1½ cups panko (Japanese-style) breadcrumbs
1 teaspoon garlic powder
½ teaspoon red pepper flakes
Ground black pepper
2 eggs
2 tablespoons butter, melted and slightly cooled
8 garlic cloves, peeled but whole
Two 4-inch sprigs fresh rosemary (leaves only)
1¼ pounds boneless, skinless chicken breasts
Balsamic vinegar, for drizzling

Heat the oven to 450°F and position one rack in the top third and one in the bottom third. Lightly coat two baking sheets with cooking spray.

Place the tomatoes in a large mesh strainer or colander set over a bowl or sink. Sprinkle ½ tablespoon of salt over them, then gently rub it through. Set the tomatoes aside for 15 minutes to drain, occasionally stirring them.

Meanwhile, in a wide, shallow bowl combine the panko, garlic powder, red pepper flakes, ¼ teaspoon black pepper, and 1 teaspoon of salt.

In a second wide, shallow bowl, whisk together the eggs and butter.

Mix the garlic, rosemary, and a bit of black pepper into the tomatoes, then transfer them to one of the prepared baking sheets. Roast on the oven's top rack for 15 minutes.

While the tomatoes roast, slice each chicken breast across the center horizontally to create two thin halves. Place each half between sheets of plastic wrap and use a meat mallet, rolling pin, or heavy skillet to pound it into an even cutlet about ¼ inch thick.

Dredge each cutlet first through the egg mixture, then through the panko mixture, turning to coat both sides. Arrange the cutlets on the second baking sheet and spritz the tops with cooking spray.

Once the tomatoes have roasted for 15 minutes, place the cutlets on the oven's bottom rack and cook for 12 minutes, or until they register 165°F on an instant-read thermometer.

To serve, spoon roasted tomatoes and garlic over each cutlet, then drizzle with balsamic vinegar.

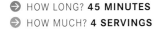 HOW LONG? **45 MINUTES**
 HOW MUCH? **4 SERVINGS**

Good gnocchi are all in the butt.

And in case we missed her point, Patrizia gave a generous side-to-side wag of her own as she pinched off a piece of tender pasta dough and rolled it across a grooved board.

She held up the gently notched gnocchi, a delicately delicious pillow of potato pasta. "You roll with your butt."

I was learning pasta making at Patrizia's school outside Pisa, Italy. The brochures had not warned that butt wagging was on the lesson plan.

Patrizia scowled at my poorly formed gnocchi. And my butt.

"Not enough butt," she scolded, grabbing my hips and forcing them back and forth as I struggled with the gnocchi.

My culinary shortcomings are many; I hadn't considered my rear among them.

Whatever the size and skill of your backside, you should make pasta from scratch at least once. It's ridiculously easy, it's a great project for the kids, and the taste is so much better than anything you can buy.

While special equipment makes it easier, you don't need it. Or even a recipe.

Here's how it works. For ingredients all you need are all-purpose flour and eggs. Each cup of flour will make enough pasta for about two people. The number of eggs will equal the number of cups of flour, plus one. So for 2 cups of flour you need 3 eggs.

To make the pasta, in a food processor combine the flour and eggs. Pulse until the mixture forms a ball of dough, then let it run for 30 seconds to knead. Place the dough on the counter and cover it with a bowl. Let it rest for 30 minutes.

That's it. You just made fresh pasta. Now all you need to do is shape it. A pasta roller/cutter (either the hand-crank style or a standing mixer attachment) makes fast and easy work of this.

Alternatively, you can roll it out like pie dough, then use a knife to cut it into long, thin strips for fettuccine. Then just boil it in salted water for a couple minutes.

I take an equally laid back approach to my pasta recipes. While I do suggest particular pastas for most dishes, when cooking for my family I take a pasta-is-pasta approach. Which is to say, I use whatever I've got on hand. Pasta dishes generally just aren't the sorts of recipes where you need to get hung up on the details.

Orecchiette Pasta with Wilted Greens

I learned this recipe in Italy, and **it has become one of my go-to dishes for company.** It's fast, easy, and adaptable, and people are always wowed by the pleasantly peppery flavors that are contrasted so nicely by the Parmesan cheese and lemon zest. If you want to make it more substantial, toss in chunks of sausage when adding the anchovies (which melt away, so set aside any anchovy anxieties).

Any hardy greens can be substituted for the kale. Try chard, arugula, spinach, dandelion greens, or broccoli raab. Likewise, any hard, assertive cheese—pecorino Romano, aged gouda, even manchego—can stand in for the Parmesan.

½-pound bunch of kale
16 ounces orecchiette pasta (or other small pasta)
3 tablespoons extra-virgin olive oil, plus more as needed
3 or 4 oil-packed anchovies
2 cloves garlic, minced
½ teaspoon red pepper flakes
Grated zest of 1 lemon
1 cup grated Parmesan cheese, plus extra for serving
Salt and ground black pepper, to taste

Bring a large saucepan of salted water to a boil.

While the water heats, use a paring knife to cut out and discard the tough center stalk from each kale leaf. Roughly chop the kale. Set aside.

Add the pasta to the water and cook according to package directions. Drain and set aside.

While the pasta cooks, in a large, deep sauté pan over medium-high heat, combine the olive oil, anchovies, garlic, and red pepper flakes. Sauté until the anchovies break down and form a paste, about 3 minutes.

Add the kale and reduce the heat to medium. Sauté for 3 minutes, or until the kale just begins to wilt. Add the pasta and toss well to combine.

Add the lemon zest and Parmesan cheese and toss until the cheese is melted. If the pasta is too dry, add additional olive oil. Season with salt and pepper. Serve topped with additional Parmesan.

➲ HOW LONG? **20 MINUTES**
➲ HOW MUCH? **6 SERVINGS**

Bow Tie Pasta with Bacon Pesto

This recipe came from **a bit of on-the-fly inspiration.** When my plans to prepare a Parmesan-laden pesto for a friend were derailed by her lactose intolerance, I scrambled for a substitute for the cheese. Bacon may seem an odd choice, but like Parmesan, it has a deep, savory flavor, takes well to being minced (think bacon bits for salads), and pairs well with peppery basil. Also try this pesto on crostini topped with tomato and fresh mozzarella.

6 slices thick-cut bacon
12 ounces bow tie pasta
2½ cups (about 4 ounces) lightly packed fresh basil
¼ cup pine nuts
3 cloves garlic
¼ cup extra-virgin olive oil
Salt and ground black pepper, to taste
1 large tomato, cored, seeded, and diced

In a large skillet over medium-high heat, cook the bacon until crisp, about 8 minutes. Use a slotted spoon to transfer it to paper towels and drain well. Let the bacon cool slightly.

Meanwhile, bring a large saucepan of salted water to a boil. Add the pasta and cook according to package directions. Reserve ¼ cup of the pasta cooking water, then drain the pasta, return it to the pot, and set aside.

In a food processor, combine the bacon, basil, pine nuts, and garlic. Pulse until well chopped. Then, with the processor running, drizzle in the olive oil until the ingredients form a thick paste. Stop the processor and scrape the sides with a rubber spatula as needed. Season with salt and pepper, then pulse again to blend.

Add the pesto to the pasta and toss well. Add just a bit of the pasta cooking water and toss again. Serve topped with diced tomato.

➲ HOW LONG? **20 MINUTES**
➲ HOW MUCH? **4 SERVINGS**

Shell Pasta with
Winter Squash and Rosemary

Sweet winter squash is a wonderful partner for spicy Italian sausage. I like butternut, but acorn or any similar hard squash works fine. Just be sure to cut the squash into small pieces for this recipe. Anything larger than about ½-inch cubes will take too long to cook.

12 ounces medium (about 1 inch) shell pasta
3 tablespoons olive oil, divided
1 medium yellow onion, thinly sliced
2 cloves garlic, minced
1 pound spicy Italian sausages, casings removed, broken into chunks
3 cups peeled and cubed winter squash
2 tablespoons chopped fresh rosemary
1 cup chicken broth
½ tablespoon cornstarch
2 tablespoons water

Bring a large saucepan of salted water to a boil. Add the pasta and cook according to package directions. Drain the pasta, return it to the pot, and toss it with 1 tablespoon of the olive oil. Set aside.

Meanwhile, in a large sauté pan over medium-high, heat the remaining 2 tablespoons of oil. Add the onion, garlic, and sausage. Sauté for 4 minutes.

Add the squash and rosemary, then sauté for another 4 minutes.

Add the chicken broth and use a wooden spoon to scrape up any browned bits from the bottom of the pan. Cover and simmer for 5 minutes.

Remove the cover and simmer for another minute, or until the squash is tender and the broth is mostly evaporated.

In a small glass, mix together the cornstarch and water, then add it to the squash and sausage mixture. Cook, stirring constantly, until thickened.

Add the pasta to the skillet and toss to combine.

⮕ HOW LONG? **20 MINUTES**
⮕ HOW MUCH? **4 SERVINGS**

Gnocchi with Cider Butter Sauce

While any pasta would work in this recipe, **the high starch content of gnocchi lends body to the sauce.** If you use another variety of pasta, don't rinse it after draining (which washes away the starch). In fact, never rinse any pasta at all.

4 tablespoons (½ stick) unsalted butter
½ cup apple cider (or apple juice plus 1 teaspoon cider vinegar)
¼ teaspoon salt
¼ teaspoon ground black pepper
10 fresh sage leaves, thinly sliced, divided
16 ounces gnocchi
¼ cup lightly toasted pine nuts
½ cup grated Parmesan cheese

In a small saucepan over medium-low heat, melt the butter. Add the cider, salt, pepper, and half of the sage, then bring to a simmer. Cook until the liquid has reduced by half, about 7 minutes.

Meanwhile, bring a large saucepan of salted water to a boil. Cook the gnocchi according to package directions (usually just until they float). Drain and transfer the gnocchi to a large serving bowl.

Pour the butter–cider sauce through a mesh strainer and discard the sage. Pour the butter reduction over the gnocchi and toss lightly.

Top the gnocchi with pine nuts, Parmesan, and the remaining sage.

HOW LONG? **20 MINUTES**
HOW MUCH? **4 SERVINGS**

Truffle Oil and Parmesan Penne

My office is a minefield of publicist debris. Cookbooks, cookware, food, wine. Most of it gets donated to charity. Which doesn't stop my son from playing with it first.

"What is that?" I asked one day when I found him smearing something across his lips.

"Nothing," he said, his lips dripping.

"What did you just put on your mouth?"

Hesitation. "Oil."

Truffle oil. **My son, then 4, had found a bottle of truffle oil, liked the smell, and started smearing it around his mouth.** The kid is odd.

This dish sounds extravagant, but the price won't bust your budget. While real truffle oil (the sort my son used as lip gloss) is pricey, truffle-flavored olive oil isn't. Look for it alongside other olive oils.

12 ounces penne pasta
1 tablespoon olive oil
1-pound bunch asparagus, bottoms trimmed,
each spear cut in half
1 cup sliced white button mushrooms
Coarse salt and ground black pepper, to taste
Truffle-flavored olive oil, to taste
½ cup grated Parmesan cheese

Bring a large saucepan of salted water to a boil. Add the pasta and cook according to package directions, then drain.

In a large skillet over medium-high heat, combine the olive oil, asparagus, and mushrooms. Sauté until the asparagus is barely tender, about 5 minutes.

Add the pasta to the skillet and toss well. Season with salt and pepper. Remove the pan from the heat, then drizzle the pasta with truffle-flavored olive oil. Toss, add the cheese, then toss again.

➡ HOW LONG? **20 MINUTES**
➡ HOW MUCH? **4 SERVINGS**

Shortcut Carbonara

My son is a fiend for carbonara. But true carbonara can be a fussy dish. Which means I never make traditional versions.

This recipe not only eliminates the fuss, it's totally forgiving. Use whatever deli meats and hard cheeses you have; it's a great way to finish up those bits and pieces in your refrigerator.

You can use the more traditional bacon, but it will take longer to cook. I prefer a combination of ham, prosciutto, and turkey breast paired with a blend of Parmesan and pecorino.

Whatever you use, **you can't mess this one up.**

2 tablespoons extra-virgin olive oil
1 pound deli meats (a blend of ham, prosciutto,
  and turkey or chicken is good), roughly chopped
12 ounces fresh fettuccine
¾ cup grated Italian cheeses (such as a blend of
  Parmesan and pecorino)
½ cup crème fraîche or plain Greek-style yogurt
Salt and ground black pepper, to taste

Bring a large saucepan of salted water to a boil.

Meanwhile, in a large skillet over medium-high, heat the oil. Add the meats and sauté until they are lightly browned and just crisp, about 6 minutes. The pan will get coated and a bit sticky. Set it aside, leaving the meat in the pan.

Add the pasta to the water and cook according to package directions. When the pasta is done, reserve ¼ cup of the cooking water, then drain and transfer the pasta to the skillet.

Return the skillet to low heat. Add the cheeses and crème fraîche, using tongs to mix and toss everything until the cheeses are melted and the pasta is coated. If the pasta is too dry, add a bit of the reserved cooking water and mix well.

Taste, then season with salt and pepper.

➔ HOW LONG? **20 MINUTES**
➔ HOW MUCH? **4 SERVINGS**

Four-Cheese Baked Gnocchi

Do I even need to say that this is a seriously rich dish? If you want to cut the fat, use low-fat versions of the sour cream, cheddar, and mozzarella. The dish will still be plenty creamy.

This one feeds a crowd, but is easily halved for smaller dinners. And if you feel like indulging, why not go for broke and make it five or six cheeses? Add ½ cup each of grated Parmesan and Monterey Jack.

1 cup sour cream
1 cup ricotta cheese
1½ cups (6-ounce package) shredded mozzarella cheese
1½ cups (6-ounce package) shredded cheddar cheese
1½ cups grated manchego cheese
½ pound prosciutto, cut into thin strips
½ teaspoon red pepper flakes
1 teaspoon salt
½ teaspoon ground black pepper
3 pounds gnocchi
½ cup pine nuts, coarsely ground
1 cup panko (Japanese-style) breadcrumbs
1 teaspoon smoked paprika
½ cup (1 stick) butter, melted

Heat the oven to 400°F. Bring a large saucepan of salted water to a boil. Lightly coat a 13-by-9-inch (3-quart) baking dish with cooking spray.

While the water heats, in a large bowl mix the sour cream, ricotta, mozzarella, cheddar, manchego, prosciutto, red pepper flakes, salt, and pepper. Set aside.

When the water is boiling, add the gnocchi and cook according to package directions (usually just until they float). Drain the gnocchi, then return them to the pan.

continued on next page

Add the cheese mixture to the gnocchi. Stir until everything is thoroughly mixed and the cheese is mostly melted. Transfer the mixture to the prepared baking dish, spreading it evenly. Set aside.

In a small bowl, mix the ground pine nuts, breadcrumbs, paprika, and butter. Sprinkle the breadcrumb mixture evenly over the gnocchi, then bake for 15 minutes, or until lightly browned.

➡ HOW LONG? **30 MINUTES (15 MINUTES ACTIVE)**
➡ HOW MUCH? **8 TO 10 SERVINGS**

PASTA PILLOWS

Gnocchi are a weeknight cook's dream pasta. Though most varieties are shelf stable (like the dry pasta they usually are sold alongside), they cook up as quickly and are as tender as refrigerated fresh pastas. And that means they are easy to keep on hand for nights when inspiration or time is lacking. Toss cooked gnocchi with salt, pepper, grated Parmesan, crushed garlic, and some baby spinach, and you have an awesome 10-minute meal.

Stovetop Brocc Mac and Cheese

After trying this dish **you'll never go back** to that wretched boxed stuff again. Because in about 15 minutes—about the same time as the box—you can have this intensely good mac and cheese.

Do anything you like to this, and it only gets better. Add cooked sausage, top it with browned ground beef or bacon, or be totally posh and mix in cooked shrimp, crabmeat, or lobster.

If you want to cut the fat, you can substitute low- or no-fat Greek-style yogurt for the crème fraîche.

12 ounces whole-wheat pasta spirals
4 cups broccoli florets
8-ounce container crème fraîche
½ teaspoon hot sauce
2½ cups grated sharp cheddar cheese
½ teaspoon garlic powder
½ teaspoon ground ginger
Ground black pepper, to taste

Bring a large saucepan of salted water to a boil.

Add the pasta and cook for 7 minutes. After that, add the broccoli and cook for another 2 minutes, or until the pasta is tender. Drain the pasta and broccoli, then set it aside.

Meanwhile, in a small saucepan over medium heat, whisk the crème fraîche and hot sauce until smooth, about 2 minutes.

Remove the pan from the heat and add the cheddar cheese, garlic powder, and ginger, then stir until melted and smooth. Season with pepper.

Divide the pasta and broccoli between serving bowls, then top with cheese sauce.

➲ HOW LONG? **15 MINUTES**
➲ HOW MUCH? **4 SERVINGS**

Meat Sauce Maximus

There is nothing subtle about this sauce. It's **all about the umami** (deep, savory flavors). The only way to make it more intense would be to add hot sauce or hot peppers. Spicy Italian sausage would be pretty great, too.

2 tablespoons olive oil
4 cloves garlic, minced
1 medium yellow onion, diced
½ teaspoon paprika
1 teaspoon dried basil
1 teaspoon dried oregano
1¼ pounds lean ground beef
½ pound prosciutto, finely chopped
28-ounce can diced tomatoes, with juices
3 tablespoons tomato paste
2 tablespoons balsamic vinegar
16 ounces pasta spirals
½ cup grated Parmesan cheese, plus extra to serve
Salt and ground black pepper, to taste

In a large saucepan over medium-high heat, combine the olive oil, garlic, onion, paprika, basil, and oregano. Sauté until the onion is tender and the seasonings are fragrant, about 5 minutes.

Add the ground beef and prosciutto. Sauté, breaking up any clumps of beef, until the beef is cooked through, about 8 minutes. Add the tomatoes, tomato paste, and vinegar, then simmer on low.

Meanwhile, heat a large saucepan of salted water to a boil. Add the pasta and cook according to package directions. Drain and return it to the pot.

Stir the Parmesan into the sauce, then season with salt and pepper. Serve the pasta topped with the sauce and additional Parmesan.

HOW LONG? **30 MINUTES**
HOW MUCH? **6 SERVINGS**

Four-Mushroom Penne
with Goat Cheese

Use this recipe as an excuse to **explore** your grocer's mushroom offerings. These days even the podunk shops where I live offer way more than just white buttons. Many varieties—such as portobello, shiitake, maitake, and lobster—have meaty, savory flavors and textures.

12 ounces penne pasta
2 tablespoons olive oil
2 cloves garlic, minced
¼ teaspoon red pepper flakes
2 cups sliced white button mushrooms
1 cup sliced baby portobello mushrooms
6 large shiitake mushroom caps, thinly sliced
1 cup sliced oyster mushrooms
1 cup fat-free half-and-half
½ cup grated Parmesan cheese
2 ounces chevre (soft goat cheese)
Splash hot sauce
1 teaspoon cool water
1½ teaspoons cornstarch
Salt and ground black pepper, to taste

Bring a large saucepan of salted water to a boil. Add the pasta and cook according to package directions. Drain and set it aside.

Meanwhile, in a large skillet over medium-high, heat the olive oil. Add the garlic and red pepper flakes, then sauté for 1 minute.

Add all 4 mushroom varieties. Sauté for 8 minutes, or until lightly browned. Reduce heat to low, add the pasta and toss well. Stir in the half-and-half, Parmesan, chevre, and hot sauce. In a small glass, mix the water and cornstarch, then add to the skillet. Cook until the sauce just thickens. Season with salt and pepper.

➔ HOW LONG? **30 MINUTES**
➔ HOW MUCH? **4 SERVINGS**

KIDS AND CUTLERY

I really did give my son a chef's knife for his second birthday. It isn't as crazy as it sounds. Getting children to appreciate and understand food means involving them from the start. I picked a short knife (five-inch blade) with a sticky, gel-coated handle (which limits slipping). I showed him how to hold it, then explained my primary rule of kids and knives—only big kids and adults are allowed to have both hands on the cutting board. When his cutting hand was on the knife, his other hand needed to be off the board and at his side. If he wanted to move the food he was cutting, the knife had to be put down first. While this approach fostered a somewhat clumsy cutting technique, there was almost no chance of him cutting himself. We've never even had a close call. Four years later he's a pro and has earned the privilege of using his second hand to hold the food as he cuts.

Stir-Fry Ravioli with Ground Turkey and Peppers

It may not seem right, but **a quick sauté such as this is all it takes to cook fresh ravioli.** And unlike boiled ravioli, these develop a crispy, meatier texture and flavor.

There isn't much "sauce" produced by this recipe. It's delicious as is, but if you prefer more liquid, stir in a bit of tomato sauce at the end and heat until just warmed.

4 tablespoons olive oil, divided
9-ounce package fresh cheese ravioli
½ teaspoon dried oregano
½ teaspoon dried basil
4 cloves garlic, minced
1 medium yellow onion, thinly sliced
1 green bell pepper, cored and thinly sliced
1 red bell pepper, cored and thinly sliced
1 pound ground turkey
¾ cup white wine
Salt and ground black pepper, to taste

In a large skillet over medium-high, heat 2 tablespoons of the oil. Add the ravioli and sauté, using tongs to move them around the pan, until lightly browned, about 4 minutes. Transfer the ravioli to a plate and set aside.

Return the skillet to the heat and add the remaining oil, the oregano, basil, garlic, onion, and both bell peppers. Sauté until the onions and peppers are tender, about 5 minutes.

Add the turkey to the onions and peppers. Sauté until browned and nearly cooked through, about 6 minutes.

Return the ravioli to the skillet. Stir in the wine, then cover and cook for 4 minutes. Uncover and simmer until the liquid has mostly evaporated, about another 2 minutes. Season with salt and pepper.

➲ HOW LONG? **20 MINUTES**
➲ HOW MUCH? **4 SERVINGS**

Linguine with Goat Cheese, Smoked Salmon, and Peas

Smoked salmon, **that wonderful friend of bagels and cream cheese,** usually is eaten uncooked. But in this dish, the heat of the pasta gently warms it, resulting in a sauce studded with wonderfully flaky salmon.

2 tablespoons olive oil
1 medium red onion, thinly sliced
3 cloves garlic, minced
¼ teaspoon red pepper flakes
12 ounces linguine
1 cup frozen peas
4-ounce package smoked salmon, cut into thin strips
4-ounce log chevre (soft goat cheese), cut into 6 chunks
½ tablespoon chopped fresh dill
Grated zest of 1 lemon
Salt and ground black pepper, to taste

Bring a large saucepan of salted water to a boil.

In a large skillet over medium-high heat, combine the olive oil, onion, garlic, and red pepper flakes. Sauté until the onion is tender, about 5 minutes.

Cook the pasta according to package directions.

Meanwhile, add the peas to the onion and sauté until the peas are heated through. Remove the skillet from the heat.

Once the pasta is done, reserve ½ cup of the cooking water, then drain the pasta. Add the pasta to the onions and peas, then toss.

Add the smoked salmon, chevre, dill, lemon zest, and ¼ cup of the reserved pasta cooking water. Toss until the cheese is melted. If the sauce is too thick, add more of the pasta cooking water. Season with salt and pepper and serve.

➲ HOW LONG? **20 MINUTES**
➲ HOW MUCH? **4 SERVINGS**

BLT Linguine

This sort of **toss-it-all-together** meal is essential to my weekday sanity. It's easy enough that I can make it while also helping my son build Lego spaceships for his toy cats, Sandwich and Scream Cheese (his names). And no, I don't know why they need spaceships.

Scallions stand in for the usual BLT greens in this pasta dish. If you're looking to trim fat, substitute low- or no-fat plain Greek-style yogurt for the cream cheese and about six pieces of thinly sliced prosciutto for the bacon.

10 slices smoked bacon, cut into 1-inch pieces
1 bunch scallions, whites and light green sections, chopped
1 pint cherry tomatoes, halved
12-ounce package fresh linguine
4 ounces cream cheese, cut into small chunks
Salt and ground black pepper, to taste

Bring a large saucepan of salted water to a boil.

While the water heats, in a large skillet over medium heat, cook the bacon until it is crisp, 6 to 7 minutes. Add the scallions and tomatoes, then sauté for 2 minutes. Use a slotted spoon to transfer the mixture to a bowl, draining any excess fat.

Cook the pasta according to package directions. Reserve ¼ cup of the cooking water, then drain the pasta and return it to the saucepan.

Add the cream cheese and half of the reserved cooking water to the pasta. Toss until the cheese is melted and forms a creamy sauce.

Add three-quarters of the bacon and tomato mixture, then toss again. If the sauce is too thick, add a bit more of the reserved cooking water. Taste and season with salt and pepper.

Divide the pasta among 4 plates, then top each serving with some of the remaining bacon and tomato mixture.

➲ HOW LONG? **20 MINUTES**
➲ HOW MUCH? **4 SERVINGS**

Linguine with Cilantro and Pepita Pesto

Pepitas (shelled pumpkin seeds) usually can be found alongside the nuts and dried fruit. Many roasted varieties are heavily salted, so be sure to adjust your seasonings accordingly.

Nearly any nut and herb can be wedded as pesto—walnuts and parsley, peanuts and basil, almonds and a blend of sage, mint, and parsley. Also experiment with the acid, traditionally lemon juice. Lime or orange juice, as well as just about any vinegar, will work well.

12 ounces linguine
4 ounces manchego cheese, cut into small chunks,
   plus extra for garnish
½ cup roasted pepitas (shelled pumpkin seeds)
1 cup packed fresh cilantro, thick stems removed
½ tablespoon jarred jalapeño pepper slices
2 cloves garlic
3 tablespoons extra-virgin olive oil
1 tablespoon lime juice
Salt and ground black pepper, to taste

Bring a large pot of salted water to a boil. Cook the pasta according to package directions. Reserve ¼ cup of the cooking water, then drain the pasta and return it to the pot.

Meanwhile, in a food processor, combine the manchego and pepitas. Pulse until finely ground. Add the cilantro, jalapeño peppers, garlic, oil, and lime juice. Process until the mixture forms fine, moist crumbs. Taste, then season with salt and pepper.

Add the pesto and the reserved cooking water to the pasta and toss well to coat and heat the pesto. Serve topped with additional manchego.

➲ HOW LONG? **20 MINUTES**
➲ HOW MUCH? **4 SERVINGS**

IT'S KIND OF SEEDY

Toasting pumpkin seeds—or any other variety of raw seed—is easy. Dump them in a dry skillet over low heat. Stir often, until they are lightly browned, usually no more than 2 or 3 minutes. Some varieties, such as pepitas, will puff or start to pop when they are ready. Transfer the seeds to a bowl or plate to cool before using them.

Chorizo and Arugula Fettuccine

Be sure to remove the casing before using chorizo, a spicy (but not searing) sausage seasoned with garlic and chili powder. If you have a choice, **opt for Spanish chorizo,** which is made from smoked pork.

This recipe calls for using tongs, rather than a strainer, to drain the pasta and transfer it to the skillet. Doing this retains more of the starchy cooking water, which helps the other ingredients in the skillet coat the pasta.

2 tablespoons extra-virgin olive oil
Pinch red pepper flakes
8 to 9 ounces chorizo, casings removed, meat crumbled
  or chopped
12-ounce package fresh fettuccine
3 cups lightly packed arugula
3 cloves garlic, minced
1 cup grated manchego cheese
Salt and ground black pepper, to taste

Bring a large saucepan of salted water to a boil.

Meanwhile, in a large skillet over medium-high, heat the oil. Add the red pepper flakes and heat for 30 seconds. Add the chorizo and sauté until browned, about 5 minutes.

When the water boils, add the pasta to the pot and cook until just al dente, 3 minutes. Instead of draining, use tongs to transfer the pasta directly from the water to the skillet with the chorizo.

Reduce the heat under the skillet to low. Toss the pasta well, then add the arugula, garlic, and cheese. Toss again until the arugula is wilted and the cheese melts, about 2 to 3 minutes. Season with salt and pepper.

➡ HOW LONG? **20 MINUTES**
➡ HOW MUCH? **4 SERVINGS**

SANDWICHED

I'm going to hell. I've been heading there since I was about five. And it's all over a hot dog.

It wasn't easy being a pudgy and reluctant Catholic school boy with a Jewish last name. The Grey Nuns of the Cross of Ottawa wouldn't even accept the donations Mom sent with me to school every month.

So instead I spent it on the handmade ice cream sandwiches sold at the candy and card shop I passed on my walk home. Thin, crisp waffle cookies that sandwiched a slab of vanilla. I'd start by nibbling away the cookies until there was just enough to hold the now softened, nearly naked, creamy middle. Then I'd slowly work my tongue around the perimeter. Not that I was obsessive.

Using God's funds for gourmand pleasures probably didn't help my chances for eternal salvation. But my more serious sin was a failure to eat hot dogs. Mom, a longtime vegetarian, wouldn't let me. And to the nuns who ran Ste. Jeanne d'Arc School—to which my mother, grandmother, and great-grandmother had gone, but who's counting?—this was nearly as bad as thinking wicked thoughts about the young and shapely Sister Maria.

Abstaining from frankfurters was an egregious display of individuality in a school where the girls dressed in upholstery-like plaid jumpers and the boys were a sea of navy polyester. The every-other-Friday-except-during-Lent Hot Dog Days were a big deal. The nuns would pilot a hot dog vendor cart otherwise reserved for craft and bake sales down the hallways, presenting greasy links classroom by classroom with about the same ceremony as Communion.

Meanwhile, I ate the same cheese and mustard on whole wheat Mom packed in my *Empire Strikes Back* lunch box every day.

Worse still, I didn't drink milk. You'd swear I was going all Martin Luther on them they way they reacted. And I wish I could blame some contrarian rebellious instincts.

Milk just wasn't a beverage in my home. You could cook with it and pour it over whole-grain, no-added-sugar breakfast cereal. And we were happy to eat it in its various frozen and coagulated forms. But drink it? Just never really occurred to us.

And so I never paid my $2.50 a week in milk money, which as with our tithing, was to be proffered in small, preprinted envelopes. Morning snack would come, and I would be passed over by the student lucky enough to be selected for milk distribution duty. I usually got eraser duty.

I still don't eat hot dogs. I still don't drink milk. And I gave up trying to win the hearts of nuns decades ago. But I have moved way beyond cheese and mustard sandwiches.

Pepper Steak Grinders
with Mango Chutney

There are plenty of ways to tart up a grinder. But sometimes old-fashioned ground black pepper is the best bet. In this case, tons of ground black pepper. Apply as much as you can handle; the mango chutney moderates the heat.

Four 6-inch sub rolls
Dijon mustard
1 cup mango chutney
3 tablespoons coarsely ground black pepper
2 tablespoons kosher salt
12 thinly sliced eye round steaks (also called steak medallions)
6 deli slices provolone cheese, halved

Heat a grill or grill pan to high.

Cut each roll in half lengthwise. Slather one half of each roll with mustard. Spread the chutney over the mustard, dividing it equally among the rolls.

Combine the pepper and salt in a shallow bowl. Firmly press one side of each steak in the salt and pepper to coat. If you like it potent, coat both sides of the steaks.

Lightly coat the grill or grill pan with cooking spray. Grill the steaks for about 1 minute then flip them and grill for another minute, or until cooked through.

Lay half a cheese slice on each steak. Cover the grill or grill pan, turn off the heat, and let the steaks sit for 1 minute, or until the cheese melts.

To assemble the grinders, set three steaks over the chutney on each roll, then top them with the other half of the roll.

➡ HOW LONG? **20 MINUTES**
➡ HOW MUCH? **4 SERVINGS**

Open-Faced Tuna and Cheddar Melt

This is what a tuna melt ought to be. Meaty, crunchy, tangy, and cheesy. If open-faced isn't your style, toss this on a roll or into a pita pocket, or rolled in a flour tortilla. But don't leave off the cheddar; it completes the over-the-top taste.

4 thick slices rustic multigrain bread
Extra-virgin olive oil
Two 6-ounce cans water-packed tuna, drained
1 small shallot, diced
⅓ cup diced Peppadew peppers (or 1 tablespoon diced jarred jalapeño peppers)
1 celery stalk, diced
2 tablespoons finely chopped fresh cilantro
⅓ cup diced bread-and-butter pickle chips
2 tablespoons Dijon mustard
2 tablespoons mayonnaise
8 slices cheddar cheese

Heat the oven to 450°F.

Arrange the bread on a rimmed baking sheet. Drizzle each slice with olive oil. Toast in the oven until just barely browned, about 5 minutes. Set aside, leaving the oven on.

Meanwhile, in a medium bowl, combine the tuna, shallot, Peppadews, celery, cilantro, and pickles. Mix well.

In a small bowl, whisk together the mustard and mayonnaise, then mix it into the tuna.

Spread a quarter of the tuna salad over each slice of bread, then top each with 2 slices of cheese. Bake for 10 minutes, or until the cheese is melted.

➲ HOW LONG? **20 MINUTES**
➲ HOW MUCH? **4 SERVINGS**

Red Curry Falafel

Yeah, *falafel* **was one of the first words my son could write**, followed closely by *sushi* and *cookies*. His last name came later.

These falafel come together in almost no time in the food processor and are quick to pan fry. They also could be baked. If you do, be sure to spritz them on all sides with cooking spray to help them crisp.

4 slices sandwich bread (about 4 ounces)
2 teaspoons Thai red curry paste
3 tablespoons chopped fresh cilantro
3 tablespoons chopped fresh flat-leaf parsley
1 teaspoon ground cumin
1 teaspoon salt
¼ teaspoon ground black pepper
Grated zest of 1 lemon
2 tablespoons olive oil
15-ounce can chickpeas, drained
2 tablespoons canola or vegetable oil, divided
3 flatbreads, warmed
Smoked paprika
1 avocado, pitted, skinned, and cut into slices
½ cup Greek-style plain yogurt
1 tablespoon chopped fresh dill
1 large tomato, cut into wedges

In a food processor, pulse the bread until it is reduced to fine crumbs. Add the red curry paste, cilantro, parsley, cumin, salt, pepper, lemon zest, and olive oil. Pulse until well combined.

Add the chickpeas and pulse until they are finely chopped but not pureed. Form the mixture into 9 patties.

In a large skillet over medium, heat 1 tablespoon of the oil. Fry half of the patties until the bottoms are lightly browned, 1 to 2 minutes.

continued on next page

Flip the patties and brown on the other side, another 1 to 2 minutes. Transfer to a paper towel–lined plate. Add the remaining oil to the skillet and repeat with the remaining patties.

To serve, arrange 3 falafel on each flatbread. Sprinkle them with paprika, then top them with avocado, yogurt, dill, and tomatoes.

➡ HOW LONG? **15 MINUTES**
➡ HOW MUCH? **3 SERVINGS**

THAI AIN'T ALL PAD

Thai red curry paste is mildly spicy and deeply flavorful. Add just a teaspoon or two to coconut milk to create easy potato, meat, or vegetable curries. Or thin it with water or chicken broth and marinate shrimp in it.

The paste is a blend of spices, including coriander, lemon grass, black pepper, galangal (a relative of ginger), and cilantro. It can be found in small jars or cans among grocers' Asian foods.

Dolmades Wraps with Feta and Fresh Mint

Fresh mint is totally underappreciated in America. **It really can have a life beyond mojitos.** Outside the U.S., it's a common addition to fresh spring rolls, salads, pestos, sandwiches, and meatballs. Pair it with a mild cheese, such as a thick slab of buffalo mozzarella, on panini with grilled chicken or deli-sliced turkey.

Dolmades (grape leaves stuffed with a flavorful blend of rice and nuts) are available alongside the hummus at most grocers.

2 large flatbreads or pita pockets
2 cups baby spinach
2 jarred roasted red peppers, patted dry and cut into thin strips
½ cup finely chopped red onion
½ cup crumbled feta cheese
10 dolmades (stuffed grape leaves)
2 tablespoons bottled Greek salad dressing or vinaigrette
1 teaspoon finely chopped fresh mint

Heat the oven to 350°F.

Set each flatbread on the counter and arrange 1 cup of spinach down the center of each. Divide the red peppers, red onion, and feta cheese between the 2 flatbreads, arranging them over the spinach. Top each with 5 dolmades.

Drizzle each wrap with 1 tablespoon of the dressing and sprinkle on a bit of the mint. Wrap the flatbread tightly around the fillings, securing the sides with a toothpick.

Place the wraps on a baking sheet and bake for 10 minutes, or until just warmed.

➡ HOW LONG? **20 MINUTES**
➡ HOW MUCH? **2 SERVINGS**

Grilled Sourdough Pizza
with Tomato Pesto

This is a cross between pizza and an open-faced sandwich. The sauce is **an intense blend of purchased pesto and tomato paste.**

As when grilling traditional pizza dough, the bread is grilled on one side before any toppings are added. The bread then is flipped, topped, and returned to the grill to toast the second side. This ensures that both sides of the bread get the benefit of the grill.

¼ cup prepared pesto
2 tablespoons tomato paste
2 large, thick slices sourdough bread
Extra-virgin olive oil
2 medium tomatoes, thickly sliced
12-ounce ball fresh mozzarella, thickly sliced
¼ cup sliced black olives
Ground black pepper, to taste
2 fresh basil leaves, thinly sliced

Heat a grill to high.

In a small bowl, whisk together the pesto and tomato paste.

Drizzle both slices of the bread on both sides with olive oil. Grill the bread until it is lightly toasted on the bottom.

Remove the bread from the grill. Spread half of the pesto mixture over the toasted side of each slice of bread.

Top the pesto with tomato slices, then mozzarella slices and black olives. Season with pepper, then return to the grill.

Cover, reduce heat to low, and grill until the bottoms are toasted and the cheese has melted, about 10 minutes. Sprinkle with basil.

➲ HOW LONG? **20 MINUTES**
➲ HOW MUCH? **2 SERVINGS**

Ginger-Teriyaki Cheeseburgers

These burgers are so delicious and so moist **no condiments** are needed beyond the Asian-seasoned broccoli slaw. The slaw, which stands in for the more traditional lettuce, is made from purchased slaw tossed with Asian-style mustard and mayonnaise.

1¼ pounds ground beef
2 tablespoons grated fresh ginger
2 garlic cloves, minced
2 tablespoons teriyaki sauce
1 teaspoon rice vinegar
½ teaspoon salt
¼ teaspoon ground black pepper
1 large red onion, cut crosswise into 4 thick slices
1 tablespoon Asian-style mustard (Chinese hot mustard)
¼ cup mayonnaise
2 cups broccoli slaw
4 hamburger buns
4-ounce log chevre (soft goat cheese)

Heat a grill to high.

In a large bowl, combine the beef, ginger, garlic, teriyaki sauce, vinegar, salt, and pepper. Use your hands to blend the ingredients, then shape the mixture into 4 patties.

When the grill is hot, lightly oil the grates. Grill the burgers for 6 to 7 minutes per side, or until desired doneness. Grill the onions for about 4 minutes per side, or until soft.

Meanwhile, in a medium bowl, mix together the mustard and mayonnaise. Add the broccoli slaw and toss well. Divide the mixture among the bottom halves of the buns.

When the burgers are done, place each on top of a coleslaw-covered bun, then use a butter knife to spread a quarter of the goat cheese onto the burger. Top with an onion slice and bun.

➲ HOW LONG? **25 MINUTES**
➲ HOW MUCH? **4 SERVINGS**

Sloppy Joes

True to their name, **these Joes are sloppy good.** Prefer your sloppies with more bite? Substitute spicy barbecue sauce for half (or more) of the ketchup. And of course ground chicken or turkey can be substituted for the beef.

1 medium yellow onion, quartered
1 tablespoon jarred jalapeño pepper slices
12-ounce jar roasted red peppers, drained
3 cloves garlic
2 tablespoons olive oil
1 teaspoon smoked paprika
1 teaspoon ground cumin
½ teaspoon chili powder
½ teaspoon dry yellow mustard
1¼ pounds ground beef
½ cup ketchup
1½ cups tomato puree
1 tablespoon cider vinegar
Salt and ground black pepper, to taste
4 hamburger buns
Bread-and-butter pickle slices, for serving

In a food processor, combine the onion, jalapeño peppers, roasted red peppers, and garlic. Pulse, scraping the bowl as needed, until minced.

In a large skillet over medium-high, heat the oil. Add the onion and pepper mixture, then sauté for 4 minutes. Add the paprika, cumin, chili powder, and mustard. Sauté for another 4 minutes.

Add the beef and sauté, breaking up the clumps with a spoon, until the meat is just browned, about another 5 minutes.

In a medium bowl, whisk together the ketchup, tomato puree, and vinegar. Add this to the meat, bring to a simmer, then lower the heat to medium. Cook, uncovered, for 10 minutes.

Season with salt and pepper. Serve on a bun with pickles.

➡ HOW LONG? **30 MINUTES**
➡ HOW MUCH? **4 SERVINGS**

Garlic Shrimp Po'boys with Cheesy Slaw

This intense take on the classic New Orleans grinder combines **pan-fried shrimp drenched in garlic and butter** with a slaw of broccoli and cheese. Swaddle the whole thing in a baguette, or whatever bread or roll you have handy, and you have a serious sandwich.

Broccoli slaw is an effortless way to add great greens to your meals. The bagged medley of slivered broccoli and other vegetables requires zero prep and can be dressed or cooked as you like. Preshredded slaw mixes are widely available in produce sections.

24-inch baguette
5.2-ounce package Boursin (or other garlic-and-herb
  soft cheese)
2 cups (about 6 ounces) broccoli slaw
2 tablespoons olive oil
2 tablespoons butter
3 cloves garlic, minced
½ small red chili, such as fresno or Thai, minced
  (more or less to taste)
1 pound shelled, veined shrimp (see sidebar)
¼ teaspoon ground black pepper
Salt, to taste

Cut the baguette into 4 sections, then split each down the center.

Place the Boursin in a medium microwave-safe bowl. Microwave on high for 20 seconds, or until the cheese is very soft but not melted.

Add the broccoli slaw to the warmed cheese, then mix well. Spread a quarter of the slaw mixture onto each baguette section.

In a large skillet over medium-high heat, combine the oil and butter. When the butter has melted, add the garlic and chili. Sauté for 30 seconds.

Add the shrimp and cook for 2 to 3 minutes, or until firm. Add the pepper and toss. Season with salt. Divide the shrimp among the baguettes.

➲ HOW LONG? **20 MINUTES**
➲ HOW MUCH? **4 SERVINGS**

SHELLFISH ON ICE

I almost always have a few bags of frozen shrimp on hand. They are a fast and easy way to get dinner—whether a stir-fry, frittata, pasta dish, or whatever—on the table. They thaw quickly under cold running water, and so long as you buy them sans veins and shells, there's no need for prep. For most of my recipes, size doesn't matter. But since most people find larger shrimp more satisfying, I always suggest buying the largest you can afford. Stir-fry them with rice and veggies, toss them in tomato soups, or skewer and grill them. As for seasonings, they particularly love garlic, butter, fresh ginger, and anything spicy.

Warmed Smoked Salmon and Bacon Bagel

Salty, creamy, and savory. It's everything a bagel was meant for. This is a pretty hefty sandwich, so you'll want to use a fresh, soft bagel.

1 bagel
¼ cup cream cheese (block-style, not whipped)
2 ounces smoked salmon
Red onion, thinly sliced, to taste
1 large tomato
Balsamic vinegar, to drizzle
Ground black pepper, to taste
1 slice bacon, cooked

Heat the oven to 350°F.

Cut the bagel in half, then spread half of the cream cheese on each side. Top one half of the bagel with the salmon and red onion slices.

Cut a thick slice out of the center of the tomato; reserve the remaining tomato for another use. Place the tomato slice over the onion, then drizzle it with a bit of balsamic vinegar. Season with pepper.

Top the tomato with the bacon, breaking the bacon into shorter lengths as needed to fit evenly. Top with the second half of the bagel, then tightly wrap the sandwich in foil.

Place in the oven for 20 minutes, or until just heated through.

➡ HOW LONG? **25 MINUTES (5 MINUTES ACTIVE)**
➡ HOW MUCH? **1 SERVING**

Smoked Turkey Breast and Apple Chutney Panini

Don't waste your money on a silly panini press. **All you really need** are two skillets, one smaller than the other. Heat the larger of the two pans, put your sandwich in it, then place the second pan on top. Place some heavy canned goods in the top pan to weigh it down. If you have a cast-iron pan, use that for the top, and you won't even need the cans.

½ small apple, peeled, cored, and diced
2 tablespoons mango chutney
2 large naan or pita pockets, halved crosswise
4 large slices extra-sharp cheddar cheese (about 3 ounces)
4 deli slices smoked turkey breast
Ground black pepper, to taste

In a small bowl, combine the apple and chutney. Spread this mixture over 2 of the bread halves. Top the chutney with cheese, turkey breast, and pepper. Top each with the second bread half.

Set a large skillet over medium heat. Spritz the pan with cooking spray, then add the panini. Place a second pan on top of the panini, weighing it down with several canned goods if it is light.

Toast the panini until the bottoms are crisp and lightly browned, 2 to 3 minutes. Remove the top pan, flip the sandwiches, replace the top pan, and toast another 2 to 3 minutes.

➡ HOW LONG? **15 MINUTES**
➡ HOW MUCH? **2 SERVINGS**

Grilled Asian Chicken Sandwich

The combination of **sesame oil, vinegar, and soy sauce is decadent** without being cloying or fatty. Add a splash of hot sauce and some chopped scallions, and you have a great dipping sauce for spring rolls or Asian-style dumplings. Or toss cubed winter squash in it, then roast and sprinkle with sesame seeds for a flavorful side dish.

2 tablespoons toasted sesame oil, divided
1 tablespoon rice vinegar or cider vinegar
1 tablespoon soy sauce
1 teaspoon garlic powder
½ teaspoon ground ginger
1 teaspoon salt
¼ teaspoon ground black pepper
1 teaspoon smoked paprika
1 boneless, skinless chicken breast
2 ciabatta or crusty rolls
1 tablespoon mayonnaise
1 tablespoon Asian-style or other hot mustard
4 to 6 leaves Bibb lettuce
2 thick slices tomato
1 scallion, chopped

In a medium bowl, whisk together 1 tablespoon of the oil, the vinegar, soy sauce, garlic powder, ginger, salt, pepper, and paprika. Set aside.

Carefully cut the chicken breast horizontally through the center to create 2 thin cutlets. Place the chicken in the bowl of marinade, turn it to coat, and set aside for 15 minutes.

Split the rolls in half. Use the remaining tablespoon of oil to lightly coat the cut sides of each bun. Remove the chicken from the marinade; discard the marinade.

Set a grill pan over medium-high heat. Lightly coat the pan with cooking spray, then add the chicken. Grill until there are prominent marks on the bottoms, 5 to 6 minutes.

Flip the chicken. Reduce the heat to medium, cover the pan, and grill for another 3 to 4 minutes, or until an instant-read thermometer inserted at the center registers 165°F. Transfer the chicken to a plate. Cover and set it aside.

Place the buns in the grill pan, cut sides down, and toast for 1 to 2 minutes.

To assemble the sandwiches, in a small bowl or cup, combine the mayonnaise and mustard. Spread half of the mixture over the bottom half of each bun.

Top each bun with lettuce, tomato, and a piece of chicken. Finish with chopped scallion.

➡ HOW LONG? **30 MINUTES**
➡ HOW MUCH? **2 SERVINGS**

Flatbread Grilled Cheese
with Spinach and Prosciutto

Use this same approach with whatever ingredients appeal to you. The trick is to **keep the toppings thin.** For example, substitute thin slices of apple for the prosciutto and crumbled blue cheese for the mozzarella. Or try roasted red peppers (drained and well dried) and gouda.

1 teaspoon diced jarred jalapeño pepper slices
1 tablespoon Dijon mustard
2 large flatbreads or flour tortillas
2 cups baby spinach
5 slices prosciutto or deli-sliced ham
1 cup shredded mozzarella cheese
Salt and ground black pepper, to taste

Heat a grill to high or set a grill pan over high heat.

In a small bowl, combine the peppers and mustard. Use a fork to mash them into a paste. Spread the mixture over one of the flatbreads.

Arrange the spinach over the mustard, then top it with the prosciutto and cheese. Season with salt and pepper, then top with the remaining flatbread.

Spritz the grill grate or pan lightly with cooking spray, then place the sandwich on it. Cook for 2 to 3 minutes, or until the bottom browns.

If you are using a grill, reduce the heat on one side to low. If you are using a grill pan, reduce the burner to low.

Spritz the top of the sandwich with cooking spray, then flip the sandwich. On the grill, move the sandwich to the cooler side.

Cover the grill or pan and cook until the cheese is melted, 3 to 4 minutes. Cut the sandwich into quarters.

➡ HOW LONG? **15 MINUTES**
➡ HOW MUCH? **2 SERVINGS**

Triple Seafood Salad
on Butter-Toasted Buns

This is one serious seafood salad. **I've jammed it with shrimp, crab, and lobster** (okay, imitation lobster, but for a salad, who's counting?). For crunch and a hint of sweetness, I added diced apple, jicama, and celery. And the whole thing is tossed with a tangy, creamy dressing. Add buttered rolls, and you've got summer in a sandwich.

I'm not normally a fan of imitation seafood (it's still "real" seafood, it just isn't lobster), but it kind of belongs in seafood salad. It's like California rolls, which simply aren't legit without the imitation crab.

If you can't find the jicama (it resembles a big, ugly potato) just up the other crunchy ingredients—the celery, red bell pepper, and apple.

3 to 4 tablespoons mayonnaise
1 tablespoon whole-grain mustard
½ teaspoon garlic powder
Pinch celery seeds
Ground black pepper, to taste
Hot sauce, to taste
1 stalk celery, finely chopped
1 small red bell pepper, cored and finely chopped
1 cup peeled and finely chopped jicama
1 medium green apple, peeled and diced
½ pound cooked shrimp, peeled and roughly chopped
½ pound crabmeat, picked over for shells
½ pound imitation lobster meat, roughly chopped or
  pulled apart
2 tablespoons butter
6 to 8 hamburger or hot dog buns

In a large bowl, whisk together the mayonnaise, mustard, garlic powder, celery seeds, and pepper. Add hot sauce, mix well, then taste and adjust the pepper and hot sauce as desired.

Add the celery, bell pepper, jicama, and apple, then toss well to coat. Add the shrimp, crabmeat, and imitation lobster meat. Toss until just coated. Set aside.

In a large skillet over medium-low heat, melt the butter. Add the buns (split open if hamburger, on their sides if hot dog) and toast them until they are lightly browned and crispy.

Serve the seafood salad in the toasted buns.

➡ HOW LONG? **20 MINUTES**
➡ HOW MUCH? **6 TO 8 SERVINGS**

Roasted Tomato and Ricotta Bruschetta

Roasting tomatoes—especially out-of-season ones—caramelizes their natural sugars, giving them a **serious flavor boost.** And the same technique works with most vegetables, especially winter squash.

If you'd like to simplify this recipe, you could use just ricotta or goat, though the combination of tangy, soft cheeses works especially nicely here. If you want to up the flavor even more, you could mash roasted garlic cloves into the cheese blend.

2 pints cherry or grape tomatoes, halved
3 tablespoons olive oil, divided
1 teaspoon kosher salt
¼ teaspoon ground black pepper
½ teaspoon dried oregano
½ cup balsamic vinegar
6 thick slices sourdough bread
2 cloves garlic
¾ cup ricotta cheese
8 ounces chevre (soft goat cheese)
1 tablespoon fresh thyme leaves

Heat the oven to 400°F.

In a medium bowl, combine the tomatoes, 2 tablespoons of the olive oil, the salt, pepper, and oregano. Toss to coat evenly.

Transfer the tomatoes, along with any oil in the bowl, to a rimmed baking sheet. Roast for 35 minutes, or until the tomatoes are lightly browned and wrinkled.

While the tomatoes roast, in a small saucepan over medium heat, bring the balsamic vinegar to a simmer and let it reduce by half, about 5 to 8 minutes. Set aside.

During the final 10 minutes of roasting, place the bread in the oven and toast until it is just lightly browned.

Remove the tomatoes and bread from the oven and let the tomatoes cool slightly. While the tomatoes cool, rub the toasted bread with the garlic cloves.

In a small bowl, mix the ricotta and goat cheeses. Slather a generous layer of the cheese blend on each slice of bread, then arrange the slices on a serving platter.

Top each slice with some of the tomatoes. Sprinkle with fresh thyme, then finish with a drizzle of the reduced balsamic vinegar and remaining olive oil over each.

➡ HOW LONG? **1 HOUR (20 MINUTES ACTIVE)**
➡ HOW MUCH? **6 SERVINGS**

Soft Tacos with Spicy Lime Pulled Chicken

This boiling technique also is a great way to do pulled barbecue chicken. Prepare the chicken breasts as described below, then toss them with your favorite barbecue sauce (try the awesome sweet-and-savory barbecue sauce on page 129), then serve it on buns with tomato and pickles.

1¼ pounds boneless, skinless chicken breasts, cut into large chunks
4 large flour tortillas
16-ounce can refried beans
Juice of 1 lime
1 teaspoon garlic powder
1 teaspoon hot sauce (or more or less, to taste)
1½ cups (6 ounces) shredded mozzarella cheese
Salt and ground black pepper, to taste
3 tablespoons mayonnaise
½ teaspoon ground cumin
1½ cups shredded coleslaw mix (bagged shredded cabbage and carrots)
2 tomatoes, cut into wedges
1 avocado, peeled, pitted, and sliced
2 tablespoons chopped fresh cilantro

Bring a large saucepan of water to a boil. Add the chicken and boil until an instant-read thermometer inserted at the center of the largest piece of chicken reads 165°F, about 10 minutes.

Heat the oven to 200°F. Wrap the tortillas in foil and place them in the oven to warm.

Meanwhile, in a medium saucepan, combine the refried beans, lime juice, garlic powder, hot sauce, and cheese. Stir until the mixture is hot and the cheese has melted. Season with salt and pepper.

In a medium bowl, whisk together the mayonnaise and cumin. Season with pepper. Add the coleslaw blend, then mix well.

continued on next page

When the chicken is done, drain it, then return it to the pan. Use forks to shred the pieces. To do this, use one fork to hold each piece while using another to scrape and pull at it.

Add the refried bean mixture to the chicken and toss well. Transfer it to a serving bowl.

Let diners assemble their own tacos by filling a warmed tortilla with the coleslaw mixture and chicken, then topping it with tomatoes, avocado, and cilantro.

➡ HOW LONG? **30 MINUTES**
➡ HOW MUCH? **4 SERVINGS**

Fig, Prosciutto, and Goat Cheese Panini

Focaccia is another great bread choice for these sandwiches, which sport the terrific combination of sweet figs, salty prosciutto, and creamy goat cheese. And deli-sliced smoked turkey breast or honey-baked ham would be fine substitutes for the prosciutto.

4-ounce log chevre (soft goat cheese)
4 slices rustic multigrain bread
2 tablespoons fig jam
1 tablespoon chopped fresh oregano
4 slices prosciutto
1 tablespoon butter

Spread a quarter of the goat cheese over one side of each slice of bread. Spread 1 tablespoon fig jam over the goat cheese on 2 of the slices.

Scatter the oregano over the fig jam, then top it with prosciutto, then the remaining slices of bread, cheese side down.

In a large skillet over medium-high heat, melt the butter. Add the sandwiches, then set a heavy or weighted pan over them. Cook until the bread is lightly browned on the bottom, about 2 minutes.

Remove the top pan, flip the sandwiches, then replace the top pan and cook for about another 2 minutes.

➡ HOW LONG? **15 MINUTES**
➡ HOW MUCH? **2 SERVINGS**

Is there anything potatoes can't do?

It was Larry, screaming and laughing as bits of root vegetable shot out from under the tires of our tiny rental car, showering me with sand and potato pulp. I bet the editors at *Bon Appétit* and *Food & Wine* don't have to deal with this sort of thing.

The car groaned as its wheels spun wildly. I moaned as I heaved against the bumper.

I had told Larry, AP's food photographer and my close friend and working partner of too many years, not to take the side road. I'd pointed out the sign, which seemed pretty unambiguous to me: SOFT SAND. NO CARS BEYOND THIS POINT.

We were on assignment in Ireland and late as usual. For reasons I can only attribute to his Guinness consumption the night before, Larry saw the sign, heard my warning, then gunned the engine. The car lunged forward. Then stopped. Really, really suddenly. Obscenities were exchanged.

The tires couldn't get traction. And as we walked around the car to assess the damage, we realized we had nothing, not even floor mats, to shove under the tires. Nothing, that is, except for potatoes. It was Ireland, after all.

We'd stopped at a farm stand a short time before and bought a sack of potatoes. Larry jammed several under each tire. I pushed as he pumped the gas.

He got lucky. With a sudden lurch and a spray of vegetable matter, the tires caught on a particularly dense chunk of spud. Still laughing and screaming something about potatoes, Larry slammed on the brakes, bringing the car to a sliding halt a couple feet from a river.

This chapter offers several things to do with potatoes (as well as plenty of other ingredients). No Irish rental cars or foolish food photographers needed.

Maple-Roasted Squash with Prosciutto

This squash is **intensely smoky, sweet, savory, and salty.** A blend of smoked paprika, chopped prosciutto, and maple syrup take plain old butternut squash totally over the top. Don't substitute bacon for the prosciutto; it is too fatty for this recipe.

This assertive dish goes nicely with roasted turkey, chicken, or beef.

1 teaspoon cinnamon
¼ teaspoon ground nutmeg
1 teaspoon smoked paprika
⅔ cup maple syrup
4-pound butternut squash, peeled, seeded, and cut
**   to a ½-inch dice (about 9 cups cut)**
8 ounces prosciutto, cut or torn into small pieces
Salt and ground black pepper, to taste

Heat the oven to 400°F. Line 2 rimmed baking sheets with parchment paper.

In a small bowl, whisk together the cinnamon, nutmeg, smoked paprika, and maple syrup.

Place the squash in a large bowl, then drizzle the maple syrup mixture over it. Toss well to coat. Add the prosciutto and toss again.

Divide the squash mixture between the prepared baking sheets, arranging it in single layers. Bake for 45 to 50 minutes, or until the squash is lightly browned. Season with salt and pepper.

➡ HOW LONG? **1 HOUR (10 MINUTES ACTIVE)**
➡ HOW MUCH? **8 SERVINGS**

Green Beans with Gouda and Marcona Almonds

Marcona almonds are nothing like the brown California almonds most people are familiar with. Marconas have a rich, sweet flavor and moist, crunchy-chewy texture. They usually are roasted in oil and lightly salted. In this salad, they offer a great crispy, salty contrast to the green beans.

Aged gouda is similar to Parmesan, but with a creamy, smokier flavor. If you can't find it, substitute chunks of Parmesan or cheddar.

These green beans are seriously garlicky, making them a natural for Italian and Greek foods. Pair them with summer pasta and vegetable dishes.

1½ pounds green beans, ends trimmed
3 tablespoons extra-virgin olive oil
3 tablespoons sherry or red wine vinegar
3 cloves garlic, minced
Salt and ground black pepper, to taste
1 cup Marcona almonds, roughly chopped or crushed
¼ cup crumbled aged gouda cheese

Fill a large bowl with cold water and ice.

Bring a large saucepan of salted water to a boil. Add the green beans and blanch for 2 minutes. Drain and transfer the green beans to the ice water.

When the green beans are cool, drain them again and spread them on a kitchen towel to dry.

Meanwhile, in a medium bowl, whisk together the olive oil, vinegar, and garlic, then season with salt and pepper.

Add the green beans to the vinaigrette, tossing them to coat. Add three-quarters of the almonds and cheese, then toss. Sprinkle the remaining almonds and cheese over the top.

➲ HOW LONG? **15 MINUTES**
➲ HOW MUCH? **6 SERVINGS**

Thai Peanut Coleslaw with Pepper Jelly and Peanuts

Another example of the beauty of pairing sweet and heat. **Pepper jelly also makes a great barbecue glaze** (thin it with soy sauce and chicken broth). Or spoon some over a slab of goat cheese or cream cheese and serve it with a sliced baguette for instant party food.

Serve this slaw with grilled burgers, steaks, or poultry. The acidic sweetness of the dressing is perfect for cutting through the hearty flavors of meat.

½ pound green beans, trimmed and halved crosswise
2 tablespoons water
¾ cup pepper jelly (more or less to taste)
6 tablespoons extra-virgin olive oil
2 tablespoons cider vinegar
Salt and ground black pepper, to taste
12-ounce package broccoli slaw
10-ounce package shredded carrots
½ cup lightly crushed unsalted peanuts

Fill a large bowl with cold water and ice. Set aside.

In a large microwave-safe bowl, combine the green beans and water. Cover the bowl with plastic wrap, then microwave it on high for 1½ minutes.

Transfer the beans to the ice water. Once the beans are cool, transfer them to a kitchen towel to dry.

In a small bowl, whisk together the pepper jelly, olive oil, and vinegar. Season with salt and pepper. Set aside.

In a large serving bowl, combine the broccoli slaw and carrots. Toss to mix well. Add the green beans and toss again. Add the dressing and toss well to coat. Sprinkle with peanuts.

➲ HOW LONG? **25 MINUTES**
➲ HOW MUCH? **8 SERVINGS**

Cherry Tomato and Feta Cheese Turnovers

These turnovers are **bold enough to stand up to just about anything,** especially grilled meats or hearty pasta dishes. To make a light meal out of them, add some chopped cooked chicken or ham.

Frozen puff pastry is a breeze to work with. Just thaw, unfold, cut as desired, then top or fill and bake.

2 cups (10 ounces) cherry or grape tomatoes, halved
1 tablespoon kosher salt
½ tablespoon olive oil
2 cloves garlic, minced
1 teaspoon dried oregano
1 tablespoon balsamic vinegar
1 small red onion, diced
½ cup crumbled feta cheese
2 sheets frozen puff pastry, thawed according to package
directions (each 17.3-ounce package contains 2 sheets)
Ground black pepper, to taste
½ cup grated Parmesan cheese

Heat the oven to 375°F.

In a medium bowl, combine the tomatoes and salt, tossing to season evenly. Transfer the tomatoes to a colander or mesh strainer, then place it over a bowl or sink for 5 minutes to drain excess liquid.

Gently squeeze the tomatoes to expel and discard as much liquid as possible. Transfer the tomatoes to a clean bowl, then add the oil, garlic, oregano, vinegar, onion, and feta. Toss well, then set aside.

continued on next page

On a lightly floured counter, unfold the pastry sheets. Cut each sheet into 4 squares. Arrange the squares on a baking sheet.

Spoon an eighth of the tomato mixture into the center of each pastry square, then fold one corner over the filling to form a triangle. Use a fork to crimp the edges of the pastry.

Spritz the pastries with cooking spray, then sprinkle them with black pepper and a bit of the Parmesan. Bake for 20 minutes, or until lightly browned. Cool for 5 minutes, then serve.

➲ HOW LONG? **35 MINUTES (15 MINUTES ACTIVE)**
➲ HOW MUCH? **8 SERVINGS**

TOMATO WOES

Out-of-season tomatoes are depressingly bland. But if that's what you're limited to, buy them small (they're sweeter) and roast them (it intensifies the flavors). If you must eat them raw, it helps to sprinkle them with vinegar, especially if they are destined for a salad. Cider vinegar (a cheap and totally underappreciated workhorse of the blunt force kitchen) makes any tomato pop with flavor.

Prosciutto Potato Poppers

These bite-size potatoes combine a **crunchy, bacony exterior with a soft, baked-potato center.** Eat them as is for a side, pair them with a vegetable soup, serve them alongside a frittata (for breakfast, lunch, or dinner), or turn them into party food by serving them with ramekins of sour cream and chives for dunking.

¼ cup olive oil
½ teaspoon garlic powder
½ teaspoon kosher salt
1½ pounds new potatoes (about 20 small potatoes)
20 slices prosciutto
3 sprigs fresh rosemary, leaves only

Heat the oven to 400°F. Lightly coat a baking sheet with cooking spray.

In a large bowl, whisk together the olive oil, garlic powder, and salt. Add the potatoes, then toss well to coat.

Wrap each potato in a slice of prosciutto. To do so, place the potato at one end of the slice, then roll. Press the prosciutto to wrap it snugly around the potato.

Arrange the potatoes on the prepared baking sheet. Roast for 25 minutes. Sprinkle the potatoes with the rosemary, then bake for another 5 to 10 minutes, or until a knife easily pierces to the center of the potatoes.

➲ HOW LONG? **50 MINUTES (10 MINUTES ACTIVE)**
➲ HOW MUCH? **4 SERVINGS**

Red Beans and Rice with Sausage

This is seriously flavorful **comfort food via Louisiana.** It's great as a side to well-seasoned seafood, but also hearty enough to serve as a one-dish meal.

1 cup long-grain brown rice
2 cups water
6 slices bacon, cut into 1-inch pieces
1 medium yellow onion, diced
2 red bell peppers, cored and diced
4 cloves garlic, minced
⅛ to ¼ teaspoon cayenne powder
¼ teaspoon ground cumin
¼ teaspoon dried oregano
¼ teaspoon ground black pepper
¼ teaspoon smoked paprika
12-ounce package precooked chicken or turkey sausages
   (such as sweet Italian), cut into ½-inch chunks
15-ounce can kidney beans
Salt, to taste

In a small saucepan, combine the rice and water. Bring to a boil, then cover, reduce to a simmer, and cook for 30 minutes.

After the rice has cooked for 20 minutes, in a large skillet over medium-high heat, cook the bacon until it begins to render fat, about 2 minutes.

Add the onion, bell peppers, garlic, cayenne, cumin, oregano, black pepper, and paprika. Sauté until the onions are just tender, about 4 minutes. Add the sausage and sauté another 2 minutes.

Drain about half the liquid from the can of beans, then add the beans and remaining liquid to the skillet. When the rice is done, add it to the skillet. Mix, reduce heat to medium and cook for 10 minutes. Season with salt.

➔ HOW LONG? **40 MINUTES (20 MINUTES ACTIVE)**
➔ HOW MUCH? **4 SERVINGS**

Brown Rice Spiked with Feta, Lemon Zest, and Dried Mango

In the United States, **dried fruit** isn't common in savory cooking. Too bad. Raisins, cherries, and cranberries can be a wonderful complement to roasted meat and other savory dishes, including your Thanksgiving stuffing. In this recipe, dried mango is paired with brown rice and feta, but dried papaya or apricots would go nicely, too.

The Mediterranean flavors in this rice make it a great partner for Greek, Italian, and North African foods, especially grilled or roasted meats and vegetables. It also would go great with Middle Eastern Chicken and Veggies with Hummus on page 100.

1 cup long-grain brown rice
2 cups water
1 teaspoon garlic powder
1 teaspoon onion powder
Grated zest of ½ lemon
1 teaspoon chopped fresh oregano
⅓ cup diced dried mango
¾ cup crumbled feta cheese
Salt and ground black pepper, to taste
⅓ cup slivered almonds, roughly chopped

In a medium saucepan over high heat, combine the rice, water, garlic powder, and onion powder. Bring the mixture to a boil, then cover the pan, reduce the heat to simmer, and cook for 30 minutes.

When the rice is done, take it off the heat and let it cool for 10 minutes.

Stir the lemon zest, oregano, mango, and feta into the rice. Season with salt and pepper. Serve sprinkled with the almonds.

➲ HOW LONG? **45 MINUTES (10 MINUTES ACTIVE)**
➲ HOW MUCH? **4 SERVINGS**

Horseradish and Dill Cream Cheese Mashed Potatoes

One of AP's test cooks, Ryan King, masterminded these insanely good—and utterly artery-clogging—mashed potatoes. **Don't be intimidated by the horscradish.** It provides a mild bite that makes the other flavors pop without adding much real heat.

Serve these with meatloaf or any other dish you'd normally offer mashed taters alongside. Or just do what we all really want to: serve them as dinner all on their own.

2 pounds Yukon Gold potatoes, peeled and diced
½ cup (1 stick) butter
⅔ cup heavy cream
½ tablespoon dried dill
3 ounces cream cheese, softened
2 tablespoons bottled horseradish
Salt and ground black pepper, to taste

Place the potatoes in a large pot. Add enough water to cover the potatoes by 1 inch. Bring to a boil over high heat, then lower the temperature to medium-high to maintain a low boil. Cook until tender, about 25 minutes.

During the final 5 to 10 minutes of cooking, in a small saucepan over medium-low heat, combine the butter, cream, and dill. Once the butter melts, mix well and set aside.

Drain the potatoes. Return them to the pot and mash them.

Use an electric mixer, whisk, or masher to lightly beat the potatoes. Mix in the butter and cream mixture, then the cream cheese and horseradish. Season with salt and pepper.

➡ HOW LONG? **45 MINUTES (15 MINUTES ACTIVE)**
➡ HOW MUCH? **6 SERVINGS**

Grilled Rosemary Garlic Bread

This **pleasantly pungent rosemary garlic bread** is great on the grill, on which it is cooked upside down (trust me on that one). But there's no need to fire up the grill if the rest of the meal is being cooked inside. Just pop these under the broiler—right side up—for a minute or two.

This garlic bread is wonderful with grilled chicken, but it just begs to be with rambunctiously seasoned pasta dishes, such as my Meat Sauce Maximus on page 170.

2 sprigs fresh rosemary, leaves only
4 cloves garlic
½ cup grated Parmesan cheese
2 tablespoons extra-virgin olive oil
2 tablespoons butter
1 teaspoon kosher salt
¼ teaspoon ground black pepper
4 thick slices sourdough bread

Heat a grill to medium-high.

In a food processor, combine the rosemary, garlic, Parmesan, olive oil, butter, salt, and pepper. Process until mostly smooth.

Spread the mixture thickly over one side of each slice of bread. Set the bread, coated side down, on the grill and cook for 2 to 3 minutes, or until lightly browned.

Alternatively, the breads can be broiled (coated side up) for 1 to 2 minutes.

➡ HOW LONG? **20 MINUTES**
➡ HOW MUCH? **4 SERVINGS**

Smoky-Spicy Grilled Corn

Prefer to keep it simple? Substitute 1 or 2 tablespoons of curry powder for the seasonings called for here. The flavor won't be as smoky, but it will still be delicious. You also could substitute coconut cream for the butter.

Grilled corn is a natural with anything else that goes on the grill, such as spicy ribs, burgers, and my Sweet-and-Savory BBQ Chicken on page 129.

½ **cup (1 stick) butter, softened**
1 **tablespoon kosher salt**
1 **tablespoon ground black pepper**
1 **tablespoon smoked paprika**
½ **teaspoon ground cumin**
½ **teaspoon chili powder**
8 **ears corn, husked**

Heat a grill to medium-high.

In a small bowl, combine the butter, salt, pepper, paprika, cumin, and chili powder. Use a fork to mash everything to a smooth paste.

Rub a generous amount of the butter mixture over each ear of corn. Wrap each ear in foil, then grill for 4 to 5 minutes.

➔ HOW LONG? **10 MINUTES**
➔ HOW MUCH? **8 SERVINGS**

Fiery Fruit Salad

Trust me on this one. **Sweet and heat** are awesome together. And this brightly flavored salad will cut through anything heavy, such as barbecue chicken or mayo-heavy potato or pasta salads. If you refrigerate it, let it stand at room temperature for 15 minutes before serving.

If jalapeños aren't your thing, use thinly sliced fresh basil. The mild, peppery bite of basil is a perfect companion to fruit.

2 pints strawberries, hulled and halved
1 pint blueberries
3 apples, cored and diced
2 pears, cored and diced
2 cups seedless red grapes, halved
2 tablespoons cider vinegar
1 teaspoon finely minced jarred jalapeño pepper slices
Pinch salt

In a large bowl, combine the strawberries, blueberries, apples, pears, and grapes. Toss gently to mix. Set aside.

In a small bowl, whisk together the cider vinegar, jalapeño peppers, and salt.

Drizzle the dressing over the fruit and toss gently to coat. Serve immediately.

➔ HOW LONG? **15 MINUTES**
➔ HOW MUCH? **8 SERVINGS**

Stacked and Broiled Fresh Mozzarella with Tomatoes

No prosciutto? Bacon will taste just as good, but will take a bit longer to cook. It also will produce more fat, so be sure to pat it with paper towels after frying it.

For even stacking, select mozzarella balls that are about the same size as the tomatoes.

3 tablespoons extra-virgin olive oil, divided
2 slices prosciutto
2 large slicing tomatoes, such as beefsteak
2 medium balls fresh buffalo mozzarella (about 1 pound total)
8 large fresh basil leaves, thinly sliced
2 tablespoons balsamic vinegar
Kosher salt and ground black pepper, to taste

Place the rack in the middle position and heat the oven to broil.

In a large skillet over medium-high, heat 1 tablespoon of the olive oil. When the oil is hot, add the prosciutto and cook until well browned and crispy, about 5 minutes. Set aside to cool.

Trim and discard the ends of each tomato. Cut each tomato into 4 thick slices. Use a serrated knife to cut each ball of mozzarella into 4 slices.

Coat a rimmed baking sheet with cooking spray. Arrange 4 slices of tomato on the baking sheet, then top each with a slice of cheese.

Continue stacking, alternating tomato and cheese. Each stack should have 2 slices of tomato and 2 slices of cheese, with cheese as the final layer.

Broil the stacks until the top slices of cheese are lightly browned, 3 to 4 minutes. Transfer each stack to a serving plate.

Top each stack with basil. Crumble a bit of prosciutto over each, then drizzle with the remaining 2 tablespoons olive oil and the balsamic vinegar. Season with salt and pepper.

➲ HOW LONG? **15 MINUTES**
➲ HOW MUCH? **4 SERVINGS**

Potato Tart with Manchego, Spinach, and Thyme

Much as I love her sense of style, I had to break up with Martha Stewart a few years ago. I dumped her for Rachael Ray, who told me dirty jokes about almonds.

It seemed like a good idea at the time. Spend half a day with each of these wonderful ladies chatting about cooking up the perfect romantic dinner for two for Valentine's Day. They'd share their recipes with me, then I'd share them with you.

All was well until I got back to the test kitchen. Martha's menu for multiple soufflés and pasta with white truffles was luscious, but beyond my skills. Clearly, I never could woo Martha.

Rachael, however, was the woman for me. Her steak dinner had me in and out of the kitchen in no time.

This **easy tart** was inspired by one of Rachael's recipes. Try this alongside a steak, an omelet, or a bowl of chicken or vegetable soup.

Olive oil, for brushing, or olive oil cooking spray
1 pound Yukon Gold potatoes, peeled and thinly sliced
½ medium yellow onion, very thinly sliced
Kosher salt and ground black pepper
½ teaspoon dried thyme
2 cups baby spinach leaves
3 cups grated manchego or cheddar cheese
1 tablespoon diced jarred jalapeño pepper slices
2 slices prosciutto, finely chopped

Heat the oven to 425°F. Lightly coat a pie plate with olive oil.

Arrange a single layer of potato slices over the bottom of the pie plate, edges slightly overlapping. Lightly brush or spray the potatoes with olive oil. Place half the onions in a thin layer over the potatoes, then season with salt, pepper, and half of the thyme.

Top the onions with 1 cup of the spinach leaves, spread evenly, then sprinkle with 1 cup of the cheese. Place a second layer of potatoes over the cheese, pressing it down gently with the palm of your hand. Brush or spray on another light coat of oil.

Repeat the layering by topping the potatoes with the remaining onions, seasonings, spinach, 1 cup of the cheese, and a final layer of potatoes. Gently press down on the potatoes, coat with oil, then top with the final cup of cheese. Sprinkle the tart with the diced peppers and prosciutto.

Bake for 35 to 40 minutes, or until the edges are brown and potatoes are cooked. Let stand 5 minutes, then cut into wedges to serve.

➔ HOW LONG? **1 HOUR (20 MINUTES ACTIVE)**
➔ HOW MUCH? **4 SERVINGS**

Dessert shouldn't hurt. That's my response to the crazy stupid lengths to which some cookbooks (and, every now and again, this delusional food editor) will urge the home cook to go just to gussy up an otherwise fine recipe.

It's a lesson I should have learned the time I nearly set my dining room ablaze during a photo shoot of a brownie and ice cream flambé. Or the time my photographer set the two of us on fire during an indoor hibachi shoot. Or the time I misjudged how flame retardant peanuts are (they aren't) and set an entire pan of peanut-topped scallops on fire under the broiler.

No. For this lesson to sink in, I had to experience a hand burn serious enough to draw blood.

As host of a weekly food video segment, I sometimes recruit food celebs and experts to come on air and demo take-home tricks, sort of an evening news meets Rachael Ray (minus the war, famine, and babe factors).

For an early episode, I got a pastry chef to demonstrate spun sugar. It's a trick high-end restaurants use to make you think a twenty-dollar ball of sorbet is worth it. It involves heating sugar until it melts, then drizzling it over an overturned bowl. When it hardens, you lift off a "cage" of sugar that can be placed over a dessert. It's got a serious Wow! factor.

It's also got about 310 ripping-hot degrees behind it. Not an issue if that sugar doesn't come into contact with you.

I liked the pastry chef doing the demo. Until she splashed me. On camera. There's really no way to casually brush 310-degree sugar off your hand while maintaining lively banter about dressing up Valentine's Day desserts.

And so I say, dessert shouldn't hurt. I recall no blood being shed for these recipes.

Grilled Cinnamon-Sugar Breadsticks

Imagine a dessert with the flavor of French toast and the texture of fried dough. **It's warm and doughy and crunchy and cinnamony and sugary** all rolled together.

But be sure to cover the grill grates with foil. The butter dripping off the dough will cause flare-ups, and that leaves a nasty taste on the breadsticks.

½ cup (1 stick) butter, melted
½ teaspoon cinnamon
⅛ teaspoon ground cardamom
¼ teaspoon salt
⅔ cup sugar
20-ounce ball prepared pizza dough, room temperature
Jarred caramel topping, for drizzling (optional)

Cover the grates of a grill with foil. Heat the grill to medium-high.

In a wide, shallow bowl, whisk together the butter, cinnamon, cardamom, and salt. Place the sugar in a second wide, shallow bowl. Set both aside.

On a floured surface, roll the pizza dough into a large rectangle about 18 by 11 inches. Using a pizza wheel or knife, cut the dough in half crosswise, then cut each half lengthwise into about 7 strips.

One at a time, dunk each strip of dough first in the melted butter mixture, then in the sugar, turning as needed to coat it evenly.

Arrange the dough strips on the grill and cook them for 1 to 2 minutes per side, or until they are evenly browned. Transfer the breadsticks to a serving platter and drizzle with caramel sauce, if using.

➡ HOW LONG? **20 MINUTES**
➡ HOW MUCH? **8 SERVINGS**

Marinated Strawberries with Lemony Mascarpone

Tart, sweet, creamy, and ready in minutes. **It's a kid-friendly, weeknight-easy dessert that's still elegant enough for guests.** For extra panache, serve it in wineglasses.

The mascarpone topping can be prepared up to a day ahead, but don't toss the berries with the vinegar until shortly before serving.

**3 cups hulled and quartered strawberries
(about 1 pound before trimming)
2 tablespoons granulated sugar
1 tablespoon balsamic vinegar
Salt
8-ounce container mascarpone
3 tablespoons powdered sugar
3 tablespoons half-and-half or milk
½ teaspoon vanilla extract
Grated zest of 1 lemon**

In a small bowl, gently toss the strawberries with the granulated sugar, balsamic vinegar, and a pinch of salt. Set them aside for 15 minutes.

Meanwhile, in a medium bowl, whisk together the mascarpone, powdered sugar, half-and-half, vanilla, another pinch of salt, and three-quarters of the lemon zest.

When the strawberries are ready, divide them and any juices among 4 serving bowls. Spoon the mascarpone mixture over the berries, then garnish with the remaining lemon zest.

➡ HOW LONG? **20 MINUTES**
➡ HOW MUCH? **4 SERVINGS**

Ginger Fig Crumb Bars

These bars are **buttery, fruity, and slightly cakey.** The apricots and figs produce a thick, sweet sugar filling, while the ginger and pine nuts lend warm and nutty flavors to the crumb topping.

1¾ cups all-purpose flour
¼ cup cornmeal
¾ cup granulated sugar
¾ cup (1½ sticks) unsalted butter, softened
  and cut into small chunks
½ pound dried apricots
½ pound dried figs
¼ cup crystallized ginger (page xii)
¼ cup water
2 tablespoons packed light brown sugar
¼ cup pine nuts

Heat the oven to 350°F.

In a food processor, combine the flour, cornmeal, and granulated sugar. Pulse several times to combine. Add the butter, then pulse until the ingredients form a wet, sandy mixture, about 15 seconds.

Transfer three-quarters of the mixture to a 9-inch square pan and press it evenly across the bottom. Set the remaining flour mixture aside in a small bowl.

In the food processor, combine the apricots, figs, ginger, and water and process until the fruit forms a thick jam, about 15 seconds. Using a silicone spatula or large spoon, spread the fruit evenly over the dough in the pan.

Mix the brown sugar into the remaining flour mixture, then crumble it evenly over the fruit. Scatter pine nuts over the dough.

Bake for 25 minutes, or until the edges and pine nuts just begin to brown. Cool before serving. Cut into 9 squares.

➔ HOW LONG? **40 MINUTES (15 MINUTES ACTIVE)**
➔ HOW MUCH? **9 SERVINGS**

Apple Pie Pops

Apple pies. On a stick. It gets no better. I enlisted the help of AP's test kitchen baker, Alison Ladman, to help come up with these winners.

2 large apples, peeled, cored, and finely chopped
1 teaspoon lemon juice
¼ cup sugar, plus 2 tablespoons, divided
1½ teaspoons apple pie spice, divided
Pinch salt
1 tablespoon cornstarch
2 tablespoons water, plus 2 teaspoons, divided
15-ounce package prepared rolled pie dough (contains 2 pieces)
20 paper lollipop sticks
1 egg, separated

Heat the oven to 375°F. Line a baking sheet with parchment paper, then coat the paper with cooking spray.

In a medium skillet over medium-high heat, combine the apples, lemon juice, ¼ cup of the sugar, ½ teaspoon of apple pie spice, and salt. Sauté for 3 to 4 minutes. In a small glass, mix the cornstarch and 2 tablespoons of water. Add to the skillet and stir until thickened.

Unfold each sheet of pie dough and run a rolling pin over it several times. Use a 3-inch round cookie cutter to cut 10 circles from each sheet.

Arrange 10 rounds on the baking sheet. Firmly press a lollipop stick into the center of each. Place a scant tablespoon of filling in each.

In a small bowl, beat the egg white and 1 teaspoon of water. Use your finger to paint it around the edge of each dough circle. Place a second round of dough on top. Use a fork to crimp the edges and seal the pies.

In a small bowl, whisk together the egg yolk and 1 teaspoon of water, then brush the glaze over the tops of the pops. In a small bowl, mix together the remaining sugar and pie spice. Sprinkle over the pops.

Bake for 15 minutes, or until golden. Cool on the baking sheet.

➲ HOW LONG? **45 MINUTES (30 MINUTES ACTIVE)**
➲ HOW MUCH? **10 POPS**

Balsamic Chocolate Cookie Ice Cream

Seriously. **Just try it.** You never knew ice cream could be this intense.

½ **cup balsamic vinegar**
1 **tablespoon strawberry jam**
10 **cream-filled chocolate cookies (such as**
   Oreos or Newman-O's)
1 **pint vanilla ice cream**

In a small saucepan over medium-low heat, combine the balsamic vinegar and jam. Simmer, stirring often, until reduced by half, about 8 minutes. Set aside to cool.

Meanwhile, place the cookies in a zip-close plastic bag and gently pound with a meat mallet or rolling pin to break them into small chunks. Set aside.

Once the vinegar has cooled, soften the ice cream by microwaving it in 5-second bursts until it can easily be mixed with a spoon. It should be very soft, but not melted. Transfer the ice cream to a medium bowl.

Drizzle the vinegar into the ice cream and mix until blended. Mix in the cookies. Cover the ice cream and return it to the freezer until it is firm, 2 to 3 hours.

➔ HOW LONG? **3 HOURS (15 MINUTES ACTIVE)**
➔ HOW MUCH? **1 PINT**

Berries and Cream Tart

Nearly any cookie can be used for a tart crust such as this, so **wander the cookie aisle in search of inspiration.** I've done it with Oreos and vanilla wafers, as well as gingersnaps.

The whipped filling is made from a creamy blend of Greek-style yogurt and heavy cream. Greek-style yogurt is plain yogurt that has been strained to remove much of the water. As a result, it is much thicker and has a creamier taste (even the fat-free varieties).

10-ounce bag gingersnap cookies
1 large egg white
1 tablespoon butter, melted
1½ cups Greek-style yogurt
½ cup heavy cream
½ cup sour cream
¼ cup powdered sugar, plus extra for dusting
1 teaspoon vanilla extract
¾ cup fresh blueberries
¾ cup fresh raspberries
Grated zest of 1 lemon

Heat the oven to 350°F.

In a food processor, pulse the cookies into fine crumbs. Add the egg white and butter, then continue pulsing until the mixture resembles wet sand.

Transfer the mixture to a 9-inch round tart pan with removable bottom. Use your fingers or the bottom of a drinking glass to press the crumbs evenly across the bottom and up the sides.

Bake the tart crust for 12 to 15 minutes, or until it is slightly puffed. Set it aside for 5 minutes to cool, then place it in the freezer for 10 minutes.

Meanwhile, in a large bowl, use an electric mixer to whip the yogurt, heavy cream, sour cream, and powdered sugar until thick, soft peaks form, 3 to 4 minutes. Mix in the vanilla.

Remove the tart shell from the freezer and use a silicone spatula to transfer the whipped filling to the tart, spreading it evenly.

In a small bowl, mix the blueberries and raspberries, then gently mound them in the center of the tart, leaving about 1 inch of the filling showing around the edges. Sprinkle the fruit with the lemon zest.

Place 1 to 2 tablespoons of powdered sugar in a mesh strainer. Holding the strainer over the tart, gently tap it to lightly dust the tart.

Refrigerate until ready to serve, up to 1 day.

➡ HOW LONG? **30 MINUTES**
➡ HOW MUCH? **6 SERVINGS**

Brown Sugar and Ginger Pumpkin Bread

The brown sugar, cinnamon, ginger, and pumpkin combine here to create a **warmly spiced, incredibly moist bread.** And while it does have a fair amount of sugar in it, it's still pretty healthy thanks to the whole-wheat flour (you'll never taste it) and pumpkin.

2 cups white whole-wheat flour
1 teaspoon baking soda
1 teaspoon ground cinnamon
¼ teaspoon ground dry ginger
½ teaspoon kosher salt
1⅓ cups packed dark brown sugar
⅓ cup canola or vegetable oil
15-ounce can pumpkin puree
1 large egg
1 teaspoon ground fresh ginger (optional)

Heat the oven to 350°F. Coat a metal loaf pan with cooking spray.

In a medium bowl, whisk together the flour, baking soda, cinnamon, dry ginger, and salt.

In a large bowl, whisk together the brown sugar, oil, pumpkin, egg, and fresh ginger (if using). Whisk in the dry ingredients.

Transfer the batter to the prepared baking pan and bake for 1 hour 5 minutes, or until a toothpick inserted at the center comes out clean. Cool for 15 minutes, then remove from the pan and cool on a rack.

➡ HOW LONG? **1 HOUR 15 MINUTES (10 MINUTES ACTIVE)**
➡ HOW MUCH? **10 SERVINGS**

NO MORE WHOLE-WHEAT HORROR

White whole-wheat flour is my go-to grain for baking. It has all the nutrition of conventional whole-wheat flour, but a taste and texture similar to white. It's not magic; it's just a different variety of wheat. I use it in pancakes, breads, and muffins.

Chocolate Cherry Truffles

These are ridiculously chocolatey, creamy, tangy . . . and messy to make. As in your hands will be covered with a thick layer of delicious chocolate. It's okay to lick.

Though a couple hours' chilling is needed, the hands-on time is just a few minutes. Also, this recipe is really forgiving, so feel free to substitute other dried fruit or finely chopped nuts for the cherries.

14 ounces dark chocolate, broken into small pieces
¾ cup heavy cream
½ cup dried cherries, finely chopped
2 tablespoons balsamic vinegar
Pinch salt
½ cup cocoa powder

In a small saucepan over medium heat, combine the chocolate and cream. Stir until the chocolate is melted and smooth. Stir in the cherries, balsamic vinegar, and salt.

Pour the mixture into an 8-inch square baking pan, then refrigerate until set, about 2 hours.

After the chocolate has set, place the cocoa powder in a bowl.

Use a melon baller or sturdy 1-tablespoon measuring spoon to scoop balls of the chocolate mixture. Roll them into mostly smooth balls between your palms. It will be messy.

Roll the balls in the cocoa powder until well coated. Refrigerate the truffles for at least 2 hours before serving.

➡ HOW LONG? **2 HOURS 15 MINUTES (15 MINUTES ACTIVE)**
➡ HOW MUCH? **30 TRUFFLES**

No-Bake Blackberry, Blueberry, and Red Grape Pie

Life is too short to mess with pie crusts. I won't make them. I also won't fuss with persnickety fillings and toppings. Pies should be as easy to make as they are to eat. Which is why I love this no-bake wonder that sports an unusual blend of blackberries, blueberries, and grapes. The result is fresh, tangy, and sweet. Just about any blend of fresh berries can be substituted.

9-inch frozen pie shell, thawed
¾ cup sugar
3 tablespoons cornstarch
½ teaspoon salt
⅓ cup water
2 tablespoons lemon juice
1 cup blackberries
3½ cups blueberries, divided
1½ cups seedless red grapes, divided

Bake the empty pie shell according to package directions. This usually involves pricking the bottom of the crust all over with a fork, then baking it at 400°F for 10 to 14 minutes. Cool.

Meanwhile, in a medium saucepan over medium heat, combine the sugar, cornstarch, salt, water, lemon juice, blackberries, and ½ cup each of the blueberries and grapes.

Heat, stirring often, until bubbling. Continue to cook until very thick, 2 to 3 minutes. Set aside to cool for 5 minutes. Stir in the remaining fruit.

Transfer the fruit mixture to the pie shell, then refrigerate until the pie is cool and set.

➡ HOW LONG? **3 HOURS (15 MINUTES ACTIVE)**
➡ HOW MUCH? **8 SERVINGS**

Grilled Apples with Mascarpone

This simple, elegant dessert also can double as a side. The **creamy mascarpone, sweet fig jam, and tender, warm apples** are perfect alongside grilled or broiled meats such as pork chops or steaks. Just leave out the powdered sugar and lemon zest.

2 large, firm apples
Canola oil
¼ teaspoon salt
¼ teaspoon cinnamon
4 tablespoons mascarpone
2 tablespoons powdered sugar
4 teaspoons fig jam
Grated zest of 1 lemon

Heat a grill to high or heat the broiler.

Cut each apple in half. Use a melon baller to scoop out the core. Brush the cut sides with oil, then sprinkle with salt and cinnamon.

If you are using the grill, place the apples, cut-side down, on the grate. Cover the grill and cook until the apples have thick grill marks, about 3 minutes. Use tongs to flip the apples. Reduce the heat under the apples to low, or move them to a cooler part of the grill. Cover the grill and cook until the apples are just tender, about another 4 minutes.

If you are using the broiler, arrange the apples cut-side up in an oiled baking pan. Broil on the middle rack for 2 to 3 minutes, or until the apples begin to brown. Use tongs to flip the apples, then move the pan to the lowest rack. Broil for another 4 to 5 minutes.

In a small bowl, whisk together the mascarpone and powdered sugar.

Transfer each apple half to a serving plate. Place 1 teaspoon fig jam in the hollow of each half, then dollop 1 tablespoon of mascarpone next to it. Sprinkle with lemon zest. Serve warm.

➡ HOW LONG? **20 MINUTES**
➡ HOW MUCH? **4 SERVINGS**

Cookie Dough Apple-Peach Crisp

Nobody expects this sort of delicious intensity from an apple crisp. It gets its punch from a serious (but not overwhelming) helping of candied ginger, as well as a generous dose of sweet and tart dried cherries.

And the topping, made by combining crumbled purchased sugar cookie dough and oats, is simply the most comforting crisp topping you'll ever encounter.

2 tablespoons butter, melted and cooled
¼ cup packed light brown sugar
½ cup diced crystallized ginger (page xii)
1 teaspoon lemon juice
½ teaspoon cinnamon
¼ teaspoon ground cardamom
¼ teaspoon ground allspice
Pinch ground nutmeg
Pinch salt
2 tablespoons cornstarch
5 medium apples, peeled, cored, and chopped into
  bite-size chunks
Two 10-ounce bags frozen peaches, thawed
1 cup dried cherries
14-ounce package prepared sugar cookie dough,
  broken into chunks
1 cup rolled oats

Heat the oven to 375°F. Coat a 9-inch square casserole or baking pan with cooking spray.

In a large bowl, mix the butter, brown sugar, ginger, lemon juice, cinnamon, cardamom, allspice, nutmeg, salt, and cornstarch. Add the apples, peaches, and cherries, then toss to coat.

Transfer the fruit, using a rubber spatula to scrape the sides of the bowl, to the prepared pan. Set aside.

In a food processor, combine the cookie dough and oats. Pulse several times, or until the mixture resembles coarse, wet sand. Sprinkle the mixture over the fruit.

Bake for 20 to 25 minutes, or until the topping is lightly browned and the fruit bubbles. Cool slightly before serving.

➡ HOW LONG? **35 MINUTES (15 MINUTES ACTIVE)**
➡ HOW MUCH? **6 SERVINGS**

Chocolate Marzipan Sugar Cookies

A good sugar cookie should be just barely crackly on the outside, but soft and chewy inside. To make sure I got exactly the sort of cookie I wanted, I ground up a package of marzipan (sweetened almond paste—it's available in the baking section of most grocery stores) and mixed that into my cookie dough. The result was perfection. I also added a heap of cocoa powder for good measure.

This dough, which takes just minutes to prepare, is an excellent **do-ahead cookie.** Make it as directed, then wrap it tightly in plastic and refrigerate for up to three days. When ready to bake, let the dough stand at room temperature for a bit to make it easier to scoop.

These cookies should be very soft when they come out of the oven. Be sure to let them rest on the baking sheet for a few minutes before you move them to a wire rack.

¾ cup granulated sugar
½ cup light brown sugar
7-ounce package marzipan, cut into chunks
¾ cup (1½ sticks) unsalted butter, softened
2 teaspoons vanilla extract
1½ teaspoons baking powder
½ teaspoon baking soda
½ teaspoon salt
1 large egg
2 cups all-purpose flour
½ cup unsweetened cocoa powder
Powdered sugar, for dusting (optional)

Heat the oven to 350°F and position a rack in the lower third of the oven. Line a baking sheet with parchment paper.

In a food processor, combine both sugars and the marzipan. Process until they resemble fine sand, about 1 minute.

Transfer the mixture to a large bowl. Add the butter, vanilla, baking powder, baking soda, salt, and egg.

Use an electric mixer to beat the dough until smooth, scraping down the bowl once during mixing, about 2 minutes.

Add the flour and cocoa powder and mix until incorporated, scraping down the bowl once during mixing, about 1 minute. The dough should be very stiff.

Drop 1-tablespoon balls of dough on the prepared baking sheet, leaving about 2 inches around all sides. (You will need to bake in batches.)

Bake until the cookies are flat and have a crackled surface, about 10 minutes.

The cookies will be very soft. Let them cool for 5 minutes on the baking sheet, then transfer them to a rack to cool completely.

If desired, once the cookies are cool, dust them with powdered sugar. Store in an airtight container at room temperature.

➡ HOW LONG? **45 MINUTES (15 MINUTES ACTIVE)**
➡ HOW MUCH? **36 COOKIES**

Caramel Streusel Apple Pie Cookies

I've always been awed (and a tiny bit disturbed) by the tenacity with which Chris Kimball and his cooks pursue the perfect recipe. Chris, the man behind *Cook's Illustrated* magazine and public television's *America's Test Kitchen,* has his team test recipes dozens—sometimes hundreds—of times to fine-tune the minutiae of good eats.

But during research for my first cookbook, a brief excursion into the world of egg- and dairy-free cooking, I discovered even his patience has limits. I'd turned to him for help with a vegan chocolate cake, lamenting the lousy results.

I got no sympathy. Just a snappy "That's why God invented eggs."

Two lessons were learned. One, Chris doesn't suffer vegans lightly. And two, his try-and-try-and-try-and-try again method works. His cooks worked up a perfect vegan chocolate cake recipe for me after just two months and 101 cakes.

Guess I got off easy when perfecting this **apple-pie-in-a-cookie.** It took me just nineteen attempts.

FOR THE COOKIES:
1 cup shortening
½ cup packed light brown sugar
¾ cup powdered sugar
2 teaspoons vanilla extract
¾ teaspoon salt
½ teaspoon pumpkin pie spice
½ teaspoon cinnamon
1 large egg
2 egg yolks
1 tablespoon baking powder
2¼ cups all-purpose flour
3 medium apples, peeled, cored, and finely diced

FOR THE STREUSEL:
1½ cups rolled oats
2 teaspoons granulated sugar
2 teaspoons packed light brown sugar
¼ teaspoon cinnamon
¼ teaspoon pumpkin pie spice
4½ tablespoons melted butter
½ cup jarred caramel sundae sauce (optional)

continued on next page

To make the dough, in a large bowl, use an electric mixer to cream together the shortening, both sugars, vanilla, salt, pumpkin pie spice, and cinnamon. Scrape down the sides of the bowl with a silicone spatula as needed.

Beat in the egg and egg yolks, scraping the bowl as needed. Beat in the baking powder and flour, again scraping the bowl. Mix in the apples. Refrigerate the dough for 30 minutes.

Meanwhile, heat the oven to 375°F. Line 2 baking sheets with parchment paper or lightly coat them with baking spray.

Make the streusel topping. In a food processor, combine the rolled oats, both sugars, cinnamon, and pumpkin pie spice. Pulse 2 or 3 times, or enough to just chop the oats. Drizzle in the melted butter, then pulse 1 or 2 times to just mix. Set aside.

Drop tablespoon-size balls of the chilled dough onto the prepared baking sheets, leaving about 2 inches between them. Use your fingers to slightly flatten each cookie; they may be sticky.

Carefully sprinkle streusel mixture over each cookie. Bake for 13 to 15 minutes. Use a spatula to transfer the cookies to a wire rack to cool. Be sure to let the baking sheets cool before putting the next batch of cookies on them.

If desired, just before serving, drizzle each cookie with caramel sauce.

➡ HOW LONG? **1 HOUR**
➡ HOW MUCH? **ABOUT 4 DOZEN COOKIES**

Mango-Lemon Sorbet

Rare is the ice cream that is delicious enough for dessert, healthy enough to serve your kids for breakfast, and so easy to make it takes just 5 minutes. Summer and winter, this is our **go-to treat.** And while mango is my son's favorite, just about any bagged frozen fruit works.

10-ounce bag frozen mango chunks
1 banana
2 teaspoons lemon juice
Pinch salt

In a food processor, combine all ingredients. Process for about 2 minutes, or until very smooth and creamy. Stop to scrape down the sides of the bowl with a rubber spatula as needed.

Serve immediately. Do not freeze, or it will turn icy and be too hard to eat.

➲ HOW LONG? **5 MINUTES**
➲ HOW MUCH? **4 SERVINGS**

ACKNOWLEDGMENTS

A book may be conceived as one person's dream, but it is born the labor of many. I am lucky in ways I never imagined to be surrounded by so many people who care enough to help me succeed.

Lisa Tolin, Lou Ferrara, Sally Jacobsen, and Kathleen Carroll, my bosses at The Associated Press. You give me the freedom and responsibility to make my little corner of the world's largest news organization shine. Nothing I've done could have occurred without your support.

Diane Davis, my former boss. Shortly after she left AP, she told me I was supposed to say either "Many thanks to my wonderful editor who let me have my way with the best gig in the cooking world," or "Many thanks to the person who told me to buy any prop and ingredient I needed, even the organic stuff that costs extra money and the top-shelf booze I like." So there. I've said it. And I mean it.

Pamela Cannon, my editor. Thank you for seeing such promise in this project, then helping me make it a reality. Nevertheless, it's time you give your colored pencils to your children and embrace the digital age. Thanks also to the whole Ballantine team, especially Susan Corcoran in publicity.

Larry Crowe, AP's food photographer. Where's that radar we were talking about . . . ? After nearly a decade you still manage to make my slop look good. Sometimes. Now let's grab some of that top-shelf booze and toast to another ten years.

Joseph DeVita, Ryan King, and Alison Ladman, my test cooks. Week after week you make a wreck of the kitchen, keep my son stuffed with bacon, and consistently make it seem as though I know what I'm doing. I owe you big.

Michele Kayal, friend and fellow writer. If I didn't have somebody to bounce this insanity off of, I wouldn't have made it this far. Many thanks.

Charlie Dougiello, my publicist. It was over a cup of coffee and I think your words were, "Dude! You have got to pitch this." And so we did. My gratitude is eternal.

Eric Lupfer, my agent at William Morris Endeavor. I can be a bit of a clueless clod. Thank you so much for steering the ship and making me seem less so.

Matthew Mead, Jenny, and the rest of the gang at Matthew Mead Productions. Your photos made my ideas not just come to life, but vibrantly so. Thank you so much.

Hilary Chapman, Deb Moskey, and Karen Smith, my mommy friends. Thanks for the millions of little ways you make my life (and my son's) so much easier and more fun.

Robin, Chris, and Stephen Starr. We started as friends-of-friends, became friends, then traveling companions, and finally family. Thank you so much for riding the crazy with us.

Mom and Dad. I love you and can't thank you enough for everything you've given me. Actually, I'd have preferred "thin" genes.

Holly, my wife. Because Nigella and Katie and Rachael would never put up with me. Yet you continue to. Thank you. I love you.

INDEX

ABOUT THE AUTHOR

J. M. HIRSCH is the national food editor for The Associated Press. He oversees a team of writers, cooks, and photographers whose stories and recipes appear in thousands of newspapers and on countless websites around the globe. He lives in New Hampshire with his wife and six-year-old son.

9TH EDITION • 2008-2012

THE BOOK OF U.S. POSTAL EXAMS
& POST OFFICE JOBS

How to Be a Top Scorer on 473/473-C/460 Tests & Other Postal Exams to Get a Post Office Job

Veltisezar B. Bautista

Publisher's Cataloging-in-Publication
(Provided by Quality Books, Inc.)

Bautista, Veltisezar B., 1933-
   The book of U.S. postal exams & post office jobs :
how to be a top scorer on 473/473-C/460 tests & other
postal exams to get a post office job / Veltisezar B.
Bautista. -- 9th ed., 2008-2012.
   p. cm.
   LCCN 2008921028
   ISBN-13: 978-0-931613-21-0
   ISBN-10: 0-931613-21-3

   1. Postal service--United States--Examinations,
questions, etc. 2. Civil service--United States--
Examinations--Study guides. 3. Postal service--United
States--Employees.   I. Title.

HE6499.B38 2008   383'.145'076
                             QBI08-600047

Printed in the United States of America

Bookhaus Publishers
http://bookhaus.com
U.S.A.

Dedication

I dedicate this book to the light of my life,
Genoveva Abes-Bautista;
to my beloved children,
Hubert, Lester, Melvin, Ronald, and Janet;
to my daughter-in-law,
Maria Cecilia Asi-Bautista;
and to all job seekers who will read this book.

A Special Reminder: You now have in your possession a complete guide to scoring 95-100% on Post Office exams. The book covers exams for clerk-carrier, rural carrier, rural carrier associate, mail handler, mail processor, clerk-typist, clerk-stenographer, mark-up clerk, distribution clerk, flat sorting machine, operator, stationary engineer, electronics technician, garageman, and many more, making it the only book of its kind in the world.

The book is written in simple, easy-to-understand English. It covers in detail all the Postal exams and goings-on in the U.S. Postal Service. The book gives straight-to-the-point instructions that you can easily follow.

You can use this book as a reference not only for postal exams but also for civil service exams, so let it be a useful tool for you in this land of the survival of the fittest.

With this book, you'll know my test-taking secrets. Keep the secrets to yourself, and you and your family will always have the edge in competing for high-paying Postal jobs.

Similarities between characters in this book and persons living or dead are intentional, and not coincidental, for they are Real People like you!

Good luck!—The Author

Table of Contents

Area Maintenance Specialist; Area Maintenance Technician; Assistant Engineman; Blacksmith-Welder; Building Equipment Mechanic; Building Maintenance Custodian; Carpenter; Elevator Mechanic; Fireman; Fireman-Laborer; General Mechanic; Industrial Equipment Mechanic; Letter Box Mechanic; Machinist; Maintenance Electrician; Mason; Mechanic Helper; Oiler (MPE); Painter; Painter/Finisher; Plumber; Postal Machines Mechanic; Postal Maintenance Trainee; S Mechanic; and Stationary Engineer.

Foreword

You Can Pass ANY Post Office Exam with Flying Colors—and Get a $35,000 Job!

I know the above is a **bold** statement.

But it's 100% true.

You can get that job with the Post Office and make $35,000 a year. But first you have to pass the required examination, and this is what stops most people.

Here's why:
Although 70% is a passing score you want to make 90 to 100% because the Post Office usually hires people who score in that range. To make a high score, you need to know certain tricks of the trade.

First, let me emphasize one point:

I'm not basing my knowledge on hearsay. It's based it on my own practical experience in taking these exams. I don't brag, but I've been among the top scorers on postal exams. As a result of my hands-on-experience, I've put all the tricks of the trade, ins and outs, tips, strategies and secrets into one power-packed book called **The Book of U.S. Postal Exam & Post Office Jobs: How to Be a Top Scorer on 473/473-C/460 Tests and Other Postal Exams to Get a Post Office Jobs,** now on its 9th edition.

But before you read the book from cover to cover, let's see what life is like for a Postal Service employee.

One word describes it: *tremendous!* Did you know that postal jobs are recession-proof? As inflation rises, your cost-of-living allowance rises too? It's automatically added to your salary. (How many jobs in business give you this benefit?)

1

But that's not all--far from it.
The pay is high (the average postal employee makes $35,000 a year).

The fringe benefits are sensational. Retirement income is great. You have freedom from layoffs. In short, you've got *lifetime financial security.*

What's more, there's no age limit. As long as you're at least 18, you can take any exam and compete with people in their 40s and 50s. It's not your age or experience or education that counts. The only thing that matters is *the score you make on the exam. Period.*

Take education, for example.

I've known college-educated people who made low scores on the exam. Were they selected? No, indeed. The jobs went to high school graduates who managed a score between 90% and 100%. I can't emphasize enough how important that score is.

Making a good grade on the exam is as easy as falling off a log backwards -- *if you know how.*

Let me assure you that with my book, you'll go into any exam with all the confidence in the world. You'll already know beforehand what to expect. You'll know how to take the test. You'll know how to make that 95 to 100%.

Employment hinges on one thing and one thing only: *how well you do on the exam.*

This rule is strictly enforced with no ifs, ands, or buts. You could have a Ph.D. and still not be hired if you didn't come through on the exam. It doesn't matter whether you're a United States citizen or a permanent resident alien, man or woman, black or white, brown or yellow; you name it. *It's your exam score that counts.*

As I've said so many times, making a high score is essential.

This book is based on my success and on the systems I've worked out.

In fact, Susan L. Lindeman, Notary Public, Wayne County, Michigan, certifies that my scores on postal exams have been 78.5%, 88.5%, 95.8%, 99%, and 100's.

Notice how the scores have gone up and up--because I worked out sure-fire, can't-fail systems; the very systems I want to share with you now. Use them and you can't fail!

Veltisezar B. Bautista
Author

The U.S. Postal Service 1

A Short History of the U.S. Postal System

More than three hundred years ago, in 1657 to be exact, the Post Office of England was established as a government entity. In the same year, the Colonial Court of Virginia required every tobacco planter to convey official mail dispatches to the next plantation. This action became the first move in the colonies to transport mail from one locality to another. This service, however, was intended only for official mail. Another four years passed before the Virginia assembly required planters to forward "all letters superscribed for the service of His Majesty or publique," or to pay a fine of 350 pounds of tobacco. This step opened the service to all people in the colony.

Today, the U.S. Postal Service, a semiprivate corporation but still considered a federal agency, remains the giant in US civilian employment. Compared to previous years' employment of more than 660,000, the USPS now employs more than 900,000. The number of employees rose to this number with the hiring of a variety of categories of temporary employees. These temporary workers, many of whom are considered as not temps, number more than 186,000. They include the part-time flexible, part-time regular, and transitional employees or workers. The new employees are replacements of those who die or retire or workers who fill new positions created by expansion.

Scheduled Postal Service

Way back in 1672, the first serious attempt was made to establish scheduled postal service between several of the northern colonies. Francis Lovelace, the governor of New York, directed a man to carry letters monthly on horseback between New York and Boston. Then in 1692 Great Britain established the first national postal system for the American colonies. In 1753, Britain appointed Benjamin Franklin, then postmaster of Philadelphia, as a deputy postmaster general for all the colonies. In 1774, however, Franklin was removed from his post because of his questionable allegiance to the Crown.

New U.S. Postal System

After the colonies severed their ties to England in 1775, the Continental Congress established its own postal system and appointed Franklin as its head. On February 20, 1792, the U.S. Congress authorized the Post Office as a permanent government agency. By 1794 Congress had authorized the hiring of letter carriers and paid them a two-cent fee for every letter delivered to a business firm.

Then in 1825 the name Post Office Department acquired official sanction. In that year, Congress also authorized the delivery of mail to private homes. The carriers, however, were paid not by the government but by the addressees.

Pony Express

The famous Pony Express was established on April 3, 1860. A private postal and express system, the service ran between St. Joseph, Missouri and San Francisco, via Sacramento. Horses, running in relays at 190 stations along the 2,000-mile route, took eight to ten days to complete the delivery route. The Pony Express met its demise when telegraph lines were established between the east and the west.

By 1861 President Abraham Lincoln's postmaster general, Montgomery Blair, had introduced free city delivery, postal money orders, and railway post offices. In 1862 the first railway post office began to operate in the United States. In the 1880's the government added more postal services and established more railroad post offices.

New Services

In 1953 air mail service was begun; in 1955 the certified mail service was established. On June 30, 1971 the name of U.S. Post Office Department was changed to U.S. Postal Service. The Service became independent and is no longer supervised by the Office of Personnel Management (OPM), formerly the Civil Service Commission. Its head is still called the Postmaster General, but he is not a member of the President's Cabinet. Over 25 percent of all federal employees are paid under the coordinated Federal Wage Board System, but postal workers are paid according to wage schedules set under the Postal Pay Act.

Pay Rates

At present, the Postal Service pay scale consists of several rate schedules. These schedules cover different types and levels of postal employees such as technical, clerical, production, supervisory, mail carriers, and executive management. Pay schedules provide periodic paid cost-of-living adjustments (COLA). When inflation rises, postal COLA rises, too.

When a man or woman is hired as a postal employee, he or she may join the American Postal Workers Union (APWU), the largest postal union in the world, the National Association of Letter Carriers, or one of other post office unions.

Who Can Apply for Exams?

Qualification and Physical Requirements

Age Requirements

"The general minimum age requirement for positions in the Postal Service," according to the United States Postal Service, "is 18 at the time of employment." For high school graduates or for persons certified by local authorities as having terminated formal education for adequate reasons, the minimum age is 16. Applicants who are less than 18 years of age, who are not high school graduates, and have not terminated formal education, may participate in the examination if they will reach 18 within two years from the date of examination. For carrier positions which require driving, applicants must be 18 years of age or over. There is no maximum age limit."

If you are 18 years old and if you're really ambitious, you might already be a supervisor when you reach 30 or 35.

Citizenship

"All applicants must be citizens of or owe allegiance to the United States of America, or have been granted permanent resident alien status in the United States."

Whether you are from the Philippines, Haiti, or Nicaragua, provided you are an immigrant with permanent resident alien status, you are eligible to take a postal exam and to be employed with the USPS.

Qualification Requirements

Many positions, such as clerk and carrier, require passing an entrance exam; but some do not. To be a plumber, a machinist, or a maintenance mechanic, you have to pass a written exam. Your rating will be based both on the written test and on your qualifications. But you don't need to pass a written exam, for example, if you're a physician, a nurse, a psychologist, or a computer programmer. Your rating on these jobs will be based on your education, training, and experience. On the written tests, the passing score is 70 (excluding the extra five or 10 points for applicants entitled to veteran preference.)

Educational Requirements

The U.S. Postal Service does not indicate that you must be a high school graduate to be eligible for any position. So unless it is stated specifically that you need a college degree to be qualified for a certain position, such as a doctor, a nurse, or an engineer, you will be considered for any position if you meet the requirements and win over other competitors.

Physical Requirements

Applicants must be physically able to perform efficiently the arduous duties of any position. For instance, the physical requirements for a carrier are different from those for a maintenance electrician. The carrier must be able to carry a load of 70 pounds and must be on the road in all conditions. The electrician must be able to perform the duties of the position, which may involve standing, walking, climbing, bending, reaching, and stooping for prolonged periods of time as well as intermittent lifting and carrying of heavy tools, tool boxes, and equipment on level surfaces and up ladders and stairways.

All applicants who will be called for employment must undergo a thorough physical examination, including eye and ear tests. The Post Offices does not care whether you're the size of Tinker Belle or Mr. T.

Like your car, you should always be in top condition. No matter how cold or how hot it is, your own engine must be on the go as soon as you turn the ignition key. Your body must be in good condition to withstand the conditions of the roads and the climate. Whether you are a carrier or clerk, you must be healthy enough to carry a load of mail weighing up to 70 pounds.

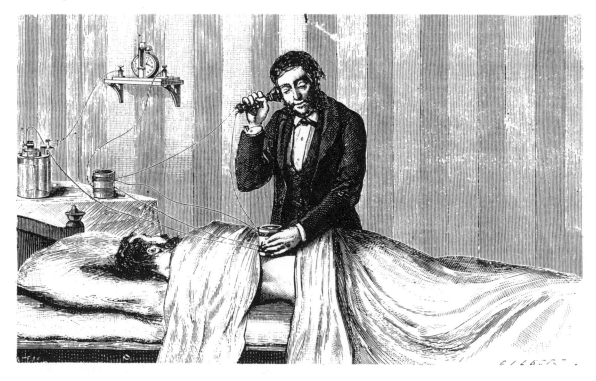

Thorough Physical Exam

It's a Test of Strength

As for the lifting or carrying a sack of mail up to seventy pounds, don't worry. Although, it's a test of strength, it's not for the championship of the world. You don't need the help of The Incredible Hulk, either. Even a thin woman can lift a seventy-pound sack of paper. If you lift weights, then you can lift it with one hand. (Look Ma, only one hand!)

Eye Examination. As regards the eye examination, the Post Office says that the requirement for distance vision is 20/40 (Snellen) in the better eye and at least 20/100 (Snellen) in the other eye. However, you are allowed to wear eyeglasses. Don't ask me what these figures mean; frankly, I don't know. I do know that during the eye test, you are asked to read some letters a few yards away, just as when you are taking eye examinations to be fitted for a new pair of glasses.

The person who gives your eye test will also determine whether you can read printing as small as a Jaeger's test, type No. 4 (whatever it is) at 14 inches with the better eye. I don't know how small this is, but as long as you can read letters and figures ordinarily written on envelopes, you'll pass the eye test.

Hearing Test. Like other applicants for any postal job, you must also have good hearing. For this reason, your ears will be tested;

you'll be wearing a headset and you'll be asked which ear hears a certain sound produced by a testing machine. Your ears must be keen enough to hear ordinary conversation; if you are an applicant for a letter carrier or a rural carrier position, you must be able to hear shouts from a distance, such as *"The dogs are coming, the dogs are coming!"*

According to USPS announcement sheets, Post Office jobs offer paid vacations, on-the-job training, liberal retirement, sick leave with pay, life insurance, low-cost health insurance, cash for suggestions, promotion opportunities, and paid holidays. Employees are paid ten percent extra for work performed between 6 p.m. and 6 a.m.

"The Dogs Are Coming! The Dogs Are Coming!"

Training Requirements

Applicants for some positions may be required to complete satisfactorily a prescribed training course or courses before assignment, reassignment, or promotion.

Operator's Permit

Some positions may require driving a government vehicle. Such positions include city carrier, rural carrier, garageman, and electronics technician.

Before you are hired for one of those jobs, you must hold a valid driver's license from the state in which the post office is located. After that you must obtain the appropriate government operator's permit.

Road Test

As an applicant for a carrier position or any other position requiring that you drive a government vehicle, you must demonstrate a safe driving record and pass a postal road test. If you fail the road test, the first time, you cannot be hired. But you may be given a second chance later. Some people who have taken this test complain that it is more difficult than the state road test. That's because safety is the name of the game in the Postal Service. To pass this road test, you must show that you follow traffic rules, drive safely, and deliver letters, magazines, and parcels to the addressees without damage.

Rates and Salaries

Under the APWU National Agreement, *(Schedule One - Salary and Rates* (Effective March 19, 2005) provided with automatic pay increases, the pay scales depending on grade levels are as follows:

Schedule One - Annual Salary & Rates (Effective 2005)

Grade 2 - (Steps D - H) $39,733 - $40,355
Grade 3 - (Steps D - H) $40,349 - $41,451
Grade 4 - (Steps D - H) $41,018 - $42,207
Grade 5 - (Steps D - H) $42,522 - $43,023
Grade 6 - (Steps D - H) $42,522 - $43,914
Grade 7 - (Steps D - H) $43,367 - $44,867

The above salaries are for regular postal employees. Part-time flexible employees at grade level receive from Grade 2 - $19.87 per hour to Grade 7 - $21.68 per hour. Part-time regular rates get from Grade 2 - $19.10 to Grade 7 - $20.85 per hour. (See the APWU Salary and Rates, *Schedule 1 and 2* on pages 412 - 415.

Schedule Two - Annual Salary & Rates (Effective (2005)

Grade 1 - (Steps BB - RC) $26,079 - $42,716
Grade 2 - (Steps BB - RC) $27,191 - $43,490
Grade 3 - (Steps BB - RC) $28,297 - $44,328
Grade 4 - (Steps A - RC) $31,871 - $45,176
Grade 5 - (Steps A- RC) $33,509 - $46,109
Grade 6 - (Steps A - RC) $35,252 - $47,132
Grade 7 - (Steps A - RC) $36,059 - $48,299
Grade 8 - (Steps A - RC) $42,033 - $49,976
Grade 9 - (Steps A - RC) $42,985 - $51,730
Grade 10 - (Steps A - RC) $43,988 - $52,906
Grade 11 - (Steps A - RC $45,047 - $54,485
Grade 12 - (Steps A - RC) $46,162 - $56,1857

For a complete schedule of salary and rates, see pages 412-415.

Postal examinations are held in testing centers throughout the United States (See Supplement B: National Directory of U.S. Postal Service Centers.) How often tests are held depends on the need for new or additional personnel. Examinations are not usually announced in the newspapers, over the radio, or on television.

Call the testing center in your area at least once a week so you won't miss any examination. The personnel department will not say whether there will be an exam any week in the future; an exam is usually announced only during the week when it accepts applications for tests. Postal exams are announced only by posting announcement sheets on postal bulletin boards; it is usually posted only for the week when it is announced. After that, the announcement is gone! If you wish to apply for any examinations in any location throughout the country, go to:

https://uspsapps.hr-services.org/

Eligibility Is Transferable

You must file an application for examinations, even if the test is for a city far from your home. In that way, you'll gain test experience. Furthermore, if you make a high score, you can request the transfer of your "eligibility" to the city where you live or to any city of your choice. The best time to transfer your eligibility is when there are "openings" in the city where you intend to move. In other words, you can take postal exams in any city of any state and if you make a high score, you can request the transfer of your eligibility to the city where you want to live and work. If your eligibility is transferred, you'll lose your eligibility in the city where you took the exam. When you are an *eligible,* you can postpone your employment in the Post Office for a certain period of time and still remain an eligible.

3

How to Get a US Postal Job

Eligibility and Employment Requirements

If doesn't matter whether you're an electrician, a professional person or just a high school graduate. It doesn't matter where you were born or where you grew up. If you're a U.S. citizen, or a permanent resident alien (immigrant), you can get a job with the U.S. Postal Service by one of two routes—either by getting high scores on postal entrance examinations or by getting a job without any examinations (if you're a doctor, nurse, or other professional).

Civil Service Eligibles

You cannot just apply for a job with the USPS without being a civil service eligible (except for technical positions). To be an eligible, you must pass the postal entrance exams. The Postal Service gives different exams for different positions, such as clerk, carrier, mail handler, mark-up clerk, distribution clerk, rural carrier, and other positions.

You can't apply for an exam if there is no opening. It's best if you have a friend or relative working in the Post Office who can tell you when an exam is forthcoming, but if you don't, you must call the personnel department of the local management sectional center. Or you may go to this website of the US Postal Service: https://uspsapps.hr-services.org/ and see where examinations are currently being held.

Post Offices throughout the country give exams to compile a *register of eligibles from* which they can take people, according to their ranking, to fill current and future vacancies. Tests are usually given by district Post Offices. For instance, the Pittsburgh (Pennsylvania) MSC gives examinations for its associate offices within the area covered by 150, 151, 153, 154, 156, and 200 (West Virginia) ZIP codes.

Although the Postal Service says that 70% is a passing score, your hair will turn grey while you wait to be called for employment if you score only in the 70's. The records show that only those who score from 90 to 100% are usually called by the Post Office, because hundreds and even thousands of people take and pass the exams and the Post Office can afford to be selective. Also, if you wish, you may request for the transfer of your eligibility to the city where you live or to any city of your choice. The best time to transfer your eligibility is when there are openings in the city where you intend to move. You can take postal exams in any city If you make a high score, request that your eligibility be transferred to the city where you want to live and work.

Route to Other Positions

When you are already employed by the Post Office, as a clerk, for instance, and you have gained enough seniority, you can submit bids for other positions. You may also take in-service examinations for other positions. The most qualified, of course, gets the job on the basis of seniority, rating, and experience. The opportunities for promotion are unlimited; it's up to you. You can be the master of your fate and the captain of your soul!

Flexible Employees

Before you obtain any of these positions, however, you start as a part-time flexible clerk or carrier. You are not yet a regular employee, but this doesn't mean that you are employed temporarily: your employment is permanent. You receive benefits similar to those given to regular employees.

"Part-time" does not mean you work only part-time. Usually you work five or six days a week. In many cases, you work six days as a part-time flexible. You are not guaranteed 40 hours' work a week, but you may sometimes work about 50 hours a week. In other words, you may work less than 40 hours a week, and sometimes more. The major difference between a part-time flexible employee and a regular is that the former does not receive any holiday pay.

All employees of the U.S. Postal Service (except those who occupy technical positions) start as part-time flexibles. From that position one moves up to a regular position with a monthly salary after six months to one or two years' employment, depending on the Post Office where one is employed. Positions become available through promotion, retirement, death, transfer, employees' leaving, and expansion of postal facilities.

Hiring Through Interviews

You can get some positions in the Postal Service without taking written examinations; these include jobs as doctors, nurses, computer analysts, psychologists, and forensic chemists. However, these jobs have to be offered first to current postal employees. For instance, if there is a vacancy for a medical officer in a certain area, the job will be offered first to insiders. Would you expect a physician working as a clerk in the Post Office? Of course not. Then, if there is no qualified person in the service, the position will be offered to an outsider through an ad in a newspaper.

My son, Lester, a computer science graduate from Michigan State University, wrote a letter to the Postal Service headquarters in Washington, DC, to inquire about postal employment. He received the following letter, which is self-explanatory:

UNITED STATES POSTAL SERVICE
475 L'Enfant Plaza, SW
Washington, DC 20260

February 23, 1987

Mr. Lester A. Bartista
Post Office Box 299
East Detroit, Michigan   48021

Dear Mr. Bartista:

Thank you for your February 16 letter seeking information concerning Postal Service employment.

The majority of professional staff positions advertised are filled by qualified applicants from within the Postal Service. However, occasionally we will be unable to fill a position from within and will subsequently advertise outside the Service, usually through advertisements in the local newspapers. Headquarters ads usually appear in the Washington Post, New York Times and Wall Street Journal.

Usually, the positions which are advertised outside the Service fall in the technical fields (computer analyst, programmer, engineer, architect, etc.). I would urge you, if you are interested in Postal Service employment in the computer field, to watch for Postal Service ads in your local paper for local positions, or the Washington Post for Headquarters positions. Your public library probably has a subscription and should have the paper available on a regular basis. In addition, I would urge you to check with the personnel office at your local post office on a periodic basis.

I hope this information is of help to you. Best wishes as you graduate and begin your career.

Sincerely,

Roberta S. Kroggel
Administrative Coordinator
Marketing Department

As indicated in the letter, if you are interested in a technical position, such as computer analyst, programmer, or engineer, watch for postal ads in the local newspapers for local positions or in the *Washington Post* for headquarters positions. If you have a friend or a relative in the local management sectional center, let him or her advise you of any vacancies for those positions. Vacancy announcements are posted on the bulletin board. In that way you'll know where the vacancies are; you may contact the local office or the headquarters, when the Postal Service advertises in the local paper for local positions or in the *Washington Post* for headquarters positions.

It's a Good Idea,
But Not in the Bag

If you're a computer programmer or an analyst and if you want to get a job in a large postal installation or at headquarters in Washington, you may take a Test 473 Exam, the test for entry-level jobs, such as mail processing clerks. When you are called for employment, accept a clerk position. When you have seniority, bid for a position as computer programmer or computer analyst or any other position. Because these jobs are offered first to insiders (like you), you have the edge in competing with outside programmers and analysts. Still, there's no guarantee that you'll get the job. Before you follow this strategy, it's best to talk with the personnel department of your local post office or the sectional center. Ask if it's really a good idea and what your chances are.

Know Where the Jobs Are

Postal Jobs for Veterans

Veteran Preference & Requirements

4

Veterans are given preference for employment in Federal jobs. If you are a veteran, a certain number of points will be added to your basic rating on the exam, so long as you make at least 70% on the exam. This is what the law dictates: if you have served in the Armed Forces of the United States, you deserve some kind of priority in government employment.

Whether you are a veteran who participated in World war II, Vietnam war, or Iraq war, you will receive this preference so long as you were honorably separated from the Armed Forces of the United States.

In the competitive tests for appointment to the positions in the Postal Service, these preference benefits are given to veterans under certain conditions.

If you are claiming the ten-point veteran disability preference, you are more fortunate than someone who is eligible for the ordinary five-point preference. Why? Because veteran eligibles who have service-connected disabilities and have extra ten points are placed first at the top of the register in the order of their scores.

That simply means that you're followed by all other eligibles, including the five-point preference veterans, who are listed according to their ratings. So if you're a ten-point preference veteran, you'll be on top of the list, even if your basic score is lower than the top scorers. You'll bump the other eligibles as if to say, "Move down, move down, move down!" The so-called *preference eligibles* who receive five points additional are listed with the other eligibles (civilians) according to scores. In other words, if you are a five-point preference veteran, it does not mean you will be ahead of those who make higher scores than yours. If you score 75, including your five points, you won't be listed above a nonpreference eligible who scores 76. However, if you are a preference eligible, you'll be listed ahead of the nonpreference eligibles who make the same scores as you.

Standard Form 15

If you're claiming veteran preference, you'll have to fill out and submit Standard Form 15 to prove that you really served in the Armed Forces.

Questions and complaints have come up because of the veteran preference. One woman who bought this book and scored 100% score on a Postal exam complained to the congressman of her district that she was discriminated against because people with lower scores than hers were appointed to positions while she was still on the waiting list. The postmaster had to explain that those who were appointed were veterans.

Because of veteran preference, many who have retired from the Army, Navy, Air Force and Marines have been appointed to postal positions after making the required scores on civil service exams.

In the competitive tests for appointment to the positions in the Postal Service, these preference benefits are given to veterans under certain conditions.

1. Five points are added to the basic rating of an examinee who scores at least 70 percent (the passing grade). If you make a score of 70, your final score will be 75; if you score 98 on the exam, your final score will be 103.
2. Ten points are added to the basic rating of an examinee who scores 70 percent or above and who is:
   a. a disabled veteran or a veteran who has received a Purple Heart award. Physical requirements are waived for persons who receive this preference, so long as they can do efficiently the duties of a postal worker.
   b. the wife of a disabled veteran if the veteran is physically disqualified by his service-connected disability for civil service appointment to positions along the line of his prewar or usual occupation.

c. the widow of a serviceman who died on active duty while serving in the Armed Forces, but only if she has not married again. (The law does not say whether she'll be disqualified if she falls in love again.)

d. The mother of a deceased or disabled veteran son or daughter, if she is either widowed, divorced, or separated, or if her present husband is permanently and totally disabled.

Veterans Preference Explained

With regard to the veterans preference, the *Postal Bulletin,* in its issue of May 30, 1985 stated:

"The following revises Handbook P-11, Personnel Operations. Section 241.31. The principal change is to incorporate the minimum 408 of *Public Law 87-300,* enacted October 14, 1982, which amended Title 38 *U.S. Code of Federal Regulations* Section 3103A. To obtain veterans preference in Federal employment, a person who enlists after September 7, 1980 (or begins active duty on or after October 14, 1982, and has not previously completed 24 months of continuous active duty), must perform active duty in the Armed Forces during a war or in a campaign or expedition for which is campaign badge has been authorized, and serve for 2 years or the full period called or ordered to active duty. The time limit does not affect eligibility for veterans preference based on peacetime service exceeding 180 days from 1955 to 1976. This change is effective immediately and will be included in a future transmittal letter."

"241.3 Kinds of Veterans Preference
.31 5-Point Preference. Five-point preference is given to honorably separated veterans (see 241.5) who served on active duty in the armed forces of the United States.

"a. During a war; or
"b. During the period April 28, 1952 to July 1, 1955; or
"c. In any campaign or expedition for which a campaign badge has been authorized (exception: a person who enlisted after September 7, 1980; or begins active duty on or after October 14, 1982, and has not previously completed 24 months of continuous active duty must perform active duty in the armed forces, during a war or in a campaign or expedition for which a campaign badge has been authorized, and serve for 2 years or the full period called or ordered for active duty. The law

excepts a person who is discharged or released from active duty (a) for a disability incurred or aggravated in the line of duty, or (b) under 10 U.S.C. 1171 or 1173 for hardship or other reasons or"

"d. For more than 180 consecutive days any part of which occurred after January 31, 1955, and before October 15, 1976. (An initial period of active duty for training under the 6-month Reserve or National Guard Program does not count.)"

City and Rural Carriers

Men and Women on the Road

5

City Carrier:

Grade 1

Salary Range: (Steps A to O) - $34,144 - $45,095 per year
Part-time Flexible: $17.07 - $22.55 per hour

Grade 2

Salary Range: (Steps A to O) - $35,865 - $48,166 per year
Part-time Flexible: $17.93 per hour

Rural Carrier:

For info, go to Internet website:
http://www.nrlca.org/PDF/25_05PAY.PDF
Part-time Flexible
Salary Range: (Grade A-C to 1 to 12): $17.58 - $23.07 per hour

Rural Carrier Associate/Rural Carrier Relief:

Salary Range: Schedule 1 - $16.45; Schedule 2 - $19.78 per hour

Persons Eligible to Apply: Open to the general public
Examination Requirement: Must pass the Postal Test 473-473-C, 460 RCA exam, and the driving test

As a carrier, (whether city or rural), you'll be required to sort, rack, and tie mail at the post office before you start making deliveries within your route or area of delivery. In sorting letters, you must arrange them in the same order as the streets occur on the route. Letters and magazines for occupants of an apartment complex must be tied together with a rubber band or a leather belt. If you make a mistake in reading an address, the letter may go into the wrong home mailbox, causing a delay in delivery. The next day, you may find a note that says, *"This is not ours. Opened by mistake."* The letter might be a "deadline" letter, an order from the court, or a warning from a creditor.

As a carrier, you'll also maintain required information, record changes of addresses, maintain other reports, and forward undeliverable-as-addressed mail.

As a carrier, you'll also maintain required information, record changes of addresses, maintain other reports, and forward undeliverable-as-addressed mail.

In some ways, a rural carrier's duty is different from that of a city carrier. If you are hired as a rural carrier or a rural carrier associate, you'll be a jack of all trades; you'll also be a "walking post office." You may carry stamps, scales, and other equipment and supplies to serve the people of the rural area you cover. For this reason, you must know how to compute the cost of a piece of mail or a package whether it's going to a neighboring city, Iraq, or the North Pole

Regular Route

Once you're a carrier, you'll have a regular route. Day in and day out, you'll walk on the same streets and open the same mailboxes. You won't get lost and you'll probably have time for a cup of coffee at McDonald's or Burger King after you've finished covering your route.

As a letter carrier you can become "the great observer." As you pound on the streets on your route, you'll notice unusual lawn ornaments, flagpoles, signs, and other out-of-the-ordinary things.

Once a letter carrier saw this sign nailed to a wooden fence: *"Dogs: Beware of Letter Carriers."*

***This is Not How
the Mail Room Looks Today***

If you're still a flexible city carrier or a rural carrier associate, that's a different story. Sometimes, as a flex, you'll cover different routes everyday. Before you go out, you'll have to look at the city map to see where you are going to so that you'll finish delivering all your mail. You'll cover the routes of carriers who are off on a particular day or who have called in sick. Don't worry—once they were flexibles, and your time will come. Seniority is the rule in the post office.

Love Notes

If you are a carrier, you must remember names as well as you can. If you don't know, you'll receive many notes and envelopes saying: "How many times have we told you that this man moved five years ago! or "I've told you a dozen times that this man has long been dead!"

Once a friend of mine who is a letter carrier found some notes on an envelope returned to him: "Gone! Not back! Not coming back anymore!"

Road Adventures

I asked my friend whether he had ever been accosted by anyone on the streets while he was covering his route.

"Yes, many times," he said

"By thieves?" I asked

"No...by retirees!" He responded.

Sometimes in the spring or the fall you'll have to bring an umbrella or a raincoast When it rains, it pours. You may also wish to put a sticker on the back bumper of your car or jeep that says, *"Warning—Give a Break to Animals."*

Undeliverable-as-Addressed (UAA) Mail

Underliverable-as-addressed mail is sent to the Computerized Forwarding System (CFS) unit in every sectional center, where the mail is processed by the mark-up clerks in every post office. Undeliverable-as-addressed mail goes to the CFS for forwarding. Changes of addresses are computerized, and every change of address (COA) is entered into the system, where it is stored on disks. When the letter, magazine, or package is keyed—that is, when the operator types in the first three letters of the last name and the last two numbers of the street address—the computer generates a corresponding change of address label.

No Record ("N") Mail

As a carrier, you will also send mail that has no change of addresses to the CFS. This mail (called "N" mail) will be returned to you for proper disposition. N mail has a "returned to sender, undeliverable as addressed" label with the letter N, meaning that there's no record of the address in the CFS or that a change of address has not been submitted to the CFS. Maybe you didn't send in the Form 3575 (change of address card), filled in properly by the one whose family moved. At times like this you will exchange some kind of note with the people in the CFS.

Once when a carrier received an N mail letter, he was angry because he had already written the word "deceased" on the envelope, but it was returned to him anyway as N mail by the CFS. He wrote a note on the envelope and sent it back to the CFS. The note said: *"This man is already dead. Where shall I deliver the mail—to hell?*

Form 3575

He might have been right. But he should have filled out Form 3575, the change-of-address card, with the name and address of the dead person and the "diseased" under "new address." This information is entered into the computer, and the mail is returned to the sender. When a CFS mark-up clerk keys this address, the label that is produced will say, *"Return to Sender, Moved. Left No Address."*

Examination Requirements

As an applicant, you have to pass an entrance examination. The Test 473/473-C and the 460 Examination are the most important exams in the Postal Service. Why? Because 80 percent of employees hired by the USPS get high scores on these tests. The 473/473-C Test consists of four parts: Part A: Address-Checking Test; Part B: Forms Completion; Part C: Coding and Memory, and Part D: Inventory of Experiences and Characteristics.The rural carrier associate Exam 460 consists of Part A: Address Checking Test; Part B: Memory-for-Address Test; Part C: Number Series Test; and Part D: Following Oral Instructions

Clerk Position

The Key to Other Postal Jobs

6

Distribution Clerk (Manual)

Grade: L-5

Salary Range: See schedule of salary & rates on pages 9 - 10; 432-435.

Persons Eligible to Apply: Open to the public

Examination Requirements: Must pass the 473 Test

A clerk may be the jack-of-all-trades position in the U.S. Postal Service. If you score high on the Test 473 and land a job in the Postal Service, you can be a manual distribution clerk.

As a distribution clerk, you'll work indoors and will handle sacks of mail weighing as heavy as 70 pounds. You'll sort mail and distribute it by using a complicated scheme, which must be memorized. You'll place letters or flats (magazines and pieces of mail in big envelopes) into the correct boxes or pigeonholes. If you make a mistake in reading addresses or numbers, the letter will go to the wrong box, thus causing a delay in delivery. Letters from different boxes in a "case" go to different routes served by carriers, who will distribute the mail door to door.

As a distribution clerk, you'll also dump sacks of mail onto conveyors for culling and sorting; you'll load and unload sacks and trays of mail on and off mail transporters, such as APCs (All-Purpose Containers) and BMCs (Bulk Mail Containers). As a clerk, you may also be assigned to a public counter or window, doing such jobs as selling stamps and weighing parcels, and you'll be personally responsible for all money and stamps.

How Not to Unload Parcels

A friend of mine who works in a post office has told me this story:

While he was still a flexible employee at the post office in Mt. Clemens, Michigan, Post Office, he was assigned to unload parcels from a BMC. He had to work fast because there were several BMCs to be unloaded. While he was unloading a big parcel, the bottom of it suddenly gave way, and hundreds of nuts poured onto the floor! He was embarrassed and had a hard time picking up the nuts, and some of the other employees helped him, too. Then on one side of the carton that had contained the nuts, my red-faced friend read a note: *Glass—please handle with care.*

Clerk-Typist

Grade: L-4 to L-6

Salary Range: See schedule of salary & rates on pages 9 - 10; 432-435.

Persons Eligible to Apply: Open to the general public.

Examination Requirements: Must pass Examination 710 and a typing test.

Duties: Originates and maintains routine records, composes memoranda and letters; acts as receptionist, answering telephone calls, talking and relaying messages and furnishing information requested; relieves office clerks; and does all other related clerical jobs.

Qualifications: Ability to read and understand instructions, to perform basic arithmetic computations, to maintain accurate records, to prepare reports and correspondence, and to operate office machines, such as calculator, adding machine, and duplicator.

Experience Requirements:
A. For PS-Level 4 or PMS-Level, 1 year
B. For PS-Level 5 or PMS-Level, 2 years
C. PS-Level 6 or PMS-level, 3 years

Substitution of Education for Experience. Successful completion of a full 4-year high school course, including credits in commercial or business subjects, such as general business education, business arithmetic, or office practice, may be substituted for 1 year of the required experience.

Study completed in a business or secretarial school or an academic institution above high school level may be substituted for a maximum of 1 year of experience on the basis of 36 weeks of study for 1 year of experience. Credit will be followed for full-time or part-time study at the rate of 20 class hours of instruction for one week of study in such subjects as business English, office machines, filing and indexing, office practice, business mathematics, and accounting or bookkeeping.

Typing Requirements: Ability to type 40 words per minute for 5 minutes with no more than two errors. This ability will be tested in the performance section of the examination.

Clerk-Stenographer

Grades: L - 5

Salary Range: See schedule of salary & rates on pages 9 - 10; 432-435.

Persons Eligible to Apply: Open to the general public

Examination Requirements: Applicants must pass Examination 710. They must also pass the Dictation test.

Duties: Same as the duties performed by a clerk-typist, except that he or she must take dictation.

Dictation Requirement: Ability to take dictation in shorthand or on a shorthand machine at 80 words per minute. This ability will be tested in the performance section of the examination.

Typing Requirement: Ability to type 40 words per minute for 5 minutes with no more than two errors. This ability will be tested in the performance section of the examination.

If There's No Opening Yet

If you're planning to take Examination 710, which is the exam for clerk-typist and clerk-stenographer, but there are no openings yet, there's an easier way to get one of those positions. Take the 473 Test and obtain a clerk position.

After you have gained enough seniority, submit your bid for a clerk-typist or clerk-stenographer position, if there are any vacancies. You won't take a written examination, but you'll have to take a typing test for a clerk-typist position, and a typing test and short-hand dictation for a clerk-stenographer position.

After you pass the test, you'll obtain the position if you win in the bidding on the basis of seniority, experience, and qualifications. Before such a position is offered to an eligible (who made a high score on an entrance exam), it is offered to an insider (like you).

Other Positions

From your clerk position, you can also transfer to any accounting technician position, if you love working with figures, or to any other available position in the Postal Service. Some positions may require you to pass "in-service" examinations or training; others do not. For instance, if you're a letter-sorting machine operator and are already tired of hitting machine keys, you can move to a manual distribution clerk position. As a distribution clerk or any other kind of clerk, you can move from one job to another (moving forward, not backward, of course) by submitting a bid and winning the job on the basis of your seniority, education, and other qualifications.

Mark-Up Clerk

The Mail Forwarder

7

Grade: L-4

Salary: See schedule of salary & rates on pages 9 - 10; 432-435.

Persons Eligible to Apply: Open to the general public

Examination Requirement: Applicants must pass the 473 Test and the typing test.

Mark-Up clerks process mail that is undeliverable as addressed. Previously they were just known as mark-up clerks, but now they are known as mark-up clerks, automated. Your duty as a mark-up clerk, automated, consists of keying on the machine, labeling, and other related jobs.

Mark-up clerks used to mark undeliverable-as-addressed mail with rubber stamps that said "Return to Sender, Address Unknown." They used to stick preprinted labels with new addresses on envelopes. These labels were inserted between change-of-addressed cards, arranged alphabetically in an index card tray.

Computerized Forwarding System Units

Today, CFS units have been installed in USPS sectional centers throughout the country. If a CFS unit is to be established by a post office, or if a CFS unit needs additional employees, postal officials will have to give a 473 Test. Those already in the service may get these jobs if they wish, by bidding for positions. But they must pass a special written exam and a typing test. Civilian employees in military headquarters or offices may also request transfer to mark-up clerks, as in other positions. But they must pass the written and typing test.

The first priority of the CFS in establishing a data bank for all changes of address in a sectional center is the conversion program (CP). All the changes of addresses in post offices under the jurisdiction of a certain sectional center is entered into the system. The

27

change-of-address notice is contained on a card known as Form 3575.

Change-of-Address Input

On the basis of the information on the change-of-address card, the mark-up clerk enters the change of address (COA) into the system.

The operator goes to the data management (DM) program. The first words to appear on the computer screen are *Zone* and *Function. Zone* means the ZIP code and the function asks if you're entering a COA for the first time or if you are modifying the file that is already in the system.

For Instance:

Zone: 48336
Extract Code: Smit431 (In entering the extract code, you type the first four letters of the family name and the last three numbers of the address. If it's a business address change, then you have to type the first four numbers of the business name and the last three numbers of the address.)

Function: ( )

A - Add
M - Modify
E - EC

Usually you'll type the A or M.

When you select the A, this will appear:

Zone:
Extraction Code:
Address Selection
1. Street Address
2. P.O. Box
3. Rural Route
4. Hwy Contract
5. General Delivery
6. Foreign

For instance, if the original (or old) address is a street, then select 1, and this information will appear:

COA Information FP4

The FP4 indicates that this is a permanent (P) address for a family (F). If it's for an individual, it should be IP4. If the change is temporary, then it should be FT4 or IT4. The 4 indicates that the address is willing to pay for 4th class mail forwarded to the new address:

Start Date:
Last Name:
First Name:
Number:
Pre-Directional:
Apt/Suite No:
DNF Code:
Additional Extraction Code:

(Note: The Last Name and the First Name will be changed to Business, if it's a business moving.)

If you are to enter the new address, this information will appear on the screen:

Number:
Pre Directional:
Street Name:
Post Directional:
Apt/Suite No.
City:
State:
ZIP:

If the person is moving from a P.O. Box and you check the selection P.O. Box, this will appear on the screen.

COA Info:
Start Date:
Last Name:
First Name:
P.O. Box
DNF Code:
Additional Extract Code:

After this, as in the street address, you must select whether the person or the business is moving to a street, a P.O. Box, a rural route, etc.

In generating labels, the mark-up clerk then goes to the Label Generation (LG) Program and the zone and extraction code questions appear. (The machinable letters pass in front of the operator (through a revolving mini-conveyor, as if asking "Where am I going?") The operator then keys the extract code (as if answering, "I Don't know") for each piece of mail passing by, typing the first four letters of the last name or first four letters of the business name and the last three numbers of the address. Then bingo! The computer automatically generates the yellow label (installed in a built-in case on the machine). This machine is different from the computer wherein COAs (changes of addresses) are entered. The letters are directed to different bins: some to the "local bin," others to the "out-of-town bin," some others to the "return-to-sender" bin, etc.

Why Do People Move?

Why do many people move so often? Because they want a change of environment or atmosphere: they seek new jobs, find new friends, and, if they are already in good financial shape, they want to live where the rich or the retirees live. Sometimes people can no longer bear the bitter cold and blizzards in northern states, so they move temporarily to places like Florida, California, or Arizona. People are like birds: they fly to certain places, depending on the season. Some of the changes are not for families, but for individuals when members of a family move to different places. For instance, two people find they no longer care for each other, so they move to different locations to try to forget each other and to find new playmates.

Extraction Codes

Why does a mark-up clerk enter additional extraction codes? The reason for this is that we think differently. An operator must type the first four letters of the family name and last three numbers of the old address to produce the label for a new address. But sometimes he or she doesn't know which is which. Hence, new additional extra codes.

Different Shifts

Mark-up clerks work in shifts: one may come at 6 a.m., another at 8 a.m., and another at 3:30 p.m.

Other Major Postal Jobs

8

5 Entry-Level Jobs

Distribution Clerk, Machine

Grade: L-5

Salary Range: See schedule of salary & rates on pages 9 - 10; 432-435.

Persons Eligible to Apply: Open to the general public

Examination Requirements: Must pass Test 473

The distribution clerk, machine, known as a Letter Sorting Machine (LSM) operator, is a clerk who operates a machine (called a console) that is attached to a giant letter-sorting machine. The console has a keyboard similar to that of a piano. Some people say that if you're a pianist or know how to play the piano, you'll be a good LSM operator.

There are two kinds of LSM operators. One is assigned to learn one or more distribution schemes; the other is assigned to key ZIP codes.

Every post office has its schemes, based on its ZIP codes. For example, Warren, Michigan has four ZIP codes: 48089, 48091, 48092, and 48093. The scheme involves the routes to which letter carriers are assigned. For instance, a carrier may be assigned to Route 38, which covers certain streets. Sometimes a street is divided into several routes. Also, letters must be diverted to their proper routes. This is the job of an LSM operator (distribution clerk, machine). A manual distribution clerk sorts letters according to their routes by putting letters into pigeonholes on a case.

If you're assigned to key schemes, you must hit the right keys (two) on the machine (all numbers) as you read the addresses on envelopes that are moving from right to left at the speed of 50 letters per minute. Your vision must not move back and forth as if you're watching a smiling John McEnroe and a frowning basketball star Magic Johnson in a tennis exhibition game. Your sight must be focused in front of you. Your eyes must be on red alert for the letters passing by, and you must hit the proper keys as soon as each letter passes. Sometimes, while you're deciding what route a letter is destined for, it's already going, going—gone! If that happens, go on to the next letter. All letters keyed wrong or unkeyed go to the nixies. You must not make many mistakes because you are allowed only a certain percentage of errors.

If you're assigned to key ZIP codes, you have to key only the first three numbers in the ZIP code. Your speed must be 60 letters per minute.

Do you think you can handle the job? Why not? They're doing it. As the saying goes, if they can do it, you can do it, too. (You must undergo training, of course, and must pass that training.)

Mail Handler

Grade: Level 4
(Full-Time Regular Employees)
Salary Range: (Steps A to O) $29,980 - $44,181) per year
Grade: Level 5
Salary Range: (Steps A to O) $31,412 - $45,120) per year
Also, go to the Internet website:
http://www.local300npmhu.org/rsc-m-09-04-04-Excel-wp.htm

Part-Time Regular Employees
Salary: (Steps A to O) - $14.41 - $21.24 per hour
Flexible Employees
Salary: (Steps A to O) - $14.99 per hour

Persons Eligible to Apply: Open to the general public

Examination Requirement: Must pass the Test 473.

If you get a job as a mail handler, you'll work mostly in the dock area, the canceling section, and the operation area. As the title indicates, you'll load and unload mail onto and off trucks and perform duties incidental to the movement and processing of mail.

As a mail handler, your duties include separating mail sacks to go to different routes or cities; canceling parcel post stamps; rewrapping parcels; and operating canceling machines, addressographs, mimeographs, and fork-lifts.

Mail Processor

Grade: L-4

Salary Range: See schedule of salary & rates on pages 9 - 10; 432-435.

Persons Eligible to Apply: Open to the general public. Occasionally, positions are open only to current employees.

Examination Requirement: Muss pass the 473 Test

If you're appointed as a mail processor, you'll process mail using a variety of automated mail processing equipment. You'll work at the optical character reader (OCR) mail processing equipment area.

Flat Sorting Machine Operator

Grade: L-5

Salary Range: See schedule of salary & rates on pages 9 - 10; 432-435.

Persons Eligible to Apply: Open to the general public

Examination Requirement: Must pass the 473 Test

As a flat-sorting machine operator, your major duty is to operate a single- or multi-position operator-faced electronic-mechanical machine in the distribution of flats. (Flats are mailed material mostly contained in manila envelopes and other self-sealed mail, and are fed to the machine by an operator to go to different cities or routes.) You may also be assigned to work in other areas as needed.

As an applicant you must have skills in operating an electromechanical machine and in the application of approved machine distribution. Heavy lifting is also required.

Data Conversion Operator

Grade: L-4

Salary Range: See schedule of salary & rates on pages 9 - 10; 432-435.

Persons Eligible to Apply: Open to the general public

Examination Requirements: Muss pass Examination 710, the Computer-Based Test 714, and a keyboard qualification test.

If you get high score on Examination 710 and pass the computer test and a keyboard qualification test, you may be hired as a data conversion operator in a Remote Encoding Center.

As a data conversion operator, you'll use a computer terminal to prepare mail for automated sorting equipment.

You'll key the essential information needed so that an address bar code can be applied to each letter.

How to Mark Circles On Answer Sheet

The Secret Way to Marking It Effectively

Your answer sheet is separate from the question sheet. This answer sheet is corrected by computer in California. The USPS furnishes lead pencils to be used during the examination; you may not use your own. You must make the pencil point broad enough to mark or darken the circle in one or two strokes.

Don't Sharpen the Point or Tip of Your Pencil.

The USPS Way

The sample below is included in a booklet published by the USPS, but it is not sent out. It is used only by organized groups that are participating in the Postal Service's affirmative action program by preparing applicants for the tests. The sample shows how an answer sheet is to be marked.

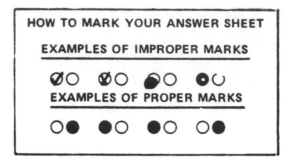

Some reviewers advise that you make this kind of mark. Others do not even discuss how a circle is to be marked.

A book on postal tests says that the instructions you receive at the time of the official test will include instructions on how to blacken the circles on the answer sheet. It reminds you to follow the instructions strictly and not to misinterpret the directions.

According to that book you are to darken completely the circle you have selected as the correct answer like this:

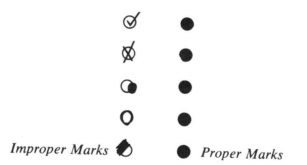

The Bautista Version

When I took an exam for the Warren (Michigan) Post Office, I tried to blacken the circles almost completely. I tried to be a Picassso; my final score was 78.5%. Then I decided to change my stroke in marking the circles after I had devised some other tests systems. I made the mark smaller; the smaller it became, the higher score I made.

Pablo R. Abesamis of Glendale, California, marked the circles better than I did (much smaller marks), and this is what he wrote to me:

"It's unbelievable! Just imagine, using your method I got five scores of 100% on postal entrance examinations. I also acquired 98.80% and 97% on two other exams. Your systems really work..."

I received flood of letters from readers, congratulating me for my efforts for showing them my own way of marking the circles. I included illustrations of how Abesamis and many others marked the circles and made high scores.

In **Booklist,** a publication of the American Library Association, a reviewer writes:

"Bautista provides valuable advice for passing the civil service exams necessary to obtain several U.S. Postal jobs...the text supplies practical background on eligibility for post office jobs, on the veteran preference system, on the actual contents of the exams, and on techniques for studying and memorization."

Here's how I made the markings.

●   ●   ●   ●   ●   ●   ●   ●   ●

Your exam score may be higher when you don't completely mark the whole circles on the answer sheet. It's simply common sense that when you compare addresses and mark the circle on a six-minute, 95-questions test, you have to work fast. To compare 95 sets of addressess in six minutes, you must take less than four seconds to answer each question, including marking the circles on the answer sheet. If you blacken the circles completely, (as advised by other postal books), you won't be able to answer all the 95 questions, but only about one-half of the items. The smaller you mark the circle, the more questions you'll answer because of the time limit.

On the basis of my experience in taking exams, the marking depends on what type of test you're taking. If you're taking the 473/473-C Test or the RCA 460 test, you can make a smaller mark; if you're taking the arithmetic and reading comprehension portions of another exam, you can make the mark bigger simply because you've the time to do it.

You can chat with your local carrier or any other current postal employee and ask him or her how he or she made the markings on the answer sheet when he or she took the exam. Maybe he or she did the right thing.

Many other people who bought my book and did what I did also made high scores on tests. When Bautista talks, people listen.

From all over the United States, readers have written to tell me that they made high marks after they had followed my step-by-step instructions on taking exams.

If You Followed My Instructions,
This Would Not Have Happened to You.

473/473-C Battery Test 10

Test for Major Entry-Level Jobs

The Postal 473/473-C Test is an exam for major entry-Level Jobs: **City Carriers, Mail Processing Clerks, Mail Handlers,** and **Sales, Services, and Distribution Associates.** It replaced the old 470 Battery Test that was first introduced in 1994.

Actually, Test 473 and Test 473-C Test are the same. However, when Test 473-C is given, it is exclusively for applicants for city carriers. Of course, a job applicant for a Test 473 who score high on the test can also be hired as a city carrier.

The duties involved in the work for these major entry-level jobs are as follows:

City Carriers: These carriers sort, rack, and tie mail at the post office before they start making deliveries within their route or area of delivery. They also maintain required information, record changes of address. maintain other reports, and forward undeliver able-as addressed mail.

Mail Processing Clerks: These clerks operate and maintain automated mail processing equipment or do manual sorting of mail. They collate, bundle, and move processed mail from one location to another.

Mail Handlers: They load and unload mail onto and off trucks and perform duties incidental to the movement and processing of mail. Duties include separating mail sacks to go to different routes or cities; cancel parcel post stamps and operate canceling machines, addressoggraphs, and fork-lifts.

Sales, Services, and Distribution Associates: They do direct sales and customer support services and distribution of mail. The associates must pass an on-the-job training program.

The 473/473-C Battery Test consists of the following Parts:

Part A: Address Checking
Part B: Forms Completion
Part C: Coding and Memory
Part D: Inventory of Personal Characteristics and Experience

When you pass the test, you'll be listed in the **Register of Eligibles.** But **although 70 is the passing score, you need to score 95-100% on the exams,** to have a better chance of being called for employment. Remember, the first to be called for employment are the ones on the top of the list.

The Test 473 requires memorizing numbers, streets, states, and ZIP codes. What you need to do is to know how to memorize these things in a very short time. Remember, this is a timed test. For example, for the Address Checking part, you need to answer 60 questions in 11 minutes; for the Coding section of the test, you are to answer 36 questions in 6 minutes. On the actual Memory section test, you have to answer 36 questions in 7 minutes. Our strategies for memorizing codes and street names and addresses will be useful to you.

Beat the Competition!

Parts of Test 473/473-C:

The test covers the following parts:

Test Unit	No. of Questions	Time Allowed	Subjects Covered
Part A Address Checking	60	11 minutes	Identify if 2 compared addresses have errors or no errors.
Part B Forms Completion	30	15 minutes	Determine if completion of form is correct.
Part C Section 1 - Coding	36	6 minutes	Create address codes to remember address range assigned to routes.
Section 2 - Memory	36	7 minutes	Use address codes to remember address range assigned to routes.
Part D Identify Job-Related Experiences & Characteristics.	236	90 minutes	Identify job-related experiences and characteristics.

Part A: Address-Checking Test

Part A of Postal Exam 473 involves 60 questions to be finished in 11 minutes, comparing two rows of addresses as quickly as possible. You have to match the *Correct List* (left column) of addresses containing numbers, names of streets, city, and state and zip codes, and the *List to Be Checked* containing the same items. You must compare the left and right rows of addresses and ZIP codes. Determine if there are **No Errors**, if there are **Errors in the Address Only**, **Errors in the ZIP Code only**, or **Errors in Both** the address and the ZIP code.

Address-Checking Sample Items

A. No Errors	B. Address Only	C: ZIP Code Only	D: Both

Correct List

Address	ZIP Code
3540 Willow Ct Sedona, AZ	86351-0001
2163 Jones Dr Palm Desert, CA	92217-2306

List to Be Checked

Address	ZIP Code
3540 Willow Ct Sedona, AZ	86451-0001
2163 Jones St Palm Desert, CA	92211-2306

As mentioned before, you must determine if there are errors in the rows of addresses and ZIP codes being compared for correctness or incorrectness of addresses and zip codes. If there are no errors in both the addresses and the ZIP codes, meaning they are exactly the same, the answer should be **A (No Errors);** if there is an error in the address only, the answer should be **B (Address Only);** if there is an error in the ZIP code only, the answer should be **C (ZIP Code Only);** and if there are errors in both address and ZIP code, the answers should be **D (Both).**

Part B: Forms Completion.

Part B involves the identification of information required to fill out or complete a Postal form for customers and Postal employees.

Part C: Coding and Memory Sections.

Part C of the new Test 473 consists of two parts or sections: the Coding Section and the Memory Section.

Part D: Inventory of Personal Experiences and Characteristics.

Part D involves the inventory of personal experiences and characteristics containing 236 test items to be finished in 90 minutes.

11

Address-Checking Strategies

Techniques for Answering Questions Instantly

The Address-Checking Test for the **Postal 473/473-C Battery Test** and the **Address-Checking Test** for the **RCA 460 Examination** have similarities and differences.

In the Address-Checking test of the **RCA 460 Examination**, you have to determine if two addresses are *Alike* or *Different*. You have to answer the questions with an "A" for Alike and a "D" for Different. In other words, there are only two choices; it's either "A" (for Alike) and "D" (for Different). However, in the Address-Checking Test of the **473/473-C Battery Test,** you have to answer the questions in different ways. What you have to do is to compare the addresses and zip codes in each row of the **List to Be Checked** with those of the **Correct List.** Decide if they are exactly alike or different (left column). You will select any of the A, B, C, or D choices; **A** for **No Errors; B** for an error in the **Address Only; C** for an error in the **ZIP Code Only;** and **D** for errors in **Both** address and ZIP code.

The Address-Checking test of the Postal 473/473-C Battery Test consists of 60 questions to be answered in 11 minutes only. So you have to compare the two addresses and zip codes quickly but accurately to score high on the exams. (On the other hand, the address-checking test of the RCA 460 examination involves 95 items to be answered in 6 minutes).

Postal 473 Battery Test
Part A: Address-Checking Test

General Techniques For Answering
Address-Checking Tests

	Correct List			List to Be Checked	
	Address	ZIP Code		Address	ZIP Code
1.	537 Richmond Dr Akron, OH	89965		337 Richmond Dr Akron, OH	89964
2.	1597 Pope Ln Douglas, GA	31535		1897 Pope Ln Douglas, GA	31535
3.	4375 Park Ave Worcester, MA	01610		4375 Park Ave Worcester, MA	01610

1. In the case of sample No. 1, the right column address is different from the left column address. The first group of numbers begins with the number 5 and the second group of numbers on the right begins with number 3. Whether the two cities/cities are alike or different, it doesn't matter. There's an error in the address. When comparing the zip codes, you'll see that the right zip code is different from the left zip code. The left zip code ends with the number 5 and the second zip codes ends with the number 4. Hence the correct answer is **D: Both.**

2. In the case of sample No. 2, the address on the right (street address and city/state) is different from those on the left. With regard to the right column zip code, it's the same as that on the left column. Therefore, the correct answer is **B. Address Only.**

3. The No. 3 sample shows that there are no errors in both addresses and Zip Codes. So, the correct answer is **A: No Errors.**

In a nutshell, you just determine whether the addresses and zip codes in the **Correct List** and **List to Be Checked** are *alike* or *different.* Each row includes the address containing numbers, street names (and abbreviations, Rd for Road, etc.), and city and state names and the ZIP codes consist of five or more numbers. Sometimes the ZIP code contains nine numbers, including the so-called ZIP plus 4 (four numbers).

Actually, it's just wise to remember that there are two columns of addresses and ZIP codes (left column or first column and right column or second column). You should not care whether any of each address or ZIP code belongs to the

Correct List or to the **List to Be Checked**. If there's any difference in any of the information in each row, there should be an error or errors. Therefore, mark **A** for **No Errors; B** for an error in the **Address Only; C** for an error in the **ZIP Code Only;** and **D** for errors in **both** address and ZIP Code. So it doesn't matter whether you read the information in each row of the addresses and ZIP codes from right to left or from left to right. Just find the error or errors in the address and ZIP code!

General Techniques
For Address-Checking Tests

Here are some strategies needed to answer all the questions within the time allocated to the items or questions.

1. Compare in groups.

Divide the address in smaller groups. For example, street number (left column to street number (right column), and zip code (left colum) to zip code (right column).

2. Use Your Fingers

In comparing addresses and zip codes (**Corrected List** and **List to Be Checked**), you can point at the numbers and streets with your fingers. Place the little finger of your nonwriting hand on one column of address and the index finger of the same hand on the other column. Move your hand downward as you make comparisons, while your writing hand marks the answers.

3. Lying Side by Side

The question sheet and the answer sheet should be lying side by side; the question sheet on your non-writing side, the answer sheet on your writing side. Don't jerk your neck from left to right as you read; just let your eyes do the sweeping. Then hold your pencil in your writing hand and don't move your non-writing hand from the question sheet. Then move it downward as you mark a circle with two or three strokes by your writing hand. Be sure that the line you are marking corresponds to the question you are answering.

4. See the Differences in Spellings and Abbreviations.

Take note of the spellings of street, city, state, and numbers in the ZIP code. There are times that the first address has a zip code such as 48012 and the second address has a ZIP code of 48021.

Most of the time, there are differences in abbreviations, such as Ave, St., or Rd. Sometimes the first address (left) is abbreviated as St and the second address (right) is Ave, or vice versa.

5. Have a Guide.

It's best to use a bookmark or some other kind of guide with your nonwriting hand: place it just below the line you are comparing and slide it straight down to the next line as you continue with the test. This prevents you from comparing the first address or number with an address or number in the wrong line. You can also place the little finger of your nonwriting hand on the left column and the index finger of the same hand on the right column of the addresses. Move your nonwriting hand downward as you make the comparisons, while you mark the answers with your writing hand.

6. Remembering This:
   You must remember that the address contains the numbers/P.O. Box, street names, and abbreviations such as St (Street), Rd (Road), or Dr (Drive), and the City/State (.
   In analyzing the numbers of streets, be sure to take note of numbers with similar shapes, such as 3 and 8 or 5, and 1 and 7, 2 and 5. Match these numbers: 29890 and 29390; 72360 and 72860; and 81939 and 87939. Did you see the errors?
   In comparing or matching addresses and zip codes in each row of the items, you should always start reading from the left. That is, compare each row of the **Correct List** with each row of the **List to be Checked.** Although the *instruction* for you is to compare the each row of the **List to Be Checked** with the **Correct List** (from right to left), it should be the other way around. **That is, you should compare** each row of the **Correct List** with each row of the **List to Be Checked.** Why? It's because it's not the usual way to look at the addresses and zip codes from the right to the left; it should be from left to right because reading is always done from left to right.

7. Speed is important.
   Since the 473-473-C exam is a timed test, you must answer the questions quickly, but correctly.

8. Right answers minus wrong answers.
   You need to be careful in answering the questions on address-checking (Part I) and Coding and Memory tests (Part C). Of course, for each right answer you get one point. But here's the rule: it's right answers minus one-third of the wrong answers. If you answer all the 60 questions, and you have a total of 15 mistakes, you will be credited only for 45 items, minus the total penalty points of 5 (1/3 of 15 = 5) In other words, 45 total correct answers minus 5 = 40. Thus, 40 is your total score on the address-taking test.

9. Which question are you answering?: Once in every five or six numbers, before you mark any *circle* for your answers, be sure that the answer corresponds to the proper *line* of each item or question. For instance, the marked circle belonging to item number 9 should answer item or question number 9. Sometimes when you're in a hurry, you may mark circles that do not correspond to the questions you're answering.

10. Be in a hurry. Skip the difficult questions you do not know, answer the ones you do know, and time permitting, return to the difficult questions you skipped.

11. No notes on palm of hand: Don't try to write down addresses or notes on the palm of your hand. You'll have no time to do that. You can try to remember only the first or two digits of the address. it's better to remember 1 or 2 digits.

12. Marking circles on answer sheet. You need to speed up to complete answering the questions or at least finish working on the questions before the time alloted lapses. One of the techniques on these tests, especially the three parts of the exams, is to know how to mark the circles on the answer sheet. (See *How to Make Circles,* page 35).

Ways of Doing the Comparison of Addresses and Zip Codes

On the 473/473-C Tests, you may memorize the following answers, whether the answer may be **A, B, C** or **D**.

A: No Errors   B: Address Only   C: Zip Code only D: Both

Here are the ways to compare the ZIP codes:

First Way: Here's the first way of comparison as contained in the following sample.

2200 Martin Ave 23221		2200 Martin Ave 23221	
Richmond, VA		Richmond, VA	

First, compare the zip code on the left to the zip code on the right. If they are alike, then remember them as *alike,* and then match the address on the left (street number, street/state/city) to the address on the left. If they are *alike,* remember them as such. Hence, both addresses and the zip codes have no errors, so the answer is **A: No Errors.**

Second Way: Here's another way of making the comparison of the two columns.

Compare the two addresses by moving your sight from left to right. It's easier to compare the address and the zip code on the left column to the address and the zip code on the right column. Here's how you can do it.

Example:

28091 Hickory Dr	48091	28097 Hickory Dr.	48091
Farmington Hills, MI		Farmington Hills, MA	

First, compare the address "Hickory" to the address "Hickory" to the right, containing numbers of street/P.O. box and names of streets, including the abbreviations, whether it's a St or a Rd. If there's a difference in the address, such as in the above example (last number of first column is different from the street number on the right, 1 and 7), then stop comparing and just remember there's a difference or error in the address. Don't continue comparing anymore, the city and state at left (which are included in the address) to the ones on the right. Now compare the zip code on the left to the zip code on the right. As you may see, there's no difference in the zip codes; the numbers are the alike or the same. Then just remember there's no error in the zip code, not making any mark to avoid waste of time. So the correct answer is "**Address Only.**"

Third Way: Here's another way of comparison as exemplified by the sample below:

Example:

3192 Aberdeen Ct.	34743	3192 Aberdeen Ct	34743
Kissimmee, FL		Kissimmee, FL	

Compare only the numbers, streets, and abbreviations such as Rd, St, Ave, and on the left to the ones on the right column. If they are alike, as indicated in the sample above, then compare the city and state on the left to the city and state on the right. Next, compare the zip codes of both columns. Since they are alike too, the correct answer is **A (No Errors).**

Fourth Way: Here's another way of comparison as contained in the following sample.

2200 Martin Ave	23221	2200 Martin Ave	23227
Richmond, VA		Richmond, VA	

First, compare the zip code on the left to the zip code on the right. If there's a difference, then remember them as different, and then match the address on the left (street number, street/state/city) with the ones on the right. If they are *alike,* remember them as such. Hence, since there's an error in the Zip Code and no errors in the addresses, the answer is **C (Zip Code Only).**

Fifth Way: Here's another way of doing it as per sample below:

3812 Bourbon Ln	60565-2101	3813 Bourbon Ln	60566-2101
Naperville, IL		Naperville, IL	

You compare the street address on the left to the street address on the right, (including the street name, and abbreviation Rd, etc.) and the ZIP codes. If there are errors, then compare the city and state names of both columns. If there are also errors as in the above sample, answer **D (Both).**

Yes, in the above example, the answer is **D (Both)**. It's because there's an error in the address (numbers 12 and 13 of the address) and there's an error in the Zip codes (60565 and 60566).

Sixth Way: The fifth way of doing it is explained as per sample below:

3590 Sonoma Ln	84770	3590 Sonoma Ln	84710
Saint George, UT		Saint George, UT	

Compare the state/city on the left column to the ones on the right. If there's no error as per sample, then compare the street/P.O. box numbers and names of streets of both columns. If there's no error as per sample, then continue comparing the zip codes. Since, the zip codes have an error, (the first one ends with the number 70 and the second one ends with the number 10) the correct answer is C: **ZIp Code Only.**

Seventh Way: The seven way of comparison is explained below:

2069 Pershing Ave	33525-3012	2066 Pershing Ave	33525-3012
Dade City, FL		Dode City, FL	

Compare the city/state of both columns. If there's a difference (the right column has a wrong city). then don't compare anymore the street address (numbers, street names, and abbreviations) of both columns. Now, match the zip codes. If there's no error (as in the case of the above sample), then answer, **B: Address Only.** (If there's an error in the Zip Code, then mark **D: Both.)**

I have presented to you the different ways of comparing the columns of addresses and zip codes. Who knows, you may also think of a better way of matching the left and the right columns of addresses. Find one, which is easier for you to use.

12

6 Exam 473 Practice Tests

Part A: Address Checking

Part A: Address-Checking Practice Test 1

This is a practice test containing 60 items or questions. You have to answer these questions in 11 minutes.

What you have to do is to compare each row of the address and zip code in the **Correct List** (left column) to those in the **List to Be Checked** (right column). Determine of they are alike or different. If there are differences, know where the errors are. Mark any of the Delivery Routes **A, B, C,** and **D: A** for **No Errors; B** for an error in the **Address Only; C** for an error in the **Zip Code Only;** and **D,** for errors in **Both** the address and ZIP code.

A. No Errors	B. Address Only	C. ZIP Code Only	D. Both

	Correct List		*List to be Checked*		
	Address	ZIP Code	Address	ZIP Code	
1.	50378 Bear Dr Park City, UT	84098-3101	50878 Bear Dr Park City, UT	84098-3101	1. ___
2.	89411 Braxton Ct Williamsburg, VA	23185-2183	39411 Braxton Ct Williamsburg, VA	23195-2183	2. ___
3.	2028 Bay Ct Pasadena, TX	77505-0109	2026 Bay Ct Pasadena, TX	77505-0109	3. ___
4.	15982 Townsend Rd Charleston, SC	29406-1102	15982 Townsed Rd Charleston, SC	29406-1102	4. ___
5.	21033 Walnut Dr Hamilton, OH	45011	21933 Walnut Dr Hamilton OH	45011	5. ___
6.	20931 Greenbriar Dr Goldsboro, NC	27534-0102	20931 Greenbriar Dr Goldsboro, NC	27534-0103	6. ___
7.	50921 Coleridge Rd Rochester, NY	14509-2302	50921 Coleridge Dr Rochester, NY	14509-2303	7. ___
8.	29105 Richmond Pl Akron, OH	44303-2109	29105 Richmond Pl Akron, OH	44303-2109	8. ___
9.	3422 Drove Dr Los Angeles, CA	90065	4322 Dove Dr Los Angeles, CA	90065	9. ___
10.	24161 Chapman Orange, CA	92868-4120	24161 Chapman Orange, CA	92868-4120	10. ___

	A. No Errors		B. Address Only		C. ZIP Code Only		D. Both

	Correct List			Correct List		
	Address	Zip Code		Address	ZIP Code	Answers
11.	70830 Pepperfield Dr Tampa, FL	33624-2309		70330 Pepperfield Dr Tampa, Fl	33624-2381	11. ____
12	9310 Tuscany Ln Griffin, GA	92868		9310 Tuscany Dr Griffin, GA	92869	12. ____
13.	28014 Madison Ct Champaign, IL	61820-2117		28015 Madison Ct Champaign, IL	61825-2117	13. ____
14.	3815 Shady Grove Rd Rockville, MD	20850-0105		3815 Shady Grove St Rockville, MD	20850-0105	14. ____
15.	3551 Pine View Ct Battle Creek, MI	49017		3551 Pineview Ct Battle Creek, MI	49017	15. ____
16.	31012 Todd St Ypsilanti, MI	48198		31012 Todd St Ypsilanti, MI	48098	16. ____
17.	4109 Mayfair St Waterloo, IA	50701-2131		4109 Mayfair St Waterloo, IA	50701-2131	17. ____
18.	7203 Rock Rd Rockville, MD	20852-4121		7203 Rock Rd Rockville, MD	20852-4122	18. ____
19.	2130 Randall Ln Bloomfield Hills, MI	48304-0120		2130 Randall Ln Bloomfield Hills, MI	48304-0220	19. ____
20	42591 Scott Loop Honolulu, HI	96818		42591 Scott Loop Honolulu, HI	96818	20. ____
21.	2131 Blanchard St Pensacola, F	32505-2109		2131 Blanchard Dr Pensacola, FL	32505-2709	21. ____
22.	7012 Old Ridge Pl Atlanta, GA	30327		7013 Old Ridge Dr Atlanta, GA	30827	22. ____
23.	20831 Princeton Ln Valdosa, GA	30327-2103		20831 Princeton Rd Valdosa, GA	30328-2103	23. ____
24.	7079 Heatherfield Dr Lafayette, IN	47909-1025		7013 Heatherfield Dr Lafayette, IN	47809-1025	24. ____
25.	10254 Thompson Ave Newport, KY	41076		10254 Thompson Rd Newport, KY	41076	25. ____
26.	40120 Bush Ave Chicopee, MA	01013-5121		40120 Bush Ave Chicopee, MA	01013-5121	26. ____
27.	4015 Yonka St Detroit, MI	48234-2120		4016 Yonka St Detroit, MI	48284-2120	27. ____
28.	8530 Thompson Ave Waterbury, CT	06708-2109		8530 Thompson Ave Waterbury, CT	06708-2109	28. ____

A. No Errors	B. Address Only	C. ZIP Code Only	D. Both

	Correct List		List to be Check		
	Address	ZIP Code	Address	ZIP Code	Answers
29.	20512 Pershing Ave Dade City, Fl	33525-3012	20812 Pershing Cir Dade City, FL	33525-3012	29. ___
30.	5021 Jones Wood Rd Monroe, GA	30655-2106	5021 Jones Wood Rd Monroe, GA	30658-2151	30. ___
31.	12698 St James Blvd Rockville, MD	20850	12898 St James Blvd Rockville, MD	20850	31. ___
32.	4345 Park Ave Worcester, MA	01610-4120	4345 Park Ave Worcester, MA	01610-4120	32. ___
33.	5598 Hanna St Fort Wayne, IN	46806-2152	5598 Hanna Rd Fort Wayne, IN	46806-2152	33. ___
34.	17332 US Hwy 60 E Owensboro, KY	42301	17832 US Hwy 60 E Owensboro, KY	42301	34. ___
35.	4638 College Rd Baltimore, MD	21229-0103	4688 College Rd Baltimore, MD	21229-0108	35. ___
36.	4347 Park Ave Worcester, MA	01610-2151	4347 Park Ave Worcester, MA	01610-2151	36. ___
37.	1223 Taylor Ave N Grand Rapids, MI	49505-1256	1223 Taylor Ave N Grand Rapids, MI	49505-1256	37. ___
38.	25980 County Rd 138 Saint Cloud, MN	56301-2051	25980 County St 138 Saint Cloud, MN	56301-2057	38. ___
39.	6298 W 4th St Hattiesburg, MS	39402-1250	6298 W 5th St Hattiesburg, MS	39402-6019	39. ___
40.	1597 Pope Ln Douglas, GA	31535	1897 Pope Ln Douglas, GA	31535	40. ___
41.	14901 Observatory Dr Orlando, FL	32818-2121	14901 Observatory Dr Orlando, FL	32818-2121	41. ___
42.	91431 Baymeadows Rd Jacksonville, FL	32256	91431 Beymeadow Rd Jacksonville, FL	32256	42. ___
43.	17398 Monitor Ave Bakersfield, CA	93307	17898 Monitor Ave Bakersfield, CA	93307	43. ___
44.	13808 Telluride St Brighton, CO	80603-2108	13808 Telluride Rd Brighton, CO	80603-2103	44. ___

A. No Errors	B. Address Only	C. ZIP Code Only	D. Both

	Correct List		List to Be Check		
	Address	ZIP Code	Address	ZIP Code	Answers
45.	16798 Ponce Leon Blvd Brooksfield, FL	34614	18798 Ponce Leon Blvd Brooksfield, FL	34614	45. ___
46.	1898 7th Ave SE Cedar Rapids, IA	52403	1898 7th Ave SW Cedar Rapids, IA	52408	46. ___
47.	3150 Skylark Ln Newport, KY	41076-0112	2150 Skylark Ln Newport, KY	41076-0115	47. ___
48.	3159 White Oak Ct Denham Springs, LA	70435	3159 White Oak Ct Denham Springs, LA	70435	48. ___
49.	18990 Elmwood Ave Detroit, MI	48207-2108	18990 Elmwood Ave Detroit, MI	48307-2108	49. ___
50.	25778 Timberline Dr Warren, MI	48091	28778 Timberline Dr Warren, MI	48091	50. ___
51.	1109 National Pkwy Fort Lauderdale, FL	33323-3107	1109 National Pkwy Fort Lauderdale, FL	33323-3107	51. ___
52	5897 "O" St Sacramento, CA	96819-3156	5397 "O" St Sacramento, CA	96819-3156	52. ___
53.	2315 Rockhurst Dr Waterbury, CT	06708-2109	2315 Rockhurst Dr Waterbury, CT	06708-2109	53. ___
54.	8805 Lee Vista Rd Orlando, FL	32829	8805 Lee Vista St Orlando, FL	32929	54. ___
55.	2497 Wallace Rd Griffin, GA	30224-4129	2497 Wallace Ave Griffin, GA	30224-4129	55. ___
56.	1425 111th St Bolingbrook, IL	60440	1625 111th St Bolingbrook, IL	60440	56. ___
57.	8298 Broadacres Rd Shreveport, LA	71119	8298 Broadacres Rd Shreveport, LA	71119	57. ___
58.	12601 Wyoming St Detroit, MI	48238-2106	12801 Wyoming St Detroit, MI	48238-2109	58. ___
59.	12579 Dorchester Ct Saint Paul MN	55124-0110	12579 Dorchester Ct Saint Paul MN	55124-0110	59. ___
60.	2301 15th Ave Longmont, CO	80501	2307 15th Ave Longmont, CO	80501	60. ___

(See the answers to the above questions on page 75.

Postal Test 473

Part A: Address-Checking Practice Test 2

This is a practice test containing 60 items or questions. You have to answer these questions in 11 minutes.

What you have to do is to compare the each row of the address and zip code in the **Correct List** (left column) to those in the **List to Be Checked** (right column). Determine of they are alike or different. If there are differences, know where the errors are. Mark any of the Delivery Routes **A, B, C,** and **D: A** for **No Errors; B** for an error in the **Address Only; C** for an error in the **Zip Code Only;** and **D,** for errors in **Both** the address and ZIP code.

A. No Errors	B. Address Only	C. ZIP Code Only	D. Both

	Correct List		List to Be Checked		
	Address	ZIP Code	Address	ZIP Code	Answers
1.	3145 Sandra Ln Corona, CA	92879-2109	3145 Sandra Ln Corona, CA	93879-2109	1. ___
2.	4402 Asbrook Ln Orlando, FL	32919	4302 Asbrook Ln Orlando, FL	32919	2. ___
3.	91201 Old Ham Dr Indianapolis, IN	46228-0122	91201 Old Ham Dr Indianapolis, IN	46228-0128	3. ___
4.	2108 Vasseur Ave Paduca, KY	42003-2102	2108 Basseur Ave Paduca, KY	42003-2102	4. ___
5.	2345 Church Rd Chesterfield, MO	63005	2435 Church Rd Chesterfield, MO	63003	5. ___
6.	21307 Bluebird Ln Naperville, IL	60565-2801	21307 Bluebird Ln Naperville, IL	60565-2801	6. ___
7.	7821 Compass Ln Tampa, FL	33611-0120	7821 Compass Rd Tampa, FL	33611-0120	7. ___
8.	17854 King St New Iberia, LA	70560	17854 King Ln New Iheria, LA	70568	8. ___
9.	3094 Oakview St Worcester, MA	01605-7021	3194 Oakview St Worcester, MA	01605-7022	9. ___
10	4129 Riverview Ave Saint Paul, MN	55107-1027	4129 Riverview Ave Saint Paul, MN	55107-1037	10. ___
11.	8129 Gladys Ct McDonough, GA	30252-2905	8128 Gladys Ct McDonough, GA	30253-2905	11. ___

A. No Errors	B. Address Only	C. ZIP Code	D. Both

	Correct List		List to Be Checked		
	Address	ZIP Code	Address	ZIP Code	Answers
12.	3451 Belvedere Dr Stratford, CT	06614-2109	3451 Belvedere Dr Stratford, CT	06615-2109	12. ___
13.	76095 Gibson Rd San Francisco, CA	94129-2160	76095 Gibson Rd San Francisco, CA	94129-2160	13. ___
14.	30591 San Juan Dr Anchorage, AK	99504-3106	30691 San Juan Dr Anchorage, AK	99504-3106	14. ___
15.	1678 Brookwood Rd Peoria, IL	61614	1778 Brookwood St Peoria, IL	61615	15. ___
16.	21595 Packard St Rochester, NY	14609-2102	21895 Packard St Rochester, NY	14608-2102	16. ___
17.	28091 Hickory St New Bern, NC	28502	28091 Hickory St New Bern, NC	28502	17. ___
18.	2121 Rolling Hills Dr Kingsport, TN	37660-8126	2121 Rolling Hills Dr Kingsport, TN	37661-8125	18. ___
19.	50605 SW Millen Dr Portland, OR	97224-2101	50605 SW Millen Dr Portland, OR	97224-2101	19. ___
20.	50672 Armstrong Dr Spartanburg, SC	29301-2106	50673 Armstrong Dr Spartanburg, NC	29301-2108	20. ___
21.	50618 Peterson Ct Fort Worth, TX	76177-0102	50618 Peterson Ct Forth Worth, TX	76117-0102	21. ___
22.	87401 Baywood Dr Harrisburgh, PA	17111	87401 Beywood Dr Harrisburgh, PA	17111	22. ___
23.	3194 Beaver Rd Columbus, OH	43213-2104	3195 Beaver Ave Columbus, OH	43213-2104	23. ___
24.	8254 Sandy Creek Raleigh, NC	27615	8254 Sandy Creek Raleigh, NC	27615	24. ___
25.	54902 Bedford Ave Middletown, NY	10940	54902 Bedford Ave Middletown, NY	10940	25. ___
26.	48125 Wisconsin St Middletown, OH	45049-2109	48125 Wisconsin Ln Middletown, OH	45049-2109	26. ___
27.	2586 Sky Park Dr Portland, OR	97504	2586 Sky Park Dr Portland, OR	97504	27. ___

| A. No Errors | B. Address Only | C. ZIP Code Only | D. Both |

	Correct List		List to Be Checked	
	Address	ZIP Code	Address	ZIP Code	Answers
28.	9321 Hudson Pl Providence, RI	02905-3102	9321 Hudson Pl Providence, RI	02905-3108	28. ___
29.	17092 Arlington Dr Johnson City, TN	37601-0120	17092 Arlington Dr Johnson City, TN	37601-0120	29. ___
30.	1021 Cypress Brook Cypress, TX 77429	88428	1021 Cypress Brook Cypress, TX	88420	30. ___
31.	10888 Edes Ave Oakland, CA	94603-0530	10888 Edes Ave Oakland, CA	94603-0530	31. ___
32.	5267 Lakesside Dr Lake Wales, FL	33898-2109	5267 Lakeside Dr Lake Wales, FL	33898-2109	32. ___
33.	1100 8th SW Fifton, GA	31794-0581	1100 8th NW Fifton, GA	31894-0581	33. ___
34.	7498 42nd St NE Cedar Rapids, IA	52411	7496 42nd St NE Cedar Rapids, IA	52412	34. ___
35.	4000 N Charles St Baltimore, MD	31535-0210	4000 N Charles St Baltimore, MD	31535-0210	35. ___
36.	4234 Adams Rd Douglas, GA	31535-0320	4238 Adams Rd Douglas, GA	31835-0320	36. ___
37.	3398 E Las Vegas St Colorado Springs, CO	80906	3396 E Las Vegas St Colorado Sprgs, CO	80908	37. ___
38.	25199 Highway 27 Lake Wales, FL	33859	25190 Highway 27 Lake Wales, FL	33859	38. ___
39.	5201 Union Ave Santa Maria, CA	93454-2106	5201 Union Ave Santa Maria, CA	93458-2106	39. ___
40.	2100 Hillside Ave Trenton, IJ	08618	2108 Hillside Rd Trenton, NJ	08614	40. ___
41.	1299 Beverly Rd Asheville, NC	28806-0310	1200 Beverly Rd Asheville, NC	28906-0310	41. ___
42.	6732 Beech St Cincinnati, OH	45217	6832 Beech St Cincinnati, OH	48217	42. ___
43.	6732 E 7th Ct Tulsa, OK	74133	6732 E 7th Ct Tulsa, OK	74133	43. ___

A. No Errors	B. Address Only	C. ZIP Code Only	D. Both

	Correct List		List to Be Checked		Answers
44.	1676 Hagood Ave Columbia, SC	29204	1778 Hagood Ave Columbia, SC	29204	44. ___
45.	899 Cates St Marysville, TN	37803-3192	899 Cates St Marysville, TN	37803-3192	45. ___
46.	31512 N Hwy 303 Grand Prairie, TX	75050	31812 N Hwy 303 Grand Prairie, TX	78050	46. ___
47.	1299 E 1040 N Orem, UT	84097	1299 E 1040 N Orem, UT	84097	47. ___
48.	7300 NE 110th St Vancouver, WA	98662	7800 NE 110th St Vancouver, WA	93662	48. ___
49.	4998 Oakfield Way San Antonio, TX	78250	4998 Oakfield Way San Antonio, TX	78250	49. ___
50.	3741 Woodcrest Ln Virginia Beach, VA	34563-3106	3741 Woodcrest Rd Virginia Beach, VA	38563-3106	50. ___
51.	15882 Paloxy Dr Tyler, TX	75703-0951	15882 Paloxy Dr Tyler, TX	85703-0951	51. ___
52.	13786 83rd Ave E Puyallup, WA	98373 -1220	19897 93rd Ave E Puyallup, WA	98373-1280	52. ___
53.	2007 Tryon St Greer, SC	29651	2008 Tryon Pl Greer, SC	29657	53. ___
54.	3298 Dunaway St Amarillo, TX	79103	3298 Dunaway St Amarillo, TX	98103	54. ___
55.	5297 NW Rogers Ln Lawton, OK	73505	5297 NW Rogers Ln Lawton, OK	73505	55. ___
56.	7398 Overton St Pittsburgh, PA	15218-2109	7399 Overton St Pittsburgh, PA	15218-2106	56. ___
57.	3120 Tudor Pl Chesapeake, VA	23320-4182	3120 Tudor Rd Chesapeake, VA	23320-4102	57. ___
58.	18197 79th Ave E Puyallup, WA	98375-0151	18197 79th Ave E Puyallup, WA	98375-0151	58. ___
59.	5926 Sandy Porks St Raleigh, NC	27615	5926 Sandy Porks St Raleigh, NC	27618	59. ___
60.	7298 E 73rd Pl Tulsa, OK	74133-2691	7299 N 73rd Pl Tulsa, OK	74138-2691	60. ___

(See the answers to the above questions on page 76)

Postal Test 473

Part A: Address-Checking Practice Test 3

This is a practice test containing 60 items or questions. You have to answer these questions in 11 minutes.

What you have to do is to compare the each row of the address and zip code in the **Correct List** (left column) to those in the **List to Be Checked** (right column). Determine of they are alike or different. If there are differences, know where the errors are. Mark any of the Delivery Routes **A, B, C,** and **D: A** for **No Errors; B** for an error in the **Address Only; C** for an error in the **Zip Code Only;** and **D,** for errors in **Both** the address and ZIP code.

A. No Errors	B. Address Only	C. ZIP Code Only	D. Both

	Correct List		*List to Be Checked*		
	Address	ZIP Code	Address	ZIP Code	Answers
1.	3182 Teakwood Dr Santa Maria, CA	93455-2102	3182 Teakwood Dr Santa Maria, CA	93455-2102	1. ___
2.	25911 Sulivan St Waterbury, CT	06708-0125	25911 Sulvan Rd Waterbury, CT	06708-0125	2. ___
3.	5209 Richmond Wy Commerce, GA	30529	5209 Richmond Rd Commerce, GA	30529	3. ___
4.	30510 Edmonton St Detroit, MI	48204	30510 Edmonton Dr Detroit, MI	48204	4. ___
5.	2812 Roundtree Blvd Ypsilanti, MI	48197-4102	2812 Roundtree Blvd Ypsilanti, MI	48197-4103	5. ___
6.	210 Grand Oak Dr Carbondale, IL	62901-0205	210 Grand Oak Dr Carbondale, IL	62901-0205	6. ___
7.	2014 Sngleton Ave Newport, KY	41076-0326	2014 Singleton Ave New Port, KY	41078-0326	7. ___
8.	38312 Paradise Way Eustis, FL	32736-0106	38312 Paradise Cir Eustia, FL	32730-0106	8. ___
9.	3054 Missouri Ave Los Angeles, CA	90025-1256	3054 Missouri Ave Los Angeles, CA	90025-1256	9. ___
10.	31561 Winnipig St Brighton, CO	80603-0127	31561 Winnipig St Brighton, CO	80803-0127	10. ___
11.	301 Shadowbrook Ct Burlington, NC	27215-0220	307 Shadowcrook Ct Burlington, NC	27215-0220	11. ___

| A. No Errors | B. Address Only | C. ZIP Code Only | D. Both |

	Correct List		Correct List	
	Address	ZIP Code	Address	ZIP Code	Answers
12.	3157 Glastonburgh Ln Portland, OR	97224-2146	3157 Glastonburg Dr Portland, OR	97224-2146	12. ___
13.	2725 Manchester Ln Chesapeake, VA	23321	2725 Manchester Rd Chesapeake, VA	23321	13. ___
14.	12254 Parryville Dr Houston, TX	77041-0109	12258 Perryville Dr Houston, TX	77041-0109	14. ___
15.	4254 Westside Dr Olympia, WA	98502-0121	4254 Westside Ln Olympia, WA	98502-0127	15. ___
16.	3152 Stonebrook Rd Charleston, WV	25314-2109	3152 Stonebrook Rd Charleston, WV	25314-2109	16. ___
17.	214 Peacock Dr Fort Worth, TX	76131-0129	214 Peacock Dr Fort Worth, TX	76137-0129	17. ___
18.	30912 Mallard Dr Pittsburg, PA	15238-2012	30912 Malard Dr Pittsburg, PA	15238-2012	18. ___
19.	3152 Bayham Dr Cincinnati, OH	45218	3152 Baham Dr Cincinnati, OH	48218	19. ___
20.	2154 Netherfield Ct Winchester, VA	22602	2154 Netherfield Dr Winchester, VA	22603	20. ___
21.	542 Auburn Dr Madison, WI	53711-0109	542 Auburn Dr Madison, MI	53811-0109	21. ___
22.	50113 NW 32nd Ave Vancouver, WA	98685-2199	50113 NW 33rd Ave Vancouver, WA	98685-2199	22. ___
23.	3452 Castlewood Dr Greenville, SC	29615-2298	3452 Castlewood Dr Greenoak, SC	29615-2298	23. ___
24.	31075 Ottawa St Pittsburg, PA	15211	31075 Ottawa St Pittsburg, PA	15212	24. ___
25.	433 Woodside Dr Oklahoma City, OK	73110-0610	423 Woodside Dr Oklahoma City, OK	73110-0610	25. ___
26.	3154 Kellwood Ct Raleigh, NC	27609-0291	3154 Kellwood Ct Raleigh, SC	27609-0291	26. ___

A. No Errors	B. Address Only	ZIP Code Only	D. Both

	Correct List		List to Be Checked		
	Address	ZIP Code	Address	ZIP Code	Answers
27.	12540 Ruthland Ave Buffalo, NY	14212-0029	12540 Ruthlan Ave Buffalo, NY	14212-0028	27. ___
28.	5409 Knoll Crest Ct Boulder, CO	80301-2158	5409 Knoll Crest Ct Boulder, CO	80307-2158	28. ___
29.	6789 S Vassar St Wichita, KS	67218	6788 S Vassar St Wichita, KS	78219	29. ___
30.	9054 Bramble Way Shreveport, LA	71118-0929	9054 Bramble Way Shreveport, LA	71118-0929	30. ___
31.	63990 Lakeside Ln Carbondale, IL	62903-2108	63998 Lakeside St Carbondale, IL	62908-2108	31. ___
32.	1015 US Hwy 319 N Fifton, GA	31794-0129	1015 US Hwy 319 N Fifton, GA	31794-0129	32. ___
33.	150 N Drake Rd Kalamazoo, MI	49009-5201	150 E Drake Rd Kalamazoo, MI	48009-5201	33. ___
34.	3015 Duncan Dr Greenville, MS	38703	3015 Duncan Dr Greenville, MS	38708	34. ___
35.	8531 Fernwood Trl Roswell, GA	30075-2105	8531 Fernwood Trl Roswell, GA	30075-2105	35. ___
36.	1900 Adams Ln Sarasota, FL	34236	1908 Adams Ln Sarasota, FL	34286	36. ___
37.	11990 Drake Rd Kalamazoo, MI	49009-4120	11990 Drake Rd Kalamzoo, MI	49009-4120	37. ___
38.	1343 Colbert Ct Florissant, MO	63031	1348 Colbert Ct Florrisant, MO	63037	38. ___
39.	5011 N Covington Ct Wichita, KS	67212-3012	5011 N Covington Ct Wichita, KS	67212-3012	39. ___
40.	499 Oliver Ct Monroe, LA	71202	499 Oliver Trl Monroe, LA	71203	40. ___
41.	1289 Windsor Rd Wesminster, MD	21158	1288 Windsor St Wesminster, MD	21158	41. ___
42.	1688 S 11th St Greenwood, IN	46526	1689 S 11th St Greenwood, IN	46528	42. ___

A. No Errors	B. Address Only	ZIP Code Only	D. Both

	Correct List		List to Be Checked		
	Address	ZIP Code	Address	ZIP Code	Answers
43.	2911 Cherry Wood Dr Buffalo, NY	142121-0102	2911 Cherry Wood Dr Buffalo, NY	142121-0102	43.___
44.	3569 Apache Dr Johnson City, TN	37604-3107	3560 Apache Dr Johnson City, TN	38604-3107	44.___
45.	29010 Woodside Dr Yorktown, VA	22191-2651	29010 Woodside Dr Yorktown, VA	22191-2651	45.___
46.	2080 Crossbow Ct Fort Worth, TX	76133	2080 Crossbow Ct Fort Worth, TX	76133	46.___
47.	4100 NE 20th St Renton, WA	98059-0621	4108 NE 20th St Renton, WA	98159-0621	47.___
48.	5990 S Rosa Rd Madison, WI	53719	5990 S Rosa Rd Madison, WI	53719	48.___
49.	2290 Crest Dr El Cajon, CA	92021-0934	2290 Crest Dr El Cajon, CA	92022-0934	49.___
50.	3901 McIntosh Plz Newark, DE	19713-0492	3901 McIntosh Pl Newark, DE	19713-0492	50.___
51.	12199 SW 8th Ave Gainsville, FL	32607	12190 SW 8th Ave Gainsville, FL	32807	51.___
52.	7703 Whipple St Chicago, IL	60652-2307	7708 Whippe St Chicago IL	60652-2308	52.___
53.	16199 Old Auburn Rd Fort Wayne, IN	46845	16199 Old Auburn Rd Fort Wayne, IN	46845	53.___
54.	16346 S Butch St Olathe, KS	47892-2109	16346 S Butch St Olathe, KS	47392-2108	54.___
55.	1398 Natchitocks St Monroe, LA	71291	1398 Natchitocks Rd Monroe, LA	71291	55.___
56.	12980 N Windsor Rd Westminster, MD	21158-0721	12980 N Windsor Rd Westminster, MD	21758-0721	56.___
57.	35981 N 32nd St Caldwell, ID	83605	38981 N 32nd St Caldwell, ID	83608	57.___
58.	5199 Sweetser Ave Evansville, IN	47715-2017	5199 Sweetser Ave Evansville, IN	47715-2017	58.___
59.	1489 Walter Jetlon St Paducan, KY	42003	1489 Walter Jetlon St Paducan, KY	42003	59.___
60.	3501 Oliver Ct Shreveport, LA	71202	3501 Oliver Ct Shreveport, LA	71202	60.___

(See the answers to the above questions on page 77.)

Part A: Address-Checking Practice Test 4

This is a practice test containing 60 items or questions. You have to answer these questions in 11 minutes.

What you have to do is to compare the each row of the address and zip code in the **Correct List** (left column) to those in the **List to Be Checked** (right column). Determine of they are alike or different. If there are differences, know where the errors are. Mark any of the Delivery Routes **A, B, C,** and **D: A** for **No Errors; B** for an error in the **Address Only; C** for an error in the **Zip Code Only;** and **D,** for errors in **Both** the address and ZIP code.

A. No Errors	B. Address Only	C. ZIP Code	D. Both

	Correct List		List to Be Checked		
	Address	Zip Code	Address	Zip Code	Answers
1.	26902 Poseidon Dr Havasa City, Al	86406-2102	28902 Poseidon Dr Havassa City, AL	86306-2102	1.___
2.	3201 Duray Pl Los Angeles, CA	90008-0731	3201 Duray Dr Los Angeles, CA	90008-0731	2.___
3.	13700 Livingston Ave Tampa, FL	33613	13700 Livingston Ave Tampa, FL	33613	3.___
4.	1973 N Collington Ave Baltimore, MD	21213-5020	1978 N Collington Ave Baltimore, MD	21218-5020	4.___
5.	1523 Heyward St Columbia, SC	29205	1523 Heyward St Columbia, SC	29208	5.___
6.	1599 S Peach Ave Tyler, TX	75701-2129	1590 S Peach Ave Tyler, TX	75701-2120	6.___
7.	13799 9th Ave W Everett, WA	98204-3109	13899 9th Ave W Everett, WA	98204-3108	7.___
8.	4211 Boxwood Dr Mesquite, TX	75180	4211 Boxwood Dr Mesquite, TX	75180	8.___
9.	5300 Lozzeles Rd Charlotte, NC	28214-5114	5800 Lozzeles Rd Charlotte, NC	28214-5115	9.___
10.	6175 Morroco St Cincinnati, OH	45230	6175 Morroco St Cincinnati, OH	45230	10.___
11.	1199 N 10th St Hagleton, PA	17103-2108	1190 E 10th St Hagleton, PA	17103-2108	11.___
12.	7391 Barnett St Rockhill, SC	29732	7391 Barnett St Rockhill, SC	29732	12.___
13.	1217 River Divide Rd Seviervill, TN	37862-0120	1217 River Divide St Seviervill, TN	37662-0120	13.___

A. No Errors	B. Address Only	C. ZIP Code Only	D. Both

	Corect List		List to Be Checked		
	Address	ZIP Code	Address	ZIP Code	Answers
14.	6408 Boat Club Rd Forth Worth, TX	76179-0197	6408 Boat Club Rd Forth Worth, TX	76179-0198	14.___
15.	7290 Bairbridge St Charlottesville, VA	22902-3023	7290 Bairbridge Rd Charlottesville, VA	22902-3023	15.___
16.	3577 S 93rd St Milwaukee, WI	53228	3577 S 93rd St Milwaukee, WI	53229	16.___
17.	62812 Merchant Way Everett, WA	98208-6109	62812 Merchant Way Everett, WA	98209-6109	17.___
18.	1100 Jeff Davis Ave Selma, AL	36703-2121	1100 Jeff Davis Ave Selma, AL	36703-2127	18.___
19.	2398 Cottonwood St Santa Ana, CA	92705-2109	2398 Cottonwood Pl Santa Ana, CA	92705-2109	19.___
20.	4364 Blackston St S Augusta, GA	30906	4364 Blackston St S Augusta, GA	30906	20.___
21.	3399 S Gayer Rd Kokomo, IN	46902-4201	3398 S Gayer Rd Kokomo, IN	46902-4207	21.___
22.	7306 Hillcrest Dr Lowell, MA	01851	7306 Hillcrest Dr Lowell, MA	01851	22.___
23.	2289 S Drake Rd Kalamazoo, MI	49009-7120	2289 N Drake Rd Kalamazoo, MI	49009-7120	23.___
24.	17990 Marina Dr Slidell, LA	70458-3106	17890 Marina Dr Slidell, LA	70459-3106	24.___
25.	1319 Park Ave Worcester, MA	01610	1319 Park Ave Worcester, MA	01610	25.___
26.	8210 Glenhaven Cir Hattiesburg, MS	39401-5212	8219 Glenhaven Cir Hattiesburg, MS	39401-5212	26.___
27.	7312 Pleasant Knoll Joliet, IL	60435	7312 Pleasant Knoll Joliet, IL	60435	27.___
28.	10597 Blue Hill Rd Baton Raton Rouge, LA	70810	10597 Blue Hill Ln Baton Raton Rouge, LA	90810	28.___
29.	73109 Puckett Pl Covington, GA	30014-7231	73109 Puckett Pl Covington, GA	30014-7237	29.___

A. No Errors	B. Address Only	C: ZIP Code Only	D. Both

	Correct List		List to Be Checked		
	Address	Zip Code	Address	Zip Code	Answers
30.	699 N Mountan Ave Montclair, NJ	07043-2106	699 S Mountain Ave Montclair, NJ	07043-2106	30.___
31.	6108 S 75th East Ave Tulsa, OK	74133-2109	6108 N 75th East Ave Tulsa, OK	74133-2109	31.___
32.	1299 Valley Rd Montclair, NJ	07043	1299 Valley Rd Montclair, NJ	07043	32.___
33.	15498 Parkview St Houston, TX	77071-2608	15498 Parkview St Houston, TX	78071-2608	33.___
34.	11497 34th St SW Seattle, WA	98146-2109	11497 34th St SW Seattle, WA	09146-2109	34.___
35.	10967 Metcalf St Escondido, CA	92026-0151	10967 Metcalf Rd Escondido, CA	92026-0751	35.___
36.	2199 E Park St Arlington Hts, IL	60004	2199 E Park St Arlington Hts, IL	60004	36.___
37.	3322 Burton St Chicopee, MA	01013	3322 Burton St Chicopee, MA	01013	37.___
38.	2201 Fuller St Hattiesburg, MS	39402-1020	2207 Fuller St Hattiesburg, MS	39408-1020	38.___
39.	69912 Ludwig Ave West Monroe, LA	71292-0129	69912 Ludwig Ave West Monroe, LA	71892-0129	39.___
40.	1700 N School St Honolulu, HI	96819-7130	1700 N School St Honolulu, HI	96819-7130	40.___
41.	10417 Old Decatur Rd Fort Wayne, IN	46806-1028	10417 Old Decator Rd Fort Wayne, IN	46906-1028	41.___
42.	1499 Walter Jetton Rd Paducan, KY	42003-2129	1490 Walter Jetton Paducan, KY	48003-2129	42.___
43.	45598 Murfield Dr Canton, MI	48188-2469	45598 Murfield Dr Canton, MI	48188-2469	43.___
44.	11203 W Florence Ln Boise, ID	48709	11203 W Florence Rd Boise, ID	48709	44.___
45.	2199 SW Filmore St. Topeka, KS	66611	2199 SW Filmore St Topeka, KS	66611	45.___

A. No Errors	B. Address Only	C. ZIP Code Only	D. Both

	Correct List		List to Be Checked		
	Address	ZIP Code	Address	ZIP Code	Answers
46.	1299 New Windsor Rd Westminster, MD	21158-0670	1299 New Windsor Rd Westminster, MD	21158-0670	46._____
47.	289 Stuyvesant Ave Brooklyn, NY	11288	280 Stuyvesant Ave Brooklyn, NY	11288	47._____
48.	1968 Old Mountain Rd Statesville, NC	28677-1020	1968 Old Mountain Ln Statesville, NC	28877-1020	48._____
49.	5797 NE Church St Portland, OR	97224-8010	5797 NE Church St Portland, OR	97224-8010	49._____
50.	1133 Hope St Providence, RI	02906-5021	1138 Hope St Providence, RI	02906-5021	50._____
51.	62980 Davis Ln Austin, TX	78749	62980 Davis Rd Austin, TX	78740	51._____
52.	2299 Wolfsnare Rd Virginia Beach, VA	23454-1030	2290 Wolfsnare Rd Virginia Beach, VA	23454-1030	52._____
53.	7993 Forest Ave Fond Du Lac, WI	54937-0950	7993 Forest Ave Fond Du Lac, WI	54937-0050	53._____
54.	586 Highland Ave Albertville, AL	35950-1020	586 Highland Ave Albertville, AL	35950-1029	54._____
55.	1478 W Emerald Ave Mesa, AZ	85202-7211	1470 W Emerald Ave Mesa, AZ	82202-7211	55._____
56.	3496 Moonbeam Dr Monterey Park, CA	91754-0106	3498 Moonbeam Dr Monterey Park, CA	97754-0106	56._____
57.	13798 Livingstone Ave Tampa, FL	33613-0710	13898 Livingstone Ave Tampa, FL	33618-0710	57._____
58.	8576 Creekview Ct Riverdale, GA	30274-1030	8576 Creekview Ct Riverdale, GA	30274-1030	58._____
59.	3598 Maple Rd Loisville, KY	40299-3341	3598 Maple Rd Loisville, KY	40299-3341	59._____
60.	8699 Military St Detroit, MI	48204	8699 Military St Detroit, MI	48205	60._____

(See the answers to the above questions on page 78)

Part A: Address-Checking Practice Test 5

This is a practice test containing 60 items or questions. You have to answer these questions in 11 minutes.

What you have to do is to compare the each row of the address and zip code in the **Correct List** (left column) to those in the **List to Be Checked** (right column). Determine of they are alike or different. If there are differences, know where the errors are. Mark any of the Delivery Routes **A, B, C,** and **D**: A for **No Errors**; B for an error in the **Address Only**; C for an error in the **Zip Code Only**; and **D,** for errors in **Both** the address and ZIP code.

A. No Errors	B. Address Only	C. ZIP Code	D. Both

	Correct List		List to Be Checked		
	Address	ZIP Code	Address	ZIP Code	Answers
1.	1598 N Emerson Ave Idaho Falls, ID	83402-0736	1598 N Emerson Ave Idaho Falls, ID	83402-0736	1.____
2.	3659 E County Rd 400 Columbus, OH	47201-2180	3659 E County Rd 400 Columbus, OH	47207-2180	2.____
3.	3099 Belle Chase Hwy Gretna, LA	70053	3090 Belle Chase Hwy Gretna, LA	70953	3.____
4.	73011 Beech St Chicopee, MA	01020-0347	73017 Beech St Chicopee, MA	01020-0347	4.____
5.	30317 Stonetree Cir Rochester, MI	48399	30317 Stonetree Cir Rochester, MI	48399	5.____
6.	12900 Michael Dr Utica, MI	48315-2106	12900 Michael Dr Utica, MI	48315-2106	6.____
7.	1350 Cannon Ave Goldsboro, NC	28143-2189	1350 Cannon Rd Goldsboro, NC	28148-2189	7.____
8.	799 Elm St Salisbury, NC	28144-3107	790 Elm St Salisbury, NC	28144-3107	8.____
9.	12100 Bangor Ave Cleveland, OH	44125	12100 Bangor Ave Cleveland, OH	44725	9.____
10.	1700 W Great Lakes Rd Enid, OK	73703-3091	1700 W Great Lakes Rd Enid, OK	73703-3091	10.____
11.	1100 Fawcett Ave Keesport, PA	15132-1461	1100 Fawcett Rd Keesport, PA	15133-1461	11.____
12.	5208 Bluebird Ln Greer, SC	29650	5208 Bluefird Ln Greer, SC	29650	12.____
13.	2699 Highland Dr Knoxville, TN	37918-0164	2699 Highland Dr Knoxville, TN	38918-0164	13.____

A. No Errors	B. Address Only	C. ZIP Code Only	D. Both

	Correct List		List to Be Checked		
	Address	ZIP Code	Address	ZIP Code	Answers
14.	3109 Winthrop Ave Fort Worth, TX	76116	3109 Winthrop Ave Fort Worth, TX	76116	14.____
15.	8991 E 46th St Ogden, UT	84403-0172	8990 E 4th St Ogden, UT	84403-0173	15.____
16.	2217 S 78th St Yakima, WA	98903-2142	2217 N 78th St Yakima, WA	98903-2143	16.____
17.	1586 S Peach Ave Tyler, TX	75701	1586 S Peach Ave Tyler, TX	75701	17.____
18.	3088 Niagara St Bellingham, WA	98226	3088 Niagara St Bellingham, WA	98226	18.____
19.	5277 Walnut Ave Long Beach, CA	90805-3172	5278 Walnut Ave Long Beach, CA	90805-3172	19.____
20.	15200 Telluride St Brighton, CO	80601-0103	15200 Telluride St Brighton, CO	80601-0103	20.____
21.	6856 N Sterling Ave Tampa, FL	33614-1420	6856 N Sterling Ave Tampa, FL	33614-1428	21.____
22.	2701 Keith Bridge Rd Cumming, GA	30041	2801 Keith Bridge Rd Cumming, GA	30047	22.____
23.	4421 N Broadway St Chicago, IL	60640-7120	4421 N Broadway St Chicago, IL	60640-7120	23.____
24.	2988 Tebbs Ave Indianapolis, IN	46221-2107	2988 Tebbs Ln Indianapolis, IN	46227-2107	24.____
25.	3011 Ford Cir Annapolis, MD	21401	3017 Ford Ctr Annapolis, MD	21409	25.____
26.	2709 Pleasantview Dr Redlands, CA	92374-8120	2709 Pleasantview Dr Redlands, CA	92374-6120	26.____
27.	11788 Eudora Ct Denver, CO	80233-2182	11788 Eudora Ct Denver, CO	80233-2182	27.____
28.	3312 Starfish St Kissimmee, FL	34744-0129	3313 Starfish St Kissimmee, FL	34744-0129	28.____
29.	2799 E Monroe St Springfield, IL	62703-4160	2799 N Monroe St Springfield, IL	62703-4160	29.____

A. No Errors	B. Address Only	C. ZIP Code Only	D. Both

	Correct List		List to Be Checked		
	Address	ZIP Code	Address	ZIP Code	Answers
30.	4731 Rock Creek Dr Jasper, AL	35504-3178	4731 Rock Creek Ln Jasper, AL	35504-3178	30.____
31.	1454 Bryant Ave Bronx, NY	10460-3109	1454 Bryant Ave Bronx, NY	10460-3109	31.____
32.	2432 Sawmill Rd Raleigh, NC	27613	2432 Sawmill Rd Raleigh, NC	27613	32.____
33.	601 E 8th St Portland, OR	97501-3172	601 N 8th St Portland, OR	97801-3172	33.____
34.	2801 Wild Field Dr Warwick, RI	02889-4187	2301 Wild Field Dr Warwick, RI	02889-4181	34.____
35.	7264 Birck Wood Ct Greer, SC	29651-0267	7268 Birch Wood Ct Greer, SC	29651-0267	35.____
36.	2178 Linden Ave Memphis, TN	38104	2178 Linden Ave Memphis, TN	39104	36.____
37.	1374 Creek Stone Ct Park City, UT	84098	1384 Creek Stone Ct Park City, UT	84098	37.____
38.	8401 S 212th St Kent, WA	98031-4122	8401 S 212th St Kent, WA	93031-4122	38.____
39.	6500 James St Mobile, AL	36608-0391	6500 James St Mobile, AL	36608-0391	39.____
40.	1479 W 14th St Wilmington, DE	19806-4121	1479 E 14th St Wilmington, DE	19806-4121	40.____
41.	19500 SW 57th Pl Dunnellon, FL	34431	19500 SW 57th Pl Dunnellon, FL	34431	41.____
42.	1311 Oxford Rd NE Atlanta, GA	30307-7186	1311 Oxford St NE Atlanta, GA	30307-7186	42.____
43.	1227 Spring Rd East Saint Louis, IL	62206-4179	1237 Spring Rd East Saint Louis, IL	62206-4178	43.____
44.	12502 Valley Wood Dr Silver Spring, MD	20906-5108	12502 Valley Wood Dr Silver Spring, MD	20906-5108	44.____
45.	4800 Aleda Ave SE Grand Rapids, MI	49508-2170	4800 Aleda Ave SW Grand Rapids, MI	49508-2170	45.____

A. No Errors	B. Address Only	C. ZIP Code Only	D. Both

	Correct List		List to Be Checked		
	Address	Zip Code	Address	Zip Code	Answers
46.	2170 Woodridge Dr Greenwood, SC	29611	2170 Woodridge Dr Greenwood, SC	29611	46.____
47.	1562 Helen Ave North Las Vegas, NV	89032-5108	1563 Helen Ave North Las Vegas, NV	89032-5108	47.____
48.	3189 Birch St Toms River, NJ	08753-2191	3189 Birth St Toms River, NJ	08753-2191	48.____
49.	24401 Grand Central Little Neck, NY	11362-4173	24401 Grand Central Little Neck, NY	11862-4173	49.____
50.	1002 E 11th St Portland, OR	97501-0320	1002 E 11th St Portland, OR	78501-0320	50.____
51.	699 Randolph St Knoxville, TN	39117	690 Randolph St Knoxville, TN	39117	51.____
52.	3059 Wynterset Cir Yorktown, VA	23692-5123	3089 Wynterset Cir Yorktown, VA	28692-5123	52.____
53.	5299 S Birchwood Dr Sioux Falls, SD	57108-0986	5299 S Birthwood Dr Sioux Falls, SD	57108-0986	53.____
54.	5600 Bull Creek Rd Austin, TX	78756-4120	5600 Bull Creek Rd Austin, TX	78756-4220	54.____
55.	4800 Center St Salt Lake City, UT	84107-3760	4300 Center St Salt Lake City, UT	84107-3860	55.____
56.	4999 14th St NW Big Harbor, WA	98329	4999 14th St NE Big Harbor, WA	98329	56.____
57.	1701 Beld St Madison, WI	53713-2170	1701 Beld St Madison, WI	53713-2170	57.____
58.	2702 Poseidon Dr Lake Havasu City, AZ	86404-7180	2702 Poseidon Dr Lake Havasu City, AZ	86404-7180	58.____
59.	2228 Monterey St Bakersfield, CA	93306	2228 Montey St Bakersfield, CA	93806	59.____
60.	2172 N 7th Ave Greeley, CO	80631-6742	2172 N 7th St Greeley, CO	80831-6742	60.____

See the answers to the above questions on page 79.

Part A: Address-Checking Practice Test 6

This is a practice test containing 60 items or questions. You have to answer these questions in 11 minutes.

What you have to do is to compare the each row of the address and zip code in the **Correct List** (left column) to those in the **List to Be Checked** (right column). Determine of they are alike or different. If there are differences, know where the errors are. Mark any of the Delivery Routes **A, B, C,** and **D: A** for **No Errors; B** for an error in the **Address Only; C** for an error in the **Zip Code Only;** and **D,** for errors in **Both** the address and ZIP code.

A. No Errors	B. Address Only	C. ZIP Code	D. Both

	Correct List		List to be Checked		
	Address	Zip Code	Address	Zip Code	Answers
1.	3149 Robin Hood Dr Modesto, CA	95350-3106	3749 Robinhood Dr Modesto, CA	95350-3106	1. ____
2.	3195 Kellwood Ct Raleigh, NC	27609-0291	3195 Kellwood Ct Raleigh, NC	27809-0291	2. ____
3.	5001 Mount Vernon Pl Rockville, MD	20850	5001 Mount Vernon Pl Rockville, MD	20850	3. ____
4.	1602 Superior Rd Ypsilanti, MI	48198-2105	1602 Superior Rd Ypsilanti, MI	48190-2105	4. ____
5.	2301 Kensington Dr Columbus, OH	43221-0321	2307 Kensington Dr Columbus, OH	43221-0321	5. ____
6.	3346 Thunderbred Ln Plano, TX	75023-0971	3546 Thunderbred Ln Plano, TX	75823-0971	6. ____
7.	3510 Whitestorm Way Virginia Beach, VA	23454-2370	3510 Whitestorm Rd Virginia Beach, WA	23454-2370	7. ____
8.	5209 Harding Pl Nashville, TN	23454	5208 Harding Place Nashville, TN	23484	8. ____
9.	4902 Brentwood Dr Greenwood, SC	29646	4902 Brentwood Dr Greenwood, NC	29846	9. ____
10.	6527 Little League Rd Williamsport, PR	17701-3172	6527 Little League Way Williamsport, PR	17701-3172	10. ____
11.	5021 Grant Ln Sevierville, TN	37876-0429	5021 Grant Ln Sevierville, TN	37876-0429	11. ____
12.	7501 Malood Ct Fontana, CA	92335-7103	7507 Malood Ct Fontana, CA	92335-7103	12. ____
13.	1730 State Ct Bridgeport, CT	06605-3102	1730 State Ct Bridgeport, CT	06605-3102	13. ____

A. No Errors	B. Address Only	C.ZIP Code Only	D. Both

	Correct List		*List to Be Checked*		
	Address	Zip Code	Address	Zip Code	Answers
14.	7381 Hucklebern Ln Lake Wales, FL	33898-5172	7381 Hucklebern Ln Lake Wales, FL	33898-5172	14. ___
15.	10570 Flat Shoals Rd Covington, GA	30051-2103	10570 Flat Shoals Dr Covington, GA	30081-2103	15. ___
16.	5598 W Jackson St Hayward, CA	94545	5598 W Jackson St Hayward, CA	94546	16. ___
17.	3891 Wall St Waterburg, CT	06704-5109	3897 Wall St Waterburg, CT	06708-5109	17. ___
18.	5721 Woodfield Rd Bloomington, IL	61704-2108	5727 Woodfield Rd Bloomington, IL	61704-2108	18. ___
19.	1900 Greyhound Pass Carmel, IN	61704	1900 Greyhound Pass Carmel, IN	61705	19. ___
20.	4311 W 110th Ter Leanwood, KS	66211-0731	4311 W 110th Ter Leanwood, KS	66211-0731	20. ___
21.	5822 Acorn St Shreveport, LA	71107-0971	5822 Acorn St Shreveport, LA	71107-0971	21. ___
22.	8522 2nd Ave Silver Spring, MD	20910-6206	8522 3rd Ave Silver Spring, MD	20970-6206	22. ___
23.	8501 Elmira St Detroit, MI	48204	8801 Elmira St Detroit, MI	48204	23. ___
24.	6003 Candlewood Dr Minneapolis, MN	55443-8120	6003 Candlewood Ln Minneapolis, MN	55443-8120	24. ___
25.	3439 Greenleaf Ln Columbus, MS	39705	3539 Greenleaf Ln Columbus, MS	39708	25. ___
26.	8402 Chef Menteur St New Orleans, LA	70127-2105	8402 Chef Menteur St New Orleans, LA	70128-2105	26. ___
27.	720 Gannet Ct Bel Air, MD	21015-4129	720 Gannet Dr Bel Air, MD	21015-4129	27. ___
28.	3912 Adams Dr Valdosa, GA	31605	3912 Adams Dr Valdosa, GA	31605	28. ___
29.	8900 220th St Queens Village, NY	11427-5026	8908 220th St Queens Village, NY	11427-5026	29. ___

A. No Errors	B. Address Only	C. ZIP Code Only	D. Both

Correct List — **List to Be Checked**

#	Address	Zip Code	Address	Zip Code	Answers
30.	2902 Burchner Blvd Bronx, NY	10465-2103	2902 Burchner Blvd Bronx, NY	10465-2102	30. ___
31.	11702 US Hwy 301 N Lumberton, NC	28358-0529	11703 US Hwy 301 N Lumberton, NC	28359-0529	31. ___
32.	3908 S 74th West Ave Tulsa, OK	74107	3908 N 74th West Ave Tulsa, OK	74108	32. ___
33.	1923 Blackfort St Chattanooga, TN	37404-0371	1928 Blackfort St Chattanooga, TN	37504-0371	33. ___
34.	3909 N Highway 360 Grand Prairie, TX	75052	3909 N Highway 360 Grand Prairie, TX	75052	34. ___
35.	3472 Fawkland Cir Boynton Beach, FL	33426-5102	3472 Fawkland Dr Boynton Beach, FL	33426-5102	35. ___
36.	1429 E Gate Shop Ctr Carbondale, IL	62902	1429 E Gate Shop Ctr Carbondale, IL	62902	36. ___
37.	2684 Armherst Ave Manhattan, KS	66502-8129	2884 Armherst Ave Manhattan, KS	68502-8129	37. ___
38.	11575 Highway Ave Silver Spring, MD	20902-3103	11575 Highway Ave Silver Spring, MD	20902-3103	38. ___
39.	22205 Hall Rd Macomb, MI	48042	22205 Hall Rd Macomb, MI	48043	39. ___
40.	2206 Main St Tupelo, MS	38804-6291	2208 Main St Tupelo, MS	38804-6291	40. ___
41.	1276 S Thomas Ave Yuma, AZ	85364-0681	1276 S Thomas Ave Yuma, CO	85364-0681	41. ___
42.	4647 E Wardlow Rd Long Beach, FL	90808	4647 E Wardlow Rd Long Beach, CA	90308	42. ___
43.	7282 W State Rd 40 Ormond Beach, FL	32174-0617	7282 N State Rd 40 Ormond Beach, FL	32174-0617	43. ___
44.	2872 W 111th Ter Leawood, KS	66211-9320	2872 N 111th Ter Leawood, KS	66211-9320	44. ___
45.	3599 Beverly Pl Shreveport, LA	77105-3177	3599 Beverly Pl Shreveport, LA	77106-3177	45. ___

A. No Errors	B. Address Only	C. ZIP Code Only	D. Both

	Correct List		List to Be Checked		D. Both
	Address	Zip Code	Address	Zip Code	Answers
46.	1998 North Ave Columbus, GA	31901-5261	1997 North Ave Columbus, GA	31901-5261	46. ___
47.	1789 W Park Ave Champaign, IL	61821-0031	1789 W Park Ave Champaign, IL	61821-0031	47. ___
48.	2700 Hanna St Fort Wayne, IN	46806-7102	2708 Hanna St Fort Wayne, IN	46806-7102	48. ___
49.	399 Langdon St Somerset, KY	42503	399 Langdon St Somerset, KY	42508	49. ___
50.	3976 Casino Ave Chicopee, MA	01013-2650	3976 Casino Ave Chicopee, MA	01013-2650	50. ___
51.	5823 W Victory Rd Boise, IN	83709-2372	5323 W Victory Rd Boise, IN	88709-2372	51. ___
52.	5001 Maple Ave Newport, KY	41071-0029	5008 Maple Ave New Port, KY	47071-0029	52. ___
53.	2238 Clifton Ave Baltimore, MD	21216	2238 Clifton Ave Baltimore, MD	21216	53. ___
54.	5386 Euclid Ave NE Albuquerque, NM	87110-2181	5886 Euclid Ave NE Albuquerque, NM	87110-2181	54. ___
55.	3029 Bethesda Rd Asheville, NC	28805	3029 Bethesda St Asheville, NC	28805	55. ___
56.	3976 Timberway Sevierville, TN	37876	3976 Timberway Sevierville, TN	37876	56. ___
57.	3741 Rosewood Ln Huntsville, TX	77340-3201	3741 Rosewood Ln Huntsville, TX	77341-3201	57. ___
58.	1827 Court St Richmond, VA	23222-7321	1827 Court Rd Richmond, VA	23322-7321	58. ___
59.	17200 W Capital Dr Brookfield, WI	53045	17200 N Capital Dr Brookfield, WI	53045	59. ___
60.	1775 Ames Ave Cheyeane, WY	82001-3203	1775 Ames Ave Cheyeane, WY	82001-3203	60. ___

(See Answers to the above questions on page 80).

Answers to Questions
Address-Checking Practice Test 1

Answers to Questions
on pages 51 - 54.

1. B		31. B
2. D		32. A
3. B		33. B
4. B		34. B
5. B		35. D
6. C		36. A
7. D		37. A
8. A		38. D
9. B		39. D
10. A		40. B
11. D		41. A
12. C		42. B
13. D		43. B
14. B		44. D
15. B		45. B
16. C		46. D
17. A		47. D
18. C		48. A
19. C		49. C
20. A		50. B
21. D		51. A
22. D		52. B
23. D		53. A
24. D		54. D
25. B		55. B
26. A		56. B
27. D		57. A
28. A		58. D
29. B		59. A
30. C		60. B

Answers to Questions
Address-Checking Practice Test 2

Answers to Questions
on pages 55 - 58

1. C	31. A
2. B	32. B
3. C	33. D
4. B	34. D
5. D	35. A
6. A	36. D
7. B	37. D
8. D	38. B
9. D	39. C
10. C	40. D
11. D	41. D
12. C	42. D
13. A	43. A
14. B	44. B
15. D	45. A
16. D	46. D
17. A	47. A
18. C	48. D
19. A	49. A
20. D	50. D
21. D	51. C
22. B	52. D
23. B	53. D
24. A	54. C
25. A	55. A
26. B	56. D
27. A	57. D
28. C	58. A
29. A	59. C
30. D	60. D

Answers to Questions
Address-Checking Practice Test 3

Answers to Questions
on page 59 - 62

1. A	31. D
2. B	32. A
3. B	33. D
4. B	34. C
5. C	35. A
6. A	36. D
7. D	37. B
8. D	38. D
9. A	39. A
10. C	40. D
11. B	41. B
12. B	42. D
13. B	43. A
14. B	44. D
15. D	45. A
16. A	46. A
17. C	47. D
18. B	48. A
19. D	49. C
20. D	50. B
21. D	51. D
22. B	52. D
23. B	53. A
24. C	54. C
25. B	55. B
26. B	56. C
27. D	57. D
28. C	58. A
29. D	59. A
30. A	60. A

Answers to Questions
Address-Checking Practice Test 4

Answers to Questions
on pages 63 - 66

1. D	31. B
2. B	32. A
3 . A	33. C
4. D	34. C
5. C	35. D
6. D	36. A
7. D	37. A
8. A	38. D
9. D	39. C
10. A	40. A
11. B	41. D
12. A	42. D
13. D	43. A
14. C	44. B
15. B	45. A
16. C	46. A
17. C	47. B
18. C	48. D
19. B	49. A
20. A	50. B
21. D	51. D
22. A	52. B
23. B	53. C
24. D	54. C
25. A	55. D
26. B	56. D
27. A	57. D
28. D	58. A
29. C	59. A
30. B	60. C

Answers to Questions
Address-Checking Practice Test 5

Answers to Questions
on pages 67 - 70

1. A	31. A
2. C	32. A
3. D	33. D
4. B	34. D
5. A	35. B
6. A	36. C
7. D	37. B
8. B	38. C
9. C	39. A
10. A	40. B
11. D	41. A
12. B	42. B
13. C	43. D
14. A	44. A
15. D	45. B
16. D	46. A
17. A	47. B
18. A	48. B
19. B	49. C
20. A	50. C
21. C	51. B
22. D	52. D
23. A	53. B
24. D	54. C
25. D	55. D
26. C	56. B
27. A	57. A
28. B	58. A
29. B	59. D
30. B	60. D

Answers to Questions
Address-Checking Practice Test 6

Answers to Questions
on pages 71- 74

1. B	31. D
2. C	32. D
3. A	33. D
4. C	34. A
5. B	35. B
6. D	36. A
7. B	37. D
8. D	38. A
9. D	39. C
10. B	40. B
11. A	41. B
12. B	42. D
13. A	43. B
14. A	44. B
15. D	45. C
16. C	46. B
17. D	47. A
18. B	48. B
19. C	49. C
20. A	50. A
21. A	51. D
22. D	52. D
23. B	53. A
24. B	54. B
25. D	55. B
26. C	56. A
27. B	57. C
28. A	58. D
29. B	59. B
30. C	60. A

13

Part B: Forms Completion

Identification of Information to Complete a Form

Part B: Forms Completion of Test 473 involves the identification of information required to fill out or complete a form. A number of forms with several items or questions, will be shown to you by the US Postal Service so that you can identify the data required to complete the form.

You will be answering 30 items or questions to be finished in 15 minutes. You have to understand the questions, and think of the correct information to complete the forms. Just understand well the questions, and see to it that you give the correctt information needed to accomplish the form.

How to Answer the Part B Test

Become familiar with forms. For instance, the USPS uses many forms in accomplishing its mission of giving satisfactory service to the American public. Before you answer any questions, look at the form briefly. You have to understand the questions being asked. To be familiar with Postal forms, go to your local Post Office, and get some forms available in the lobby.

On this part of the test, you may just use your common sense. For instance, an item merely asks you which information is needed to be entered in a box or line.

In other words, this Part II of the exam tests your ability to know the correct information to complete or fill in different forms used by the U.S. Postal Service.

Look at all the 4 answer choices marked **A, B,** and **D.** Some of the questions maybe like these:

Which of these should be the correct entry for Box 10?

Which of these should require a check mark?

Which box will tell the letter carrier when to resume delivery of mail to a certain address?

Where does the customer sign his or her name?

Which box should indicate the dates of holding mail if you're on vacation? The instruction is usually in the shaded area. Don't put the information in the wrong box or line

The correct answer to a question maybe a date, the name of the applicant or postal worker, or an address, etc.

Application Cards

Tear off this page, fill it out, and turn it in to your Post Office™.

Application for Post Office Box or Caller Service – Part 1

Customer: Complete items 1, 3-6, 14-16, and 18-19.   Post Office: Complete items 2, 7-13, 17 and 20.

1. Name(s) to Which Box Number(s) Is (are) Assigned	2. Box or Caller Numbers
	_____ through _____
3. Name of Person Applying, Title *(if representing an organization)*, and Name of Organization *(if Different From Item 1)*	4a. Will This Box Be Used for: □ Personal Use □ Business Use *(Optional)*
	4b. Email Address *(Optional)*
5. Address *(Number, street, apt. no., city, state, and ZIP Code™).* When address changes, cross out address here and put new address on back.	
	6. Telephone Number *(Include area code)*

7. Date Application Received	8. Box Size Needed	9. ID and Physical Address Verified by *(Initials)*	10. Dates of Service _____ through _____
11. **Two types of identification are required. One must contain a photograph of the adressee(s). Social Security cards, credit cards, and birth certificates are unacceptable as identification. Write in identifiying information. Subject to verification.**		12. Check Eligibility for Carrier Delivery □ a. City □ b. Rural □ c. HCR □ d. None	13. Service assigned □ a. Box □ b. Caller □ c. Reserve No.
		14. List name(s) of minors or names of other persons **receiving mail** in individual box. Other persons must present two forms of valid ID. If applicant is a firm, name each member **receiving mail**. Each member must have verifiable ID upon request. *(Continue on reverse side.)*	
WARNING: *The furnishing of false or misleading information on this form or omission of information may result in criminal sanctions (including fines and imprisonment) and/or civil sanctions (including multiple damages and civil penalties.)* (18 U.S.C. 1001)		15. Signature of Applicant *(Same as Item 3).* I agree to comply with all Postal Service® rules regarding Post Office box or caller services.	

PS Form **1093**, April 2004 *(Page 1 of 2)* (7530-02-000-7165)

Use a separate form for each number or consecutive group of numbers, and type of service. File part 1 alphabetically by customer's name.

1. Which of these should be a correct entry for Box 7?

A. $3.50
B. April 2, 2005
C. Small
D. 3 p.m.

2. Where would you enter the applicant's address?

A. Box 4b
B. Box 5
C. Box 3
D. Box 6

3. Which of these would be a correct entry for Box 8?

A. 12/02/04
B. Medium
C. 2513 Hickory Dr., Farmington Hills, MI 48333
D. $5.00

Application for Post Office™ Box or Caller Service – Part 2

Special Orders

16. Postmaster: The following named persons or representatives of the organization listed below are authorized to **accept** mail addressed to this (these) Post Office box(es) or caller number(s). All names listed must have verifiable ID. *(Continue on reverse side.)*

a. Name of Box Customer *(Same as item 1)*

b. Name(s) of Applicant(s) *(Same as item 3)*

c. Other Authorized Representative

d. Other Authorized Representative

17. Box or Caller Number to Which This Card Applies

18. Will this box be used for Express Mail® reshipment? *(Check one)*

   a. Yes ☐   b. No ☐

Customer Note:

The Postal Service® may consider it valid evidence that a person is authorized to remove mail from the box if that person possesses a key or combination to the box.

20. Post Office Date Stamp

19. Signature of Applicant *(Same as Item 3).* I agree to comply with all Postal Service® rules regarding Post Office box or caller services.

WARNING: The furnishing of false or misleading information on this form or omission of material may result in criminal sanctions (including fines and imprisonment) and/or civil sanctions (including multiple damages and civil penalties.) (18 U.S.C. 1001)

Use a separate form for each number or consecutive group of numbers, and type of service. File part 2 by box or caller number.

PS Form **1093,** April 2004 *(Detached from Page 1 of 2)* (7530-02-000-7165)

The above is Part II of an Application for Post Office Box or Caller Service. Here are some questions to be answered.

1. Which of these would require a check mark?

A. Box C
B. Box 20
C. Box 18
D. Box D

2. Where would you enter the names of persons authorized to remove or get the mail from the box?

A. Box 17
B. Box A
C. Box B
D. Boxes C and D

3. Which of these would be a correct entry for Box 18?

A. 2 p.m.
B. 05/29/04
C. 2
D. A check mark

14

Part C: Coding and Memory

The Way to Assign Addresses to Delivery Routes

Postal Test 473 is similar in some ways to the old **470 Battery Test**. The **Memory-for-Address Test** of the old **470 Test** consisted of two Parts: Part A, Practice Test, and Part B: The Actual Test.

Now, the **Part C** of the new Test 473 consists of two sections: the **Coding Section** and the **Memory Section**. The Coding Section contains 36 items to be answered or completed in 6 minutes while the Memory Section contains 36 items to be answered in 7 minutes.

During the test, you will be presented with a **Coding Guide**, the first column of which consists of **Address Range** and the second column, **Delivery Route**, represented by letters **A, B, C,** and **D.** You must decide which correct code (or route lettered A, B, C, and D), is assigned to each item or address range (containing numbers and names of streets).

You must work on the items as fast and as accurate as you can. But the most important thing to remember is to be able to memorize address ranges containing numbers and names of streets and the delivery routes.

During the first section **(Coding)** of the Part C Test, you will be allowed to look at the coding guide while you are assigning codes, (A, B, C, and D, to each item of the addresses. But you won't be allowed to look at the coding guide while doing the second section **(Memory)** of the Part C Test.

Here's a sample Coding Guide.

Coding Guide	
Address Range	Delivery Route
200 - 4999 Mayfair Rd 61 - 498 Seaweed St 400 - 1399 Oakwood Dr	A
5000 - 6599 Mayfair Rd 500 - 1699 Seaweed St	B
1 - 199 Hill Ct **1400**- 7998 Oakwood Dr 200 - 499 Lebanon Blvd	C
All mail matters that don't fall in one of the address ranges listed above.	D

The Coding Guide that the Post Office will give you will be used during the Coding Section test and the Memory Section test of the Part C Test. Create address codes to remember address ranges assigned to routes.

You must memorize the address ranges to be assigned to delivery routes, marked A, B, C, and D. In the above example, all numbers ranging from 200-4999 Mayfair Rd are assigned to Delivery Route "A." All numbers ranging from 5000 - 6599 Mayfair Rd, are assigned to Delivery Route "B."

In remembering the address ranges on Mayfair Rd which are 200 - 4999 Mayfair Rd and **5000** - 6599 Mayfair Rd, make the number **5000** as the **boundary** between Routes A and B. Any address from 200 to 4999 Mayfair is assigned to Route A. Then any address from 5000 to 65999 Mayfair is assigned to Route B.

In memorizing the address ranges on Oakwood which are 400-1399 Oakwood for Route A, and **1400** - 7998 Oakwood for Route C, make the number **1400** as the boundary between Route A and Route C (eliminating the numbers 1399). We chose 1400 because it's easier to remember than 1399. That is, any address on Oakwood Dr from 400 to 1399 is assigned to Route A. Then, any address on Oakwood Dr from 1400 to 7998 Oakwood is assigned to Route C.

If there's an address such as 600 Oakwood (between the numbers 400 and 1400 Oakwood), the mail goes to Delivery Route "A." And the list goes on and on.

With regard to addresses that are not extended to another route, such as, 1 - 199 Hill and 200 - 499 Lebanon, just remember the two address ranges as belonging to **HllLe** (combination of **Hill** and **Le**banon). The problem with this strategy is, you'll miss the "D" answers. (All mail matters that don't fall in one of the address ranges listed above are assigned to Route D). Of course, if you can memorize the address ranges, then it's good for you.

For strategies for **Coding and Memory Section Tests**, see the next page.

15

Strategies for Coding-Memory Test
Techniques for Memorizing Coding Guides

The **Part C** of the Test 473 consists of two sections: the **Coding Section** which contains 36 items to be answered or completed in 6 minutes.and the **Memory Section** which contains 36 items to be finished in 7 minutes.

During the test, you will be presented with a **Coding Guide**, the first column of which consists of **Address Range** and the second column, **Delivery Route**, represented by letters **A, B, C,** and **D.** You must decide which correct code (or route lettered A, B, C, or D, is assigned to each item or address range (containing numbers and names of streets).

Actually, techniques for the **Coding-Memory Test** of the Postal 473/473/-C Test and the **Memory-for-Address Test** of the RCA 460 Exam have similarities and differences.

In the **Coding-Memory Test** of the 473/473-C Test, you have four choices in answering the questions: Delivery Routes A, B, C, and D. You must determine which route the address range is assigned to. In other words, you will be given numbers of streets that are within certain address ranges. And then identify if the address belongs to Delivery Routes A, B, C, or D. If the address is not within the given address range, then the answer should be D. That is, all mail matters that don't fall in one of the address ranges listed in the Coding Guide, are covered by Route D, which is served by a particular letter carrier.

In the **Memory-for-Address Test** of the 460 RCA examination, you have to memorize the locations of addresses (numbers and street names) contained in boxes marked A, B, C, D, and E. You will be given an address range such as 4700-5599 Table and you must determine to which box the address range belongs. For instance, the address range 4700-5599 Table may be assigned to Box B. This Memory-for-Address test of the 460 RCA exam is easier than the Coding and Memory Section Test of the Postal 473 Battery Test. Why? Because on the 460 RCA exam, the selection of the answer will be the exact address contained in each box. On the other hand, in the Coding-Memory test of the 473 Battery Test, the numbers given are almost always not the exact numbers mentioned in Coding Guide. The numbers given may just be within the address range. In addition, you must determine if the numbers really fall in any of the address ranges listed.

Here's a sample Coding Guide:

Coding Guide	
Address Range	Delivery Route
200-4999 Mayfair Rd 61- 498 Seaweed St 400 - 1399 Oakwood Dr	A
5000 - 6599 Mayfair Rd 500 -1699 Seaweed St	B
1 - 199 Oven Hill 1400 - 7998 Oakwood Dr 200 - 499 Lebanon Blvd	C
All mail matters that don't fall in one of the address ranges listed above.	D

The Coding Guide that the Post Office will be used during the **Coding** section and the **Memory** section test. Create address codes to remember address ranges assigned to routes.

You must memorize the address ranges to be assigned to a delivery route to be served by a city or rural letter carrier. In the above example, any address from **200- 4999 Mayfair Rd** is assigned to Delivery Route "A."

In the same example, any address from **5000 - 6599 Mayfair Rd,** is covered by Delivery Route "B".

Memorizing the Codes

There are different ways you can do to memorize the codes. Remember, there's a limited time in memorizing the codes and completing the items or questions.

Again, devote most of the 2 minutes and 1 1/2 minutes allowed to the practice test to memorization of the coding guide since this part of the test is not scored. Then you will also be given 3 minutes to memorize the Coding Guide. You will be given 7 minutes to answer the 36 items in the Memory Section part of the Part C test.

Here's a short cut to memorizing the codes.

From top to bottom, first memorize the names of the streets (excluding the word "Rd" or "St." or the letter "S" (for South).

Coding Guide	
Address Range	Delivery Route
200 - 4999 **Mayfair** Rd 61 - 499 **Seaweed** St 400 - 1399 **Oakwood** Dr	A
5000 - 6599 Mayfair Rd 500 - 1699 Seaweed St	B
1 - 199 Oven Hill 1400 - 7998 Oakwood Dr 200 - 499 Lebanon Blvd	C
All mail matters that don't fall in one of the address ranges listed above.	D

To remember the names, associate **Mayfair, Seaweed,** and **Oakwood,** you may think of things or objects you know. For instance, imagine some things such as you saw the Broadway show *Mayfair*, then you went to get a string of *seaweeds*, after which you proceeded to the *Oakwood* Hospital. You can do the same with the other names of streets. Things or objects that are imagined are easily remembered or recalled.

You may also combine **May**fair, **Sea**weed and **Oak**wood as one word **"May-seaoak",** combining the three names into one, just using the first syllable of each word. You can do the same thing with the other addresses

Address Ranges

In seeing the increasing numbers with regard to address ranges, let's have the following example:

61 - 499 Seaweed St
500 - 1699 Seaweed St

In remembering the address ranges on Seaweed which are 61 - 499 Seaweed for Route A, and **500** - 1699 Seaweed for Route B, make the number **500** as the **boundary** between Route A and Route B. We chose 500 because it's easier to remember than 499. That is, any address on Seaweed St from 61 to 499 is assigned to Route A.

Moreover, any address on Seaweed from 500 to 1699 Seaweed is assigned to Route B. In other words, make the code with this kind of arrangement:

Code: Seaweed 61 - 500 - 1699

Generally, an address range group of numbers end with the number 98 or 99. For instance, the group of numbers for Route B of Seaweed ends with the number 99 (as seen above). So in memorizing the above code, you remember the code as 61-500-1699 (remembering the number 61 as the age of your father or whoever he is, gathering seaweeds and the number 16 as the age of your daughter or sister or whatever. Then you may recall the 99 as 1999 as the date of your trip to the sea or somewhere else. Create events in your imagination.

To explain further, any address below 61 Seaweed is assigned to Route D. Also, any address above 1699 belongs to Route D. In other words, all mail matters that don't fall in one of the address ranges listed in the Coding Guide are assigned to Route D.

You can do the same technique in determining the address ranges on other addresses stated in the Coding Guide.

It's common that the last number of the first address range of a street ends with a 9 or 99 or an 8 or 98; for instance 1299 or 1398. Also, the last 2 numbers of the first string of numbers of address range (same street) will naturally end with two zeroes (00), for instance 13**99** - 25**00**; if the first strings of numbers end with two zeroes, the next address range will start with the number **01** (such as in the number 25**01** and again the next string of numbers will end with the number 9 or **99**, such as in the number 25**99**, or **8 or 98**.

To remember numbers and places, associate them with things or places you know or familiar with you. For instance, you may associate any number or numbers such as street number 1956 as the year you were born or the year you visited your relatives in Haiti or Rome. You may associate the street name Venice being the city where you took a vacation in the year 2000 or whatever date. It all depends on events or happenings that took or taking place in your life. Everyone will have his or her own codes to remember or recall things or places. Creating codes to recall things is the instrument to easily recalling numbers, events, things, and places. Things imagined are easily remembered by your own biocomputer.

See another sample Coding Guide on the next page.

Coding Guide	
Address Range	Delivery Route
100 - 2999 **Se**minol Ln 51 - 298 **Ford** Pkwy 4001 - 1399 **Cam**bridge Dr	A
3000 - 6599 **Se**minol Ln 501- 2000 **Sum**merview Dr	B
1 - 199 **Ha**milton Blvd 300 - 2798 **Ford** Pkwy 201 - 3000 **Jeff**erson Cir	C
All mail matters that don't fall in one of the address ranges listed above.	D

You can see in the above sample Coding Code the following streets that are covered by different routes (A, B, C, and D): Seminol, Ford, Cambridge, Summerview, Hamilton, and Jefferson. Listed twice are Seminole and Ford. Each route, A, B, or C includes street names mentioned only once: Cambridge, Summerview, and Jefferson.

From top to bottom (Routes A, B, and C), you may combine the first syllables of the streets in the following manner: **SeFordCam** (Route A), **SeSum** (Route B), and **HaFordJeff** (Route C).

The combined syllables of the above streets are considered as your codes for remembering the streets. In the case of streets such as Seminol Ln, Ford Pkwy, Cambridge Dr., etc., forget about whether the street name is a Ln, Pkwy, Dr or an Ave. Just remember Seminol, Ford, and Cambridge.

Address Ranges

Here's another sample of address ranges:

51 - 299 Ford Pkwy
300 - 2798 Ford Pkwy

In remembering the address ranges on Ford Pkwy which are 51 - 299 Ford Parkway for Route A, and 300 - 2798 Ford Pkwy for Route C, make the numbers **300** as the dividing line between Route A and Route C. We selected 300 because it's easier to remember than 299. That is, any address on Ford Parkway from 51 to 299 is assigned to Route A. Moreover, any address on Ford Parkway between 300 and 2798 Seaweed St is assigned to Route C.

Then create the code with this kind of arrangement:

Then create the code with this kind of arrangement:

Code: Ford Parkwy 51 - 300 - 2798

Furthermore, any address below 51 is assigned to Route D. Also, any address above 2798 Ford Pkwy belongs to Route D. In other words, all mail matters that don't fall in one of the address ranges listed in the coding guide are assigned to Route D.

You must remember the code as follows:

You may recall 51 as the day Ford had a grandson or what; recall 300 as the number of wedding visitors of his daughter. You may divide 2798 into two string of numbers, such as 27 and 98. You may link the number 27 and 98 to things you know; for instance, remembering 27 as the year you got married, and recalling 98 (or 1998) as the year your son went to Paris or wherever. Use your imagination! Create images and happenings or events to remember things, such as numbers. Remembering images make recalling easier to do.

16

4 Exam 473 Practice Tests

Part C: Coding-Memory Test

Part C of the new Test 473 consists of two sections: the Coding Section and the Memory Section. The Coding section contains 36 items to be answered or completed in 6 minutes while the Memory Section contains 36 items to be answered in 7 minutes.

It is important to note that you will be presented with a Coding Guide. The first column of the guide consists of Address Range and the second column contains the Delivery Route, represented by letters A, B, C, and D. The procedure is to decide which correct route (marked A, B, C, or D), is assigned to each addresss range (consisting of numbers and names of streets.)

You'll be using the same guide throughout both sections of the Part C Test. Each item or question is an address. You must decide which delivery route serves the address.

Coding Section

The first section of the Part C Test, called Coding Section, actually consists of three segments:

Segment 1: You are given 2 minutes within which to study or memorize the Coding Guide. Also, you have to answer four items as a practice test. Since this is not counted, you may answer only one question and use the time in memorizing the code. You are allowed to look at the Coding Guide as you answer the questions. The same Coding Guide will be used throughout the Coding and Memory tests.

Segment 2: You'll be given 1 1/2 minutes to answer 8 questions on this part of the test. Since this is not scored, you may answer only 2 or 3 questions. You better use the time in memorizing the coding guide.

Segment 3: You have 6 minutes to answer 36 questions. This part of the test is scored or counted. You must mark the circles on the official answer sheet. You'll still be allowed to look at the coding guide as you answer the questions.

When you work on the first section, Coding, of the test, you are allowed to look at the coding guide while you are assigning codes, (A, B, C, and D), to each item of the addresses. However, when you work on the second section (memory), you won't be allowed to look at the coding guide. In other words, memorize the coding guide.

As mentioned, you are given 2 minutes in Segment 1 and another 1 1/2 minutes in Segment 2 (total of 3 1/2 minutes to memorize and answer 4 questions (Segment 1) and 8 questions (Segment 2). After that you are allowed to answer the 36 items in 6 minutes. Since Segment 1 and Segment 2 are not counted or scored, why not use the 3 1/2 minutes to memorize the guiding code? Answers to questions or items (Segment 1 and Segment 2) should be marked on the sample answer sheet at the bottom of the question page. The 36 questions (Segment 3) should, however, be answered on the official answer sheet. After that comes the Memory Test.

Practice Test 1
Part C: Coding and Memory

Segment 1 of Coding Section

Instructions

Segment 1 of the Coding Section test is a 2-minute exercise for memorizing the Coding Guide to be used in answering the questions on this test. Also, you have these 2 minutes to answer 4 questions. Since this part of the test is not scored, you should not work on all of the questions. Just memorize the guide using the techniques mentioned in Chapter 15: **Strategies for the Coding-Memory Test** on pages 87-92. Turn the page to see the Coding Guide.

Part C: Coding & Memory

Segment 1 of Coding Section

Coding Guide	
Address Range	Delivery Route
10 - 299 SW **2nd** St 300 - 399 **Sun**set Dr 1 - 2498 **Wet**son Rd	A
300 - 899 SW **2nd** St 600 - 999 **Pine** Ridge Dr	B
200 - 1399 **Shot**gun Rd **400** - 899 **Sun**set Dr 1 - 1099 S **Pros**pect Ter	C
All mail that doesn't fall in one of the address ranges listed above	D

There are several ways of remembering the above address ranges in different boxes assigned to any of the delivery routes, **A, B, C,** and **D.** We should create so-called extract codes to easily memorize the above numbers and streets. You may combine the **first syllables** of the streets.

The codes may be created (from top to bottom) as **2ndSunWet** for SW **2nd, Sun**set, and **Wet**son (Box A). For the second box, it should be **2ndPine** for SW **2nd** and **Pine** Ridge. For the third box it should be **ShotSunPros** for **Shot**gun, **Sun**set and **Pros**pect.

In memorizing address ranges on 10 - 299 SW 2nd St (Route A) and 300 - 899 SW 2nd St (Route B), make the number **300** as the boundary or dividing line between Route A and Route B. We chose the round figure 300 because it's easier to remember than 299. Any address from 10 to 299 is assigned to Route A and any address from 300 (the boundary) to to 899 belongs to Route B.). Then any address below 10 or any address above 899 doesn't not fall in any of the addresss ranges. Therefore, any of the address is assigned to Route D.

In the above Coding Guide, three street address ranges don't extend to another route. They are 1 - 2498 **Wet**son, 600 - 999 **Pine** Ridge, 200 - 1399 **Shot**gun, and 1-1099 S **Pros**pect. To remember them, you may combine the four street names into one, using the first syllable of each name, such as **WetPineShotPros.** You may also disregard the address ranges and just remember the name **WetPineShotPros** representing the four streets, if you have trouble remembering the address ranges. However, again, you may miss the "D" answers (any mail that doesn't fall in any of the address ranges listed above). Of course, it would be better, if you could memorize the address ranges (or numbers) to increase your number of correct answers..

Part C: Coding and Memory
Practice Test 1

Segment 1 of Coding Section

Questions

Address	Delivery Route			
1. 200 SW 2nd St	A	B	C	D
2. 900 Sunset Dr	A	B	C	D
3. 970 Pine Ridge Dr	A	B	C	D
4. 14000 Shotgun Rd	A	B	C	D

Sample Answer Sheet

1. Ⓐ Ⓑ Ⓒ Ⓓ

2. Ⓐ Ⓑ Ⓒ Ⓓ

3. Ⓐ Ⓑ Ⓒ Ⓓ

4. Ⓐ Ⓑ Ⓒ Ⓓ

The correct answers are 1-A, 2-D, 3-B, and 4-D

Part C: Coding and Memory

Segment 2 of Coding Section

Instructions

Segment 2 of the Coding Section has 8 questions to be answered in 1 1/2 minutes. Of course, you can look at the Coding Guide. Since this part of the test is not scored, you can just answer 2 or 3 questions, then use the time to memorize the guide. You have to mark your answers at the bottom of the sample question page, not on the official answer sheets.

For Segment 2 of the Coding Section, which serves as a practice test, turn the page.

Part C: Coding & Memory

Segment 2 of Coding Section

Coding Guide	
Address Range	Delivery Route
10 - 299 SW **2nd** St 300 - 399 **Sun**set Dr 1 - 2498 **Wet**son Rd	A
300 - 899 SW **2nd** St 600 - 999 **Pine** Ridge Dr	B
200 - 1399 **Shot**gun Rd **400** - 899 **Sun**set Dr 1 - 1099 S **Pros**pect Ter	C
All mail that doesn't fall in one of the address ranges listed above	D

There are several ways of remembering the above address ranges in different boxes assigned to the delivery routes, **A, B, C,** and **D.** We should create so-called **extract codes** to easily memorize the above addresses.

The address coding guide is as follows:

10 - **300** - 899 SW **2nd** (Routes A & B)
300 - **400** - 899 **Sun**set (Routes A & C)
1 - 2498 **Wet**son (Route A)
600 - 999 **Pine** Ridge (Route B)
200 - 1399 **Shot**gun) (Route C)
1 - 1099 S **Pros**pect (Route C)

Usually, an address range ends with the number "98" or "99." or with the number "00." For the purpose of short cutting, you may eliminate the numbers 98, 99, and 00 in remembering the addresses, if you wish. It's just understood that the numbers are there.

Part C: Coding and Memory
Practice Test 1

Segment 2 of Coding Section

Questions

Addresses	Delivery Route				Answers
1. 601 Pine Ridge Dr	A	B	C	D	1. ___
2. 900 Sunset Dr	A	B	C	D	2. ___
3. 350 Wetson Rd	A	B	C	D	3. ___
4. 550 S Prospect Ter	A	B	C	D	4. ___
5. 950 SW 2nd St	A	B	C	D	5. ___
6. 1250 Shotgun Rd	A	B	C	D	6. ___
7. 340 Wetson Rd	A	B	C	D	7. ___
8. 700 Sunset Dr	A	B	C	D	8. ___

Sample Answer Sheet

1. Ⓐ Ⓑ Ⓒ Ⓓ   5. Ⓐ Ⓑ Ⓒ Ⓓ

2. Ⓐ Ⓑ Ⓒ Ⓓ   6. Ⓐ Ⓑ Ⓒ Ⓓ

3. Ⓐ Ⓑ Ⓒ Ⓓ   7. Ⓐ Ⓑ Ⓒ Ⓓ

4. Ⓐ Ⓑ Ⓒ Ⓓ   8. Ⓐ Ⓑ Ⓒ Ⓓ

The correct answers are 1-B, 2-D, 3-A, 4-C, 5-D, 6-C, 7-A, and 8-C

Part C: Coding and Memory

Segment 3 of Coding Section

Instructions

Segment 3 of the Coding Section, Practice Test 1 has 36 questions to be answered in 6 minutes. You can still look at the Coding Guide. It's the real test, therefore, this part of the test is scored. In other words, correct answers are counted. Answer the questions in 6 minutes. You have to mark your answers on the official answer sheets.

For Segment 3 of the Coding Section, go to the next page.

Part C: Coding & Memory

Segment 3 of Coding Section

Coding Guide	
Address Range	Delivery Route
10 - 299 SW 2nd St 300 - 399 Sunset Dr 1 - 2498 Wetson Rd	A
300 - 899 SW 2nd St 600 - 999 Pine Ridge Dr	B
200 - 1399 Shotgun Rd 400 - 899 Sunset Dr 1 - 1099 S Prospect Ter	C
All mail that doesn't fall in one of the address ranges listed above	D

Part C: Coding and Memory
Practice Test 1

Segment 3 of Coding Section

Questions

Address	Delivery Route				Answers
1. 299 SW 2nd St	A	B	C	D	1. ___
2. 870 SW 2nd St	A	B	C	D	2. ___
3. 400 Sunset Dr	A	B	C	D	3. ___
4. 890 Pine Ridge Dr	A	B	C	D	4. ___
5. 1000 S Prospect Ter	A	B	C	D	5. ___
6. 460 Wetson Rd	A	B	C	D	6. ___
7. 1250 Shotgun Rd	A	B	C	D	7. ___
8. 400 Sunset Dr	A	B	C	D	8. ___
9. 2399 Wetson Rd	A	B	C	D	9. ___
10. 780 SW 2nd St	A	B	C	D	10. ___
11. 998 S Prospect Ter	A	B	C	D	11. ___
12. 335 Sunset Dr	A	B	C	D	12. ___
13. 59 S Prospect Ter	A	B	C	D	13. ___
14. 50 SW 2nd St	A	B	C	D	14. ___
15. 800 SW 2nd St	A	B	C	D	15. ___
16. 400 Sunset Dr	A	B	C	D	16. ___
17. 780 Wetson Rd	A	B	C	D	17. ___
18. 959 Shotgun Rd	A	B	C	D	18. ___

Continued on the next page.

Part C: Coding & Memory

Segment 3 of Coding Section

Coding Guide	
Address Range	Delivery Route
10 - 299 SW 2nd St 300 - 399 Sunset Dr 1 - 2498 Wetson Rd	A
300 - 899 SW 2nd St 600 - 999 Pine Ridge Dr	B
200 - 1399 Shotgun Rd 400 - 899 Sunset Dr 1 - 1099 S Prospect Ter	C
All mail that doesn't fall in one of the address ranges listed above	D

Part C: Coding and Memory
Practice Test 1
Continuation

Segment 3 of Coding Section

Questions

Address	Delivery Route				Answers
19. 1299 Shotgun Rd	A'	B	C	D	19. ___
20. 1950 Wetson Rd	A	B	C	D	20. ___
21. 500 SW 2nd St	A	B	C	D	21. ___
22. 1000 Pine Ridge Dr	A	B	C	D	22. ___
23. 275 SW 2nd St	A	B	C	D	23. ___
24. 900 SW 2nd St	A	B	C	D	24. ___
25. 1199 Shotgun Rd	A	B	C	D	25. ___
26. 389 Sunset Dr	A	B	C	D	26. ___
27. 998 S Prospect Ter	A	B	C	D	27. ___
28. 2399 Wetson Rd	A	B	C	D	28. ___
29. 785 Sunset Dr	A	B	C	D	29. ___
30. 400 SW 2nd St	A	B	C	D	30. ___
31. 890 S Prospect Ter	A	B	C	D	31. ___
32. 750 Pine Ridge Dr	A	B	C	D	32. ___
33. 259 SW 2nd St	A	B	C	D	33. ___
34. 55 S Prospect Ter	A	B	C	D	34. ___
35. 95 Wetson Rd	A	B	C	D	35. ___
36. 800 Pine Ridge Dr	A	B	C	D	36. ___

See the answers to the above questions on the next page.

Part C: Coding & Memory

Coding Section

Answers to Questions
Practice Test 1

Segment 3 of Coding Section, 105-107

1. A
2. B
3. C
4. B
5. C
6. A
7. C
8. C
9. A
10. B
11. C
12. A
13. C
14. A
15. B
16. C
17. A
18. C
19. C
20. A
21. B
22. D
23. A
24. D
25. C
26. A
27. C
28. A
29. C
30. B
31. C
32. B
33. A
34. C
35. A
36. B

Part C: Coding and Memory

Memory Section

The second section of Part C, called Memory Section, is composed of four segments, which are as follows:

Segment 1: You'll have 3 minutes to memorize the Coding Guide.

Segment 2: You have 1 1/2 minutes to memorize the Coding Guide and answer the questions. There are 8 questions to be answered. Since this part of the test is not counted or scored, you may just answer 2 or 3 questions. Instead, use the 1 1/2 minutes allowed to this part of the test in memorizing the Coding Guide.

Segment 3: This part of the test gives you 5 minutes to memorize the guide. There are no questions to be answered on this part of the exam.

Segment 4: This is the part that is important. You have 7 minutes to answer 36 questions, without any Coding Guide to look at. You must answer the questions from memory. Also, you must mark the circles for your answers on the official answer sheet, (not on the sample answer sheet on the question page).

As you can see, you have a total of 9 1/2 minutes to memorize the Coding Guide. That's enough time in memorizing the same code. As you may remember, you also have 3 1/2 minutes time to memorize the Coding Guide on the Coding Section of Part C Test.

For **Strategies for Coding-Memory Test,** see page 87-92.

Part C - Coding & Memory
Practice Test #1

Segment 1 of Memory Section

Instructions

Segment 1 of the Memory Section test gives you 3 minutes to memorize the Coding Guide. There will be no questions to be answered. Memorize the guide using the techniques mentioned in Chapter 15: **Strategies for the Coding-Memory Test** on pages 87-92. This same Coding Guide is used throughout this Practice 1 of this Coding and Memory Test. Now, memorize the Coding Code on the next page.

Part C: Coding & Memory
Segment 1 of Memory Section

Coding Guide	
Address Rage	Delivery Route
10 - 299 SW **2nd** St 300 - 399 **Sun**set Dr 1 - 2498 ***Wet***son Rd	A
300 - 899 SW **2nd** St 600 - 999 ***Pine*** Ridge Dr	B
200 - 1399 ***Shot***gun Rd **400** - 899 **Sun**set Dr 1 - 1099 S ***Pros***pect Ter	C
All mail that doesn't fall in one of the address ranges listed above	D

You must memorize the address ranges to be assigned to delivery routes, marked **A, B, C,** and **D.** In the above example, any address from 300 - 399 **Sun**set is assigned to Delivery Route "A." Any address from 400 to 899 **Sun**set, is assigned to Delivery Route "B."

To memorize the address ranges on SW **2nd** which are 10 - 299 SW **2nd** (Route A) and 300 - 899 SW **2nd**, make the number **300** as the boundary between Route A and Route B. Thus, any address from 10 to 299 SW 2nd belongs to Route A. And, any address from 300 to 899 is assigned to Route B.

To remember the address ranges on **Sun**set which are 300 - 399 **Sun**set (Route A) and **400** - 899 **Sun**set (Route C)**,** make the number **400** as the boundary between Routes A and C. Any address from 300 to under 400 **Sun**set is assigned to Route A.Then any address from 400 to 899 **Sun**set is assigned to Route C.

If there's an address such as 450 **Sun**set *(between* 400 and 899 Sunset), the mail goes to Delivery Route "C." And the list goes on and on.

With regard to addresses that are not extended to another route, such as, 1 - 2498 **Wet**son; 600 - 999 **Pine** Ridg; 200 - 1399 **Shot**gun; and 1 - 1099 S. **Pros**pect, just remember the four addresses ranges as belonging to ***WetPineShotPros,*** (combination of **Wet**son (Route 1), **Pine** Ridge (Route B, **Shot**gun (Route C) and S **Pros**pect (Route C). Each of the address ranges consists addresses in a single route. The problem with this strategy is, you'll miss the "D" answers. Any mall that doesn't fall in one of the address ranges listed above is assigned to Route D). Of course, if you can memorize the address ranges, then it's good for you.

Part C: Coding and Memory
Segment 2 of Memory Section

Instructions

Segment 2 of the Memory Section has 8 questions to be answered in 1 1/2 minutes. Of course, you can't look at the Coding Guide. You have to answer the questions from memory. Since this part of the test is not scored, you can just answer 2 or three questions. Instead, use the time to memorize the guide. You have to mark your answers at the bottom of the sample question page, not on the official answer sheets.

For Segment 2 of the Coding Section, which serves as a practice test, turn the next page.

Part C: Coding and Memory
Practice Test 1

Segment 2 of Memory Section

Questions

Address	Delivery Route	Answers
1. 597 S Prospect Ter	A B C D	1. ___
2. 650 Sunset Dr	A B C D	2. ___
3. 2500 Wetson Rd	A B C D	3. ___
4. 900 Sunset Dr	A B C D	4. ___
5. 499 SW 2nd St	A B C D	5. ___
6. 2298 Wetson Rd	A B C D	6. ___
7. 288 SW 2nd St	A B C D	7. ___
8. 870 Pine Ridge Dr	A B C D	8. ___

Sample Answer Sheet

1. (A) (B) (C) (D)

2. (A) (B) (C) (D)

3. (A) (B) (C) (D)

4. (A) (B) (C) (D)

5. (A) (B) (C) (D)

6. (A) (B) (C) (D)

7. (A) (B) (C) (D)

8. (A) (B) (C) (D)

The correct answers are 1-C; 2-C; 3-D; 4-D; 5- B; 6-A; 7-A and 8-B

Part C: Coding and Memory
Segment 3 of Memory Section

Instructions

On Segment 3 of the Memory Section test, you have 5 minutes to memorize the address ranges and routes of the Coding Guide. See it on the next page. There will be no questions to be answered during this memorization period. For the next test, (Segment 4) you don't have to look at the Coding Guide. In other words, you have to answer the questions from memory.

Part C: Coding & Memory
Segment 3 of Memory Section

Coding Guide	
Address Rage	Delivery Route
10 - 299 SW **2nd** St 300 - 399 **Sun**set Dr 1 - 2498 **Wet**son Rd	A
300 - 899 SW **2nd** St 600 - 999 **Pine** Ridge Dr	B
200 - 1399 **Shot**gun Rd **400** - 899 **Sun**set Dr 1 - 1099 S **Pros**pect Ter	C
All mail that doesn't fall in one of the address ranges listed above	D

There are several ways of remembering the above address ranges in different boxes assigned to the delivery routes, **A, B, C,** and **D.** We should create so-called **extract codes** to easily remember the above addresses.

The address coding guide is as follows:

10 - **300** - 899 SW **2nd** (Routes A & B)
300 - **400** - 899 **Sun**set (Routes A & C)
1 - 2498 **Wet**son (Route A)
600 - 999 **Pine** Ridge (Route B)
200 - 1399 **Shot**gun (Route C)
1 - 1099 S **Pros**pect (Route C)

Usually, an address range ends with the number "98" or "99." or with the number 00. For the purpose of short cutting, you may eliminate the numbers 98, 99, and 00 in remembering the addresses, if you wish. It's just understood that the numbers are there.

Part C: Coding and Memory

Segment 4 of Memory Section

Instructions

Segment 4 of the Memory Section is the real test. This part is scored and the score adds to your total Test 473 score. You will have 36 questions to be answered in 7 minutes. You should mark the answers on the official answer sheet. Segment 4 of the Memory Section prohibits you from looking at the Coding Guide. You have to answer the questions from memory.

Part C: Coding and Memory
Practice Test 1

Segment 4 of Memory Section

Questions

Address	Delivery Route				Answers
1. 399 Sunset Dr	A	B	C	D	1. ___
2. 1400 Shotgun Rd	A	B	C	D	2. ___
3. 799 Sunset Dr	A	B	C	D	3. ___
4. 690 SW 2nd St	A	B	C	D	4. ___
5. 2000 Wetson Rd	A	B	C	D	5, ___
6. 379 Sunset Dr	A	B	C	D	6. ___
7. 89 S Prospect Ter	A	B	C	D	7. ___
8. 49 Wetson Rd	A	B	C	D	8. ___
9. 1000 Pine Ridge Dr	A	B	C	D	9. ___
10. 170 SW 2nd St	A	B	C	D	10. ___
11. 389 Sunset Dr	A	B	C	D	11. ___
12. 150 SW 2nd St	A	B	C	D	12. ___
13. 1199 Shotgun Rd	A	B	C	D	13. ___
14. 950 Sunset Dr	A	B	C	D	14. ___
15. 198 Wetson Rd	A	B	C	D	15. ___
16. 299 Sunset Dr	A	B	C	D	16. ___
17. 850 Pine Ridge Dr	A	B	C	D	17. ___
18. 89 S Prospect Ter	A	B	C	D	18. ___

Part C: Coding and Memory
Practice Test 1
Continuation

Segment 4 of Memory Section

Questions

Address	Delivery Route				Answers
19. 95 S Prospect Ter	A	B	C	D	19. ___
20. 2398 Wetson Rd	A	B	C	D	20. ___
21. 490 Pine Ridge Dr	A	B	C	D	21. ___
22. 199 SW 2nd St	A	B	C	D	22. ___
23. 1200 S Prospect Ter	A	B	C	D	23. ___
24. 1200 Wetson Rd	A	B	C	D	24. ___
25. 299 Sunset Dr	A	B	C	D	25. ___
26. 799 Sunset Dr	A	B	C	D	26. ___
27. 2199 Wetson Rd	A	B	C	D	27. ___
28. 56 S Prospect Ter	A	B	C	D	28. ___
29. 780 SW 2nd St	A	B	C	D	29. ___
30. 301 Sunset Dr	A	B	C	D	30. ___
31. 450 S Prospect Ter	A	B	C	D	31. ___
32. 899 Pine Ridge Dr	A	B	C	D	32. ___
33. 900 Sunset Dr	A	B	C	D	33. ___
34. 89 Wetson Rd	A	B	C	D	34. ___
35. 699 SW 2nd St	A	B	C	D	35. ___
36. 1000 Pine Ridge Dr	A	B	C	D	36. ___

See the answers to the above questions on the next page

Part C: Coding & Memory

Memory Section

Answers to Questions
Practice Test 1

Segment 4 of Memory Section, p. 118-119

1. A
2. D
3. C
4. B
5. A
6. A
7. C
8. A
9. D
10. A
11. A
12. A
13. C
14. D
15. A
16. D
17. B
18. C
19. C
20. A
21. D
22. A
23. D
24. A
25. D
26. C
27. A
28. C
29. B
30. A
31. C
32. B
33. D
34. A
35. B
36. D

Practice Test 2
Part C - Coding & Memory

Coding Section

The first section of the Part C Test, called Coding Section, actually consists of three segments:

Segment 1: You are given 2 minutes within which to study or memorize the Coding Guide. Also, you have to answer four items as a practice test. Since this is not counted, you may answer only one question and use the time in mcmorizing the code. You are allowed to look at the Coding Guide as you answer the questions. The same Coding Guide will be used throughout the Coding and Memory tests.

Segment 2: You'll be given 1 1/2 minutes to answer 8 questions on this part of the test. Since this is not scored, you may answer only 2 or 3 questions. You better use the time in memorizing the coding guide.

Segment 3: You have 6 minutes to answer 36 questions. This part of the test is scored or counted. You'll still be allowed to look at the coding guide as you answer the questions. You must mark the circles on the official answer sheet.

When you work on the first section, Coding, of the test, you are allowed to look at the coding guide while you are assigning codes, (A, B, C, and D), to each item of the addresses. However, when you work on the second section (memory), you won't be allowed to look at the coding guide. In other words, memorize the coding guide.

Part C - Coding & Memory

Segment 1 of Coding Section

Instructions

Segment 1 of the Coding Section test is a 2-minute exercise for memorizing the Coding Guide to be used in answering the questions on this test. Also, you have these 2 minutes to answer 4 questions. Since this part of the test is not scored, you should not work on all of the questions. Just memorize the guide using the techniques mentioned in Chapter 18: **Strategies for the Coding-Memory Test** on pages 87-92. Turn the page to see the Coding Guide.

Part C: Coding & Memory

Segment 2 of Coding Section

Coding Guide	
Address Range	Delivery Route
601 - 1299 **Chrys**ler Dr 800 - 999 **De**cator St 85 - 2499 *Bir*wood Rd	A
1300 - 1599 **Chrys**ler Dr 12601 - 13599 *Black*stone St	B
1 - 1299 *Clair*mont St **1000** - 2999 **De**cator St 1 - 1399 *Wood*ward Ave	C
All mail that doesn't fall in one of the address ranges listed above	D

There are several ways of remembering the above address ranges in different boxes assigned to the delivery routes, **A, B, C,** and **D.** We should create so-called **extract codes** to easily remember the above addresses. You may combine the **first syllables** of the streets.

The codes may be created (from top to bottom) as **ChrysDeBir** for **Chrys**ler, **De**cator and **Bir**wood. For the second box, it should be **ChrysBlack** for **Chrys**ler and **Black**stone. For the third box it should be **ClairDeWood** for **Clair**mont, **De**cator and **Wood**ward. Disregard the Dr, St, Ave, etc.

To remember the address ranges on 601 - 1299 **Chrys**ler (Route A) and 1300 - 1599 **Chrys**ler (Route B), make the number **1300** as the boundary between Routes A and B. Any address *from* 601 to 1299 **Chrys**ler is assigned to Route A and any address from 1300 - 1599 Chrysler is covered by Route B.

To memorize the address ranges on 800 - 999 **De**cator (Route A) and 1000 - 2999 **De**cator (Route C), make the number **1000** as the boundary between Route A and Route C. That is, any address from 800 to 999 **De**cator belongs to Route A. And, of course, any address from 1000 to 2999 **De**cactor belongs to Route C.

Part C: Coding and Memory
Practice Test 2

Segment 1 of Coding Section

Questions

Address	Delivery Route			
1. 1199 Chrysler Dr	A	B	C	D
2. 1011 Decator St	A	B	C	D
3. 1299 Birwood Rd	A	B	C	D
4. 590 Woodward Ave	A	B	C	D

Sample Answer Sheet

1. (A) (B) (C) (D)

2. (A) (B) (C) (D)

3. (A) (B) (C) (D)

4. (A) (B) (C) (D)

The correct answers are 1-A; 2-C; 3-A; and 4-C.

Part C: Coding and Memory
Segment 2 of Coding Section

Instructions

Segment 2 of the Coding Section has 8 questions to be answered in 1 1/2 minutes. Of course, you can look at the Coding Guide. Since this part of the test is not scored, you can just answer 2 or 3 questions, then use the time to memorize the guide. You have to mark your answers at the bottom of the sample question page, not on the official answer sheets.

For Segment 2 of the Coding Section, which serves as a practice test, turn the page.

Part C: Coding & Memory

Segment 2 of Coding Section

Coding Guide	
Address Range	Delivery Route
601 - 1299 **Chrys**ler Dr 800 - 999 **De**cator St 85 - 2499 *Bir*wood Rd	A
1300 - 1599 **Chrys**ler Dr 12601 - 13599 *Black*stone St	B
1 - 1299 *Clair*mont St 1000 - 29*99* **De**cator *St* *1 - 1399* **Wood**ward Ave	C
All mail that doesn't fall in one of the address ranges listed above	D

You must memorize the address ranges to be assigned to delivery routes, marked **A, B, C,** and **D.** In the above example, *all* numbers from 601 - 1299 **Chrys**ler, are assigned to Delivery Route "A." Any address from 1300 - 1599 **Chrys**ler is assigned to Route "B."

To memorize the address ranges on **Chrys**ler which are 601 - 1299 **Chrys**ler and 1300 - 1599 **Chrys**ler, make the number **1300** as the boundary between Route A and Route B Thus, any address from 601 to 1299 Chrysler is covered by Route A. And, any address from 1300 to 1599 **Chrys**ler is assigned to Route B.

To remember the address ranges on **De**cator, which are 800 - 999 **De**cator (Route A) and **1000** - 2999 **De**cator (Route C; make the number **1000** as the boundary between Routes A and C. Any address from 800 to 999 **De**cator is assigned to Route A. Then, any address from 1000 to 2999 Decator is assigned to Route C.

If there's an address such as 700 (between 601 and 1299 **Chry**sler, the mail goes to Delivery Route "A." And the list goes on and on.

With regard to addresses that are not extended to another route, such as, 85 - 2499 **Bir**wood, 12601 - 13599 **Black**stone, 1 - 1299 **Clair**mont, and 1 - 1399 **Wood**ward, just remember the four addresses ranges as belonging to ***BirBlackClairWood,*** (combination of **Bir**wood (Route 1), **Black**stone ((Route B) **Clair**mont and **Wood**ward (Route C). Each of the address ranges consists of addresses in a single route. The problem with this strategy is, you'll miss the "D" answers. But of course, you may try to memorize the address ranges.

Part C: Coding & Memory
Practice Test 2

Segment 2 of Coding Section

Questions

Address	Delivery Route				Answers
1. 3000 Decator St	A	B	C	D	1. ___
2. 1199 Chrysler Dr	A	B	C	D	2. ___
3. 1100 Clairmont St	A	B	C	D	3. ___
4. 96 Woodward Ave	A	B	C	D	4. ___
5. 12900 Blackstone St	A	B	C	D	5. ___
6. 59 Woodward Ave	A	B	C	D	6. ___
7. 3002 Decator St	A	B	C	D	7. ___
8. 1500 Birwood Rd	A	B	C	D	8. ___

Sample Answer Sheet

1. Ⓐ Ⓑ Ⓒ Ⓓ

2. Ⓐ Ⓑ Ⓒ Ⓓ

3. Ⓐ Ⓑ Ⓒ Ⓓ

4. Ⓐ Ⓑ Ⓒ Ⓓ

5. Ⓐ Ⓑ Ⓒ Ⓓ

6. Ⓐ Ⓑ Ⓒ Ⓓ

7. Ⓐ Ⓑ Ⓒ Ⓓ

8. Ⓐ Ⓑ Ⓒ Ⓓ

The correct answers are 1-D; 2-A; 3-C; 4-C; 5-B; 6-C; 7-D; and 8-A.

Part C: Coding and Memory

Segment 3 of Coding Section

Instructions

Segment 3 of the Coding Section, Practice Test 1 has 36 questions to be answered in 6 minutes. You can still look at the Coding Guide. It's the real test, therefore, this part of the test is scored. In other words, correct answers are counted. Answer the questions in 6 minutes. You have to mark your answers on the official answer sheets.

For Segment 3 of the Coding Section, go to the next page.

Part C: Coding and Memory

Segment 3 of Coding Section

Coding Guide	
Address Range	Delivery Route
601 - 1299 Chrysler Dr 800 - 999 Decator St 85 - 2499 Birwood Rd	A
1300 - 1599 Chrysler Dr 12601 - 13599 Blackstone St	B
1 - 1299 Clairmont St 1000 - 2999 Decator St 1 - 1399 Woodward Ave	C
All mail that doesn't fall in one of the address ranges listed above	D

Part C: Coding and Memory
Practice Test 2

Segment 3 of Coding Section

Questions

Address	Delivery Route	Answers
1. 1199 Chrysler Dr	A B C D	1. ___
2. 1400 Woodward Ave	A B C D	2. ___
3. 2299 Birwood Rd	A B C D	3. ___
4. 955 Chrysler Dr	A B C D	4. ___
5. 12900 Blackstone St	A B C D	5. ___
6. 95 Clairmont St	A B C D	6. ___
7. 950 Woodward Ave	A B C D	7. ___
8. 1500 Chrysler Dr	A B C D	8. ___
9. 1298 Woodward Ave	A B C D	9. ___
10. 899 Decator St	A B C D	10. ___
11. 2197 Birwood Rd	A B C D	11. ___
12. 759 Decator St	A B C D	12. ___
13. 1198 Clairmont St	A B C D	13. ___
14. 2398 Birwood Rd	A B C D	14. ___
15. 1159 Decator St	A B C D	15. ___
16. 1300 Chrysler Dr	A B C D	16. ___
17. 12700 Blackstone St	A B C D	17. ___
18. 1500 Birwood Rd	A B C D	18. ___

Practice Test 2
Part C: Coding and Memory
Continuation

Segment 3 of Coding Section

Coding Guide	
Address Range	Delivery Route
601 - 1299 Chrysler Dr 800 - 999 Decator St 85 - 2499 Birwood Rd	A
1300 - 1599 Chrysler Dr 12601 - 13599 Blackstone St	B
1 - 1299 Clairmont St 1000 - 2999 Decator St 1 - 1399 Woodward Ave	C
All mail that doesn't fall in one of the address ranges listed above	D

Part C: Coding and Memory
Practice Test 2
Continuation

Segment 3 of Coding Section

Questions

Address	Delivery Route				Answers
19. 11599 Blackstone St	A	B	C	D	19. ___
20. 1298 Woodward Ave	A	B	C	D	20. ___
21. 95 Birwood Rd	A	B	C	D	21. ___
22. 2897 Decator St	A	B	C	D	22. ___
23. 1499 Chrysler Dr	A	B	C	D	23. ___
24. 12599 Blackstone St	A	B	C	D	24. ___
25. 2798 Decator St	A	B	C	D	25. ___
26. 59 Woodward Ave	A	B	C	D	26. ___
27. 1399 Chrysler Dr	A	B	C	D	27. ___
28. 12798 Blackstone St	A	B	C	D	28. ___
29. 79 Clairmont St	A	B	C	D	29. ___
30. 1199 Chrysler Dr	A	B	C	D	30. ___
31. 900 Decator St	A	B	C	D	31. ___
32. 95 Woodward Ave	A	B	C	D	32. ___
33. 2500 Birwood Rd	A	B	C	D	33. ___
34. 12909 Blackstone St	A	B	C	D	34. ___
35. 89 Clairmont St	A	B	C	D	35. ___
36. 890 Woodward Ave	A	B	C	D	36. ___

See the answers to the above questions on the next page.

Part C: Coding & Memory

Coding Section

Answers to Questions
Practice Test 2

Segment 3 of Coding Section, 133-135

1. A
2. D
3. A
4. A
5. B
6. C
7. C
8. B
9. C
10. A
11. A
12. D
13. C
14. A
15. C
16. B
17. B
18. A
19. D
20. C
21. A
22. C
23. B
24. B
25. C
26. C
27. B
28. B
29. C
30. A
31. A
32. C
33. D
34. B
35. C
36. C

Practice Test 2
Part C: Coding and Memory

Memory Section

The second section of Part C, called Memory Section, is composed of four segments, which are as follows:

Segment 1: You'll have 3 minutes to memorize the Coding Guide.

Segment 2: You have 1 1/2 minutes to memorize the Coding Guide and answer the questions. There are 8 questions to be answered. Since this part of the test is not counted or scored, you may just answer 2 or 3 questions. Instead, use the 1 1/2 minutes allowed to this part of the test in memorizing the Coding Guide.

Segment 3. This part of the test gives you 5 minutes to memorize the guide. There are no questions to be answered on this part of the exam.

Segment 4: This is the segment that is scored or counted. You have 7 minutes to answer 36 questions, without any Coding Guide to look at. You must answer the questions from memory. Also, you must mark the circles for your answers on the official answer sheet, not on the sample answer sheet on the question page.

As you can see, you have a total of 9 1/2 minutes to memorize the Coding Guide. That's enough time in memorizing the code. As you may remember, you also have 3 1/2 minutes time to memorize the Coding Guide on the Coding Section of Part C Test.

For **Strategies for Coding-Memory Test,** see pages 85-90.

Part C: Coding and Memory

Segment 1 of Memory Section

Instructions

Segment 1 of the Memory Section test gives you 3 minutes to memorize the Coding Guide. There will be no questions to be answered. Memorize the guide using the techniques mentioned in Chapter 15: **Strategies for the Coding-Memory Test** on pages 87-92. This same Coding Guide is used throughout this Practice 1 of this Coding and Memory Test. Now, memorize the Coding Code on the next page.

Part C: Coding and Memory

Segment 2 of Memory Section

Coding Guide	
Address Range	Delivery Route
601 - 1299 **Chrys**ler Dr 800 - 999 **De**cator St 85 - 2499 **Bir**wood Rd	A
1300 - 1599 **Chrys**ler Dr 12601 - 13599 **Black**stone St	B
1 - 1299 **Clair**mont St **1000** - 2999 **De**cator St 1 - 1399 **Wood**ward Ave	C
All mail that doesn't fall in one of the address ranges listed above	D

There are several ways of remembering the above address ranges in different boxes assigned to the delivery routes, **A, B, C,** and **D.** We should create so-called **extract codes** to easily remember the above addresses.

The address coding guide is as follows:

601 - **1300** - 1599 **Chrys**ler (Routes A & B)
800 - **1000** - 2999 **De**cator (Routes A & C)
85 - 2499 **Bir**wood (Route A)
12601 - 13599 **Black**stone (Route B)
1 - 1299 **Clair**mont (Route C)
1 - 1399 **Wood**ward (Route C)

Usually, an address range ends with the number "98" or "99", or with the number "00". For the purpose of short cutting, you may eliminate the numbers 98, 99, and 00 in remembering them, if you wish. It's just understood that the numbers are there.

Part C: Coding and Memory

Segment 2 of Memory Section

Instructions

Segment 2 of the Memory Section has 8 questions to be answered in 1 1/2 minutes. Of course, you can't look at the Coding Guide. You have to answer the questions from memory. Since this part of the test is not scored, you can just answer 2 or 3 questions. Instead, use the time to memorize the guide. You have to mark your answers at the bottom of the sample question page, not on the official answer sheets.

For Segment 2 of the Coding Section, which serves as a practice test, turn the next page.

Part C: Coding and Memory
Practice Test 2

Segment 2 of Memory Section

Questions

Address	Delivery Route				Answers
1. 1200 Woodward Ave	A	B	C	D	1. ___
2. 1399 Chrysler Dr	A	B	C	D	2. ___
3. 2499 Decator St	A	B	C	D	3. ___
4. 99 Clairmont St	A	B	C	D	4. ___
5. 1500 Birwood Rd	A	B	C	D	5. ___
6. 99 Clairmont St	A	B	C	D	6. ___
7. 870 Decator St	A	B	C	D	7. ___
8. 1600 Chrysler Dr	A	B	C	D	8. ___

Sample Answer Sheet

1. Ⓐ Ⓑ Ⓒ Ⓓ

2. Ⓐ Ⓑ Ⓒ Ⓓ

3. Ⓐ Ⓑ Ⓒ Ⓓ

4. Ⓐ Ⓑ Ⓒ Ⓓ

5. Ⓐ Ⓑ Ⓒ Ⓓ

6. Ⓐ Ⓑ Ⓒ Ⓓ

7. Ⓐ Ⓑ Ⓒ Ⓓ

8. Ⓐ Ⓑ Ⓒ Ⓓ

The correct answers are: 1-C; 2-B; 3-C; 4-C; 5-A; 6-C; 7-A; and 8-D.

Part C: Coding and Memory

Segment 3 of Memory Section

Instructions

On Segment 3 of the Memory Section test, you have 5 minutes to memorize the address ranges and routes of the Coding Guide. See it on the next page. There will be no questions to be answered during this memorization period. For the next test, (Segment 4) you don't have to look at the Coding Guide. In other words, you have to answer the questions from memory.

Part C: Coding & Memory

Segment 3 of Memory Section

Coding Guide	
Address Range	Delivery Route
601 - 1299 **Chrys**ler Dr 800 - 999 **De**cator St 85 - 2499 **Bir**wood Rd	A
1300 - 1599 **Chrys**ler Dr 12601 - 13599 **Black**stone St	B
1 - 1299 **Clair**mont St **1000** - 2999 **De**cator St 1 - 1399 **Wood**ward Ave	C
All mail that doesn't fall in one of the address ranges listed above	D

There are addresses that start with the number 1; for instance, two of the above address ranges: 1 - 12**99** Clairmont and 1 - 13**99** Woodward. In the case of these addresses, you must just remember the addresses 1299 Clairmont and 1399 Wooodward, forgetting about the number 1. In other words, the address 1299 Clairmont and the addresses below it are assigned to Route C, and the address 1399 Woodward and the addressses below it are also covered by Route C. All address above the two addresses, 1299 Clairmont and 1399 Wooodward, are covered by Route D. Why? Because all mail matters that don't fall in one of the address ranges as listed above are assigned to Route D.

Furthermore, associate the numbers 1299 and 1399 to places or things you are familiar with. For example, you may remember 1299 in this way: you have 12 years of schooling, and you graduated in college in 1999. You may remember 1399 as the model of your HP computer or whatever. You may associate the numbers to other significant events in your life. Use your imagination.

Part C: Coding and Memory

Segment 4 of Memory Section

Instructions

Segment 4 of the Memory Section is the real test. This part is scored and the score adds to your total Test 473 score. You will have 36 questions to be answered in 7 minutes. You should mark the answers on the official answer sheet. Segment 4 of the Memory Section prohibits you from looking at the Coding Guide. You have to answer the questions from memory.

Part C: Coding and Memory
Practice Test 2

Segment 4 of Memory Section

Questions

Address	Delivery Route				Answers
1. 1299 Clairmont St	A	B	C	D	1. ___
2. 14000 Blackstone St	A	B	C	D	2. ___
3. 45 Clairmont St	A	B	C	D	3. ___
4. 1500 Decator St	A	B	C	D	4. ___
5. 1200 Birwood Rd	A	B	C	D	5. ___
6. 14000 Blackstone St	A	B	C	D	6. ___
7. 750 Chrysler Dr	A	B	C	D	7. ___
8. 1400 Birwood Rd	A	B	C	D	8. ___
9. 1100 Clairmont St	A	B	C	D	9. ___
10. 89 Woodward Ave	A	B	C	D	10. ___
11. 1300 Chrysler Dr	A	B	C	D	11. ___
12. 1499 Birwood Rd	A	B	C	D	12. ___
13. 3000 Decator St	A	B	C	D	13. ___
14. 12900 Blackstone St	A	B	C	D	14 ___
15. 2300 Birwood Rd	A	B	C	D	15. ___
16. 1000 Decator St	A	B	C	D	16. ___
17. 70 Woodward Ave	A	B	C	D	17. ___
18. 1350 Chrysler Dr	A	B	C	D	18. ___

Part C: Coding and Memory
Practice Test 2
Continuation

Segment 4 of Memory Section

Questions

Address	Delivery Route				Answers
19. 1199 Chrysler Dr	A	B	C	D	19. ___
20. 14000 Blackstone St	A	B	C	D	20. ___
21. 59 Woodward Ave	A	B	C	D	21. ___
22. 1400 Chrysler Dr	A	B	C	D	22. ___
23. 95 Birwood Rd	A	B	C	D	23. ___
24. 881 Decator St	A	B	C	D	24. ___
25. 85 Clairmont St	A	B	C	D	25. ___
26. 2285 Birwood Rd	A	B	C	D	26. ___
27. 87 Woodward Ave	A	B	C	D	27. ___
28. 2288 Birwood Rd	A	B	C	D	28. ___
29. 1200 Decator St	A	B	C	D	29. ___
30. 99 Clairmont St	A	B	C	D	30. ___
31. 1100 Chrysler Dr	A	B	C	D	31. ___
32. 2398 Birwood Rd	A	B	C	D	32. ___
33. 12700 Blackstone St	A	B	C	D	33. ___
34. 801 Decator St	A	B	C	D	34. ___
35. 1100 Woodward Ave	A	B	C	D	35. ___
36. 95 Birwood Rd	A	B	C	D	36. ___

For answer to the above items, turn the page.

Part C: Coding & Memory
Memory Section

Answers to Questions
Practice Test 2

Segment 4 of Memory Section, 146-147

1. C
2. D
3. C
4. C
5. A
6. D
7. A
8. A
9. C
10. C
11. B
12. A
13. D
14. B
15. A
16. C
17. C
18. B
19. A
20. D
21. C
22. B
23. A
24. A
25. C
26. A
27. C
28. A
29. C
30. C
31. A
32. A
33. B
34. A
35. C
36. A

Practice Test 3
Part C: Coding and Memory

Coding Section

The first section of the Part C Test, called Coding Section, actually consists of three parts:

Segment 1: You are given 2 minutes within which to study or memorize the Coding Guide. Also, you have to answer four items as a practice test. Since this is not counted, you may answer only one question and use the time in memorizing the code. You are allowed to look at the Coding Guide as you answer the questions. The same Coding Guide will be used throughout the Coding and Memory tests.

Segment 2: You'll be given 1 1/2 minutes to answer 8 questions on this part of the test. Since this is not scored, you may answer only 2 or 3 questions. You better use the time in memorizing the coding guide.

Segment 3: You have 6 minutes to answer 36 questions. This part of the test is scored or counted. You must mark the circles on the official answer sheet. You'll still be allowed to look at the coding guide as you answer the items.

When you work on the first section, Coding, of the test, you are allowed to look at the coding guide while you are assigning delivery routes, (A, B, C, and D), to each address range. However, when you work on the second section (memory), you won't be allowed to look at the coding guide. In other words, memorize the coding guide.

Part C: Coding and Memory

Segment 1 of Coding Section

Instructions

Segment 1 of the Coding Section test is a 2-minute exercise for memorizing the Coding Guide to be used in answering the questions on this test. Also, you have these 2 minutes to answer 4 questions. Since this part of the test is not scored, you should not work on all of the questions. Just memorize the guide using the techniques mentioned in Chapter 18: **Strategies for the Coding-Memory Test** on pages 87-92. Turn the page to see the Coding Guide.

Part C: Coding and Memory

Segment 1 of Coding Section

Coding Guide	
Address Range	Delivery Route
50 - 1799 **Clark** St 100 - 1499 **Wal**ter Jetton Blvd 2800 - 3098 **Wash**ington St	A
1800 - 2999 **Clark** St 300 - 3099 **Staff**ord St	B
1 - 2299 **Lar**go Rd 100 - 4899 **East**lawn St **1500 -** 1999 **Wal**ter Jetton Blvd	C
All mail that doesn't fall in one of the address ranges listed above	D

You must memorize the address ranges to be assigned to delivery routes, marked **A, B, C,** and **D.** In the above example, any address from 50 - 1799 **Clark** is designated to Delivery Route "A." Any address from 1800 - 2999 **Clark** is assigned to Route "B."

To memorize the address ranges on **Clark** which are 50 - 1799 **Clark** (Route A) and 1800 - 2999 **Clark** (Route B), make the number **1800** as the dividing line between Route A and Route B. Thus, any address from 50 to 1799 **Clark** belongs to Route A. And, any address from 1800 to 2999 Clark is assigned to Route B.

To remember the address ranges on **Wal**ter, which are 100 - 1499 **Wal**ter (Route A) and **1500** - 1999 **Wal**ter (Route C, make the number **1500** as the boundary between Routes A and C. Any address to 100 to 1499 **Wal**ter Jetton is assigned to Route A. Then, any address from 1500 to 1999 **Wal**ter is covered by Route C.

If there's an address such as 71 (between 50 and 1800 **Clark**, the mail goes to Delivery Route "A." And the list goes on and on.

With regard to addresses that are not extended to another route, such as, 2800 - 3098 **Wash**ington; 300 - 3099 **Staff**ord; 1 - 2299 **Lar**go; and 100 - 4899 **East**lawn, just remember the four addresses ranges as belonging to **WashStaffLarEast,** (combination of **Wash**ington (Route 1), **Staff**ord ((Route B) and **Lar**go and **East**lawn. (Route C). Each of the address ranges consists of addresses in a single route. The problem with this strategy is, you'll miss the "D" answers. But of course, you may try to memorize the address ranges.

Any address outside the address ranges is assigned to Route D.

Part C: Coding and Memory
Practice Test 3

Segment 1 of Coding Section

Questions

Address	Delivery Route			
1. 80 Clark St	A	B	C	D
2. 3599 Eastlawn St	A	B	C	D
3. 1500 Stafford St	A	B	C	D
4. 4000 Washington St	A	B	C	D

Sample Answer Sheet

1. (A)(B)(C)(D)

2. (A)(B)(C)(D)

3. (A)(B) (C) (D)

4. (A)(B) (C)(D)

The correct answers are: 1-A; 2-C; 3-B, & 4-D.

Part C: Coding and Memory

Segment 2 of Coding Section

Instructions

Segment 2 of the Coding Section has 8 questions to be answered in 1 1/2 minutes. Of course, you can look at the Coding Guide. Since this part of the test is not scored, you can just answer 2 or 3 questions, then use the time to memorize the guide. You have to mark your answers at the bottom of the sample question page, not on the official answer sheets.

For Segment 2 of the Coding Section, which serves as a practice test, turn the page.

Part C: Coding and Memory

Segment 2 of Coding Section

Coding Guide	
Address Range	Delivery Route
50 - 1799 **Clark** St 100 - 1499 **Wal**ter Jetton Blvd 2800 - 3098 **Wash**ington St	A
1800 - 2999 *Clark St* *300 - 3099 **Staff**ord St*	B
1 - 2299 *Lar*go Rd 100 - 4899 **East**lawn St **1500 -** 1999 **Wal**ter Jetton Blvd	C
All mail that doesn't fall in one of the address ranges listed above	D

There are several ways of remembering the above address ranges in different boxes assigned to the delivery routes, **A, B, C,** and **D.** We should create so-called **extract codes** to easily remember the above addresses.

The address coding guide is as follows:

50 - **1800** - 2999 **Clark** (Routes A & B)
100 - **1500** - 1999 **Wal**ter Jetton (Routes A & C)
2800 - 3098 **Wash**ington (Route A)
300 - 3099 S**taff**ord (Route B)
1 - 2299 **Lar**go (Route C)
100 - 4899 **East**lawn (Route C)

Usually, an address range ends with a "98" or "99." or with a   "00." For the purpose of short cutting, you may eliminate the 98, 99, and 00 in remembering the addresses, if you wish. It's just understood that the numbers are there.

Part C: Coding and Memory
Practice Test 3

Segment 2 of Coding Section

Questions

	Address	Delivery Route				Answers
1.	2000 Walter Jetton Blvd	A	B	C	D	1. ___
2.	1650 Clark St	A	B	C	D	2. ___
3.	1099 Largo Rd	A	B	C	D	3. ___
4.	1889 Walter Jetton Blvd	A	B	C	D	4. ___
5.	2995 Stafford St	A	B	C	D	5. ___
6.	2889 Washington St	A	B	C	D	6. ___
7.	4809 Eastlawm St	A	B	C	D	7. ___
8.	79 Largo Rd	A	B	C	D	8. ___

Sample Answer Sheet

1. Ⓐ Ⓑ Ⓒ Ⓓ
2. Ⓐ Ⓑ Ⓒ Ⓓ
3. Ⓐ Ⓑ Ⓒ Ⓓ
4. Ⓐ Ⓑ Ⓒ Ⓓ
5. Ⓐ Ⓑ Ⓒ Ⓓ
6. Ⓐ Ⓑ Ⓒ Ⓓ
7. Ⓐ Ⓑ Ⓒ Ⓓ
8. Ⓐ Ⓑ Ⓒ Ⓓ

The correct answers are: 1-D; 2-A; 3-C; 4-C; 5-B; 6-A; 7-C; & 8-C.

Part C: Coding and Memory

Segment 3 of Coding Section

Instructions

Segment 3 of the Coding Section, Practice Test 1 has 36 questions to be answered in 6 minutes. You can still look at the Coding Guide. It's the real test, therefore, this part of the test is scored. In other words, correct answers are counted. Answer the questions in 6 minutes. You have to mark your answers on the official answer sheets.

For Segment 3 of the Coding Section, go to the next page.

Part C: Coding and Memory
Segment 3 of Coding Section

Coding Guide	
Address Range	Delivery Route
50 - 1799 Clark St 100 - 1499 Walter Jetton Blvd 2800 - 3098 Washington St	A
1800 - 2999 Clark St 300 - 3099 Stafford St	B
1 - 2299 Largo Rd 100 - 4899 Eastlawn St 1500 - 1999 Walter Jetton Blvd	C
All mail that doesn't fall in one of the address ranges listed above	D

Part C: Coding and Memory
Practice Test 3

Segment 3 of Coding Section

Questions

Address	Delivery Route				Answers
1. 870 Walter Jetton Blvd	A	B	C	D	1. ___
2. 4999 Eastlawn St	A	B	C	D	2. ___
3. 2000 Largo Rd	A	B	C	D	3. ___
4. 3100 Stafford St	A	B	C	D	4. ___
5. 1550 Largo Rd	A	B	C	D	5. ___
6. 1900 Walter Jetton Blvd	A	B	C	D	6. ___
7. 2098 Washington St	A	B	C	D	7. ___
8. 75 Largo Rd	A	B	C	D	8. ___
9. 2095 Walter Jetton Blvd	A	B	C	D	9. ___
10 1800 Clark St	A	B	C	D	10. ___
11. 500 Eastlawn St	A	B	C	D	11. ___
12. 1759 Clark St	A	B	C	D	12. ___
13. 670 Eastlawn St	A	B	C	D	13. ___
14. 1300 Walter Jetton Blvd	A	B	C	D	14. ___
15. 90 Largo Rd	A	B	C	D	15. ___
16. 4000 Washington St	A	B	C	D	16. ___
17. 900 Stafford St	A	B	C	D	17. ___
18. 799 Eastlawn St	A	B	C	D	18. ___

Part C: Coding and Memory

Segment 3 of Coding Section

Coding Guide	
Address Range	Delivery Route
50 - 1799 Clark St 100 - 1499 Walter Jetton Blvd 2800 - 3098 Washington St	A
1800 - 2999 Clark St 300 - 3099 Stafford St	B
1 - 2299 Largo Rd 100 - 4899 Eastlawn St 1500 - 1999 Walter Jetton Blvd	C
All mail that doesn't fall in one of the address ranges listed above	D

Part C: Coding and Memory
Practice Test 3
Continuation

Segment 3 of Coding Section

Questions

	Address	Delivery Route				Answers
19.	1900 Walter Jetton Blvd	A	B	C	D	19. ___
20.	1699 Clark St	A	B	C	D	20. ___
21.	2189 Largo Rd	A	B	C	D	21. ___
22.	2000 Walter Jetton Blvd	A	B	C	D	22. ___
23.	3100 Washington St	A	B	C	D	23. ___
24.	3789 Eastlawn St	A	B	C	D	24. ___
25.	2299 Stafford St	A	B	C	D	25. ___
26.	3030 Clark St	A	B	C	D	26. ___
27.	1900 Largo Rd	A	B	C	D	27. ___
28.	2998 Washington St	A	B	C	D	28. ___
29.	2050 Walter Jetton Blvd	A	B	C	D	29. ___
30.	4000 Stafford St	A	B	C	D	30. ___
31.	2199 Largo Rd	A	B	C	D	31. ___
32.	4000 Washington St	A	B	C	D	32. ___
33.	5000 Eastlawn St	A	B	C	D	33. ___
34.	2999 Clark St	A	B	C	D	34. ___
35.	1400 Walter Jetton Blvd	A	B	C	D	35. ___
36.	2998 Washington St	A	B	C	D	36. ___

See the answers to the above questions on the next page.

Part C: Coding & Memory

Coding Section

Answers to Questions
Practice Test 3

Segment 3 of Coding Section, p. 161-163

1. A
2. D
3. C
4. D
5. C
6. C
7. D
8. C
9. D
10. B
11. C
12. A
13. C
14. A
15. C
16. D
17. B
18. C
19. C
20. A
21. C
22. D
23. D
24. C
25. B
26. D
27. C
28. A
29. D
30. D
31. C
32. D
33. D
34. B
35. A
36. A

Part C: Coding and Memory
Practice Test 3

Memory Section

The second section of Part C, called Memory Section, is composed of four parts, which are as follows:

Segment 1: You'll have 3 minutes to memorize the Coding Guide.

Segment 2: You have 1 1/2 minutes to memorize the Coding Guide and answer the questions. There are 8 questions to be answered. Since this part of the test is not counted or scored, you may just answer 2 or 3 questions. Instead, use the 1 1/2 minutes allowed to this part of the test in memorizing the Coding Guide.

Segment 3. This part of the test gives you 5 minutes to memorize the guide. There are no questions to be answered on this part of the exam.

Segment 4: This is the part that counts. You have 7 minutes to answer 36 questions, without any Coding Guide to look at. You must answer the questions from memory. Also, you must mark the circles for your answers on the official answer sheet, not on the sample answer sheet on the question page.

As you can see, you have a total of 9 1/2 minutes to memorize the Coding Guide. That's enough time in memorizing the same code. As you may remember, you also have 3 1/2 minutes time to memorize the Coding Guide on the Coding Section of Part C Test.

For **Strategies for Coding-Memory Test,** see pages 85-90.

Part C: Coding and Memory

Segment 1 of Memory Section

Instructions

Segment 1 of the Memory Section test gives you 3 minutes to memorize the Coding Guide. There will be no questions to be answered. Memorize the guide using the techniques mentioned in Chapter 15: **Strategies for the Coding-Memory Test** on pages 87-92. This same Coding Guide is used throughout this Practice 1 of this Coding and Memory Test. Now, memorize the Coding Code on the next page.

Part C: Coding and Memory

Segment 1 of Memory Section

Coding Guide	
Address Range	Delivery Route
50 - 1799 **Clark** St 100 - 1499 **Wal**ter Jetton Blvd 2800 - 3098 **Wash**ington St	A
1800 - 2999 **Clark** St 300 - 3099 **Staff**ord St	B
1 - 2299 **Lar**go Rd 100 - 4899 **East**lawn St **1500** - 1999 **Wal**ter Jetton Blvd	C
All mail that doesn't fall in one of the address ranges listed above	D

You must memorize the address ranges to be assigned to delivery routes, marked **A, B, C,** and **D.** In the above example, any address from 50 - 1799 **Clark**, is covered by Delivery Route "A." And any address from 1800 - 2999 **Clark** is assigned to Route "B."

To memorize the address ranges on **Clark** which are 50 - 1799 **Clark** (Route A) and 1800 - 2999 **Clark** (Route B). make the number 1800 as the boundary between Route A and Route B. Thus, any address from 50 to 1799 **Clark** belongs to Route A. And, any address from 1800 to 2999 Clark is assigned to Route B.

To remember the address ranges on **Wal**ter, which are 100 - 1499 **Wal**ter (Route A) and **1500** - 1999 **Wal**ter (Route C) make the number **1500** as the boundary between Routes A and C. Any address from 100 to 1499 Walter is assigned to Route A. Then, any address from 1500 to 1999 **Wal**ter is assigned to Route C.

If there's an address such as *71 (*between 50 and 1800 **Clark)**, the mail goes to Delivery Route "A." And the list goes on and on.

With regard to addresses that are not extended to another route, such as, 2800 - 3098 **Wash**ington; 300 - 3099 **Staff**ord; 1 - 2299 **Lar**go; and 100 - 4899 **East**lawn, just remember the four addresses as belonging to *WashStaffLarEast,* (combination of **Wash**ington (Route 1), **Staff**ord ((Route B) and **Lar**go and **East**lawn. (Route C). Each of the address ranges consists of addresses in a single route. The problem with this strategy is, you'll miss the "D" answers. (But of course, you may try to memorize the address ranges.)

All numbers outside the address ranges are assigned to Route D.

Part C: Coding and Memory

Segment 2 of Memory Section

Instructions

Segment 2 of the Memory Section has 8 questions to be answered in 1 1/2 minutes. Of course, you can't look at the Coding Guide. You have to answer the questions from memory. Since this part of the test is not scored, you can just answer 2 or three questions. Instead, use the time to memorize the guide. You have to mark your answers at the bottom of the sample question page, not on the official answer sheets.

For Segment 2 of the Coding Section, which serves as a practice test, turn the next page.

Part C: Coding and Memory
Practice Test 3

Segment 2 of Memory Section

Questions

Address	Delivery Route				Answers
1. 2290 Walter Jetton Blvd	A	B	C	D	1. ___
2. 1995 Clark St	A	B	C	D	2. ___
3. 1595 Walter Jetton Blvd	A	B	C	D	3. ___
4. 750 Stafford St	A	B	C	D	4. ___
5. 2950 Washington St	A	B	C	D	5. ___
6. 50 Largo Rd	A	B	C	D	6. ___
7. 1699 Clark St	A	B	C	D	7. ___
8. 600 Eastlawn St	A	B	C	D	8. ___

Sample Answer Sheet

1. Ⓐ Ⓑ Ⓒ Ⓓ

2. Ⓐ Ⓑ Ⓒ Ⓓ

3. Ⓐ Ⓑ Ⓒ Ⓓ

4. Ⓐ Ⓑ Ⓒ Ⓓ

5. Ⓐ Ⓑ Ⓒ Ⓓ

6. Ⓐ Ⓑ Ⓒ Ⓓ

7. Ⓐ Ⓑ Ⓒ Ⓓ

8. Ⓐ Ⓑ Ⓒ Ⓓ

The correct answers are: 1-D; 2-B; 3-C; 4-B; 5-A; 6-C; 7-A; & 8-C

Part C: Coding and Memory

Segment 3 of Memory Section

Instructions

On Segment 3 of the Memory Section test, you have 5 minutes to memorize the address ranges and routes of the Coding Guide. See it on the next page. There will be no questions to be answered during this memorization period. For the next test, (Segment 4) you don't have to look at the Coding Guide. In other words, you have to answer the questions from memory.

Part C: Coding and Memory

Segment 3 of Memory Section

Coding Guide	
Address Range	Delivery Route
50 - 1799 **Clark** St 100 - 1499 **Wal**ter Jetton Blvd 2800 - 3098 **Wash**ington St	A
1800 - 2999 **Clark** St 300 - 3099 Stafford St	B
1 - 2299 **Lar**go Rd 100 - 4899 **East**lawn St **1500** - 1999 **Wal**ter Jetton Blvd	C
All mail that doesn't fall in one of the address ranges listed above	D

There are addresses that start with the number 1; for instance, one of the above address ranges: 1 - 2299 **Lar**go. In the case of this address, you may just remember 2299 **Lar**go, *forgetting about the number 1*. In other words, the address 2299 **Lar**go and addresses below it are assigned to Route C. And any address above it is covered by Route D. Why? Because any mail that doesn't fall in one of the address ranges as listed above is assigned to Route D.

Furthermore, associate the number 2299 to places or things you are familiar with. For example, you may remember 2299 in this way: you have 22 years of living in the United States, and you went home to the Philippines for the first time in 1999. You may remember 2299 as the model of your HP computer or whatever. You may associate the numbers to other significant events in your life. Use your imagination!

Part C: Coding and Memory

Segment 4 of Memory Section

Instructions

Segment 4 of the Memory Section is the real test. This part is scored and the score adds to your total Test 473 score. You will have 36 questions to be answered in 7 minutes. You should mark the answers on the official answer sheet. Segment 4 of the Memory Section prohibits you from looking at the Coding Guide. You have to answer the questions from memory.

Part C: Coding and Memory
Practice Test 3

Segment 4 of Memory Section

Questions

Address	Delivery Route				Answers
1. 951 Stafford St	A	B	C	D	1. ___
2. 399 Walter Jetton Blvd	A	B	C	D	2. ___
3. 487 Eastlawn St	A	B	C	D	3. ___
4. 2999 Washington St	A	B	C	D	4. ___
5. 2800 Clark St	A	B	C	D	5. ___
6. 80 Largo Rd	A	B	C	D	6. ___
7. 2000 Walter Jetton Blvd	A	B	C	D	7. ___
8. 2997 Stafford St	A	B	C	D	8. ___
9. 289 Stafford St	A	B	C	D	9. ___
10. 4890 Eastlawn St	A	B	C	D	10. ___
11. 1700 Walter Jetton Blvd	A	B	C	D	11. ___
12. 4799 Eastlawn St	A	B	C	D	12. ___
13. 49 Clark St	A	B	C	D	13. ___
14 400 Stafford St	A	B	C	D	14. ___
15. 2900 Washington St	A	B	C	D	15. ___
16. 2300 Eastlawn St	A	B	C	D	16. ___
17 1398 Walter Jetton Blvd	A	B	C	D	17. ___
18. 95 Clark St	A	B	C	D	18. ___

Part C: Coding and Memory
Practice Test 3
Continuation

Segment 4 of Memory Section

Questions

Address	Delivery Route				Answers
19. 3500 Washington St	A	B	C	D	19. ___
20. 395 Stafford St	A	B	C	D	20. ___
21. 89 Largo Rd	A	B	C	D	21. ___
22. 129 Walter Jetton Blvd	A	B	C	D	22. ___
23. 47 Clark St	A	B	C	D	23. ___
24. 2000 Walter Jetton Blvd	A	B	C	D	24. ___
25. 19 Largo Rd	A	B	C	D	25. ___
26. 50 Clark St	A	B	C	D	26. ___
27. 3198 Eastlawn St	A	B	C	D	27. ___
28. 500 Stafford St	A	B	C	D	28. ___
29. 3199 Clark St	A	B	C	D	29. ___
30. 2905 Washington St	A	B	C	D	30. ___
31. 180 Clark St	A	B	C	D	31. ___
32. 3000 Walter Jetton Blvd	A	B	C	D	32. ___
33. 1500 Clark St	A	B	C	D	33. ___
34 300 Eastlawn St	A	B	C	D	34. ___
35. 2596 Stafford St	A	B	C	D	35. ___
36. 85 Largo Rd	A	B	C	D	36. ___

See the answers to the above questions on the next page.

Part C: Coding & Memory

Memory Section

Answers to Questions
Practice Test 3

Segment 4 of Memory Section, p. 174-175

1. B
2. A
3. C
4. A
5. B
6. C
7. D
8. B
9. D
10. C
11. C
12. C
13. D
14. B
15. A
16. C
17. A
18. A
19. D
20. B
21. C
22. A
23. D
24. D
25. C
26. A
27. C
28. B
29. D
30. A
31. A
32. D
33. A
34. C
35. B
36. C

Practice Test 4
Part C: Coding and Memory

Coding Section

The first section of the Part C Test, called Coding Section, actually consists of three segments:

Segment 1: You are given 2 minutes within which to study or memorize the Coding Guide. Also, you have to answer four items as a practice test. Since this is not counted, you may answer only one question and use the time in mcmorizing the code. You are allowed to look at the Coding Guide as you answer the questions. The same Coding Guide will be used throughout the Coding and Memory tests.

Segment 2: You'll be given 1 1/2 minutes to answer 8 questions on this part of the test. Since this is not scored, you may answer only 2 or 3 questions. You better use the time in memorizing the coding guide.

Segment 3: You have 6 minutes to answer 36 questions. This part of the test is scored or counted. You must mark the circles on the official answer sheet.

When you work on the first section, Coding, of the test, you are allowed to look at the Coding Guide while you are assigning address ranges to delivery routes, (A, B, C, and D). However, when you work on the second section (memory), you won't be allowed to look at the Coding Guide. In other words, memorize the coding guide.

Part C: Coding and Memory

Segment 1 of Coding Section

Instructions

Segment 1 of the Coding Section test is a 2-minute exercise for memorizing the Coding Guide to be used in answering the questions on this test. Also, you have these 2 minutes to answer 4 questions. Since this part of the test is not scored, you should not work on all of the questions. Just memorize the guide using the techniques mentioned in Chapter 18: **Strategies for the Coding-Memory Test** on pages 87-92. Turn the page to see the Coding Guide.

Part C: Coding and Memory

Segment 1 of Coding Section

Coding Guide	
Address Range	Delivery Route
20 - 899 **Has**ting St 1- 799 **Far**well Dr 6000 - 10099 **High** St	A
900 - 1899 **Has**ting St 201 - 900 **Lum**ber St	B
1- 500 **Lau**rel St **800** - 999 **Far**well Dr 81 - 2000 **High**way 41 N	C
All mail that doesn't fall in one of the address ranges listed above	D

You must memorize the address ranges to be assigned to delivery routes, marked **A, B, C,** and **D.** In the above example, any address from 20 - 899 **Has**ting is covered by Delivery Route "A." Any address from 900 - 1899 **Has**ting is assigned to Route "B."

To memorize the address ranges on **Has**ting which are 20 - 899 Hasting (Route A) and 900 - 1899 **Has**ting (Route B). make the number **900** as the boundary between Route A and Route B (eliminating 1899 **Has**ting). Thus, any address from 20 to 899 belongs to Route A. And, any address from 900 - 1899 Hasting is covered by Route B.

To remember the address ranges on 1 - 799 **Far**well (Route A), and 800 - 999 **Far**well, (Route C) make the number **800** as the boundary between Routes A and C. Any address from 1 and 799 **Far**well is assigned to Route A. Then, any address from 800 to 999 **Far**well, is covered by Route C.

If there's an address such as 70 (between 1 and 800 **Far**well), the mail goes to Delivery Route "A." And the list goes on and on.

With regard to **addresses** that are not extended to another route, such as, 6000 - 10099 **High;** 201 - 900 **Lum**ber; and 1- 500 **Lau**rel and 81 - 2000 **High**way 41, just remember the four addresses ranges as belonging to **HighLumLauHigh** (combination of **High** (Route A), **Lum**ber (Route B) and **Lau**rel and **High**way **41** (Route C). Each of the address ranges consists of addresses in a single route. The problem with this strategy is, you'll miss the "D" answers. But of course, you may try to memorize all the address ranges.

All addresses outside the address ranges are assigned to Route D.

Part C: Coding and Memory
Practice Test 4

Segment 1 of Coding Section

Questions

Address	Delivery Route			
1. 37 Hasting St	A	B	C	D
2. 22 Laurel St	A	B	C	D
3. 300 Farwell Dr	A	B	C	D
4. 1997 Highway 41 N	A	B	C	D

Sample Answer Sheet

1. Ⓐ Ⓑ Ⓒ Ⓓ

2. Ⓐ Ⓑ Ⓒ Ⓓ

3. Ⓐ Ⓑ Ⓒ Ⓓ

4. Ⓐ Ⓑ Ⓒ Ⓓ

The correct answers are: 1-A; 2-C; 3-A; & 4-C.

Part C: Coding and Memory

Segment 2 of Coding Section

Instructions

Segment 2 of the Coding Section has 8 questions to be answered in 1 1/2 minutes. Of course, you can look at the Coding Guide. Since this part of the test is not scored, you can just answer 2 or 3 questions, then use the time to memorize the guide. You have to mark your answers at the bottom of the sample question page, not on the official answer sheets.

For Segment 2 of the Coding Section, which serves as a practice test, turn the page.

Part C: Coding and Memory

Segment 2 of Coding Section

Coding Guide	
Address Range	Delivery Route
20 - 899 **Has**ting St 1 - 799 **Far**well Dr 6000 - 10099 ***High*** St	A
900 - 1899 **Has**ting St 201 - 900 ***Lum***ber St	B
1 - 500 ***Lau***rel St **800** - 999 **Far**well Dr 81 - 2000 ***High***way 41 N	C
All mail that doesn't fall in one of the address ranges listed above	D

There are several ways of remembering the above address ranges in different boxes assigned to the delivery routes, **A, B, C,** and **D.** We should create so-called **extract codes** to easily remember the above addresses. You may combine the **first syllables** of the streets.

The address coding guide is as follows:

20 - **900** - 1899 **Has**ting (Routes A & B)
1 - **800** - 999 **Far**well (Routes A & C)
6000 - 10099 **High** (Route A)
201 - 900 **Lum**ber (Route B)
1 - 500 **Lau**rel (Route C)
81 - 2000 **High**way 41 N (Route C)

Usually, an address range ends with a "98" or "99." or with a "00." For the purpose of short cutting, you may eliminate the 98, 99, and 00 in remembering them, if you wish. It's just understood that the numbers are there.

Part C: Coding and Memory
Practice Test 4

Segment 2 of Coding Section

Questions

Address	Delivery Route				Answers
1. 90 Farwell Dr	A	B	C	D	1. __
2. 278 Hasting St	A	B	C	D	2. __
3. 395 Laurel St	A	B	C	D	3. __
4. 295 Highway 41 N	A	B	C	D	4. __
5. 38 Farwell Dr	A	B	C	D	5. __
6. 231 Laurel St	A	B	C	D	6. __
7. 2001 Highway 41 N	A	B	C	D	7. __
8. 899 Lumber St	A	B	C	D	8. __

Sample Answer Sheet

1. Ⓐ Ⓑ Ⓒ Ⓓ

2. Ⓐ Ⓑ Ⓒ Ⓓ

3. Ⓐ Ⓑ Ⓒ Ⓓ

4. Ⓐ Ⓑ Ⓒ Ⓓ

5. Ⓐ Ⓑ Ⓒ Ⓓ

6. Ⓐ Ⓑ Ⓒ Ⓓ

7. Ⓐ Ⓑ Ⓒ Ⓓ

8. Ⓐ Ⓑ Ⓒ Ⓓ

The correct answers are: 1-A; 2-A; 3-C; 4-C; 5-A; 6-C; 7-D; and 8-B

Part C: Coding and Memory

Segment 3 of Coding Section

Instructions

Segment 3 of the Coding Section, Practice Test 1 has 36 questions to be answered in 6 minutes. You can still look at the Coding Guide. It's the real test, therefore, this part of the test is scored. In other words, correct answers are counted. Answer the questions in 6 minutes. You have to mark your answers on the official answer sheets.

For Segment 3 of the Coding Section, go to the next page.

Part C: Coding and Memory

Segment 3 of Coding Section

Coding Guide	
Address Range	Delivery Route
20 - 899 Hasting St 1 - 799 Farwell Dr 6000 - 10099 High St	A
900 - 1899 Hasting St 201 - 900 Lumber St	B
1 - 500 Laurel St 800 - 999 Farwell Dr 81 - 2000 Highway 41 N	C
All mail that doesn't fall in one of the address ranges listed above	D

Part C: Coding and Memory
Practice Test 4

Segment 3 of Coding Section

Questions

Address	Delivery Route				Answers
1. 801 Farwell Dr	A	B	C	D	1. ___
2. 6700 High St	A	B	C	D	2. ___
3. 299 Lumber St	A	B	C	D	3. ___
4. 800 Laurel St	A	B	C	D	4. ___
5. 1998 Hasting St	A	B	C	D	5. ___
6. 899 Farwell Dr	A	B	C	D	6. ___
7. 701 Lumber St	A	B	C	D	7. ___
8. 1788 Hasting St	A	B	C	D	8. ___
9. 1800 Highway 41 N	A	B	C	D	9. ___
10. 750 Farwell Dr	A	B	C	D	10. ___
11. 1501 Highway 41 N	A	B	C	D	11. ___
12. 1999 Hasting St	A	B	C	D	12. ___
13. 801 Farwell Dr	A	B	C	D	13. ___
14. 786 Lumber St	A	B	C	D	14. ___
15. 901 Farwell Dr	A	B	C	D	15. ___
16. 10100 High St	A	B	C	D	16. ___
17. 899 Lumber St	A	B	C	D	17. ___
18. 2001 Highway 41 N	A	B	C	D	18. ___

Part C: Coding and Memory

Segment 3 of Coding Section

Coding Guide	
Address Range	Delivery Route
20 - 899 Hasting St 1 - 799 Farwell Dr 6000 - 10099 High St	A
900 - 1899 Hasting St 201 - 900 Lumber St	B
1 - 500 Laurel St 800 - 999 Farwell Dr 81 - 2000 Highway 41 N	C
All mail that doesn't fall in one of the address ranges listed above	D

Part C: Coding and Memory
Practice Test 4
Continuation

Segment 3 of Coding Section

Questions

Address	Delivery Route				Answers
19. 223 Hasting St	A	B	C	D	19. ___
20. 9000 High St	A	B	C	D	20. ___
21. 2002 Highway 41 N	A	B	C	D	21. ___
22. 801 Lumber St	A	B	C	D	22. ___
23. 699 Farwell Dr	A	B	C	D	23. ___
24. 2010 Highway 41 N	A	B	C	D	24. ___
25. 778 Lumber St	A	B	C	D	25. ___
26. 800 Hasting St	A	B	C	D	26. ___
27. 400 Laurel St	A	B	C	D	27. ___
28. 476 Farwell Dr	A	B	C	D	28. ___
29. 1799 Hasting St	A	B	C	D	29. ___
30. 21 Laurel St	A	B	C	D	30. ___
31. 11500 High St	A	B	C	D	31. ___
32. 94 Highway 41 N	A	B	C	D	32. ___
33. 1999 Hasting St	A	B	C	D	33. ___
34. 300 Lumber St	A	B	C	D	34. ___
35. 27 Hasting St	A	B	C	D	35. ___
36. 1500 Highway 41 N	A	B	C	D	36. ___

See the answers to the above questions on the next page.

Part C: Coding & Memory

Coding Section

Answers to Questions
Practice Test 4

Segment 3 of Coding Section, p. 189-191

1. C
2. A
3. B
4. D
5. D
6. C
7. B
8. B
9. C
10. A
11. C
12. D
13. C
14. B
15. C
16. D
17. B
18. D
19. A
20. A
21. D
22. B
23. A
24. D
25. B
26. A
27. C
28. A
29. B
30. C
31. D
32. C
33. D
34. B
35. A
36. C

Practice Test 4
Part C: Coding and Memory

Memory Section

The second section of Part C, called Memory Section, is composed of four parts or segments, which are as follows:

Segment 1: You'll have 3 minutes to memorize the Coding Guide.

Segment 2: You have 1 1/2 minutes to memorize the Coding Guide and answer the questions. There are 8 questions to be answered. Since this part of the test is not counted or scored, you may just answer 2 or 3 questions. Instead, use the 1 1/2 minutes allowed to this part of the test in memorizing the Coding Guide.

Segment 3. This segment is a 5-minute study time to memorize the guide. There are no questions to be answered on this part of the exam.

Segment 4: This is the part that counts. You have 7 minutes to answer 36 questions, without any Coding Guide to look at. You must answer the questions from memory. Also, you must mark the circles for your answers on the official answer sheet.

As you can see, you have a total of 9 1/2 minutes to memorize the Coding Guide. That's enough time in memorizing the same code. As you may remember, you also have 3 1/2 minutes time to memorize the Coding Guide on the Coding Section of Part C Test.

For **Strategies for Memory Section Test,** see pages 87-92.

Part C: Coding and Memory

Segment 1 of Memory Section

Instructions

Segment 1 of the Memory Section test gives you 3 minutes to memorize the Coding Guide. There will be no questions to be answered. Memorize the guide using the techniques mentioned in Chapter 15: **Strategies for the Coding-Memory Test** on pages 87-92. This same Coding Guide is used throughout this Practice 1 of this Coding and Memory Test. Now, memorize the Coding Code on the next page.

Part C: Coding and Memory

Segment 1 of Memory Section

Coding Guide	
Address Range	Delivery Route
20 - 899 **Has**ting St 1 - 799 **Far**well Dr 6000 - 10099 *High* St	A
900 - 1899 **Has**ting St 201 - 900 *Lum*ber St	B
1 - 500 *Lau*rel St **800** - 999 **Far**well Dr 81 - 2000 *High*way 41 N	C
All mail that doesn't fall in one of the address ranges listed above	D

There are several ways of remembering the above address ranges in different boxes assigned to the delivery routes, **A, B, C,** and **D.** We should create so-called **extract codes** to easily remember the above addresses. You may combine the **first syllables** of the streets.

The address coding guide is as follows:

20 - **900** - 1899 **Has**ting (Routes A & B)
1 - **800** - 999 **Far**well (Routes A & C)
6000 - 10099 **High** (Route A)
201 - 900 **Lum**ber (Route B)
1 - 500 **Lau**rel (Route C)
81 - 2000 **High**way 41 N (Route C)

Usually, an address range ends with a "98" or "99." or with a   "00." For the purpose of short cutting, you may eliminate the 98, 99, and 00 in remembering the address, if you wish. It's just understood that the numbers are there.

Part C: Coding and Memory

Segment 2 of Memory Section

Instructions

Segment 2 of the Memory Section has 8 questions to be answered in 1 1/2 minutes. Of course, you can't look at the Coding Guide. You have to answer the questions from memory. Since this part of the test is not scored, you can just answer 2 or three questions. Instead, use the time to memorize the guide. You have to mark your answers at the bottom of the sample question page, not on the official answer sheets.

For Segment 2 of the Coding Section, which serves as a practice test, turn the next page.

Part C: Coding and Memory
Practice Test 4

Segment 2 of Memory Section

Questions

Address	Delivery Route				Answers
1. 36 Hasting St	A	B	C	D	1. ___
2. 600 Laurel St	A	B	C	D	2. ___
3. 1599 Highway 41 N	A	B	C	D	3. ___
4. 351 Lumber St	A	B	C	D	4. ___
5. 81 Farwell Dr	A	B	C	D	5. ___
6. 6100 High St	A	B	C	D	6. ___
7. 1900 Hasting St	A	B	C	D	7. ___
8. 59 Laurel St	A	B	C	D	8. ___

Sample Answer Sheet

1. Ⓐ Ⓑ Ⓒ Ⓓ

2. Ⓐ Ⓑ Ⓒ Ⓓ

3. Ⓐ Ⓑ Ⓒ Ⓓ

4. Ⓐ Ⓑ Ⓒ Ⓓ

5. Ⓐ Ⓑ Ⓒ Ⓓ

6. Ⓐ Ⓑ Ⓒ Ⓓ

7. Ⓐ Ⓑ Ⓒ Ⓓ

8. Ⓐ Ⓑ Ⓒ Ⓓ

The correct answers are: 1-A; 2-D; 3-C; 4-B; 5-A; 6-A; 7-D; and 8-C.

Part C: Coding and Memory

Segment 3 of Memory Section

Instructions

On Segment 3 of the Memory Section test, you have 5 minutes to memorize the address ranges and routes of the Coding Guide. See it on the next page. There will be no questions to be answered during this memorization period. For the next test, (Segment 4) you don't have to look at the Coding Guide. In other words, you have to answer the questions from memory.

Part C: Coding and Memory

Segment 3 of Memory Section

Coding Guide	
Address Range	Delivery Route
20 - 899 Hasting St 1 - 799 Farwell Dr 6000 - 10099 High St	A
900 - 1899 Hasting St 201 - 900 Lumber St	B
1 - 500 Laurel St 800 - 999 Farwell Dr 81 - 2000 Highway 41 N	C
All mail that doesn't fall in one of the address ranges listed above	D

Part C: Coding and Memory

Segment 4 of Memory Section

Instructions

Segment 4 of the Memory Section is the real test. This part is scored and the score adds to your total Test 473 score. You will have 36 questions to be answered in 7 minutes. You should mark the answers on the official answer sheet. Segment 4 of the Memory Section prohibits you from looking at the Coding Guide. You have to answer the questions from memory.

Part C: Coding and Memory Practice Test 4

Segment 4 of Memory Section

Questions

Address	Delivery Route				Answers
1. 801 Lumber St	A	B	C	D	1. ___
2. 899 Farwell Dr	A	B	C	D	2. ___
3. 7000 High St	A	B	C	D	3. ___
4. 1000 Highway 41 N	A	B	C	D	4. ___
5. 11099 High St	A	B	C	D	5. ___
6. 87 Highway 41 N	A	B	C	D	6. ___
7. 1599 Hasting St	A	B	C	D	7. ___
8. 650 Farwell Dr	A	B	C	D	8. ___
9. 401 Laurel St	A	B	C	D	9. ___
10. 1000 Farwell Dr	A	B	C	D	10. ___
11. 395 Lumber St	A	B	C	D	11. ___
12. 798 Hasting St	A	B	C	D	12. ___
13. 491 Laurel St	A	B	C	D	13. ___
14. 1050 Lumber St	A	B	C	D	14. ___
15. 50 Laurel St	A	B	C	D	15. ___
16. 1777 Hasting St	A	B	C	D	16. ___
17. 1700 Highway 41 N	A	B	C	D	17. ___
18. 1070 Farwell Dr	A	B	C	D	18. ___

Part C: Coding and Memory
Practice Test 4
Continuation

Segment 4 of Memory Section
Continuation

Questions

Address		Delivery Route				Answers
19. 800 Farwell Dr	A	B	C	D		19. ___
20. 2001 Highway 41 N	A	B	C	D		20. ___
21. 900 Lumber St	A	B	C	D		21. ___
22. 590 Laurel St	A	B	C	D		22. ___
23. 651 Farwell Dr	A	B	C	D		23. ___
24. 1999 Hasting St	A	B	C	D		24. ___
25. 600 Laurel St	A	B	C	D		25. ___
26. 95 Highway 41 N	A	B	C	D		26. ___
27. 10100 High St	A	B	C	D		27. ___
28. 401 Lumber St	A	B	C	D		28. ___
29. 1001 Farwell Dr	A	B	C	D		29. ___
30. 1700 Hasting St	A	B	C	D		30. ___
31. 50 Laurel St	A	B	C	D		31. ___
32. 801 Farwell Dr	A	B	C	D		32. ___
33. 899 Hasting St	A	B	C	D		33. ___
34. 901 Lumber St	A	B	C	D		34. ___
35. 995 Farwell Dr	A	B	C	D		35. ___
36. 7000 High St	A	B	C	D		36. ___

See the answers to the above questions on the next page.

Part C: Coding & Memory

Memory Section

Answers to Questions
Practice Test 4

Segment 4 of Memory Section, p. 202-203

1. B
2. C
3. A
4. C
5. D
6. C
7. B
8. A
9. C
10. D
11. B
12. A
13. C
14. D
15. C
16. B
17. C
18. D
19. C
20. D
21. B
22. D
23. A
24. D
25. D
26. C
27. D
28. B
29. D
30. B
31. C
32. C
33. A
34. D
35. C
36. A

17

Part D. Inventory of Personal

Characteristics And Experiences

Part B that involves **inventory of personal experiences and characteristics** contains 236 test items to be finished in 90 minutes. That's one and a half hours of evaluating personal characteristics, experiences, tendencies or feelings as related to doing work as an employee of the United States Postal Service.

This portion of the test is divided into three sections. Each section contains several items with response choices. For instance, the **first section** may contain items with response choices, such as "Strongly Agree" to "Strongly Disagree". The **second section** may have items with four response choices, from "Very" Often" to "Rarely or Never". And the **third section** may consist of items with four to nine response choices.

Strategies for Answering the Part D Test Questions

There are several strategies for answering the Part D Test questions. Here are some of them:

■ **No correct or wrong answers? Really?** On the Part D Test, some postal book reviewer say that there are no correct and wrong answers. But we must realize that strictly speaking, on any test, especially on multiple-choice exams, there should be one "best" answer among several questions. In the case of the Part D Test, you have to choose the "best' or "most appropriate" answer that will evaluate your personality. That is, the test is intended to measure your reactions to certain work situations.

■ **Figure out the correct way of answering the questions.** The questions, which are actually statements, as stated above, ask the test taker to select the best or most appropriate answer.

■ You should just answer the statements "honestly" or "truthfully" based on your opinions, ideas, feelings, preferences, personality, and experiences.

■ Don't create an ideal personality profile that is most likely appropriate for a particular job. Just be consistent in your answers. Nobody knows how the U.S. Postal Service scores the Part D: Inventory of Personal Characteristics and Experiences test. And you must remember that personality questionnaires are administered by trained staff, and they know how to trick test takers.

■ Memorize the 3 segments of the test. Remember that the segments of the Part D Test are 1. Agree/Disagree Section, 2. Frequency Section, and 3. Experience Section.

■ **Use your common sense.** As stated, there are no correct or incorrect answers. Just base your answer on how you may reflect your feelings based on your own personal characteristics and experiences that may relate to what's happening in a Postal work setting. Or you may mark the answer that may reflect what your reactions will be to certain situations in the work place such as dealings with other Postal workers. In other words, you are psychologically tested in evaluating what will be your opinions on·and reactions to certain situational cases.

■ **Use your imagination.** Imagine what you may do in a certain situations in the Postal work setting, and think what your opinion will be on any issue. Just imagine how you would describe yourself to a postal interviewer or official.

■ **Be positive.** When you describe yourself, don't present a profile that is too good to be true. But don't be too hard on yourself, either. Just be yourself, and select the best answer that reflect your opinions or feelings on a certain work situation. Or how you would react in dealings with fellow employees in a work setting.

■ **Be Aware of the time allotted to answer the questions.** You must remember that you are given 90 minutes to answer 236 items. So you need answer the items within the alloted time, averaging between 2 and 3 items per minute.

■ **Be aware of confusing words.** In the Experience part of the test, the answer choices usually contain words, such as *most* or *least, like* or *dislike,* and *do* or *don't.* So beware of the items that contains confusing double negatives, such as, *prefer the least, dislike the most,* and *don't dislike.* They can give you trouble.

■ **Read carefully the answer choices in the Experience segment of the Part D Test.** Certain questions may contain any of the following answer choices, usually appearing as the last response choice.:

None of the above
All of the above
Two of the above
Two or more of the above
Not sure

Usually, when you can't figure out the "best" answer, you may just pick the answer choice that contains these words:

Not sure.

However, as in any other multiple-choice test, beware of answer choices that contain the words, *all, only, never, always, none, etc.* Generally, they are not the correct or best answer.

In narrowing down your answer choice to a single best or most appropriate one, do the following:

Single out first the 2 inappropriate answers. In other words, cross out first the answer choices that you think are definitely not the best answers, until you reach the point of having only 2 possible most appropriate answers. These last 2 answer choices, may have similar in meaning. So be careful in selecting the best one.

Sample Questions: Part D
Personal Characteristics and Experience Inventory

Although there should be no practice test for the Part D: test, I would like to familiarize you with the types of questions you may encounter on this part of the test. Of course, you will be given different questions during the test.

Here are some sample questions:

I. Agree/Disagree Section

1. You do not like other workers to intervene in your work.
A. Strongly Agree
B. Agree
C. Disagree
D. Strongly Disagree

2. Family problems should not be discussed in the work place.

A. Strongly Agree
B. Agree
C. Disagree
D. Strongly Disagree

II. Frequency Section

1. You schedule your work ahead of time.

A. Very Often
B. Often
C. Sometimes
D. Rarely

2. There should be a division of labor in the work place, doing your own things.

A. Very often
B. Often
C. Sometimes
D. Rarely

III. Experience Section

1. What type of work do you like best?

A. Work that requires physical efforts.
B. Work that needs stretching of hands and feet.
C. Work that requires you doing your own while sitting or standing.
D. Doing the same work every day.
E. Would not mind doing any of these.
F. Not sure

2. What type of work do you like the least?

A. Work that requires a lot of time standing.
B. Work that requires a lot of time sitting down.
C. Work that needs too much concentration
D. Doing the same tasks every day.
E. Doesn't care doing any of these.
F. Not sure

460 RCA Examination

Test for Rural Carrier Associate Applicants

The 460 Examination is a test for Rural Carrier Associate applicants. The rural carrier associates are substitutes of regular rural carriers serving the remote areas of the United States.

Regular rural carriers mostly come from the ranks of rural carrier associates who take Exam 460. That is, rural carrier associates, who substitute during vacations or absences of regular or permanent rural carriers, are promoted to the positions of regular carriers when positions become available due to retirement, death, or transfer of regular rural carriers.

Exam 460 covers the following parts:

Part A: Address Checking
Part B: Memory for Address
Part C: Number Series
Part D: Following Oral Instructions

Part A: Address-Checking Test

In this part of the test, you will have to determine whether two addresses are alike (Letter "A" for Alike) or different (Letter "D" for Different) You have to select one answer from two choices. On the other hand, in the Address-Checking Test of Exam 473/473-C Battery Test, you have to select one answer from a selection of four choices, answering the questions with "A" for "No Errors"; "B" for "Address Only Errors"; "C" for "Zip Code Only" and "D" for Both (Address and ZIP Code errors). Thus, the two address-checking tests have similarities and differences. It is interesting to note that the address-checking test for RCA 460 Test is easier than the 473/473-C Battery Test because in the 460 Test, you have to answer the question with only two choices, "A" or "D".

Part B: Memory-for-Address Test

In this part of the test, you will have to memorize the locations of names of streets and numbers (A, B, C, D, or E) of 25 addresses shown in five boxes. You will be given a list of street names and numbers with address ranges, and you have to determine in which box the street name or address is contained.

Part C: Number Series Test

For each series of question, there is at the left a series of numbers which follow some definite order and at the right five sets of two numbers. You are to see the numbers in the series at the left and find out what order they follow. You then may decide what the two numbers in that series would be if the same order were continued.

Part D: Following Oral Instructions

In this part of the test, you will be instructed to follow some directions by writing in a test booklet and then on an actual answer sheet.

Sample Questions
460 Rural Carrier Associate Exam
U.S. Postal Service

TEST INSTRUCTIONS

During the test session, it will be your responsibility to pay close attention to what the examiner has to say and to follow all instructions. One of the purposes of the test is to see how quickly and accurately you can work. Therefore, each part of the test will be carefully timed. You will not START until being told to do so. Also, when you are told to STOP, you must immediately STOP answering the questions. When you are told to work on a particular part of the examination, regardless of which part, you are to work on that part ONLY. If you finish a part before time is called, you may review your answers for that part, but you will not go on or back to any other part. Failure to follow ANY directions given to you by the examiner may be grounds for disqualification. Instructions read by the examiner are intended to ensure that each applicant has the same fair and objective opportunity to compete in the examination.

SAMPLE QUESTIONS

Study carefully before the examination.

The following questions are like the ones that will be on the test. Study these carefully. This will give you practice with the different kinds of questions and show you how to mark your answers.

Part A: Address Checking

In this part of the test, you will have to decide whether two addresses are alike or different. If the two addresses are exactly *Alike* in every way, darken circle A for the question. If the two addresses are *Different* in any way, darken circle D for the question.

Mark your answers to these sample questions on the Sample Answer Grid at the right.

1...2134 S 20th St   2134 S 20th St

Since the two addresses are exactly alike, mark A for question 1 on the Sample Answer Grid.

Sample Answer Grid		
1	Ⓐ	Ⓓ
2	Ⓐ	Ⓓ
3	Ⓐ	Ⓓ
4	Ⓐ	Ⓓ
5	Ⓐ	Ⓓ

2...4608 N Warnock St   4806 N Warnock St

3...1202 W Girard Dr   1202 W Girard Rd

4...Chappaqua NY 10514   Chappaqua NY 10514

5...2207 Markland Ave   2207 Markham Ave

The correct answers to questions 2 to 5 are: 2D, 3D, 4A, and 5D.

Your score on Part A of the actual test will be based on the number of wrong answers as well as on the number of right answers. Part A is scored right answers minus wrong answers. Random guessing should not help your score. For the Part A test, you will have six minutes to answer as many of the 95 questions as you can. It will be to your advantage to work as quickly and as accurately as possible. You will not be expected to be able to answer all the questions in the time allowed.

Part B: Memory for Addresses

In this part of the test, you will have to memorize the locations (A, B, C, D, or E) of 25 addresses shown in five boxes, like those below. For example, "Sardis" is in Box C, "6800-6999 Table" is in Box B, etc. (The addresses in the actual test will be different.)

A	B	C	D	E
4700-5599 Table	6800-6999 Table	5600-6499 Table	6500-6799 Table	4400-4699 Table
Lismore	Kelford	Joel	Tatum	Ruskin
5600-6499 West	6500-6799 West	6800-6999 West	4400-4699 West	4700-5599 West
Hesper	Musella	Sardis	Porter	Nathan
4400-4699 Blake	5600-6499 Blake	6500-6799 Blake	4700-5599 Blake	6800-6999 Blake

Study the locations of the addresses for five minutes. As you study, silently repeat these to yourself. Then cover the boxes and try to answer the questions below. Mark your answers for each question by darkening the circle as was done for questions 1 and 2.

1. Musella	5. 4400-4699 Blake	9. 6500-6799 Blake	13. Porter
2. 4700-5599 Blake	6. Hesper	10. Joel	14. 6800-6999 Blake
3. 4700-5599 Table	7. Kelford	11. 4400-4699 Blake	
4. Tatum	8. Nathan	12. 6500-6799 West	

Sample Answer Grid

1	Ⓐ ● Ⓒ Ⓓ Ⓔ	5	Ⓐ Ⓑ Ⓒ Ⓓ Ⓔ	9	Ⓐ Ⓑ Ⓒ Ⓓ Ⓔ	13	Ⓐ Ⓑ Ⓒ Ⓓ Ⓔ
2	Ⓐ Ⓑ Ⓒ ● Ⓔ	6	Ⓐ Ⓑ Ⓒ Ⓓ Ⓔ	10	Ⓐ Ⓑ Ⓒ Ⓓ Ⓔ	14	Ⓐ Ⓑ Ⓒ Ⓓ Ⓔ
3	Ⓐ Ⓑ Ⓒ Ⓓ Ⓔ	7	Ⓐ Ⓑ Ⓒ Ⓓ Ⓔ	11	Ⓐ Ⓑ Ⓒ Ⓓ Ⓔ	
4	Ⓐ Ⓑ Ⓒ Ⓓ Ⓔ	8	Ⓐ Ⓑ Ⓒ Ⓓ Ⓔ	12	Ⓐ Ⓑ Ⓒ Ⓓ Ⓔ	

The correct answers for questions 3 to 14 are: 3A, 4D, 5A, 6A, 7B, 8E, 9C, 10C, 11A, 12B, 13D, and 14E.

During the examination, you will have three practice exercises to help you memorize the location of addresses shown in five boxes. After the practice exercises, the actual test will be given. Part B is scored right answers minus one-fourth of the wrong answers. Random guessing should not help your score. But, if you can eliminate one or more alternatives, it is to your advantage to guess. For the Part B test, you will have five minutes to answer as many of the 88 questions as you can. It will be to your advantage to work as quickly and as accurately as you can. You will not be expected to be able to answer all the questions in the time allowed.

Part C: Number Series

For each *Number Series* question there is at the left a series of numbers which follow some definite order and at the right five sets of two numbers each. You are to look at the numbers in the series at the left and find out what order they follow. Then decide what the next two numbers in that series would be if the same order were continued. Mark your answers on the Sample Answer Grid.

1. 1 2 3 4 5 6 7 .... A) 1 2   B) 5 6   C) 8 9   D) 4 5   E) 7 8

The numbers in this series are increasing by 1. If the series were continued for two more numbers, it would read: 1 2 3 4 5 6 7 8 9. Therefore the correct answer is 8 and 9 and you should have darkened C for question 1.

2. 15 14 13 12 11 10 9 .... A) 2 1   B) 17 16   C) 8 9   D) 8 7   E) 9 8

The numbers in this series are decreasing by 1. If the series were continued for two more numbers, it would read: 15 14 13 12 11 10 9 8 7. Therefore the correct answer is 8 and 7 and you should have darkened D for question 2.

3. 20 20 21 21 22 22 23 .... A) 23 23   B) 23 24   C) 19 19   D) 22 23   E) 21 22

Each number in this series is repeated and then increased by 1. If the series were continued for two more numbers, it would read: 20 20 21 21 22 22 23 23 24. Therefore the correct answer is 23 and 24 and you should have darkened B for question 3.

4. 17 3 17 4 17 5 17 .... A) 6 17   B) 6 7   C) 17 6   D) 5 6   E) 17 7

This series is the number 17 separated by numbers increasing by 1, beginning with the number 3. If the series were continued for two more numbers, it would read: 17 3 17 4 17 5 17 6 17. Therefore the correct answer is 6 and 17 and you should have darkened A for question 4.

5. 1 2 4 5 7 8 10 .... A) 11 12   B) 12 14   C) 10 13   D) 12 13   E) 11 13

The numbers in this series are increasing first by 1 (plus 1) and then by 2 (plus 2). If the series were continued for two more numbers, it would read: 1 2 4 5 7 8 10 (plus 1) *11* and (plus 2) 13. Therefore the correct answer is 11 and 13 and you should have darkened E for question 5.

Now read and work sample questions 6 through 10 and mark your answers on the Sample Answer Grid.

6. 21 21 20 20 19 19 18 .... A) 18 18   B) 18 17   C) 17 18   D) 17 17   E) 18 19

7. 1 22 1 23 1 24 1 .... A) 26 1   B) 25 26   C) 25 1   D) 1 26   E) 1 25

8. 1 20 3 19 5 18 7 .... A) 8 9   B) 8 17   C) 17 10   D) 17 9   E) 9 18

9. 4 7 10 13 16 19 22 .... A) 23 26   B) 25 27   C) 25 26   D) 25 28   E) 24 27

10. 30 2 28 4 26 6 24 .... A) 23 9   B) 26 8   C) 8 9   D) 26 22   E) 8 22

Sample Answer Grid			
6 Ⓐ Ⓑ Ⓒ Ⓓ Ⓔ	8 Ⓐ Ⓑ Ⓒ Ⓓ Ⓔ	9 Ⓐ Ⓑ Ⓒ Ⓓ Ⓔ	10 Ⓐ Ⓑ Ⓒ Ⓓ Ⓔ
7 Ⓐ Ⓑ Ⓒ Ⓓ Ⓔ			

The correct answers to sample questions 6 to 10 are: 6B, 7C, 8D, 9D and 10E. Explanations follow.

6. Each number in the series repeats itself and then decreases by 1 or minus 1; *21* (repeat) *21* (minus 1) *20* (repeat) *20* (minus 1) *19* (repeat) *19* (minus 1) *18* (repeat) *?* (minus 1) *?*

7. The number 1 is separated by numbers which begin with 22 and increased by 1; *1 22 1* (increase 22 by 1) *23 1* (increase 23 by 1) *24 1* (increase ?4 by 1) *?*

8. This is best explained by two alternating series — one series starts with 1 and increases by 2 or plus 2; the other series starts with 20 and decreases by 1 or minus 1.

$$1 \quad {}^{\wedge} \quad 3 \quad {}^{\wedge} \quad 5 \quad {}^{\wedge} \quad 7 \quad {}^{\wedge} \quad ?$$
$$20 \qquad 19 \qquad 18 \qquad ?$$

9. This series of numbers increases by 3 (plus 3) beginning with the first number — *4 7 10 13 16 19 22 ? ?*

10. Look for two alternating series — one series starts with 30 and decreases by 2 (minus 2); the other series starts with 2 and increases by 2 (plus 2).

Now try questions 11 to 15.

11. 5 6 20 7 8 19 9 . . . .   A) 10 18   B) 18 17   C) 10 17   D) 18 19   E) 10 11

12. 4 6 9 11 14 16 19 . . . .   A) 21 24   B) 22 25   C) 20 22   D) 21 23   E) 22 24

13. 8 8 1 10 10 3 12 . . . .   A) 13 13   B) 12 5   C) 12 4   D) 13 5   E) 4 12

14. 10 12 50 15 17 50 20 . . . .   A) 50 21   B) 21 50   C) 50 22   D) 22 50   E) 22 24

15. 20 21 23 24 27 28 32 33 38 39 .   A) 45 46   B) 45 52   C) 44 45   D) 44 49   E) 40 46

Sample Answer Grid			
11 Ⓐ Ⓑ Ⓒ Ⓓ Ⓔ	13 Ⓐ Ⓑ Ⓒ Ⓓ Ⓔ	14 Ⓐ Ⓑ Ⓒ Ⓓ Ⓔ	15 Ⓐ Ⓑ Ⓒ Ⓓ Ⓔ
12 Ⓐ Ⓑ Ⓒ Ⓓ Ⓔ			

The correct answers to the sample questions above are: 11A, 12A, 13B, 14D and 15A.

It will be to your advantage to answer every question in Part C that you can, since your score on this part of the test will be based on the number of questions that you answer correctly. Answer first those questions which are easiest for you. For the Part C test, you will have 20 minutes to answer as many of the 24 questions as you can.

Part D: Following Oral Instructions

In this part of the test, you will be told to follow directions by writing in a test booklet and then on an answer sheet. The test booklet will have lines of material like the following five samples:

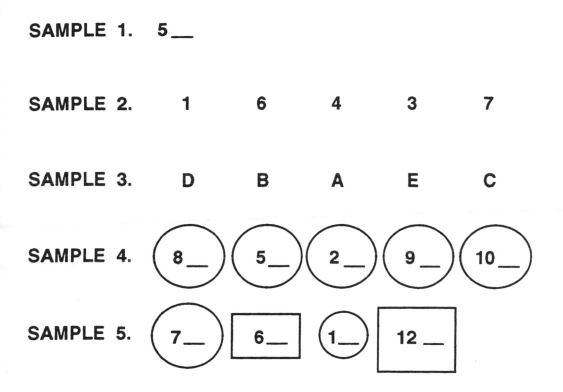

SAMPLE 1.   5 __

SAMPLE 2.   1   6   4   3   7

SAMPLE 3.   D   B   A   E   C

SAMPLE 4.   (8 __) (5 __) (2 __) (9 __) (10 __)

SAMPLE 5.   (7 __) [6 __] (1 __) [12 __]

To practice this part of the test, tear off page 11. Then have somebody read the instructions to you and you follow the instructions. When he or she tells you to darken the space on the Sample Answer Grid, use the one on this page.

Sample Answer Grid			
1 Ⓐ Ⓑ Ⓒ Ⓓ Ⓔ	4 Ⓐ Ⓑ Ⓒ Ⓓ Ⓔ	7 Ⓐ Ⓑ Ⓒ Ⓓ Ⓔ	10 Ⓐ Ⓑ Ⓒ Ⓓ Ⓔ
2 Ⓐ Ⓑ Ⓒ Ⓓ Ⓔ	5 Ⓐ Ⓑ Ⓒ Ⓓ Ⓔ	8 Ⓐ Ⓑ Ⓒ Ⓓ Ⓔ	11 Ⓐ Ⓑ Ⓒ Ⓓ Ⓔ
3 Ⓐ Ⓑ Ⓒ Ⓓ Ⓔ	6 Ⓐ Ⓑ Ⓒ Ⓓ Ⓔ	9 Ⓐ Ⓑ Ⓒ Ⓓ Ⓔ	12 Ⓐ Ⓑ Ⓒ Ⓓ Ⓔ

Your score for part D will be based on the number of questions that you answer correctly. Therefore, if you are not sure of an answer, it will be to your advantage to guess. Part D will take about 25 minutes.

KEEP THESE INSTRUCTIONS FOR FUTURE REFERENCE. YOUR PARTICIPATION AND COOPERATION IN THIS POSTAL EXAM IS APPRECIATED.

Instructions to be read **(the words in parentheses should NOT be read aloud)**

You are to follow the instructions that I shall read to you. I cannot repeat them.

Look at the samples. Sample 1 has a number and a line beside it. On the line write A as in ace. **(Pause 2 seconds.)** Now on the Sample Answer Grid, find the number 5 **(pause 2 seconds)** and darken the letter you just wrote on the line. **(Pause 2 seconds.)**

Look at Sample 2. **(Pause slightly.)** Draw a line under the third number. **(Pause 2 seconds.)** Now look on the Sample Answer Grid, find the number under which you just drew a line and darken B as in boy. **(Pause 5 seconds.)**

Look at the letters in Sample 3. **(Pause slightly.)** Draw a line under the third letter in the line. **(Pause 2 seconds.)** Now on your Sample Answer Grid, find number 9 **(pause 2 seconds)** and darken the letter under which you drew a line. **(Pause 5 seconds.)**

Look at the five circles in Sample 4. **(Pause slightly.)** Each circle has a number and a line in it. Write D as in dog on the line in the last circle. **(Pause 2 seconds.)** Now on the Sample Answer Grid, darken the number-letter combination that is in the circle you just wrote in. **(Pause 5 seconds.)**

Look at Sample 5. **(Pause slightly.)** There are two circles and two boxes of different sizes with numbers in them. **(Pause slightly.)** If 4 is more than 2 and if 5 is less than 3, write A as in ace in the smaller circle. **(Pause slightly.)** Otherwise write C as in car in the larger box. **(Pause 2 seconds.)** Now on the Sample Grid, darken the number-letter combination in the box or circle in which you just wrote. **(Pause 5 seconds.)**

Now look at the Sample Answer Grid. **(Pause slightly.)** You should have darkened 4B, 5A, 9A, 10D, and 12C on the Sample Answer Grid. **(If the person preparing to take the examination made any mistakes, try to help him or her see why he or she made the wrong marks.)**

19

Techniques for Address-Checking

And Practice Tests

The *Address-Checking Test* forms Part A of the 460 examination. This test is given to applicants for rural carriere associates. On this test, you must determine whether two addresses are *alike* or *different.* It's like comparing sexy Sharon Stone with sassy Drew Barrymore, the size of their bodies, the shape of their legs or noses, and so on. In comparing addresses, too, you are to see how they are alike or different. If they are alike in numbers, roads, streets, or spelling, you answer **A** (for alike); if they are different in numbers, roads, streets, or spelling, you answer **D** (for different).

You're Not a Walkathon Participant

If you had plenty of time to take this test, as if participating in a walkhathon, you might score 100%. But you are racing against time; there is a time limit to answer the items or questions. You must compare 95 sets of addresses in only 6 minutes. In other words, you are like in a participant in a Grand Prix race. Your eyes must zoom from left to right in seconds! To finish comparing the 95 sets of addresses, you must take less than 4 seconds to answer each question, including the marking of circles on the answer sheet. (See **How to Mark Circles on the Answer Sheet**, page 35.) The examiner may tell you, however, that you don't have to answer all the questions (few do) to make a high score.

Let Your Fingers Do the Walking

In comparing addresses (in two columns), you can point at the streets and the numbers with your fingers. Place the little finger of your nonwriting hand on one column of addresses and your index finger of the same hand on the other column. Move your hand downward as you make comparisons, while your right hand marks the answer sheets.

Widen the Focus of Your Eyes!

Pretend that you're driving a car. Your sight is focused to the front as far as you can see, but you can still see to your left and to your right. You don't need the eyes of an E.T. to do this, but do remember that comparing addresses is faster than the so-called speed reading. If possible, just make one or two "eye sweeps" of the addresses.

Things to Do, In a Nutshell

■ Compare the two addresses (left and right) by one or two eye sweeps of the line. It's also a good idea to fold the paper so that the number, for instance, "2134" of the second address will be near the "St." or "Rd." of the first address (on the same line, of course). It's like taking a photo of an excited Bill Clinton and Hillary Rodman at their anniversary ball—you want them to be close together so that you can get a good close-up shot. The question sheet and the answer sheet should be lying side by side; the question sheet on your non-writing side, the answer sheet on your writing side. In this way, your sight doesn't travel too far. Don't jerk your neck from left to right as you read; just let your eyes do the sweeping. While you do this, hold your pencil in your writing hand and don't move your nonwriting hand from the answer sheet. Then move it downward as you mark a circle with two or three strikes by your writing hand. Be sure that the line you are marking corresponds to the question you are answering.

■ **Spellings:** Note the spellings of street, city, state, and numbers in the ZIP code. Sometimes the first address has a ZIP code of 48012 and the second address has a ZIP code of 48021.

■ **Differences:** Most of the time there are differences in abbreviations, such as St., Rd., or Ave. Sometimes the first address (left) is abbreviated as St. and the second address (right) is abbreviated as Rd., or vice versa.

■ **Guide:** It's best to use a bookmark or some other kind of guide with your nonwriting hand: place it just below the line you are comparing and slide it straight down to the next line as you continue with the test. This prevents you from comparing the first address or number with an address or number in the wrong line. You can also place the little finger of your nonwriting hand on the left column and the index finger of the same hand on the right column of addresses. Move your nonwriting hand downward as you make the comparisons, while you mark the answers with your writing hand.

How to Compare the Addresses

There are four ways to compare the addresses. Use whichever is most comfortable for you:

First Way: Compare the two addresses by moving your eyes from left to right; that is, compare the address on the left to the one on the right. Make *one* or *two* "eye sweeps" of the addresses. It's like sweeping snow from your car, but you do it in a snap. If possible, the "eye sweep" should be faster than the speed of sound.

Example:

2134 S 20th St   2134 S 20th St

Since the addresses are alike, the answer is *A*.

Second Way: Focus your sight on the space between the two addresses. You can look at the addresses simultaneously from the center. With this method you can get a complete view of both addresses, like looking at Bo Derek and Raquel Welch at the same time while they are smiling at you.

Example:

7507 Wyngate Dr ● 7505 Wyngate Dr

Since the street numbers are different, the answer is *D*.

Third Way: First, compare only the street name and the abbreviations: *St, Rd,* or *Ave.* If they are alike, then compare the street numbers on the left to the numbers on the right. If they are alike, answer *A*.

Example:

2207 Markland Ave   2207 Markham

When you use the third way in this example, first compare the street name and the abbreviation *Rd* or *Ave*. Since there's a difference in street names (one is Mark*land* and the other is Mark*ham*), you immediately mark circle *D*, meaning that they are different. Do not continue comparing anymore, but proceed at once to the next line or number. If the street names are alike, then compare the left-hand numbers to the numbers on the right. If they are still alike, answer *A*; if the figures are different, answer *D*.

Fourth Way: This can be discussed by analyzing the example below.

Example:

5428 N Shelbourne Rd   5482   N   Shelbourne   Rd

You compare the numbers at the left to the numbers at right, ignoring the initial, street name, and abbreviation (Rd. etc.). Once you see a difference (*28* and *82*) darken circle *D* right away. Do not go on to compare the street names because you've already found a difference between the *two* addresses. In a nutshell, differences may occur in numbers, abbreviations, or names.

Address-Checking Practice Test

Work—6 Minutes

These addresses are like the ones in the address-checking test.

Decide whether the two addresses are *Alike* or *Different*. If they are *Alike,* darken or mark space A; if they are *Different,* darken space D. Mark the answers on the answer sheet to the right. Work as fast as you can without making too any errors. Work exactly 6 minutes.

ANSWER SHEET

			Test A	Test B
1.	1405 Hickory Rd NW	1504 Hickory Rd NW	1 Ⓐ Ⓓ	1 Ⓐ Ⓓ
2.	1354 Central Park W	1354 Central Park W	2 Ⓐ Ⓓ	2 Ⓐ Ⓓ
3.	500 Court Rd NE	500 Court RD NW	3 Ⓐ Ⓓ	3 Ⓐ Ⓓ
4.	East Point, MI 48021	East Pointe, MI 48031	4 Ⓐ Ⓓ	4 Ⓐ Ⓓ
5.	35016 S Main St	35015 S Main St	5 Ⓐ Ⓓ	5 Ⓐ Ⓓ
6.	Bay Pines, FL 33503	Bay Pines, FL 33503	6 Ⓐ Ⓓ	6 Ⓐ Ⓓ
7.	3653 Peasant Run Ave	3653 Pleasant Run Ave	7 Ⓐ Ⓓ	7 Ⓐ Ⓓ
8.	154 S Washington Sq	154 N Washington Sq	8 Ⓐ Ⓓ	8 Ⓐ Ⓓ
9.	3531 McWeeney Rd	3531 McWeeney Rd	9 Ⓐ Ⓓ	9 Ⓐ Ⓓ
10.	7535 Cedar Ln	7535 Cedar St	10 Ⓐ Ⓓ	10 Ⓐ Ⓓ
11.	Meridian, Idaho 83645	Meridian, Idaho 83345	11 Ⓐ Ⓓ	11 Ⓐ Ⓓ
12.	Manson, NC 27553	Manson, NC 27553	12 Ⓐ Ⓓ	12 Ⓐ Ⓓ
13.	2105 W 18th Ave	2103 W 18th Ave	13 Ⓐ Ⓓ	13 Ⓐ Ⓓ
14.	3153 Carter Dr	3157 Carter Dr	14 Ⓐ Ⓓ	14 Ⓐ Ⓓ
15.	98354 Hopeville Ln	98354 Hopeville Ln	15 Ⓐ Ⓓ	15 Ⓐ Ⓓ
16.	15315 N Audrey Rd	15815 N Audrey Rd	16 Ⓐ Ⓓ	16 Ⓐ Ⓓ
17.	31543 Stony Brook	31543 Stony Brook	17 Ⓐ Ⓓ	17 Ⓐ Ⓓ
18.	Southfield, MI 48075	Southfield, MI 48073	18 Ⓐ Ⓓ	18 Ⓐ Ⓓ
19.	11359 N Tulipe St	11359 S Tulipe St	19 Ⓐ Ⓓ	19 Ⓐ Ⓓ
20.	31547 Country Club Rd	31547 Country Club Rd	20 Ⓐ Ⓓ	20 Ⓐ Ⓓ
21.	80329 Guillian Rdg	80329 Guillian Rdg	21 Ⓐ Ⓓ	21 Ⓐ Ⓓ
22.	93178 Herschel Plaza	98178 Hershel Plaza	22 Ⓐ Ⓓ	22 Ⓐ Ⓓ
23.	5462 Audobon Ct	5462 Audobon Ct	23 Ⓐ Ⓓ	23 Ⓐ Ⓓ
24.	89354 Ocean Blvd	19354 Ocean Blvd	24 Ⓐ Ⓓ	24 Ⓐ Ⓓ
25.	77331 SW Teppert St	77381 SW Teppert St	25 Ⓐ Ⓓ	25 Ⓐ Ⓓ
26.	315 Bensen Pky	315 Bensen Pky	26 Ⓐ Ⓓ	26 Ⓐ Ⓓ
27.	20361 Alexander St	20361 Alexander Ave	27 Ⓐ Ⓓ	27 Ⓐ Ⓓ
28.	3154 S Colorado Rd	3154 N Colorado Rd	28 Ⓐ Ⓓ	28 Ⓐ Ⓓ
29.	9156 N Placid Ln	9156 S Placid Ln	29 Ⓐ Ⓓ	29 Ⓐ Ⓓ
30.	1120 Kenilworth Ct	1120 Kenilworth Ct	30 Ⓐ Ⓓ	30 Ⓐ Ⓓ
31.	87104 Tulip Pky	87104 Tulip Rd	31 Ⓐ Ⓓ	31 Ⓐ Ⓓ
32.	2465 Cornplakes Sq	2465 Cornplakes Sq	32 Ⓐ Ⓓ	32 Ⓐ Ⓓ
33.	9037 Delaware Ave	9038 Delaware Ave	33 Ⓐ Ⓓ	33 Ⓐ Ⓓ
34.	3154 N Lancaster	3154 N Lancaster	34 Ⓐ Ⓓ	34 Ⓐ Ⓓ
35.	3698 Stonybrook Sq	3698 Stonybrook Sq	35 Ⓐ Ⓓ	35 Ⓐ Ⓓ
36.	3154 E Jefferson St	3154 E Jefferson St	36 Ⓐ Ⓓ	36 Ⓐ Ⓓ
37.	8634 19th Ave SW	8634 19th Ave SE	37 Ⓐ Ⓓ	37 Ⓐ Ⓓ
38.	2654 Avenue NW	3645 Avenue NW	38 Ⓐ Ⓓ	38 Ⓐ Ⓓ
39.	3545 Monticello Ct	3545 Montecello Ct	39 Ⓐ Ⓓ	39 Ⓐ Ⓓ
40.	46017 Thunder Hill	46017 Thunder Hill	40 Ⓐ Ⓓ	40 Ⓐ Ⓓ

Go on to the next number on the next page.

41. 8761 Woodridge Ave	8761 Woodrige Rd	41 Ⓐ Ⓓ	41 Ⓐ Ⓓ
42, 11253 Lovers Ln	11253 Lovers Ln	42 Ⓐ Ⓓ	42 Ⓐ Ⓓ
43. 7718 Rolling Hills NW	7718 Rolling Hills SE	43 Ⓐ Ⓓ	43 Ⓐ Ⓓ
44. 3838 Edgecom View	3383 Edgecom View	44 Ⓐ Ⓓ	44 Ⓐ Ⓓ
45. 7634 5th Ave S	7634 5th Ave S	45 Ⓐ Ⓓ	45 Ⓐ Ⓓ
46. 1873 7th St SW	1878 7th St SW	46 Ⓐ Ⓓ	46 Ⓐ Ⓓ
47. 3838 Oceanside Blvd	3838 Oceanside Blvd	47 Ⓐ Ⓓ	47 Ⓐ Ⓓ
48. 9835 Frescot Ct E	9835 Frescot CT W	48 Ⓐ Ⓓ	48 Ⓐ Ⓓ
49. 43735 Belleview N	43735 Belleview N	49 Ⓐ Ⓓ	49 Ⓐ Ⓓ
50. 3549 Eastland Dr E	3549 Eastland Dr W	50 Ⓐ Ⓓ	50 Ⓐ Ⓓ
51. 860 Rolling Acres W	860 Rolling Acres W	51 Ⓐ Ⓓ	51 Ⓐ Ⓓ
52. 9117 Surf St	9117 Surf St	52 Ⓐ Ⓓ	52 Ⓐ Ⓓ
53. 3938 Woodridge Ct	3938 Woodridge Ct	53 Ⓐ Ⓓ	53 Ⓐ Ⓓ
54. 9304 Yarbu St	9304 Yarbugh St	54 Ⓐ Ⓓ	54 Ⓐ Ⓓ
55. 11397 Edgeman Blvd S	11395 Edgeman Blvd S	55 Ⓐ Ⓓ	55 Ⓐ Ⓓ
56. 62660 High Noon Rd	62669 High Noon Rd	56 Ⓐ Ⓓ	56 Ⓐ Ⓓ
57. 2951 Lamaro Cove	2551 Lamaro Cove	57 Ⓐ Ⓓ	57 Ⓐ Ⓓ
58. 5066 Laurel Cir	5066 Laurel Cir	58 Ⓐ Ⓓ	58 Ⓐ Ⓓ
59. Ashburn, Virginia 22111	Ashburne, Virginia 22111	59 Ⓐ Ⓓ	59 Ⓐ Ⓓ
60. 1703 Allensville St	1708 Allensville St	60 Ⓐ Ⓓ	60 Ⓐ Ⓓ
61. 58356 Deerfield Cir	58356 Deerfield Cir	61 Ⓐ Ⓓ	61 Ⓐ Ⓓ
62. 3259 Rolling Stone Ct	3259 Rolling Stone Ct	62 Ⓐ Ⓓ	62 Ⓐ Ⓓ
63. 9306 High St SW	9307 High St SW	63 Ⓐ Ⓓ	63 Ⓐ Ⓓ
64. 305 Kentucky Ave	305 Kentucky Ave	64 Ⓐ Ⓓ	64 Ⓐ Ⓓ
65. 2548 Redesco Rd	2548 Redesco Sq	65 Ⓐ Ⓓ	65 Ⓐ Ⓓ
66. 2088 N Melendreso St	2089 N Melendreso St	66 Ⓐ Ⓓ	66 Ⓐ Ⓓ
67. 5983 Aroma Blvd	5983 Aroma Blvd	67 Ⓐ Ⓓ	67 Ⓐ Ⓓ
68. 3784 Lincoln Ave	3785 Lincoln Ave	68 Ⓐ Ⓓ	68 Ⓐ Ⓓ
69. 7835 Malcom Rd	7838 Malcom Rd	69 Ⓐ Ⓓ	69 Ⓐ Ⓓ
70. 2549 Montgomery Ave	2549 Montgomery Cir	70 Ⓐ Ⓓ	70 Ⓐ Ⓓ
71. 250 Virginia St W	250 Virginia St W	71 Ⓐ Ⓓ	71 Ⓐ Ⓓ
72. 13286 E Ausburn St	13286 W Ausburne St	72 Ⓐ Ⓓ	72 Ⓐ Ⓓ
73. 934 Lenoxin Cir SW	934 Lenoxin Cir SW	73 Ⓐ Ⓓ	73 Ⓐ Ⓓ
74. 1035 Lovers Ln W	1085 Lovers Ln W	74 Ⓐ Ⓓ	74 Ⓐ Ⓓ
75. 937 W Waterford Rd	937 W Waterford Rd	75 Ⓐ Ⓓ	75 Ⓐ Ⓓ
76. 3087 E Bellevue Hill	3087 W Bellevue Hill	76 Ⓐ Ⓓ	76 Ⓐ Ⓓ
77. 6943 6th Ave N	6948 6th Ave N	77 Ⓐ Ⓓ	77 Ⓐ Ⓓ
78 . 2052 Hubert Ave	2052 Hubert Ave	78 Ⓐ Ⓓ	78 Ⓐ Ⓓ
79. 983 SW Campbell Rd	983 SW Campbell Rd	79 Ⓐ Ⓓ	79 Ⓐ Ⓓ
80. 4088 4th Ave W	4088 4th Ave SE	80 Ⓐ Ⓓ	80 Ⓐ Ⓓ
81. 22011 Crossroad Ave	22011 Crossroad Ave	81 Ⓐ Ⓓ	81 Ⓐ Ⓓ
82. 1342 Northwest St	1342 Northeast St	82 Ⓐ Ⓓ	82 Ⓐ Ⓓ
83. 2057 Tender Rd	2057 Tender Rd	83 Ⓐ Ⓓ	83 Ⓐ Ⓓ
84. 3522 Bleeker Cove	3522 Bleeker Cove	84 Ⓐ Ⓓ	84 Ⓐ Ⓓ
85. 3154 Pittsburg Ct	3134 Pitsburg Ct	85 Ⓐ Ⓓ	85 Ⓐ Ⓓ
86. 5497 Gilmore Sq	5495 Gilmore Sq	86 Ⓐ Ⓓ	86 Ⓐ Ⓓ
87. 3921 Melendres Ave	3921 Melendres Ave	87 Ⓐ Ⓓ	87 Ⓐ Ⓓ
88. 5834 SW 7th Ave	5835 SW 7th Ave	88 Ⓐ Ⓓ	88 Ⓐ Ⓓ
89. 8640 Cherry Hill	8640 Cherry Hill	89 Ⓐ Ⓓ	89 Ⓐ Ⓓ

Go on to the next number on the next page.

90. 306 Calihan Ave E	306 Calihan Ave W	90 Ⓐ Ⓓ	90 Ⓐ Ⓓ
91. 3040 Makiling Ct	3040 Makiling Sq	91 Ⓐ Ⓓ	91 Ⓐ Ⓓ
92. 1555 Rectory Pl	1555 Rectory Pl	92 Ⓐ Ⓓ	92 Ⓐ Ⓓ
93. 3056 Bradley Ave	3056 Bradley Ave	93 Ⓐ Ⓓ	93 Ⓐ Ⓓ
94. 3054 Gangho Cir W	3054 Gangho Cir E	94 Ⓐ Ⓓ	94 Ⓐ Ⓓ
95. 97711 Acres Rd	97711 Acres Rd	95 Ⓐ Ⓓ	95 Ⓐ Ⓓ

STOP

If you finish before the time is up, check your answers for Part A.

Do not go to any other part.

(See the correct answers on the next page.)

Correct Answers

Address-Checking Test

1. D	25. D	49. A	73. A
2. A	26. A	50. D	74. D
3. D	27. D	51. A	75. A
4. D	28. D	52. A	76. D
5. D	29. D	53. A	77. D
6. A	30. A	54. D	78. A
7. D	31. D	55. D	79. A
8. D	32. A	56. D	80. D
9. A	33. D	57. D	81. A
10. D	34. A	58. A	82. D
11. D	35. A	59. D	83. A
12. A	36. A	60. D	84. A
13. D	37. D	61. A	85. D
14. D	38. D	62. A	86. D
15. A	39. D	63. D	87. A
16. D	40. A	64. A	88. D
17. A	41. D	65. D	89. A
18. D	42. A	66. D	90. D
19. D	43. D	67. A	91. D
20. A	44. D	68. D	92. A
21. A	45. A	69. D	93. A
22. D	46. D	70. D	94. D
23. A	47. A	71. A	95. A
24. D	48. D	72. D	

Address-Checking Practice Test

Work—6 Minutes

These addresses are like the ones in the adress-checking test.

Decide whether the two addresses are *Alike* or *Different*. If they are Alike, darken or mark space A; if they are *Different*, darken space D. Mark the answers on the answer sheet to the right. Work as fast as you can without making too many errors. Work exactly 6 minutes.

ANSWER SHEET

			Test A	Test B
1.	1545 Harrison Ave	1543 Harrison Ave	1 Ⓐ Ⓓ	1 Ⓐ Ⓓ
2.	94375 Forrest Pl SW	94375 Forrest Pl SW	2 Ⓐ Ⓓ	2 Ⓐ Ⓓ
3.	3598 Lassie Rd W	3598 Lassie Rd W	3 Ⓐ Ⓓ	3 Ⓐ Ⓓ
4.	5071 Nesika Bay Sq	5077 Nesika Bay SQ	4 Ⓐ Ⓓ	4 Ⓐ Ⓓ
5.	3857 Blackberry Ln E	5857 Blackberry Ln W	5 Ⓐ Ⓓ	5 Ⓐ Ⓓ
6.	3547 Sherman Oaks St	3547 Sherman Oaks St	6 Ⓐ Ⓓ	6 Ⓐ Ⓓ
7.	9763 Clay Pky W	8653 Ckay Pkwy W	7 Ⓐ Ⓓ	7 Ⓐ Ⓓ
8.	308 S Lincolnside Dr	308 S Lincolnside Dr	8 Ⓐ Ⓓ	8 Ⓐ Ⓓ
9.	836 Sundae Sq N	836 Sundae Sq S	9 Ⓐ Ⓓ	9 Ⓐ Ⓓ
10.	3547 E Brighton Rd	3547 E Brighton Rd	10 Ⓐ Ⓓ	10 Ⓐ Ⓓ
11.	9836 W Falkner St	9836 E Falkner St	11 Ⓐ Ⓓ	11 Ⓐ Ⓓ
12.	5945 Stevens Rd	4945 Stevens Rd	12 Ⓐ Ⓓ	12 Ⓐ Ⓓ
13.	9003 Underwood St	9003 Underwood St	13 Ⓐ Ⓓ	13 Ⓐ Ⓓ
14.	4846 Blanchard Ave	4846 Glanchard Ave	14 Ⓐ Ⓓ	14 Ⓐ Ⓓ
15.	93658 Mt. Elena Sq	93658 Mt. Elena Dr	15 Ⓐ Ⓓ	15 Ⓐ Ⓓ
16.	354 W Boston Way	354 E Boston Way	16 Ⓐ Ⓓ	16 Ⓐ Ⓓ
17.	1919 Sievers Pky	1919 Stevers Pkwy	17 Ⓐ Ⓓ	17 Ⓐ Ⓓ
18.	3785 Apache Drum Rd	3785 Apache Dr Rd	18 Ⓐ Ⓓ	18 Ⓐ Ⓓ
19.	301 Bryan Ct	301 Bryan Ct	19 Ⓐ Ⓓ	19 Ⓐ Ⓓ
20.	9381 Agatha Pass Way	9331 Agatha Pass Way	20 Ⓐ Ⓓ	20 Ⓐ Ⓓ
21.	3547 Brownsville St	3547 Bronsville St	21 Ⓐ Ⓓ	21 Ⓐ Ⓓ
22.	3078 13th Ave SW	3073 13th Ave SW	22 Ⓐ Ⓓ	22 Ⓐ Ⓓ
23.	234 Creol Pass	234 Creole Pass	23 Ⓐ Ⓓ	23 Ⓐ Ⓓ
24.	7878 Burnett Dr	7878 Burnett Dr	24 Ⓐ Ⓓ	24 Ⓐ Ⓓ
25.	235 Dixon	235 Dixon	25 Ⓐ Ⓓ	25 Ⓐ Ⓓ
26.	9478 Wicker Way	9478 Wicker Way	26 Ⓐ Ⓓ	26 Ⓐ Ⓓ
27.	3054 17th St	3054 17th St	27 Ⓐ Ⓓ	27 Ⓐ Ⓓ
28.	37854 Bonn Ave	37854 Bonn Ave	28 Ⓐ Ⓓ	28 Ⓐ Ⓓ
29.	9076 Bingham Dr	9076 Bighan Dr	29 Ⓐ Ⓓ	29 Ⓐ Ⓓ
30.	3175 Walnut	3175 Walnut	30 Ⓐ Ⓓ	30 Ⓐ Ⓓ
31.	347 Bridgeview Ave	347 Bridgeview Rd	31 Ⓐ Ⓓ	31 Ⓐ Ⓓ
32.	9048 3rd Avenue SE	9048 3rd Avenue SE	32 Ⓐ Ⓓ	32 Ⓐ Ⓓ
33.	3250 Grant S	3250 Grant W	33 Ⓐ Ⓓ	33 Ⓐ Ⓓ
34.	1867 Pinecone Creek	1867 Pinecone Creek	34 Ⓐ Ⓓ	34 Ⓐ Ⓓ
35.	3065 Simon Blvd	3065 Simon Blvd	35 Ⓐ Ⓓ	35 Ⓐ Ⓓ
36.	3545 Armstrong Rd	3545 Armstrong Rdg	36 Ⓐ Ⓓ	36 Ⓐ Ⓓ
37.	16459 Rudolf Rdg	16459 Rudolf Rdg	37 Ⓐ Ⓓ	37 Ⓐ Ⓓ
38.	3649 Campbell Way	3669 Campbell Way	38 Ⓐ Ⓓ	38 Ⓐ Ⓓ
39.	3965 Simon Ave	9363 Simon Ave	39 Ⓐ Ⓓ	39 Ⓐ Ⓓ
40.	3548 Walnut Rd	3548 Walnut Rd	40 Ⓐ Ⓓ	40 Ⓐ Ⓓ

Go on to the next nmber on the next page.

41. 35646 W Armstrong St	35648 W Armstrong Sq	41 Ⓐ Ⓓ	41 Ⓐ Ⓓ
42. 3759 N Ford	3759 N Ford	42 Ⓐ Ⓓ	42 Ⓐ Ⓓ
43. 3584 Rose S	3584 Rose N	43 Ⓐ Ⓓ	43 Ⓐ Ⓓ
44. 40647 S Philips	40647 S Philips	44 Ⓐ Ⓓ	44 Ⓐ Ⓓ
45. 4657 Scotts Bluff	4657 Scotts Bluff	45 Ⓐ Ⓓ	45 Ⓐ Ⓓ
46. 9486 Beechnut St	9486 Beechnut Ct	46 Ⓐ Ⓓ	46 Ⓐ Ⓓ
47. 7786 Maleroy Ct	7788 Maleroy Ct	47 Ⓐ Ⓓ	47 Ⓐ Ⓓ
48. 36547 Keyport Rd	36547 Keyport Rd	48 Ⓐ Ⓓ	48 Ⓐ Ⓓ
49. 6458 47th Ave W	6458 47th Ave W	49 Ⓐ Ⓓ	49 Ⓐ Ⓓ
50. 308 King Dr	308 King Dr	50 Ⓐ Ⓓ	50 Ⓐ Ⓓ
51. 5496 Franklin Cove	5496 Franklin Cove	51 Ⓐ Ⓓ	51 Ⓐ Ⓓ
52. 8745 Cactus Ave	8745 Cactus Ave S	52 Ⓐ Ⓓ	52 Ⓐ Ⓓ
53. 35648 W Glenn	35648 S. Glenn	53 Ⓐ Ⓓ	53 Ⓐ Ⓓ
54. 8475 E Cherokee	8475 E Cherokee	54 Ⓐ Ⓓ	54 Ⓐ Ⓓ
55. 48757 Roxbury Sq	48757 Roxbury Sq	55 Ⓐ Ⓓ	55 Ⓐ Ⓓ
56. 9475 Lawrence Ct	9473 Lawrence Ct	56 Ⓐ Ⓓ	56 Ⓐ Ⓓ
57. 35548 Bauxitc Sq	35548 Bauxite Sq	57 Ⓐ Ⓓ	57 Ⓐ Ⓓ
58. 3756 Pearl Bay	3756 Pearl Bay	58 Ⓐ Ⓓ	58 Ⓐ Ⓓ
59. 30657 Plymouth Rock	30655 Plymouth Rock	59 Ⓐ Ⓓ	59 Ⓐ Ⓓ
60. 9486 Pleasant Rdg	9486 Pleasant Rd	60 Ⓐ Ⓓ	60 Ⓐ Ⓓ
61. 32875 Clifton Blvd	32875 Clifton Blvd	61 Ⓐ Ⓓ	61 Ⓐ Ⓓ
62. 307 Paramount W	307 Paramount W	62 Ⓐ Ⓓ	62 Ⓐ Ⓓ
63. 9468 Cottonwood Cove	9463 Cottonwood Sq	63 Ⓐ Ⓓ	63 Ⓐ Ⓓ
64. 3757 E Atchinson	3757 E Atchinson	64 Ⓐ Ⓓ	64 Ⓐ Ⓓ
65. 3756 Sheridan St	3758 Sheridan St	65 Ⓐ Ⓓ	65 Ⓐ Ⓓ
66. 5476 Bloomfield Rd	5476 Bloomfield Rd	66 Ⓐ Ⓓ	66 Ⓐ Ⓓ
67. 396547 Highland	396547 Highland	67 Ⓐ Ⓓ	67 Ⓐ Ⓓ
68. 5430 Shellfield SW	5430 Shellfield SW	68 Ⓐ Ⓓ	68 Ⓐ Ⓓ
69. 37546 Taft Ave E	37546 Taft Ave W	69 Ⓐ Ⓓ	69 Ⓐ Ⓓ
70. 307 Panama Park	307 Panama Park	70 Ⓐ Ⓓ	70 Ⓐ Ⓓ
71. 68456 Bayview St.	68456 Bayview St	71 Ⓐ Ⓓ	71 Ⓐ Ⓓ
72. 305 Ballard Sq E	305 Ballard Sq E	72 Ⓐ Ⓓ	72 Ⓐ Ⓓ
73. 38656 Rose Rd	38656 Rose Rd	73 Ⓐ Ⓓ	73 Ⓐ Ⓓ
74. 9357 Armstrong Ave	9357 Armstrong Ave	74 Ⓐ Ⓓ	74 Ⓐ Ⓓ
75. 3547 Madonna Way	3547 Madonna Way	75 Ⓐ Ⓓ	75 Ⓐ Ⓓ
76. 39658 Victor Sq	39658 Victor Sq	76 Ⓐ Ⓓ	76 Ⓐ Ⓓ
77. 458 N Hermosillo Ct	458 N Hemosillo Ct	77 Ⓐ Ⓓ	77 Ⓐ Ⓓ
78. 3233 Teppert	3233 Teppert	78 Ⓐ Ⓓ	78 Ⓐ Ⓓ
79. 3065 Salty Bay Sq	3063 Salty Bay Sq	79 Ⓐ Ⓓ	79 Ⓐ Ⓓ
80. 9654 Audubon Blvd	9654 Audubon Blvd	80 Ⓐ Ⓓ	80 Ⓐ Ⓓ
81. 3054 Sleepy Hollow	3054 Sleep Holly	81 Ⓐ Ⓓ	81 Ⓐ Ⓓ
82. 3258 Pine Way St	3253 Pine Way St	82 Ⓐ Ⓓ	82 Ⓐ Ⓓ
83. 3547 Bums Ct W	3547 Bums Ct W	83 Ⓐ Ⓓ	83 Ⓐ Ⓓ
84. 30645 Mountainside View	30643 Mountainside View	84 Ⓐ Ⓓ	84 Ⓐ Ⓓ
85. 354 Carlson St W	354 Carlson St W	85 Ⓐ Ⓓ	85 Ⓐ Ⓓ
86. 659 Brooks Shield N	659 Brooks Shield N	86 Ⓐ Ⓓ	86 Ⓐ Ⓓ
87. 3645 Stevens Rd	3647 Stevesn Rd W	87 Ⓐ Ⓓ	87 Ⓐ Ⓓ
88. 3547 Alderwood W	3547 Alderwood W	88 Ⓐ Ⓓ	88 Ⓐ Ⓓ
89. 3543 Pineapple Cove	3543 Pineapple Cove	89 Ⓐ Ⓓ	89 Ⓐ Ⓓ

Go on the next number on the next page.

90.	3540 Francisco Sq	3540 Francisco Sq	90	Ⓐ Ⓓ	90	Ⓐ Ⓓ
91.	6486 Pleasan Rd	8486 Pleasant Sq	91	Ⓐ Ⓓ	91	Ⓐ Ⓓ
92.	3547 Sutter Ave	3547 Sutter Ave	92	Ⓐ Ⓓ	92	Ⓐ Ⓓ
93.	3547 Mango Sq	3547 Mango Sq	93	Ⓐ Ⓓ	93	Ⓐ Ⓓ
94.	54 5 Marina Dr	545 Marina St	94	Ⓐ Ⓓ	94	Ⓐ Ⓓ
95.	65406 Marine Way	65406 Marine Way	95	Ⓐ Ⓓ	95	Ⓐ Ⓓ

STOP

If you finish before the time is up, check your answers for Part A

Do not go to any other part.

(See the correct answers on the next page.)

Correct Answers

Address-Checking Test

1. D	25. A	49. A	73. A
2. A	26. A	50. A	74. A
3. A	27. A	51. A	75. A
4. D	28. A	52. D	76. A
5. D	29. D	53. D	77. D
6. A	30. A	54. A	78. A
7. D	31. D	55. A	79. D
8. A	32. A	56. D	80. A
9. D	33. D	57. A	81. D
10. A	34. A	58. A	82. D
11. D	35. A	59. D	83. A
12. D	36. D	60. D	84. D
13. A	37. A	61. A	85. A
14. D	38. D	62. A	86. A
15. D	39. D	63. D	87. D
16. D	40. A	64. A	88. A
17. D	41. D	65. D	89. A
18. D	42. A	66. A	90. A
19. A	43. D	67. A	91. D
20. D	44. A	68. A	92. A
21. D	45. A	69. D	93. A
22. D	46. D	70. A	94. D
23. D	47. D	71. A	95. A
24. A	48. A	72. A	

Address-Checking Practice Test

Work—6 Minutes

These addresses are like the ones in the address-checking test.

Decide whether the two addresses are *Alike* or *Different*. If they are *Alike*, darken or mark space A; if they are *Different*, darken space D. Mark the answers on the answer sheet to the right. Work as fast as you can without making too many errors. Work Exactly 6 minutes.

			Test A		Test B	
1.	3854 Carson S	3854 Carson S	1	Ⓐ Ⓓ	1	Ⓐ Ⓓ
2.	9046 Los Padres Cir	9048 Los Padres Cir	2	Ⓐ Ⓓ	2	Ⓐ Ⓓ
3.	354 S Luverne Rd	354 S Luverne Rd	3	Ⓐ Ⓓ	3	Ⓐ Ⓓ
4.	3548 Kimberly Sq	3548 Kimberly Sq	4	Ⓐ Ⓓ	4	Ⓐ Ⓓ
5.	253 Larami Rd N	258 Larami Rd N	5	Ⓐ Ⓓ	5	Ⓐ Ⓓ
6.	9461 S Audubon	9461 S Audubon	6	Ⓐ Ⓓ	6	Ⓐ Ⓓ
7.	3547 La Cross Dr	3547 La Cross Dr	7	Ⓐ Ⓓ	7	Ⓐ Ⓓ
8.	547 Salty Bay Rd	547 Salty Bay Rd	8	Ⓐ Ⓓ	8	Ⓐ Ⓓ
9.	36548 Harrison Cir	36543 Harrison Cir	9	Ⓐ Ⓓ	9	Ⓐ Ⓓ
10.	547 S Gregory Park	547 S Gregory Park	10	Ⓐ Ⓓ	10	Ⓐ Ⓓ
11.	658 S Salem Ln	658 S Salem Ln	11	Ⓐ Ⓓ	11	Ⓐ Ⓓ
12.	7845 S Liberty Pl	7845 N Liberty Pl	12	Ⓐ Ⓓ	12	Ⓐ Ⓓ
13.	745 Olympic Way	745 Olympic Way	13	Ⓐ Ⓓ	13	Ⓐ Ⓓ
14.	5478 Monterrey Rd	5478 Monterrey Rd	14	Ⓐ Ⓓ	14	Ⓐ Ⓓ
15	986 S Ocean Blvd	986 N Ocean Blvd	15	Ⓐ Ⓓ	15	Ⓐ Ⓓ
16.	389 S Placid Plaza	389 N Placid Plaza	16	Ⓐ Ⓓ	16	Ⓐ Ⓓ
17.	9475 Olympic Cove	7475 Olympic Cove	17	Ⓐ Ⓓ	17	Ⓐ Ⓓ
18.	346 S Blanchard Ct	346 S Blanchard Ct	18	Ⓐ Ⓓ	18	Ⓐ Ⓓ
19.	8764 Jensen Way	3764 Jensen Way	19	Ⓐ Ⓓ	19	Ⓐ Ⓓ
20.	3754 Hayes Point	8754 Hayes Point	20	Ⓐ Ⓓ	20	Ⓐ Ⓓ
21.	8457 Galveston Blvd	8457 Galveston Hwy	21	Ⓐ Ⓓ	21	Ⓐ Ⓓ
22.	8475 NE Wilmoth	8475 NE Wilmont	22	Ⓐ Ⓓ	22	Ⓐ Ⓓ
23.	3503 O'Neal Rd	3503 O'Neal Rd	23	Ⓐ Ⓓ	23	Ⓐ Ⓓ
24.	1057 S Pierce Ct	1057 N Pierce Ct	24	Ⓐ Ⓓ	24	Ⓐ Ⓓ
25 .	3854 Monroe NW	3854 Monroe NW	25	Ⓐ Ⓓ	25	Ⓐ Ⓓ
26.	79845 Bonn Blvd	79845 Bonn Blvd	26	Ⓐ Ⓓ	26	Ⓐ Ⓓ
27.	3015 Holiday Inn Dr	3015 Holiday Inn Dr	27	Ⓐ Ⓓ	27	Ⓐ Ⓓ
28.	4961 Warner St	8961 Warner St	28	Ⓐ Ⓓ	28	Ⓐ Ⓓ
29.	5488 Wellington Way	5488 Wellington Way	29	Ⓐ Ⓓ	29	Ⓐ Ⓓ
30.	466 S Terrace	466 S Terrace	30	Ⓐ Ⓓ	30	Ⓐ Ⓓ
31.	4466 Jackson Rd W	4466 Jackson Rd E	31	Ⓐ Ⓓ	31	Ⓐ Ⓓ
32.	4455 Concord Blvd	4455 Concord Pky	32	Ⓐ Ⓓ	32	Ⓐ Ⓓ
33.	776 Symington St	767 Symington St	33	Ⓐ Ⓓ	33	Ⓐ Ⓓ
34.	8811 Carver Cove	8811 Carver Cove	34	Ⓐ Ⓓ	34	Ⓐ Ⓓ
35.	8835 Joplin Ct	8885 Joplin Ct	35	Ⓐ Ⓓ	35	Ⓐ Ⓓ
36.	9947 S Lighthouse Ln	9947 S Lighthouse Ln	36	Ⓐ Ⓓ	36	Ⓐ Ⓓ
37.	6649 Main St	6649 Main St	37	Ⓐ Ⓓ	37	Ⓐ Ⓓ
38.	9488 32nd Ave S	9483 32nd Ave S	38	Ⓐ Ⓓ	38	Ⓐ Ⓓ
39.	1143 S Greenbriar Ct	1149 S Greenbriar Ct	39	Ⓐ Ⓓ	39	Ⓐ Ⓓ
40.	766 Hazel Park	766 Hazel Park	40	Ⓐ Ⓓ	40	Ⓐ Ⓓ

Go on to the next number on the next page.

41.	8976 S Lester	8976 S Lester	41	Ⓐ Ⓓ	41	Ⓐ Ⓓ
42.	389 Hubert Rd	389 Hubert Rd	42	Ⓐ Ⓓ	42	Ⓐ Ⓓ
43.	8881 Melvin Way	8881 Melvin Way	43	Ⓐ Ⓓ	43	Ⓐ Ⓓ
44.	76459 Ronald St	76459 Ronald Dr	44	Ⓐ Ⓓ	44	Ⓐ Ⓓ
45.	3887 Saint Peter Dr	3887 Saint Peter Dr	45	Ⓐ Ⓓ	45	Ⓐ Ⓓ
46.	4152 Melrose Park	4152 Melrose Park	46	Ⓐ Ⓓ	46	Ⓐ Ⓓ
47.	4648 Crestwood N	4643 Crestwood N	47	Ⓐ Ⓓ	47	Ⓐ Ⓓ
48.	37647 Stables St	37647 Stables Rd	48	Ⓐ Ⓓ	48	Ⓐ Ⓓ
49.	3754 S Belair Blvd	3754 S Belaire Blvd	49	Ⓐ Ⓓ	49	Ⓐ Ⓓ
50.	370 E Essex St	370 W Essex St	50	Ⓐ Ⓓ	50	Ⓐ Ⓓ
51.	3654 S Mathews	3654 S Mathew	51	Ⓐ Ⓓ	51	Ⓐ Ⓓ
52.	94745 Severance Ct	94745 Severance Ct	52	Ⓐ Ⓓ	52	Ⓐ Ⓓ
53.	4538 Wheeler Way	4538 Wheeler Way	53	Ⓐ Ⓓ	53	Ⓐ Ⓓ
54.	794 Norfolk Ave	794 Norfolk Ave	54	Ⓐ Ⓓ	54	Ⓐ Ⓓ
55.	578 7th Ave NW	578 7th Ave SW	55	Ⓐ Ⓓ	55	Ⓐ Ⓓ
56.	3904 12th St. SW	3904 12th St SE	56	Ⓐ Ⓓ	56	Ⓐ Ⓓ
57.	3547 S Wendover	3547 S Wendover	57	Ⓐ Ⓓ	57	Ⓐ Ⓓ
58.	448 E Lincoln Sq	448 E Lincoln Sq	58	Ⓐ Ⓓ	58	Ⓐ Ⓓ
59.	354 St. Peter St E	354 St Peter St E	59	Ⓐ Ⓓ	59	Ⓐ Ⓓ
60.	3308 Essex Ct	3308 Essex Ct	60	Ⓐ Ⓓ	60	Ⓐ Ⓓ
61.	947 E Amherst	947 W Amherst	61	Ⓐ Ⓓ	61	Ⓐ Ⓓ
62.	7987 Elizabeth Ln	7987 Elizabeth Ln	62	Ⓐ Ⓓ	62	Ⓐ Ⓓ
63.	3649 Montrose Rd	3649 Montrose Rd	63	Ⓐ Ⓓ	63	Ⓐ Ⓓ
64.	396 Montreal Pl	3946 Montreal Pl	64	Ⓐ Ⓓ	64	Ⓐ Ⓓ
65.	4497 Clayton Ct	4497 Clayton St	65	Ⓐ Ⓓ	65	Ⓐ Ⓓ
66.	436 Ontario Way	486 Ontario Way	66	Ⓐ Ⓓ	66	Ⓐ Ⓓ
67.	94876 S Olmstead	94876 N Olmstead	67	Ⓐ Ⓓ	67	Ⓐ Ⓓ
68.	3540 Brooks Shield	3540 Brooks Shield	68	Ⓐ Ⓓ	68	Ⓐ Ⓓ
69.	9887 Cortland Dr	9837 Cortland Dr	69	Ⓐ Ⓓ	69	Ⓐ Ⓓ
70.	397 S Hamilton Ln	397 S Hamilton Ln	70	Ⓐ Ⓓ	70	Ⓐ Ⓓ
71.	547 E Vernon	547 S Vernon	71	Ⓐ Ⓓ	71	Ⓐ Ⓓ
72.	7845 S Perry Dr	7845 N Perry Dr	72	Ⓐ Ⓓ	72	Ⓐ Ⓓ
73.	4457 Old Hickory	4487 Old Hickory	73	Ⓐ Ⓓ	73	Ⓐ Ⓓ
74.	5645 N Dolomite Dr	5645 S Dolomite Dr	74	Ⓐ Ⓓ	74	Ⓐ Ⓓ
75.	3540 S Hampstead Pl	3540 S Hampstead Pl	75	Ⓐ Ⓓ	75	Ⓐ Ⓓ
76.	35489 E Clinton Sq	85489 E Clinton Sq	76	Ⓐ Ⓓ	76	Ⓐ Ⓓ
77.	3548 Bush Hwy	3548 Bush Hwy	77	Ⓐ Ⓓ	77	Ⓐ Ⓓ
78.	3540 S Kendall	3540 S Kendall	78	Ⓐ Ⓓ	78	Ⓐ Ⓓ
79.	3540 Battlecreek Rd	354 Battlecreeek Rd	79	Ⓐ Ⓓ	79	Ⓐ Ⓓ
80.	5469 Bismark Park	5489 Bismark Park	80	Ⓐ Ⓓ	80	Ⓐ Ⓓ
81.	84645 Pocahontas Hwy	84645 Pocahontas Hwy	81	Ⓐ Ⓓ	81	Ⓐ Ⓓ
82.	3954 Wasbash Rd	3854 Wasbash Rd	82	Ⓐ Ⓓ	82	Ⓐ Ⓓ
83.	4965 Bancroft Pky	4965 Gancroft Pky	83	Ⓐ Ⓓ	83	Ⓐ Ⓓ
84.	3547 S Windsor Ave	3547 S Windsor Ave	84	Ⓐ Ⓓ	84	Ⓐ Ⓓ
85.	6947 Hiawatha Way	6947 Hiawatha Way	85	Ⓐ Ⓓ	85	Ⓐ Ⓓ
86.	3540 E Lucerne Dr	3540 E Lucerne Dr	86	Ⓐ Ⓓ	86	Ⓐ Ⓓ
87.	4645 Marshall Park	4645 Marshal Park	87	Ⓐ Ⓓ	87	Ⓐ Ⓓ
88.	3545 Janet Pl	3548 Janet Pl	88	Ⓐ Ⓓ	88	Ⓐ Ⓓ
89.	9943 Lucern Way	9943 Lucern Way	89	Ⓐ Ⓓ	89	Ⓐ Ⓓ

Go on to the next number on the next page.

90. 3369 S Laverne Rd	3369 S Laverne St	90 Ⓐ Ⓓ	90 Ⓐ Ⓓ
91. 6536 Sta. Ana Rd	6536 Sta. Ana St	91 Ⓐ Ⓓ	91 Ⓐ Ⓓ
92. 7659 5th Ave SW	7659 5th Ave SE	92 Ⓐ Ⓓ	92 Ⓐ Ⓓ
93. 36450 S Marshall	36450 S Marshall	93 Ⓐ Ⓓ	93 Ⓐ Ⓓ
94. 4783 Randolph Hwy	4783 Randolf Hwy	94 Ⓐ Ⓓ	94 Ⓐ Ⓓ
95. 6459 Bismark Cove	6459 Bismark Cove	95 Ⓐ Ⓓ	95 Ⓐ Ⓓ

STOP

If you finish before the time is up, check your answers for Part A.

Do not go to any other part.

(See the correct answers on the next page.)

Correct Answers

Address-Checking Test

1. A	25. A	49. D	73. D
2. D	26. A	50. D	74. D
3. A	27. A	51. D	75. A
4. A	28. D	52. A	76. D
5. D	29. A	53. A	77. A
6. A	30. A	54. A	78. A
7. A	31. D	55. D	79. D
8. A	32. D	56. D	80. D
9. D	33. D	57. A	81. A
10. A	34. A	58. A	82. D
11. A	35. D	59. A	83. D
12. D	36. A	60. A	84. A
13. A	37. A	61. D	85. A
14. A	38. D	62. A	86. A
15. D	39. D	63. A	87. D
16. D	40. A	64. D	88. D
17. D	41. A	65. D	89. A
18. A	42. A	66. D	90. D
19. D	43. A	67. D	91. D
20. D	44. D	68. A	92. D
21. D	45. A	69. D	93. A
22. D	46. A	70. A	94. D
23. A	47. D	71. D	95. A
24. D	48. D	72. D	

Address-Checking Practice Test

Work—6 Minutes

These addresses are like the ones in the address-checking test.

Decide whether the two addresses are *Alike* or *Different*. if they are *Alike*, darken or mark space A; if they are *Different* darken Space D. Mark the answers on the answer sheet to the right. Work as fast as you can without making too many errors. Work exactly 6 minutes.

			Test A	Test B
1.	3540 Willow SW	3540 Willo SE	1 Ⓐ Ⓓ	1 Ⓐ Ⓓ
2.	3548 Santa Cruz Bay	3548 Santa Cruz Bay	2 Ⓐ Ⓓ	2 Ⓐ Ⓓ
3.	9375 Hollister Rd	9375 Hollister St	3 Ⓐ Ⓓ	3 Ⓐ Ⓓ
4.	65499 Grandview Dr	65499 Grandview Dr	4 Ⓐ Ⓓ	4 Ⓐ Ⓓ
5.	385 Evangeline St	385 Evangeline St	5 Ⓐ Ⓓ	5 Ⓐ Ⓓ
6.	9354 Briarcliff View	9354 Briarcliff View	6 Ⓐ Ⓓ	6 Ⓐ Ⓓ
7.	39547 Memphis Rd	39547 Memphis St	7 Ⓐ Ⓓ	7 Ⓐ Ⓓ
8.	1978 Briarwood Cir	1978 Briarwood Cir	8 Ⓐ Ⓓ	8 Ⓐ Ⓓ
9.	3954 Peppermint	3954 Peppermint	9 Ⓐ Ⓓ	9 Ⓐ Ⓓ
10.	3549 Woodward Ave	3549 Woodward Ave	10 Ⓐ Ⓓ	10 Ⓐ Ⓓ
11.	23323 Teppert St	23328 Teppert St	11 Ⓐ Ⓓ	11 Ⓐ Ⓓ
12.	4488 Campbell	4488 Campbell	12 Ⓐ Ⓓ	12 Ⓐ Ⓓ
13.	8745 S Copper Creek	8745 N Copper Creek	13 Ⓐ Ⓓ	13 Ⓐ Ⓓ
14.	865 12th Mile S	865 12th Mile S	14 Ⓐ Ⓓ	14 Ⓐ Ⓓ
15.	647 Morning Breeze	647 Morning Breese	15 Ⓐ Ⓓ	15 Ⓐ Ⓓ
16.	9481 Bownsville Cove	9481 Brownsville Cove	16 Ⓐ Ⓓ	16 Ⓐ Ⓓ
17.	1054 Gainsville Rd	1054 Gainsville Rd	17 Ⓐ Ⓓ	17 Ⓐ Ⓓ
18.	6493 Parker Cir	6493 Parker Cir	18 Ⓐ Ⓓ	18 Ⓐ Ⓓ
19.	9454 Alexandria St	9454 Alexandra Dr	19 Ⓐ Ⓓ	19 Ⓐ Ⓓ
20.	7845 Crescent View	7845 Crescent View	20 Ⓐ Ⓓ	20 Ⓐ Ⓓ
21.	9450 Darwin St	9450 Darwin Sq	21 Ⓐ Ⓓ	21 Ⓐ Ⓓ
22.	390 Pandora Rd	390 Pandora Rd	22 Ⓐ Ⓓ	22 Ⓐ Ⓓ
23.	5403 Gilbert St	5408 Gilbert St	23 Ⓐ Ⓓ	23 Ⓐ Ⓓ
24.	38545 Santa Fe Cir	33545 Santa Fe Cir	24 Ⓐ Ⓓ	24 Ⓐ Ⓓ
25.	3054 S Daytona St	3054 S Daytona St	25 Ⓐ Ⓓ	25 Ⓐ Ⓓ
26.	9467 Guadalupe Loop	9467 Guadalupe Loop	26 Ⓐ Ⓓ	26 Ⓐ Ⓓ
27.	10545 Tallahasse Ln	10548 Tallsahasse Ln	27 Ⓐ Ⓓ	27 Ⓐ Ⓓ
28.	54065 Redfield SW	54065 Redfield SW	28 Ⓐ Ⓓ	28 Ⓐ Ⓓ
29.	8351 Greenfield Sq	3351 Greenfield Sq	29 Ⓐ Ⓓ	29 Ⓐ Ⓓ
30.	8354 52nd Ave S	8354 52nd Ave S	30 Ⓐ Ⓓ	30 Ⓐ Ⓓ
31.	8540 Sleepy Hollow	8540 Sleepy Hollow	31 Ⓐ Ⓓ	31 Ⓐ Ⓓ
32.	3954 Hubert Dr	3954 Hubert Dr	32 Ⓐ Ⓓ	32 Ⓐ Ⓓ
33.	5482 Durhamn Rd	5482 Durham Rd	33 Ⓐ Ⓓ	33 Ⓐ Ⓓ
34.	9354 Maleroy	9354 Maleroy	34 Ⓐ Ⓓ	34 Ⓐ Ⓓ
35.	3367 Franklin S	3367 Franklin N	35 Ⓐ Ⓓ	35 Ⓐ Ⓓ
36.	3954 E Beechnut	3954 E Beechnut	36 Ⓐ Ⓓ	36 Ⓐ Ⓓ
37.	9461 Falcon Crest	9461 Falcon Crest	37 Ⓐ Ⓓ	37 Ⓐ Ⓓ
38.	94564 Carver Pl	94564 Carver Pl	38 Ⓐ Ⓓ	38 Ⓐ Ⓓ
39.	7735 Keyport Point	7733 Keyport Point	39 Ⓐ Ⓓ	39 Ⓐ Ⓓ
40.	9454 Scotts Bluff N	9454 Scotts Bluff S	40 Ⓐ Ⓓ	40 Ⓐ Ⓓ

Go on to the next number on the next page.

41.	3300 Boston Harbor	3300 Boston Harbor	41 Ⓐ Ⓓ	41 Ⓐ Ⓓ
42.	93547 St John	93547 St John	42 Ⓐ Ⓓ	42 Ⓐ Ⓓ
43.	9476 Eagle View	9476 Eagle View	43 Ⓐ Ⓓ	43 Ⓐ Ⓓ
44.	3054 Blanchard Dr	3054 Blanchard Cir	44 Ⓐ Ⓓ	44 Ⓐ Ⓓ
45.	3377 Alderwood Ln	3377 Alderwood Ln	45 Ⓐ Ⓓ	45 Ⓐ Ⓓ
46.	5667 Sievers Rd	5661 Sievers Rd	46 Ⓐ Ⓓ	46 Ⓐ Ⓓ
47.	9457 S Burnett	9457 N Burnett	47 Ⓐ Ⓓ	47 Ⓐ Ⓓ
48.	6573 Dixon Rd	6573 Dixon Rd	48 Ⓐ Ⓓ	48 Ⓐ Ⓓ
49.	8477 Covington Ln	8477 Covington Ln	49 Ⓐ Ⓓ	49 Ⓐ Ⓓ
50.	3549 E Amhurst Creek	3549 W Amherst Creek	50 Ⓐ Ⓓ	50 Ⓐ Ⓓ
51.	9474 Melbourne Ave	9474 Melborne Ave	51 Ⓐ Ⓓ	51 Ⓐ Ⓓ
52.	3549 Granite View	3549 Gratite View	52 Ⓐ Ⓓ	52 Ⓐ Ⓓ
53.	3047 Diamond Crest	3047 Diamond Crest	53 Ⓐ Ⓓ	53 Ⓐ Ⓓ
54.	39540 Central Plaza	30540 Central Plaza	54 Ⓐ Ⓓ	54 Ⓐ Ⓓ
55.	3540 Blake Rd	3540 Blake Rd	55 Ⓐ Ⓓ	55 Ⓐ Ⓓ
56.	3054 Cooper SW	3054 Cooper SE	56 Ⓐ Ⓓ	56 Ⓐ Ⓓ
57.	745 Knoll IIwy	745 Knoll Hwy	57 Ⓐ Ⓓ	57 Ⓐ Ⓓ
58.	5400 Birmingham Park	5400 Biningham Park	58 Ⓐ Ⓓ	58 Ⓐ Ⓓ
59.	3954 Grant Pl	3954 Grant Pl	59 Ⓐ Ⓓ	59 Ⓐ Ⓓ
60.	45451 7th Ave SW	45451 7th Ave SE	60 Ⓐ Ⓓ	60 Ⓐ Ⓓ
61.	3054 Bridgeview St	3054 Bridgeview St	61 Ⓐ Ⓓ	61 Ⓐ Ⓓ
62.	3954 Armistice	3954 Armistice	62 Ⓐ Ⓓ	62 Ⓐ Ⓓ
63.	541 S Averley	541 N Averley	63 Ⓐ Ⓓ	63 Ⓐ Ⓓ
64.	3005 Flint SW	8005 Flint SW	64 Ⓐ Ⓓ	64 Ⓐ Ⓓ
65.	39651 Chrysler Rd	39651 Chrysler Rd	65 Ⓐ Ⓓ	65 Ⓐ Ⓓ
66.	3301 Ford Pky	3301 Ford Pky	66 Ⓐ Ⓓ	66 Ⓐ Ⓓ
67.	7731 Armstrong Dr	7731 Armstrong Dr	67 Ⓐ Ⓓ	67 Ⓐ Ⓓ
68.	33901 King St	33907 King Sq	68 Ⓐ Ⓓ	68 Ⓐ Ⓓ
69.	310 Amapola Rd	310 Anapola Rd	69 Ⓐ Ⓓ	69 Ⓐ Ⓓ
70.	3016 Straton Lake	3016 Straton Lake	70 Ⓐ Ⓓ	70 Ⓐ Ⓓ
71.	3011 Belmont Way	3011 Belmont Way	71 Ⓐ Ⓓ	71 Ⓐ Ⓓ
72.	318 S Marine	318 N Marine	72 Ⓐ Ⓓ	72 Ⓐ Ⓓ
73.	3105 N Foster Ave	3105 N Foster Ave	73 Ⓐ Ⓓ	73 Ⓐ Ⓓ
74.	3016 Knottingham	3016 Knottingham	74 Ⓐ Ⓓ	74 Ⓐ Ⓓ
75.	7861 Bell St	7861 Bell St	75 Ⓐ Ⓓ	75 Ⓐ Ⓓ
76.	3810 Jerriman S	3810 Jerriman N	76 Ⓐ Ⓓ	76 Ⓐ Ⓓ
77.	3106 Knickerbocker	3106 Knickerbocker	77 Ⓐ Ⓓ	77 Ⓐ Ⓓ
78.	1154 R Johnston	1154 R Johnston	78 Ⓐ Ⓓ	78 Ⓐ Ⓓ
79.	31545 Dorchester	31545 Darchester	79 Ⓐ Ⓓ	79 Ⓐ Ⓓ
80.	3154 Ft. Hamilton	3154 Ft Hamilton	80 Ⓐ Ⓓ	80 Ⓐ Ⓓ
81.	3190 S Boulder	3190 S Boulder	81 Ⓐ Ⓓ	81 Ⓐ Ⓓ
82.	3106 NW 157th St	8315 SW 157th St	82 Ⓐ Ⓓ	82 Ⓐ Ⓓ
83.	3154 Evergreen	3154 Evergreen	83 Ⓐ Ⓓ	83 Ⓐ Ⓓ
84.	3154 Rosengarden	3154 Rosengarden	84 Ⓐ Ⓓ	84 Ⓐ Ⓓ
85.	3965 Lumberville N	3965 Lumberville S	85 Ⓐ Ⓓ	85 Ⓐ Ⓓ
86.	316 Markham S	316 Markam S	86 Ⓐ Ⓓ	86 Ⓐ Ⓓ
87.	3188 Warnock Creek	3188 Warnock Creek	87 Ⓐ Ⓓ	87 Ⓐ Ⓓ
88.	3110 Kessler Nook	3110 Kessler Nook	88 Ⓐ Ⓓ	88 Ⓐ Ⓓ
89.	3388 Ovington Park	3388 Ovington Park	89 Ⓐ Ⓓ	89 Ⓐ Ⓓ

Go on to the next number on the next page.

90. 3100 Catalina Cir	3100 Catalina Cir	90	Ⓐ Ⓓ	90	Ⓐ Ⓓ
91. 9615 Dorchester	9615 Darchester	91	Ⓐ Ⓓ	91	Ⓐ Ⓓ
92. 3110 Blake E	3110 Blake S	92	Ⓐ Ⓓ	92	Ⓐ Ⓓ
93. 3174 Empire St	8174 Empire St	93	Ⓐ Ⓓ	93	Ⓐ Ⓓ
94. 1947 Hampton Ave	1847 Hampton Ave	94	Ⓐ Ⓓ	94	Ⓐ Ⓓ
95. 31054 Hancock	31054 Hamcock	95	Ⓐ Ⓓ	95	Ⓐ Ⓓ

STOP

If you finish before the time is up, check your answers for Part A.

Do not go to any other part.

(See the correct answers on the next page.)

Correct Answers

Address-Checking Test

1. D		49. A	73. A
2. A	25. A	50. D	74. A
3. D	26. A	51. D	75. A
4. A	27. D	52. D	76. D
5. A	28. A	53. A	77. A
6. A	29. D	54. D	78. A
7. D	30. A	55. A	79. D
8. A	31. A	56. D	80. A
9. A	32. A	57. A	81. A
10. A	33. D	58. D	82. D
11. D	34. A	59. A	83. A
12. A	35. D	60. D	84. A
13. D	36. A	61. A	85. D
14. A	37. A	62. A	86. D
15. D	38. A	63. D	87. A
16. D	39. D	64. D	88. A
17. A	40. D	65. A	89. A
18. A	41. A	66. A	90. A
19. D	42. A	67. A	91. D
20. A	43. A	68. D	92. D
21. D	44. D	69. D	93. D
22. A	45. A	70. A	94. D
23. D	46. D	71. A	95. D
24. D	47. D	72. D	
	48. A		

Address-Checking Practice Test

Work—6 Minutes

These addresses are like the ones in the address-checking test.

Decide whether the two addresses are *Alike* or *Different*. If they are *Alike*, darken or mark space A; if they are *Different*, darken space D. Mark the answers on the answer sheet to the right. Work as fast as you can without making too many errors. Work exactly 6 minutes.

#	Address 1	Address 2	Test A	Test B
1.	76386 Island Park	76386 Island Park	1 Ⓐ Ⓓ	1 Ⓐ Ⓓ
2.	3540 S Hotel Rd	9540 S Hotel Rd	2 Ⓐ Ⓓ	2 Ⓐ Ⓓ
3.	3964 Missouri Ct	3964 Misouri Ct	3 Ⓐ Ⓓ	3 Ⓐ Ⓓ
4.	93645 Harness St	93647 Harness St	4 Ⓐ Ⓓ	4 Ⓐ Ⓓ
5.	3540 Raffles Blvd	3540 Raffles Blvd	5 Ⓐ Ⓓ	5 Ⓐ Ⓓ
6.	350 N Westminster	350 N Westminster	6 Ⓐ Ⓓ	6 Ⓐ Ⓓ
7.	3064 Columbia Dr	3064 Columbia Dr	7 Ⓐ Ⓓ	7 Ⓐ Ⓓ
8.	5400 Cordelia NW	5400 Cordelia NE	8 Ⓐ Ⓓ	8 Ⓐ Ⓓ
9.	1649 Kauai Rd	1649 Kauai Rd	9 Ⓐ Ⓓ	9 Ⓐ Ⓓ
10.	3540 Cadiz Way	3540 Cadiz Way	10 Ⓐ Ⓓ	10 Ⓐ Ⓓ
11.	3889 Stockbridge S	3839 Stockbridge S	11 Ⓐ Ⓓ	11 Ⓐ Ⓓ
12.	4401 E Cadiz Ln	4401 S Cadiz Ln	12 Ⓐ Ⓓ	12 Ⓐ Ⓓ
13.	35400 Morris Ave	35400 Morris Ave	13 Ⓐ Ⓓ	13 Ⓐ Ⓓ
14.	3054 Hampton Rd	3054 Hanpton Rd	14 Ⓐ Ⓓ	14 Ⓐ Ⓓ
15.	3358 Marina Rd	3353 Marina Rd	15 Ⓐ Ⓓ	15 Ⓐ Ⓓ
16.	30658 Windmill Ave	30658 Windmill Ave	16 Ⓐ Ⓓ	16 Ⓐ Ⓓ
17.	7883 Markham Way	7883 Markhan Way	17 Ⓐ Ⓓ	17 Ⓐ Ⓓ
18.	30654 Warnock St	30654 Warnock St	18 Ⓐ Ⓓ	18 Ⓐ Ⓓ
19.	5400 Berkshire Sq	5400 Berkshire Sq	19 Ⓐ Ⓓ	19 Ⓐ Ⓓ
20.	9365 Columbia Dr	9365 Columbia Ave	20 Ⓐ Ⓓ	20 Ⓐ Ⓓ
21.	8835 Doughty Hwy	8835 Doughty Hwy	21 Ⓐ Ⓓ	21 Ⓐ Ⓓ
22.	3047 Jerriman Pky	3047 Jerriman Pky	22 Ⓐ Ⓓ	22 Ⓐ Ⓓ
23.	6589 Nautilus Castle	6539 Nautilus Castle	23 Ⓐ Ⓓ	23 Ⓐ Ⓓ
24.	4054 Red Light	4058 Red Light	24 Ⓐ Ⓓ	24 Ⓐ Ⓓ
25.	385 S Blue Moon	385 S Blue Moon	25 Ⓐ Ⓓ	25 Ⓐ Ⓓ
26.	3054 Green Lagoon	3058 Green Lagoon	26 Ⓐ Ⓓ	26 Ⓐ Ⓓ
27.	3064 Kalamazoo Rd	3064 Kalamazoo St	27 Ⓐ Ⓓ	27 Ⓐ Ⓓ
28.	6540 Catalunia Dr	6540 Catalunia Dr	28 Ⓐ Ⓓ	28 Ⓐ Ⓓ
29.	9463 Delaware Creek	9469 Delaware Creek	29 Ⓐ Ⓓ	29 Ⓐ Ⓓ
30.	3054 LaSalle Village	3054 LaSale Village	30 Ⓐ Ⓓ	30 Ⓐ Ⓓ
31.	5405 Hamilton Way	5405 Hamilton Way	31 Ⓐ Ⓓ	31 Ⓐ Ⓓ
32.	5481 Montana Dr	5481 Montana Dr	32 Ⓐ Ⓓ	32 Ⓐ Ⓓ
33.	8954 Doughty Way	8957 Doughty Hwy	33 Ⓐ Ⓓ	33 Ⓐ Ⓓ
34.	3054 Christy St	3054 Christy St	34 Ⓐ Ⓓ	34 Ⓐ Ⓓ
35.	3437 Glendale Rd	5437 Glendale St	35 Ⓐ Ⓓ	35 Ⓐ Ⓓ
36.	43065 7th Ave W	40368 7th Ave W	36 Ⓐ Ⓓ	36 Ⓐ Ⓓ
37.	3054 MacDonald Vlg	3054 MacDonald Vlg	37 Ⓐ Ⓓ	37 Ⓐ Ⓓ
38.	30547 Keating E	30547 Keating W	38 Ⓐ Ⓓ	38 Ⓐ Ⓓ
39.	3054 Carter Dr	3057 Carter Dr	39 Ⓐ Ⓓ	39 Ⓐ Ⓓ
40.	3068 E Evanston	3063 Evanston	40 Ⓐ Ⓓ	40 Ⓐ Ⓓ

Go on to the next number on the next page.

41. 64506 Pittmar Dr	64506 Pittmar Dr	41 Ⓐ Ⓓ	41 Ⓐ Ⓓ	
42. 3540 Chamber Ln	3540 Chamber Ln	42 Ⓐ Ⓓ	42 Ⓐ Ⓓ	
43. 3954 Central Sq	3954 Central Sq	43 Ⓐ Ⓓ	43 Ⓐ Ⓓ	
44. 944 S Apple Rdge	944 S Apple Rdg	44 Ⓐ Ⓓ	44 Ⓐ Ⓓ	
45. 4867 Tripp Rd	4887 Tripp Rd	45 Ⓐ Ⓓ	45 Ⓐ Ⓓ	
46. 1469 Brayton Cir	1469 Brytom Cir	46 Ⓐ Ⓓ	46 Ⓐ Ⓓ	
47. 4954 Crestlane Rd	4954 Crestlane Rd	47 Ⓐ Ⓓ	47 Ⓐ Ⓓ	
48. 3054 Wilmington Pl	3054 Wilmington Pl	48 Ⓐ Ⓓ	48 Ⓐ Ⓓ	
49. 7697 Brooklyn Bridge	7697 Brooklyn Bridge	49 Ⓐ Ⓓ	49 Ⓐ Ⓓ	
50. 85349 Williston St	85349 Williston St	50 Ⓐ Ⓓ	50 Ⓐ Ⓓ	
51. 5831 Medford Dr	5831 Melford Dr	51 Ⓐ Ⓓ	51 Ⓐ Ⓓ	
52. 9485 Tuyvesant Way	9485 Tuysevent Way	52 Ⓐ Ⓓ	52 Ⓐ Ⓓ	
53. 5948 Briarcliff St	5948 Briarcliff St	53 Ⓐ Ⓓ	53 Ⓐ Ⓓ	
54. 4057 59th St W	4057 59th St E	54 Ⓐ Ⓓ	54 Ⓐ Ⓓ	
55. 57849 Prince Rd	57849 Prince Rd	55 Ⓐ Ⓓ	55 Ⓐ Ⓓ	
56. 4857 Welch Sq	4857 Welch Sq	56 Ⓐ Ⓓ	56 Ⓐ Ⓓ	
57. 59846 Interlaken	53846 Interlaken	57 Ⓐ Ⓓ	57 Ⓐ Ⓓ	
58. 3857 Rugby St	3857 Rugby St	58 Ⓐ Ⓓ	58 Ⓐ Ⓓ	
59. 4395 Boutinville	4395 Boutinville	59 Ⓐ Ⓓ	59 Ⓐ Ⓓ	
60. 294 76th Ave SW	294 76th Ave SW	60 Ⓐ Ⓓ	60 Ⓐ Ⓓ	
61. 8823 Pleasant Run	8828 Pleasant Run	61 Ⓐ Ⓓ	61 Ⓐ Ⓓ	
62. 4867 Old Coral Rd	4867 Old Coral Rd	62 Ⓐ Ⓓ	62 Ⓐ Ⓓ	
63. 4856 Chessnut Way	4356 Chessnut Way	63 Ⓐ Ⓓ	63 Ⓐ Ⓓ	
64. 475 Penn Sq	475 Penn Sq	64 Ⓐ Ⓓ	64 Ⓐ Ⓓ	
65. 4057 Mountainville	4057 Mountainville	65 Ⓐ Ⓓ	65 Ⓐ Ⓓ	
66. 4005 Bryant Rd	4008 Bryant Rd	66 Ⓐ Ⓓ	66 Ⓐ Ⓓ	
67. 4481 Carmen Cove	4482 Carmen Cove	67 Ⓐ Ⓓ	67 Ⓐ Ⓓ	
68. 497 S Elmhurst	497 S Elmhurst	68 Ⓐ Ⓓ	68 Ⓐ Ⓓ	
69. 3751 Spring Valley	3751 Spring Valley	69 Ⓐ Ⓓ	69 Ⓐ Ⓓ	
70. 4477 Sycamore Rd	4477 Sycamore St	70 Ⓐ Ⓓ	70 Ⓐ Ⓓ	
71. 8845 Massachusettes	8848 Massachusettes	71 Ⓐ Ⓓ	71 Ⓐ Ⓓ	
72. 405 SE Griffin Way	405 SW Griffin Way	72 Ⓐ Ⓓ	72 Ⓐ Ⓓ	
73. 4054 Crossroad Pky	4054 Crossroad Pky	73 Ⓐ Ⓓ	73 Ⓐ Ⓓ	
74. 4976 Kempner Dr	4976 Kempner Sq	74 Ⓐ Ⓓ	74 Ⓐ Ⓓ	
75. 9451 Stephenway Hwy	9451 Stephenway Pky	75 Ⓐ Ⓓ	75 Ⓐ Ⓓ	
76. 8830 Runyon Way	8830 Runyon Way	76 Ⓐ Ⓓ	76 Ⓐ Ⓓ	
77. 7740 Sedgewick St	7740 Sedgewick St	77 Ⓐ Ⓓ	77 Ⓐ Ⓓ	
78. 8847 Upper Loop Dr	8347 Upper Loop Dr	78 Ⓐ Ⓓ	78 Ⓐ Ⓓ	
79. 3754 Westchester Rd	3754 Westchester Rd	79 Ⓐ Ⓓ	79 Ⓐ Ⓓ	
80. 9973 Bisbee Creek	9973 Bisbeek Creek	80 Ⓐ Ⓓ	80 Ⓐ Ⓓ	
81. 4956 Kneeland Way S	4956 Kneeland Way S	81 Ⓐ Ⓓ	81 Ⓐ Ⓓ	
82. 6947 LeRoy Rdg	6947 LeRoy Brdg	82 Ⓐ Ⓓ	82 Ⓐ Ⓓ	
83. 4954 Honeybee Cir	4954 Honebee Cir	83 Ⓐ Ⓓ	83 Ⓐ Ⓓ	
84. 7745 Kneeland Ct	7745 Kneeland Ct	84 Ⓐ Ⓓ	84 Ⓐ Ⓓ	
85. 3354 Upperhill Way	3354 Uppperhill Hwy	85 Ⓐ Ⓓ	85 Ⓐ Ⓓ	
86. 46549 Moseman Rd	46549 Moseman Rd	86 Ⓐ Ⓓ	86 Ⓐ Ⓓ	
87. 449 17th Ave SW	449 17th Ave SE	87 Ⓐ Ⓓ	87 Ⓐ Ⓓ	
88. 5478 Curtis Way	5478 Curtis Way	88 Ⓐ Ⓓ	88 Ⓐ Ⓓ	
89. 54854 Gedney Rd	54854 Gedney Rd	89 Ⓐ Ⓓ	89 Ⓐ Ⓓ	

Go on to the next number on the next page.

90. 68893 Hudson Bay	68893 Hudson Bay	90 Ⓐ Ⓓ	90 Ⓐ Ⓓ
91. 44054 Palmer Rd	44054 Palmer Rd	91 Ⓐ Ⓓ	91 Ⓐ Ⓓ
92. 9943 Evangeline Sq	9943 Evangeline Sq	92 Ⓐ Ⓓ	92 Ⓐ Ⓓ
93. 4467 Lorezo Rd	4467 Lorenzo Rd	93 Ⓐ Ⓓ	93 Ⓐ Ⓓ
94. 9947 Robbin W	9847 Robbin W	94 Ⓐ Ⓓ	94 Ⓐ Ⓓ
95. 4471 S Lawton Sq	4471 N Lawton Sq	95 Ⓐ Ⓓ	95 Ⓐ Ⓓ

If you finish before the time is up, check your answers for Part A.

STOP

If you finish before the time is up, check your answers for Part A.

Do not go to any other part.

(See the correct answers on the next page.)

Correct Answers

Address-Checking Test

1. A	25. A	49. A	73. A
2. D	26. D	50. A	74. D
3. D	27. D	51. D	75. D
4. D	28. A	52. D	76. A
5. A	29. D	53. A	77. A
6. A	30. D	54. D	78. D
7. A	31. A	55. A	79. A
8. D	32. A	56. A	80. D
9. A	33. D	57. D	81. A
10. A	34. A	58. A	82. D
11. D	35. D	59. A	83. D
12. D	36. D	60. A	84. A
13. A	37. A	61. D	85. D
14. D	38. D	62. A	86. A
15. D	39. D	63. D	87. D
16. A	40. D	64. A	88. A
17. D	41. A	65. A	89. A
18. A	42. A	66. D	90. A
19. A	43. A	67. D	91. A
20. D	44. A	68. A	92. A
21. A	45. D	69. A	93. D
22. A	46. D	70. D	94. D
23. D	47. A	71. D	95. D
24. D	48. A	72. D	

Address-Checking Practice Test

Work—6 Minutes

These addresses are like the ones in the address-checking test.

Decide whether the two addresses are *Alike* or *Different*. If they are *Alike*, darken or mark space A; if they are *Different*, darken space D. Mark the answers on the answer sheet to the right. Work as fast as you can without making too many errors. Work exactly 6 minutes.

ANSWER SHEET

#	Address 1	Address 2	Test A	Test B
1.	405 Winter Rd NW	405 Winter Rd NW	Ⓐ Ⓓ	Ⓐ Ⓓ
2.	607 S Calaveras Rd	607 S Calaveras Rd	Ⓐ Ⓓ	Ⓐ Ⓓ
3.	8406 La Casa St	8406 La Cosa St	Ⓐ Ⓓ	Ⓐ Ⓓ
4.	121 N Rippon St	121 N Rippon St	Ⓐ Ⓓ	Ⓐ Ⓓ
5.	Wideman Ark	Wiseman Ark	Ⓐ Ⓓ	Ⓐ Ⓓ
6.	Sodus NY 14551	Sodus NY 14551	Ⓐ Ⓓ	Ⓐ Ⓓ
7.	3429 Hermosa Dr	3429 Hermoso Dr	Ⓐ Ⓓ	Ⓐ Ⓓ
8.	3628 S Zeeland St	3268 S Zealand St	Ⓐ Ⓓ	Ⓐ Ⓓ
9.	1330 Cheverly Ave NE	1330 Cheverly Ave NE	Ⓐ Ⓓ	Ⓐ Ⓓ
10.	1689 N Derwood Dr	1689 N Derwood Dr	Ⓐ Ⓓ	Ⓐ Ⓓ
11.	3886 Sunrise Ct	3886 Sunrise Ct	Ⓐ Ⓓ	Ⓐ Ⓓ
12.	635 La Calle Mayor	653 La Calle Mayor	Ⓐ Ⓓ	Ⓐ Ⓓ
13.	2560 Lansford Pl	2560 Lansford St	Ⓐ Ⓓ	Ⓐ Ⓓ
14.	4631 Central Ave	4631 Central Ave	Ⓐ Ⓓ	Ⓐ Ⓓ
15.	Mason City Iowa 50401	Mason City Iowa 50401	Ⓐ Ⓓ	Ⓐ Ⓓ
16.	758 Los Arboles Ave SE	758 Los Arboles Ave SW	Ⓐ Ⓓ	Ⓐ Ⓓ
17.	3282 E Downington St	3282 E Dunnington St	Ⓐ Ⓓ	Ⓐ Ⓓ
18.	7117 N Burlingham Ave	7117 N Burlingham Ave	Ⓐ Ⓓ	Ⓐ Ⓓ
19.	32 Oaklawn Blvd	32 Oakland Blvd	Ⓐ Ⓓ	Ⓐ Ⓓ
20.	1274 Manzana Rd	1274 Manzana Rd	Ⓐ Ⓓ	Ⓐ Ⓓ
21.	4598 E Kenilworth Dr	4598 E Kenilworth Dr	Ⓐ Ⓓ	Ⓐ Ⓓ
22.	Dayton Okla 73449	Dagton Okla 73449	Ⓐ Ⓓ	Ⓐ Ⓓ
23.	1172 W 83rd Ave	1127 W 83rd Ave	Ⓐ Ⓓ	Ⓐ Ⓓ
24.	6434 E Pulaski St	6434 E Pulaski Ct	Ⓐ Ⓓ	Ⓐ Ⓓ
25.	2764 N Rutherford Pl	2764 N Rutherford Pl	Ⓐ Ⓓ	Ⓐ Ⓓ
26.	565 Greenville Blvd SE	565 Greenview Blvd SE	Ⓐ Ⓓ	Ⓐ Ⓓ
27.	Washington DC 20013	Washington DC 20018	Ⓐ Ⓓ	Ⓐ Ⓓ
28.	3824 Massasoit St	3824 Massasoit St	Ⓐ Ⓓ	Ⓐ Ⓓ
29.	22 Sagnaw Pkwy	22 Saganaw Pkwy	Ⓐ Ⓓ	Ⓐ Ⓓ
30.	Byram Conn 10573	Byram Conn 10573	Ⓐ Ⓓ	Ⓐ Ⓓ
31.	1928 S Fairfield Ave	1928 S Fairfield St	Ⓐ Ⓓ	Ⓐ Ⓓ
32.	36218 Overhills Dr	36218 Overhills Dr	Ⓐ Ⓓ	Ⓐ Ⓓ
33.	516 Avenida de Las Am	516 Avenida de Las Am	Ⓐ Ⓓ	Ⓐ Ⓓ
34.	7526 Naraganset Pl SW	7526 Naraganset Pl SW	Ⓐ Ⓓ	Ⓐ Ⓓ
35.	52626 W Ogelsby Dr	52626 W Ogelsby Dr	Ⓐ Ⓓ	Ⓐ Ⓓ
36.	1003 Winchester Rd	1003 Westchester RD	Ⓐ Ⓓ	Ⓐ Ⓓ
37.	3478 W Cavanaugh Ct	3478 W Cavenaugh Ct	Ⓐ Ⓓ	Ⓐ Ⓓ
38.	Kendall Calif 90551	Kendell Calif 90551	Ⓐ Ⓓ	Ⓐ Ⓓ
39.	225 El Camino Blvd	225 El Camino Ave	Ⓐ Ⓓ	Ⓐ Ⓓ
40.	7310 Via delos Pisos	7310 Via de los Pinos	Ⓐ Ⓓ	Ⓐ Ⓓ

Go on to the next number on the next page.

41.	1987 Wellington Ave SW	1987 Wellington Ave SW	41 ⒶⒹ	41 ⒶⒹ
42.	3124 S 71st St	3142 S 71st St	42 ⒶⒹ	42 ⒶⒹ
43.	729 Lincolnwood Blvd	729 Lincolnwood Blvd	43 ⒶⒹ	43 ⒶⒹ
44.	1166 N Beaumont Dr	1166 S Beaumont Dr	44 ⒶⒹ	44 ⒶⒹ
45.	3224 W Winecona Pl	3224 W Winecona Pl	45 ⒶⒹ	45 ⒶⒹ
46.	608 Calle Bienvenida	607 Calle Bienvenida	46 ⒶⒹ	46 ⒶⒹ
47.	La Molte Iowa 52045	La Molte Iowa 52045	47 ⒶⒹ	47 ⒶⒹ
48.	8625 Armitage Ave NW	8625 Armitage Ave NW	48 ⒶⒹ	48 ⒶⒹ
49.	2343 Broadview Ave	2334 Broadview Ave	49 ⒶⒹ	49 ⒶⒹ
50.	4279 Sierra Grande Ave	4279 Sierra Grande Dr	50 ⒶⒹ	50 ⒶⒹ
51.	165 32nd Ave	165 32nd Ave	51 ⒶⒹ	51 ⒶⒹ
52.	12742 N Deerborn St	12724 N Deerborn St	52 ⒶⒹ	52 ⒶⒹ
53.	114 Estancia Ave	141 Estancia Ave	53 ⒶⒹ	53 ⒶⒹ
54.	351 S Berwyn Rd	351 S Berwyn Pl	54 ⒶⒹ	54 ⒶⒹ
55.	7732 Avenida Manana SW	7732 Avenida Manana SW	55 ⒶⒹ	55 ⒶⒹ
56.	6337 C St SW	6337 G St SW	56 ⒶⒹ	56 ⒶⒹ
57.	57895 E Drexyl Ave	58795 E Drexyl Ave	57 ⒶⒹ	57 ⒶⒹ
58.	Altro Tex 75923	Altra Tex 75923	58 ⒶⒹ	58 ⒶⒹ
59.	3465 S Nashville St	3465 N Nashville St	59 ⒶⒹ	59 ⒶⒹ
60.	1226 Odell Blvd NW	1226 Oddell Blvd NW	60 ⒶⒹ	60 ⒶⒹ
61.	94002 Chappel Ct	94002 Chappel Ct	61 ⒶⒹ	61 ⒶⒹ
62.	512 La Vega Dr	512 La Veta Dr	62 ⒶⒹ	62 ⒶⒹ
63.	8774 W Winona Pl	8774 R Winona	63 ⒶⒹ	63 ⒶⒹ
64.	6431 Ingleside St SE	6431 Ingleside St SE	64 ⒶⒹ	64 ⒶⒹ
65.	2270 N Leanington St	2270 N Leanington St	65 ⒶⒹ	65 ⒶⒹ
66.	235 Calle de Vecinos	235 Calle de Vecinos	66 ⒶⒹ	66 ⒶⒹ
67.	3987 E Westwood Ave	3987 W Westwood Ave	67 ⒶⒹ	67 ⒶⒹ
68.	Skamokawa Wash	Skamohawa Wash	68 ⒶⒹ	68 ⒶⒹ
69.	2674 E Champlain Cir	2764 E Champlain Cir	69 ⒶⒹ	69 ⒶⒹ
70.	8751 Elmhurst Blvd	8751 Elmwood Blvd	70 ⒶⒹ	70 ⒶⒹ
71.	6649 Solano Dr	6649 Solana Dr	71 ⒶⒹ	71 ⒶⒹ
72.	4423 S Escenaba St	4423 S Escenaba St	72 ⒶⒹ	72 ⒶⒹ
73.	1198 N St NW	1198 M St NW	73 ⒶⒹ	73 ⒶⒹ
74.	Sparta GA	Sparta Va	74 ⒶⒹ	74 ⒶⒹ
75.	96753 Wrightwood Ave	96753 Wrightwood Ave	75 ⒶⒹ	75 ⒶⒹ
76.	2445 Sangamow Ave SE	2445 Sangamow Ave SE	76 ⒶⒹ	76 ⒶⒹ
77.	5117 E 67 Pl	5171 E 67 Pl	77 ⒶⒹ	77 ⒶⒹ
78.	847 Mesa Grande Pl	847 Mesa Grande Ct	78 ⒶⒹ	78 ⒶⒹ
79.	1100 Cermaken St	1100 Cermaker St	79 ⒶⒹ	79 ⒶⒹ
80.	321 Tijeras Ave NW	321 Tijeras Ave NW	80 ⒶⒹ	80 ⒶⒹ
81.	3405 Prospect St	3405 Prospect St	81 ⒶⒹ	81 ⒶⒹ
82.	6643 Burlington Pl	6643 Burlingtown Pl	82 ⒶⒹ	82 ⒶⒹ
83.	851 Esperanza Blvd	851 Esperanza Blvd	83 ⒶⒹ	83 ⒶⒹ
84.	Jenkinjones W Va	Jenkinjones W Va	84 ⒶⒹ	84 ⒶⒹ
85.	1006 Pennsylvania Ave	1008 Pennsylvania Ave	85 ⒶⒹ	85 ⒶⒹ
86.	2924 26th St N	2929 26th St N	86 ⒶⒹ	86 ⒶⒹ
87.	7115 Highland Dr	7115 Highland Dr	87 ⒶⒹ	87 ⒶⒹ
88.	Chaptico MD	Chaptica MD	88 ⒶⒹ	88 ⒶⒹ
89.	3508 Camron Mills Rd	3508 Camron Mills Rd	89 ⒶⒹ	89 ⒶⒹ

Go on to the next number on the next page.

90. 67158 Capston Dr	67158 Capston Dr	90 Ⓐ Ⓓ	90 Ⓐ Ⓓ
91. 3613 S Taylor Ave	3631 S Taylor Ave	91 Ⓐ Ⓓ	91 Ⓐ Ⓓ
92. 2421 Menokin Dr	2421 Menokin Dr	92 Ⓐ Ⓓ	92 Ⓐ Ⓓ
93. 3226 M St NW	3226 N St NW	93 Ⓐ Ⓓ	93 Ⓐ Ⓓ
94. 1201 S Court House Rd	1201 S Court House Rd	94 Ⓐ Ⓓ	94 Ⓐ Ⓓ
95. Findlay Ohio 45840	Findley Ohio 45840	95 Ⓐ Ⓓ	95 Ⓐ Ⓓ

STOP
**If you finish before the time is up, check your answers for Part A.
Do not go to any other part.**

(See the correct answers on the next page.)

Correct Answers

Address-Checking Test

1. A	25. A	49. D	73. D
2. A	26. D	50. D	74. D
3. D	27. D	51. A	75. A
4. A	28. A	52. D	76. A
5. D	29. D	53. D	77. D
6. A	30. A	54. D	78. D
7. D	31. D	55. A	79. D
8. D	32. A	56. D	80. A
9. A	33. A	57. D	81. A
10. A	34. A	58. D	82. D
11. A	35. A	59. D	83. A
12. D	36. D	60. D	84. A
13. D	37. D	61. A	85. D
14. A	38. D	62. D	86. D
15. A	39. D	63. D	87. A
16. D	40. D	64. A	88. D
17. D	41. A	65. A	89. A
18. A	42. D	66. A	90. A
19. D	43. A	67. D	91. D
20. A	44. D	68. D	92. A
21. A	45. A	69. D	93. D
22. D	46. D	70. D	94. A
23. D	47. A	71. D	95. D
24. D	48. A	72. A	

20

Memory-for-Address Test

Tips, Strategies & Practice Tests

The *Memory-for-Address Test* forms Part B of the **460 Battery Test.** In this part of the test, you must memorize the locations (A, B, C, D, or E) of 25 addresses shown in 5 boxes. You'll be sent a sample test when you file an application for examinations. But the addresses in the actual test will be different from your sample test.

In determining in which box each address is located, you must memorize every address in the 5 boxes. The location of the addresses is easy to memorize if you use some strategies. Based on my experience in postal test taking, I have developed the following strategies for memory-for-address test:

■ **Shortcut:** Just remember the *first two numbers* in each address in a box and the *first syllable* of each name in the same box. For examples, Hubert and Lester are *Hu-Les* when combined. In answering, read only the first two numbers of each address and the first syllable of the name of street, and answer the question by marking the correct circle. Proceed immediately to the next number: You don't have to use a bookmark or any guide in your nonwriting hand. Just point the index finger of that hand to the name or address you are working on. Immediately place the tip of your pencil in your writing hand on the next line on the answer sheet, as you move your nonwriting hand's index finger downward.

■ **Caution:** Once in every five or six numbers, before you mark the circle, be sure that the *circle* corresponds to the proper *line.* That is, the circle belonging to item number 9, for instance, should answer question number 9. Sometimes when you're in a hurry, you may mark circles that do not correspond to the questions you're answering. That happened to me once.

■ **Be in a hurry:** Skip the questions you don't know. Go back to them, however, if you finish working on the test early.

■ **Memorization:** Don't try to write down addresses or notes on your palm. You'll have no time to do that. You can try to remember only the *first digit* of each address, but the trouble is that sometimes the first digits are the same. It's better to remember *two* numbers.

■ **Side by side:** Don't place the question sheet and the answer sheet far from each other or far from your body. Your eyes must not travel long distances. If you don't follow this advice, it's like traveling to Africa instead of to California!

Memory-for-Address Test

In the example below, there are various techniques for memorizing the names and addresses in five minutes.

A	B	C	D	E
1700-2599 Wood Dushore 8500-8699 Lang Lott 6200-6399 James	2700-3299 Wood Jeriel 8700-9399 Lang Vanna 5700-6199 James	1300-1699 Wood Levering 9400-9499 Lang Ekron 6400-6499 James	3300-3599 Wood Bair 8000-8499 Lang Viborg 5000-5699 James	2600-2699 Wood Danby 9500-9999 Lang Lycan 4700-4999 James

The best thing to do is to remember only *two* numbers, the *first two* digits of the addresses. Combine the *first* syllables of the two names in each box, to make it only one name; example, *DusLot (Dushore and Lott.)*

For Box A	Box B	Box C	Box D	Box E
17	27	13	33	26
85	87	94	80	95
62	57	64	50	47

To remember the names:

Box A	Box B	Box C	Box D	Box E
DusLot	JeVa	LeEk	BaVi	DanLy

Decide which is the best way for you to memorize the numbers above: from **top** to **bottom** or from **left to right.**

One way is from **top** to **botttom,** by boxes.

A	B	C	D	E
17 ⬇	27 ⬇	13 ⬇	33 ⬇	26 ⬇
85 ⬇	87 ⬇	94 ⬇	80 ⬇	95 ⬇
62 ⬇	57 ⬇	64 ⬇	50 ⬇	47 ⬇
DusLot ⬇	JeVa ⬇	LeEk ⬇	BaVi ⬇	DanLy ⬇

Memorize the combined names from **left to right.**

Another way is to memorize A and B **vertically** and C, D, and E **horizontally.**

A	B	C	D	E
17 ⬇	27 ⬇	13 ⬇	33 ⬇	26
85 ⬇	87 ⬇	94 ⬇	80 ⬇	95
62 ⬇	57 ⬇	64 ⬇	50 ⬇	47
DusLot ⬇	JeVa ⬇	LeEk ⬇	BaVi ⬇	DanLy

Important! Important! Important!

Lately, the U.S. Postal Service has been including two or three "same numbers" in the addresses in the five boxes (Memory-for-Address test).

This creates confusion. (You cannot just remember the *first two numbers*. You must remember the *first two numbers*, along with the name of the *street*.

Part B: Memory for Addresses

In this part of the test, you will have to memorize the locations (A, B, C, D, or E) of 25 addresses shown in five boxes, like those below. For example, "Sardis" is in Box C, "6800-6999 Table" is in Box B, etc. (The addresses in the actual test will be different.)

A	B	C	D	E
4700-5599 Table	6800-6999 Table	5600-6499 Table	6500-6799 Table	4400-4699 Table
Lismore	Kelford	Joel	Tatum	Ruskin
5600-6499 West	6500-6799 West	6800-6999 West	4400-4699 West	4700-5599 West
Hesper	Musella	Sardis	Porter	Nathan
4400-4699 Blake	5600-6499 Blake	6500-6799 Blake	4700-5599 Blake	6800-6999 Blake

If you examine the boxes above, you'll see the identical numbers:

1. Three 4700-5599s:

4700-5599 Table (Box A), 4700-5599 Blake (Box D), and 4700-5599 Table (Box E);

2. Three 5600-6499s:

5600-6499 West (A), 5600-6499 Blake (B), and 5600-6499 Table (C);

3. Three 4400-4699s:

4400-4699 Blake (A), 4400-4699 West (D), 4400-4699 Table (E);

4. Three 6800-6999s:

6800-6999 Table (B), 6800-6999 West (C), and 6800-6999 Blake (E).

5. And three 6500-6799s:

6500-6799 West (B), 6500-6799 Blake (C) and 6500-6799 Table (D).

Instruction: To avoid confusion and to remember to which box the numbers belong, remember the *first two numbers* along with the name of the *streets*:

Example: 47 Table (Box A); 47 Blake (Box D) and 47 West (Box E).

For Box A, for instance, you may remember the numbers and names of streets as follows (Box A):

A	B	C	D	E
47 Table	68 Table	56 Table	65 Table	44 Table
56 West	65 West	68 West	44 West	47 West
44 Blake	56 Blake	65 Blake	47 Blake	68 Blake
LisHe	KelMu	JoSar	TaPor	RusNa

LisHe (Combination of the first syllables of Lismore and Hesper.)

You may memorize the *first two numbers* vertically; for example, 47, 56, 44. Then remember that in every box the *first street* is **Table**; the *second*, **West**, and the *third*, **Blake.** Or you may find your own way of memorizing them.

How to Remember
Names and Numbers

In memorizing numbers or names, associate them with numbers or names familiar to you, so that you can retrieve them instantly from your mind. Visualize! A thing visualized is not usually forgotten. That is, create key words or extraction codes. In entering information into a computer, you need to have a *code* so that you can retrieve the information. Without it, you cannot retrieve the facts and figures you stored on the disk. Your brain, which is your own computer, operates in the same way.

Use Your Imagination

To memorize Box A, for example, I'll remember *17* as the age of a beautiful teenaged girl living in the neighborhood; I'll remember *85* (1985) as the year I invaded Grenada; and *62* (1962) as the year my wife and I promised to each other "*to love and cherish, for better or worse, till death do us part.*" I'll remember *Dus-Lot* by visualizing that I'll go to the *lot* which is full of *dust* to play games.

Since you have to memorize the names and addresses in five boxes in five minutes, you'll have to memorize each box in sixty seconds. Actually, you'll do the memorization in eight minutes, including the three minutes for the practice test. But don't rely on that. Count on only five minutes. I have done it and many of my students have done it. If the computer can do it, your brain can do it, too!

In your case, think of years or numbers that you can associate with the numbers in Box A. For example, your youngest brother or sister may be *17* years old (or make him or her 17), you visited Beirut in year *85 (1985)*, and for *62*, you may remember that the Texas Rangers won the World Series in 1962. You may remember *Dus-Lot* by recalling the name *Dusty* Baker, who has a *lot* of chewing gum in his mouth. Or you may recall names of your friends which sound like *Dus* or *Lot*.

Associate Numbers
with Things or Events

You can think of many things. Associate numbers with age, weight, height, numbers of floors in buildings, dates, or events. Associate names with well-known personalities: actors, actresses, politicians, athletes, and others.

When you see the number, you can associate it easily with things familiar to you. Associate it with the first thing that comes into your mind. Different people will usually have different key numbers or key words.

In a nutshell, you'll have to remember only the first two numbers of addresses and the first syllables of two names. Forget about the street names, such as Wood or Lang. *Combine two names* into *one* and kill two birds with one stone. Imagine too that you're writing numbers and names on an invisible computer screen!

Combine Two Names Into One.

Memory-for-Address Test

Work—3 Minutes

Answer each question on a piece of paper to show the letter of the box in which the address belongs.
Try to remember the location of as many addresses as you can. If you are not sure of an address, guess.
Work only three minutes.

A	B	C	D	E
1800-2499 Wood Lott 7500-8799 Lang Dushore 6400-6599 James	2200-3199 Wood Vanna 8600-9299 Lang Jeriel 5400-6299 James	1200-1599 Wood Ekron 7400-9399 Lang Levering 6100-6499 James	3100-3699 Wood Viborg 8000-8299 Lang Valley 5500-5899 James	2700-2799 Wood Lycan 5600-9999 Lang Danby 4500-4699 James

1. 1800-2499 Wood
2. 2700-2799 Wood
3. Danby
4. 8600-9299 Lang
5. Lott
6. 6400-6599 James
7. Vanna
8. 6100-6499James
9. 8000-8299 Lang
10. Levering
11. 5600-9999 Lang
12. 8600-9299 Lang
13. Lott
14. 4500-4699 James
15. Ekron
16. 5500-5899 James
17. Jeriel
18. Dushore
19. 6400-6599 James
20. Viborg
21. 7500-8799 Lang
22. Danby
23. 4500-4699 James
24. 5500-5899 James

25. 2200-3199 Wood
26. Viborg
27. 7500-8799 Lang
28. Lycan
29. 5600-9999 Lang
30. 2200-3199 Wood
31. Levering
32. 2700-2799 Wood
33. 5500-5899 James
34. Vanna
35. 4500-4699 James
36. Dushore
37. 7500-8799 Lang
38. 6400-6599 James
39. 2700-2799 Wood
40. Valley
41. 8600-9299 Lang
42. Lycan
43. Vanna
44. 8000-8299 Lang
45. 2700-2799 Wood
46. Valley
47. Dushore
48. 7500-8799 Lang

49. Levering
50. 6400-6599 James
51. 5600-9999 Lang
52. 4500-4699 James
53. Jeriel
54. 7400-9399 Lang
55. Dushore
56. 3100-3699 Wood
57. 2200-3199 Wood
58. Valley
59. 6400-6599 James
60. Danby
61. 7400-9399 Lang
62. 5500-5899 James
63. Jeriel
64. 2200-3199 Wood
65. Viborg
66. 8000-8299 Lang
67. Ekron
68. 5400-6299 James
69. 5600-9999 Lang
70. 6400-6599 James
71. 2700-2799 Wood
72. Valley

73. Lott
74. Danby
75. 1800-2499 Wood
76. 8600-9299 Lang
77. 6100-6499 James
78. Lycan
79. 5400-6299 James
80. 6100-6499 James
81. Vanna
82. 7400-9399 Lang
83. 3100-3699 Wood
84. 4500-4699 James
85. 2200-3199 Wood
86. 6400-6599 james
87. Ekron
88. 8600-9299 Lang

STOP

When the time is up, go on to the next page for the correct answers.

(**Author's Note:** The sample test above is known as the memory-for-address test in the 470 Battery Test and the 460 Rural Carrier Associate Exam. This Part B is considered as a practice test. You'll be allowed to look at the names and addresses in the boxes, as you are instructed to answer as many questions as possible in three minutes. In the next part, however, you will be asked to answer all the 88 questions in five minutes and you won't be allowed to look at the names and addresses. During the three-minute practice test, answer only a few questions. Spend most of the three minutes in memorizing the placement of numbers and names (just the first two numbers of each address and the first syllables of names, combining two syllables into one. Now, answer a few questions and memorize the names and addresses in preparation for the next part. (**See Memory-for-Address Test: Tips & Strategies, pages 249-254.**)

Correct Answers

Memory-for-Address Test

1. A	31. C	61. C
2. E	32. E	62. D
3. E	33. D	63. B
4. B	34. B	64. B
5. A	35. E	65. D
6. A	36. A	66. D
7. B	37. A	67. C
8. C	38. A	68. B
9. D	39. E	69. E
10. C	40. D	70. A
11. E	41. B	71. E
12. B	42. E	72. D
13. A	43. B	73. A
14. E	44. D	74. E
15. C	45. E	75. A
16. D	46. D	76. B
17. B	47. A	77. C
18. A	48. A	78. E
19. A	49. C	79. B
20. D	50. A	80. C
21. A	51. E	81. B
22. E	52. E	82. C
23. E	53. B	83. D
24. D	54. C	84. E
25. B	55. A	85. B
26. D	56. D	86. A
27. A	57. B	87. C
28. E	58. D	88. B
29. E	59. A	
30. B	60. E	

Memory-for-Address Test

Work—5 Minutes

This is the section that counts.

Decide in which box each name or address belongs. Don't look back at the boxes with the addresses in them. Work 5 minutes. For each question, mark the answers on the answer sheet to the right.

ANSWER SHEET

	Test A	Test B
1. Ekron	1 Ⓐ Ⓑ Ⓒ Ⓓ Ⓔ	1 Ⓐ Ⓑ Ⓒ Ⓓ Ⓔ
2. 4500-4699 James	2 Ⓐ Ⓑ Ⓒ Ⓓ Ⓔ	2 Ⓐ Ⓑ Ⓒ Ⓓ Ⓔ
3. 1800-2499 Wood	3 Ⓐ Ⓑ Ⓒ Ⓓ Ⓔ	3 Ⓐ Ⓑ Ⓒ Ⓓ Ⓔ
4. Dushore	4 Ⓐ Ⓑ Ⓒ Ⓓ Ⓔ	4 Ⓐ Ⓑ Ⓒ Ⓓ Ⓔ
5. 8600-9299 Lang	5 Ⓐ Ⓑ Ⓒ Ⓓ Ⓔ	5 Ⓐ Ⓑ Ⓒ Ⓓ Ⓔ
6. 5400-5899 James	6 Ⓐ Ⓑ Ⓒ Ⓓ Ⓔ	6 Ⓐ Ⓑ Ⓒ Ⓓ Ⓔ
7. Levering	7 Ⓐ Ⓑ Ⓒ Ⓓ Ⓔ	7 Ⓐ Ⓑ Ⓒ Ⓓ Ⓔ
8. 6400-6599 James	8 Ⓐ Ⓑ Ⓒ Ⓓ Ⓔ	8 Ⓐ Ⓑ Ⓒ Ⓓ Ⓔ
9. Viborg	9 Ⓐ Ⓑ Ⓒ Ⓓ Ⓔ	9 Ⓐ Ⓑ Ⓒ Ⓓ Ⓔ
10. 2200-3199 Wood	10 Ⓐ Ⓑ Ⓒ Ⓓ Ⓔ	10 Ⓐ Ⓑ Ⓒ Ⓓ Ⓔ
11. 5400-6299 James	11 Ⓐ Ⓑ Ⓒ Ⓓ Ⓔ	11 Ⓐ Ⓑ Ⓒ Ⓓ Ⓔ
12. Lycan	12 Ⓐ Ⓑ Ⓒ Ⓓ Ⓔ	12 Ⓐ Ⓑ Ⓒ Ⓓ Ⓔ
13. 6400-6599 James	13 Ⓐ Ⓑ Ⓒ Ⓓ Ⓔ	13 Ⓐ Ⓑ Ⓒ Ⓓ Ⓔ
14. 8000-8299 Lang	14 Ⓐ Ⓑ Ⓒ Ⓓ Ⓔ	14 Ⓐ Ⓑ Ⓒ Ⓓ Ⓔ
15. 8600-9299 Lang	15 Ⓐ Ⓑ Ⓒ Ⓓ Ⓔ	15 Ⓐ Ⓑ Ⓒ Ⓓ Ⓔ
16. Dushore	16 Ⓐ Ⓑ Ⓒ Ⓓ Ⓔ	16 Ⓐ Ⓑ Ⓒ Ⓓ Ⓔ
17. 1200-1599 Wood	17 Ⓐ Ⓑ Ⓒ Ⓓ Ⓔ	17 Ⓐ Ⓑ Ⓒ Ⓓ Ⓔ
18. Levering	18 Ⓐ Ⓑ Ⓒ Ⓓ Ⓔ	18 Ⓐ Ⓑ Ⓒ Ⓓ Ⓔ
19. 8600-9299 Lang	19 Ⓐ Ⓑ Ⓒ Ⓓ Ⓔ	19 Ⓐ Ⓑ Ⓒ Ⓓ Ⓔ
20. 1200-1599 Wood	20 Ⓐ Ⓑ Ⓒ Ⓓ Ⓔ	20 Ⓐ Ⓑ Ⓒ Ⓓ Ⓔ
21. Danby	21 Ⓐ Ⓑ Ⓒ Ⓓ Ⓔ	21 Ⓐ Ⓑ Ⓒ Ⓓ Ⓔ
22. 2700-2799 Wood	22 Ⓐ Ⓑ Ⓒ Ⓓ Ⓔ	22 Ⓐ Ⓑ Ⓒ Ⓓ Ⓔ
23. Vanna	23 Ⓐ Ⓑ Ⓒ Ⓓ Ⓔ	23 Ⓐ Ⓑ Ⓒ Ⓓ Ⓔ
24. 6400-6599 James	24 Ⓐ Ⓑ Ⓒ Ⓓ Ⓔ	24 Ⓐ Ⓑ Ⓒ Ⓓ Ⓔ
25. Levering	25 Ⓐ Ⓑ Ⓒ Ⓓ Ⓔ	25 Ⓐ Ⓑ Ⓒ Ⓓ Ⓔ
26. 3100-3699 Wood	26 Ⓐ Ⓑ Ⓒ Ⓓ Ⓔ	26 Ⓐ Ⓑ Ⓒ Ⓓ Ⓔ
27. Lott	27 Ⓐ Ⓑ Ⓒ Ⓓ Ⓔ	27 Ⓐ Ⓑ Ⓒ Ⓓ Ⓔ
28. 1800-2499 Wood	28 Ⓐ Ⓑ Ⓒ Ⓓ Ⓔ	28 Ⓐ Ⓑ Ⓒ Ⓓ Ⓔ
29. 7400-9399 Lang	29 Ⓐ Ⓑ Ⓒ Ⓓ Ⓔ	29 Ⓐ Ⓑ Ⓒ Ⓓ Ⓔ
30. Jeriel	30 Ⓐ Ⓑ Ⓒ Ⓓ Ⓔ	30 Ⓐ Ⓑ Ⓒ Ⓓ Ⓔ
31. 5400-6299 James	31 Ⓐ Ⓑ Ⓒ Ⓓ Ⓔ	31 Ⓐ Ⓑ Ⓒ Ⓓ Ⓔ
32. 4500-4699 James	32 Ⓐ Ⓑ Ⓒ Ⓓ Ⓔ	32 Ⓐ Ⓑ Ⓒ Ⓓ Ⓔ
33. 5600-9999 Lang	33 Ⓐ Ⓑ Ⓒ Ⓓ Ⓔ	33 Ⓐ Ⓑ Ⓒ Ⓓ Ⓔ
34. 7400-9399 Lang	34 Ⓐ Ⓑ Ⓒ Ⓓ Ⓔ	34 Ⓐ Ⓑ Ⓒ Ⓓ Ⓔ
35. 8600-9299 Lang	35 Ⓐ Ⓑ Ⓒ Ⓓ Ⓔ	35 Ⓐ Ⓑ Ⓒ Ⓓ Ⓔ
36. Viborg	36 Ⓐ Ⓑ Ⓒ Ⓓ Ⓔ	36 Ⓐ Ⓑ Ⓒ Ⓓ Ⓔ
37. 5600-9999 Lang	37 Ⓐ Ⓑ Ⓒ Ⓓ Ⓔ	37 Ⓐ Ⓑ Ⓒ Ⓓ Ⓔ
38. Jeriel	38 Ⓐ Ⓑ Ⓒ Ⓓ Ⓔ	38 Ⓐ Ⓑ Ⓒ Ⓓ Ⓔ
39. 1800-2499 Wood	39 Ⓐ Ⓑ Ⓒ Ⓓ Ⓔ	39 Ⓐ Ⓑ Ⓒ Ⓓ Ⓔ
40. 8000-8299 Lang	40 Ⓐ Ⓑ Ⓒ Ⓓ Ⓔ	40 Ⓐ Ⓑ Ⓒ Ⓓ Ⓔ

Go on to the next number on the next page.

41. Danby	41 Ⓐ Ⓑ Ⓒ Ⓓ Ⓔ	41 Ⓐ Ⓑ Ⓒ Ⓓ Ⓔ
42. 5400-6299 James	42 Ⓐ Ⓑ Ⓒ Ⓓ Ⓔ	42 Ⓐ Ⓑ Ⓒ Ⓓ Ⓔ
43. Ekron	43 Ⓐ Ⓑ Ⓒ Ⓓ Ⓔ	43 Ⓐ Ⓑ Ⓒ Ⓓ Ⓔ
44. 8000-8299 Lang	44 Ⓐ Ⓑ Ⓒ Ⓓ Ⓔ	44 Ⓐ Ⓑ Ⓒ Ⓓ Ⓔ
45. Lott	45 Ⓐ Ⓑ Ⓒ Ⓓ Ⓔ	45 Ⓐ Ⓑ Ⓒ Ⓓ Ⓔ
46. 5500-9999 Lang	46 Ⓐ Ⓑ Ⓒ Ⓓ Ⓔ	46 Ⓐ Ⓑ Ⓒ Ⓓ Ⓔ
47. Ekron	47 Ⓐ Ⓑ Ⓒ Ⓓ Ⓔ	47 Ⓐ Ⓑ Ⓒ Ⓓ Ⓔ
48. 8000-8299 Lang	48 Ⓐ Ⓑ Ⓒ Ⓓ Ⓔ	48 Ⓐ Ⓑ Ⓒ Ⓓ Ⓔ
49. 5400-6299 James	49 Ⓐ Ⓑ Ⓒ Ⓓ Ⓔ	49 Ⓐ Ⓑ Ⓒ Ⓓ Ⓔ
50. 2200-3199 Wood	50 Ⓐ Ⓑ Ⓒ Ⓓ Ⓔ	50 Ⓐ Ⓑ Ⓒ Ⓓ Ⓔ
51. Valley	51 Ⓐ Ⓑ Ⓒ Ⓓ Ⓔ	51 Ⓐ Ⓑ Ⓒ Ⓓ Ⓔ
52. 1800-2499 Wood	52 Ⓐ Ⓑ Ⓒ Ⓓ Ⓔ	52 Ⓐ Ⓑ Ⓒ Ⓓ Ⓔ
53. 7500-8799 Lang	53 Ⓐ Ⓑ Ⓒ Ⓓ Ⓔ	53 Ⓐ Ⓑ Ⓒ Ⓓ Ⓔ
54. 8000-8299 Lang	54 Ⓐ Ⓑ Ⓒ Ⓓ Ⓔ	54 Ⓐ Ⓑ Ⓒ Ⓓ Ⓔ
55. Levering	55 Ⓐ Ⓑ Ⓒ Ⓓ Ⓔ	55 Ⓐ Ⓑ Ⓒ Ⓓ Ⓔ
56. 8000-8299 Lang	56 Ⓐ Ⓑ Ⓒ Ⓓ Ⓔ	56 Ⓐ Ⓑ Ⓒ Ⓓ Ⓔ
57. 5500-5899 James	57 Ⓐ Ⓑ Ⓒ Ⓓ Ⓔ	57 Ⓐ Ⓑ Ⓒ Ⓓ Ⓔ
58. 3100-3699 Wood	58 Ⓐ Ⓑ Ⓒ Ⓓ Ⓔ	58 Ⓐ Ⓑ Ⓒ Ⓓ Ⓔ
59. 5400-6299 James	59 Ⓐ Ⓑ Ⓒ Ⓓ Ⓔ	59 Ⓐ Ⓑ Ⓒ Ⓓ Ⓔ
60. 3100-3699 Wood	60 Ⓐ Ⓑ Ⓒ Ⓓ Ⓔ	60 Ⓐ Ⓑ Ⓒ Ⓓ Ⓔ
61. 4500-4699 James	61 Ⓐ Ⓑ Ⓒ Ⓓ Ⓔ	61 Ⓐ Ⓑ Ⓒ Ⓓ Ⓔ
62. 2700-2799 Wood	62 Ⓐ Ⓑ Ⓒ Ⓓ Ⓔ	62 Ⓐ Ⓑ Ⓒ Ⓓ Ⓔ
63. 1200-1599 Wood	63 Ⓐ Ⓑ Ⓒ Ⓓ Ⓔ	63 Ⓐ Ⓑ Ⓒ Ⓓ Ⓔ
64. Valley	64 Ⓐ Ⓑ Ⓒ Ⓓ Ⓔ	64 Ⓐ Ⓑ Ⓒ Ⓓ Ⓔ
65. 7500-8799 Lang	65 Ⓐ Ⓑ Ⓒ Ⓓ Ⓔ	65 Ⓐ Ⓑ Ⓒ Ⓓ Ⓔ
66. 6100-6499 James	66 Ⓐ Ⓑ Ⓒ Ⓓ Ⓔ	66 Ⓐ Ⓑ Ⓒ Ⓓ Ⓔ
67. 8000-8299 Lang	67 Ⓐ Ⓑ Ⓒ Ⓓ Ⓔ	67 Ⓐ Ⓑ Ⓒ Ⓓ Ⓔ
68. 5600-9999 Lang	68 Ⓐ Ⓑ Ⓒ Ⓓ Ⓔ	68 Ⓐ Ⓑ Ⓒ Ⓓ Ⓔ
69. Levering	69 Ⓐ Ⓑ Ⓒ Ⓓ Ⓔ	69 Ⓐ Ⓑ Ⓒ Ⓓ Ⓔ
70. 7400-9399 Lang	70 Ⓐ Ⓑ Ⓒ Ⓓ Ⓔ	70 Ⓐ Ⓑ Ⓒ Ⓓ Ⓔ
71. Valley	71 Ⓐ Ⓑ Ⓒ Ⓓ Ⓔ	71 Ⓐ Ⓑ Ⓒ Ⓓ Ⓔ
72. 5400-6299 James	72 Ⓐ Ⓑ Ⓒ Ⓓ Ⓔ	72 Ⓐ Ⓑ Ⓒ Ⓓ Ⓔ
73. 3100-3699 Wood	73 Ⓐ Ⓑ Ⓒ Ⓓ Ⓔ	73 Ⓐ Ⓑ Ⓒ Ⓓ Ⓔ
74. 6400-6599 James	74 Ⓐ Ⓑ Ⓒ Ⓓ Ⓔ	74 Ⓐ Ⓑ Ⓒ Ⓓ Ⓔ
75. 5400-6299 James	75 Ⓐ Ⓑ Ⓒ Ⓓ Ⓔ	75 Ⓐ Ⓑ Ⓒ Ⓓ Ⓔ
76. 2200-3199 Wood	76 Ⓐ Ⓑ Ⓒ Ⓓ Ⓔ	76 Ⓐ Ⓑ Ⓒ Ⓓ Ⓔ
77. 5600-9999 Lang	77 Ⓐ Ⓑ Ⓒ Ⓓ Ⓔ	77 Ⓐ Ⓑ Ⓒ Ⓓ Ⓔ
78. Dushore	78 Ⓐ Ⓑ Ⓒ Ⓓ Ⓔ	78 Ⓐ Ⓑ Ⓒ Ⓓ Ⓔ
79. 3100-3699 Wood	79 Ⓐ Ⓑ Ⓒ Ⓓ Ⓔ	79 Ⓐ Ⓑ Ⓒ Ⓓ Ⓔ
80. 2200-3199 Wood	80 Ⓐ Ⓑ Ⓒ Ⓓ Ⓔ	80 Ⓐ Ⓑ Ⓒ Ⓓ Ⓔ
81. 8600-9299 Lang	81 Ⓐ Ⓑ Ⓒ Ⓓ Ⓔ	81 Ⓐ Ⓑ Ⓒ Ⓓ Ⓔ
82. Lycan	82 Ⓐ Ⓑ Ⓒ Ⓓ Ⓔ	82 Ⓐ Ⓑ Ⓒ Ⓓ Ⓔ
83. 7400-9399 Lang	83 Ⓐ Ⓑ Ⓒ Ⓓ Ⓔ	83 Ⓐ Ⓑ Ⓒ Ⓓ Ⓔ
84. 5600-9999 Lang	84 Ⓐ Ⓑ Ⓒ Ⓓ Ⓔ	84 Ⓐ Ⓑ Ⓒ Ⓓ Ⓔ
85. 7400-9399 Lang	85 Ⓐ Ⓑ Ⓒ Ⓓ Ⓔ	85 Ⓐ Ⓑ Ⓒ Ⓓ Ⓔ
86. 4500-4699 James	86 Ⓐ Ⓑ Ⓒ Ⓓ Ⓔ	86 Ⓐ Ⓑ Ⓒ Ⓓ Ⓔ
87. 8600-9299 Lang	87 Ⓐ Ⓑ Ⓒ Ⓓ Ⓔ	87 Ⓐ Ⓑ Ⓒ Ⓓ Ⓔ
88. Viborg	88 Ⓐ Ⓑ Ⓒ Ⓓ Ⓔ	88 Ⓐ Ⓑ Ⓒ Ⓓ Ⓔ

Correct Answers

Memory-for-Address Test

1. C	31. B	61. E
2. E	32. E	62. E
3. A	33. E	63. C
4. A	34. C	64. D
5. B	35. B	65. A
6. B	36. D	66. C
7. C	37. E	67. D
8. A	38. B	68. E
9. D	39. A	69. C
10. B	40. D	70. C
11. B	41. E	71. D
12. E	42. B	72. B
13. A	43. C	73. D
14. D	44. D	74. A
15. B	45. A	75. B
16. A	46. E	76. B
17. C	47. C	77. E
18. C	48. D	78. A
19. B	49. B	79. D
20. C	50. B	80. B
21. E	51. D	81. B
22. E	52. A	82. E
23. B	53. A	83. C
24. A	54. D	84. E
25. C	55. C	85. C
26. D	56. D	86. E
27. A	57. D	87. B
28. A	58. D	88. D
29. C	59. B	
30. B	60. D	

Memory-for-Address Test

Work—3 Minutes

Answer each question on a piece of paper to show the letter of the box in which the address belongs. Try to remember the location of as many addresses as you can. If you are not sure of an address, guess. Work only three minutes.

A	B	C	D	E
1500-2599 Blake Cathy 5500-8799 Beach Baker 3400-6599 Walker	1200-3599 Blake Cedar 4600-9599 Beach Forter 1400-2299 Walker	3200-1899 Blake Halstead 6400-9599 Beach Winter 5500-6499 Walker	2100-3599 Blake Hotel 7000-8599 Beach Central 1500-1899 Walker	3500-2999 Blake Tatum 7500-9999 Beach River 2500-4999 Walker

1. 5500-8799 Beach
2. Winter
3. 3200-1899 Blake
4. River
5. 3500-2999 Blake
6. 1400-2299 Walker
7. Baker
8. 3200-1899 Blake
9. 2500-4999 Walker
10. Halsted
11. 700-8599 Beach
12. 5500-4999 Walker
13. Cedar
14. 4600-9599 Beach
15. Cathy
16. 2100-3599 Blake
17. 7500-9999 Beach
18. 4600-9599 Beach
19. 7000-8599 Beach
20. 3400-6599 Walker
21. 3200-1899 Blake
22. Halsted
23. 3500-2999 Blake
24. 1400-2299 Walker

25. 6400-9599 Beach
26. 5500-6499 Walker
27. 3500-2999 Blake
28. Halsted
29. 1400-2299 Walker
30. 1500-2599 Blake
31. Forter
32. 7000-8599 Beach
33. Tatum
34. 3200-1899 Blake
35. Cedar
36. 7000-8599 Beach
37. Winter
38. 1200-3599 Blake
39. Central
40. 4600-9599 Beach
41. Hotel
42. 7500-9999 Beach
43. 1400-2299 Walker
44. 1500-2599 Blake
45. 2100-3599 Blake
46. 7500-9999 Beach
47. 6400-9599 Beach
48. River

49. 7500-9999 Beach
50. 1500-2599 Blake
51. 1200-3599 Blake
52. 1500-1899 Walker
53. 3500-299 Blakel
54. Baker
55. Cedar
56. 1400-2299 Walker
57. 2100-3599 Blake
58. 4600-9599 Beach
59. Cathy
60. 2500-4999 Walker
61. 1200-3599 Blake
62. Forter
63. 3400-6599 Walker
64. 7000-8599 Beach
65. 1400-2299 Walker
66. 3500-2999 Blake
67. Baker
68. 1500-2599 Blake
69. Halsted
70. 5500-6499 Walker
71. 7500-9999 Beach
72. 1200-3599 Blake

73. River
74. 7000-8599 Beach
75. 1400-2299 Walker
76. 3400-6599 Walker
77. Cedar
78. Hotel
79. 3400-6599 Walker
80. Halsted
81. 1200-3599 Blake
82. 5500-6499 Walker
83. 7500-9999 Beach
84. Forter
85. Winter
86. 1500-2599 Blake
87. 3400-6599 Walker
88. 7000-8599 Beach

STOP

When the time is up, go on to the next page for the correct answers.

(**Author's Note:** The sample test above is known as the memory-for-address test in the 470 Battery Test and the 460 Rural Carrier Associate Exam. This Part B is considered as a practice test. You'll be allowed to look at the names and addresses in the boxes, as you are instructed to answer as many questions as possible in three minutes. In the next part, however, you will be asked to answer all the 88 questions in five minutes and you won't be allowed to look at the names and addresses. During the three-minute practice test, answer only a few questions. Spend most of the three minutes in memorizing the placement of numbers and names (just the first two numbers of each address and the first syllables of names, combining two syllables into one. Now, answer a few questions and memorize the names and addresses in preparation for the next part. (**See Memory-for-Address Test: Tips & Strategies, pages 249-254.**)

Correct Answers

Memory-for-Address Test

1. A	31. B	61. B
2. C	32. D	62. B
3. C	33. E	63. A
4. E	34. C	64. D
5. E	35. B	65. B
6. B	36. D	66. E
7. A	37. C	67. A
8. C	38. B	68. A
9. E	39. D	69. C
10. C	40. B	70. C
11. D	41. D	71. E
12. E	42. E	72. B
13. B	43. B	73. E
14. B	44. A	74. E
15. A	45. D	75. B
16. D	46. E	76. A
17. E	47. C	77. B
18. B	48. E	78. D
19. D	49. E	79. A
20. A	50. A	80. C
21. C	51. B	81. B
22. C	52. D	82. C
23. E	53. E	83. E
24. B	54. A	84. B
25. C	55. B	85. C
26. C	56. B	86. A
27. E	57. D	87. A
28. C	58. B	88. D
29. B	59. A	
30. A	60. E	

Memory-for-Address Test

Work—5 Minutes

This is the section that counts.

Decide in which box each name or address belongs. Don't look back at the boxes with the addresses in them. Work 5 minutes. For each question, mark the answers on the answer sheet to the right.

ANSWER SHEET

		Test A	Test B
1.	7500-9999 Beach	1 ⒶⒷⒸⒹⒺ	1 ⒶⒷⒸⒹⒺ
2.	Cathy	2 ⒶⒷⒸⒹⒺ	2 ⒶⒷⒸⒹⒺ
3.	2100-3599 Blake	3 ⒶⒷⒸⒹⒺ	3 ⒶⒷⒸⒹⒺ
4.	7500-9999 Beach	4 ⒶⒷⒸⒹⒺ	4 ⒶⒷⒸⒹⒺ
5.	3400-6599 Walker	5 ⒶⒷⒸⒹⒺ	5 ⒶⒷⒸⒹⒺ
6.	Halsted	6 ⒶⒷⒸⒹⒺ	6 ⒶⒷⒸⒹⒺ
7.	1400-2299 Walker	7 ⒶⒷⒸⒹⒺ	7 ⒶⒷⒸⒹⒺ
8.	Tatum	8 ⒶⒷⒸⒹⒺ	8 ⒶⒷⒸⒹⒺ
9.	3200-1899 Blake	9 ⒶⒷⒸⒹⒺ	9 ⒶⒷⒸⒹⒺ
10.	River	10 ⒶⒷⒸⒹⒺ	10 ⒶⒷⒸⒹⒺ
11.	3400-6599 Walker	11 ⒶⒷⒸⒹⒺ	11 ⒶⒷⒸⒹⒺ
12.	7000-8599 Beach	12 ⒶⒷⒸⒹⒺ	12 ⒶⒷⒸⒹⒺ
13.	Winter	13 ⒶⒷⒸⒹⒺ	13 ⒶⒷⒸⒹⒺ
14.	4600-9599 Beach	14 ⒶⒷⒸⒹⒺ	14 ⒶⒷⒸⒹⒺ
15.	6400-9599 Beach	15 ⒶⒷⒸⒹⒺ	15 ⒶⒷⒸⒹⒺ
16.	Cathy	16 ⒶⒷⒸⒹⒺ	16 ⒶⒷⒸⒹⒺ
17.	2100-3599 Blake	17 ⒶⒷⒸⒹⒺ	17 ⒶⒷⒸⒹⒺ
18.	7000-8599 Beach	18 ⒶⒷⒸⒹⒺ	18 ⒶⒷⒸⒹⒺ
19.	Cedar	19 ⒶⒷⒸⒹⒺ	19 ⒶⒷⒸⒹⒺ
20.	1400-2299 Walker	20 ⒶⒷⒸⒹⒺ	20 ⒶⒷⒸⒹⒺ
21.	River	21 ⒶⒷⒸⒹⒺ	21 ⒶⒷⒸⒹⒺ
22.	2100-3599 Blake	22 ⒶⒷⒸⒹⒺ	22 ⒶⒷⒸⒹⒺ
23.	5500-6499 Walker	23 ⒶⒷⒸⒹⒺ	23 ⒶⒷⒸⒹⒺ
24.	2100-3599 Blake	24 ⒶⒷⒸⒹⒺ	24 ⒶⒷⒸⒹⒺ
25.	7500-9999 Beach	25 ⒶⒷⒸⒹⒺ	25 ⒶⒷⒸⒹⒺ
26.	Winter	26 ⒶⒷⒸⒹⒺ	26 ⒶⒷⒸⒹⒺ
27.	4600-9599 Beach	27 ⒶⒷⒸⒹⒺ	27 ⒶⒷⒸⒹⒺ
28.	3200-1899 Blake	28 ⒶⒷⒸⒹⒺ	28 ⒶⒷⒸⒹⒺ
29.	Central	29 ⒶⒷⒸⒹⒺ	29 ⒶⒷⒸⒹⒺ
30.	Forter	30 ⒶⒷⒸⒹⒺ	30 ⒶⒷⒸⒹⒺ
31.	7500-9999 Beach	31 ⒶⒷⒸⒹⒺ	31 ⒶⒷⒸⒹⒺ
32.	2100-3599 Blake	32 ⒶⒷⒸⒹⒺ	32 ⒶⒷⒸⒹⒺ
33.	1500-2599 Blake	33 ⒶⒷⒸⒹⒺ	33 ⒶⒷⒸⒹⒺ
34.	7000-8599 Beach	34 ⒶⒷⒸⒹⒺ	34 ⒶⒷⒸⒹⒺ
35.	7500-9999 Beach	35 ⒶⒷⒸⒹⒺ	35 ⒶⒷⒸⒹⒺ
36.	1500-1899 Walker	36 ⒶⒷⒸⒹⒺ	36 ⒶⒷⒸⒹⒺ
37.	5500-8799 Beach	37 ⒶⒷⒸⒹⒺ	37 ⒶⒷⒸⒹⒺ
38.	Hotel	38 ⒶⒷⒸⒹⒺ	38 ⒶⒷⒸⒹⒺ
39.	1200-3599 Blake	39 ⒶⒷⒸⒹⒺ	39 ⒶⒷⒸⒹⒺ
40.	River	40 ⒶⒷⒸⒹⒺ	40 ⒶⒷⒸⒹⒺ

Go on to the next number on the next page.

41. 2500-4999 Walker	41 Ⓐ Ⓑ Ⓒ Ⓓ Ⓔ	41 Ⓐ Ⓑ Ⓒ Ⓓ Ⓔ
42. Forter	42 Ⓐ Ⓑ Ⓒ Ⓓ Ⓔ	42 Ⓐ Ⓑ Ⓒ Ⓓ Ⓔ
43. Central	43 Ⓐ Ⓑ Ⓒ Ⓓ Ⓔ	43 Ⓐ Ⓑ Ⓒ Ⓓ Ⓔ
44. 1400-2299 Walker	44 Ⓐ Ⓑ Ⓒ Ⓓ Ⓔ	44 Ⓐ Ⓑ Ⓒ Ⓓ Ⓔ
45. 7500-9999 Beach	45 Ⓐ Ⓑ Ⓒ Ⓓ Ⓔ	45 Ⓐ Ⓑ Ⓒ Ⓓ Ⓔ
46. 2100-3599 Blake	46 Ⓐ Ⓑ Ⓒ Ⓓ Ⓔ	46 Ⓐ Ⓑ Ⓒ Ⓓ Ⓔ
47. 6400-9599 Beach	47 Ⓐ Ⓑ Ⓒ Ⓓ Ⓔ	47 Ⓐ Ⓑ Ⓒ Ⓓ Ⓔ
48. Halsted	48 Ⓐ Ⓑ Ⓒ Ⓓ Ⓔ	48 Ⓐ Ⓑ Ⓒ Ⓓ Ⓔ
49. Baker	49 Ⓐ Ⓑ Ⓒ Ⓓ Ⓔ	49 Ⓐ Ⓑ Ⓒ Ⓓ Ⓔ
50. 1200-3599 Blake	50 Ⓐ Ⓑ Ⓒ Ⓓ Ⓔ	50 Ⓐ Ⓑ Ⓒ Ⓓ Ⓔ
51. 1500-1899 Walker	51 Ⓐ Ⓑ Ⓒ Ⓓ Ⓔ	51 Ⓐ Ⓑ Ⓒ Ⓓ Ⓔ
52. 1400-2299 Walker	52 Ⓐ Ⓑ Ⓒ Ⓓ Ⓔ	52 Ⓐ Ⓑ Ⓒ Ⓓ Ⓔ
53. 3200-1899 Blake	53 Ⓐ Ⓑ Ⓒ Ⓓ Ⓔ	53 Ⓐ Ⓑ Ⓒ Ⓓ Ⓔ
54. Central	54 Ⓐ Ⓑ Ⓒ Ⓓ Ⓔ	54 Ⓐ Ⓑ Ⓒ Ⓓ Ⓔ
55. 4600-9599 Beach	55 Ⓐ Ⓑ Ⓒ Ⓓ Ⓔ	55 Ⓐ Ⓑ Ⓒ Ⓓ Ⓔ
56. Tatum	56 Ⓐ Ⓑ Ⓒ Ⓓ Ⓔ	56 Ⓐ Ⓑ Ⓒ Ⓓ Ⓔ
57. Baker	57 Ⓐ Ⓑ Ⓒ Ⓓ Ⓔ	57 Ⓐ Ⓑ Ⓒ Ⓓ Ⓔ
58. 5500-6499 Walker	58 Ⓐ Ⓑ Ⓒ Ⓓ Ⓔ	58 Ⓐ Ⓑ Ⓒ Ⓓ Ⓔ
59. 3400-6599 Walker	59 Ⓐ Ⓑ Ⓒ Ⓓ Ⓔ	59 Ⓐ Ⓑ Ⓒ Ⓓ Ⓔ
60. 6400-9599 Beach	60 Ⓐ Ⓑ Ⓒ Ⓓ Ⓔ	60 Ⓐ Ⓑ Ⓒ Ⓓ Ⓔ
61. Halsted	61 Ⓐ Ⓑ Ⓒ Ⓓ Ⓔ	61 Ⓐ Ⓑ Ⓒ Ⓓ Ⓔ
62. 5500-6499 Walker	62 Ⓐ Ⓑ Ⓒ Ⓓ Ⓔ	62 Ⓐ Ⓑ Ⓒ Ⓓ Ⓔ
63. 7500-9999 Beach	63 Ⓐ Ⓑ Ⓒ Ⓓ Ⓔ	63 Ⓐ Ⓑ Ⓒ Ⓓ Ⓔ
64. Forter	64 Ⓐ Ⓑ Ⓒ Ⓓ Ⓔ	64 Ⓐ Ⓑ Ⓒ Ⓓ Ⓔ
65. 3500-2999 Blake	65 Ⓐ Ⓑ Ⓒ Ⓓ Ⓔ	65 Ⓐ Ⓑ Ⓒ Ⓓ Ⓔ
66. 3400-6599 Walker	66 Ⓐ Ⓑ Ⓒ Ⓓ Ⓔ	66 Ⓐ Ⓑ Ⓒ Ⓓ Ⓔ
67. Cedar	67 Ⓐ Ⓑ Ⓒ Ⓓ Ⓔ	67 Ⓐ Ⓑ Ⓒ Ⓓ Ⓔ
68. 7500-9999 Beach	68 Ⓐ Ⓑ Ⓒ Ⓓ Ⓔ	68 Ⓐ Ⓑ Ⓒ Ⓓ Ⓔ
69. River	69 Ⓐ Ⓑ Ⓒ Ⓓ Ⓔ	69 Ⓐ Ⓑ Ⓒ Ⓓ Ⓔ
70. 6400-9599 Beach	70 Ⓐ Ⓑ Ⓒ Ⓓ Ⓔ	70 Ⓐ Ⓑ Ⓒ Ⓓ Ⓔ
71. 3500-2999 Blake	71 Ⓐ Ⓑ Ⓒ Ⓓ Ⓔ	71 Ⓐ Ⓑ Ⓒ Ⓓ Ⓔ
72. 1400-2299 Walker	72 Ⓐ Ⓑ Ⓒ Ⓓ Ⓔ	72 Ⓐ Ⓑ Ⓒ Ⓓ Ⓔ
73. Winter	73 Ⓐ Ⓑ Ⓒ Ⓓ Ⓔ	73 Ⓐ Ⓑ Ⓒ Ⓓ Ⓔ
74. 1400-2299 Walker	74 Ⓐ Ⓑ Ⓒ Ⓓ Ⓔ	74 Ⓐ Ⓑ Ⓒ Ⓓ Ⓔ
75. 3400-6599 Walker	75 Ⓐ Ⓑ Ⓒ Ⓓ Ⓔ	75 Ⓐ Ⓑ Ⓒ Ⓓ Ⓔ
76. 6400-9599 Beach	76 Ⓐ Ⓑ Ⓒ Ⓓ Ⓔ	76 Ⓐ Ⓑ Ⓒ Ⓓ Ⓔ
77. Tatum	77 Ⓐ Ⓑ Ⓒ Ⓓ Ⓔ	77 Ⓐ Ⓑ Ⓒ Ⓓ Ⓔ
78. 1200-3599 Blake	78 Ⓐ Ⓑ Ⓒ Ⓓ Ⓔ	78 Ⓐ Ⓑ Ⓒ Ⓓ Ⓔ
79. 7500-9999 Beach	79 Ⓐ Ⓑ Ⓒ Ⓓ Ⓔ	79 Ⓐ Ⓑ Ⓒ Ⓓ Ⓔ
80. Forter	80 Ⓐ Ⓑ Ⓒ Ⓓ Ⓔ	80 Ⓐ Ⓑ Ⓒ Ⓓ Ⓔ
81. River	81 Ⓐ Ⓑ Ⓒ Ⓓ Ⓔ	81 Ⓐ Ⓑ Ⓒ Ⓓ Ⓔ
82. 5500-8799 Beach	82 Ⓐ Ⓑ Ⓒ Ⓓ Ⓔ	82 Ⓐ Ⓑ Ⓒ Ⓓ Ⓔ
83. 2100-3599 Blake	83 Ⓐ Ⓑ Ⓒ Ⓓ Ⓔ	83 Ⓐ Ⓑ Ⓒ Ⓓ Ⓔ
84. 1400-2299 Walker	84 Ⓐ Ⓑ Ⓒ Ⓓ Ⓔ	84 Ⓐ Ⓑ Ⓒ Ⓓ Ⓔ
85. 7500-9999 Beach	85 Ⓐ Ⓑ Ⓒ Ⓓ Ⓔ	85 Ⓐ Ⓑ Ⓒ Ⓓ Ⓔ
86. Baker	86 Ⓐ Ⓑ Ⓒ Ⓓ Ⓔ	86 Ⓐ Ⓑ Ⓒ Ⓓ Ⓔ
87. 1200-3599 Blake	87 Ⓐ Ⓑ Ⓒ Ⓓ Ⓔ	87 Ⓐ Ⓑ Ⓒ Ⓓ Ⓔ
88. 2500-49999 Walker	88 Ⓐ Ⓑ Ⓒ Ⓓ Ⓔ	88 Ⓐ Ⓑ Ⓒ Ⓓ Ⓔ

Go on to the next number on the next page.

STOP

If you finish before the time is up,

go back and check your answers.

(See the correct answers on the next page.)

Correct Answers

Memory-for-Address Test

1. E	31. E	61. C
2. A	32. D	62. C
3. D	33. A	63. E
4. E	34. D	64. B
5. A	35. E	65. E
6. C	36. D	66. A
7. B	37. A	67. B
8. E	38. D	68. E
9. C	39. B	69. E
10. E	40. E	70. C
11. A	41. E	71. E
12. D	42. B	72. B
13. C	43. D	73. C
14. B	44. B	74. B
15. C	45. E	75. A
16. A	46. D	76. C
17. D	47. C	77. E
18. D	48. C	78. B
19. B	49. A	79. E
20. B	50. B	80. B
21. E	51. D	81. E
22. D	52. B	82. A
23. C	53. C	83. D
24. D	54. D	84. B
25. E	55. B	85. E
26. C	56. E	86. A
27. B	57. A	87. B
28. C	58. C	88. E
29. D	59. A	
30. B	60. C	

Memory-for-Address Test

Work—3 Minutes

Answer each question on a piece of paper to show the letter of the box in which the address belongs. Try to remember the location of as many addresses as you can. If you are not sure of an address, guess. Work only three minutes.

A	B	C	D	E
1200-2599 Drake Weber 1500-1799 Palmer Dewey 4400-6599 Pine	2400-3599 Drake Baker 3600-4599 Palmer Madison 1400-2599 Pine	3200-5599 Drake Hillside 1640-2599 Palmer Dexter 4500-6599 Pine	2100-3599 Drake Ceres 6000-7599 Palmer Bayview 4200-5999 Pine	1700-2599 Drake Girard 3500-9999 Palmer Herald 3400-4599 Pine

1. Hillside
2. 2100-3599 Drake
3. 3500-9999 Palmer
4. 3600-4599 Palmer
5. 4500-6599 Pine
6. 1500-1799 Palmer
7. 3200-5599 Drake
8. Madison
9. 6000-7599 Palmer
10. 1400-2599 Pine
11. 3400-4599 Pine
12. 2400-3599 Drake
13. Dewey
14. Baker
15. 1700-2599 Drake
16. 1400-2599 Pine
17. 4400-6599 Pines
18. 3200-5599 Drake
19. 1500-1799 Palmer
20. Hillside
21. Ceres
22. 2400-3599 Drake
23. 4400-6599 Pine
24. Girard

25. 1640-2599 Palmer
26. 3200-5599 Drake
27. Baker
28. 3500-9999 Palmer
29. 4400-6599 Pine
30. Weber
31. 1400-2599 Pine
32. 2400-3599 Drake
33. 3400-4599 Pine
34. Dewey
35. 3600-4599 Palmer
36. 4400-6599 Pine
37. 2100-3599 Drake
38. 3400-4599 Pine
39. Baker
40. 1200-2599 Drake
41. 2400-3599 Drake
42. Madison
43. 6000-7599 Palmer
44. 2400-3599 Drake
45. Dexter
46. 1700-2599 Drake
47. Madison
48. Bayview

49. 3500-9999 Palmer
50. 4400-6599 Pine
51. 1640-2599 Palmer
52. 3600-4599 Palmer
53. 1700-2599 Drake
54. 2400-3599 Drake
55. 1400-2599 Pine
56. 4400-6599 Pine
57. Baker
58. 3600-4599 Palmer
59. 4400-6599 Pine
60. 3600-4599 Palmer
61. 3500-9999 Palmer
62. Dewey
63. 4200-5999 Pine
64. Hillside
65. 3200-5599 Drake
66. Dewey
67. 4400-6599 Pine
68. 1200-2599 Drake
69. Herald
70. Dexter
71. 2100-3599 Drake
72. 1700-2599 Drake

73. Bayview
74. 2400-3599 Drake
75. 1400-2599 Pine
76. Weber
77. Hillside
78. 4500-6599 Pine
79. 3500-9999 Palmer
80. 1400-2599 Pine
81. 3200-5599 Drake
82. 1500-1799 Palmer
83. 2100-3599 Drake
84. 1640-2599 Palmer
85. Ceres
86. 3600-4599 Palmer
87. Girard
88. 3200-5599 Drake

STOP

When the time is up, go on to the next page for the correct answers.

(**Author's Note:** The sample test above is known as the memory-for-address test in the 470 Battery Test and the 460 Rural Carrier Associate Exam. This Part B is considered as a practice test. You'll be allowed to look at the names and addresses in the boxes, as you are instructed to answer as many questions as possible in three minutes. In the next part, however, you will be asked to answer all the 88 questions in five minutes and you won't be allowed to look at the names and addresses. During the three-minute practice test, answer only a few questions. Spend most of the three minutes in memorizing the placement of numbers and names (just the first two numbers of each address and the first syllables of names, combining two syllables into one. Now, answer a few questions and memorize the names and addresses in preparation for the next part. (**See Memory-for-Address Test: Tips & Strategies, pages 249-254.**)

Correct Answers

Memory-for-Address Test

1. C	31. B	61. E
2. D	32. B	62. A
3. E	33. E	63. D
4. B	34. A	64. C
5. C	35. B	65. C
6. A	36. A	66. A
7. C	37. D	67. A
8. B	38. E	68. A
9. D	39. B	69. F.
10. B	40. A	70. C
11. E	41. B	71. D
12. B	42. B	72. E
13. A	43. D	73. D
14. B	44. B	74. B
15. E	45. C	75. B
16. B	46. E	76. A
17. A	47. B	77. C
18. C	48. D	78. C
19. A	49. E	79. E
20. C	50. A	80. B
21. D	51. C	81. C
22. B	52. B	82. A
23. A	53. E	83. D
24. E	54. B	84. C
25. C	55. B	85. D
26. C	56. A	86. B
27. B	57. B	87. E
28. E	58. B	88. C
29. A	59. A	
30. A	60. B	

Memory-for-Address Test

Work—5 Minutes

This is the section that counts.

Decide in which box each name or address belongs. Don't look back at the boxes with the addresses in them. Work 5 minutes. For each question, mark the answers on the answer sheet to the right.

ANSWER SHEET

		Test A	Test B
1.	1700-2599 Drake	1 Ⓐ Ⓑ Ⓒ Ⓓ Ⓔ	1 Ⓐ Ⓑ Ⓒ Ⓓ Ⓔ
2.	Bayview	2 Ⓐ Ⓑ Ⓒ Ⓓ Ⓔ	2 Ⓐ Ⓑ Ⓒ Ⓓ Ⓔ
3.	1500-1799 Palmer	3 Ⓐ Ⓑ Ⓒ Ⓓ Ⓔ	3 Ⓐ Ⓑ Ⓒ Ⓓ Ⓔ
4.	4200-4599 Pine	4 Ⓐ Ⓑ Ⓒ Ⓓ Ⓔ	4 Ⓐ Ⓑ Ⓒ Ⓓ Ⓔ
5.	Baker	5 Ⓐ Ⓑ Ⓒ Ⓓ Ⓔ	5 Ⓐ Ⓑ Ⓒ Ⓓ Ⓔ
6.	1640-2599 Palmer	6 Ⓐ Ⓑ Ⓒ Ⓓ Ⓔ	6 Ⓐ Ⓑ Ⓒ Ⓓ Ⓔ
7.	Girard	7 Ⓐ Ⓑ Ⓒ Ⓓ Ⓔ	7 Ⓐ Ⓑ Ⓒ Ⓓ Ⓔ
8.	4400-6599 Pine	8 Ⓐ Ⓑ Ⓒ Ⓓ Ⓔ	8 Ⓐ Ⓑ Ⓒ Ⓓ Ⓔ
9.	2100-3599 Drake	9 Ⓐ Ⓑ Ⓒ Ⓓ Ⓔ	9 Ⓐ Ⓑ Ⓒ Ⓓ Ⓔ
10.	2400-3599 Drake	10 Ⓐ Ⓑ Ⓒ Ⓓ Ⓔ	10 Ⓐ Ⓑ Ⓒ Ⓓ Ⓔ
11.	Herald	11 Ⓐ Ⓑ Ⓒ Ⓓ Ⓔ	11 Ⓐ Ⓑ Ⓒ Ⓓ Ⓔ
12.	4200-5999 Pine	12 Ⓐ Ⓑ Ⓒ Ⓓ Ⓔ	12 Ⓐ Ⓑ Ⓒ Ⓓ Ⓔ
13.	3600-4599 Palmer	13 Ⓐ Ⓑ Ⓒ Ⓓ Ⓔ	13 Ⓐ Ⓑ Ⓒ Ⓓ Ⓔ
14.	Hillside	14 Ⓐ Ⓑ Ⓒ Ⓓ Ⓔ	14 Ⓐ Ⓑ Ⓒ Ⓓ Ⓔ
15.	2400-3599 Drake	15 Ⓐ Ⓑ Ⓒ Ⓓ Ⓔ	15 Ⓐ Ⓑ Ⓒ Ⓓ Ⓔ
16.	4400-6599 Pine	16 Ⓐ Ⓑ Ⓒ Ⓓ Ⓔ	16 Ⓐ Ⓑ Ⓒ Ⓓ Ⓔ
17.	Ceres	17 Ⓐ Ⓑ Ⓒ Ⓓ Ⓔ	17 Ⓐ Ⓑ Ⓒ Ⓓ Ⓔ
18.	3500-9999 Palmer	18 Ⓐ Ⓑ Ⓒ Ⓓ Ⓔ	18 Ⓐ Ⓑ Ⓒ Ⓓ Ⓔ
19.	4400-6599 Pine	19 Ⓐ Ⓑ Ⓒ Ⓓ Ⓔ	19 Ⓐ Ⓑ Ⓒ Ⓓ Ⓔ
20.	3600-4599 Palmer	20 Ⓐ Ⓑ Ⓒ Ⓓ Ⓔ	20 Ⓐ Ⓑ Ⓒ Ⓓ Ⓔ
21.	6000-7599 Palmer	21 Ⓐ Ⓑ Ⓒ Ⓓ Ⓔ	21 Ⓐ Ⓑ Ⓒ Ⓓ Ⓔ
22.	1700-2599 Drake	22 Ⓐ Ⓑ Ⓒ Ⓓ Ⓔ	22 Ⓐ Ⓑ Ⓒ Ⓓ Ⓔ
23.	1400-2599 Pine	23 Ⓐ Ⓑ Ⓒ Ⓓ Ⓔ	23 Ⓐ Ⓑ Ⓒ Ⓓ Ⓔ
24.	Dexter	24 Ⓐ Ⓑ Ⓒ Ⓓ Ⓔ	24 Ⓐ Ⓑ Ⓒ Ⓓ Ⓔ
25.	4200-5999 Pine	25 Ⓐ Ⓑ Ⓒ Ⓓ Ⓔ	25 Ⓐ Ⓑ Ⓒ Ⓓ Ⓔ
26.	Baker	26 Ⓐ Ⓑ Ⓒ Ⓓ Ⓔ	26 Ⓐ Ⓑ Ⓒ Ⓓ Ⓔ
27.	1400-2599 Pine	27 Ⓐ Ⓑ Ⓒ Ⓓ Ⓔ	27 Ⓐ Ⓑ Ⓒ Ⓓ Ⓔ
28.	1640-2599 Palmer	28 Ⓐ Ⓑ Ⓒ Ⓓ Ⓔ	28 Ⓐ Ⓑ Ⓒ Ⓓ Ⓔ
29.	Herald	29 Ⓐ Ⓑ Ⓒ Ⓓ Ⓔ	29 Ⓐ Ⓑ Ⓒ Ⓓ Ⓔ
30.	4500-6599 Pine	30 Ⓐ Ⓑ Ⓒ Ⓓ Ⓔ	30 Ⓐ Ⓑ Ⓒ Ⓓ Ⓔ
31.	3200-5599 Drake	31 Ⓐ Ⓑ Ⓒ Ⓓ Ⓔ	31 Ⓐ Ⓑ Ⓒ Ⓓ Ⓔ
32.	4200-5999 Pine	32 Ⓐ Ⓑ Ⓒ Ⓓ Ⓔ	32 Ⓐ Ⓑ Ⓒ Ⓓ Ⓔ
33.	2400-3599 Drake	33 Ⓐ Ⓑ Ⓒ Ⓓ Ⓔ	33 Ⓐ Ⓑ Ⓒ Ⓓ Ⓔ
34.	1640-2599 Palmer	34 Ⓐ Ⓑ Ⓒ Ⓓ Ⓔ	34 Ⓐ Ⓑ Ⓒ Ⓓ Ⓔ
35.	Dexter	35 Ⓐ Ⓑ Ⓒ Ⓓ Ⓔ	35 Ⓐ Ⓑ Ⓒ Ⓓ Ⓔ
36.	1400-2599 Pine	36 Ⓐ Ⓑ Ⓒ Ⓓ Ⓔ	36 Ⓐ Ⓑ Ⓒ Ⓓ Ⓔ
37.	3400-4599 Pine	37 Ⓐ Ⓑ Ⓒ Ⓓ Ⓔ	37 Ⓐ Ⓑ Ⓒ Ⓓ Ⓔ
38.	1500-1799 Palmer	38 Ⓐ Ⓑ Ⓒ Ⓓ Ⓔ	38 Ⓐ Ⓑ Ⓒ Ⓓ Ⓔ
39.	3600-4599 Palmer	39 Ⓐ Ⓑ Ⓒ Ⓓ Ⓔ	39 Ⓐ Ⓑ Ⓒ Ⓓ Ⓔ
40.	1500-1799 Palmer	40 Ⓐ Ⓑ Ⓒ Ⓓ Ⓔ	40 Ⓐ Ⓑ Ⓒ Ⓓ Ⓔ

Go on to the next number on the next page.

41. Ceres	41 Ⓐ Ⓑ Ⓒ Ⓓ Ⓔ	41 Ⓐ Ⓑ Ⓒ Ⓓ Ⓔ
42. Madison	42 Ⓐ Ⓑ Ⓒ Ⓓ Ⓔ	42 Ⓐ Ⓑ Ⓒ Ⓓ Ⓔ
43. Girard	43 Ⓐ Ⓑ Ⓒ Ⓓ Ⓔ	43 Ⓐ Ⓑ Ⓒ Ⓓ Ⓔ
44. 3600-4599 Palmer	44 Ⓐ Ⓑ Ⓒ Ⓓ Ⓔ	44 Ⓐ Ⓑ Ⓒ Ⓓ Ⓔ
45. 4400-6599 Pine	45 Ⓐ Ⓑ Ⓒ Ⓓ Ⓔ	45 Ⓐ Ⓑ Ⓒ Ⓓ Ⓔ
46. 3200-5599 Drake	46 Ⓐ Ⓑ Ⓒ Ⓓ Ⓔ	46 Ⓐ Ⓑ Ⓒ Ⓓ Ⓔ
47. 1700-2599 Drake	47 Ⓐ Ⓑ Ⓒ Ⓓ Ⓔ	47 Ⓐ Ⓑ Ⓒ Ⓓ Ⓔ
48. 3400-4599 Pine	48 Ⓐ Ⓑ Ⓒ Ⓓ Ⓔ	48 Ⓐ Ⓑ Ⓒ Ⓓ Ⓔ
49. 4500-6599 Pine	49 Ⓐ Ⓑ Ⓒ Ⓓ Ⓔ	49 Ⓐ Ⓑ Ⓒ Ⓓ Ⓔ
50. 3600-4599 Palmer	50 Ⓐ Ⓑ Ⓒ Ⓓ Ⓔ	50 Ⓐ Ⓑ Ⓒ Ⓓ Ⓔ
51. 4400-6599 Pine	51 Ⓐ Ⓑ Ⓒ Ⓓ Ⓔ	51 Ⓐ Ⓑ Ⓒ Ⓓ Ⓔ
52. 2100-3599 Drake	52 Ⓐ Ⓑ Ⓒ Ⓓ Ⓔ	52 Ⓐ Ⓑ Ⓒ Ⓓ Ⓔ
53. 1640-2599 Palmer	53 Ⓐ Ⓑ Ⓒ Ⓓ Ⓔ	53 Ⓐ Ⓑ Ⓒ Ⓓ Ⓔ
54. Dewey	54 Ⓐ Ⓑ Ⓒ Ⓓ Ⓔ	54 Ⓐ Ⓑ Ⓒ Ⓓ Ⓔ
55. Madison	55 Ⓐ Ⓑ Ⓒ Ⓓ Ⓔ	55 Ⓐ Ⓑ Ⓒ Ⓓ Ⓔ
56. 1500-1799 Palmer	56 Ⓐ Ⓑ Ⓒ Ⓓ Ⓔ	56 Ⓐ Ⓑ Ⓒ Ⓓ Ⓔ
57. 2100-3599 Drake	57 Ⓐ Ⓑ Ⓒ Ⓓ Ⓔ	57 Ⓐ Ⓑ Ⓒ Ⓓ Ⓔ
58. Herald	58 Ⓐ Ⓑ Ⓒ Ⓓ Ⓔ	58 Ⓐ Ⓑ Ⓒ Ⓓ Ⓔ
59. 1640-2599 Palmer	59 Ⓐ Ⓑ Ⓒ Ⓓ Ⓔ	59 Ⓐ Ⓑ Ⓒ Ⓓ Ⓔ
60. Dexter	60 Ⓐ Ⓑ Ⓒ Ⓓ Ⓔ	60 Ⓐ Ⓑ Ⓒ Ⓓ Ⓔ
61. 1400-2599 Pine	61 Ⓐ Ⓑ Ⓒ Ⓓ Ⓔ	61 Ⓐ Ⓑ Ⓒ Ⓓ Ⓔ
62. 2100-3599 Drake	62 Ⓐ Ⓑ Ⓒ Ⓓ Ⓔ	62 Ⓐ Ⓑ Ⓒ Ⓓ Ⓔ
63. Herald	63 Ⓐ Ⓑ Ⓒ Ⓓ Ⓔ	63 Ⓐ Ⓑ Ⓒ Ⓓ Ⓔ
64. 3200-5599 Drake	64 Ⓐ Ⓑ Ⓒ Ⓓ Ⓔ	64 Ⓐ Ⓑ Ⓒ Ⓓ Ⓔ
65. 4500-6599 Pine	65 Ⓐ Ⓑ Ⓒ Ⓓ Ⓔ	65 Ⓐ Ⓑ Ⓒ Ⓓ Ⓔ
66. 6000-7599 Palmer	66 Ⓐ Ⓑ Ⓒ Ⓓ Ⓔ	66 Ⓐ Ⓑ Ⓒ Ⓓ Ⓔ
67. 1640-2599 Palmer	67 Ⓐ Ⓑ Ⓒ Ⓓ Ⓔ	67 Ⓐ Ⓑ Ⓒ Ⓓ Ⓔ
68. 4500-6599 Pine	68 Ⓐ Ⓑ Ⓒ Ⓓ Ⓔ	68 Ⓐ Ⓑ Ⓒ Ⓓ Ⓔ
69. Dewey	69 Ⓐ Ⓑ Ⓒ Ⓓ Ⓔ	69 Ⓐ Ⓑ Ⓒ Ⓓ Ⓔ
70. 1200-2599 Drake	70 Ⓐ Ⓑ Ⓒ Ⓓ Ⓔ	70 Ⓐ Ⓑ Ⓒ Ⓓ Ⓔ
71. 3500-9999 Palmer	71 Ⓐ Ⓑ Ⓒ Ⓓ Ⓔ	71 Ⓐ Ⓑ Ⓒ Ⓓ Ⓔ
72. 1700-2599 Drake	72 Ⓐ Ⓑ Ⓒ Ⓓ Ⓔ	72 Ⓐ Ⓑ Ⓒ Ⓓ Ⓔ
73. 4200-5999 Pine	73 Ⓐ Ⓑ Ⓒ Ⓓ Ⓔ	73 Ⓐ Ⓑ Ⓒ Ⓓ Ⓔ
74. Madison	74 Ⓐ Ⓑ Ⓒ Ⓓ Ⓔ	74 Ⓐ Ⓑ Ⓒ Ⓓ Ⓔ
75. 1200-2599 Drake	75 Ⓐ Ⓑ Ⓒ Ⓓ Ⓔ	75 Ⓐ Ⓑ Ⓒ Ⓓ Ⓔ
76. Hillside	76 Ⓐ Ⓑ Ⓒ Ⓓ Ⓔ	76 Ⓐ Ⓑ Ⓒ Ⓓ Ⓔ
77. 3600-4599 Palmer	77 Ⓐ Ⓑ Ⓒ Ⓓ Ⓔ	77 Ⓐ Ⓑ Ⓒ Ⓓ Ⓔ
78. Bayview	78 Ⓐ Ⓑ Ⓒ Ⓓ Ⓔ	78 Ⓐ Ⓑ Ⓒ Ⓓ Ⓔ
79. 3600-4599 Palmer	79 Ⓐ Ⓑ Ⓒ Ⓓ Ⓔ	79 Ⓐ Ⓑ Ⓒ Ⓓ Ⓔ
80. 2100-3599 Drake	80 Ⓐ Ⓑ Ⓒ Ⓓ Ⓔ	80 Ⓐ Ⓑ Ⓒ Ⓓ Ⓔ
81. 4400-6599 Pine	81 Ⓐ Ⓑ Ⓒ Ⓓ Ⓔ	81 Ⓐ Ⓑ Ⓒ Ⓓ Ⓔ
82. 1640-2599 Palmer	82 Ⓐ Ⓑ Ⓒ Ⓓ Ⓔ	82 Ⓐ Ⓑ Ⓒ Ⓓ Ⓔ
83. 1700-2599 Drake	83 Ⓐ Ⓑ Ⓒ Ⓓ Ⓔ	83 Ⓐ Ⓑ Ⓒ Ⓓ Ⓔ
84. Madison	84 Ⓐ Ⓑ Ⓒ Ⓓ Ⓔ	84 Ⓐ Ⓑ Ⓒ Ⓓ Ⓔ
85. 4500-6599 Pine	85 Ⓐ Ⓑ Ⓒ Ⓓ Ⓔ	85 Ⓐ Ⓑ Ⓒ Ⓓ Ⓔ
86. Girard	86 Ⓐ Ⓑ Ⓒ Ⓓ Ⓔ	86 Ⓐ Ⓑ Ⓒ Ⓓ Ⓔ
87. 2400-3599 Drake	87 Ⓐ Ⓑ Ⓒ Ⓓ Ⓔ	87 Ⓐ Ⓑ Ⓒ Ⓓ Ⓔ
88. Dewey	88 Ⓐ Ⓑ Ⓒ Ⓓ Ⓔ	88 Ⓐ Ⓑ Ⓒ Ⓓ Ⓔ

Go on to the next number on the next page.

STOP

If you finish before the time is up,

go back and check your answers.

(See the correct answers on the next page.)

Correct Answers

Memory-for-Address Test

1. E	31. C	61. B
2. D	32. D	62. D
3. A	33. B	63. E
4. D	34. C	64. C
5. B	35. C	65. C
6. C	36. B	66. D
7. E	37. E	67. C
8. A	38. A	68. C
9. D	39. B	69. A
10. B	40. A	70. A
11. E	41. D	71. E
12. D	42. B	72. E
13. B	43. E	73. D
14. C	44. B	74. B
15. B	45. A	75. A
16. A	46. C	76. C
17. D	47. E	77. B
18. E	48. E	78. D
19. A	49. C	79. B
20. B	50. B	80. D
21. D	51. A	81. A
22. E	52. D	82. C
23. B	53. C	83. E
24. C	54. A	84. B
25. D	55. B	85. C
26. B	56. A	86. E
27. B	57. D	87. B
28. C	58. E	88. A
29. E	59. C	
30. C	60. C	

Memory-for-Address Test

Work—3 Minutes

Answer each question on a piece of paper to show the letter of the box in which the address belongs.
Try to remember the location of as many addresses as you can. If you are not sure of an address, guess.
Work only three minutes.

A	B	C	D	E
1500-2399 Bell Cadiz 5500-8599 Carter Wilton 3300-3589 Huber	2500-3599 Bell Windell 1600-2499 Carter Vernon 8100-8499 Huber	2200-2699 Bell Madison 3700-9899 Carter Atlantic 6500-6499 Huber	3400-3699 Bell Alden 7099-8999 Carter Lucy 4400-5399 Huber	7200-8799 Bell Livonia 4500-9999 Carter Perry 3500-4699 Huber

1. 2500-3599 Bell
2. 7099-8999 Carter
3. Lucy
4. Wilton
5. 3500-4699 Huber
6. 1600-2499 Carter
7. Lucy
8. 3500-4699 Huber
9. 2500-3599 Bell
10. 1600-2499 Carter
11. Alden
12. 3400-3699 Bell
13. 1600-2499 Carter
14. 3700-9899 Carter
15. 8100-8499 Huber
16 Perry
17. Madison
18. 2500-3599 Bell
19. 3300-3589 Huber
20. 3700-9899 Carter
21. 2500-3599 Bell
22. 1600-2499 Carter
23. 7200-8799 Bell
24. 7099-8999 Carter

25. Livonia
26. 4400-5399 Hubert
27. Windell
28. 1500-2399 Bell
29. 2200-2699 Bell
30. 5500-8599 Carter
31. 4500-9999 Carter
32. 8100-8499 Huber
33. 7099-9899 Carter
34. 7200-8799 Bell
35. Madison
36. Vernon
37. 3400-3699 Bell
38. Windell
39. 3300-3589 Huber
40. 5500-8599 Carter
41. 2500-3599 Bell
42. 3400-3699 Bell
43. Lucy
44. 7200-8799 Bell
45. 3500-6499 Huber
46. 8100-8499 Huber
47. Windell
48. 2200-2699 Bell

49. Cadiz
50. Vernon
51. 3700-9899 Carter
52. Lucy
53. 3500-4699 Huber
54. 6500-6499 Huber
55. 3400-3699 Bell
56. 3300-3589 Huber
57. 7099-8999 Carter
58. 4500-9999 Carter
59. Vernon
60. 2200-2699 Bell
61. 7099-8999 Carter
62. 4500-9999 Carter
63. 2200-2699 Bell
64. 3700-9899 Carter
65. 4400-5399 Huber
66. 5500-8599 Carter
67. 3400-3699 Bell
68 . 4500-9999 Carter
69. 2500-3599 Bell
70. Atlantic
71. 3300-3589 Huber
72. Alden

73. 7200-8799 Bell
74. Lucy
75. 2200-2699 Bell
76. Vernon
77. 7099-8999 Carter
78. 6500-6499 Huber
79. 4400-5399 Huber
80. 7200-8799 Bell
81. 2500-3599 Bell
82. 8100-8499 Huber
83. Alden
84. 3400-3699 Bell
85. 3500-4699 Huber
86. 1500-2399 Bell
87. Atlantic
88. 1600-2499 Carter

STOP

When the time is up, go on to the next page for the correct answers.

(**Author's Note:** The sample test above is known as the memory-for-address test in the 470 Battery Test and the 460 Rural Carrier Associate Exam. This Part B is considered as a practice test. You'll be allowed to look at the names and addresses in the boxes, as you are instructed to answer as many questions as possible in three minutes. In the next part, however, you will be asked to answer all the 88 questions in five minutes and you won't be allowed to look at the names and addresses. During the three-minute practice test, answer only a few questions. Spend most of the three minutes in memorizing the placement of numbers and names (just the first two numbers of each address and the first syllables of names, combining two syllables into one. Now, answer a few questions and memorize the names and addresses in preparation for the next part. (**See Memory-for-Address Test: Tips & Strategies, pages 249-254.**)

Correct Answers

Memory-for-Address Test

1. B	31. E	61. D
2. D	32. B	62. E
3. D	33. D	63. C
4. A	34. E	64. C
5. E	35. C	65. D
6. B	36. B	66. A
7. D	37. D	67. D
8. E	38. B	68. E
9. B	39. A	69. B
10. B	40. A	70. C
11. D	41. B	71. A
12. D	42. D	72. D
13. B	43. D	73. E
14. C	44. E	74. D
15. B	45. E	75. C
16. E	46. B	76. B
17. C	47. B	77. D
18. B	48. C	78. C
19. A	49. A	79. D
20. C	50. B	80. E
21. B	51. C	81. B
22. B	52. D	82. B
23. E	53. E	83. D
24. D	54. C	84. D
25. E	55. D	85. E
26. D	56. A	86. A
27. B	57. D	87. C
28. A	58. E	88. B
29. C	59. B	
30. A	60. C	

Memory-for-Address Test

Work—5 Minutes

This is the section that counts.

Decide in which box each name or address belongs. Don't look back at the boxes with the addresses in them. Work 5 minutes. For each question, mark the answers on the answer sheet to the right.

ANSWER SHEET

		Test A	Test B
1.	7200-8799 Bell	1 Ⓐ Ⓑ Ⓒ Ⓓ Ⓔ	1 Ⓐ Ⓑ Ⓒ Ⓓ Ⓔ
2.	Atlantic	2 Ⓐ Ⓑ Ⓒ Ⓓ Ⓔ	2 Ⓐ Ⓑ Ⓒ Ⓓ Ⓔ
3.	1500-2399 Bell	3 Ⓐ Ⓑ Ⓒ Ⓓ Ⓔ	3 Ⓐ Ⓑ Ⓒ Ⓓ Ⓔ
4.	4400-5399 Huber	4 Ⓐ Ⓑ Ⓒ Ⓓ Ⓔ	4 Ⓐ Ⓑ Ⓒ Ⓓ Ⓔ
5.	Livonia	5 Ⓐ Ⓑ Ⓒ Ⓓ Ⓔ	5 Ⓐ Ⓑ Ⓒ Ⓓ Ⓔ
6.	1600-2499 Carter	6 Ⓐ Ⓑ Ⓒ Ⓓ Ⓔ	6 Ⓐ Ⓑ Ⓒ Ⓓ Ⓔ
7.	Madison	7 Ⓐ Ⓑ Ⓒ Ⓓ Ⓔ	7 Ⓐ Ⓑ Ⓒ Ⓓ Ⓔ
8.	3300-3589 Huber	8 Ⓐ Ⓑ Ⓒ Ⓓ Ⓔ	8 Ⓐ Ⓑ Ⓒ Ⓓ Ⓔ
9.	1600-2499 Carter	9 Ⓐ Ⓑ Ⓒ Ⓓ Ⓔ	9 Ⓐ Ⓑ Ⓒ Ⓓ Ⓔ
10.	Perry	10 Ⓐ Ⓑ Ⓒ Ⓓ Ⓔ	10 Ⓐ Ⓑ Ⓒ Ⓓ Ⓔ
11.	4400-5399 Huber	11 Ⓐ Ⓑ Ⓒ Ⓓ Ⓔ	11 Ⓐ Ⓑ Ⓒ Ⓓ Ⓔ
12.	4500-9999 Carter	12 Ⓐ Ⓑ Ⓒ Ⓓ Ⓔ	12 Ⓐ Ⓑ Ⓒ Ⓓ Ⓔ
13.	2500-3599 Bell	13 Ⓐ Ⓑ Ⓒ Ⓓ Ⓔ	13 Ⓐ Ⓑ Ⓒ Ⓓ Ⓔ
14.	Vernon	14 Ⓐ Ⓑ Ⓒ Ⓓ Ⓔ	14 Ⓐ Ⓑ Ⓒ Ⓓ Ⓔ
15.	3300-3589 Huber	15 Ⓐ Ⓑ Ⓒ Ⓓ Ⓔ	15 Ⓐ Ⓑ Ⓒ Ⓓ Ⓔ
16.	3400-3699 Bell	16 Ⓐ Ⓑ Ⓒ Ⓓ Ⓔ	16 Ⓐ Ⓑ Ⓒ Ⓓ Ⓔ
17.	4500-9999 Carter	17 Ⓐ Ⓑ Ⓒ Ⓓ Ⓔ	17 Ⓐ Ⓑ Ⓒ Ⓓ Ⓔ
18.	4400-5399 Huber	18 Ⓐ Ⓑ Ⓒ Ⓓ Ⓔ	18 Ⓐ Ⓑ Ⓒ Ⓓ Ⓔ
19.	Madison	19 Ⓐ Ⓑ Ⓒ Ⓓ Ⓔ	19 Ⓐ Ⓑ Ⓒ Ⓓ Ⓔ
20.	Wilton	20 Ⓐ Ⓑ Ⓒ Ⓓ Ⓔ	20 Ⓐ Ⓑ Ⓒ Ⓓ Ⓔ
21.	5500-8599 Carter	21 Ⓐ Ⓑ Ⓒ Ⓓ Ⓔ	21 Ⓐ Ⓑ Ⓒ Ⓓ Ⓔ
22.	3700-9899 Carter	22 Ⓐ Ⓑ Ⓒ Ⓓ Ⓔ	22 Ⓐ Ⓑ Ⓒ Ⓓ Ⓔ
23.	7200-8799 Bell	23 Ⓐ Ⓑ Ⓒ Ⓓ Ⓔ	23 Ⓐ Ⓑ Ⓒ Ⓓ Ⓔ
24.	Atlantic	24 Ⓐ Ⓑ Ⓒ Ⓓ Ⓔ	24 Ⓐ Ⓑ Ⓒ Ⓓ Ⓔ
25.	3300-3589 Huber	25 Ⓐ Ⓑ Ⓒ Ⓓ Ⓔ	25 Ⓐ Ⓑ Ⓒ Ⓓ Ⓔ
26.	3500-4699 Huber	26 Ⓐ Ⓑ Ⓒ Ⓓ Ⓔ	26 Ⓐ Ⓑ Ⓒ Ⓓ Ⓔ
27.	1500-2399 Bell	27 Ⓐ Ⓑ Ⓒ Ⓓ Ⓔ	27 Ⓐ Ⓑ Ⓒ Ⓓ Ⓔ
28.	7099-8999 Carter	28 Ⓐ Ⓑ Ⓒ Ⓓ Ⓔ	28 Ⓐ Ⓑ Ⓒ Ⓓ Ⓔ
29.	3500-4699 Huber	29 Ⓐ Ⓑ Ⓒ Ⓓ Ⓔ	29 Ⓐ Ⓑ Ⓒ Ⓓ Ⓔ
30.	3700-9899 Carter	30 Ⓐ Ⓑ Ⓒ Ⓓ Ⓔ	30 Ⓐ Ⓑ Ⓒ Ⓓ Ⓔ
31.	Vernon	31 Ⓐ Ⓑ Ⓒ Ⓓ Ⓔ	31 Ⓐ Ⓑ Ⓒ Ⓓ Ⓔ
32.	3300-3589 Huber	32 Ⓐ Ⓑ Ⓒ Ⓓ Ⓔ	32 Ⓐ Ⓑ Ⓒ Ⓓ Ⓔ
33.	Alden	33 Ⓐ Ⓑ Ⓒ Ⓓ Ⓔ	33 Ⓐ Ⓑ Ⓒ Ⓓ Ⓔ
34.	3500-4699 Huber	34 Ⓐ Ⓑ Ⓒ Ⓓ Ⓔ	34 Ⓐ Ⓑ Ⓒ Ⓓ Ⓔ
35.	Windell	35 Ⓐ Ⓑ Ⓒ Ⓓ Ⓔ	35 Ⓐ Ⓑ Ⓒ Ⓓ Ⓔ
36.	6500-6499 Huber	36 Ⓐ Ⓑ Ⓒ Ⓓ Ⓔ	36 Ⓐ Ⓑ Ⓒ Ⓓ Ⓔ
37.	3400-3699 Bell	37 Ⓐ Ⓑ Ⓒ Ⓓ Ⓔ	37 Ⓐ Ⓑ Ⓒ Ⓓ Ⓔ
38.	1600-2499 Carter	38 Ⓐ Ⓑ Ⓒ Ⓓ Ⓔ	38 Ⓐ Ⓑ Ⓒ Ⓓ Ⓔ
39.	Atlantic	39 Ⓐ Ⓑ Ⓒ Ⓓ Ⓔ	39 Ⓐ Ⓑ Ⓒ Ⓓ Ⓔ
40.	8100-8499 Huber	40 Ⓐ Ⓑ Ⓒ Ⓓ Ⓔ	40 Ⓐ Ⓑ Ⓒ Ⓓ Ⓔ

Go on to the next number on the next page.

41. 3400-3699 Bell	41 Ⓐ Ⓑ Ⓒ Ⓓ Ⓔ	41 Ⓐ Ⓑ Ⓒ Ⓓ Ⓔ
42. 3700-9899 Carter	42 Ⓐ Ⓑ Ⓒ Ⓓ Ⓔ	42 Ⓐ Ⓑ Ⓒ Ⓓ Ⓔ
43. Alden	43 Ⓐ Ⓑ Ⓒ Ⓓ Ⓔ	43 Ⓐ Ⓑ Ⓒ Ⓓ Ⓔ
44. Wilton	44 Ⓐ Ⓑ Ⓒ Ⓓ Ⓔ	44 Ⓐ Ⓑ Ⓒ Ⓓ Ⓔ
45. 7099-8999 Carter	45 Ⓐ Ⓑ Ⓒ Ⓓ Ⓔ	45 Ⓐ Ⓑ Ⓒ Ⓓ Ⓔ
46. 8100-8499 Huber	46 Ⓐ Ⓑ Ⓒ Ⓓ Ⓔ	46 Ⓐ Ⓑ Ⓒ Ⓓ Ⓔ
47. 4500-9999 Carter	47 Ⓐ Ⓑ Ⓒ Ⓓ Ⓔ	47 Ⓐ Ⓑ Ⓒ Ⓓ Ⓔ
48. 7200-8799 Bell	48 Ⓐ Ⓑ Ⓒ Ⓓ Ⓔ	48 Ⓐ Ⓑ Ⓒ Ⓓ Ⓔ
49. Atlantic	49 Ⓐ Ⓑ Ⓒ Ⓓ Ⓔ	49 Ⓐ Ⓑ Ⓒ Ⓓ Ⓔ
50. Windell	50 Ⓐ Ⓑ Ⓒ Ⓓ Ⓔ	50 Ⓐ Ⓑ Ⓒ Ⓓ Ⓔ
51. 3300-3589 Huber	51 Ⓐ Ⓑ Ⓒ Ⓓ Ⓔ	51 Ⓐ Ⓑ Ⓒ Ⓓ Ⓔ
52. 3400-3699 Bell	52 Ⓐ Ⓑ Ⓒ Ⓓ Ⓔ	52 Ⓐ Ⓑ Ⓒ Ⓓ Ⓔ
53. 6500-6499 Huber	53 Ⓐ Ⓑ Ⓒ Ⓓ Ⓔ	53 Ⓐ Ⓑ Ⓒ Ⓓ Ⓔ
54. Lucy	54 Ⓐ Ⓑ Ⓒ Ⓓ Ⓔ	54 Ⓐ Ⓑ Ⓒ Ⓓ Ⓔ
55. 4400-5399 Huber	55 Ⓐ Ⓑ Ⓒ Ⓓ Ⓔ	55 Ⓐ Ⓑ Ⓒ Ⓓ Ⓔ
56. 2200-2699 Bell	56 Ⓐ Ⓑ Ⓒ Ⓓ Ⓔ	56 Ⓐ Ⓑ Ⓒ Ⓓ Ⓔ
57. Perry	57 Ⓐ Ⓑ Ⓒ Ⓓ Ⓔ	57 Ⓐ Ⓑ Ⓒ Ⓓ Ⓔ
58. 4400-5399 Huber	58 Ⓐ Ⓑ Ⓒ Ⓓ Ⓔ	58 Ⓐ Ⓑ Ⓒ Ⓓ Ⓔ
59. 6500-6499 Huber	59 Ⓐ Ⓑ Ⓒ Ⓓ Ⓔ	59 Ⓐ Ⓑ Ⓒ Ⓓ Ⓔ
60. 7200-8799 Bell	60 Ⓐ Ⓑ Ⓒ Ⓓ Ⓔ	60 Ⓐ Ⓑ Ⓒ Ⓓ Ⓔ
61. 4400-5399 Huber	61 Ⓐ Ⓑ Ⓒ Ⓓ Ⓔ	61 Ⓐ Ⓑ Ⓒ Ⓓ Ⓔ
62. 6500-6499 Huber	62 Ⓐ Ⓑ Ⓒ Ⓓ Ⓔ	62 Ⓐ Ⓑ Ⓒ Ⓓ Ⓔ
63. 3400-3699 Bell	63 Ⓐ Ⓑ Ⓒ Ⓓ Ⓔ	63 Ⓐ Ⓑ Ⓒ Ⓓ Ⓔ
64. Livonia	64 Ⓐ Ⓑ Ⓒ Ⓓ Ⓔ	64 Ⓐ Ⓑ Ⓒ Ⓓ Ⓔ
65. 3700-9899 Carter	65 Ⓐ Ⓑ Ⓒ Ⓓ Ⓔ	65 Ⓐ Ⓑ Ⓒ Ⓓ Ⓔ
66. Vernon	66 Ⓐ Ⓑ Ⓒ Ⓓ Ⓔ	66 Ⓐ Ⓑ Ⓒ Ⓓ Ⓔ
67. 3700-9899 Carter	67 Ⓐ Ⓑ Ⓒ Ⓓ Ⓔ	67 Ⓐ Ⓑ Ⓒ Ⓓ Ⓔ
68. 2500-3599 Bell	68 Ⓐ Ⓑ Ⓒ Ⓓ Ⓔ	68 Ⓐ Ⓑ Ⓒ Ⓓ Ⓔ
69. 3400-3699 Bell	69 Ⓐ Ⓑ Ⓒ Ⓓ Ⓔ	69 Ⓐ Ⓑ Ⓒ Ⓓ Ⓔ
70. 5500-8599 Carter	70 Ⓐ Ⓑ Ⓒ Ⓓ Ⓔ	70 Ⓐ Ⓑ Ⓒ Ⓓ Ⓔ
71. 1600-2499 Carter	71 Ⓐ Ⓑ Ⓒ Ⓓ Ⓔ	71 Ⓐ Ⓑ Ⓒ Ⓓ Ⓔ
72. Atlantic	72 Ⓐ Ⓑ Ⓒ Ⓓ Ⓔ	72 Ⓐ Ⓑ Ⓒ Ⓓ Ⓔ
73. 3300-3589 Huber	73 Ⓐ Ⓑ Ⓒ Ⓓ Ⓔ	73 Ⓐ Ⓑ Ⓒ Ⓓ Ⓔ
74. 7099-8999 Carter	74 Ⓐ Ⓑ Ⓒ Ⓓ Ⓔ	74 Ⓐ Ⓑ Ⓒ Ⓓ Ⓔ
75. 4500-9999 Carter	75 Ⓐ Ⓑ Ⓒ Ⓓ Ⓔ	75 Ⓐ Ⓑ Ⓒ Ⓓ Ⓔ
76. 2500-3599 Bell	76 Ⓐ Ⓑ Ⓒ Ⓓ Ⓔ	76 Ⓐ Ⓑ Ⓒ Ⓓ Ⓔ
77. 8100-8499 Huber	77 Ⓐ Ⓑ Ⓒ Ⓓ Ⓔ	77 Ⓐ Ⓑ Ⓒ Ⓓ Ⓔ
78. Alden	78 Ⓐ Ⓑ Ⓒ Ⓓ Ⓔ	78 Ⓐ Ⓑ Ⓒ Ⓓ Ⓔ
79. 3300-3589 Huber	79 Ⓐ Ⓑ Ⓒ Ⓓ Ⓔ	79 Ⓐ Ⓑ Ⓒ Ⓓ Ⓔ
80. Lucy	80 Ⓐ Ⓑ Ⓒ Ⓓ Ⓔ	80 Ⓐ Ⓑ Ⓒ Ⓓ Ⓔ
81. 4500-9999 Carter	81 Ⓐ Ⓑ Ⓒ Ⓓ Ⓔ	81 Ⓐ Ⓑ Ⓒ Ⓓ Ⓔ
82. 4400-5399 Huber	82 Ⓐ Ⓑ Ⓒ Ⓓ Ⓔ	82 Ⓐ Ⓑ Ⓒ Ⓓ Ⓔ
83. 6500-6499 Huber	83 Ⓐ Ⓑ Ⓒ Ⓓ Ⓔ	83 Ⓐ Ⓑ Ⓒ Ⓓ Ⓔ
84. 5500-8599 Carter	84 Ⓐ Ⓑ Ⓒ Ⓓ Ⓔ	84 Ⓐ Ⓑ Ⓒ Ⓓ Ⓔ
85. 7099-8999 Carter	85 Ⓐ Ⓑ Ⓒ Ⓓ Ⓔ	85 Ⓐ Ⓑ Ⓒ Ⓓ Ⓔ
86. 4500-9999 Carter	86 Ⓐ Ⓑ Ⓒ Ⓓ Ⓔ	86 Ⓐ Ⓑ Ⓒ Ⓓ Ⓔ
87. 3500-4699 Huber	87 Ⓐ Ⓑ Ⓒ Ⓓ Ⓔ	87 Ⓐ Ⓑ Ⓒ Ⓓ Ⓔ
88. 2500-3599 Bell	88 Ⓐ Ⓑ Ⓒ Ⓓ Ⓔ	88 Ⓐ Ⓑ Ⓒ Ⓓ Ⓔ

Go on to the next number on the next page.

STOP

If you finish before the time is up,

go back and check your answers.

(See the correct answers on the next page.)

Correct Answers

Memory-for-Address Test

1. E	31. B	61. D
2. C	32. A	62. C
3. A	33. D	63. D
4. D	34. E	64. E
5. E	35. B	65. C
6. B	36. C	66. B
7. C	37. D	67. C
8. A	38. B	68. B
9. B	39. C	69. D
10. E	40. B	70. A
11. D	41. D	71. B
12. E	42. C	72. C
13. B	43. D	73. A
14. B	44. A	74. D
15. A	45. D	75. E
16. D	46. B	76. B
17. E	47. E	77. B
18. D	48. E	78. D
19. C	49. C	79. A
20. A	50. B	80. D
21. A	51. A	81. E
22. C	52. D	82. D
23. E	53. C	83. C
24. C	54. D	84. A
25. A	55. D	85. D
26. E	56. C	86. E
27. A	57. E	87. E
28. D	58. D	88. B
29. E	59. C	
30. C	60. E	

Number Series Test 21

Series of Numbers That Progresses and Follows Definite Order

The *Number Series Test* involves a series of numbers that follows some definite pattern. For each number series question, there is a series of numbers that progresses from left to right and follows some definite order. All you must do is to determine what the next two last numbers or the last two pairs of numbers will be if the same order is continued. The test, which is considered nonverbal, measures your ability to find the "missing link."

Here are some strategies:

Strategy 1: Find the rule that creates the series of numbers.

Strategy 2: Found out which number comes next or is missing.

Strategy 3: Find the patterns used.

In this test, you'll discover that the pattern or the relationship may involve the use of the following:

- addition
- subtraction
- multiplication
- division
- squaring
- cubing
- square root
- cube root

At first, the sequence of numbers is easier to determine. For instance, the number may increase by 2, 4, 5, etc.; sometimes, the number may decrease by 1, 3, 5, etc. But sometimes, the series involves the alternating uses of addition and subtraction, which may appear a little more complex.

Simple Number Series. Each of the three sample questions below gives a series of seven numbers. Each number follows a certain pattern or order. Choose what will be the next one or two numbers in that series if the pattern is continued.

1. 6   8   10   12   14   16   18   ....

A) 22
B) 20
C) 24
D) 21
E) 23

In this question, the pattern is to add 2 to each number: 6 + 2 = 8; 8 + 2 = 10; 10 + 2 = 12; 12 + 2 14; 14 + 2 = 16; 16 + 2 = 18. The next number in the series is 18 + 2 which equals 20. B is the correct answer. Here's how it's done:

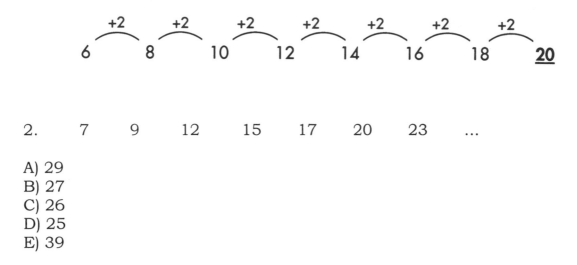

2.   7   9   12   15   17   20   23   ...

A) 29
B) 27
C) 26
D) 25
E) 39

In this question, the pattern is to add 2 to the first number (7 + 2 = 9); add 3 to the second number (9 + 3 = 12; add 3 to the third number (12 + 3 = 15); add 2 to the fourth number (15 + 2 = 17); add 3 to the fifth number (17 + 3 = 20); add 3 to the sixth number (20 + 3) = 23). To continue the series, add 2 to the next number (23 + 2) = 25). D is the correct answer. Here's how it's done:

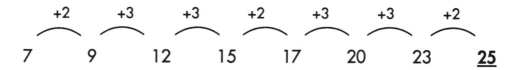

As you can see, the order or pattern is to add 2 once, then add 3 twice. Get it?

3.   9   10   8   9   7   8   6   ...   ...

A) 7
B) 5
C) 9

D) 8
E) 6

In this question, the pattern is to add 1 to the first number, subtract 2 from the next, add 1, subtract 2, and so on. (9 + 1 = 10; 10 - 2 = 8; 8 + 1 = 9; 9 - 2 = 7; 7 + 1 = 8; 8 - 2 = 6; 6 + 1 = 7). Thus A is the correct answer. Here's how it's done:

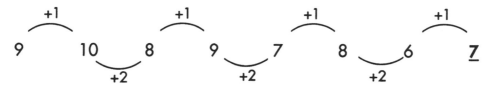

Complex Number Series. These questions are more difficult and the correct answer must be chosen from sets of two numbers. Your job is to select the correct set of two numbers.

The technique used in this type of question is to compare the first number to the third number, the second to the fourth, the third to the fifth, and so on. To make it easier, draw lines to join the numbers as you analyze the pattern. So that you won't be confused, draw the lines both above and below the numbers. (When you finish answering the questions, you may erase these lines on the question or answer sheet. It's as simple as connecting Monday to Wednesday, Wednesday to Friday, Tuesday to Thursday, and Thursday to Saturday. Then all you have to do is find the pattern within each group of numbers.

1. 7   13   8   15   10   17   13   19   17   ...   ...

A) 23   24
B) 21   22
C) 25   26
D) 27   28
E) 28   30

There two patterns in this series. Add 2 to the second, fourth, sixth, and the eight numbers and add to the first, third, fifth, seventh, and ninth numbers as follows: + 1, + 2, +3, +4, +5. B is the correct answer. Here's how it's done:

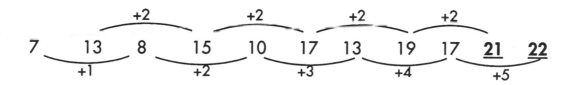

2.   1   7   2   6   4   5   7   4   ...   ...

A) 13 3
B) 15 2
C) 11 3
D) 17 2
E) 12 2

For the first, third, fifth, and seventh numbers, you must to add 1, add 2, add 3, and add 4. For the second, fourth, sixth, and eight numbers, subtract 1 each time. C is the correct answer. Here's how it's done:

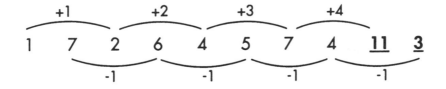

In this test, you are allotted 20 minutes to complete 24 number series questions. In other words, if you have a hard time on a particular question, skip it and go to the next number, etc. Then if you have enough time left, go back to any of the unanswered questions.

Number Series
Practice Test

1. 8 14 9 16 11 18 14 20 18 ... ...   1.   ....

   A) 24 22   C) 22 30   E) 20 23
   B) 22 23   D) 16 22

2. 12 17 12 16 12 15 12   ... ...   2.   ....

   A) 12 13   C) 14 12   E) 14 13
   B) 12 14   D) 13 14

3. 12 3 4 12 5 6 12 ... ...   3.   ....

   A) 6 7   C) 7 8   E) 7 12
   B) 7 7   D) 12 7

4. 1 5 3 7 5 9 7 ... ...   4.   ....

   A) 5 3   C) 11 15   E) 5 9
   B) 11 9   D) 9 11

5. 5 8 10 13 15 18 ... ...   5.   ....

   A) 21 24   C) 20 22   E) 19 21
   B) 20 23   D) 21 23

6. 20 7 17 19 6 16 18 ... ...   6.   ....

   A) 5 17   C) 17 5   E) 5 15
   B) 4 14   D) 15 17

7. 8 9 10 6 7 8 4 ... ...   7.   ....

   A) 5 6   C) 6 7   E) 5 3
   B) 6 4   D) 4 5

8. 17 4 5 17 6 7 17 ... ...   8.   ....

   A) 8 9   C) 17 6   E) 17 8
   B) 8 8   D) 7 8

9. 19 8 7 18 9 8 17 10 9 ... ...   9.   ....

   A) 16 9   C) 18 11   E) 16 11
   B) 18 10   D) 18 9

10. 11 18 12 19 13 20 14 ... ...   10.   ....

   A) 21 15   C) 14 21   E) 15 16
   B) 14 15   D) 15 21

11. 18 17 11 16 15 12 14 ... ...   11.   ....

   A) 11 13   C) 13 13   E) 13 11
   B) 15 11   D) 11 15

12. 15 7 14 8 13 9 12 ... ...   12.   ....

   A) 10 13   C) 12 11   E) 11 10
   B) 10 12   D) 10 11

13. 15 26 24 23 21 20 18 ... ...   13.   ....

   A) 17 15   C) 16 15   E) 13 14
   B) 16 14   D) 19 17

14. 23 29 28 21 27 20 18 25 24 14 23 ... ... 14.   ....

   A) 18 17   C) 13 12   E) 22 9
   B) 24 10   D) 23 21

15. 10 8 13 11 16 14 19 17 22 ... ...15.   ....

   A) 25 20   C) 20 25   E) 23 26
   B) 20 23   D) 25 28

(See the correct answers on page 286.)

Number Series Practice Test

Here's how it's done.

1. 8 14 9 16 11 18 14 20 18 **22** **23**
    (+2 between 14, 16, 18, 20, 22; +1, +2, +3, +4, +5 between 8, 9, 11, 14, 18)

2. 12 17 12 16 12 15 12 **14** **12**
    (-1 between 17, 16, 15, 14)

3. 12 3 4 12 5 6 12 **7** **8**
    (+2; +2; +2)

4. 1 5 3 7 5 9 7 **11** **9**
    (+2 top; +2 bottom)

5. 5 8 10 13 15 18 **20** **23**
    (+5 top; +5 bottom)

6. 20 7 17 19 6 16 18 **5** **15**
    (-1 top; -1 bottom)

7. 8 9 10 6 7 8 4 **5** **6**
    (-2 top; -2 bottom)

8. 17 4 5 17 6 7 17 **8** **9**
    (+2 top; +2 bottom)

9.   19   8   7   18   9   8   17   10   9   **16**   **11**

10.   11   18   12   19   13   20   14   **21**   **15**

11.   18   17   11   16   15   12   14   **13**   **13**

12.   15   7   14   8   13   9   12   **10**   **11**

13.   15   26   24   23   21   20   18   **17**   **15**

14.   23   29   28   21   27   26   18   25   24   14   23   **22**   **9**

15.   10   8   13   11   16   14   19   17   22   **20**   **25**

Correct Answers

Number Series Test

1. 22   23
2. 14   12
3. 7   8
4. 11   9
5. 20   23
6. 5   15
7. 5   6

8. 8   9
9. 16   11
10. 21   15
11. 13   13
12. 10   11
13. 17   15
14. 22   9
15. 20   25

22

Following Oral Instructions Test

Instructions to Be Followed by Job Applicants

Part D of the 460 RCA Exam consists of the *Following Oral Instructions Test* that involves directions to be given by the examiner to job applicants. When the examiner talks, you listen. If you don't, that's the end of the story; you will fail on this exam. It's because during the test, direction for answering questions will be given orally, and if you miss those questions, the examiner will not repeat them. You better listen carefully to the instructions, and follow them.

The suggested answers to each questions are lettered. You choose the *best* answer, whichever it is.

To practice for the test, you might have a friend read the directions to you, while you mark your answers on the sample answer sheet on page 2.

You will be told to follow directions by writing in a test booklet and then on an answer sheet. The test booklet will have lines of material like the following four samples:

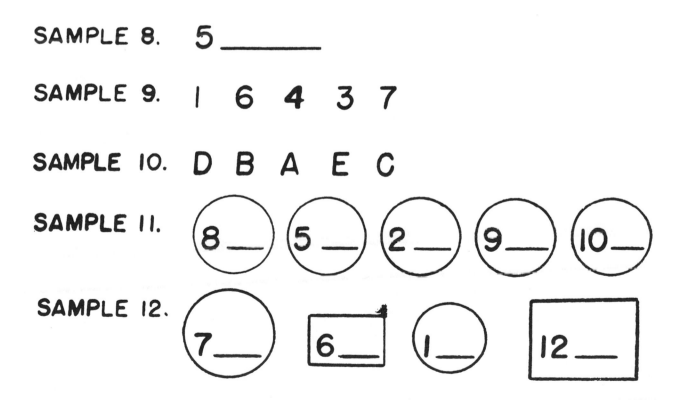

SAMPLE 8.   5 _____

SAMPLE 9.   1   6   4   3   7

SAMPLE 10.   D B A E C

SAMPLE 11.   8__ 5__ 2__ 9__ 10__

SAMPLE 12.   7__ 6__ 1__ 12__

To practice this test, tear off page 3. Then have somebody read the instructions to you. When you are told to darken a space on the sample answer sheet, use the one on this page.

Sample Answer Sheet	
1 Ⓐ Ⓑ Ⓒ Ⓓ Ⓔ	7 Ⓐ Ⓑ Ⓒ Ⓓ Ⓔ
2 Ⓐ Ⓑ Ⓒ Ⓓ Ⓔ	8 Ⓐ Ⓑ Ⓒ Ⓓ Ⓔ
3 Ⓐ Ⓑ Ⓒ Ⓓ Ⓔ	9 Ⓐ Ⓑ Ⓒ Ⓓ Ⓔ
4 Ⓐ Ⓑ Ⓒ Ⓓ Ⓔ	10 Ⓐ Ⓑ Ⓒ Ⓓ Ⓔ
5 Ⓐ Ⓑ Ⓒ Ⓓ Ⓔ	11 Ⓐ Ⓑ Ⓒ Ⓓ Ⓔ
6 Ⓐ Ⓑ Ⓒ Ⓓ Ⓔ	12 Ⓐ Ⓑ Ⓒ Ⓓ Ⓔ

Instructions to be read (the words in parentheses should not be read aloud):

You are to follow the instructions that I shall read to you. I cannot repeat them.

Look at the samples. Sample 1 has a number and a line beside it. On the line write an A. (Pause 2 seconds.) Now on the sample answer sheet, find number 5 (pause 2 seconds) and darken the space for the letter you just wrote on the line. (Pause 2 seconds.)

Look at Sample 2. (Pause slightly.) Draw a line under the third number. (Pause 2 seconds.) Now look on the sample answer sheet, find the number under which you just drew a line, and darken space B as in "baker" for that number. (Pause 5 seconds.)

Look at Sample 3. (Pause slightly.) Draw a line under the third letter in the line. (Pause 2 seconds.) Now on your answer sheet, find number 9 (pause 2 seconds) and darken the space for the letter under which you drew a line. (Pause 5 seconds.)

Look at the five circles in Sample 4. (Pause slightly.) Each circle has a number and a line in it. Write D as in "dog" on the blank in the last circle. (Pause 2 seconds.) Now on the sample answer sheet, darken the space for the number-letter combination that is in the circle you just wrote in (pause 5 seconds.)

Now look at the sample answer sheet. (Pause slightly.) You should have darkened spaces 4B, 5A, 9A, and 10D on the sample answer sheet. (If the person preparing to take the examination made any mistakes, try to help him see why he made wrong marks.)

Examination 710   23

Data Conversion Operator, Clerk-Typist & Clerk Stenographer

(Data Conversion Operator, Clerk-Typist, Clerk Stenographer)

The following questions are samples of the types of questions that will be used on Examination 710. Study these questions carefully. Each question has several suggested answers. You are to decide which one is the **best answer**. Next, on the Sample Answer Sheet below, find the answer space that is numbered the same number as the question, then darken the space that is lettered the same as the answer you have selected. After you have answered all the questions, compare your answers with the ones given in the Correct Answers to Sample Questions below the Sample Answer Sheets.

Sample Questions 1 through 14 - **Clerical Aptitude**

In Sample Questions 1 through 3 below, there is a name or code in a box at the left, and four other names or codes in alphabetical or numerical order at the right. Find the correct space for the boxed name or number so that it will be in alphabetical and/or numerical order with the others and mark the letter of that space as your answer on your Sample Answer Sheet below.

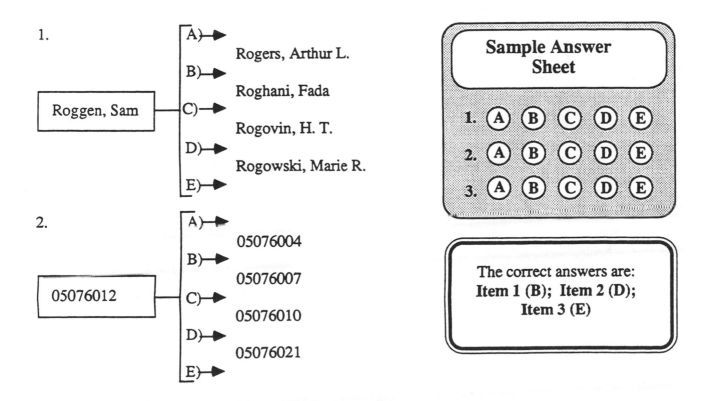

1.
A) ➡
    Rogers, Arthur L.
B) ➡
    Roghani, Fada

[Roggen, Sam] C) ➡
    Rogovin, H. T.
D) ➡
    Rogowski, Marie R.
E) ➡

Sample Answer Sheet

1. Ⓐ Ⓑ Ⓒ Ⓓ Ⓔ
2. Ⓐ Ⓑ Ⓒ Ⓓ Ⓔ
3. Ⓐ Ⓑ Ⓒ Ⓓ Ⓔ

2.
A) ➡
    05076004
B) ➡
    05076007

[05076012] C) ➡
    05076010
D) ➡
    05076021
E) ➡

The correct answers are:
Item 1 (B); Item 2 (D);
Item 3 (E)

289

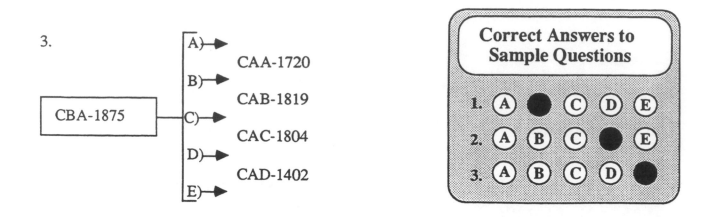

3.

CBA-1875

A) → CAA-1720
B) → CAB-1819
C) → CAC-1804
D) → CAD-1402
E) →

Correct Answers to Sample Questions

1. (A) ● (C) (D) (E)
2. (A) (B) (C) ● (E)
3. (A) (B) (C) (D) ●

Sample Questions 4 through 8 require you to compare names, addresses, or codes. In each line across the page, there are three names, addresses or codes that are much alike. Compare the three and decide which ones are exactly alike. On the Sample Answer Sheet at the bottom, mark the answers:

A   if **ALL THREE** names, addresses, or codes are exactly **ALIKE**
B   if only the **FIRST** and **SECOND** names, addresses, or codes are exactly **ALIKE**
C   if only the **FIRST** and **THIRD** names, addresses, or codes are exactly **ALIKE**
D   if only the **SECOND** and **THIRD** names, addresses, or codes are exactly **ALIKE**
E   if **ALL THREE** names, addresses, or codes are **DIFFERENT**

4.   Helene Bedell   Helene Beddell   Helene Beddell

5.   F. T. Wedemeyer   F. T. Wedemeyer   F. T. Wedmeyer

6.   3214 W. Beaumont St.   3214 Beaumount St.   3214 Beaumont St.

7.   BC 3105T-5   BC 3015T-5   BC 3105T-5

8.   4460327   4460327   4460327

For the next two questions, find the correct spelling of the word and darken the appropriate answer space on your Sample Answer Sheet. If none of the alternatives are correct, darken Space D.

9.   A) accomodate
     B) acommodate
     C) accommadate
     D) none of the above

10.   A) manageble
      B) manageable
      C) manegeable
      D) none of the above

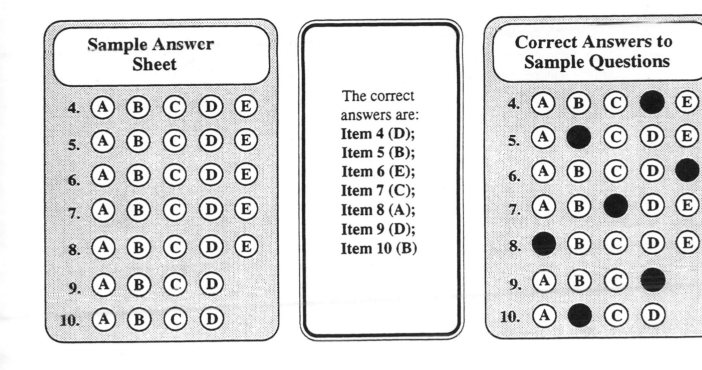

Sample Answer Sheet

4. (A) (B) (C) (D) (E)
5. (A) (B) (C) (D) (E)
6. (A) (B) (C) (D) (E)
7. (A) (B) (C) (D) (E)
8. (A) (B) (C) (D) (E)
9. (A) (B) (C) (D)
10. (A) (B) (C) (D)

The correct answers are:
Item 4 (D);
Item 5 (B);
Item 6 (E);
Item 7 (C);
Item 8 (A);
Item 9 (D);
Item 10 (B)

Correct Answers to Sample Questions

4. (A) (B) (C) ● (E)
5. (A) ● (C) (D) (E)
6. (A) (B) (C) (D) ●
7. (A) (B) ● (D) (E)
8. ● (B) (C) (D) (E)
9. (A) (B) (C) ●
10. (A) ● (C) (D)

For Questions 11 through 14, perform the computation as indicated in the question and find the answer among the list of alternative responses. Mark your Sample Answer Sheet A, B, C, or D for the correct answer; or, if your answer is not among these, mark E for that question.

Sample Answer Sheet

11. (A) (B) (C) (D) (E)
12. (A) (B) (C) (D) (E)
13. (A) (B) (C) (D) (E)
14. (A) (B) (C) (D) (E)

11.   32 + 26 =

    A) 69
    B) 59
    C) 58
    D) 54
    E) none of the above

12.   57 - 15 =

    A) 72
    B) 62
    C) 54
    D) 44
    E) none of the above

The correct answers are:
Item 11 (C); Item 12 (E);
Item 13 (B); Item 14 (A)

13.   23 x 7 =

    A) 164
    B) 161
    C) 154
    D) 141
    E) none of the above

Correct Answers to Sample Questions

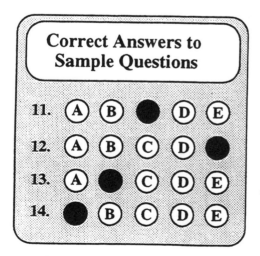

11. (A) (B) ● (D) (E)
12. (A) (B) (C) (D) ●
13. (A) ● (C) (D) (E)
14. ● (B) (C) (D) (E)

14.   160 / 5 =

    A) 32
    B) 30
    C) 25
    D) 21
    E) none of the above

Sample Questions 15 through 22 - **Verbal Abilities**

Sample items 15 through 17 below test the ability to follow instructions. They direct you to mark a specific number and letter combination on your Sample Answer Sheet. The answers that you are instructed to mark are, for the most part, NOT in numerical sequence (·i.e., you would not use Number 1 on your answer sheet to answer Question 1; Number 2 for Question 2, etc.). Instead, you must mark the number and space specifically designated in each test question.

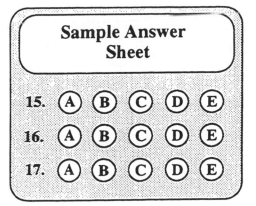

15.   Look at the letters below. Draw a circle around the middle letter. Now, on your Sample Answer Sheet, find Number 16 and darken the space for the letter you just circled.

R   C   H

16.   Draw a line under the number shown below that is more than 10 but less than 20. Find that number on your Sample Answer Sheet, and darken Space A.

5   9   17   22

17.   Add the numbers 11 and 4 and write your answer on the blank line below. Now find this number on your Sample Answer Sheet and darken the space for the second letter in the alphabet.

_____

The correct answers are:
**Item 15 (B); Item 16 (C);
Item 17 (A)**

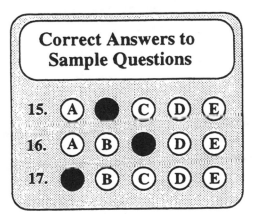

Answer the remaining Sample Test Questions on the Sample Answer Sheet in numerical sequence (i.e., Number 18 on the Sample Answer Sheet for Question 18; Number 19 for Question 19, etc.).

Select the sentence below which is most appropriate with respect to grammar, usage, and punctuation suitable for a formal letter or report.

18.   A) He should of responded to the letter by now.
      B) A response to the letter by the end of the week.
      C) The letter required his immediate response.
      D) A response by him to the letter is necessary.

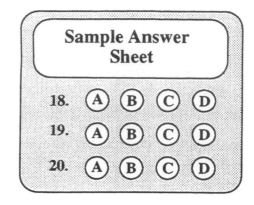

In questions 19 and 20 below, you will be asked to decide what the highlighted word means.

19.   The payment was **authorized** yesterday. **Authorized** most nearly means

      A) expected
      B) approved
      C) refunded
      D) received

The correct answers are:
Item 18 (C); Item 19 (B);
Item 20 (D)

20.   Please **delete** the second paragraph. **Delete** most nearly means

      A) type
      B) read
      C) edit
      D) omit

In questions 21 and 22 below, you are asked to read a paragraph, then answer the question that follows it.

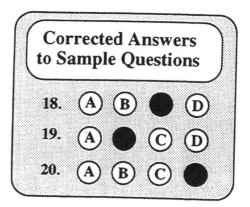

21. "Window Clerks working for the Postal Service have direct financial responsibility for the selling of postage. In addition, they are expected to have a thorough knowledge concerning the acceptability of all material offered by customers for mailing. Any information provided to the public by these employees must be completely accurate."

The paragraph best supports the statement that Window Clerks

A) must account for the stamps issued to them for sale

B) have had long training in other Postal Service jobs

C) must help sort mail to be delivered by carriers

D) inspect the contents of all packages offered for mailing

22. "The most efficient method for performing a task is not always easily determined. That which is economical in terms of time must be carefully distinguished from that which is economical in terms of expended energy. In short, the quickest method may require a degree of physical effort that may be neither essential nor desirable."

The paragraph best supports the statement that

A) it is more efficient to perform a task slowly than rapidly

B) skill in performing a task should not be acquired at the expense of time

C) the most efficient execution of a task is not always the one done in the shortest time

D) energy and time cannot both be considered in the performance of a single task

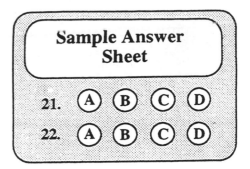

Sample Answer Sheet

21. A B C D
22. A B C D

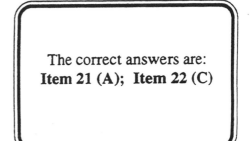

The correct answers are:
Item 21 (A); Item 22 (C)

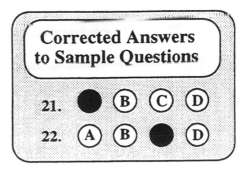

Corrected Answers to Sample Questions

21. ● B C D
22. A B ● D

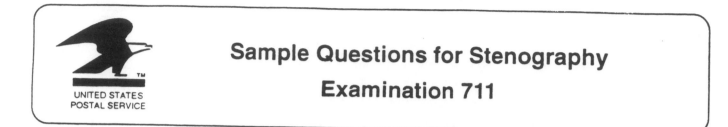

**Sample Questions for Stenography
Examination 711**

UNITED STATES
POSTAL SERVICE

The sample below shows the length of material dictated. Have someone dictate the passage to you so that you can see how well prepared you are to take dictation at 80 words a minute. Each pair of lines is dictated in 10 seconds. Dictate periods, but not commas. Read the exercise with the expression the punctuation indicates.

I realize that this practice dictation is not a part of the examination	10 sec.
proper and is not to be scored.(Period) When making a study of the private	20 sec.
pension structure and its influence on turnover, the most striking feature is its	30 sec.
youth.(Period) As has been shown, the time of greatest growth began just a few years	40 sec.
ago.(Period) The influence that this growth has had on the labor market and	50 sec.
worker attitudes is hard to assess, partly because the effects have not yet fully	1 min.
evolved and many are still in the growing stage.(Period) Even so, most pension	10 sec.
plans began with much more limited gains than they give now.(Period) For example,	20 sec.
as private plans mature they grant a larger profit and a greater range of gains to	30 sec.
more workers and thereby become more important.(Period) Plans which protect accrued pension	40 sec.
credits are rather new and are being revised in the light of past trends.(Period)	50 sec.
As informal and formal information on pension plans spreads, the workers become more	2 min.
aware of the plans and their provisions increase, their impact on employee attitudes	10 sec.
and decisions will no doubt become stronger.(Period) Each year, more and more workers	20 sec.
will be retiring with a private pension, their firsthand knowledge of the benefits to	30 sec.
be gained from private pensions will spread to still active workers.(Period) Thus, workers	40 sec.
may less often view pensions as just another part of the security package	50 sec.
based on service and more often see them as unique benefits.(Period)	3 min.

On the back page, the TRANSCRIPT and WORD LIST for part of the above dictation are similar to those each competitor will receive for the dictation test. Many words have been omitted from the TRANSCRIPT. Compare your notes with it. When you come to a blank space in the TRANSCRIPT, decide which word (or words) belongs in the space. Look for the missing word in the WORD LIST. Notice what letter is printed beside the word. Write that letter in the blank. B is written in blank 1 to show how you are to record your choice. Write E if the exact answer is NOT in the WORD LIST. You may also write the word (or words) or the shorthand for it, if you wish. The same choice may belong in more than one blank.

EFFECTIVE APRIL 1993

ALPHABETIC WORD LIST

Write E if the answer is NOT listed.

at - D	make - A
attitudes - C	making - B
be - B	market - B
been - C	markets - D
began - D	marking - D
being - A	never - B
completely - A	not - D
examination - A	over - C
examine - B	part - C
examining - D	partly - D
feat - A	pension - C
feature - C	practical - C
full - B	practice - B
fully - D	private - D
greater - D	proper - C
grow - B	section - D
growing - C	so - B
had - D	still - A
has - C	structure - D
has been - B	structured - B
has had - A	to - D
has made - A	to be - C
in - C	trial - A
in part - B	turn - D
influence - A	turnover - B
labor - C	values - A
main - B	yet - C

TRANSCRIPT

I realize that this ----- dictation is ----- a ----- of the
                    B
1   2   3

----- ----- and is ----- ----- scored.
4   5   6   7

When ----- a ----- of the ----- ----- ----- and its
      8   9   10   11   12

----- on -----, the most striking ----- is its youth. As
13   14   15

----- shown, the time of ----- growth began just a few
16   17

years ago. The ----- that this growth ----- on the labor
                18   19

----- and worker ----- is hard to assess, ----- because
20   21   22

the effects have not yet ----- evolved and many are ----
                          23   24

in the ----- stage....
        25

(For the next sentences there would be another WORD
LIST, if the entire sample dictation were transcribed.)

You will be given an answer sheet like the sample at the left, below, on which your answers can be scored by machine.
Each number on the answer sheet stands for the blank with the same number in the transcript. Darken the space
below the letter that is the same as the letter you wrote in the transcript. If you have not finished writing letters in the
blanks in the transcript, or if you wish to make sure that you have lettered them correctly, you may continue to use
your notes after you begin marking the answer sheet.

Answer Sheet for Sample Transcript

Correct Answers for Sample Transcript

24

Analyzing Examination 710
Clerical Aptitude, Verbal Abilities & Typing Test

I. Clerical Aptitude

Sample Questions 1 through 14

In sample questions 1 through 3, there is a name or a code in a box at the left. There are also four other names or codes in alphabetical or numeral order at the right. All you have to do is find out the appropriate place (A to D) at right, so that it will be in alphabetical and/or numerical order with the others. Mark the letter of that space as your answer on the sample answer sheet. In other words, know how to alphabetize or do numerical arrangement.

You are required by sample questions 4 through 8 to compare names, addresses, and codes. In each line across the page, there are three names, addresses, or codes that are much alike. You must compare the three and decide which ones are exactly alike or the same. You must answer A, B, C, D, or E.

On the same sample answer sheet at the right, mark the answer as follows:

A   If **ALL THREE** names, addresses, or codes are exactly **ALIKE**
B   If only the **FIRST** and **SECOND** names, addresses, or codes are exactly **ALIKE**
C   If only the **FIRST** and **THIRD** names, addresses, or codes are exactly **ALIKE**
D   If only the **SECOND** and **THIRD** names, addresses, or codes are exactly **ALIKE**
E   If **ALL THREE** names, addresses, or codes are **DIFERENT**

To make it easier for me to answer the questions, I developed my own system of memorization and comparison. Here is my code, which is easy to remember.

A = 123 (first, second, and third alike)
B = 12 (first and second alike)
C = 13 (first and third alike)
D = 23 (second and third alike)
E =   0 (all different)

(Note: This examination is for Data Conversion Operator, Clerk-Typist, and Clerk-Stenographer)

It is to be emphasized that you'll look for names, addresses, and codes that are ALIKE, except answer E. In other words, in answering E, you look for those names, and addresses, and codes that are all different. Memorize and use my code for this kind of test.

Examples:

4. Helene Bedell	Helene Beddell	Helene Beddell
5. F. T. Wedemeyer	F. T. Wedemeyer	F. T. Wedmeyer
6. 3214 W. Beaumont St.	3214 Beaumount St.	3214 Beaumont St.
7. BC 3105T-5	BC 3015T-5	BC 3105T-5
8. 4460327	4460327	4460327

General Rule: In comparing names or numbers, compare the first column with the second column, then the second with the third. So that you won't get confused, place a minus sign (- for different) or a plus sign (+ for alike) between the first column and the second column and between the second column and the third column. These plus and minus signs are my own codes, not the Postal Service's.

Example 1: (No. 4)

Helen Bedell   -   Helene Beddell   +   Helene Beddell

The code is 23 (second and third alike), so the answer is D.

In the above example, the first and second columns are different (the first column has one *d*, while the second column has a double *d*) and the second and third columns are alike (both have a double *d*). You must not compare the third and first columns to see whether they are different or alike. In short, the third and first columns are different. Hence, the answer is D (code 23).

Example 2: (No. 5)

F. T. Wedemeyer   +   F. T. Wedemeyer   -   F. T. Wedmeyer

In the above example, the first and second columns are alike (with a plus sign) and the second and third columns are different, the third column having only three *e*'s (with a minus sign). You don't need to compare the third column with the first. It is understood that they are different.

The code is 12 (first and second columns are alike). The correct answer is B.

Example 3: (No.6)

3214 W. Beaumont St.   -   3214 Beaumount St.   -   3214 Beaumont St.

If the first and the second columns are different (with a minus sign), and the third and second columns, are different, the code is 0 (all are different). As you can see, the first column has a direction, which is W (West), while the second and third columns have different spellings of streets. The second street is spelled "Beau*mount*) while the third is spelled "Beau*mont*." The correct answer is E, the code being 0.

Example 4: (No. 7)

BC 3105T-5   -   BC 3015T-5   -   BC 3105T-5

In the above example, the first and second columns are different (with a minus sign) and the second and third are different (with a minus sign). You still need to compare the third column with the first, to see if there is any similarity or difference. The first and third columns have the same letters and figures. So the code is 13 (first and third are alike). Therefore, the correct answer is C.

Example 5: (No.) 8

4460327   +   4460327   +   4460327

As you can see, the first and second columns (with a plus sign) are alike and the second and third columns are alike (with a plus sign). Since they are alike, the code is 123 (first, second, and third columns are alike). So the correct answer is A.

As explained in the above examples, you have to know which columns are alike.

After writing the answers, you should erase the plus and minus signs you made on the question sheet. However, if you have no more time to do it, then leave them alone.

Spelling

(See **Spelling Techniques**.)

For the next two questions, find the correct spelling of the word and darken the appropriate answer space on your sample answer sheet. If none of the alternatives are correct, darken Space D.

9.
A) accomodate
B) acommodate
C) accommadate
D) none of the above

10.
A) manageble
B) manageable
C) manegeable
D) none of the above

.If you are practicing speed reading, you can glance at the words from A to D in a snap in the above example (question 9). You can immediately disregard A, B, and C because merely by looking at them you'll know they are awkwardly spelled. Pronounce the words to yourself and you'll know what I mean. D is the correct answer. As to question 10, B is the correct answer. The words *manage* and *able* are combined.

Arithmetic

For questions 11 through 14, perform the computation as indicated in the question and find the answer among the list of alternative responses. Mark your sample answer sheet A, B, C, or D for the correct answer; or if your answer is not among these, mark E for that question.

11.

32 + 26 =

A) 69
B) 59
C) 58
D) 54
E) none of the above

12.

57 - 15 =

A) 72
B) 62
C) 54
D) 44
E) none of the above

13.

23 x 7 =

A) 164
B) 161
C) 154
D) 141
E) none of the above

14.

160/5 =

A) 32
B) 30
C) 25
D) 21
E) none of the above

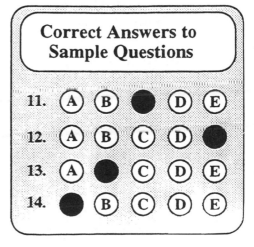

Sample Answer Sheet

11. Ⓐ Ⓑ Ⓒ Ⓓ Ⓔ
12. Ⓐ Ⓑ Ⓒ Ⓓ Ⓔ
13. Ⓐ Ⓑ Ⓒ Ⓓ Ⓔ
14. Ⓐ Ⓑ Ⓒ Ⓓ Ⓔ

Now, for the analyses of questions 11 to 14.

You don't need to be an Einstein to score high on arithmetic tests. What you need to do is use some techniques and try them out with your own biocomputer. The Postal Service gives only simple mathematical problems, and you can surely make a perfect score if you have enough time to answer the questions. The problem is that time is limited, so you have to use some techniques to beat the system.

The correct answers are:
Item 11 (C);   Item 12 (E);
Item 13 (B);   Item 14 (A)

11. Addition problem (32 + 26):

```
  32
+ 26
  58
```

The numbers 32 and 26 are to be added together. The solution to the addition, 58 in this case, is called the "sum."

If the problem is as simple as this, without any carrying, you can simply add the numbers mentally from left to right—not

Correct Answers to Sample Questions

11. Ⓐ Ⓑ ● Ⓓ Ⓔ
12. Ⓐ Ⓑ Ⓒ Ⓓ ●
13. Ⓐ ● Ⓒ Ⓓ Ⓔ
14. ● Ⓑ Ⓒ Ⓓ Ⓔ

from right to left, which is taught in school. It's much simpler and faster from left to right.

12. Subtraction problem (57 - 15):

```
  57
- 15
  42
```

The number 15 is to be subtracted from 57. Simply deduct 1 from 5 and 5 from 7 (starting from the left, because you don't need borrowing. If you need to borrow, then start from right to left).

13. In the multiplication problem (23 x 7):

```
  23
 x 7
 161
```

In a simple multiplication problem like this, try to work mentally to save time. (When you write it down, you spend several seconds. Think to yourself, 7 x 3 = 21 (just remember 1 and carry 2): 7 x 2 = 14 + 2 = 16. Put the 1 after 16 and the answer is 161 or B.

14. Division problem (160/5):

5/160 = 32

The division given in the sample test is as simple as this, but remember, there's a time limit. You can do the division mentally, too by dividing 16 by 5 = 3 (with the extra 1). Place the extra 1 before 0 and the answer is 10. Dividing 10 by 5 = 2. Put 2 after 3 and the answer is 32 or A.

*(Also see **Numbers and Mathematics,** and **Strategies for Standardized Tests,** Solving Mathematics Problems.)*

II. Verbal Abilities

Sample questions 15 through 22

Sample questions 15 through 17 below tests the ability to follow instructions. They direct you to mark a specific number and letter combination on your sample answer sheet. The answers that you are instructed to mark are, for the most part, NOT in numerical sequence (i.e., you would not use number 1 on your answer sheet to answer question 1; number 2 for question 2, etc.). Instead, you must mark the number and space specifically designated in each test question, as specified in the following sample questions:

15. Look at the letters below. Draw a circle around the middle letter. Now, on your sample answer sheet, find Number 16 and darken the space for the letter you just circled.

R   C   H

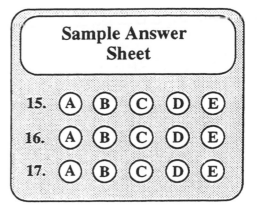

So you darken the circle with letter C on number 16. In other words, you are not told to darken the letter C on number 15. The answer to question 15 is to be marked on number 16. So number 16 has C as the answer. How about the answer to number 15? Just continue.

16. Draw a line under the number shown below that is more than 10 but less than 20. Find that number on your sample sheet, and darken space A.

5   9   17   22

So the answer to question number 16 is to be marked on question number 17, which is A. So darken space A on Number 17. In other words, the answer to question number 16 is A, which happened to be on number 17.

17. Add the numbers 11 and 4 and write your answer on the blank line below. Now find this number on your sample answer sheet and darken the space for the second letter in the alphabet.

_____

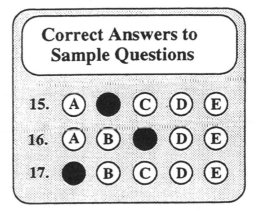

Add 11 and 4 and the answer is 15. So find number 15 on the sample answer sheet. Darken the second letter in the alphabet, which happens to be B. So darken space B on number 15.

In other words, the darkening of spaces started from number 16, then to number 17 and back to number 15. As you can see, the questions are easy to answer but the Postal Service is trying to confuse you and me!

Answer the remaining sample test questions on the sample answer sheet in numerical sequence (i.e., number 18 on the sample answer sheet for question 18; number 19 for question 19, etc.).

Select the sentence below that is the most appropriate with respect to grammar, usage, and punctuation for a formal letter or report.

18.

A) He should be of responded to the letter by now.
B) A response to the letter by the end of the week.
C) The letter required his immediate response.
D) A response by him to the letter is necessary.

If you analyze the sentences, you'll see the question A is awkward and question B is incomplete. So neither of them is the answer. C is grammatically correct. D, although a complete sentence, seems to be awkward, too. So C is the answer. Darken space C.

In questions 19 and 20 below, you'll be asked to decide what the highlighted word means:

19. The payment was **authorized** yesterday. **Authorized** means

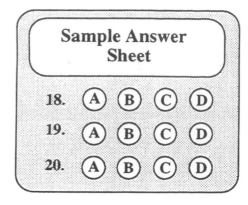

Sample Answer Sheet

18. Ⓐ Ⓑ Ⓒ Ⓓ
19. Ⓐ Ⓑ Ⓒ Ⓓ
20. Ⓐ Ⓑ Ⓒ Ⓓ

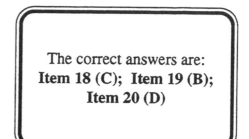

The correct answers are:
Item 18 (C); Item 19 (B);
Item 20 (D)

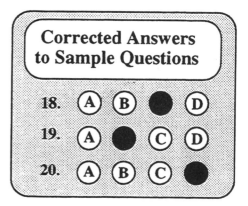

Corrected Answers to Sample Questions

18. Ⓐ Ⓑ ● Ⓓ
19. Ⓐ ● Ⓒ Ⓓ
20. Ⓐ Ⓑ Ⓒ ●

A) expected
B) approved
C) refunded
D) received

In an instance, you'll know that *approved* (B) is the answer. Why? Because *expected, refunded,* and *received,* mean something else.

20. Please *delete* the second paragraph. *Delete* most nearly means

A) type
B) read
C) edit
D) omit

The letters *de* before *lete* indicate a negative action. That is, *de* means *from* which may mean take it out or away from something. So naturally, omit or D is the correct answer.

In questions 21 and 22 below, you are asked to read a paragraph, then answer the question that follows it:

21. "Window clerks working for the Postal Service have direct financial responsibility for the selling of postage. In addition, they are expected to have a thorough knowledge concerning the acceptability of all material offered by customers for mailing. Any information provided to the public by these employees must be completely accurate."

The paragraph best supports the statement that window clerks

A) must account for stamps issued to them for sale
B) have had long training in other Postal Service jobs
C) must help sort mail to be delivered by carriers
D) inspect the contents of all packages offered for mailing

(Reading Comprehension)

In choosing answers to reading comprehension questions, look for the main idea in the statement. In question 20, look for the main idea in the statement "Window clerks...." If you read it carefully, you'll see that the main point in the paragraph is the financial responsibility for the selling of postage. Hence, "A) must account for the stamps issued to them for sale" best supports the statement about Window Clerks.

22. "The most efficient method for performing a task is not always easily determined. That which is economical in terms of time must be carefully distinguished from that which is economical in terms of expended energy. In short, the quickest method may require a degree of physical effort that may be neither essential nor desirable."

The paragraph best supports the statement that

A) it is more efficient to perform a task slowly than rapidly

B) skill in performing a task should not be acquired at the expense of time

C) the most efficient execution of a task is not always the one done in the shortest time

D) energy and time cannot both be considered in the performance of a single task

If you analyze the statement in question 22, the sentence "the most efficient method for performing a task is not always easily determined" clearly indicates that it is the main idea in the statement. As you'll note, there's the word *efficient* in the first sentence of the statement and there's also the word *efficient* in two answer choices: "A) it is more efficient to perform a task slowly than rapidly" and "C) the most efficient execution of a task is not always the one done in the shortest time." So the correct answer is from either these two choices. And it is. C is the correct answer.

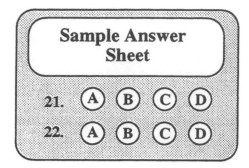

Sample Answer Sheet

21. (A) (B) (C) (D)
22. (A) (B) (C) (D)

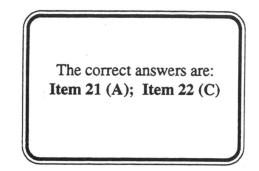

The correct answers are:
Item 21 (A); Item 22 (C)

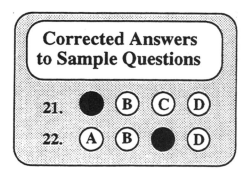

Corrected Answers to Sample Questions

21. ● (B) (C) (D)
22. (A) (B) ● (D)

Typing Test

As an applicant, you must show that you can type forty words per minute for five minutes with no more than two errors. Space, paragraph, spell, punctuate, capitalize, and begin and end each line precisely as shown in the exercise.

In the examination, you will have five minutes in which to copy the test exercise. When you complete the exercise, simply double space and begin again. In the test you must type at least sixteen lines to be eligible in speed. At that minimum speed, your paper should not have more than two errors. The number of errors permitted increases with the number of words typed.

Below is an example of the type of material that appears on the typing test:

> This is an example of the type of material which will be presented to you as the actual typewriting examination. Each competitor will be required to typewrite the practice material exactly as it appears on the copy. You are to space, capitalize, punctuate, spell, and begin and end each line exactly as it is presented in the copy. Each time you reach the end of the paragraph you should begin again and continue to practice typing the practice paragraph on scratch paper until the examiner tells you to stop. You are advised that it is more important to type accurately than to type rapidly.

I must repeat that to be a clerk-typist or mark-up clerk, automated, you should type at least forty words per minute and pass the last part of the exam: the typing test. I usually type fifty to sixty words per minute accurately, so whenever I take this typing test, and I have already made one mistake, I try to increase my speed to type more words. For example, when I took an automated mark-up clerk exam in Michigan (including the typing test), I increased my speed as soon as I knew I had made one error. I typed about sixty words per minute with only two errors. You are allowed more errors if you type more than forty words per minute.

Techniques

Try to be at the examination room at least thirty minutes before the test time. Select a typewriter that you like; remember, it will be your word processor, which will produce at least forty words per minute.

From the looks of the machine, you'll know whether you like it and it likes you. Check out the size and shape. Place your fingers in the proper places; see if they fit the keys. See if all the parts work: release the margins and make new ones, especially for the paragraph. How about the spaces? Is the typewriter set for the single space? How about the ribbon? Is it new? If the typewriter is an electric one, it might have a film ribbon, which is no problem.

Gentle Touch

Now feel the keys; be gentle with them. Feel how they react to your touch; touch every part, including the carriage return. Do you like the way it responds to your touch?

Probably, you are now breathing fast. Try typing some words, slowly. Then make a few strong strokes; see if the keys respond quickly to your strokes, or if they like your touch. Now you know your partner; you know which parts are sensitive and which aren't. You know where to touch it and when to touch it.

Now you are ready for your test. Concentrate hard and don't look at any other typewriter. Stare at your typewriter as if it's staring at you too. Say to your partner, "We'll make it."

Take Your Time

When the examiner says "Start!" don't rush and type at full speed. Although your fingers may be trembling and you may be breathing fast, make your every move correct and don't let your fingers slip from the keys. Be gentle with them, and as you become familiar with your typewriter's sensitiveness, you'll know when and how fast to make your move. Little by little, as you make your strokes, you'll notice that you are moving *with* your typewriter.

Little by little, you can increase your speed, but try to be accurate. You have now regained your composure and confidence.

Type in small groups of letters: example: ma-te-ri-al, ex-am-in-a-tion, par-a-graph, im-por-tune. (Forget the hyphen; it's invisible.) Now you are on the way to your destiny!

Answer Want Ads

To become an expert in taking typing tests, answer want ads for typists in the newspapers and tell the advertiser you want to take a typing test. Take the tests for practice only. Make it a routine until you don't get nervous anymore.

When the time comes for your postal typing test, tell yourself, "This is *not* a test. This is the real thing. This is it!"

CB Test 714

Exam for Data Conversion Operators

(Data Conversion Operator)

SAMPLE ITEMS FOR COMPUTER BASED TEST 714

The CB 714 is a computer administered and scored exam. Applicants are assisted with the start-up of the exam and with the exam instructions. **You do not need prior experience on a computer terminal to take this test.**

The exam contains a list of alphanumeric postal data entry items just as you see in the sample items below. Applicants must demonstrate that they can type these items on the computer terminal at the following rate(s) based on the requirements of the position. The lower level passing rate is 5 correct lines per minute. The higher level passing rate is 7 correct lines per minute. Credit is given only for correctly typed lines. Practice for the exam by typing the sample provided below.

Type each line as shown in the exercise, beginning with the first column. You may use lower-case or capital letters when typing the sample exercise. When you reach the end of a line, single space and begin typing the next line. If you reach the end of the sample items in the first column, continue with the items in the second column. If you finish both columns, simply begin again with the first column and continue to type until the five minutes have elapsed.

See whether you can copy the entire Sample Test once in a five minute timing. Now count the number of lines you typed correctly and divide this number by five to determine your per minute score. Correctly typing only the items in column 1 is approximately equal to typing 5 correct lines per minute. Correctly typing all of the items in both columns is approximately equal to typing 7 correct lines per minute.

In the exam you will have five minutes in which to type the test material. Keep in mind that in order to pass the test you must type both rapidly and accurately.

(See Data Conversion Operator, page 283.)

SAMPLE TEST COPY

```
  4.90 STEERING DAMPER        18.25 DOWN SPRING
16.55 REAR DOOR LATCH          3.10 UC GASKET
23.80 TIMING CHAIN            35.45 ROCKER ARM
8721 8906                     4973 5261
2013 2547                     6057 7382
5972 6841                     2783 4195
HANOVER RD. 600 - 699         GREENBRIAR DR. 1100 - 1399
ARKANSAS AVE. 4000 - 4199     MADISON ST. 3700 - 3799
SO. MAIN ST. 1200 - 1299      BRUNSWICK AVE. 8100 - 8199
CAPITOL DR. 500 - 599         INDUSTRIAL RD. 2300 - 2499
L ON MAPLEWOOD PL.
RETRACE TO 421
R ON MOHICAN TO TOWER
4478267 LSM/LSM
4478271 MPLSM
4478289 EGR SECONDARY
KNIGHT, J.R. 04/17/67
CHARLES, S.M. 11/19/68
JEFFERSON, W.A. 08/20/69
SPRINGFIELD 07215
GREENSBORO 07098
LEXINGTON 07540
FOURTH CLASS 363
INTN. SECTION 27
200 BOX 10
```

Examination 715

26

Typing Test for Mark-Up Clerks

(Sample Typing Test for Mark-Up Clerk)

Examination 715 is a computer administered and scored exam. Applicants are assisted with the start-up of the exam and with the exam instructions. You do *not* need prior experience on a computer terminal to take this test.

The exam contains a list of seven digit mail codes each consisting of four letters and three numbers just as you see in the sample items below. To pass this test, applicants must show that they can type these codes on the computer terminal at a rate of 14 correct lines per minute. Credit is given only for correctly typed lines. Practice for the exam by typing the sample provided below.

Type each line as shown in the exercise using lower case or capital letters. When you reach the end of a line, single space and begin typing the next line. When you reach the end of the sample items, simply begin again with the first line and continue to type until the five minutes have elapsed.

See whether you can copy it three times in a five-minute timing. Now count the number of lines you typed correctly and divide this number by five to determine your per minute score.

In the examination you will have five minutes in which to type the test material. Keep in mind that in order to pass the test you must type both rapidly and accurately.

Sample Test Copy

KATZ204
CURR907
ADAM101
BONN530
GORD223
OWEN241
SCHN421
HALL375
LOGU779
ROSE995
USHER963
MART895
KATA854
SHAN289
JAME409
CHER103
LINC510
MOSI521
NORM486
SALY541
MCNE326
PATS293
PRIN815
KAPL337
DUNN919

Practice Typing Test

Work—5 Minutes

As the Post Office instructs, type each line as shown in the exercise using lower case or capital letters. It's easier for you to use the upper case because you won't have to hit the "shift" key every time to capitalize any letter. Just set the Caps lock, and that's it. Type the sample material below in five minutes. When you reach the end of the sample items, simply begin again with the first line and continue to type until the five minutes have elapsed. See whether you can copy it three times in a five-minute timing. Afterwards, count the number of lines you typed correctly and divide this number by five to determine your per minute store. In order to pass the test, you must type both quickly and accurately. However, before typing the sample codes below, learn the technique for fast and accurate typing of the items. Also, see why these codes are typed by mark-up clerks.

Typing Techniques. When you type the line, MARC891. you divide the line into two parts: MAR-891. First, type the letters MARC and then 891. As you type the lines below, you'll notice that you'll gain your own rhythm. That is, you type the lines as if you were hearing music. Or better still, listen to a radio station playing music.

Actually as a mark-up clerk, you'll be typing these codes. The codes as shown below representing the first four letters of a family name or last name and the first three number of a street or a P.O. box address. These codes are used by mark-up clerks to enter names and addresses of people moving to other addresses. Change of address cards are sent by letter carriers within a certain area consisting of several Post Offices to so-called Computerized Forwarding System Units of a Postal Sectional Center, such as the Royal Oak Post Office. In the Royal Oak area, letter carriers from associate Post Offices send their Change-of-address cards and all mail to be forwarded to the CFS Unit of the Royal Oak Post Office which is on the corner of American Way and Minnesota St. in Troy, Michigan. In the Detroit area, letter carriers from the associate Post Offices send their mail and change-of-address cards to the U.S. Postal Service building on Fort Street in Detroit, Michigan. Clerks in CFS units enter these addresses into the systems. Once entered, when a mark-up clerk keys the codes such as HARR541, the computer will generate labels, automatically attached to letters passing by through a mini-conveyor in front of a clerk's typing the codes on the computer terminal. Other mail, with unknown forwarding addresses are returned to senders. The computer also attaches the corresponding label for mail with notes: "Return to Sender." That's why

mark-up clerks should type rapidly and accurately "to process" more mails to be forwarded to new addresses.

Now, type the example test below:

HARR541
BAUT215
REYE041
ALVE915
POOL412
MARC286
CART316
REYE981
PAJA315
BURN886
WOOD451
ASIR199
CLAR773
CRUZ839
DERR321
MARV315
PADI315
NATI384
MARR310
RAVA938
ABDU336
MANG991
CORR327
MARR387
LEON447

As indicated above, you must type the above lines at least three times in five minutes.

Examination 911

Cleaner, Custodian, & Custodial Laborer Test

27

The positions of cleaner, custodian, and custodial laborer are exclusively for veterans and present employees. Only individuals entitled to veteran preference are eligible to take this entrance exam.

Cleaner

Grade: L-2

Salary Range: See schedule of salary & rates on pages 412-415.

Persons Eligible to Apply: Open to veterans only

Examination Requirements: All applicants will be required to take Examination M/N 911 to test their ability to interpret and follow instructions. The test and completion of the forms will require approximately 1 1/2 hours. Competitors will be rated on a scale of 100 and must score 70 to be eligible.

Duties: Performs light and heavy manual cleaning and housekeeping at a postal facility.

Custodian

Grade: L-2

Salary Range: See schedule of salary & rates on pages 412-415.

Persons Eligible to Apply: Open to veterans only

Examination Requirements: Applicants will be required to take Examination M/N 911 to test their ability to interpret and follow instructions.

Duties: Performs heavier manual cleaning, housekeeping, and buildings and grounds maintenance tasks at a postal facility.

Custodial Laborer

Grade: L-3

Salary Range: See schedule of salary & rates on pages 412-415.

Persons Eligible to Apply: Open to veterans only

Examination Requirements: Must pass Examination M/N 911 to determine the ability to interpret and follow instructions.

Duties: Performs manual labor in maintaining and cleaning buildings and grounds of a postal facility.

Examination 911

United States Postal Service

Sample Questions

STUDY CAREFULLY BEFORE YOU GO TO THE EXAMINATION ROOM

The purpose of this booklet is to illustrate the types of questions you will use in Examination M/N 911. It also shows you how the questions are to be answered.

The suggested answers to each question are lettered. Select the *best* answer, and make a heavy pencil mark in the space on the sample answer sheet by darkening the space for the best answer to that question. Each mark must be dense black. Each mark must cover more than half of the area of the space, and must not extend into neighboring spaces. If the answer to sample 1 is B, you would mark the sample answer sheet like this:

Record your answers to each sample question. Then compare your answers with those given in the sample question instructions.

During the test, directions for answering questions will be given orally. You are to listen closely to the directions and follow them. To practice for the test, you might have a friend read the directions to you while you mark your answers on the sample answer sheet on the next page.

You will be told to follow directions by writing in a test booklet and then on an answer sheet. The test booklet will have lines of material like the following four samples:

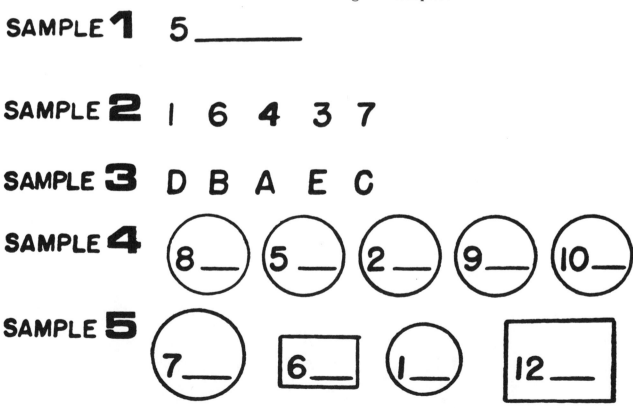

To practice this test, tear off page 3. Then have somebody read the instructions to you. When you are told to darken a space on the sample answer sheet, use the one on this page.

```
┌─────────────────────────────────────────────────────┐
│                  Sample Answer Sheet                  │
│   1 Ⓐ Ⓑ Ⓒ Ⓓ Ⓔ    5 Ⓐ Ⓑ Ⓒ Ⓓ Ⓔ    9 Ⓐ Ⓑ Ⓒ Ⓓ Ⓔ    │
│                                                       │
│   2 Ⓐ Ⓑ Ⓒ Ⓓ Ⓔ    6 Ⓐ Ⓑ Ⓒ Ⓓ Ⓔ   10 Ⓐ Ⓑ Ⓒ Ⓓ Ⓔ    │
│                                                       │
│   3 Ⓐ Ⓑ Ⓒ Ⓓ Ⓔ    7 Ⓐ Ⓑ Ⓒ Ⓓ Ⓔ   11 Ⓐ Ⓑ Ⓒ Ⓓ Ⓔ    │
│                                                       │
│   4 Ⓐ Ⓑ Ⓒ Ⓓ Ⓔ    8 Ⓐ Ⓑ Ⓒ Ⓓ Ⓔ   12 Ⓐ Ⓑ Ⓒ Ⓓ Ⓔ    │
└─────────────────────────────────────────────────────┘
```

Instructions to be read (the words in parentheses should not be read aloud):

You are to follow the instructions that I shall read to you. I cannot repeat them.

Look at the samples. Sample 1 has a number and a line beside it. On the line write an A. (Pause 2 seconds.) Now on the sample answer sheet, find number 5 (pause 2 seconds) and darken the space for the letter you just wrote on the line. (Pause 2 seconds.)

Look at Sample 2. (Pause slightly.) Draw a line under the third number. (Pause 2 seconds.) Now look on the sample answer sheet, find the number under which you just drew a line, and darken space B, as in "baker" for that number. (Pause 5 seconds.)

Look at Sample 3. (Pause slightly.) Draw a line under the third letter in the line. (Pause 2 seconds.) Now on your answer sheet find number 9 (pause 2 seconds) and darken the space for the letter under which you drew a line. (Pause 5 seconds.)

Look at the five circles in Sample 4. (Pause slightly.) Each circle has a number and a line in it. Write D, as in "dog," on the blank in the last circle. (Pause 2 seconds.) Now on the sample answer sheet, darken the space for the number-letter combination that is in the circle you just wrote in (pause 5 seconds).

Now look at the sample answer sheet. (Pause slightly.) You should have darkened spaces 4B, 5A, 9A, and 10D on the sample answer sheet. (If the person preparing to take the examination made any mistakes, try to help him see why he made wrong marks.)

Postal Test 91   28

Garageman, Motor Vehicle & Tractor-Trailer Operators Exam

Applicants for these positions will take a written test, Examination M/N 91, to measure their ability to understand instructions. The exam will last for approximately two hours, including filling out forms. (See **Who Is Qualified to Apply for Exams?** on pages 5-10 and **Strategies for Standardized Tests,** pages 253.258.)

The job descriptions of the these positions are as follows:

Garageman

Grade: L-5

Salary Range: See schedule of salary & rates on pages 432-435 .

Persons Eligible to Apply: Open to the general public

Examination Requirements: Applicants must pass the written test and the road test.

Duties: Lubricates, services, and cleans trucks; drives trucks to and from the garage; assists automotive mechanics; cleans garage and washroom.

Qualifications: Ability to service trucks, to understand written instructions, and to fill out forms; ability to work independently and to help mechanics.

Motor Vehicle Operator

Grade: L-5

Salary Range: See schedule of salary & rates on pages 432-435

Persons Eligible to Apply: Open to the general public

Examination Requirements: Must pass the written test and road test.

Duties: Operates trucks and performs related work.

Qualifications: At least one year's experience in driving trucks of at least 5-ton capacity or buses of 24-passenger capacity or over. Ability to drive safely and with a satisfactory driving record; to drive under local driving conditions; to follow instructions and to prepare trip and other reports. Experience in driving pickups, vans, jeeps, step-in vans, etc. does not qualify.

Tractor-Trailer Operator

Grade: L-6

Salary Range: See schedule of salary & rates on pages **432-435**

Persons Eligible to Apply: Open to the general public

Examination Requirements: Applicants must pass the written test and road test.

Duties: Operates heavy-duty tractor-trailers and performs related work.

Qualifications: Must have at least one year's experience in driving trucks of at least 5-ton capacity or buses of 24-passenger capacity or over, of which at least 6 months' experience must be in driving tractor-trailers.

U.S. Postal Service
Sample Questions for Test 91

The sample questions in this booklet show the kinds of questions that you will find in the written test. By reading and answering these questions, you will find out how to answer the questions in the test and about how hard the questions will be.

Read the questions carefully. Be sure you know what the questions are about and then answer the questions in the way you are told to do. If you are told the answer to a question, be sure you understand why the answer is right.

Here are the sample questions for you to answer.

Question 1 is about picture 1, below. Look at the picture.

Picture 1

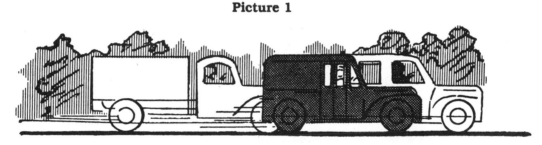

1. How many vehicles are shown in the picture?

(Write your answer for question 1 here.)

GO ON TO THE NEXT PAGE

Question 2 and 3 are about picture 2, below. Look at the picture.

Picture 2

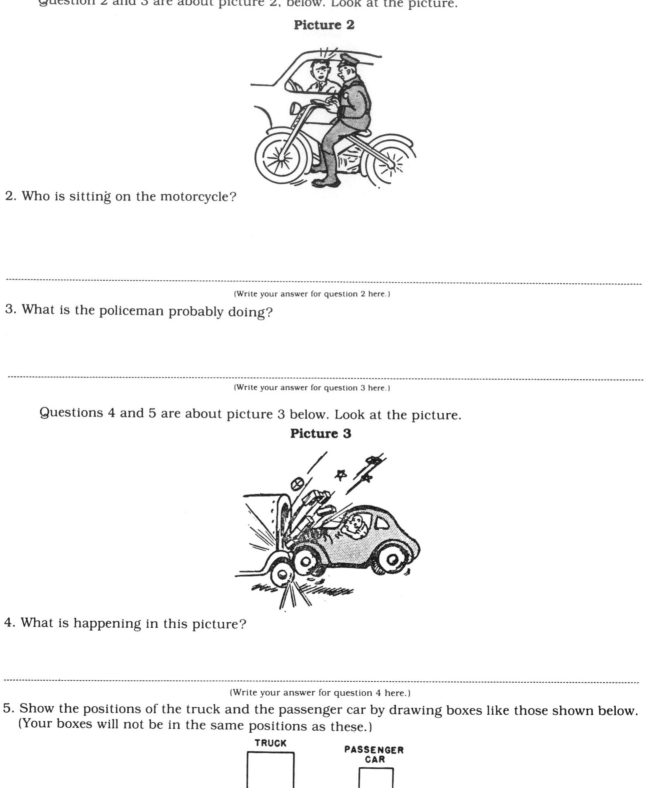

2. Who is sitting on the motorcycle?

(Write your answer for question 2 here.)

3. What is the policeman probably doing?

(Write your answer for question 3 here.)

Questions 4 and 5 are about picture 3 below. Look at the picture.

Picture 3

4. What is happening in this picture?

(Write your answer for question 4 here.)

5. Show the positions of the truck and the passenger car by drawing boxes like those shown below. (Your boxes will not be in the same positions as these.)

TRUCK

PASSENGER CAR

Draw your boxes in the space below.

GO ON TO THE NEXT PAGE

Questions 6 and 7 are about pictures of oilcans. Each picture has a letter. You are to tell what each picture shows by writing a short description of the picture on the answer line that goes with the question.

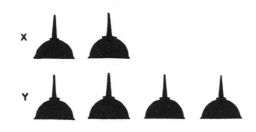

Now look at picture X.

6. What does picture X show?

(Write your answer for question 6 here.)

Picture X shows two oilcans. So you should have written something like "two oilcans" on the line under question 6.

   Now look at picture Y.

7. What does picture Y show?

(Write your answer for question 7 here.)

Question 8 is filling in a chart. You are given the following information to put in the chart.

Truck, license number 48-7128, had its oil changed last at speedometer reading 96,005. Truck, license number 858-232, was greased last at speedometer reading 89,564.

Look at the chart below. The information for the first truck has already been filled in. For question 8, fill in the information for the other truck. You are to show in the proper columns the license number of the truck, the kind of service, and the speedometer reading when serviced.

CHART

Truck License Number	Kind of Service	Speedometer Reading When Serviced
48-7128	Oil Change	96,005

(For question 8, write the information for the second truck in the proper columns above.)

GO ON TO THE NEXT PAGE

Question 9 and 10 are about words that might appear on traffic signs.

In questions like 9, there is one numbered line and then, just below that line, four other lines which are lettered A, B, C, and D. Read the first line. Then read the other four lines. Decide which line—A, B, C, or D—means most nearly the same as the first line in the question. Write the letter of the line that means the same as the numbered line in the answer space.

Here is an example.

9. Speed Limit—20 Miles

   A) Do not exceed 20 Miles per Hour

   B) Railroad Crossing

   C) No Turns

   D) Dangerous Intersection   ---
                                (Write letter of answer here for question 9.)

The first line says "Speed Limit—20 Miles." Line A says "Do Not Exceed 20 Miles per Hour." B says "Railroad Crossing." C says "No Turns." D says "Dangerous Intersection." The line that says almost the same thing as the first line is line A. That is, the one that most nearly means "Speed Limit—20 Miles" is "Do not Exceed 20 Miles per Hour." The answer to question 9 is A. You should have marked A on the answer line for question 9.

Here is another example.

10. Dead End

   A) Merging Traffic

   B) No U-Turns

   C) Turn on Red

   D) No Through Traffic   ---
                            (Write your answer here for question 10.)

GO ON TO THE NEXT PAGE

After you answer questions like the ones you have just finished, you will be asked other questions to see how well you understand what you have written. To answer the next questions, you will use the information that you wrote for the first 10 questions. Mark your answers to the next questions on the sample answer sheet on the next page.

The sample answer sheet has spaces that look like these:

1 Ⓐ Ⓑ Ⓒ Ⓓ Ⓔ

2 Ⓐ Ⓑ Ⓒ Ⓓ Ⓔ

If you wanted to mark D for your answer to question 1, you would mark it like this:

1 Ⓐ Ⓑ Ⓒ ● Ⓔ

If you wanted to mark C for your answer to question 2, you would mark it like this:

2 Ⓐ Ⓑ ● Ⓓ Ⓔ

Each of the questions in the next part is about something you should have written on your answer lines.

In answering the next questions you may look back to what you have already written as often as you wish. You may look back while you are marking the sample answer sheet. In the actual test, the pictures and their questions will be taken away from you before you mark the answer sheet, but you will keep what you wrote about the pictures while marking the answer sheet. So for this practice, try not to look at the pictures but look at what you wrote about them.

Answer each of the following questions by darkening completely space A, B, C, D, or E beside the number that you are told in the question. Mark all your answers on the sample answer sheet.

Question 11 is about question 1. Use what you wrote under question 1 to answer question 11. Mark your answer on the sample answer sheet.

11. For number 1 on the sample answer sheet,
    mark space A if only one vehicle is shown in the picture
    mark space B if only two vehicles are shown in the picture
    mark space C if only three vehicles are shown in the picture
    mark space D if only four vehicles are shown in the picture
    mark space E if only five vehicles are shown in the picture

If you look at the answer you gave for question 1, you will see that you wrote that three vehicles were shown in the picture. The question above tells you to mark space C on the sample answer sheet if only three vehicles are shown. So you should have marked space C for number 11 on the sample answer sheet.

Question 12 below is about question 2, and question 13 below is about question 3.

12. For number 12 on the sample answer sheet, mark space
    A if a policeman is sitting on the motorcycle
    B if a man in overalls is sitting on the motorcycle
    C if a boy in a sport shirt is sitting on the motorcycle
    D if a nurse is sitting on the motorcycle
    E if a man with a white beard is sitting on the motorcycle

Be sure to mark your answer on the sample answer sheet.

13. For number 13 on the sample answer sheet, mark space
    A if the policeman is probably fixing a tire
    B if the policeman is probably using a telephone
    C if the policeman is probably taking off his cap
    D if the policeman is probably blowing a whistle
    E if the policeman is probably writing a "ticket"

GO ON TO THE NEXT PAGE

Question 14 below is about question 4, and question 15 below is about question 5.

14. For number 14 on the sample answer sheet, mark space
    A if a bus is passing a fire truck
    B if a motorcycle is hitting a fence
    C if a truck is backing up to a platform
    D if a passenger car is getting gas
    E if a passenger car is hitting a truck

15. Look at the boxes you drew for question 5. For number 15 on the sample answer sheet, mark space

    A if a truck is on a ramp and a passenger car is on the street
    B if a truck is to the rear of a passenger car
    C if the front bumpers of a passenger car and a truck are in line
    D if a passenger car is to the rear of a truck
    E if a motorcycle is between a truck and a passenger car

Question 16 below is about question 6 under picture X, and question 17 below is about question 7 under picture Y.

16. For number 16 on the sample answer sheet, mark space

    A if there is only one oilcan in picture X
    B if there are only two oilcans in picture X
    C if there are only three oilcans in picture X
    D if there are only four oilcans in picture X
    E if there are only five oilcans in picture X

17. For number 17 on the sample answer sheet, mark space
    A if there is only one oilcan in picture Y
    B if there are only two oilcans in picture Y
    C if there are only three oilcans in picture Y
    D if there are only four oilcans in picture Y
    E if there are only five oilcans in picture Y

Question 18 below is about the chart you filled in. For this question, mark on the sample answer sheet the letter of the suggested answer—A, B, C, D, or E— that answers the question best.

18. What is the license number of the truck that was greased? (Look at what you wrote on the chart. Don't answer from memory.)
    A) 89,564
    B) 48-7128
    C) 858-232
    D) 96,005

For number 19 on the sample answer sheet, mark the space that has the same letter as the letter you wrote on the answer line for question 9.

For number 20 on the sample answer sheet, mark the space that has the same letter as the letter you wrote on the answer line for question 10.

(See the correct answers on page 327.)

Correct Answers

Sample Questions

11.	C	16.	B
12.	A	17.	D
13.	E	18.	C
14.	E	19.	A
15.	D	20.	D

Examination 924

Maintenance Mechanic Test

29

The test for maintenance mechanic consists of two parts: Part I, a multiple-choice test dealing with basic mechanics, electricity, and electronics and with the use of hand and portable power tools and test equipment; and Part II, a multiple-choice test dealing with basic mathematical computations, reading comprehension, and how to follow verbal instructions. Each part of the exam takes about four hours. (See **Who Can Apply for Exams?**, page 5.)

For the reading comprehension and multiple-choice test, see **Analyzing Examination 710**—*Clerical and Verbal Abilities,* page 293), and **Strategies for Standardized Test**, page 393.)

As an applicant, you must have knowledge of basic mechanics, basic electricity, basic electronics, safety procedures, and equipment; you must know how to perform basic and complex mathematical computations, apply theory, detect patterns, use reference materials, communicate orally and in writing, use hand and power tools, use shop power equipment, and use technical drawings and test equipment.

If you are hired, you'll perform preventive maintenance and repair work at the journeyman level on the mechanical, electrical, electronic, pneumatic, or hydraulic controls and on the operating mechanisms of mail processing equipment.

T0478 00 00 00   **United States Postal Service**   SG-924

Maintenance Mechanic

STUDY CAREFULLY BEFORE YOU GO TO THE EXAMINATION ROOM

Sample Questions

Part I

The purpose of this booklet is to illustrate the types of questions you will see in Examination M/N 924. It also shows you how the questions are to be answered.

Examination M/N 924 measures the knowledge and ability areas which are described in this booklet. First read the definition to get a general idea of the test content. Then answer the sample questions on the sample answer sheet.

The suggested answers to each question are lettered. Select the *best* answer, and make a heavy pencil mark in the space on the sample answer sheet by darkening the space of the best answer to that question. Each mark must be dense black. Each mark must cover more than half of the area of the space, and must not extend into neighboring spaces. If the answer to sample 1 is B, you would mark the sample answer sheet like this:

Record your answers to each sample question. Then compare your answers with those given in the correct answers to sample questions.

85280

The following categories are covered by Examination M/N 924:

1. **Knowledge of basic mechanics** refers to the theory of operation, terminology, usage, and characteristics of basic mechanical principles as they apply to such things as gears, pulleys, cams, pawls, power transmissions, linkages, fasteners, chains, sprockets, and belts; and including hoisting, rigging, roping, and pneumatic and hydraulic devices.

2. **Knowledge of lubrication materials and procedures** refers to the terminology, characteristics, storage, preparation, disposal, and usage techniques involved with lubrication materials such as oils, greases, and other types of lubricants.

3. **Knowledge of basic electricity** refers to the theory, terminology, usage, and characteristics of basic electrical principles such as Ohm's Law, Kirchoff's Law, and magnetism, as they apply to such things as AC-DC circuitry and hardware, relays, switches, and circuit breakers.

4. **Knowledge of basic electronics** refers to the theory, terminology, usage, and characteristics of basic electronic principles concerning such things as solid-state devices, vacuum tubes, coils, capacitors, resistors, and basic logic circuitry.

5. **Knowledge of safety procedures and equipment** refers to the knowledge of industrial hazards (e.g., mechanical, chemical, electrical, electronic) and procedures and techniques established to avoid injuries to self and others such as lock-out devices, protective clothing, and waste disposal techniques.

6. **Ability to apply theoretical knowledge to practical applications** refers to the ability to recall specific theoretical knowledge and apply it to mechanical, electrical, or electronic maintenance applications such as inspection, troubleshooting, equipment repair and modification, preventive maintenance, and installation of electrical equipment.

7. **Ability to use hand tools** refers to the knowledge of, and proficiency with, various hand tools. This ability involves the safe and efficient use and maintenance of such tools as screwdrivers, wrenches, hammers, pliers, chisels, punches, taps, dies, rules, gauges, and alignment tools.

8. **Ability to use portable power tools** refers to the knowledge of, and proficiency with, various power tools. This ability involves the safe and efficient use and maintenance of power tools such as drills, saws, sanders, and grinders.

9. **Ability to solder** refers to the knowledge of, and the ability to apply safely and effectively, the appropriate soldering techniques.

10. **Ability to use test equipment** refers to the knowledge of, and proficiency with, various types of mechanical, electrical, and electronic test equipment such as VOMS, oscilloscopes, circuit tracers, amprobes, and RPM meters.

(Author's Note: See **Strategies for Standardized Tests,** *multiple choice,* pages 399-402 and review any books about basic mechanics, basic electricity, and basic electronics.)

1. The primary function of a take-up pulley in a belt conveyor is to

   A) carry the belt on the return trip
   B) track the belt
   C) maintain proper belt tension
   D) change the direction of the belt
   E) regulate the speed of the belt

2. Which device is used to transfer power and rotary mechanical motion from one shaft to another?

   A) bearing
   B) lever
   C) idler roller
   D) gear
   E) bushing

3. What special care is required in the storage of hard steel roller bearings? They should be

   A) cleaned and spun dry with compressed air
   B) oiled once a month
   C) stored in a humid place
   D) wrapped in oiled paper
   E) stored at temperatures below 90° F

4. Which is the correct method to lubricate a roller chain?

   A) use brush to apply lubricant while chain is in motion
   B) use squirt can to apply lubricant while chain is in motion
   C) use brush to apply lubricant while chain is not in motion
   D) soak chain in pan of lubricant and hang to allow excess to drain
   E) chains do not need lubrication

5. A circuit has two resistors of equal value in series. The voltage and current in the circuit are 20 volts and 2 amps respectively. What is the value of *each* resistor?

   A) 5 ohms
   B) 10 ohms
   C) 15 ohms
   D) 20 ohms
   E) Not enough information given

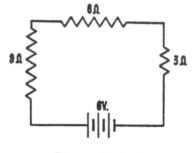

Figure III-A-22

6. Which of the following circuits is shown in Figure III-A-22?

   A) series circuit
   B) parallel circuit
   C) series, parallel circuit
   D) solid state circuit
   E) none of the above

7. What is the total net capacitance of two 60-farad capacitors connected in series?

   A) 30 F
   B) 60 F
   C) 90 F
   D) 120 F
   E) 360 F

8. If two 30-mH inductors are connected in series, what is the total net inductance of the combination?

   A) 15 mH
   B) 20 mH
   C) 30 mH
   D) 45 mH
   E) 60 mH

Figure 75-25-1

9. Crowbars, light bulbs, and vacuum bags are to be stored in the cabinet shown in Figure 75-25-1. Considering the balance of weight, what would be the safest arrangement?

A) top drawer   — crowbars
middle drawer   — light bulbs
bottom drawer   — vacuum bag

B) top drawer   — crowbars
middle drawer   — vacuum bag
bottom drawer   — light bulbs

C) top drawer   — vacuum bag
middle drawer   — crowbars
bottom drawer   — light bulbs

D) top drawer   — vacuum bag
middle drawer   — light bulbs
bottom drawer   — crowbars

E) top drawer   — light bulbs
middle drawer   — vacuum bag
bottom drawer   — crowbars

10. Contaminants have caused bearings to fail prematurely. Which pair of the items listed below should be kept away from the bearings?

A) dirt and oil
B) grease and water
C) oil and grease
D) dirt and moisture
E) water and oil

11. The electrical circuit term *open circuit* refers to a closed loop being opened. When an ohmmeter is connected into this type of circuit, one can expect the meter to

A) read infinity
B) read infinity and slowly return to *zero*
C) read *zero*
D) read *zero* and slowly return to infinity
E) none of the above

12. Which is most appropriate for pulling a heavy load?

A) electric lift
B) fork lift
C) tow conveyor
D) dolly
E) pallet truck

13. In order to operate a breast drill, in which direction should you turn it?

A) clockwise
B) counterclockwise
C) up and down
D) back and forth
E) right, then left

14. Which is the correct tool for tightening or loosening a water pipe?

A) slip joint pliers
B) household pliers
C) monkey wrench
D) water pump pliers
E) pipe wrench

15. What is one purpose of a chuck key?

A) open doors
B) remove drill bits
C) remove screws
D) remove set screws
E) unlock chucks

16. When smoke is generated as a result of using a portable electric drill for cutting holes into a piece of angle iron, one should

    A) use a fire watch
    B) cease the drilling operation
    C) use an exhaust fan to remove smoke
    D) use a prescribed coolant solution to reduce friction
    E) call the fire department

17. The primary purpose of soldering is to

    A) melt solder to a molten state
    B) heat metal parts to the right temperature to be joined
    C) join metal parts by melting the parts
    D) harden metal
    E) join metal parts

18. Which of the following statements is correct of a soldering gun?

    A) tip is not replaceable
    B) cannot be used in cramped places
    C) heats only when trigger is pressed
    D) not rated by the number of watts they use
    E) has no light

19. What unit of measurement is read on a dial torque wrench?

    A) pounds
    B) inches
    C) centimeters
    D) foot-pounds
    E) degrees

20. Which instrument is used to test insulation breakdown of a conductor?

    A) ohmmeter
    B) ammeter
    C) megger
    D) wheatstone bridge
    E) voltmeter

(See the correct answers on the next page.)

Correct Answers

Sample Questions

Part I

1. C	11. A
2. D	12. E
3. D	13. A
4. D	14. E
5. A	15. B
6. A	16. D
7. A	17. E
8. E	18. C
9. E	19. D
10. D	20. C

T0472 00 00 00

United States Postal Service

SQ-912

Maintenance Mechanic
Sample Questions
Part II

STUDY CAREFULLY BEFORE YOU GO TO THE EXAMINATION ROOM

The purpose of this booklet is to illustrate the types of questions you will see in Examination M/N 912. It also shows you how the questions are to be answered.

At the beginning of each set of sample questions you will find the definition of a question category which the test measures. First read the definition to get a general idea of the test content. Then answer the sample questions on the sample answer sheet at the bottom of the page.

The suggested answers to each question are lettered. Select the *best* answer, and make a heavy pencil mark in the space on the sample answer sheet by darkening the space of the best answer to that question. Each mark must be dense black. Each mark must cover more than half of the area of the space, and must not extend into neighboring spaces. If the answer to sample 1 is B, you would mark the sample answer sheet like this:

Record your answers to each sample question. Then compare your answers with those given in the correct answers to sample questions.

During the test, directions for answering questions in the last category will be given orally, either by a cassette tape or by the examiner. You are to listen closely to the directions and follow them. To practice for this part of the test you might have a friend read the directions to you while you mark your answers on the sample answer sheet.

85280

Ability to perform basic mathematical computations refers to the ability to perform basic calculations such as addition, subtraction, multiplication, and division with whole numbers, fractions, and decimals. Perform the computations required by each problem. Decide which answer (A, B, C, D, or E) is correct and mark it on the sample answer sheet. If the correct answer is not provided, mark E (none of the above).

Author's Note: See **Strategies for Standardized Tests,** *solving mathematics problems,* pages 399-402 and review any books about basic mechanics, basic electricity, and basic electronics.

---

1) 23 + 34 =

A) 46
B) 47
C) 56
D) 57
E) 66

2) 2.6 − .5 =

A) 2.0
B) 2.1
C) 3.1
D) 3.3
E) none of the above

3) ½ of ¼ =

A) $\frac{1}{12}$
B) ⅛
C) ¼
D) ½
E) 8

4) 168 ÷ 8 =

A) 20
B) 22
C) 24
D) 26
E) none of the above

```
+-----------------------+
|        SAMPLE         |
|     ANSWER SHEET      |
|                       |
|   1 Ⓐ Ⓑ Ⓒ Ⓓ Ⓔ      |
|                       |
|   2 Ⓐ Ⓑ Ⓒ Ⓓ Ⓔ      |
|                       |
|   3 Ⓐ Ⓑ Ⓒ Ⓓ Ⓔ      |
|                       |
|   4 Ⓐ Ⓑ Ⓒ Ⓓ Ⓔ      |
+-----------------------+
```

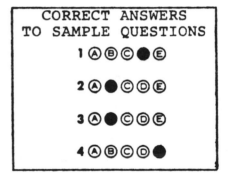

Ability to perform more complex mathematics refers to the ability to perform calculations such as basic algebra, geometry, scientific notation, and number conversions, as applied to mechanical, electrical, and electronic applications. For each problem, decide which is the correct answer (i.e., A, B, C, D, E) and mark it on the sample answer sheet. If the correct answer is not provided mark E (none of the above).

1) Simplify the following expression in terms of amps:

$$563 \times 10^{-6}$$

A) 563,000,000 amps
B) 563,000 amps
C) .563 amps
D) .000563 amps
E) .000000563 amps

2) Solve the power equation

$P = I^2 R$ for R

A) $R = EI$
B) $R = I^2 P$
C) $R = PI$
D) $R = P/I^2$
E) $R = E/I$

3) The product of 3 kilo ohms times 3 micro ohms is

A) 6×10^{-9} ohms
B) 6×10^{-3} ohms
C) 9×10^3 ohms
D) 9×10^{-6} ohms
E) 9×10^{-3} ohms

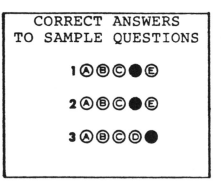

Ability to detect patterns refers to the ability to observe and analyze qualitative and quantitative factors such as number progressions, spatial relationships, and auditory and visual patterns. This includes combining information and determining how a given set of numbers, objects, or sounds are related to each other. Solve each problem below and mark the correct answer on the sample answer sheet on the next page.

1) Select from the drawings of objects labeled A, B, C, and D the one that would have the top, front, and right views shown in the drawing at the left.

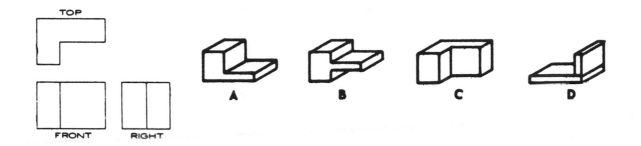

2) In the problem below there is at the left a drawing of a flat piece of paper and at the right four figures labeled A, B, C, and D. When the paper is bent on the dotted lines, it will form one of the figures at the right. Decide which figure can be formed from the flat piece.

In each of the sample questions, look at the symbols in the first two boxes. Something about the three symbols in the first box makes them alike; something about the two symbols in the other box with the question mark makes them alike. Look for some characteristic that is common to all symbols in the same box, yet makes them different from the symbols in the other box. Among the five answer choices, find the symbol that can best be substituted for the question mark, because it is *like* the symbols in the second box, and, *for the same reason,* different from those in the first box.

3.

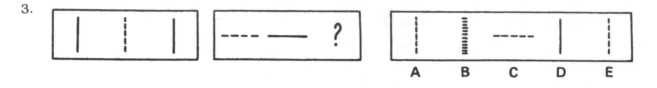

In the sample question 3, all the symbols in the first box are vertical lines. The second box has two lines, one broken and one solid. Their *likeness* to each other consists of their being horizontal; and their being horizontal makes them *different* from the vertical lines in the other box. The answer must be the only one of the five lettered choices that is a horizontal line, either broken or solid. *Note:* There is not supposed to be a *series* or progression in these symbol questions. If you look for a progression in the first box and try to find the missing figure to fill out a similar progression in the second box, you will be wasting time. Remember to look for a *likeness* within each box and a *difference* between the two boxes. Now answer sample questions 4 and 5.

4.

5.

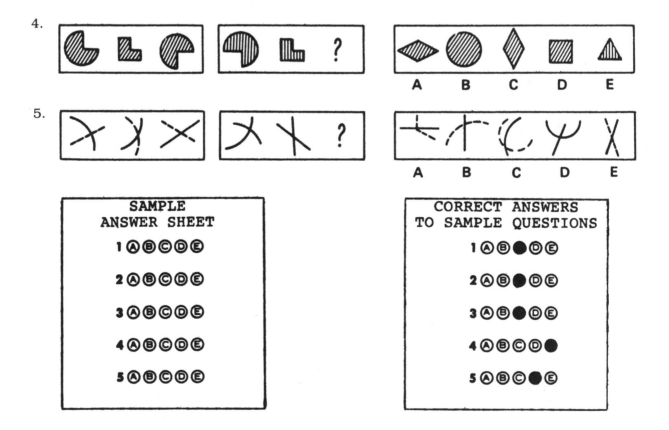

Ability to use written reference materials refers to the ability to locate, read, and comprehend text material such as handbooks, manuals, bulletins, directives, checklists, and route sheets. Read the following paragraph, determine the answer which is most nearly correct (A, B, C, D, or E), and mark it on the sample answer sheet.

1) "Prior to 1870, a conveyor that made use of rollers was developed for transporting clay. This construction substituted rolling friction at the idler bearing points for the sliding friction of the slider bed. A primitive type of troughing belt conveyor was developed about the same time for the handling of grain. This design was improved during the latter part of the century when the troughing idler was developed."

Author s Note: See **Analyzing Examination 710,** *Clerical and Verbal Abilies,* pages 299-310.

According to the above paragraph, which of the following statements is *most* nearly correct?

A) The troughing belt conveyor was developed about 1870 to handle clay and grain.

B) Rolling friction construction was replaced by the sliding friction construction prior to 1870.

C) In the late nineteenth century, conveyors were improved with the development of the troughing idler.

D) The troughing idler, a significant design improvement for the conveyors, was developed in the early nineteenth century.

E) Conveyor belts were invented and developed in the 1800's.

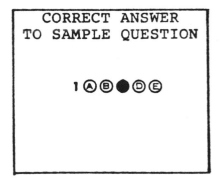

Ability to use technical drawings refers to the ability to read and comprehend technical materials such as diagrams, schematics, flow charts, and blueprints. For each problem, decide which is the correct answer.

1) In Figure 3-8-6, what is the measurement of dimension F?

A) 1 ¾ inches
B) 2 ¼ inches
C) 2 ½ inches
D) 3 ¾ inches
E) none of the above

2) In Figure 612.160-57, what is the current flow through R_3 when V = 50 volts, R_1 = 25 ohms, R_2 = 25 ohms, R_3, R_4, and R_5 each equal 50 ohms, and the current through the entire circuit totals one amp?

A) 0.5 amp
B) 5.0 amps
C) 5.0 milliamps
D) 50.0 milliamps
E) none of the above

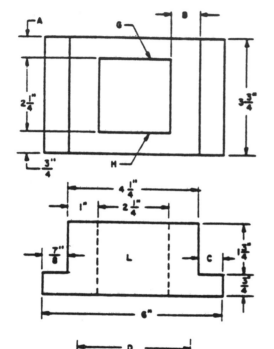

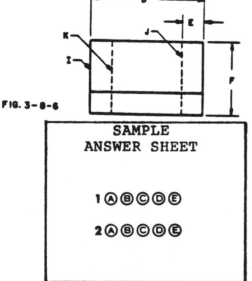

FIG. 3-8-6

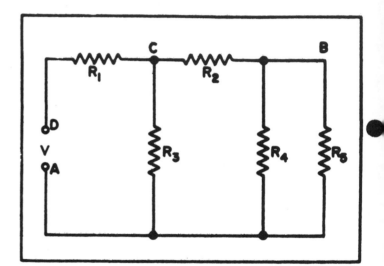

Fig. 612. 160—57

SAMPLE ANSWER SHEET
1 Ⓐ Ⓑ Ⓒ Ⓓ Ⓔ
2 Ⓐ Ⓑ Ⓒ Ⓓ Ⓔ

CORRECT ANSWER TO SAMPLE QUESTION
1 Ⓐ Ⓑ ● Ⓓ Ⓔ
2 ● Ⓑ Ⓒ Ⓓ Ⓔ

Ability to follow instructions refers to the ability to comprehend and execute written and oral instructions such as work orders, checklists, route sheets, and verbal directions and instructions. The previous questions tested your ability to follow written instructions. The remaining items test your ability to follow instructions given verbally.

You will be told to follow directions by writing in a test booklet and then on an answer sheet. The test booklet will have lines of material like the five samples:

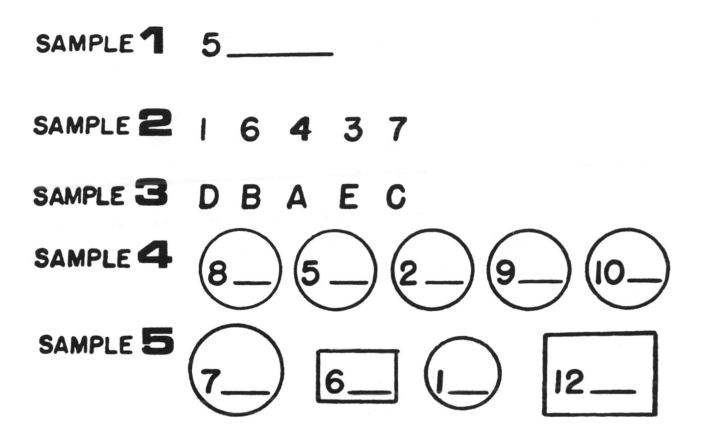

To practice this test, have somebody read the instructions to you and you follow the instructions. When he or she tells you to darken the space on the sample answer sheet, use the one on this page.

Instructions to be read (the words in parentheses should not be read aloud).

You are to follow the instructions that I shall read to you. I cannot repeat them.

Look at the samples. Sample 1 has a number and a line beside it. On the line write an A. (Pause 2 seconds.) Now on the sample answer sheet, find number 5 (pause 2 seconds) and darken the space for the letter you just wrote on the line. (Pause 2 seconds.)

Look at sample 2. (Pause slightly.) Draw a line under the third number. (Pause 2 seconds.) Now look on the sample answer sheet, find the number under which you just drew a line and darken space B as in baker for that number. (Pause 5 seconds.)

Look at sample 3. (Pause slightly.) Draw a line under the third letter in the line. (Pause 2 seconds). Now on your answer sheet, find number 9 (pause 2 seconds) and darken the space for the letter which you drew a line. (Pause 5 seconds.)

Look at the five circles in sample 4. (Pause slightly.) Each circle has a number and a line in it. Write D as in dog on the blank in the last circle. (Pause 2 seconds.) Now on the sample answer sheet, darken the space for the number-letter combination in the box or circle in which you just wrote. (Pause 5 seconds.)

Look at sample 5. (Pause slightly.) There are two circles and two boxes of different sizes with numbers in them. (Pause slightly.) If 4 is more than 2 and if 5 is less than 3, write A in the smaller circle. (Pause slightly.) Otherwise, write C in the larger box. (Pause 2 seconds.) Now on the sample answer sheet, darken the space for the number-letter combination in the box or circle in which you just wrote. (Pause 5 seconds.)

Now look at the sample answer sheet. (Pause slightly.) You should have darkened spaces 4B, 5A, 9A, 10D, and 12C on the sample answer sheet. (If the person preparing to take the examination made any mistakes, try to help him see why he made the wrong marks.)

Examination 914

Electronics Technician Test

30

The test for electronics technician is broken down into two parts: Part I deals with basic mechanics, basic, electricity, and basic electronics; Part II deals with Mathematical computations and how to follow instructions. (See **Who Can Apply for Exams?**, pages 5-10, and **Strategies for Standardized Tests,** *multiple choice and vocabulary* tests and *solving mathematics problems,* pages 399-402.

If you are hired as an electronics technician, you'll carry out what the post office calls "well-documented phases of maintenance, testing, and troubleshooting and knowledge of solid state electronics." To do this job, you must have the knowledge of basic mechanics, basic electricity, and basic electronics, and you should be familiar with such things as gears, pulleys, linkages, belts, magnetism, switches, circuit breakers, coils, capacitors, and resistors.

As an applicant, you must be able to solve problems in basic algebra and geometry, understand scientific notation, and number conversions as applied to mechanical, electrical, and electronic problems. You must also have knowledge of industrial hazards (mechanical, chemical, electrical, and electronics), and understand devices, protective clothing, and waste disposal techniques.

T0474 00 00 00   **SQ-914**

United States Postal Service

Electronics Technician

STUDY CAREFULLY BEFORE YOU GO TO THE EXAMINATION ROOM

Sample Questions

Part I

The purpose of this booklet is to illustrate the types of questions you will see in Examination M/N 914. It also shows you how the questions are to be answered.

Examination M/N 914 measures the knowledge and ability areas which are described in this booklet. First read the definition to get a general idea of the test content. Then answer the sample questions on the sample answer sheet.

The suggested answers to each question are lettered. Select the *best* answer, and make a heavy pencil mark in the space on the sample answer sheet by darkening the space of the best answer to that question. Each mark must be dense black. Each mark must cover more than half of the area of the space, and must not extend into neighboring spaces. If the answer to sample 1 is B, you would mark the sample answer sheet like this:

Record your answers to each sample question. Then compare your answers with those given in the correct answers to sample questions.

Note: See **Strategies for Standardized Tests,** *multiple choice test techniques,* pages 393-396, and review any books about basic mechanics, basic electricity, and basic electronics.

1. The primary function of a take-up pulley in a belt conveyor is to

   A) carry the belt on the return trip
   B) track the belt
   C) maintain proper belt tension
   D) change the direction of the belt
   E) regulate the speed of the belt

2. Which device is used to transfer power and rotary mechanical motion from one shaft to another?

   A) bearing
   B) lever
   C) idler roller
   D) gear
   E) bushing

3. A circuit has two resistors of equal value in series. The voltage and current in the circuit are 20 volts and 2 amps respectively. What is the value of *each* resistor?

   A) 5 ohms
   B) 10 ohms
   C) 20 ohms
   D) not enough information given

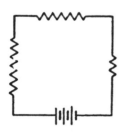

Figure III-A-22

4. Which of the following circuits is shown in Figure III-A-22?

   A) series circuit
   B) parallel circuit
   C) series, parallel circuit
   D) solid state circuit
   E) none of the above

5. What is the total net capacitance of two 60-farad capacitors connected in series?

   A) 30 farads
   B) 60 farads
   C) 90 farads
   D) 120 farads
   E) 360 farads

6. If two 30-mH inductors are connected in series, what is the total net inductance of the combination?

   A) 15 mH
   B) 20 mH
   C) 30 mH
   D) 45 mH
   E) 60 mH

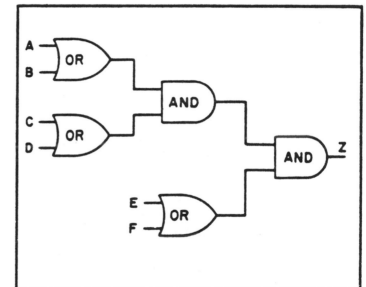

Figure 79-4-17B

7. Select the Boolean equation that matches the circuit diagram in Figure 79-4-17B.

   A) $Z = AB + CD + EF$
   B) $Z = (A + B)(C + D)(E + F)$
   C) $Z = A + B + C + D + EF$
   D) $Z = ABCD(E + F)$

8. In pure binary the decimal number 6
would be expressed as

A) 001
B) 011
C) 110
D) 111

Figure 75-25-1

FIGURE 75-8-11

9. In Figure 75-8-11, which of the following
scores will be printed?

A) all scores > 90 and < 60
B) all scores < 90
C) all scores < 90 and > 60
D) all scores < 60

10. Crowbars, light bulbs, and vacuum bags
are to be stored in the cabinet shown in
Figure 75-25-1. Considering the balance
of weight, what would be the safest
arrangement?

A) top drawer   — crowbars
   middle drawer   — light bulbs
   bottom drawwer   — vacuum bag

B) top drawer   — crowbars
   middle drawer   — vacuum bag
   bottom drawer   — light bulbs

C) top drawer   — vacuum bag
   middle drawer   — crowbars
   bottom drawer   — light bulbs

D) top drawer   — vacuum bag
   middle drawer   — light bulbs
   bottom drawer   — crowbars

E) top drawer   — light bulbs
   middle drawer   — vacuum bag
   bottom drawer   — crowbars

11. Which is most appropriate for pulling a heavy load?

    A) electric lift
    B) fork lift
    C) tow conveyor
    D) dolly
    E) pallet truck

12. The electrical circuit term *open circuit* refers to a closed loop being opened. When an ohmmeter is connected into this type of circuit, one can expect the meter to

    A) read infinity
    B) read infinity and a slowly return to *zero*
    C) read *zero*
    D) read *zero* and slowly return to infinity
    E) none of the above

13. Contaminants have caused bearings to fail prematurely. Which pair of the items listed below should be kept away from bearings?

    A) dirt and oil
    B) grease and water
    C) oil and grease
    D) dirt and moisture
    E) water and oil

14. In order to operate a breast drill, in which direction should you turn it?

    A) clockwise
    B) counterclockwise
    C) up and down
    D) back and forth
    E) right, then left

15. Which is the correct tool for tightening or loosening a water pipe?

    A) slip joint pliers
    B) household pliers
    C) monkey wrench
    D) water pump pliers
    E) pipe wrench

16. What is the purpose of a chuck key?

    A) open doors
    B) remove drill bits
    C) remove screws
    D) remove chucks
    E) remove set screws

17. When smoke is generated as a result of cutting holes into a piece of angle iron using a portable electric drill, one should

    A) use a fire watch
    B) cease the drilling operation
    C) use an exhaust fan to remove smoke
    D) use a prescribed coolant solution to reduce friction
    E) call the fire department

18. The primary purpose of soldering is to

    A) melt solder to a molten state
    B) heat metal parts to the right temperature to be joined
    C) join metal parts by melting the parts
    D) to harden the metal
    E) join metal parts

19. Which of the following statements is correct about a soldering gun?

    A) tip is not replaceable
    B) cannot be used in cramped places
    C) heats only when trigger is pressed
    D) not rated by the number of watts they use
    E) has no light

20. What unit of measurement is read on a dial torque wrench?

    A) pounds
    B) inches
    C) centimeters
    D) foot-pounds
    E) degrees

21. Which instrument is used to test insulation breakdown of a conductor?

    A) ohmmeter
    B) ammeter
    C) megger
    D) wheatstone bridge
    E) voltmeter

(See the correct answers on the next page.)

Correct Answers

Sample Questions

Part I

1.	C	11.	E
2.	D	12.	A
3.	A	13.	.D
4.	A	14.	A
5.	A	15.	E
6.	E	16.	B
7.	B	17.	D
8.	C	18.	E
9.	C	19.	C
10.	E	20.	D
		21.	C

Sample Questions
Part II

Note: Part II of the electronics exam is the same as Part II of the maintenance mechanic exam. See **Maintenance Mechanic Exam,** pages 336-344. For the reading comprehension part of the test (Part II), see **Analyzing Examination 710** - *Clerical and Verbal Abilities,* pages 299-308.

Examination 940

31

Automotive Mechanic Test

Automotive Mechanic

Grade: L-6

Salary Range: $27,619 - $37,827

Persons Eligible to Apply: Open to the general public

Examination Requirement: Applicants must pass Examination V/N 940. The test and completion of forms will require approximately 1 1/2 hours. Competitions must score 70, exclusive of veteran preference points, to be eligible. (See **Who Is Qualified to Apply for Exams?** on pages 5-10 and **Veterans in the U.S. Postal Service,** pages 15-18.)

To make a high score on this test, read books on tools and shop equipment, brakes, steering and suspension systems, automatic transmissions and torque converters, manual transmissions, and rear axles.

To qualify as an automotive mechanic in the U.S. Postal Service you must know how to diagnose mechanical and operating difficulties of vehicles; adjust and tune engines and clean fuel pumps, carburetors, and radiators.

You must also know how to regulate timing and make other necessary adjustments to maintain trucks that are in service in proper operating condition. In addition, you must know how to repair and replace automotive electrical equipment such as generators, starters, ignition systems, distributors, and wiring; install new spark plugs; conduct road tests of vehicles after repairs, noting performance of engine, clutch, transmission, brakes, and other parts.

As an automotive mechanic, you may also perform any of the following duties: remove, disassemble, and install entire engines; overhaul transmissions, rear end assemblies, and braking systems; straighten frames and axles; make road calls to obtain emergency repairs; and make required truck inspections.

Note: See **Strategies for Standardized Tests,** *multiple-choice test techniques,* pages 399-402 and review any books about basic mechanics, basic electricity, and basic electronics.

U.S. Postal Service

Automotive Mechanic Exam

Sample Questions for Examination V/N 940

The following samples show the types of questions that will be used in the written automotive mechanic examination. They will show how the questions are to be answered by those who take the test and the approximate difficulty of the test. Read the directions below; then look over these questions carefully and try to answer them. Record your answers on the sample answer sheet. Then check your answers with the correct answers.

Each sample question has a number of suggested answers, lettered A, B, C, etc. Decide which one is the *best* answer to the question. Then on the sample answer sheet, find the answer space numbered to correspond with the number of the question and *blacken* the space lettered the same as the suggested answer you consider best.

Here are the sample questions for you to answer on the sample answer sheet.

1. During a cylinder leakage test, what is indicated when air escapes through the radiator from two adjacent cylinders?

   A) Leaking intake valves
   B) Worn piston rings
   C) Burnt exhaust valves
   D) Defective cylinder head gasket
   E) Worn cylinder walls

2. Which of the following would cause a soft, spongy brake pedal?

   A) Master cylinder not returning to proper stop
   B) A brake disc with excessive runout
   C) Out-of-round brake drums
   D) Air in the hydraulic system
   E) Bent brake shoe hold-down pins

3. What is wrong during a compression test, if a low compression reading goes up after a small amount of oil is squirted into a spark plug hole?

   A) Cracked cylinder head
   B) A burnt valve
   C) Worn rings
   D) A blown cylinder head gasket
   E) Valves adjusted too tightly

4. For which of the following should a torque wrench be used?

   A) Measuring engine torque at a specific engine r.p.m.
   B) Tightening automatic transmission valve body bolts
   C) Checking a hydraulic lifter clearance in its bore
   D) Measuring distributor point gap to check swell
   E) Correctly identifying threads per inch on large-diameter bolts

5. Which of the following conditions will result when a brake drum is out of round?

   A) A spongy pedal
   B) A pulsating pedal
   C) A hard pedal
   D) A high pedal
   E) A low pedal

6. A vacuum gauge connected to a well-tuned engine should show a steady reading between which of the following during engine idle?

   A) 5" - 9"
   B) 10" - 13"
   C) 14" - 22"
   D) 23" - 27"
   E) 28" - 30"

7. Which one of the following emission control systems is common to all automobiles and light trucks manufactured at the present time in the United States?

A) CAS — Cleaner Air System
B) CCS — Controlled Combustion System
C) ImCo — Improved Combustion
D) PCV — Positive Crankcase Ventilation
E) AIR — Air Injection Reaction

8. A PCV valve is controlled by which of the following?

A) Throttle linkage
B) Engine temperature
C) Exhaust pressure or flow
D) Engine vacuum
E) Valve lifter or rocker arm

9. Which of the following is used to adjust the up-and-down clearance between an I-beam or solid front axle and the steering knuckle?

A) King pin bushings
B) King pin
C) Draw key
D) Thrust bearing
E) Spacer shims

10. Using Figure 613.180-10, determine which unit is defective when the vehicle will not move in *Drive* or *Low* but moves in *Reverse.*

A) Rear band
B) Front clutch
C) Front band
D) One-way clutch
E) Rear clutch

11. In an automatic transmission, which of the following is part of a planetary gear set?

A) Pinion
B) Stator support
C) Modulator
D) Impeller
E) Rotor support

12. The front band of an automatic transmission is applied through which of the following?

A) Front clutch
B) One-way clutch
C) Input shaft bushing
D) Servo lever
E) Sun gear

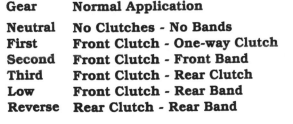

Gear	Normal Application
Neutral	No Clutches - No Bands
First	Front Clutch - One-way Clutch
Second	Front Clutch - Front Band
Third	Front Clutch - Rear Clutch
Low	Front Clutch - Rear Band
Reverse	Rear Clutch - Rear Band

Fig. 613.180-10

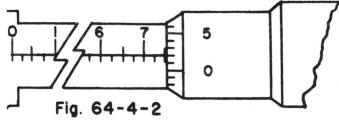

Fig. 64-4-2

13. The reading shown in Fig. 64-4-2 is

A) 0.722
B) 0.742
C) 0.752
D) 0.7112
E) 1.6722

Correct Answers

1. D
2. D
3. C
4. B
5. B
6. C
7. D

8. D
9. E
10. B
11. A
12. D
13. C

United States Postal Service
Sample Questions

The following positions use Test M/N 931:

Area Maintenance Specialist	**Letter Box Mechanic**
Area Maintenance Technician	**Machinist**
Assistant Engineman	**Maintenance Electrician**
Blacksmith-Welder	**Mason**
Building Equipment Mechanic	**Mechanic Helper**
Building Maintenance Custodian	**Oiler, MPE**
Carpenter	**Painter**
Elevator Mechanic	**Painter/Finisher**
Engineman	**Plumber**
Fireman	**Postal Machines Mechanic**
Fireman-Laborer	**Postal Maintenance Trainee**
General Mechanic	**Scale Mechanic**
Industrial Equipment Mechanic	**Stationary Engineer**

The examination, which is known as Examination 931, is given to applicants for the above positions. The exam consists of Part I, Following Oral Instructions; and Part II, which involves basic mechanics, basic electricity, and basic electronics. See **Who Can Apply for Exams?**, pages 5-10; **Analyzing Examination 710**, pages 299-310; and **Strategies for Standardized Tests,** *multiple choice, vocabulary,* and *solving mathematics problems*, pages 399-402. The total qualifications of an applicant will be evaluated based on the results of the written test and the review panel evaluation.

Sample Answer Sheet

Test M/N 931 measures 16 Knowledge, Skills, and Abilities (KSAs) used by a variety of maintenance positions. Exhibit A lists the actual KSAs that are measured. However, not all KSAS that are measured in this test are scored for every position listed. The qualification standard for each position lists the KSAs required for the position. Only those questions that measure KSAs required for the position(s) for which you are applying will be scored for the position(s).

The suggested answers to each question are lettered A, B, C, etc. Select the *best* answer and make a heavy pencil mark in the corresponding space on the sample answer sheet. Each mark must be dense black. Each mark must cover more than half the space and must not extend into neighboring spaces. If the answer to Sample 1 is B, you would make the sample answer sheet like this:

After recording your answers, compare them with those in the correct answers to sample questions. If they do not agree, carefully reread the questions that were missed to get a clear understanding of what each question is asking.

During the test, directions for answering questions in Part I will be given orally, either by a cassette tape or by the examiner. You are to listen closely to the directions and follow them. To practice for this part of the test you might have a friend read the direction to you while you mark your answers on the sample answer sheet. Directions for answering questions in Part II will be completely described in the test booklet.

STUDY CAREFULLY BEFORE YOU GO TO THE EXAMINATION ROOM

PART I

In Part I of the test, you will be told to follow directions by writing in a test booklet and then on an answer sheet. The test booklet will have lines of material like the following five samples.

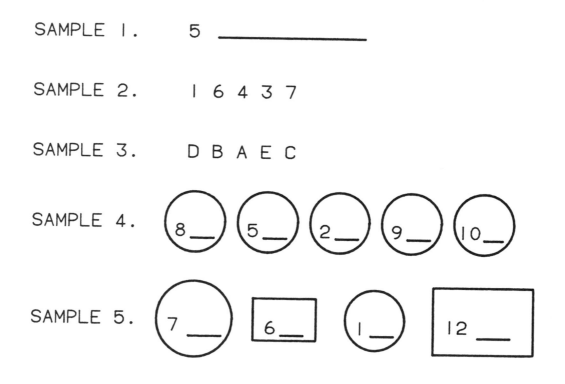

To practice this test, have someone read the instructions on the next page to you and you follow the instructions. When they tell you to darken the space on the sample answer sheet, use the one on this page.

Instructions to be read (the words in parentheses should not be read aloud).

You are to follow the instructions that I shall read to you. I cannot repeat them.

Look at the samples. Sample 1 has a number and a line beside it. On the line write an A. (Pause 2 seconds.) Now on the sample answer sheet, find numbers 5 (pause 2 seconds) and darken the space for the letter you just wrote on the line. (Pause 2 seconds.)

Look at Sample 2. (Pause slightly.) Draw a line under the third number. (Pause 2 seconds.) Now look on the sample answer sheet, find the number under which you just drew a line and darken space B as in baker for that number. (Pause 5 seconds.)

Look at Sample 3. (Pause slightly.) Draw a line under the third letter in the line. (Pause 2 seconds.) Now on your sample answer sheet, find number 9 (pause 2 seconds) and darken the space for the letter under which you drew a line. (Pause 5 seconds.)

Look at the five circles in Sample 4. (Pause slightly.) Each circle has a number and a line in it. Write D as in dog on the blank in the last circle. (Pause 2 seconds.) Now on the sample answer sheet, darken the space for the number-letter combination that is in the circle you just wrote in. (Pause 5 seconds.)

Look at Sample 5. (Pause slightly.) There are two circles and two boxes of different sizes with numbers in them. (Pause slightly.) If 4 is more than 2 and if 5 is less than 3, write A in the smaller circle. (Pause slightly.) Otherwise write C in the larger box. (Pause 2 seconds.) Now on the sample answer sheet, darken the space for the number-letter combination in the circle or box in which you just wrote. (Pause 5 seconds.)

Now look at the sample answer sheet. (Pause slightly.) You should have darkened spaces 4B, 5A, 9A, 10D, and 12C on the sample answer sheet. (If the person preparing to take the examination made any mistakes, try to help him or her understand why the answers are wrong.)

Note: See **Strategies for Standardized Tests,** *multiple-choice test techniques,* pages 399-402 and review any books about basic mechanics, basic electricity, and basic electronics.

Part II

1. Which device is used to transfer power and rotary mechanical motion from one shaft to another?

    A) bearing
    B) lever
    C) idler roller
    D) gear
    E) bushing

2. Lead anchors are usually mounted in

    A) steel paneling
    B) drywall construction
    C) masonry construction
    D) wood construction
    E) gypsum board

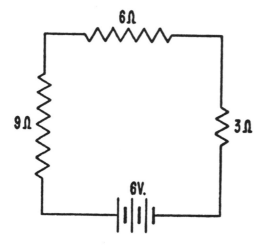

Figure III-A-22

3. Which of the following circuits is shown in Figure III-A-22?

    A) series circuit
    B) parallel circuit
    C) series, parallel circuit
    D) solid state circuit
    E) none of the above

4. Which component would *best* simulate the actions of the photocell in Figure 24-3-1?

    A) variable resistor
    B) variable capacitor
    C) variable inductor
    D) autotransformer
    E) battery

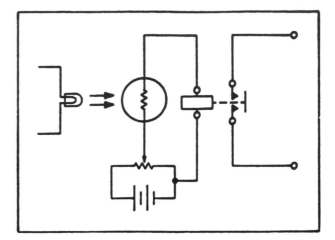

Figure 24-3-1

5. The semi-conductor materials contained in a transistor are designated by the letter(s)

    A) Q
    B) N, P
    C) CR
    D) M, P, M
    E) none of the above

6. Which of the following circuits or devices always has inductance?

    A) rectifier
    B) coil
    C) current limiter
    D) condenser
    E) filter

7. Crowbars, light bulbs, and vacuum bags are to be stored in the cabinet shown in Figure 75-25-1. Considering the balance of weight, what would be the safest arrangement?

A) top drawer — crowbars
   middle drawer — light bulbs
   bottom drawer — vacuum bags

B) top drawer — crowbars
   middle drawer — vacuum bags
   bottom drawer — light bulbs

C) top drawer — vacuum bags
   middle drawer — crowbars
   bottom drawer — light bulbs

D) top drawer — vacuum bags
   middle drawer — light bulbs
   bottom drawer — crowbars

E) top drawer — light bulbs
   middle drawer — vacuum bags
   bottom drawer — crowbars

Figure 75-25-1

8. Which is most appropriate for pulling a heavy load?

A) electric lift
B) fork lift
C) tow conveyor
D) dolly
E) pallet truck

9. What measuring device is illustrated in Figure 75-26-1?

A) screw pitch gage
B) vernier calipers
C) inside calipers
D) outside calipers
E) outside micrometer

Figure 75-26-1

10. A screw pitch gage can be used for

A) determining the pitch and number of internal threads
B) measuring the number of gages available for use
C) measuring the depth of a screw hole
D) checking the thread angle
E) cleaning the external threads

11. What measuring device is illustrated in Figure 75-20-17?

A) screw pitch gage
B) vernier caliper
C) inside calipers
D) outside calipers
E) outside micrometer

12. One characteristic of the breast drill is that it

A) is gearless
B) is hand operated
C) has a 3 ¼ hp motor
D) has 4 speeds
E) is steam powered

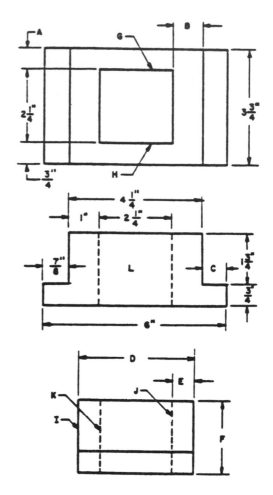

Figure 3-8-6

Figure 75-20-17

13. In Figure 3-8-6, what is the measurement of dimension F?

A) 1 ¾ inches
B) 2 ¼ inches
C) 2 ½ inches
D) 3 ¾ inches
E) none of the above

14. The device pictured in Figure 36 is in a rest position. Which position, if any, is the normal closed?

A) A
B) B
C) C
D) devices of this sort have no normal closed position
E) the normal closed is not shown in this diagram

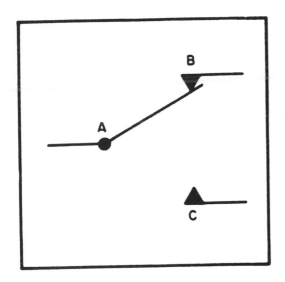

Figure 36

15. Which of the following test equipment would most likely be used in determining amplifier band width?

A) clamp-on ammeter
B) tube tester
C) watt meter
D) frequency analyzer
E) sweep frequency generator

16. Which instrument is used to test insulation breakdown of a conductor?

A) ohmmeter
B) ammeter
C) megger
D) wheatstone bridge
E) voltmeter

17. The primary purpose of soldering is to

A) melt solder to a molten state
B) heat metal parts to the right temperature to be joined
C) join metal parts by melting the parts
D) harden metal
E) join metal parts

18. Which of the following statements is correct of a soldering gun?

A) tip is not replaceable
B) cannot be used in cramped places
C) heats only when trigger is pressed
D) not rated by the number of watts they use
E) has no light

19. Contaminants have caused bearings to fail prematurely. Which pair of the items listed below should be kept away from bearings?

A) dirt and oil
B) grease and water
C) oil and grease
D) dirt and moisture
E) water and oil

20. The electrical circuit term *open circuit* refers to a closed loop being opened. When an ohmmeter is connected into this type of circuit, one can expect the meter to

A) read infinity
B) read infinity and slowly return to *zero*
C) read *zero*
D) read *zero* and slowly return to infinity
E) none of the above

21. A change from refrigerant vapor to liquid while the temperature stays constant results in a

A) latent pressure loss
B) sensible heat loss
C) sensible pressure loss
D) latent heat loss
E) super heat loss

22. The mediums normally used in condensing refrigerants are

A) air and water
B) air and vapor
C) water and gas
D) liquid and vapor
E) vapor and gas

23. Most condenser problems are caused by

A) high head pressure
B) high suction pressure
C) low head pressure
D) low suction pressure
E) line leaks

24. Most air conditioners with motors of 1 horsepower, or less, operate on which type of source?

A) 110-volt, single-phase
B) 110-volt, three-phase
C) 220-volt, single-phase
D) 220-volt, three-phase
E) 220-440-volt, three-phase

25. $2.6 - .5 =$

A) 2.0
B) 2.1
C) 3.1
D) 3.3
E) None of the above

26. $\frac{1}{2}$ of $\frac{1}{4}$ is

A) $\frac{1}{12}$
B) $\frac{1}{8}$
C) $\frac{1}{4}$
D) $\frac{1}{2}$
E) 8

27. A drawing of a certain large building is 10 inches by 15 inches. On this drawing, 1 inch represents 5 feet. If the same drawing had been made 20 inches by 30 inches, 1 inch on the drawing would represent

A) 2 1/2 feet
B) 3 $\frac{1}{3}$ feet
C) 5 feet
D) 7 1/2 feet
E) 10 feet

28. In a shipment of bearings, 51 were defective. This is 30 percent of the total number of bearings ordered. What was the total number of bearings ordered?

A) 125
B) 130
C) 153
D) 171
E) None of the above

Note: To answer the question that follow, see **Analyzing Examination 710,** *Reading Comprehension,* pages 299-310.

In sample questions 29 below, select the statement which is most nearly correct according to the paragraph.

"Without accurate position descriptions, it is difficult to have proper understanding of who is to do what and when. As the organization obtains newer and different equipment and as more and more data are accumulated to help establish proper preventive maintenance routines, the organization will change. When changes occur, it is important that the organization charts and the position descriptions are updated to reflect them."

29. According to the above paragraph, which of the following statements is most nearly correct?

A) Job descriptions should be general in nature to encourage job flexibility.
B) The organizational structure is not dependent upon changes in preventive maintenance routines.
C) As long as supervisory personnel are aware of organizational changes, there is no need to constantly update the organization chart.
D) Organizational changes can result from procurement of new, advanced equipment.
E) Formal job descriptions are not needed for an office to function on a day-to-day basis. The supervisor knows who is to do what and when.

30. A small crane was used to raise the heavy part. Raise *most* nearly means

A) lift
B) drag
C) drop
D) deliver
E) guide

31. Short *most* nearly means

A) tall
B) wide
C) brief
D) heavy
E) dark

In each of the sample questions below, look at the symbols in the first two boxes. Something about the three symbols in the first box makes them alike; something about the two symbols in the other box with the question mark makes them alike. Look for some characteristics that is common to all symbols in the same box, yet makes them different from the symbols in the other box. Among the five answer choices, find the symbol that can best be substituted for the question mark, because it is *like* the symbols in the second box, and, *for the same reason,* different from those in the first box.

32.

In the sample question above, all the symbols in the first box are vertical lines. The second box has two lines, one broken and one solid. Their *likeness* to each other consists in their being horizontal; and their being horizontal makes them *different* from the vertical lines in the other box. The answer must be the only one of the five lettered choices that is a horizontal line, either broken or solid. NOTE: There is not supposed to be a series of progression in these symbol questions. If you look for a progression in the first box and the second box, you will be wasting time. Remember, look for a *likeness* within each box and a *difference* between the two boxes. Now do sample question 33.

33.

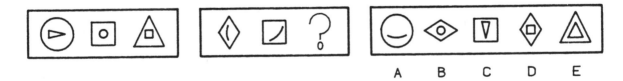

In sample question 34 below, there is at the left a drawing of a flat piece of paper and at the right, four figures labeled A, B, C, and D. When the paper is rolled, it will form one of the figures at its right. Decide which figure can be formed from the flat piece. Then on the answer sheet darken the space which has the same letter as your answer.

34.

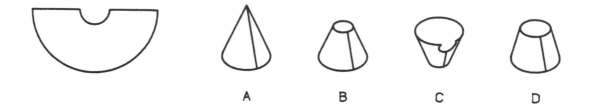

A   B   C   D

Correct Answers

Sample Questions

Part I

1. D		18. C
2. C		19. D
3. A		20. A
4. A		21. D
5. B		22. A
6. B		23. A
7. E		24. A
8. E		25. B
9. C		26. B
10. A		27. A
11. E		28. E
12. B		29. D
13. C		30. A
14. B		31. C
15. D		32. C
16. C		33. A
17. E		34. B

Test 916

33

Custodial Maintenance Exam

(Sample questions only, no answers are provided)

The purpose of this section is to illustrate the types of questions that will be used in Test 916. The samples will also show how the questions in the test are to be answered.

The test questions are designed to evaluate the following subject areas:

VOCABULARY AND READING: These questions test your ability to read and understand written materials as used in reading product label instructions and warnings, material safety data sheets (MSDS), equipment operating instructions, and cleaning route sheets.

BASIC SAFETY: These questions test your knowledge of basic safety principles and practices such as proper lifting techniques, use of personal protective equipment, and awareness of electrical, chemical, and other health hazards in the area of cleaning and building maintenance.

GENERAL CLEANING: These questions test your knowledge of general cleaning and disinfecting materials, techniques, equipment, and tools commonly used by custodians.

FOLLOWING WRITTEN INSTRUCTIONS: These questions test your ability to understand and carry out instructions similar to those you might receive on the job.

The suggested answers to each question are lettered A, B, C, D, and E. Select the BEST answer and make a heavy pencil mark in the corresponding space on the Sample Answer Sheet. Each mark must be dense black. Each mark must cover more than half the space and must not extend into neighboring spaces. If the answer to Sample 1 is B, you would mark the Sample Answers Sheet like this:

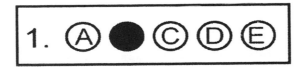

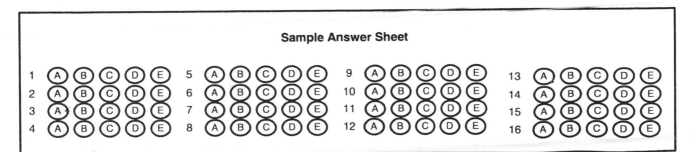

365

DIRECTIONS AND SAMPLE QUESTIONS

Study sample questions 1 through 12 carefully. Each question has several alternative responses. Decide from among the alternatives which is the best response. Find the question number on the Sample Answer Sheet on Page 7 and mark your answer to the question by completely darkening the space corresponding to the letter you have chosen.

VOCABULARY AND READING

1. Avoid **inhaling** the fumes from this product. Inhaling most nearly means:

A) Diluting
B) Expelling
C) Breathing
D) Vaporizing
E) Ventilating

2. The contents of this load are **fragile** and require special handling. Fragile most nearly means:

A) Durable
B) Delicate
C) Valuable
D) Jagged
E) Greasy

3. Safety goggles are **mandatory** when handling corrosive chemicals. Mandatory most nearly means:

A) Essential
B) Awkward
C) Optional
D) Useless
E) Foolproof

4. "Although mixing cleaners can be risky, there are many products that can be harmful on their own. They range from window cleaners to all-purpose scrubs. Even liquid soap containing ammonia can be toxic. Ammonia can cause dizziness, and mixed with certain types of bleach, can create deadly fumes."

The quotation best supports the statement that:

A) Gases can be detected by their color
B) All-purpose cleaners are rarely effective
C) Chemicals should never be mixed with water
D) Cleaners can be toxic even when used alone
E) Combining products will improve air quality

BASIC SAFETY

5. Which of the following lists information on the health hazards of cleaning products?

    A) Lockout/tagout fact sheet
    B) National Electrical Code (NEC)
    C) National Building Code (NBC)
    D) Better Business Bureau (BBB)
    E) Material Safety Data Sheet (MSDS)

6. What should be done if an electrical cord is defective, damaged, or frayed?

    A) Splice to a one-pronged plug
    B) Apply finish to maintain appearance
    C) Use only when working near water
    D) Have the cord replaced at once
    E) Run the electrical cord under a rug

7. Which of the following is a general rule of safe manual lifting?

    A) Use the back to bear the entire load
    B) Bend the back with knees straight
    C) Keep the load close to one's body
    D) Lift alone, no matter how heavy the load
    E) Twist at the waist while carrying loads

8. Which of the following makes it unsafe to stand directly under ladders, lifts, and scaffolds?

    A) Radiant energy
    B) Falling tools or debris
    C) Dog and insect bites
    D) Cross-breeze venting
    E) Stiff neck syndrome

9. Which of the following is used to apply cleaning solution to a painted wall?

    A) Sponge
    B) Spatula
    C) Scraper
    D) Wire brush
    E) Drop cloth

10. Which of the following is used to clean inside a toilet?

    A) Treated dust cloth
    B) Bowl brush
    C) Chamois cloth
    D) Feather duster
    E) HEPA vacuum

11. What is the primary purpose of a disinfectant?

    A) Freshen air
    B) Prevent fires
    C) Flavor foods
    D) Stain fabrics
    E) Destroy germs

12. Which of the following is used to sweep dust and dirt from smooth floors?

    A) Push broom
    B) Sponge cloth
    C) Floor stripper
    D) Counter brush
    E) Pressure washer

GENERAL CLEANING

FOLLOWING INSTRUCTIONS

Sample items 13 through 16 below test your ability to follow instructions.

Read each item carefully. Following the instructions in each item will lead you to identify or create a letter-number combination (e.g., P1, S4, Q10, T6). Next, go to the "Look-Up Table" to find the specific letter ("P" through "T") and number (1 through 10) from the combination you identified or created. Locate the intersection of this letter-number combination on the table to find your answer of A, B, C, D, or E. After you have found an answer, darken the corresponding space on your Sample Answer Sheet on Page 7.

For example, if you came up with P1 for Item 1, then your answer from the Look-Up Table would be "A", and you would darken "A" for question 1 on your Sample Answer Sheet. If you came up with T4 as the letter-number combination, then your answer would be "C" and you would darken "C" on your answer sheet, and so on. Apply these instructions when answering sample items 13 through 16.

LOOK-UP TABLE

	P	Q	R	S	T
1	A	B	C	D	E
2	B	C	D	E	A
3	C	D	E	A	B
4	D	E	A	B	C
5	E	A	B	C	D
6	A	B	C	D	E
7	B	C	D	E	A
8	C	D	E	A	B
9	D	E	A	B	C
10	E	A	B	C	D

13. Look at the letter-number combinations below. Draw a line under the second letter-number combination from the left. Write the letter-number combination you drew a line under here: __ __.

$$Q4 \qquad P3 \qquad R4 \qquad S9 \qquad T5$$

14. Draw a line under each letter in the line below that is <u>not</u> a "P" or "S". Write the letter under which you drew the lines and the number of lines you drew here: __ __.

$$P \quad S \quad Q \quad P \quad S \quad S \quad P \quad Q \quad P \quad S \quad P \quad Q$$

15. Look at the circles below. The number inside each circle represents the number of light bulbs in a container. Write the letter "Q" below the container with the most bulbs.

16. Look at the list of hand tools below. Circle the tool with the fewest letters. Count the number of letters in that word. Now write that number and the first letter of that tool here: __ __.

SHOVEL   EDGER   RAKE   SCRAPER   SHEARS

(These are sample questions only, no answers are provided)

Examination 410

Postal Center Technician Test

The following samples show the types of questions you will see in the written test. They also show how the questions in the test are to be answered. Test 410 contains questions which test the ability to read and understand technical information, questions on mechanical and electrical principals and applications, and questions on arithmetic. The sample questions illustrate these types of questions.

The suggested answers to each question are lettered A, B, C, D, and E. Select the BEST answer and make a heavy pencil mark in the corresponding space on the Sample Question Answer Sheet. Each mark must be dense black. Each mark must cover more than half the space and must not extend into neighboring spaces. If the answer to Sample 1 is B, you would mark the Sample Question Answer Sheet like this:

After recording your answers compare them with those in the Correct Answers to sample questions.

SAMPLE QUESTIONS

USE THE FOLLOWING PASSAGE TO ANSWER QUESTION 1.

Coins inserted into the machine are registered by the recorder and are in the escrow area of the coin unit. When the coin return lever (scavenger bar) is depressed, the upper cancel switch is moved to the N.O. position, thereby removing the selector switch series from the circuit. This prevents simultaneous vend and coin return.

1. When a customer wants his money back, he pushes the coin return lever. What protection is there against his also getting merchandise as well as return of his money?

   A) The scavenger bar is also depressed
   B) The escrow area prevents vending
   C) The coin return is registered by the recorder
   D) The selector switches are cut out of the circuit
   E) All of the above

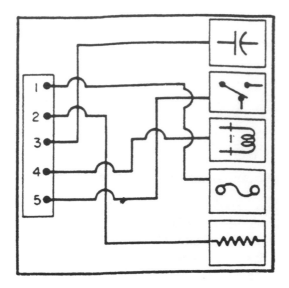

Figure 1

2. Wire 1 connects to which of the following in the diagram shown in Figure 1?

   A) Transformer
   B) Fuse
   C) Switch
   D) Battery
   E) Resistor

3. What is the total cost of a coil of 29-cent stamps, a coil of 8-cent stamps, and a coil of 1-cent stamps, if there are 500 stamps to a coil?

   A) $ 59.50
   B) $180.00
   C) $190.00
   D) $595.00
   E) None of these

4. A Technician paid $25.50 for 3 boxes of envelopes. Each box contained 25 envelopes. What was the cost for each envelope?

   A) $ .34
   B) $ .35
   C) $1.02
   D) $3.40
   E) None of these

Figure 2

5. The proper method to tighten the item shown in Figure 2 is to use

    A) slip-joint pliers
    B) spanner wrench
    C) thumb and forefinger
    D) spin-type socket
    E) mechanical finger

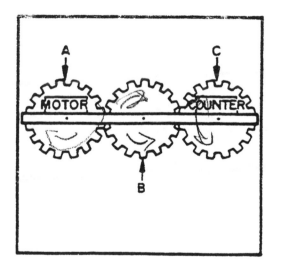

Figure 3

6. In Figure 3, gears A, B, and C are the same size. If gear A is moving in a clockwise direction, which of the following describes the action of gear C?

    A) Turns counterclockwise slower than gear A
    B) Turns clockwise slower than gear A
    C) Turns counterclockwise at the same speed as gear A
    D) Turns clockwise faster than gear A
    E) Turns clockwise at the same speed as gear A

Examination 932

Test For Electronics Group

35

United States Postal Service
Sample Questions

The following positions use Examination 932:

Electronics Technician 8 (Register Number M26)
Electronics Technician 9 (Register Number M27)
Electronics Technician 10 (Register Number M28)

This examination, which is known as Examination 932, is given to applicants for the above positions. This exam consists of Part I, *Following Oral Instructions;* and Part II - *Multiple Choice Test,* which involves basic mechanics, basic electricity, and basic electronics and with the use of hand and portable power tools and test equipment. Study books on basic mechanics, basic electricity, and basic electronics in your local library. (See **Who Can Apply for Exams?**, pages 5-10; **Analyzing Examination 710,** pages 299-310 ; and **Strategies for Standardized Tests**, *multiple choice, vocabulary* and *solving mathematics problems,* pages 399-402 . The total qualifications for an application will be evaluated based on the results of the written test and the review panel evaluation.

Test M/N 932 measures 16 Knowledge, Skills, and Abilities (KSAs) used by a variety of maintenance positions. Exhibit A lists the actual KSAs that are measured, and Exhibit B lists the positions that use this examination. However, not all KSAs that are measured in this test are scored for every position listed.   The qualification standard for each position lists the KSAs required for the position. Only those questions that measure KSAs required for the position(s) for which you are applying will be scored for the position(s).

The suggested answers to each question are lettered A, B, C, etc. Select the BEST answer and make a heavy pencil mark in the corresponding space on the Sample Answer Sheet. Each mark must be dense black. Each mark must cover more than half the space and must not extend into neighboring spaces. If the answer to Sample 1 is B, you would mark the Sample Answer Sheet like this:

After recording your answers, compare them with those in the Correct Answers to Sample Questions. If they do not agree, carefully re-read the questions that were missed to get a clear understanding of what each question is asking.

During the test, directions for answering questions in Part I will be given orally, either by a cassette tape or by the examiner. You are to listen closely to the directions and follow them. To practice for this part of the test you might have a friend read the direction to you while you mark your answers on the Sample Answer Sheet. Directions for answering questions in Part II will be completely described in the test booklet.

STUDY CAREFULLY BEFORE YOU GO TO THE EXAMINATION ROOM

PART I

In Part I of the test, you will be told to follow directions by writing in a test booklet and then on an answer sheet. The test booklet will have lines of material like the following five samples:

SAMPLE QUESTIONS

SAMPLE 1.   5 _____

SAMPLE 2.   1 6 4 3 7

SAMPLE 3.   D B A E C

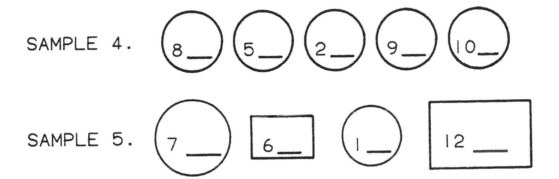

SAMPLE 4.

SAMPLE 5.

To practice this test, have someone read the instructions on the next page to you and you follow the instructions. When they tell you to darken the space on the Sample Answer Sheet, use the one on this page.

SAMPLE ANSWER SHEET

1 Ⓐ Ⓑ Ⓒ Ⓓ Ⓔ   5 Ⓐ Ⓑ Ⓒ Ⓓ Ⓔ   9 Ⓐ Ⓑ Ⓒ Ⓓ Ⓔ

2 Ⓐ Ⓑ Ⓒ Ⓓ Ⓔ   6 Ⓐ Ⓑ Ⓒ Ⓓ Ⓔ   10 Ⓐ Ⓑ Ⓒ Ⓓ Ⓔ

3 Ⓐ Ⓑ Ⓒ Ⓓ Ⓔ   7 Ⓐ Ⓑ Ⓒ Ⓓ Ⓔ   11 Ⓐ Ⓑ Ⓒ Ⓓ Ⓔ

4 Ⓐ Ⓑ Ⓒ Ⓓ Ⓔ   8 Ⓐ Ⓑ Ⓒ Ⓓ Ⓔ   12 Ⓐ Ⓑ Ⓒ Ⓓ Ⓔ

<u>Instructions to be read</u> (the words in parentheses should not be read aloud).

You are to follow the instructions that I shall read to you. I cannot repeat them.

Look at the samples. Sample 1 has a number and a line beside it. On the line write an A. (Pause 2 seconds.) Now on the Sample Answer Sheet, find number 5 (pause 2 seconds) and darken the space for the letter you just wrote on the line. (Pause 2 seconds.)

Look at Sample 2. (Pause slightly.) Draw a line under the third number. (Pause 2 seconds.) Now look on the Sample Answer Sheet, find the number under which you just drew a line and darken space B as in baker for that number. (Pause 5 seconds.)

Look at Sample 3. (Pause slightly.) Draw a line under the third letter in the line. (Pause 2 seconds.) Now on your Sample Answer Sheet, find number 9 (pause 2 seconds) and darken the space for the letter under which you drew a line. (Pause 5 seconds.)

Look at the five circles in Sample 4. (Pause slightly.) Each circle has a number and a line in it. Write D as in dog on the blank in the last circle. (Pause 2 seconds.) Now on the Sample Answer Sheet, darken the space for the number-letter combination that is in the circle you just wrote in. (Pause 5 seconds.)

Look at Sample 5. (Pause slightly.) There are two circles and two boxes of different sizes with numbers in them. (Pause slightly.) If 4 is more than 2 and if 5 is less than 3, write A in the smaller circle. (Pause slightly.) Otherwise write C in the larger box. (Pause 2 seconds.) Now on the Sample Answer Sheet, darken the space for the number-letter combination in the circle or box in which you just wrote. (Pause 5 seconds.)

Now look at the Sample Answer Sheet. (Pause slightly.) You should have darkened spaces 4B, 5A, 9A, 10D, and 12C on the Sample Answer Sheet. (If the person preparing to take the examination made any mistakes, try to help him or her understand why the mistakes are wrong.)

SAMPLE ANSWER QUESTIONS

1 Ⓐ Ⓑ Ⓒ Ⓓ Ⓔ	18 Ⓐ Ⓑ Ⓒ Ⓓ Ⓔ
2 Ⓐ Ⓑ Ⓒ Ⓓ Ⓔ	19 Ⓐ Ⓑ Ⓒ Ⓓ Ⓔ
3 Ⓐ Ⓑ Ⓒ Ⓓ Ⓔ	20 Ⓐ Ⓑ Ⓒ Ⓓ Ⓔ
4 Ⓐ Ⓑ Ⓒ Ⓓ Ⓔ	21 Ⓐ Ⓑ Ⓒ Ⓓ Ⓔ
5 Ⓐ Ⓑ Ⓒ Ⓓ Ⓔ	22 Ⓐ Ⓑ Ⓒ Ⓓ Ⓔ
6 Ⓐ Ⓑ Ⓒ Ⓓ Ⓔ	23 Ⓐ Ⓑ Ⓒ Ⓓ Ⓔ
7 Ⓐ Ⓑ Ⓒ Ⓓ Ⓔ	24 Ⓐ Ⓑ Ⓒ Ⓓ Ⓔ
8 Ⓐ Ⓑ Ⓒ Ⓓ Ⓔ	25 Ⓐ Ⓑ Ⓒ Ⓓ Ⓔ
9 Ⓐ Ⓑ Ⓒ Ⓓ Ⓔ	26 Ⓐ Ⓑ Ⓒ Ⓓ Ⓔ
10 Ⓐ Ⓑ Ⓒ Ⓓ Ⓔ	27 Ⓐ Ⓑ Ⓒ Ⓓ Ⓔ
11 Ⓐ Ⓑ Ⓒ Ⓓ Ⓔ	28 Ⓐ Ⓑ Ⓒ Ⓓ Ⓔ
12 Ⓐ Ⓑ Ⓒ Ⓓ Ⓔ	29 Ⓐ Ⓑ Ⓒ Ⓓ Ⓔ
13 Ⓐ Ⓑ Ⓒ Ⓓ Ⓔ	30 Ⓐ Ⓑ Ⓒ Ⓓ Ⓔ
14 Ⓐ Ⓑ Ⓒ Ⓓ Ⓔ	31 Ⓐ Ⓑ Ⓒ Ⓓ Ⓔ
15 Ⓐ Ⓑ Ⓒ Ⓓ Ⓔ	32 Ⓐ Ⓑ Ⓒ Ⓓ Ⓔ
16 Ⓐ Ⓑ Ⓒ Ⓓ Ⓔ	33 Ⓐ Ⓑ Ⓒ Ⓓ Ⓔ
17 Ⓐ Ⓑ Ⓒ Ⓓ Ⓔ	34 Ⓐ Ⓑ Ⓒ Ⓓ Ⓔ

1. The primary function of a take-up pulley in a belt conveyor is to

   A) carry the belt on the return trip.
   B) track the belt.
   C) maintain proper belt tension
   D) change the direction of the belt

2. Which device is used to transfer power and rotary mechanical motion from one shaft to another?

   A) Bearing
   B) Lever
   C) Idler roller
   D) Gear
   E) Bushing

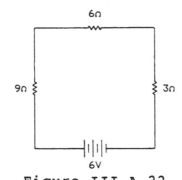

Figure III-A-22

3. Which of the following circuits is shown in Figure III-A-22?

   A) Series circuit
   B) Parallel circuit
   C) Series, parallel circuit
   D) Solid state circuit
   E) None of the above

4. A circuit has two resistors of equal value in series. The voltage and current in the circuit are 20 volts and 2 amps respectively. What is the value of EACH resistor?

   A) 5 ohms
   B) 10 ohms
   C) 20 ohms
   D) Not enough information given

PART II

5. What is the total net capacitance of two 60-farad capacitors connected in series?

   A) 30 farads
   B) 60 farads
   C) 90 farads
   D) 120 farads
   E) 360 farads

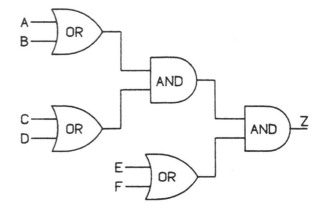

FIGURE 79-4-17B

6. Select the Boolean equation that matches the circuit diagram in Figure 79-4-17B.

   A) Z = AB+CD+EF
   B) Z = (A+B) (C+D) (E+F)
   C) Z = A+B+C+D+EF
   D) Z = ABCD(E+F)

7. If two 30-mH inductors are connected in series, what is the total net inductance of the combination?

   A) 15 mH
   B) 20 mH
   C) 30 mH
   D) 45 mH
   E) 60 mH

8. In pure binary the decimal number 6 would be expressed as

A)   001
B)   011
C)   110
D)   111

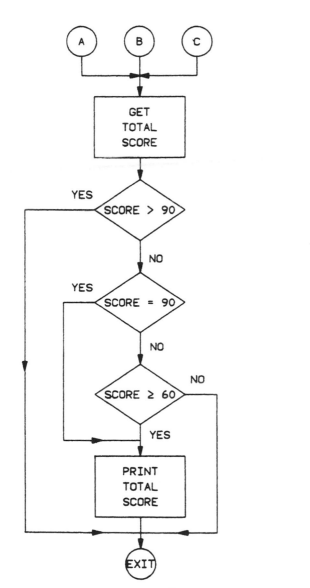

FIGURE /5-8-11

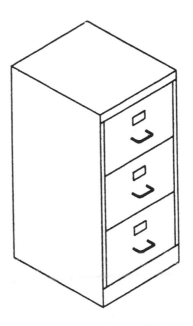

Figure 75-25-1

9. In Figure 75-8-11, which of the following scores will be printed?

A)   All scores > 90 and < 60

B)   All scores < 90

C)   All scores ≤ 90 and ≥ 60

D)   All scores < 60

10. Crowbars, light bulbs and vacuum bags are to be stored in the cabinet shown in Figure 75-25-1. Considering the balance of weight, what would be the safest arrangement?

A)   Top Drawer – Crowbars
      Middle Drawer – Light Bulbs
      Bottom Drawer – Vacuum bags
B)   Top Drawer – Crowbars
      Middle Drawer – Vacuum bags
      Bottom Drawer – Light Bulbs
C)   Top Drawer – Vacuum Bags
      Middle Drawer – Crowbars
      Bottom Drawer – Light Bulbs
D)   Top Drawer – Vacuum Bags
      Middle Drawer – Light Bulbs
      Bottom Drawer – Crowbars
E)   Top Drawer – Light Bulbs
      Middle Drawer – Vacuum Bags
      Bottom Drawer – Crowbars

11. Which is most appropriate for pulling a heavy load?

A) Electric lift
B) Fork lift
C) Tow Conveyor
D) Dolly
E) Pallet truck

12. The electrical circuit term "open circuit" refers to a closed loop being opened. When an ohmmeter is connected into this type of circuit, one can expect the meter to

A) Read infinity
B) Read infinity and slowly return to ZERO
C) Read ZERO
D) Read ZERO and slowly return to infinity
E) None of the above

13. Contaminants have caused bearings to fail prematurely. Which pair of the items listed below should be kept away from bearings?

A) Dirt and oil
B) Grease and water
C) Oil and grease
D) Dirt and moisture
E) Water and oil

14. In order to operate a breast drill, which direction should you turn it?

A) Clockwise
B) Counterclockwise
C) Up and down
D) Back and forth
E) Right, then left

15. Which is the correct tool for tightening or loosening a water pipe?

A) Slip joint pliers
B) Household pliers
C) Monkey wrench
D) Water pump pliers
E) Pipe wrench

16. What is one purpose of a chuck key?

A) Open doors
B) Remove drill bits
C) Remove screws
D) Remove set screws
E) Unlock chucks

17. When smoke is generated as a result of using a portable electric drill for cutting holes into a piece of angle iron, one should

A) use a fire watch.
B) cease the drilling operation.
C) use an exhaust fan to remove smoke.
D) use a prescribed coolant solution to reduce friction.
E) call the Fire Department.

18. The primary purpose of soldering is to

A) melt solder to a molten state.
B) heat metal parts to the right temperature to be joined.
C) join metal parts by melting the parts.
D) harden metal.
E) join metal parts.

19. Which of the following statements is correct of a soldering gun?

A) Tip is not replaceable
B) Cannot be used in cramped places
C) Heats only when trigger is pressed
D) Not rated by the number of watts they use
E) Has no light

20. What unit of measurement is read on a dial torque wrench?
A) Pounds
B) Inches
C) Centimeters
D) Foot-pounds
E) Degrees

21. Which instrument is used to test insulation breakdown of a conductor?

A) Ohmmeter
B) Ammeter
C) Megger
D) Wheatstone bridge
E) Voltmeter

22.   1/2 of 1/4 =

   A) 1/12
   B) 1/8
   C) 1/4
   D) 1/2
   E) 8

23.   2.6 - .5 =

   A) 2.0
   B) 2.1
   C) 3.1
   D) 3.3
   E) None of the above

24.   Simplify the following
      expression in terms of amps:

   563×10^{-6}

   A)   563,000,000 amps
   B)   563,000 amps
   C)   .563 amps
   D)   .000563 amps
   E)   .000000563 amps

25.   Solve the power equation

   $P = I^2R$ for R

   A) R = EI

   B) $R = I^2P$

   C) R = PI

   D) $R = P/I^2$

   E) R = E/I

26.   The product of 3 kilo ohms
      times 3 micro ohms is

   A) 6×10^{-9} ohms

   B) 6×10^{-3} ohms

   C) 9×10^3 ohms

   D) 9×10^{-6} ohms

   E) 9×10^{-3} ohms

In sample question 25 below, select the statement which is most nearly correct according to the paragraph.

"Prior to 1870, a conveyor that made use of rollers was developed for transporting clay. This construction substituted rolling friction at the idler bearing points for the sliding friction of the slider bed. A primitive type of troughing belt conveyor was developed about the same time for the handling of grain. This design was improved during the latter part of the century when the troughing idler was developed."

27. <u>According to the above paragraph</u>, which of the following statements is most nearly correct?

    A)   The troughing belt conveyor was developed about 1870 to handle clay and grain.

    B)   Rolling friction construction was replaced by sliding friction construction prior to 1870.

    C)   In the late nineteenth century, conveyors were improved with the development of the troughing idler.

    D)   The troughing idler, a significant design improvement for conveyors, was developed in the early nineteenth century.

    E)   Conveyor belts were invented and developed in the 1800's.

For sample question 28 below, select from the drawings of objects on the right labeled A, B, C, and D, the one that would have the TOP, FRONT, and RIGHT views shown in the drawing at the left

28.

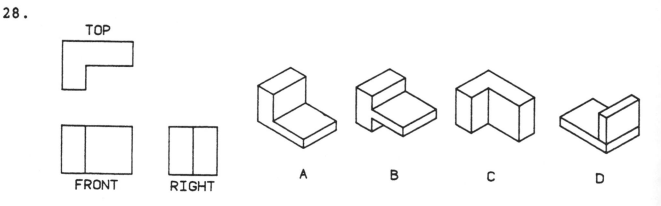

TOP

FRONT   RIGHT

A   B   C   D

In sample question 29 below, there is, on the left, a drawing
of a flat piece of paper and, on the right, four figures
labeled A, B, C, and D. When the paper is bent on the dotted
lines it will form one of the figures on the right. Decide
which alternative can be formed from the flat piece.

29.
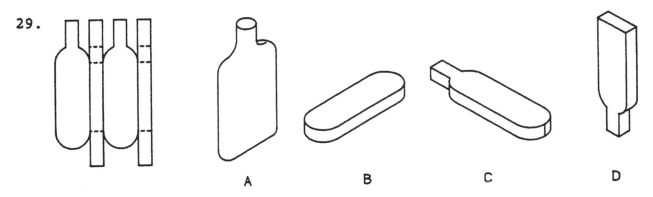

In each of the sample questions below, look at the symbols in
the first two boxes. Something about the three symbols in
the first box makes them alike; something about the two
symbols in the other box with the question mark makes them
alike. Look for some characteristic that is common to all
symbols in the same box, yet makes them different from the
symbols in the other box. Among dthe five answer choices,
find the symbol that can best be substituted for the question
mark, because it is <u>like</u> the symbols in the second box, and,
<u>for the same reason</u>, different from those in the first box.

30.
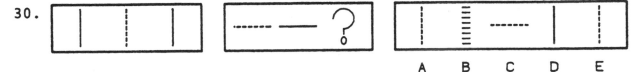

In sample question 30 above, all the symbols in the first box
are vertical lines. The second box has two lines, one broken
and one solid. Their <u>likeness</u> to each other consists in
their being horizontal; and their being horizontal makes them
<u>different</u> from the vertical lines in the other box. The
answer must be the only one of the five lettered choices that
is a horizontal line, either broken or solid. NOTE: There
is not supposed to be a series or progression in these symbol
questions. If you look for a progression in the first box
and the second box, you will be wasting time. Remember, look
for a <u>likeness</u> within each box and a <u>difference</u> between the
two boxes.

Now do sample questions 31 and 32.

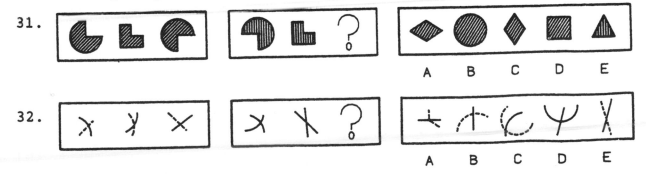

33. In Figure 3-8-6 below, what is the measurement of Dimension F? Drawing is not actual size.

   A) 1 3/4 inches
   B) 2 1/4 inches
   C) 2 1/2 inches
   D) 3 3/4 inches
   E) None of the above

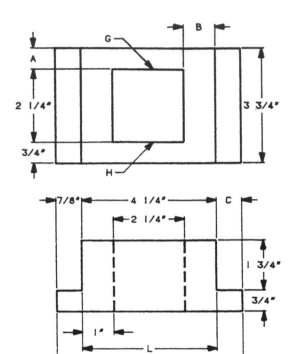

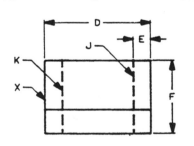

Figure 3-8-6

34. In Figure 160-57 below, what is the current flow through R_3 when:

   V = 50 volts

   R_1 = 25 ohms

   R_2 = 25 ohms

   R3 = 50 ohms

   R_4 = 50 ohms

   R_5 = 50 ohms

and the current through the entire circuit totals one amp?

   A) 0.5 amp
   B) 5.0 amps
   C) 5.0 milliamps
   D) 50.0 milliamps
   E) None of the above

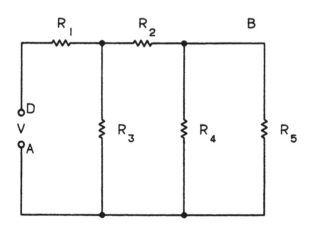

Figure 160-57

CORRECT ANSWERS TO
SAMPLE QUESTIONS

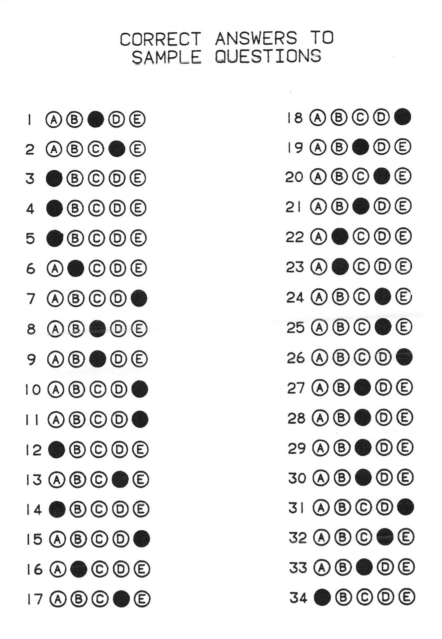

1 Ⓐ Ⓑ ● Ⓓ Ⓔ
2 Ⓐ Ⓑ Ⓒ ● Ⓔ
3 ● Ⓑ Ⓒ Ⓓ Ⓔ
4 ● Ⓑ Ⓒ Ⓓ Ⓔ
5 ● Ⓑ Ⓒ Ⓓ Ⓔ
6 Ⓐ ● Ⓒ Ⓓ Ⓔ
7 Ⓐ Ⓑ Ⓒ Ⓓ ●
8 Ⓐ Ⓑ ● Ⓓ Ⓔ
9 Ⓐ Ⓑ ● Ⓓ Ⓔ
10 Ⓐ Ⓑ Ⓒ Ⓓ ●
11 Ⓐ Ⓑ Ⓒ Ⓓ ●
12 ● Ⓑ Ⓒ Ⓓ Ⓔ
13 Ⓐ Ⓑ Ⓒ ● Ⓔ
14 ● Ⓑ Ⓒ Ⓓ Ⓔ
15 Ⓐ Ⓑ Ⓒ Ⓓ ●
16 Ⓐ ● Ⓒ Ⓓ Ⓔ
17 Ⓐ Ⓑ Ⓒ ● Ⓔ

18 Ⓐ Ⓑ Ⓒ Ⓓ ●
19 Ⓐ Ⓑ ● Ⓓ Ⓔ
20 Ⓐ Ⓑ Ⓒ ● Ⓔ
21 Ⓐ Ⓑ ● Ⓓ Ⓔ
22 Ⓐ ● Ⓒ Ⓓ Ⓔ
23 Ⓐ ● Ⓒ Ⓓ Ⓔ
24 Ⓐ Ⓑ Ⓒ ● Ⓔ
25 Ⓐ Ⓑ Ⓒ ● Ⓔ
26 Ⓐ Ⓑ Ⓒ Ⓓ ●
27 Ⓐ Ⓑ ● Ⓓ Ⓔ
28 Ⓐ Ⓑ ● Ⓓ Ⓔ
29 Ⓐ Ⓑ ● Ⓓ Ⓔ
30 Ⓐ Ⓑ ● Ⓓ Ⓔ
31 Ⓐ Ⓑ Ⓒ Ⓓ ●
32 Ⓐ Ⓑ Ⓒ ● Ⓔ
33 Ⓐ Ⓑ ● Ⓓ Ⓔ
34 ● Ⓑ Ⓒ Ⓓ Ⓔ

Examination 933

Test for Mail Processing Equipment Group

36

United States Postal Service
Sample Questions

The following positions use Examination 933:

Maintenance Mechanic, MPE 06 (Register Number 32)
Maintenance Mechanic, MPE/07 (Register Number M33)
Overhaul Specialist (Register Number M34)

This examination, which is known as Examination 933, is given to applicants for the above positions. This exam consists of Part I, *Following Oral Instructions;* and Part II - *Multiple Choice Test,* which involves basic mechanics, basic electricity, and basic electronics and with the use of hand and portable power tools and test equipment. Study books on basic mechanics, basic electricity, and basic electronics in your local library. (See **Who Can Apply for Exams?**, pages 5-10; **Analyzing Examination 710,** pages 299-310 ; and **Strategies for Standardized Tests**, *multiple choice, vocabulary* and *solving mathematics problems,* pages 399-402 . The total qualifications for an application will be evaluated based on the results of the written test and the review panel evaluation.

PART I

In Part I of the test, you will be told to follow directions by writing in a test booklet and then on an answer sheet. The test booklet will have lines of material like the following five samples:

SAMPLE QUESTIONS

SAMPLE 1.   5 _____

SAMPLE 2.   1 6 4 3 7

SAMPLE 3.   D B A E C

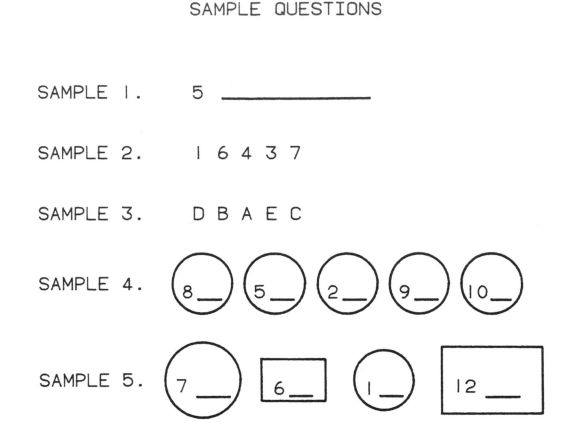

SAMPLE 4.

SAMPLE 5.

To practice this test, have someone read the instructions on the next page to you and you follow the instructions. When they tell you to darken the space on the Sample Answer Sheet, use the one on this page.

SAMPLE ANSWER SHEET

1 Ⓐ Ⓑ Ⓒ Ⓓ Ⓔ	5 Ⓐ Ⓑ Ⓒ Ⓓ Ⓔ	9 Ⓐ Ⓑ Ⓒ Ⓓ Ⓔ
2 Ⓐ Ⓑ Ⓒ Ⓓ Ⓔ	6 Ⓐ Ⓑ Ⓒ Ⓓ Ⓔ	10 Ⓐ Ⓑ Ⓒ Ⓓ Ⓔ
3 Ⓐ Ⓑ Ⓒ Ⓓ Ⓔ	7 Ⓐ Ⓑ Ⓒ Ⓓ Ⓔ	11 Ⓐ Ⓑ Ⓒ Ⓓ Ⓔ
4 Ⓐ Ⓑ Ⓒ Ⓓ Ⓔ	8 Ⓐ Ⓑ Ⓒ Ⓓ Ⓔ	12 Ⓐ Ⓑ Ⓒ Ⓓ Ⓔ

Instructions to be read (the words in parentheses should not be read aloud).

You are to follow the instructions that I shall read to you. I cannot repeat them.

Look at the samples. Sample 1 has a number and a line beside it. On the line write an A. (Pause 2 seconds.) Now on the Sample Answer Sheet, find number 5 (pause 2 seconds) and darken the space for the letter you just wrote on the line. (Pause 2 seconds.)

Look at Sample 2. (Pause slightly.) Draw a line under the third number. (Pause 2 seconds.) Now look on the Sample Answer Sheet, find the number under which you just drew a line and darken space B as in baker for that number. (Pause 5 seconds.)

Look at Sample 3. (Pause slightly.) Draw a line under the third letter in the line. (Pause 2 seconds.) Now on your Sample Answer Sheet, find number 9 (pause 2 seconds) and darken the space for the letter under which you drew a line. (Pause 5 seconds.)

Look at the five circles in Sample 4. (Pause slightly.) Each circle has a number and a line in it. Write D as in dog on the blank in the last circle. (Pause 2 seconds.) Now on the Sample Answer Sheet, darken the space for the number-letter combination that is in the circle you just wrote in. (Pause 5 seconds.)

Look at Sample 5. (Pause slightly.) There are two circles and two boxes of different sizes with numbers in them. (Pause slightly.) If 4 is more than 2 and if 5 is less than 3, write A in the smaller circle. (Pause slightly.) Otherwise write C in the larger box. (Pause 2 seconds.) Now on the Sample Answer Sheet, darken the space for the number-letter combination in the circle or box in which you just wrote. (Pause 5 seconds.)

Now look at the Sample Answer Sheet. (Pause slightly.) You should have darkened spaces 4B, 5A, 9A, 10D, and 12C on the Sample Answer Sheet. (If the person preparing to take the examination made any mistakes, try to help him or her understand why the mistakes are wrong.)

SAMPLE ANSWER QUESTIONS

1 (A) (B) (C) (D) (E)　　18 (A) (B) (C) (D) (E)

2 (A) (B) (C) (D) (E)　　19 (A) (B) (C) (D) (E)

3 (A) (B) (C) (D) (E)　　20 (A) (B) (C) (D) (E)

4 (A) (B) (C) (D) (E)　　21 (A) (B) (C) (D) (E)

5 (A) (B) (C) (D) (E)　　22 (A) (B) (C) (D) (E)

6 (A) (B) (C) (D) (E)　　23 (A) (B) (C) (D) (E)

7 (A) (B) (C) (D) (E)　　24 (A) (B) (C) (D) (E)

8 (A) (B) (C) (D) (E)　　25 (A) (B) (C) (D) (E)

9 (A) (B) (C) (D) (E)　　26 (A) (B) (C) (D) (E)

10 (A) (B) (C) (D) (E)　　27 (A) (B) (C) (D) (E)

11 (A) (B) (C) (D) (E)　　28 (A) (B) (C) (D) (E)

12 (A) (B) (C) (D) (E)　　29 (A) (B) (C) (D) (E)

13 (A) (B) (C) (D) (E)　　30 (A) (B) (C) (D) (E)

14 (A) (B) (C) (D) (E)　　31 (A) (B) (C) (D) (E)

15 (A) (B) (C) (D) (E)　　32 (A) (B) (C) (D) (E)

16 (A) (B) (C) (D) (E)　　33 (A) (B) (C) (D) (E)

17 (A) (B) (C) (D) (E)　　34 (A) (B) (C) (D) (E)

PART II

1. The primary function of a take-up pulley in a belt conveyor is to

   A) carry the belt on the return trip.
   B) track the belt.
   C) maintain proper belt tension.
   D) change the direction of the belt.
   E) regulate the speed of the belt.

2. Which device is used to transfer power and rotary mechanical motion from one shaft to another?

   A) Bearing
   B) Lever
   C) Idler roller
   D) Gear
   E) Bushing

3. What special care is required in the storage of hard steel roller bearings? They should be

   A) cleaned and spun dry with compressed air.
   B) oiled once a month.
   C) stored in a humid place.
   D) wrapped in oiled paper.
   E) stored at temperatures below 90 degrees Fahrenheit.

4. Which is the correct method to lubricate a roller chain?

   A) Use brush to apply lubricant while chain is in motion
   B) Use squirt can to apply lubricant while chain is in motion
   C) Use brush to apply lubricant while chain is not in motion
   D) Soak chain in pan of lubricant and hang to allow excess to drain
   E) Chains do not need lubrication

5. A circuit has two resistors of equal value in series. The voltage and current in the circuit are 20 volts and 2 amps respectively. What is the value of EACH resistor?

   A) 5 ohms
   B) 10 ohms
   C) 15 ohms
   D) 20 ohms
   E) Not enough information given

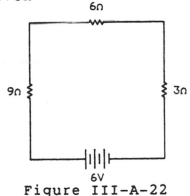

Figure III-A-22

6. Which of the following circuits is shown in Figure III-A-22?

   A) Series circuit
   B) Parallel circuit
   C) Series, parallel circuit
   D) Solid state circuit
   E) None of the above

7. What is the total net capacitance of two 60 farad capacitors connected in series?

   A) 30 F
   B) 60 F
   C) 90 F
   D) 120 F
   E) 360 F

8. If two 30 mH inductors are connected in series, what is the total net inductance of the combination?

   A) 15 mH
   B) 20 mH
   C) 30 mH
   D) 45 mH
   E) 60 mH

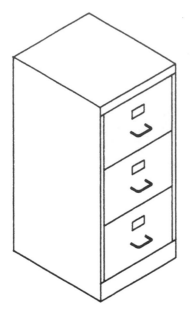

Figure 75-25-1

9. Crowbars, light bulbs and vacuum bags are to be stored in the cabinet shown in Figure 75-25-1. Considering the balance of weight, what would be the safest arrangement?

A) Top drawer - Crowbars
   Middle drawer - Light bulbs
   Bottom drawer - Vacuum bags
B) Top drawer - Crowbars
   Middle drawer - Vacuum bags
   Bottom drawer - Light bulbs
C) Top drawer - Vacuum bags
   Middle drawer - Crowbars
   Bottom drawer - Light bulbs
D) Top drawer - Vacuum bags
   Middle drawer - Light bulbs
   Bottom drawer - Crowbars
E) Top drawer - Light bulbs
   Middle drawer - Vacuum bags
   Bottom drawer - Crowbars

10. Contaminants have caused bearings to fail prematurely. Which pair of the items listed below should be kept away from bearings?

A) Dirt and oil
B) Grease and water
C) Oil and grease
D) Dirt and moisture
E) Water and oil

11. The electrical circuit term "open circuit" refers to a closed loop being opened. When an ohmmeter is connected into this type of circuit, one can expect the meter to

A) read infinity.
B) read infinity and slowly return to ZERO.
C) read ZERO.
D) read ZERO and slowly return to infinity.
E) None of the above

12. Which is most appropriate for pulling a heavy load?

A) Electric lift
B) Fork lift
C) Tow conveyor
D) Dolly
E) Pallet truck

13. In order to operate a breast drill, which direction should you turn it?

A) Clockwise
B) Counterclockwise
C) Up and down
D) Back and forth
E) Right, then left

14. Which is the correct tool for tightening or loosening a water pipe?

A) Slip joint pliers
B) Household pliers
C) Monkey wrench
D) Water pump pliers
E) Pipe wrench

15. What is one purpose of a chuck key?

A) Open doors
B) Remove drill bits
C) Remove screws
D) Remove set screws
E) Unlock chucks

16. When smoke is generated as a result of using a portable electric drill for cutting holes into a piece of angle iron, one should

A) use a fire watch.
B) cease the drilling operation.
C) use an exhaust fan to remove smoke.
D) use a prescribed coolant solution to reduce friction.
E) call the Fire Department.

17. The primary purpose of soldering is to

A) melt solder to a molten state.
B) heat metal parts to the right temperature be be joined.
C) join metal parts by melting the parts.
D) harden metal.
E) join metal parts.

18. Which of the following statements is correct concerning a soldering gun?

A) Tip is not replaceable
B) Cannot be used in cramped places
C) heats only when trigger is pressed
D) Not rated by the number of watts it uses
E) Has no light

19. What unit of measurement is read on a dial torque wrench?

A) Pounds
B) Inches
C) Centimeters
D) Foot-pounds
E) Degrees

20. Which instrument is used to test insulation breakdown of a conductor?

A) Ohmmeter
B) Ammeter
C) Megger
D) Wheatstone bridge
E) Voltmeter

21. 1/2 of 1/4 =

A) 1/12
B) 1/8
C) 1/4
D) 1/2
E) 8

22. 2.6 – .5 =

A) 2.0
B) 2.1
C) 3.1
D) 3.3
E) None of the above

23. Solve the power equation

$$P = I^2R \text{ for } R$$

A) $R = EI$

B) $R = I^2P$

C) $R = PI$

D) $R = P/I^2$

E) $R = E/I$

24. The product of 3 kilo ohms times 3 micro ohms is

A) 6×10^{-9} ohms

B) 6×10^{-3} ohms

C) 9×10^3 ohms

D) 9×10^{-6} ohms

E) 9×10^{-3} ohms

In sample question 25 below, select the statement which is most nearly correct according to the paragraph.

"Prior to 1870, a conveyor that made use of rollers was developed for transporting clay. This construction substituted rolling friction at the idler bearing points for the sliding friction of the slider bed. A primitive type of troughing belt conveyor was developed about the same time for the handling of grain. This design was improved during the latter part of the century when the troughing idler was developed."

25.   According to the above paragraph, which of the following statements is most nearly correct?

A)   The troughing belt conveyor was developed about 1870 to handle clay and grain.

B)   Rolling friction construction was replaced by sliding friction construction prior to 1870.

C)   In the late nineteenth century, conveyors were improved with the development of the troughing idler.

D)   The troughing idler, a significant design improvement for conveyors, was developed in the early nineteenth century.

E)   Conveyor belts were invented and developed in the 1800's.

26. A small crane was used to raise the heavy part. Raise MOST nearly means

A)   lift
B)   drag
C)   drop
D)   deliver
E)   guide

27. Short MOST nearly means

A)   tall
B)   wide
C)   brief
D)   heavy
E)   dark

For sample question 28 below, select from the drawings of objects on the right labeled A, B, C, and D, the one that would have the TOP, FRONT, and RIGHT views shown in the drawing at the left

28.

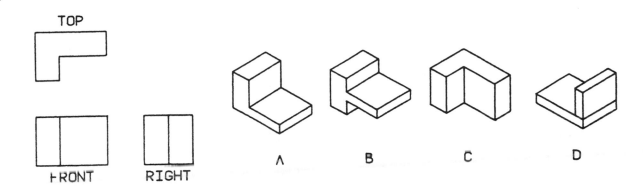

In sample question 29 below, there is, on the left, a drawing of a flat piece of paper and, on the right, four figures labeled A, B, C, and D. When the paper is bent on the dotted lines it will form one of the figures on the right. Decide which alternative can be formed from the flat piece.

29.

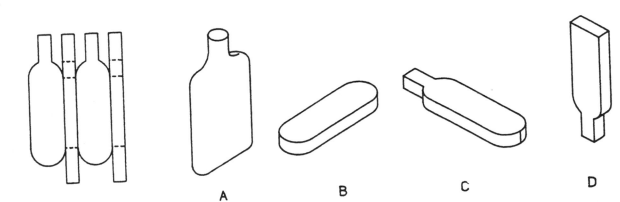

In each of the sample questions below, look at the symbols in the first two boxes. Something about the three symbols in the first box makes them alike; something about the two symbols in the other box with the question mark makes them alike. Look for some characteristic that is common to all symbols in the same box, yet makes them different from the symbols in the other box. Among dthe five answer choices, find the symbol that can best be substituted for the question mark, because it is <u>like</u> the symbols in the second box, and, <u>for the same reason</u>, different from those in the first box.

30.

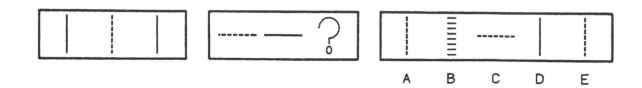

                                          A   B   C   D   E

In sample question 30 above, all the symbols in the first box are vertical lines. The second box has two lines, one broken and one solid. Their <u>likeness</u> to each other consists in their being horizontal; and their being horizontal makes them <u>different</u> from the vertical lines in the other box. The answer must be the only one of the five lettered choices that is a horizontal line, either broken or solid. NOTE: There is not supposed to be a series or progression in these symbol questions. If you look for a progression in the first box and the second box, you will be wasting time. Remember, look for a <u>likeness</u> within each box and a <u>difference</u> between the two boxes.

Now do sample questions 31 and 32.

31.

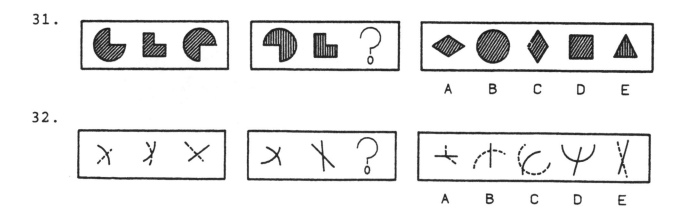

32.

33. In Figure 160-57 below, what is the current flow through R_3 when:

  V = 50 volts

  R_1 = 25 ohms

  R_2 = 25 ohms

  R3 = 50 ohms

  R_4 = 50 ohms

  R_5 = 50 ohms

and the current through the entire circuit totals one amp?

A) 0.5 amp
B) 5.0 amps
C) 5.0 milliamps
D) 50.0 milliamps
E) None of the above

34. In Figure 3-8-6 below, what is the measurement of Dimension F? Drawing is not actual size.

A) 1 3/4 inches
B) 2 1/4 inches
C) 2 1/2 inches
D) 3 3/4 inches
E) None of the above

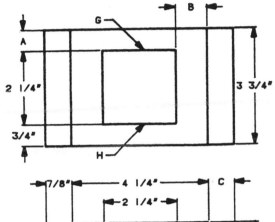

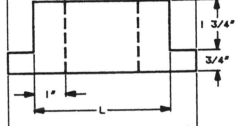

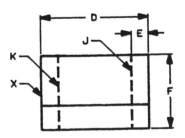

Figure 3-8-6

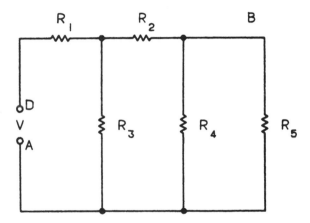

Figure 160-57

CORRECT ANSWERS TO
SAMPLE QUESTIONS

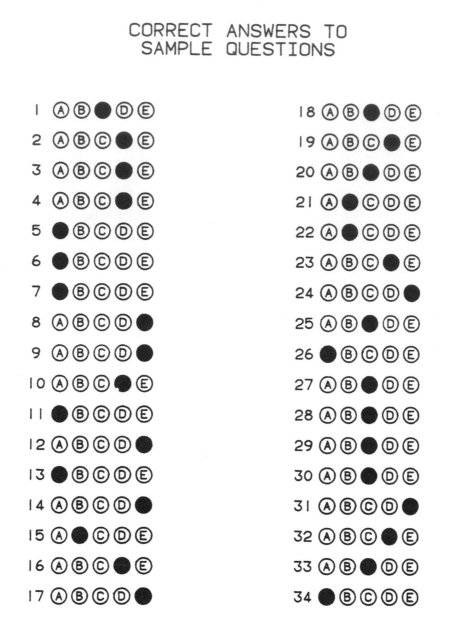

1 Ⓐ Ⓑ ● Ⓓ Ⓔ
2 Ⓐ Ⓑ Ⓒ ● Ⓔ
3 Ⓐ Ⓑ Ⓒ ● Ⓔ
4 Ⓐ Ⓑ Ⓒ ● Ⓔ
5 ● Ⓑ Ⓒ Ⓓ Ⓔ
6 ● Ⓑ Ⓒ Ⓓ Ⓔ
7 ● Ⓑ Ⓒ Ⓓ Ⓔ
8 Ⓐ Ⓑ Ⓒ Ⓓ ●
9 Ⓐ Ⓑ Ⓒ Ⓓ ●
10 Ⓐ Ⓑ Ⓒ ● Ⓔ
11 ● Ⓑ Ⓒ Ⓓ Ⓔ
12 Ⓐ Ⓑ Ⓒ Ⓓ ●
13 ● Ⓑ Ⓒ Ⓓ Ⓔ
14 Ⓐ Ⓑ Ⓒ Ⓓ ●
15 Ⓐ ● Ⓒ Ⓓ Ⓔ
16 Ⓐ Ⓑ Ⓒ ● Ⓔ
17 Ⓐ Ⓑ Ⓒ Ⓓ ●

18 Ⓐ Ⓑ ● Ⓓ Ⓔ
19 Ⓐ Ⓑ Ⓒ ● Ⓔ
20 Ⓐ Ⓑ ● Ⓓ Ⓔ
21 Ⓐ ● Ⓒ Ⓓ Ⓔ
22 Ⓐ ● Ⓒ Ⓓ Ⓔ
23 Ⓐ Ⓑ Ⓒ ● Ⓔ
24 Ⓐ Ⓑ Ⓒ Ⓓ ●
25 Ⓐ Ⓑ ● Ⓓ Ⓔ
26 ● Ⓑ Ⓒ Ⓓ Ⓔ
27 Ⓐ Ⓑ ● Ⓓ Ⓔ
28 Ⓐ Ⓑ ● Ⓓ Ⓔ
29 Ⓐ Ⓑ ● Ⓓ Ⓔ
30 Ⓐ Ⓑ ● Ⓓ Ⓔ
31 Ⓐ Ⓑ Ⓒ Ⓓ ●
32 Ⓐ Ⓑ Ⓒ ● Ⓔ
33 Ⓐ Ⓑ ● Ⓓ Ⓔ
34 ● Ⓑ Ⓒ Ⓓ Ⓔ

Standardized Test

Tips, Techniques, & Strategies

37

Standardized tests, prepared in standard patterns and ways, are time tested. That is, a time limit is set for each test. For example, Part A should be finished in five minutes and Part B should be finished in six.

There are strategies you can use to attack the questions. A test is a game; if you take a standardized test, you are a football quarterback and the testmaker is the opposing team: you read the defense, anticipating what kind of defense the opponent has formed and deciding what to do, whether to throw the ball to a wide receiver or give it to a fullback for a touchdown. If you aren't sure, at least make a guess.

Since postal tests are standardized, you can become an exam expert and make a high score on any test once you master the types of questions which have been asked in past years.

I. Multiple-Choice Test Strategies

One of the most common types of examination is the multiple-choice test, in which you select one correct answer from four or five choices. Some questions contain more than one correct answer.

Here are some strategies you can use in answering multiple-choice tests.

■ **Tactic 1:** Answer the sample questions for practice.

■ **Tactic 2:** Answer the easy questions first and the tough questions last.

■ **Tactic 3:** Evaluate the questions and see how they are designed. For example, questions within each test usually progress in difficulty from easy to hard.

■ **Tactic 4:** Search for hints. Some clues will help you find the right answer. Testmakers, for instance, usually use correct grammar in the correct answers and sometimes use incorrect grammar in the wrong answers without knowing it, because of their speed in preparing the other answers.

■ **Tactic 5:** If you're sure of a correct answer, select it and don't look for any traps.

■ **Tactic 6:** If you can't figure out the correct answer to a question, pick one. Make a little mark alongside the number with your pencil, and tell yourself, "I shall return!" (That is, if you have the time to do so.)

■ **Tactic 7:** Be on the lookout for choices like "all of the above" and "none of the above"; usually they are not the right answers. If the first three choices are right, for instance, and if the fourth is wrong, and if the fifth is "all of the above," don't select number 4 or 5. Choose among 1, 2, and 3.

■ **Tactic 8:** Watch out for sentences that contain words such as *all, only, none, never, always, usually, generally.* Often these words are traps; they do not belong to the correct answers. Unless you're sure that it's the right answer. don't select it.

■ **Tactic 9:** Most often, two out of the four or five choices are obvious wrong answers; so eliminate them first. In other words, eliminate the answers which are clearly wrong until you come to a point where you are to choose between the two best choices.

■ **Tactic 10.** Follow your first hunch on a particular answer; don't change it unless you're certain that you're making the right move.

■ **Tactic 11:** When two answers have opposite meanings, usually one of them is the right answer; when two answers express the same thing, usually one of the pair is the right answer.

■ **Tactic 12:** Guess if you don't know the answer, but be careful when the test score is calculated by subtracting the wrong answers from the right answers.

II. Vocabulary Test Strategies

■ **Tactic 1:** Watch out for traps. For example, if the question and one of the answers sound alike or look alike, it may be a trap, and most often it's not the right answer.

■ **Tactic 2:** Eliminate wrong parts of speech. If the word you are to define is a noun, the correct answer will be a noun; if it's a verb, the answer will be a verb. If you aren't sure whether a word is a noun or a verb, place "the" before the word. If it looks or sounds right, it's a noun. Place "to" before a word that may be a verb. If it sounds okay, it's a verb.

■ **Tactic 3:** Read a lot and look up every unfamiliar word in the dictionary. Learning vocabulary is a continuing education.

III. Solving Mathematics Problems

You can find the answers to math problems, no matter how complicated they are, by addition, subtraction, multiplication, and division, or by conversion of millimeters into centimeters, ounces into pounds, and so on. First, though, you must know whether you're going east or west. If you don't know, you're lost.

■ **Tactic 1:** The first time you're faced with a math problem, figure out how you're going to solve it. You must know the following:

- What you are supposed to find out.
- The given numbers.
- The principles or formulas needed to solve the problems.

■ **Tactic 2:** Write the numbers carefully. Be extra careful in writing 0 so that it doesn't look like a 6 or 8, and vice versa. Don't write a 3 that looks like a 5 or a 1 that looks like a 7, or vice versa. The columns should be in straight lines so that you don't make mistakes in addition or subtraction.

■ **Tactic 3:** Be sure to check the units of measurement. If they are not in the proper units, convert them into the correct units, such as millimeters into centimeters, ounces into pounds, or kilometers into miles. Don't try to add pounds to ounces, for example.

■ **Tactic 4:** Use diagrams such as squares, triangles and other shapes as much as possible. Label all the given numbers if such diagrams are needed to simplify solving.

■ **Tactic 5:** In solving any problem, particularly in a multiple-choice math test, don't glance at the choices (A, B, C, D, E) before you work on the problem. Work on the problem first, and when you have an answer, see if it matches any of the given numbers. It's like comparing your numbers with the numbers in a lottery; if your numbers don't match the winning numbers, you didn't win and you must try another time. So if your answer is not among the choices, it's not the correct answer.

■ **Tactic 6:** If you don't really know how to solve the problem, you'd better guess; that's better than leaving the question unanswered. Use the following elimination system:

- First eliminate the least probable answers.
- Eliminate the lowest and highest values among the remaining answers.
- Then select the most likely answer from the answers that remain.

Math Test techniques

Thomas F. Ewald, a former college instructor, gives the following advice on multiplication problems:

Solve the following multiplication problem:

$$3453 \times 4376 =$$

A) 15,112,432   C) 15,110,328
B) 15,121,324   D) 15,432,222

How long did it take you? If it took more than five seconds, you need this technique!

Take the last digit of each of the numbers to be multiplied against each other; now find the product of these two digits (that is, multiply them against each other): $3 \times 6 = 18$. Now notice the last digit of the correct answer above, Answer C. (You did get the right answer, didn't you?) It's 8. What was the last digit of the simple problem we just did (3×6)? That was also 8. It's not a coincidence. It will happen every time! As long as only one answer is given with the correct last digit, it's easy to pick the right answer!

If more than one answer ends in the correct digit, you'll have to do the actual multiplication. Also, my advice won't work if "none of the above" is given as an option. But it will help some of the time and can save precious seconds, or even minutes.

On some tests, such as the SAT, speed is extra important. Tactics like the one above helped me achieve a perfect score on the math portion of the SAT! It can be done!

38

What and Where the Jobs Are

Good Job Choices throughout the U.S.

Before we discuss what and where the jobs are, it would be best to take a look at the organization of the U.S. Postal Service. Headed by the Postmaster General, the USPS has its general headquarters at 475 L'Enfant Plaza SW, Washington, DC 20260.

The USPS is divided into four regions: Western, Southern, Northeastern, and Central. The regions are divided into divisions and the divisions are divided into Management Sectional Centers (MSC's) and General Mail Facilities (GMF's) that manage associate offices.

The Detroit division, for instance, includes the Detroit General Mail Facilities (GMF) and the Royal Oak Post Office Sectional Center whose general office is situated in Troy, Michigan. In the Royal Oak sectional center, mail from all cities whose ZIP codes begin with 480 or 483 is brought for processing and forwarding. In the sectional such as this, mail is processed through letter sorting machines (LSM's) and optical character reader machines (OCR's). There, the mail is postmarked, sorted and sent back to different local post offices for distribution. (Mail for out-of-state post offices is forwarded from sectional centers directly to its destination.)

Openings for most Postal Service jobs are not restricted to particular states or divisional or regional areas; rather, they are distributed in direct proportion to the volume of mail processed, or the size of a particular area or city. You can expect to find more letter carriers in thickly populated states like California, New York, Texas, or Florida. You can also expect large numbers of distribution clerks (machine), mail handlers, mark-up clerks (automated), and mail processors to be concentrated in GMF's and MSC's.

Technical Positions

For technical positions such as computer programmer, computer analyst, engineer, or architect, you'll have a better chance of being employed with the Postal Service Headquarters in Washington DC. These technical jobs are offered first to current career employees through vacancy announcement sheets, which are distributed throughout the post offices, particularly GMF's and MSC's. If the positions can't be filled up by qualified "insiders," then they are advertised in newspapers, particularly in the *Washington Post,* which may be available in your local library. Technical jobs in your area are advertised in the local newspapers.

If you want to live and work in any of the states but can't get a postal job there, take postal exams and get a job in the state where you live. Then, after one or two years, request a transfer to the city where you want to live. To increase your chances of getting a postal job anywhere, you must take as many exams as possible. But before you do so, you must be prepared to score high on these exams and beat the competition. You must remember that thousands of people take a single exam but only a small number will be called for immediate employment. The rest will be placed on the waiting list.

To know about scheduled postal exams, call several or many MSC's and GM'S (see Supplement A: *National Directory of U.S. Postal Service Examination Centers*). You can also go to the U.S. Postal Service websites at:

http://usps.com

When you are on the site (to find where postal entrance exams are being currently held) type the word, job

on the http://usps.com (research tool):.

From the page you can select which exams for jobs you would want to apply for (whether it's a position for Maintenance, Operations, Transportation, or Services). Yes, you can apply for exams for any job which you are interested in. However, for some technical positions, you need to have some knowledge of or experience in such jobs.

You can also get a technical job, not only with the headquarters in Washington DC, but also in field regions and divisions. For instance, computer programmers are hired at the Software Branch Systems Data Operations Divisions. In San Mateo, California, and in St. Louis. Computer system analysts are hired in the Rates and Classification Center in the Eastern Region in Philadelphia, Pennsylvania. Telecommunications hardware technicians are hired at the Network Operation Branches such as that in Network Communications Division, National Information Systems Development Center in Raleigh, North California.

Mail processing maintenance mechanics, letter box mechanics, electronic technicians, blacksmith/welders, and other skilled or semi-skilled workers are hired in sectional centers.

The best plan is to be hired by the Postal Service, as a clerk, a carrier, or whatever. Once you're in, you'll get a better view of the service, and through vacancy announcements you'll know where the jobs are. As I said before, other jobs in the postal service are offered first to "insiders".

So whether you're a mechanic, a plumber, or a computer expert, get a postal job first. As the saying goes, "If you can't beat them, join them."

Listing of Post Office Jobs

Here is an incomplete listing of U.S. Postal Service Jobs to give you an idea on job positions at the Postal Service offices throughout the country. To be filled up, many of these jobs require passing entrance examinations, while many others are filled up through promotions of current employees or by hiring professional outsiders. .

A

Accountant
Accounting Assistant
Accounting Associate
Accounting Officer
Accountant, Postal
    Facilities
Accountant, Senior
Accounts Payable
    Branch Manager,
    EAS 20
Address Information
    Systems Supervisor
Administrative Specialist
Advertising Specialist
Air Taxi and Highway
    Superintendent
Area Maintenance Specialist
Area Maintenance
    Technician
Area Manager, Stations
Area Maintenance
    Technician
Architect/Engineer,
    Senior
Architect/Engineer,
    Staff
Assistant Engineman
Associate Office Coordinator

Audiovisual Production Branch Manager
Automotive Mechanic

B

Body and Fender
    Repairman
Budget and Cost Analyst
Budget and Cost Analyst, Principal
Budget and Cost Analyst, Senior
Budget Specialist
Building Equipment
    Mechanic
Building Maintenance
    Custodian
Bulk Mail Clerk

C

Carpenter
City Operations Director
Classification Support
    Specialist, Associate
Classification Support
    Specialist, Senior
Cleaner
Clerk
Clerk Stenographer
Clerk Typist

Commercial Accounts
    Manager
Communications Manager
Communications Specialist
Compensation Services Specialist
Computer Programer
Computer Programmer,
    Senior
Computer Programmer/Software Specialist
Computer Programmer
    Software Specialist,
    Senior
Computer Systems
    Administrator
Computer Systems
    Analyst
Computer Systems
    Analyst, Senior
Computer Systems
    Analyst/Programmer
Computer Systems
    Scheduler
Confidential Secretary
Console Operator
Correspondence Center Supervisor
Conveyor Mechanic

Criminal Investigation Evaluator

Curriculum Planning and Evaluation Specialist, Sr

Curriculum and Planning Specialist

Custodial Laborer

Custodian

Customer Services Manager

D

Data Administrator, Principal

Data Base Designer

Data Base Management Program Manager

Data Base Software Specialist

Data Collection Supervisor

Data Conversion Operator

Data Operations and Fulfillment Supervisor

Data Systems Management Officer

Delivery and Collection Manager

Delivery and Collection Supervisor

Delivery Operations Specialist

Delivery and Retail Programs Manager

Design and Construction Branch Manager

Director, Analysis Specialist

Director, City Operations

Director, Employee and Labor Relations

Director, Operations Services

Director, Mail Processing

Director, Plant Maintenance (Bulk Mail)

Director, Stations Administration

Director, Support, Bulk Mail Center

Distribution Clerk, (Machine)

Distribution Clerk (Manual)

Distribution Manager

Distribution Procedures Analyst

Distribution Program Specialist

Distribution Window Clerk

Drafting Clerk

E

Economist

Economist, Senior

Economist, Staff

Editor, Technical Manuals

EDP Systems Operations Supervisor

Electronic Engineer (Program Engineer)

Electronics Technician

Elevator and Boiler Inspector

Elevator Mechanic

Employee Assistance Program Coordinator

Employee and Labor Relations Director

Employee Relations Specialist

Employment and Development Manager

Engineman

Express Mail Manager

Express Mail Technician

F

Facilities Contract Specialist

Facilities Contract Technician, Senior

Facilities Engineer

Facilities Specialist

Facility Design Estimator

Field Manager, National Test Administration Center

Financial Analyst

Financial Analyst (Headquarters)

Financial Analyst, Senior

Financial Systems Analyst, Principal

Fireman

Fireman-Laborer

Flat-Sorter Machine Operator

Fleet Operations Manager
Forensic Chemist
Forms Control Analyst, Staff

G

Garageman
General Manager, Mail Processing Facility
General Mechanic
General Supervisor, Delivery and Collection
General Supervisor, Mails
General Supervisor, Vehicle Maintenance
Government Relations Specialist

H

Human Resource Specialist

I

Industrial Equipment Mechanic
Industrial Engineer
Industrial Engineer, Program Engineer
Industrial Engineer, Senior Associate
Industrial Engineer Senior (Field)
Industrial Engineer, Staff
Industrial Engineering Coordinator

Industrial Equipment Mechanic
Information Services Specialist
Information System Analyst
Information Systems Coordinator
Information Systems Coordinator, Associate
Information Systems Coordinator, Senior
Information Systems Specialist, Junior
Information Systems Specialist, Senior
Injury Compensation Program Supervisor
Instructor, Technical Training
Instructor, Technical Training, Senior

L

Labor Relations Manager
Labor Relations, Representative, (Field)
Labor Relations Specialist
Letter Box Mechanic
Letter Carrier
Logistics & Distribution Systems Manager
Logistics Planning Specialist
Logistics Program Manager
LSM Operator

M

Machinist
Mail Equipment, Handler
Mail Handler
Mail Processing Director
Mail Processing Program Coordinator
Mail Processor
Maintenance Control Supervisor
Maintenance Electrician
Maintenance Engineering Analyst
Maintenance Mechanic
Maintenance Program Specialist
Management Analyst Program Manager
Management Analyst, Senior
Management Education Specialist
Management Sectional Center Director, City Operations
Management Sectional Center Director, Field Operations
Management Sectional Center Director, Finance
Management Sectional Center, Director, Finance
Manager, Accounts Payable Branch
Manager, Address Info Center

Manager, Budget and Financial Analyst

Manager, Commercial Accounts

Manager, Communications (B)

Manager, Communications (D)

Manager, Costumer Service (B)

Manager, Delivery and Collection (A)

Manager, Delivery and Collection (B)

Manager, Delivery and Retail Programs

Manager, Design and Construction Branch

Manager, Distribution (B)

Manager, Distribution (C)

Manager Employment and Development

Manager, Employment and Training

Manager, Equal Employment Opportunity Complaints Processing

Manager, Engineering Technical Unit

Manager, Fleet Operation (A)

Manager, Fleet Operations (C)

Manager, Fleet Operations (d)

Manager, General Mail Facility Operations

Manager, General Mail Facility (B)

Manager, Labor Relations

Manager, Logistics and Distribution Systems

Manager, Mail Requirements (B)

Manager, Material Management Operations Branch

Manager, Overhaul Support (A)

Manager, Personnel Services (A)

Manager, Plant and Equipment Engineering

Manager, Plant Maintenance (A) and (E)

Manager, Public and Employee Communications

Manager, Quality Assurance Branch

Manager Realty Management Branch

Manager, Retail Sales and Services (A) and (B)

Manager, Safety (A) and (B)

Manager, Safety and Health Services

Manager, Support Services (A)

Manager, Systems Compliance (B)

Manager, Training

Marketing Specialist, Senior

Mark-Up Clerk

Mason

Mechanic Helper

Mechanical Engineer

Mechanical Engineer, Program Engineer

Mechanical Engineer, Project Engineer

Mechanical Engineer, Senior

Media Relations Representative

Medical Officer, Field Division

Motor Vehicle Operator

N

Nurse

O

Occupation Specialist

Office Clerk

Office Systems Coordinator

Oiler MPE

Operating Engineer

Operating Policies and Programs Analyst, Principal]

Operations Research Analyst, Senior

Operations Specialist (Delivery)

Operations Specialist, Senior (Delivery)

Overhaul Specialist

P

Painter

Personnel Services Manager

Philatelic Design Program Manager

Philatelic Programs Specialist, Senior

Planning Analyst, Principal (Region)

Plant and Equipment Engineering Manager

Plant Maintenance Director

Plant Maintenance Manager

Plumber

Plumber Helper

Postal Center Technician

Postal Equipment Overhaul Supervisor

Postal Inspector

Postal Machines Mechanic

Postal Maintenance Mechanic

Postal Operations Analyst (C)

Postal Operations Superintendent

Postal Operations Specialist, Senior

Postal Service Data Technician

Postmaster

Postmaster General

Printing Contract Specialist

Procurement Specialist

Procurement Specialist, Senior

Procurement Specialist, Staff

Process Control Systems Supervisor

Procurement Clerk

Procurement Quality Assurance Program Manager

Procurement and Supply Compliance Specialist

Professional Specialist Trainee (Data Base Specialist)

Professional/Specialist Trainee (Industrial Engineer)

Professional/Specialist Trainee (Mechanical Engineer)

Program Analyst

Program Coordinator, Mail Processing

Program Manager, Data Base Management

Program Manager, Design and Construction

Program Manager, Facility Requirements

Program Manager, Logistics

Program Manager, Mechanization Maintenance

Program Manager, Philatelic Design

Program Manager, Procurement Quality Assurance

Program Manager, Software Systems Administration

Project Manager, Facility Design and Construction

Psychologist

Psychologist, Senior

Public and Employee Administration Manager

Purchasing Specialist

Q

Quality Control Specialist

Quality Control Analyst

Quality Assurance Specialist

R

Real Estate Specialist (Career Ladder)

Real Estate Specialist, Staff

Realty Acquisitions Branch Manager

Records Management Analyst

Regional Labor Relations Executive

Resource Specialist

Retail Specialist

Retail Sales and Services Manager
Rural Carrier
Rural Carrier Associate

S

Safety Engineer, Service Center
Safety Specialist
Scale Mechanic
Scheme Operator
Secretary
Secretary (A)
Secretary Typist
Sectional Center Director, Customer Services
Sectional Center Director, Customer Services
Sectional Center Director, Customer Services
Security Electronics Specialist
Senior Equipment Specialist
Senior Instructor, Delivery and Vehicle Services
Senior Mathematical Statistician
Senior Management Analyst
Senior Psychologist
Senior Statistician
Senior Typist
Service Center Safety Engineer
Shipping Engineer

Stamp Supervising Clerk
Stationary Engineer
Statistical Programs Analyst, Senior
Statistical Programs Coordinator
Superintendent, Accountable Paper Depository
Superintendent, Building Equipment Maintenance
Superintendent, Postal Operations
Superintendent, Support Services
Supervisor Address Information Systems
Supervisor, Analysis and Programming
Supervisor, Audiovisual Production Branch
Supervisor, Building Equipment Maintenance
Supervisor, Compensation and Staffing
Supervisor, Computer Operations
Supervisor, Computer Systems Operations
Supervisor, Correspondence Center
Supervisor, Data Collection
Supervisor, Data Operations and Fulfillment

Supervisor, Delivery and Collection
Supervisor, Disbursing Supervisor, EDP Systems Operations
Supervisor, Electronics Technician
Supervisor, Employee Assistance Program
Supervisor, Employment and Placement
Supervisor, Injury Compensation Programs
Supervisor, Mails and Delivery
Supervisor, Maintenance Mail Processing Equipment
Supervisor, Postal Equipment
Supervisor, Postal Equipment Mechanic (Overhaul)
Supervisor, Process Control System
Supervisor, Transportation (TMSC)
Support Service Information Specialist
Support Services Manager
Systems Analysis Program Manager
Systems Compliance Manager

T

Technical Training Instructor
Technical Writer

Telecommunications Hardware Technician

Telecommunications Program Manager

Telecommunication System Specialist

Telephone Operator

Text and Data Service Assistant

Timekeeper

Tour Superintendent, Bulk Mail Center

Tour Superintendent, Equipment Maintenance

Tour Superintendent, Mails

Tour Superintendent (Designated Area)

Tour Superintendent (Maintenance Operations

Tour Supervisor, Mails (MPLSM)

Tractor-Trailer Operator

Traffic Management Specialist

Training Manager

Training Technician

Transportation Analyst

Transportation and Equipment Specialist (TMSC)

Transportation Procurement Analyst

Transportation Requirement Analyst

Transportation Specialist (TMSC)

Transportation Specialist, Senior

Treasurer

Typist

W

Welder

Window Clerk

Z

Zip Code Operator

39

Wanted: U.S. Postal Inspectors

Only the Exceptional May Apply

Postal inspectors are federal law enforcement officers with investigative jurisdiction in all criminal matters involving the integrity of the mail and the security of the U.S. Postal Service.

U.S. Postal Inspectors

Postal inspectors, among others, investigate criminal and civil violations of postal laws and protect the revenue and assets of the U.S. Postal Service. They are authorized to carry firearms, make arrests, and they testify in court, serve subpoenas, and write comprehensive reports.

It was only January 8, 2003, that the U.S. Postal Inspection Service began recruiting college graduates who don't have previous work experience. Just in case you don't meet one of the special requirements listed in the Application for U.S. Inspectors, but have either a conferred, four-year college degree with a minimum GPA of 3.0 or an advance degree, you may apply for a Postal Inspector job, by submitting the *Application for U.S. Postal Inspector,* with a copy of your college transcript. Or write to: **U.S. Postal Inspection Service,** Office of Recruitment, 9600 Newbridge Drive, Potomac, MD 20854-4436. Or call the office at 301-983-7400.

Other U.S. Postal Inspection Service Jobs

From time to time, the U.S. Postal Inspection Service also recruits for other positions such as:

- Postal Police Officers
- Forensic Scientists
- Information Technology Specialists
- Security Electronic Technicians
- Administration Support Specialists

Excerpted from the U.S. Postal Inspection Service Website:
http://usps.com/postalinspectors/employmt.htm

Requirements for U.S. Postal Inspectors

U.S. Postal Inspectors are federal law enforcement officers. They investigate criminal, civil, and administrative violations of postal laws and are responsible for protecting the revenue and assets of the Postal Service. Inspectors are required to carry firearms, make arrests, testify in court, serve subpoenas, and write comprehensive reports. They must operate motor vehicles and may undergo moderate to arduous physical exertion under unusual environmental conditions. It is essential that Inspectors be in sound physical condition and be capable of performing vigorous physical activities on a sustained basis. The activities may require Inspectors to perform the following: climb ladders; work long and irregular hours; occupy cramped or crowded spaces for extended periods of time; exert physical force in the arrest, search, pursuit, and restraint of another person; and protect themselves and others from imminent danger.

The duties of the position require the ability to communicate with people from all walks of life, be proficient with firearms, have skills in self-defense, and have the ability to exercise good judgment. Inspectors may be relocated according to the needs of the Service.

The recruitment process is extremely thorough, and there is intense competition for relatively few positions. The recruitment and selection process must be completed prior to the applicant's 37th birthday.

This position is exempt from the Fair Labor Standards Act (FLSA) and does not qualify for overtime compensation. Postal Inspector salaries are based on the Inspection Service Law Enforcement (ISLE) pay system. The ISLE pay grades and steps correspond to the General Schedule (GS) pay scale for law enforcement officers.

Selection procedures include the following:

- Completion of this application.
- Written examination, including a business writing test and the 620 Entry Examination (cognitive abilities).
- Language proficiency test, if applicable.
- Completion of the *Comprehensive Application Packet.*
- Assessment Center evaluation of knowledge, skills, and abilities.
- Medical examination
- Polygraph examination.
- Background suitability investigation.
- Management interview.
- Drug screening.
- Residential basic training program at Potomac, Maryland.
- Six-month probation period for nonpostal and nonfederal law enforcement applicants.

Recruiting Standards

Applicants must be U.S. citizen between 21 and 36 years of age and meet all the General Requirements to apply for the position of U.S. Postal Inspector. The Postal Inspection Service is currently seeking individuals who meet the General Requirements, as well as at least one of the Special Requirements, listed below. Applications that do not contain one of the Special Requirements will be kept on file for two years and then purged. If an applicant's skills change during the two-year period, the applicant should contact the Postal Inspection Service.

General Requirements

Applicants must meet the requirements below and undergo a full medical suitability exam to determine fitness to perform the duties of a Postal Inspector, including, but not limited to, the following:

- A conferred-four-year degree from an accredited college or university.
- Binocular vision must test 20/40 (Snellen) without corrective lens. Unconnected vision must test at least 20/100 in each eye. Each eye must be corrected to 20/20, with good color identification and discrimination, depth perception, and normal peripheral vision. Radial keratotomy or orthokeratology are not acceptable.
- Hearing loss, as measured by an audiometer, must not exceed 30 decibels (A.S.A. or equivalent I.S.O.) in either ear in the 500, 1,000, and 2,000 Hz ranges. The applicant must have the ability to perceive normal speech discrimination.
- In good physical condition (weight proportional to height) and possessing emotional and mental stability. Manual dexterity with comparatively free motion of fingers, wrists, elbows, shoulders, hips, and knee joints. Arms, hands, legs, and feet must be sufficiently intact and functioning in order to perform duties satisfactorily.
- No felony convictions (felony charges may also render applicant ineligible.)
- No misdemeanor conviction of domestic violence (other misdemeanor charges or convictions may also render applicant ineligible).
- A current, valid state driver's license, held for at least two years.
- Ability to demonstrate these attributes, as measured by the Assessment Center:

  - Write and speak English clearly.

  - Schedule and complete activities in a logical, timely sequence.
  - Comprehend and execute instructions written and spoken in English.
  - Think clearly and comprehend verbal and nonverbal information.
  - Interact with others to obtain or exchange information or services.
  - Perceive or identify relevant details and associate them with other facts.

Special Requirements

Language Skills

Applicants seeking to enter the recruitment process under the language skills track must have advanced competency in a foreign language deemed as needed by the Postal Inspection Service to meet its investigative mission. The current list is as follows:

Arabic
Czech
French Creole

Hebrew
Italian
Mandarin
Punjabi
Spanish
Thai
Vietnamese
Armenian
Dutch
German
Hindi
Japanese
Norwegian
Russian
Swahili
Turkish
Cambodian
Egyptian
Greek (Modern)
Hmong
Korean
Polish
Serbo-Croatian
Swedish
Ukranian
Cantonese
Farsi (Persian)
Haitian
Indonesian
Lao
Portuguese
Slovak
Tagalog
Urdu

Applicants must pass a formal proficiency test administered by a contractor of the Postal Inspection Service. In addition to the language requirement, applicants in this track must have one year of full-time work experience with the same company or firm within two years of the date of their application.

Specialized Postal Experience

Applicants entering through the specialized postal experience track must be currently employed by the U.S. Postal Service and have at least one year of full-time work experience in one of the postal functional areas designated as critical to the needs of the Postal Inspection Service. Currently, critical needs exist in the following areas:

■ Business Mail Entry
■ Computer Analysis

- EEO Investigation
- Finance/Budget/Revenue Assurance
- Industrial Engineering
- Information/Computer/LAN Systems
- In-Plant Support
- Labor Relations/Workplace Intervention
- Media Relations
- Operations Support
- Safety/Health/Security/Injury Compensation

In addition, Postal Service supervisors in any functional area (including acting supervisors) with at least one year of supervisory experience will also be eligible under this entry track. A letter from he applicant's immediate supervisor must verify that the applicant has been a supervisor for at least one year. Also, Postal Inspection Service employees and/or contract employees with one year of full-time work experience with the Postal Inspection Service would qualify under this skill track.

Specialized Nonpostal Experience

Applicants seeking consideration under the specialized nonpostal skill track must have experience in one of the areas of expertise designated as critical to the needs of the Postal Inspection Service. The areas are as follows:

Law Degree. Candidates must have a Juris Doctorate degree and one year of full-time work experience with the same company or firm within two years of the date of their application.

Certification in auditing or investigations. Candidates with certifications in accounting, such as Certified Public Accountant (CPA), Certified Management Accountant (CMA), Certified Internal Auditor (CIA), and Certified Information Systems examination, such as Certified Protection Professional (CPP) and Certified Fraud Examiner (CFE), are accepted under this skills track. Applicants in this track must have a one year of full-time work experience with the same company or firm within two years of the date of their application. Applicants must also provide proof of certification.

Specialized computer education. Candidates with a four-year degree in one of the following fields: computer science, computer engineering, telecommunications, management information systems, electronic commerce, decision and information science, or computer information systems. Applicants in this track must have one year of full-time work experience with the same company or firm within two years of the date of their application.

Specialized computer expertise. Candidates who are currently employed (and have been employed for at least one year) in a position(s) specialized in one of the following computer forensics, internet investigations, internet security, network security, or information systems security. Applicants in this track must have one year of full-time work experience with the same company or firm within two years of the date of their application.

Certification in computer systems. Candidates with one of the following certifications and one year of work experience with the same firm within two years of the date of their application: Microsoft Certified Systems Engineer (MCSE), Microsoft Certified Professional +_ Internet (MCP+I), Cisco Certified Network Professional (CCNP), Certified Novell Engineer (CNE), A+ Certified Computer Technician, Certified Information Systems Security Professional (CISSP), Linux certification, or Sun Systems Certified Administrator.

Law enforcement. Candidates with at least one year of full-time work experience, within the last two years, in the law enforcement field. This includes detectives, criminalists, and polygraph examiners, and patrol, probation, correction, and parole officers. This track excludes clerical or other technical support personnel. Applicants must provide examples of the type of work conducted.

Diversified Experience

To increase competitiveness and acquire a more diversified candidate pool, applicants may enter the recruitment process along a fourth track, which combines higher education and work experience, including:

■ Bachelor's degree (B.A. or B.S. in any field) plus two years of full-time work experience.

■ Advanced degree (M.A., or Ph.D. in any field) plus one year of full-time work experience.

Applicants entering the recruitment process under the diversified experience entry track must have completed at least one year of full-time work experience with the same company or firm within two years of the date of their application. This includes U.S. Postal Service employees who have a four-year degree and meet the required minimum work experience.

Excerpted from the U.S. Postal Inspection Service Website:
http://usps.com/postalinspectors/employmt.htm

For information on other postal jobs, go to:
tp://usps.com/employment/welcome.htm?from=global&page=employment

How to Score 95-100% on the Scheme Test

40

A newly hired distribution clerk who is in training with full hourly pay is required to pass the *scheme* test. If he or she cannot pass this test within a certain period of time, he cannot qualify for the position of distribution clerk or scheme LSM operator. He can be a letter carrier or mail handler, though. In order to pass this test, he needs to score 95% or higher.

As I mentioned earlier, every post office has its own schemes, based on its zip codes. For example, Mt. Clemens (MI) has four zip codes: 48043, 48044, 48045, and 48046. The *scheme* is based on the numbers of streets and street names. For zip code 48043, for example, you must study and memorize street names and their numbers typed on more than 600 cards (at the time this book was written). You must know this scheme by heart, because when you sort letters, you must know to what box or route they should go. There are about fifty letter-carrier routes in the 48043 zip code area.

As I mentioned in previous instructions, you should associate names of streets and numbers with well-known personalities, places, things, or events.

To see how a scheme can be prepared for memorization, let's take a look at the Mt. Clemens and Warren (Michigan) Post Office schemes. Like the weather, schemes change. When the following "stories" were written, the schemes were up to date, but I cannot guarantee that they will still be up to date by the time you read this book. However, the technique for memorizing streets and numbers remains the same; once you know the system, you'll know how to memorize them easily and score 95 to 100% on scheme exams.

Mt. Clemens Scheme
(Zip codes 48043, 48044-45, 48046)

According to this city's scheme (48043), La Belle Street is route 42, so you must think of a name similar to La Belle and 42. You can choose an event. Example: Belle Island (Detroit) was established in 42 (1942). It's not true, but imagine Belle Island and you cannot forget this number. This is easy because you need only remember the name of the street (La Belle). All letters addressed to this street go to route 42 (box 42 on the case for zip code 48043).

You'll encounter difficulties, though, when there are so-called "breaks" in a street.

Examples:	Route
Euclid Ave. 1 - 99	-28 (4328)

All letters for Euclid Ave. from 1 to 99 go to box no. 28 or route 28. Only one letter carrier takes charge of this route.

Euclid Ave. 100 - 199	-10
Euclid Ave. 200 - out (all numbers over 200)	-09

If I were to remember these routes, 28, 10, and 09, this is how I would do it:

Euclid Ave. 1-99 (I'm going to *Euclid Ave.* at the corner of *28th* St. and Pontiac via I-*99*, not I-94.)   -28

Euclid Ave. 100 - 199 (Before I go there, I'll call *10-01-99* at *10* a.m.)   -10

Euclid Ave. 200 - out (The crowd at *Euclid* is composed of *200* people, questioned by agent *09*, Dirty Harry.)   -09

As you can see, I created a story about Euclid Avenue and its numbers. You cannot forget numbers when you associate them with names and things that you visualize.

Here are some other examples:

	Route No.
Coleman 19000 - 19699	-38
Coleman 19700 - out (all numbers over 19700)	-27

Here's my memory code:

Coleman 19000 - 19699   (Mayor *Coleman* Young of Detroit got elected at age *38.*)   -38

Coleman 19700 - out   (Mayor Young got married at age *27.*)   -27

Roslyn (11 numbers)   *Rosalyn* was courted at the age of *16* by Jimmy Who).   -16

Warren (Michigan) Scheme
(Zip codes 48089, 48090, 48091, 48092, 48093)

Warner St.
20700 - 21699 - 34   All numbers between 20700 - 21700 go to route 34.

It's easy to remember Warner if you think of actor Robert Wagner or Warner Brothers or something else. It's up to you.

Now, let's take this example:

20700 - 21699 - (Route 34)

Robert Wagner was earning *$20,700* per picture at age *34*.   -34

21700 - 22999 - 01

He was receiving *$21,700* per picture when he got married to only *01* woman, Natalie Wood.   *-01*

23000 - 23499 - 10

Then, he was receiving *$23,000* per picture. They remained married for *10* years.   *-10*

23500 - 23999 - 02

When Wagner was earning *$23,500* per picture, Natalie Wood had *02* daughters.   *-02*

24000 - 25999 - 21

When Wagner was receiving *$24,000* per picture, he fell in love with a *21*-year-old girl, and he and Natalie got divorced.   *-21*

26000 - 26999 - 31

When Wagner was receiving *$26,000* to *$26,999* per picture, he and Natalie got married again. Natalie was *31*.   *-31*

And so on.

When you have written stories such as those mentioned, you can record them on cassette tapes and listen to them when you are driving, when you are watching a football game on TV (with one earphone plugged into one of your ears and the other ear is listening to the game), and before you sleep.

With a guide like this one, you can easily score 95 to 100% on scheme tests. You can create your own stories. But don't worry yet. You will take this test only when you are already in training to be a distribution clerk. First, score in the 90s on exams and get employed. That's the key to postal employment, as St. Peter is the key to Heaven.

I'm confident you can make it because I've shown you the way.

Step-by-step Instructions

Supplement A

National Directory of U.S. Postal Service Examination Centers

Copyright 2008 by Veltisezar B. Bautista. The following testing centers are main offices generally known as District Offices, General Mail facilities (GMF), Sectional Center Facilities (SCF), and Management Sectional Centers (MSC). Needless to say, this directory is very valuable for finding a Post Office Job. If you want a postal job, call all the testing centers in your state, especially those in your area, at least once a week to find out if there are any examinations coming up. If you are thinking of moving to another state, call the testing centers in that state at least once a week. Always reach out and touch someone! If there are openings in another city, fly there and apply for examinations. Go where the action is! Here are the addresses and telephone numbers of the USPS testing centers.

ALABAMA

U.S. Postal Service
351 24th Street N
Birmingham, AL 35203-9998
(205) 521-0251
Job Hotline
(205) 521-0214

ALASKA

U.S. Postal Service
4141 Postmark Drive
Anchorage, AK 99599-9998
(Job Hotline
(907) 564-2962

ARIZONA

U.S. Postal Service
1441 East Buckeye Road
Phoenix, AZ 85026-9998
(602) 223-3631
Job Hotline
(602) 223-3624

ARKANSAS

U.S. Postal Service
4700 E McCain Boulevard
Little Rock, AR 72231-9998
(501) 945-6665

CALIFORNIA

U.S. Postal Service
300 Long Beach Boulevard
Long Beach, CA 90809-9998
(562) 983-3072
Job Hotline
(562) 435-4529

U.S. Postal Service
7001 S Central Avenue
Los Angeles, CA 90052-9998
(323) 586-1340
Job Hotline
(323) 586-1351

U.S. Postal Service
1675 7th Street
Oakland, CA 94615-9998
(510) 874-8344
Job Hotline
(510) 251-3040

U.S. Postal Service
11251 Rancho Carmel Drive
San Diego, CA 92199-9998
(619) 674-0430
Job Hotline
(619) 674-0577
(619) 674-2690

U.S. Postal Service
1300 Evans Avenue
San Francisco, CA 94188-9998
Job Hotline
(415) 550-5534

U.S. Postal Service
1750 Lunday Avenue
San Jose, CA 95101-0086
(408) 437-6925

Job Hotline
(408) 437-6986

U.S. Postal Service
3101 W Sunflower Avenue
Santa Ana, CA 92799-9998
Job Hotline
(714) 662-6375
U.S. Postal Service
28201 Franklin Parkway
Santa Clarita, CA 91383-9461
(661) 775-7040
Job Hotline
(661) 294-7680

U.S. Postal Service
3775 Industrial Boulevard
West Sacramento, CA 95799-0062
(916) 373-8686
Job Hotline
(916) 373-8448

COLORADO

U.S. Postal Service
7500 E 53rd Place Rm 2204
Denver, CO 80266-2204
(303) 853-6132
Job Hotline
(303) 853-6060

CONNECTICUT

U.S. Postal Service
141 Weston Street
Hartford, CT 06101-9998
(860) 524-6110

FLORIDA

U.S. Postal Service
1100 Kings Road
Jacksonville, FL 32203-9998
(904) 359-2921
Job Hotline
(904) 359-2737

U.S. Postal Service
800 Rinehart Road
Lake Mary, FL 32799-9421
(407) 444-2012
Job Hotline
1-888-771-9056
(407) 444-2029

U.S. Postal Service
2200 NW 72nd Avenue
Pembroke Pines, FL 33082-9990
(305) 470-0705
Job Hotline
(305) 470-0412
1-888-725-7295

U.S. Postal Service
5201 W Spruce Street
Tampa, FL 33630-9998
(813) 877-0318
Job Hotline
(813) 877-0381

GEORGIA

U.S. Postal Service
3900 Crown Road Rm. 272
Atlanta, GA 30304-9998
(404) 765-7200

U.S. Postal Service
451 College Street, -9998
(912) 752-8467
Job Hotline
(912) 752-8465

HAWAII

U.S. Postal Service
3600 Aolele Street
Honolulu, HI 96820-9998
Job Hotline
(808) 423-3690

ILLINOIS

U.S. Postal Service
6801 W 73rd Street
Bedford Park, IL 60499-9998
(708) 563-7493

U.S. Postal Service
500 E Fullerton Avenue
Carol Stream, IL 60099-9998
(630) 260-5153
Job Hotline
(630) 260-5200

U.S. Postal Service
433 W Harrison
Chicago, IL 60607-3905
(312) 983-8542

INDIANA

U.S. Postal Service
3939 Bincennes Rd
Indianapolis, IN 46298-9998
(317) 870-8551
Job Hotline

(317) 870-8500

IOWA

U.S. Postal Service
1165 2nd Avenue
Des Moines, IA 50318-7900
(515) 251-2201
Job Hotline
(515) 251-2061

KENTUCKY

U.S. Postal Service
1420 Gardiner Lane, Rm 320
Louisville, KY 40231-9998
(502) 454-1817
Job Hotline
(502) 454-1625

LOUISIANA

U.S. Postal Service
701 Loyola Avenue Rm. T2009
New Orleans, LA 70113-9998
(504) 589-1171
Job Hotline
(504) 589-1660

MAINE

380 Riverside Street
Portland, ME 041013-9998
Job Hotline
(207) 828-8520

MARYLAND

U.S. Postal Service
900 E Fayette Street
Baltimore, MD 21233-9998

(410) 347-4278
Job Hotline
(410) 347-4320

MASACHUSSETTE

U.S. Postal Service
25 Dorchester Avenue
Boston, MA 02205-9998
(617) 654-5500
Job Hotline
 (617) 654-5569

U.S. Postal Service
74 Main Street
North Reading, MA 01889
(978) 664-7079
Job Hotline
(978) 664-7665

U.S. Postal Service
1883 Main St
Springfield, MA 01101
(413) 785-6263
Job Hotline
(413) 731-0425

MICHIGAN

U.S. Postal Service
1401 W Fort Street, Rm 201
Detroit, MI 48233-9998
(313) 226-8259
(313) 226-8490
Job Hotline
1-888-442-5361

U.S. Postal Service
222 Michigan Street, NW
Grand Rapids, MI 49599-9998

(616) 776-1426
Job Hotline
(616) 776-1835

U.S. Postal Service
200 West 2nd Street
Royal Oak, MI 48068-9998
(810) 546-7106
Job Hotline
(810) 546-7104

MINNESOTA

U.S. Postal Service
180 E Kellog Boulevard
St Paul, MN 55101-9997
(651) 293-3036
Job Hotline
(651) 293-3364

U.S. Postal Service
315 W Pershing Road, Rm 572
Kansas City, MO 64108-9998
(816) 374-9310
Job Hotline
(816) 374-9346

MISSOURI

U.S. Postal Service
1720 Market Street, Rm 3027
St Louis, MO 63155-9998
(314) 436-3852
Job Hotline
(314) 436-3855

MISSISSIPPI

U.S. Postal Service
401 E South Street
Jackson, MS 39201-9998

(601) 351-7270
Job Hotline
(601) 351-7099

MONTANA

U.S. Postal Service
841 S 26th Street
Billings, MT 59101-9998
(406) 255-6427
Job Hotline
(406) 657-5763

NEBRASKA

U.S. Postal Service
1124 Pacific Street, Rm 325
Omaha NE 68108-0421
(402) 348-2506
Job Hotline
(402) 348-2523

NEW HAMPSHIRE

U.S. Postal Service
955 Goffs Falls Road
Manchester, NH 03103-9998
Job Hotline
(603) 644-4065

NEW JERSEY

U.S. Postal Service
501 Benigno Boulevard
Bellmawr, NJ 08099-9998
Job Hotline
(609) 933-4314

U.S. Postal Service
21 Kilmer Road

Edison, NJ 08901-9998
(732) 819-3272

U.S. Postal Service
2 Federal Square
Newark, NJ 07102-9998
(973) 693-5200

NEW MEXICO

U.S. Postal Service
1135 Broadway Boulevard, NE, Rm 230
Albuquerque, NM 87101-9998
(505) 245-9518
Job Hotline
(505) 245-9517

NEVADA

U.S. Postal Service
1001 E Sunset Road
Las Vegas, NV 89199-9998
(702) 361-9375
Job Hotline
(702) 361-9564

NEW YORK

U.S. Postal Service
30 Old Karmer Road
Albany, NY 12288-9998
Job Hotline
(518) 452-2445

U.S. Postal Service
1200 William Street
Buffalo, NY 14240-9998
(716) 846-2470
Job Hotline
(716) 846-2478

U.S. Postal Service
142-02 20th Avenue
Flushing, NY 11351-9998
(718) 321-5170
Job Hotline
(718) 529-7000

U.S. Postal Service
1377 Motor Parkway
Hauppauge, NY 11760-9998
(516) 582-7416
Job Hotline
(516) 582-7530

U.S. Postal Service
421 8th Avenue, Rm 3018
New York, NY 10199-9998
(212) 330-3600
(212) 330-2907

U.S. Postal Service
1000 Westchester Avenue
White Plains, NY 10610-9800
(914) 697-7190
(914) 967-8585

NORTH CAROLINA

U.S. Postal Service
2901 S Interstate 85 Service Road
Charlotte, NC 28228-9962
(704) 393-4495
Job Hotline
(704) 393-4490

U.S. Postal Service
900 Market Street, Rm 232
Greensboro, NC 27498-0001
(336) 669-1214
Job Hotline

(336) 271-5573

NORTH DAKOTA

(Same as South Dakota)

OHIO

U.S. Postal Service
675 Wolfledges Parkway
Akron, OH 44309-9998
(330) 996-9501
Job Hotline
(330) 996-9530

U.S. Postal Service
1591 Dalton Avenue, 2nd Floor
Cincinnati, OH 45234-9998
(513) 684-5451
(513) 684-5449

U.S. Postal Service
2200 Orange Avenue
Cleveland, OH 44104-9998
(216) 443-4339

U.S. Postal Service
850 Twin Rivers Drive
Columbus, OH 43216-9998
(614) 469-4357
Job Hotline
(614) 469-4356

OKLAHOMA

U.S. Postal Service
3030 NW Expressway Street, Ste 1042
Oklahoma City, OK 73198-9420
(405) 553-6172

OREGON
U.S. Postal Service
715 NW Hoyt Street
Portland, OR 97208-9999
(503) 294-2277
1-800-275-8777
Job Hotline
(503) 294-2270

PENNSYLVANIA

U.S. Postal Service
2108 E 38th Street
Erie, PA 16515-9998
(814) 898-7031
Job Hotline
(814) 899-0354

U.S. Postal Service
1425 Crooked Hill Road
Harrisburg, PA 17107-9998
(717) 257-2250
Job Hotline
(717) 390-7400

U.S. Postal Service
1400 Harrisburg Pike
Lancaster, PA 17602-9998
(717) 390-7460
Job Hotline
(717) 390-7400

U.S. Postal Service
2970 Market Street
Philadelphia, PA 19104-9422
Job Hotline
(800) 276-5627

U.S. Postal Service
1001 California Avenue
Pittsburgh, PA 15290-9998
(412) 359-7688
Job Hotline
(412) 359-7516

PUERTO RICO

U.S. Postal Service
P O. Box 363367
San Juan, PR 00936-9998
787-767-3351

RHODE ISLAND

U.S. Postal Service
24 Corliss Street
Providence, RI 02904
(401) 276-6845
Job Hotline
(401) 276-6844

SOUTH CAROLINA

U.S. Postal Service
P O. Box 29292
Columbia, SC 29292
(803) 926-6437
Job Hotline
(803) 926-6400

SOUTH DAKOTA

320 S Second Avenue
Sioux Falls, SD 57104-7554
(605) 357-5032

TENNESSEE

U.S. Postal Service
525 Royal Parkway, Rm 207
Nashville, TN 37229-9998
(615) 885-9962
Job Hotline
(615) 885-9190

TEXAS

U.S. Postal Service
951 W Bethel Road
Chappell, TX 75099-9998
Job Hotline
(214) 760-4531

U.S. Postal Service
4600 Mark IV Parkway
Fort Worth, TX 7616-9998
(817) 317-3350
Job Hotline
(817) 317-3366

U.S. Postal Service
1002 Washington Avenue
Houston, TX 77201 -9701
Job Hotline
(713) 226-3872

U.S. Postal Service
10410 Perin Beitel Road
San Antonio, TX 78284-9998
Job Hotline
(210) 368-8400

UTAII
U.S. Postal Service
1760 West 2100, S
Salt Lake City, UT 84199-9998
(801) 974-2210
Job Hotline
(801) 974-2209

VIRGINIA

U.S. Postal Service
8409 Lee Highway
Merrifield, VA 22081-9998
(703) 698-6438
Job Hotline
(703) 698-6561

U.S. Postal Service
1801 Brook Road
Richmond, VA 23232-9998
(804) 775-6196

WASHINGTON

U.S. Postal Service
415 1st Avenue N
Seattle, WA 98109-9998
(206) 442-6236
Job Hotline
(206) 442-6240

U.S. Postal Service
707 W Main Avenue
Spokane, WA 99202-9998
(509) 626-6824
Job Hotline
(509) 626-6896

WASHINGTON, DC

U.S. Postal Service
3300 V Street, NE
Washington, DC 20018-1527
Job Hotline
(202) 636-1537

WEST VIRGINIA

U.S. Postal Service
10002 Lee Street, E
Charleston, WV 25301-9998
Job Hotline
(304) 357-0648

WISCONSIN

U.S. Postal Service
245 W Saint Paul Avenue, 5th Floor
Milwaukee, WI 53203-9998
(414) 287-1834
Job Hotline
(414) 287-1835

APWU National Agreement
Schedule One — Salary and Rates
Effective March 19, 2005

Grade and Step		Full-time Regular Rates				CSRS			FERS		FERS — Thrift Savings Plan					
		Annual Salary	Biweekly Pay	Straight Time	Night Differential	7% CSRS	1.45% Medicare	Maximum 10% TSP	0.8% FERS	7.65% FICA	1% USPS Minimum	3% Employee	3% USPS	5% Employee	5% USPS	15% Employee Maximum
2	D	39,733	1,528.19	19.1024	1.37	106.97	22.16	152.82	12.23	116.91	15.28	45.85	61.13	76.41	76.41	229.23
	E	39,987	1,537.96	19.2245	1.38	107.66	22.30	153.80	12.30	117.65	15.38	46.14	61.52	76.90	76.90	230.69
	F	40,242	1,547.77	19.3471	1.39	108.34	22.44	154.78	12.38	118.40	15.48	46.43	61.91	77.39	77.39	232.17
	G	40,496	1,557.54	19.4692	1.40	109.03	22.58	155.75	12.46	119.15	15.58	46.73	62.30	77.88	77.88	233.63
	H	40,755	1,567.50	19.5938	1.41	109.73	22.73	156.75	12.54	119.91	15.68	47.03	62.70	78.38	78.38	235.13
3	D	40,349	1,551.89	19.3986	1.39	108.63	22.50	155.19	12.42	118.72	15.52	46.56	62.08	77.59	77.59	232.78
	E	40,624	1,562.46	19.5308	1.40	109.37	22.66	156.25	12.50	119.53	15.62	46.87	62.50	78.12	78.12	234.37
	F	40,903	1,573.19	19.6649	1.41	110.12	22.81	157.32	12.59	120.35	15.73	47.20	62.93	78.66	78.66	235.98
	G	41,175	1,583.66	19.7957	1.42	110.86	22.96	158.37	12.67	121.15	15.84	47.51	63.35	79.18	79.18	237.55
	H	41,451	1,594.27	19.9284	1.43	111.60	23.12	159.43	12.75	121.96	15.94	47.83	63.77	79.71	79.71	239.14
4	D	41,018	1,577.62	19.7202	1.42	110.43	22.88	157.76	12.62	120.69	15.78	47.33	63.10	78.88	78.88	236.64
	E	41,313	1,588.96	19.8620	1.43	111.23	23.04	158.90	12.71	121.56	15.89	47.67	63.56	79.45	79.45	238.34
	F	41,615	1,600.58	20.0072	1.44	112.04	23.21	160.06	12.80	122.44	16.01	48.02	64.02	80.03	80.03	240.09
	G	41,912	1,612.00	20.1500	1.45	112.84	23.37	161.20	12.90	123.32	16.12	48.36	64.48	80.60	80.60	241.80
	H	42,207	1,623.34	20.2918	1.46	113.63	23.54	162.33	12.99	124.19	16.23	48.70	64.93	81.17	81.17	243.50
5	D	41,742	1,605.46	20.0683	1.45	112.38	23.28	160.55	12.84	122.82	16.05	48.16	64.22	80.27	80.27	240.82
	E	42,062	1,617.77	20.2221	1.46	113.24	23.46	161.78	12.94	123.76	16.18	48.53	64.71	80.89	80.89	242.67
	F	42,383	1,630.11	20.3764	1.47	114.11	23.64	163.01	13.04	124.70	16.30	48.90	65.20	81.51	81.51	244.52
	G	42,700	1,642.30	20.5288	1.48	114.96	23.81	164.23	13.14	125.64	16.42	49.27	65.69	82.12	82.12	246.35
	H	43,023	1,654.73	20.6841	1.50	115.83	23.99	165.47	13.24	126.59	16.55	49.64	66.19	82.74	82.74	248.21
6	D	42,522	1,635.46	20.4433	1.48	114.48	23.71	163.55	13.08	125.11	16.35	49.06	65.42	81.77	81.77	245.32
	E	42,869	1,648.81	20.6101	1.49	115.42	23.91	164.88	13.19	126.13	16.49	49.46	65.95	82.44	82.44	247.32
	F	43,219	1,662.27	20.7784	1.50	116.36	24.10	166.23	13.30	127.16	16.62	49.87	66.49	83.11	83.11	249.34
	G	43,564	1,675.54	20.9442	1.52	117.29	24.30	167.55	13.40	128.18	16.76	50.27	67.02	83.78	83.78	251.33
	H	43,914	1,689.00	21.1125	1.53	118.23	24.49	168.90	13.51	129.21	16.89	50.67	67.56	84.45	84.45	253.35
7	D	43,367	1,667.96	20.8495	1.51	116.76	24.19	166.80	13.34	127.60	16.68	50.04	66.72	83.40	83.40	250.19
	E	43,742	1,682.38	21.0298	1.52	117.77	24.39	168.24	13.46	128.70	16.82	50.47	67.30	84.12	84.12	252.36
	F	44,116	1,696.77	21.2096	1.54	118.77	24.60	169.68	13.57	129.80	16.97	50.90	67.87	84.84	84.84	254.52
	G	44,491	1,711.19	21.3899	1.55	119.78	24.81	171.12	13.69	130.91	17.11	51.34	68.45	85.56	85.56	256.68
	H	44,867	1,725.66	21.5707	1.57	120.80	25.02	172.57	13.81	132.01	17.26	51.77	69.03	86.28	86.28	258.85

PART-TIME FLEXIBLE RATES	Grade	Pay Steps				
		D	E	F	G	H
	2	19.87	19.99	20.12	20.25	20.38
	3	20.17	20.31	20.45	20.59	20.73
	4	20.51	20.66	20.81	20.96	21.10
	5	20.87	21.03	21.19	21.35	21.51
	6	21.26	21.43	21.61	21.78	21.96
	7	21.68	21.87	22.06	22.25	22.43

APWU SALARY AND RATES
Schedule 1 and 2

PART-TIME REGULAR RATES	Grade	Pay Steps				
		D	E	F	G	H
	2	19.10	19.22	19.35	19.47	19.59
	3	19.40	19.53	19.66	19.80	19.93
	4	19.72	19.86	20.01	20.15	20.29
	5	20.07	20.22	20.38	20.53	20.68
	6	20.44	20.61	20.78	20.94	21.11
	7	20.85	21.03	21.21	21.39	21.57

AMERICAN POSTAL WORKERS UNION, AFL-CIO
1300 L STREET, NW, WASHINGTON, DC 20005

APWU National Agreement
Schedule Two — Salary and Rates

Effective March 19, 2005

Grade	Step	Full-time Regular Rates: Annual Salary	Biweekly Pay	Straight Time	Night Differential	BIWEEKLY DEDUCTIONS — CSRS: 7% CSRS	1.45% Medicare	Maximum 10% TSP	FERS: 0.80% FERS	7.65% FICA	FERS — THRIFT SAVINGS PLAN: 1% USPS Minimum	3% Employee	3% USPS	5% Employee	5% USPS	15% Employee Maximum
1	BB	26,079	1,003.04	12.5380	0.84	70.21	14.54	100.30	8.02	76.73	10.03	30.09	40.12	50.15	50.15	150.46
	AA	27,041	1,040.04	13.0005	0.88	72.80	15.08	104.00	8.32	79.56	10.40	31.20	41.60	52.00	52.00	156.01
	A	28,003	1,077.04	13.4630	0.92	75.39	15.62	107.70	8.62	82.39	10.77	32.31	43.08	53.85	53.85	161.56
	B	28,965	1,114.04	13.9255	0.95	77.98	16.15	111.40	8.91	85.22	11.14	33.42	44.56	55.70	55.70	167.11
	C	29,927	1,151.04	14.3880	0.99	80.57	16.69	115.10	9.21	88.05	11.51	34.53	46.04	57.55	57.55	172.66
	D	30,889	1,188.04	14.8505	1.03	83.16	17.23	118.80	9.50	90.89	11.88	35.64	47.52	59.40	59.40	178.21
	E	31,851	1,225.04	15.3130	1.07	85.75	17.76	122.50	9.80	93.72	12.25	36.75	49.00	61.25	61.25	183.76
	F	32,813	1,262.04	15.7755	1.11	88.34	18.30	126.20	10.10	96.55	12.62	37.86	50.48	63.10	63.10	189.31
	G	33,775	1,299.04	16.2380	1.15	90.93	18.84	129.90	10.39	99.38	12.99	38.97	51.96	64.95	64.95	194.86
	H	34,737	1,336.04	16.7005	1.18	93.52	19.37	133.60	10.69	102.21	13.36	40.08	53.44	66.80	66.80	200.41
	I	35,699	1,373.04	17.1630	1.22	96.11	19.91	137.30	10.98	105.04	13.73	41.19	54.92	68.65	68.65	205.96
	J	36,661	1,410.04	17.6255	1.26	98.70	20.45	141.00	11.28	107.87	14.10	42.30	56.40	70.50	70.50	211.51
	K	37,623	1,447.04	18.0880	1.30	101.29	20.98	144.70	11.58	110.70	14.47	43.41	57.88	72.35	72.35	217.06
	L	38,585	1,484.04	18.5505	1.34	103.88	21.52	148.40	11.87	113.53	14.84	44.52	59.36	74.20	74.20	222.61
	M	39,547	1,521.04	19.0130	1.37	106.47	22.06	152.10	12.17	116.36	15.21	45.63	60.84	76.05	76.05	228.16
	N	40,509	1,558.04	19.4755	1.41	109.06	22.59	155.80	12.46	119.19	15.58	46.74	62.32	77.90	77.90	233.71
	O	41,754	1,605.92	20.0740	1.45	112.41	23.29	160.59	12.85	122.85	16.06	48.18	64.24	80.30	80.30	240.89
	RC	42,716	1,642.92	20.5365	1.46	115.00	23.82	164.29	13.14	125.68	16.43	49.29	65.72	82.15	82.15	246.44
2	BB	27,191	1,045.81	13.0726	0.88	73.21	15.16	104.58	8.37	80.00	10.46	31.37	41.83	52.29	52.29	156.87
	AA	28,143	1,082.42	13.5303	0.92	75.77	15.70	108.24	8.66	82.81	10.82	32.47	43.30	54.12	54.12	162.36
	A	29,095	1,119.04	13.9880	0.95	78.33	16.23	111.90	8.95	85.61	11.19	33.57	44.76	55.95	55.95	167.86
	B	30,047	1,155.66	14.4457	0.99	80.90	16.76	115.57	9.25	88.41	11.56	34.67	46.23	57.78	57.78	173.35
	C	30,999	1,192.27	14.9034	1.03	83.46	17.29	119.23	9.54	91.21	11.92	35.77	47.69	59.61	59.61	178.84
	D	31,951	1,228.89	15.3611	1.07	86.02	17.82	122.89	9.83	94.01	12.29	36.87	49.16	61.44	61.44	184.33
	E	32,903	1,265.50	15.8188	1.11	88.59	18.35	126.55	10.12	96.81	12.66	37.97	50.62	63.28	63.28	189.83
	F	33,855	1,302.11	16.2764	1.14	91.15	18.88	130.21	10.42	99.61	13.02	39.06	52.08	65.11	65.11	195.32
	G	34,807	1,338.73	16.7341	1.18	93.71	19.41	133.87	10.71	102.41	13.39	40.16	53.55	66.94	66.94	200.81
	H	35,759	1,375.34	17.1918	1.22	96.27	19.94	137.53	11.00	105.21	13.75	41.26	55.01	68.77	68.77	206.30
	I	36,711	1,411.96	17.6495	1.26	98.84	20.47	141.20	11.30	108.01	14.12	42.36	56.48	70.60	70.60	211.79
	J	37,663	1,448.58	18.1072	1.29	101.40	21.00	144.86	11.59	110.82	14.49	43.46	57.94	72.43	72.43	217.29
	K	38,615	1,485.19	18.5649	1.33	103.96	21.54	148.52	11.88	113.62	14.85	44.56	59.41	74.26	74.26	222.78
	L	39,567	1,521.81	19.0226	1.37	106.53	22.07	152.18	12.17	116.42	15.22	45.65	60.87	76.09	76.09	228.27
	M	40,519	1,558.42	19.4803	1.41	109.09	22.60	155.84	12.47	119.22	15.58	46.75	62.34	77.92	77.92	233.76
	N	41,471	1,595.04	19.9380	1.44	111.65	23.13	159.50	12.76	122.02	15.95	47.85	63.80	79.75	79.75	239.26
	O	42,538	1,636.08	20.4510	1.48	114.53	23.72	163.61	13.09	125.16	16.36	49.08	65.44	81.80	81.80	245.41
	RC	43,490	1,672.70	20.9087	1.49	117.09	24.25	167.27	13.38	127.96	16.73	50.18	66.91	83.63	83.63	250.90
3	BB	28,297	1,088.34	13.6043	0.93	76.18	15.78	108.83	8.71	83.26	10.88	32.65	43.53	54.42	54.42	163.25
	AA	29,240	1,124.62	14.0577	0.97	78.72	16.31	112.46	9.00	86.03	11.25	33.74	44.98	56.23	56.23	168.69
	A	30,183	1,160.89	14.5111	1.00	81.26	16.83	116.09	9.29	88.81	11.61	34.83	46.44	58.04	58.04	174.13
	B	31,126	1,197.15	14.9644	1.04	83.80	17.36	119.72	9.58	91.58	11.97	35.91	47.89	59.86	59.86	179.57
	C	32,069	1,233.42	15.4178	1.08	86.34	17.88	123.34	9.87	94.36	12.33	37.00	49.34	61.67	61.67	185.01
	D	33,012	1,269.70	15.8712	1.11	88.88	18.41	126.97	10.16	97.13	12.70	38.09	50.79	63.48	63.48	190.45
	E	33,955	1,305.96	16.3245	1.15	91.42	18.94	130.60	10.45	99.91	13.06	39.18	52.24	65.30	65.30	195.89
	F	34,898	1,342.23	16.7779	1.18	93.96	19.46	134.22	10.74	102.68	13.42	40.27	53.69	67.11	67.11	201.33
	G	35,841	1,378.50	17.2313	1.22	96.50	19.99	137.85	11.03	105.46	13.79	41.36	55.14	68.93	68.93	206.78
	H	36,784	1,414.77	17.6846	1.26	99.03	20.51	141.48	11.32	108.23	14.15	42.44	56.59	70.74	70.74	212.22
	I	37,727	1,451.04	18.1380	1.29	101.57	21.04	145.10	11.61	111.00	14.51	43.53	58.04	72.55	72.55	217.66
	J	38,670	1,487.30	18.5913	1.33	104.11	21.57	148.73	11.90	113.78	14.87	44.62	59.49	74.37	74.37	223.10
	K	39,613	1,523.58	19.0447	1.37	106.65	22.09	152.36	12.19	116.55	15.24	45.71	60.94	76.18	76.18	228.54
	L	40,556	1,559.85	19.4981	1.40	109.19	22.62	155.98	12.48	119.33	15.60	46.80	62.39	77.99	77.99	233.98
	M	41,499	1,596.11	19.9514	1.44	111.73	23.14	159.61	12.77	122.10	15.96	47.88	63.84	79.81	79.81	239.42
	N	42,442	1,632.38	20.4048	1.47	114.27	23.67	163.24	13.06	124.88	16.32	48.97	65.30	81.62	81.62	244.86
	O	43,385	1,668.66	20.8582	1.51	116.81	24.20	166.87	13.35	127.65	16.69	50.06	66.75	83.43	83.43	250.30
	RC	44,328	1,704.92	21.3115	1.52	119.34	24.72	170.49	13.64	130.43	17.05	51.15	68.20	85.25	85.25	255.74
4	A	31,871	1,225.81	15.3226	1.06	85.81	17.77	122.58	9.81	93.77	12.26	36.77	49.03	61.29	61.29	183.87
	B	32,758	1,259.92	15.7490	1.10	88.19	18.27	125.99	10.08	96.38	12.60	37.80	50.40	63.00	63.00	188.99
	C	33,645	1,294.04	16.1755	1.13	90.58	18.76	129.40	10.35	98.99	12.94	38.82	51.76	64.70	64.70	194.11
	D	34,532	1,328.15	16.6019	1.17	92.97	19.26	132.82	10.63	101.60	13.28	39.84	53.13	66.41	66.41	199.22
	E	35,419	1,362.27	17.0284	1.20	95.36	19.75	136.23	10.90	104.21	13.62	40.87	54.49	68.11	68.11	204.34
	F	36,306	1,396.38	17.4548	1.24	97.75	20.25	139.64	11.17	106.82	13.96	41.89	55.86	69.82	69.82	209.46
	G	37,193	1,430.50	17.8813	1.27	100.14	20.74	143.05	11.44	109.43	14.31	42.92	57.22	71.53	71.53	214.58
	H	38,080	1,464.62	18.3077	1.31	102.52	21.24	146.46	11.72	112.04	14.65	43.94	58.58	73.23	73.23	219.69
	I	38,967	1,498.73	18.7341	1.34	104.91	21.73	149.87	11.99	114.65	14.99	44.96	59.95	74.94	74.94	224.81
	J	39,854	1,532.85	19.1606	1.38	107.30	22.23	153.28	12.26	117.26	15.33	45.99	61.31	76.64	76.64	229.93
	K	40,741	1,566.96	19.5870	1.41	109.69	22.72	156.70	12.54	119.87	15.67	47.01	62.68	78.35	78.35	235.04
	L	41,628	1,601.08	20.0135	1.45	112.08	23.22	160.11	12.81	122.48	16.01	48.03	64.04	80.05	80.05	240.16
	M	42,515	1,635.19	20.4399	1.48	114.46	23.71	163.52	13.08	125.09	16.35	49.06	65.41	81.76	81.76	245.28
	N	43,402	1,669.30	20.8663	1.52	116.85	24.20	166.93	13.35	127.70	16.69	50.08	66.77	83.47	83.47	250.40
	O	44,289	1,703.42	21.2928	1.55	119.24	24.70	170.34	13.63	130.31	17.03	51.10	68.14	85.17	85.17	255.51
	RC	45,176	1,737.54	21.7192	1.56	121.63	25.19	173.75	13.90	132.92	17.38	52.13	69.50	86.88	86.88	260.63
5	A	33,509	1,288.81	16.1101	1.12	90.22	18.69	128.88	10.31	98.59	12.89	38.66	51.55	64.44	64.44	193.32
	B	34,349	1,321.11	16.5139	1.15	92.48	19.16	132.11	10.57	101.07	13.21	39.63	52.84	66.06	66.06	198.17
	C	35,189	1,353.42	16.9178	1.19	94.74	19.62	135.34	10.83	103.54	13.53	40.60	54.14	67.67	67.67	203.01
	D	36,029	1,385.73	17.3216	1.22	97.00	20.09	138.57	11.09	106.01	13.86	41.57	55.43	69.29	69.29	207.86
	E	36,869	1,418.04	17.7255	1.25	99.26	20.56	141.80	11.34	108.48	14.18	42.54	56.72	70.90	70.90	212.71
	F	37,709	1,450.34	18.1293	1.28	101.52	21.03	145.03	11.60	110.95	14.50	43.51	58.01	72.52	72.52	217.55
	G	38,549	1,482.66	18.5332	1.32	103.79	21.50	148.27	11.86	113.42	14.83	44.48	59.31	74.13	74.13	222.40
	H	39,389	1,514.96	18.9370	1.35	106.05	21.97	151.50	12.12	115.89	15.15	45.45	60.60	75.75	75.75	227.24
	I	40,229	1,547.27	19.3409	1.38	108.31	22.44	154.73	12.38	118.37	15.47	46.42	61.89	77.36	77.36	232.09
	J	41,069	1,579.58	19.7447	1.42	110.57	22.90	157.96	12.64	120.84	15.80	47.39	63.18	78.98	78.98	236.94
	K	41,909	1,611.89	20.1486	1.45	112.83	23.37	161.19	12.90	123.31	16.12	48.36	64.48	80.59	80.59	241.78
	L	42,749	1,644.19	20.5524	1.48	115.09	23.84	164.42	13.15	125.78	16.44	49.33	65.77	82.21	82.21	246.63
	M	43,589	1,676.50	20.9563	1.51	117.36	24.31	167.65	13.41	128.25	16.77	50.30	67.06	83.83	83.83	251.48
	N	44,429	1,708.81	21.3601	1.55	119.62	24.78	170.88	13.67	130.72	17.09	51.26	68.35	85.44	85.44	256.32
	O	45,269	1,741.11	21.7639	1.58	121.88	25.25	174.11	13.93	133.20	17.41	52.23	69.64	87.06	87.06	261.17
	RC	46,109	1,773.42	22.1678	1.60	124.14	25.71	177.34	14.19	135.67	17.73	53.20	70.94	88.67	88.67	266.01

APWU National Agreement
Schedule Two — Salary and Rates
Effective March 19, 2005

Grade and Step	Full-time Regular Rates				CSRS			FERS		FERS — THRIFT SAVINGS PLAN					
	Annual Salary	Biweekly Pay	Straight Time	Night Differential	7% CSRS	1.45% Medicare	Maximum 10% TSP	0.80% FERS	7.65% FICA	1% USPS Minimum	3% Employee	3% USPS	5% Employee	5% USPS	15% Employee Maximum
6 A	35,252	1,355.85	16.9481	1.19	94.91	19.66	135.58	10.85	103.72	13.56	40.68	54.23	67.79	67.79	203.38
B	36,044	1,386.30	17.3288	1.22	97.04	20.10	138.63	11.09	106.05	13.86	41.59	55.45	69.32	69.32	207.95
C	36,836	1,416.77	17.7096	1.25	99.17	20.54	141.68	11.33	108.38	14.17	42.50	56.67	70.84	70.84	212.52
D	37,628	1,447.23	18.0904	1.28	101.31	20.98	144.72	11.58	110.71	14.47	43.42	57.89	72.36	72.36	217.08
E	38,420	1,477.70	18.4712	1.32	103.44	21.43	147.77	11.82	113.04	14.78	44.33	59.11	73.88	73.88	221.65
F	39,212	1,508.15	18.8519	1.35	105.57	21.87	150.82	12.07	115.37	15.08	45.24	60.33	75.41	75.41	226.22
G	40,004	1,538.62	19.2327	1.38	107.70	22.31	153.86	12.31	117.70	15.39	46.16	61.54	76.93	76.93	230.79
H	40,796	1,569.08	19.6135	1.41	109.84	22.75	156.91	12.55	120.03	15.69	47.07	62.76	78.45	78.45	235.36
I	41,588	1,599.54	19.9942	1.44	111.97	23.19	159.95	12.80	122.36	16.00	47.99	63.98	79.98	79.98	239.93
J	42,380	1,630.00	20.3750	1.47	114.10	23.64	163.00	13.04	124.70	16.30	48.90	65.20	81.50	81.50	244.50
K	43,172	1,660.46	20.7558	1.50	116.23	24.08	166.05	13.28	127.03	16.60	49.81	66.42	83.02	83.02	249.07
L	43,964	1,690.92	21.1365	1.54	118.36	24.52	169.09	13.53	129.36	16.91	50.73	67.64	84.55	84.55	253.64
M	44,756	1,721.38	21.5173	1.57	120.50	24.96	172.14	13.77	131.69	17.21	51.64	68.86	86.07	86.07	258.21
N	45,548	1,751.85	21.8981	1.60	122.63	25.40	175.18	14.01	134.02	17.52	52.56	70.07	87.59	87.59	262.78
O	46,340	1,782.30	22.2788	1.63	124.76	25.84	178.23	14.26	136.35	17.82	53.47	71.29	89.12	89.12	267.35
RC	47,132	1,812.77	22.6596	1.64	126.89	26.29	181.28	14.50	138.68	18.13	54.38	72.51	90.64	90.64	271.92
7 A	36,059	1,386.89	17.3361	1.22	97.08	20.11	138.69	11.10	106.10	13.87	41.61	55.48	69.34	69.34	208.03
B	36,875	1,418.27	17.7284	1.25	99.28	20.56	141.83	11.35	108.50	14.18	42.55	56.73	70.91	70.91	212.74
C	37,691	1,449.66	18.1207	1.28	101.48	21.02	144.97	11.60	110.90	14.50	43.49	57.99	72.48	72.48	217.45
D	38,507	1,481.04	18.5130	1.32	103.67	21.48	148.10	11.85	113.30	14.81	44.43	59.24	74.05	74.05	222.16
E	39,323	1,512.42	18.9053	1.35	105.87	21.93	151.24	12.10	115.70	15.12	45.37	60.50	75.62	75.62	226.86
F	40,139	1,543.81	19.2976	1.38	108.07	22.39	154.38	12.35	118.10	15.44	46.31	61.75	77.19	77.19	231.57
G	40,955	1,575.19	19.6899	1.41	110.26	22.84	157.52	12.60	120.50	15.75	47.26	63.01	78.76	78.76	236.28
H	41,771	1,606.58	20.0822	1.45	112.46	23.30	160.66	12.85	122.90	16.07	48.20	64.26	80.33	80.33	240.99
I	42,587	1,637.96	20.4745	1.48	114.66	23.75	163.80	13.10	125.30	16.38	49.14	65.52	81.90	81.90	245.69
J	43,403	1,669.34	20.8668	1.51	116.85	24.21	166.93	13.35	127.70	16.69	50.08	66.77	83.47	83.47	250.40
K	44,219	1,700.73	21.2591	1.54	119.05	24.66	170.07	13.61	130.11	17.01	51.02	68.03	85.04	85.04	255.11
L	45,035	1,732.11	21.6514	1.57	121.25	25.12	173.21	13.86	132.51	17.32	51.96	69.28	86.61	86.61	259.82
M	45,851	1,763.50	22.0438	1.61	123.45	25.57	176.35	14.11	134.91	17.64	52.91	70.54	88.18	88.18	264.53
N	46,667	1,794.89	22.4361	1.64	125.64	26.03	179.49	14.36	137.31	17.95	53.85	71.80	89.74	89.74	269.23
O	47,483	1,826.27	22.8284	1.67	127.84	26.48	182.63	14.61	139.71	18.26	54.79	73.05	91.31	91.31	273.94
RC	48,299	1,857.66	23.2207	1.69	130.04	26.94	185.77	14.86	142.11	18.58	55.73	74.31	92.88	92.88	278.65
8 D	42,033	1,616.66	20.2082	1.45	113.17	23.44	161.67	12.93	123.67	16.17	48.50	64.67	80.83	80.83	242.50
E	42,644	1,640.15	20.5019	1.48	114.81	23.78	164.02	13.12	125.47	16.40	49.20	65.61	82.01	82.01	246.02
F	43,255	1,663.66	20.7957	1.50	116.46	24.12	166.37	13.31	127.27	16.64	49.91	66.55	83.18	83.18	249.55
G	43,866	1,687.15	21.0894	1.53	118.10	24.46	168.72	13.50	129.07	16.87	50.61	67.49	84.36	84.36	253.07
H	44,477	1,710.66	21.3832	1.55	119.75	24.80	171.07	13.69	130.87	17.11	51.32	68.43	85.53	85.53	256.60
I	45,088	1,734.15	21.6769	1.58	121.39	25.15	173.42	13.87	132.66	17.34	52.02	69.37	86.71	86.71	260.12
J	45,699	1,757.66	21.9707	1.60	123.04	25.49	175.77	14.06	134.46	17.58	52.73	70.31	87.88	87.88	263.65
K	46,310	1,781.15	22.2644	1.62	124.68	25.83	178.12	14.25	136.26	17.81	53.43	71.25	89.06	89.06	267.17
L	46,921	1,804.66	22.5582	1.65	126.33	26.17	180.47	14.44	138.06	18.05	54.14	72.19	90.23	90.23	270.70
M	47,532	1,828.15	22.8519	1.67	127.97	26.51	182.82	14.63	139.85	18.28	54.84	73.13	91.41	91.41	274.22
N	48,143	1,851.66	23.1457	1.70	129.62	26.85	185.17	14.81	141.65	18.52	55.55	74.07	92.58	92.58	277.75
O	48,754	1,875.15	23.4394	1.72	131.26	27.19	187.52	15.00	143.45	18.75	56.25	75.01	93.76	93.76	281.27
P	49,365	1,898.66	23.7332	1.74	132.91	27.53	189.87	15.19	145.25	18.99	56.96	75.95	94.93	94.93	284.80
RC	49,976	1,922.15	24.0269	1.76	134.55	27.87	192.22	15.38	147.04	19.22	57.66	76.89	96.11	96.11	288.32
9 D	42,985	1,653.27	20.6659	1.50	115.73	23.97	165.33	13.23	126.48	16.53	49.60	66.13	82.66	82.66	247.99
E	43,630	1,678.08	20.9760	1.52	117.47	24.33	167.81	13.42	128.37	16.78	50.34	67.12	83.90	83.90	251.71
F	44,275	1,702.89	21.2861	1.55	119.20	24.69	170.29	13.62	130.27	17.03	51.09	68.12	85.14	85.14	255.43
G	44,920	1,727.70	21.5962	1.57	120.94	25.05	172.77	13.82	132.17	17.28	51.83	69.11	86.38	86.38	259.15
H	45,565	1,752.50	21.9063	1.60	122.68	25.41	175.25	14.02	134.07	17.53	52.58	70.10	87.63	87.63	262.88
I	46,210	1,777.30	22.2163	1.62	124.41	25.77	177.73	14.22	135.96	17.77	53.32	71.09	88.87	88.87	266.60
J	46,855	1,802.11	22.5264	1.65	126.15	26.13	180.21	14.42	137.86	18.02	54.06	72.08	90.11	90.11	270.32
K	47,500	1,826.92	22.8365	1.67	127.88	26.49	182.69	14.62	139.76	18.27	54.81	73.08	91.35	91.35	274.04
L	48,145	1,851.73	23.1466	1.70	129.62	26.85	185.17	14.81	141.66	18.52	55.55	74.07	92.59	92.59	277.76
M	48,790	1,876.54	23.4567	1.72	131.36	27.21	187.65	15.01	143.56	18.77	56.30	75.06	93.83	93.83	281.48
N	49,435	1,901.34	23.7668	1.75	133.09	27.57	190.13	15.21	145.45	19.01	57.04	76.05	95.07	95.07	285.20
O	50,080	1,926.15	24.0769	1.77	134.83	27.93	192.62	15.41	147.35	19.26	57.78	77.05	96.31	96.31	288.92
P	50,725	1,950.96	24.3870	1.80	136.57	28.29	195.10	15.61	149.25	19.51	58.53	78.04	97.55	97.55	292.64
RC	51,370	1,975.77	24.6971	1.82	138.30	28.65	197.58	15.81	151.15	19.76	59.27	79.03	98.79	98.79	296.37

1. CSRS. The Civil Service Retirement System requires a 7% deduction from biweekly basic pay. In addition, there is a 1.45% deduction for Medicare. Total deductions are then 8.45%. Basic pay includes COLAs. The CSRS deduction is based on straight-time wages which includes COLAs, but does not include overtime, night differential, etc. The Medicare deduction is based on gross pay and may be higher than reported here. CSRS employees can contribute up to 10% to the Thrift Savings Plan. As of April 15, 2005, postal workers will be allowed to make changes to their TSP accounts at any time. **2.** FERS. The Federal Employees Retirement System requires a 0.8% deduction from biweekly straight-time pay. In addition there is a 7.65% deduction for Social Security including Medicare. Total deduction is then 8.45%. The FICA deduction is based on gross pay and may be higher than reported here. **3.** TSP. CSRS employee may contribute up to 10% to the Thrift Savings Plan without a USPS match. FERS employees can contribute up to 15% to TSP. Employees over 49 may make "catch-up" contributions of up to $4,000 in 2005. The Postal Service automatically contributes 1% for all FERS employees and matches employee contributions up to 5%. The Service matches every dollar up to 3% plus the 1% USPS minimum. So the 3% USPS match shown here is 4%. A FERS employee who contributes 3% actually banks 7% with the USPS contribution. The Service contributes 50¢ on every employee dollar between 3% and 5%.

APWU National Agreement
Schedule Two — Salary and Rates

Effective March 19, 2005

Grade and Step	Full-time Regular Rates				CSRS			FERS		FERS — THRIFT SAVINGS PLAN					
	Annual Salary	Biweekly Pay	Straight Time	Night Differential	7% CSRS	1.45% Medicare	Maximum 10% TSP	0.80% FERS	7.65% FICA	1% USPS Minimum	3% Employee	3% USPS	5% Employee	5% USPS	15% Employee Maximum
0 D	43,988	1,691.85	21.1481	1.54	118.43	24.53	169.18	13.53	129.43	16.92	50.76	67.67	84.59	84.59	253.78
E	44,674	1,718.23	21.4779	1.56	120.28	24.91	171.82	13.75	131.44	17.18	51.55	68.73	85.91	85.91	257.73
F	45,360	1,744.62	21.8077	1.59	122.12	25.30	174.46	13.96	133.46	17.45	52.34	69.78	87.23	87.23	261.69
G	46,046	1,771.00	22.1375	1.62	123.97	25.68	177.10	14.17	135.48	17.71	53.13	70.84	88.55	88.55	265.65
H	46,732	1,797.38	22.4673	1.64	125.82	26.06	179.74	14.38	137.50	17.97	53.92	71.90	89.87	89.87	269.61
I	47,418	1,823.77	22.7971	1.67	127.66	26.44	182.38	14.59	139.52	18.24	54.71	72.95	91.19	91.19	273.57
J	48,104	1,850.15	23.1269	1.70	129.51	26.83	185.02	14.80	141.54	18.50	55.50	74.01	92.51	92.51	277.52
K	48,790	1,876.54	23.4567	1.72	131.36	27.21	187.65	15.01	143.56	18.77	56.30	75.06	93.83	93.83	281.48
L	49,476	1,902.92	23.7865	1.75	133.20	27.59	190.29	15.22	145.57	19.03	57.09	76.12	95.15	95.15	285.44
M	50,162	1,929.30	24.1163	1.78	135.05	27.97	192.93	15.43	147.59	19.29	57.88	77.17	96.47	96.47	289.40
N	50,848	1,955.70	24.4462	1.80	136.90	28.36	195.57	15.65	149.61	19.56	58.67	78.23	97.78	97.78	293.35
O	51,534	1,982.08	24.7760	1.83	138.75	28.74	198.21	15.86	151.63	19.82	59.46	79.28	99.10	99.10	297.31
P	52,220	2,008.46	25.1058	1.86	140.59	29.12	200.85	16.07	153.65	20.08	60.25	80.34	100.42	100.42	301.27
RC	52,906	2,034.85	25.4356	1.88	142.44	29.51	203.48	16.28	155.67	20.35	61.05	81.39	101.74	101.74	305.23
1 D	45,047	1,732.58	21.6572	1.58	121.28	25.12	173.26	13.86	132.54	17.33	51.98	69.30	86.63	86.63	259.89
E	45,773	1,760.50	22.0063	1.61	123.24	25.53	176.05	14.08	134.68	17.61	52.82	70.42	88.03	88.03	264.08
F	46,499	1,788.42	22.3553	1.64	125.19	25.93	178.84	14.31	136.81	17.88	53.65	71.54	89.42	89.42	268.26
G	47,225	1,816.34	22.7043	1.66	127.14	26.34	181.63	14.53	138.95	18.16	54.49	72.65	90.82	90.82	272.45
H	47,951	1,844.27	23.0534	1.69	129.10	26.74	184.43	14.75	141.09	18.44	55.33	73.77	92.21	92.21	276.64
I	48,677	1,872.19	23.4024	1.72	131.05	27.15	187.22	14.98	143.22	18.72	56.17	74.89	93.61	93.61	280.83
J	49,403	1,900.11	23.7514	1.75	133.01	27.55	190.01	15.20	145.36	19.00	57.00	76.00	95.01	95.01	285.02
K	50,129	1,928.04	24.1005	1.78	134.96	27.96	192.80	15.42	147.50	19.28	57.84	77.12	96.40	96.40	289.21
L	50,855	1,955.96	24.4495	1.81	136.92	28.36	195.60	15.65	149.63	19.56	58.68	78.24	97.80	97.80	293.39
M	51,581	1,983.89	24.7986	1.83	138.87	28.77	198.39	15.87	151.77	19.84	59.52	79.36	99.19	99.19	297.58
N	52,307	2,011.81	25.1476	1.86	140.83	29.17	201.18	16.09	153.90	20.12	60.35	80.47	100.59	100.59	301.77
O	53,033	2,039.73	25.4966	1.89	142.78	29.58	203.97	16.32	156.04	20.40	61.19	81.59	101.99	101.99	305.96
P	53,759	2,067.66	25.8457	1.92	144.74	29.98	206.77	16.54	158.18	20.68	62.03	82.71	103.38	103.38	310.15
RC	54,485	2,095.58	26.1947	1.94	146.69	30.39	209.56	16.76	160.31	20.96	62.87	83.82	104.78	104.78	314.34
2 D	46,162	1,775.46	22.1933	1.62	124.28	25.74	177.55	14.20	135.82	17.75	53.26	71.02	88.77	88.77	266.32
E	46,933	1,805.11	22.5639	1.65	126.36	26.17	180.51	14.44	138.09	18.05	54.15	72.20	90.26	90.26	270.77
F	47,704	1,834.77	22.9346	1.68	128.43	26.60	183.48	14.68	140.36	18.35	55.04	73.39	91.74	91.74	275.22
G	48,475	1,864.42	23.3053	1.71	130.51	27.03	186.44	14.92	142.63	18.64	55.93	74.58	93.22	93.22	279.66
H	49,246	1,894.08	23.6760	1.74	132.59	27.46	189.41	15.15	144.90	18.94	56.82	75.76	94.70	94.70	284.11
I	50,017	1,923.73	24.0466	1.77	134.66	27.89	192.37	15.39	147.17	19.24	57.71	76.95	96.19	96.19	288.56
J	50,788	1,953.38	24.4173	1.80	136.74	28.32	195.34	15.63	149.43	19.53	58.60	78.14	97.67	97.67	293.01
K	51,559	1,983.04	24.7880	1.83	138.81	28.75	198.30	15.86	151.70	19.83	59.49	79.32	99.15	99.15	297.46
L	52,330	2,012.70	25.1587	1.86	140.89	29.18	201.27	16.10	153.97	20.13	60.38	80.51	100.63	100.63	301.90
M	53,101	2,042.34	25.5293	1.89	142.96	29.61	204.23	16.34	156.24	20.42	61.27	81.69	102.12	102.12	306.35
N	53,872	2,072.00	25.9000	1.92	145.04	30.04	207.20	16.58	158.51	20.72	62.16	82.88	103.60	103.60	310.80
O	54,643	2,101.66	26.2707	1.95	147.12	30.47	210.17	16.81	160.78	21.02	63.05	84.07	105.08	105.08	315.25
P	55,414	2,131.30	26.6413	1.98	149.19	30.90	213.13	17.05	163.04	21.31	63.94	85.25	106.57	106.57	319.70
RC	56,185	2,160.96	27.0120	2.01	151.27	31.33	216.10	17.29	165.31	21.61	64.83	86.44	108.05	108.05	324.14

PART-TIME FLEXIBLE RATES

Grade	BB	AA	A	B	C	D	E	F	G	H	I	J	K	L	M	N	O	P	RC
1	13.04	13.52	14.00	14.48	14.96	15.44	15.93	16.41	16.89	17.37	17.85	18.33	18.81	19.29	19.77	20.25	20.88		21.36
2	13.60	14.07	14.55	15.02	15.50	15.98	16.45	16.93	17.40	17.88	18.36	18.83	19.31	19.78	20.26	20.74	21.27		21.75
3	14.15	14.62	15.09	15.56	16.03	16.51	16.98	17.45	17.92	18.39	18.86	19.34	19.81	20.28	20.75	21.22	21.69		22.16
4			15.94	16.38	16.82	17.27	17.71	18.15	18.60	19.04	19.48	19.93	20.37	20.81	21.26	21.70	22.14		22.59
5			16.75	17.17	17.59	18.01	18.43	18.85	19.27	19.69	20.11	20.53	20.95	21.37	21.79	22.21	22.63		23.05
6			17.63	18.02	18.42	18.81	19.21	19.61	20.00	20.40	20.79	21.19	21.59	21.98	22.38	22.77	23.17		23.57
7			18.03	18.44	18.85	19.25	19.66	20.07	20.48	20.89	21.29	21.70	22.11	22.52	22.93	23.33	23.74		24.15
8						21.02	21.32	21.63	21.93	22.24	22.54	22.85	23.16	23.46	23.77	24.07	24.38	24.68	24.99
9						21.49	21.82	22.14	22.46	22.78	23.11	23.43	23.75	24.07	24.40	24.72	25.04	25.36	25.69
10						21.99	22.34	22.68	23.02	23.37	23.71	24.05	24.40	24.74	25.08	25.42	25.77	26.11	26.45
11						22.52	22.89	23.25	23.61	23.98	24.34	24.70	25.06	25.43	25.79	26.15	26.52	26.88	27.24
12						23.08	23.47	23.85	24.24	24.62	25.01	25.39	25.78	26.17	26.55	26.94	27.32	27.71	28.09

PART-TIME REGULAR RATES

Grade	BB	AA	A	B	C	D	E	F	G	H	I	J	K	L	M	N	O	P	RC
1	12.54	13.00	13.46	13.93	14.39	14.85	15.31	15.78	16.24	16.70	17.16	17.63	18.09	18.55	19.01	19.48	20.07		20.54
2	13.07	13.53	13.99	14.45	14.90	15.36	15.82	16.28	16.73	17.19	17.65	18.11	18.56	19.02	19.48	19.94	20.45		20.91
3	13.60	14.06	14.51	14.96	15.42	15.87	16.32	16.78	17.23	17.68	18.14	18.59	19.04	19.50	19.95	20.40	20.86		21.31
4			15.32	15.75	16.18	16.60	17.03	17.45	17.88	18.31	18.73	19.16	19.59	20.01	20.44	20.87	21.29		21.72
5			16.11	16.51	16.92	17.32	17.73	18.13	18.53	18.94	19.34	19.74	20.15	20.55	20.96	21.36	21.76		22.17
6			16.95	17.33	17.71	18.09	18.47	18.85	19.23	19.61	19.99	20.38	20.76	21.14	21.52	21.90	22.28		22.66
7			17.34	17.73	18.12	18.51	18.91	19.30	19.69	20.08	20.47	20.87	21.26	21.65	22.04	22.44	22.83		23.22
8						20.21	20.50	20.80	21.09	21.38	21.68	21.97	22.26	22.56	22.85	23.15	23.44	23.73	24.03
9						20.67	20.98	21.29	21.60	21.91	22.22	22.53	22.84	23.15	23.46	23.77	24.08	24.39	24.70
10						21.15	21.48	21.81	22.14	22.47	22.80	23.13	23.46	23.79	24.12	24.45	24.78	25.11	25.44
11						21.66	22.01	22.36	22.70	23.05	23.40	23.75	24.10	24.45	24.80	25.15	25.50	25.85	26.19
12						22.19	22.56	22.93	23.31	23.68	24.05	24.42	24.79	25.16	25.53	25.90	26.27	26.64	27.01

Transitional Employee Rates Effective 11/27/2004

Grade	Rate
1	10.85
2	11.01
3	11.19
4	12.43
5	13.21
6	14.03

AMERICAN POSTAL WORKERS UNION, AFL-CIO

William Burrus, President
1300 L Street, NW
Washington, DC 20005